OFFICIAL REPORTS

OF

BATTLES.

PUBLISHED BY ORDER OF CONGRESS.

RICHMOND, VA.:
ENQUIRER BOOK AND JOB PRESS.
1862.

SOUTHERN HISTORY OF THE WAR.

OFFICIAL REPORTS

OF

BATTLES,

AS PUBLISHED BY ORDER OF THE CONFEDERATE CONGRESS AT RICHMOND.

NEW YORK:
CHARLES B. RICHARDSON,
594 & 596 BROADWAY.
1864.

REPORT OF GENERAL BEAUREGARD OF THE BATTLE OF MANASSAS.

HEAD-QUARTERS FIRST CORPS ARMY OF THE POTOMAC,
MANASSAS, August 26, 1861.

GENERAL:— * * * The War Department having been informed by me, by telegraph on the 17th of July, of the movement of Gen. McDowell, Gen. Johnston was immediately ordered to form a junction of his army corps with mine, should the movement, in his judgment, be deemed advisable. Gen. Holmes was also directed to push forward with two regiments, a battery, and one company of cavalry.

In view of these propositions, approaching reinforcements modifying my plan of operations so far as to determine on attacking the enemy at Centreville as soon as I should hear of the near approach of the two reinforcing columns, I sent one of my aids, Col. Chisholm, of South Carolina, to meet and communicate my plans to Gen. Johnston, and my wish that one portion of his force should march by the way of Aldie, and take the enemy on his right flank and in the rear at Centreville. Difficulties, however, of an insuperable character in connection with means of transportation, and the marching condition of his troops, made this impracticable, and it was determined our forces should be united within the lines of Bull Run, and thence advance to the attack of the enemy.

Gen. Johnston arrived here about noon on the 20th July, and being my senior in rank he necessarily assumed command of all the forces of the Confederate States, then concentrating at this point. Made acquainted with my plan of operations and dispositions to meet the enemy, he gave them his entire approval, and generously directed their execution under my command.

In consequence of the untoward detention, however, of some five thousand (5000) of Gen. Johnston's army corps, resulting from the inadequate and imperfect means of transportation for so many troops at the disposition of the Manassas Gap Railroad, it became necessary, on the morning of the 21st, before daylight, to modify the plan accepted to suit the contingency of an immediate attack on our lines by the main force of the enemy, then plainly at hand.

The enemy's forces, reported by their best-informed journals to be 55,000 strong, I had learned from reliable sources, on the night of the 20th, were being concentrated in and around Centreville, and along the Warrenton turnpike-road, to Bull Run, near which our respective pickets were in immediate proximity. This fact, with the conviction that, after his signal discomfiture on the 18th of July, before Blackburn's Ford—the centre of my lines—he would not renew the attack in that quarter, induced me at once to look for an attempt on my left flank, resting on the Stone Bridge, which was but weakly guarded by men, as well as but slightly provided with artificial defensive appliances and artillery.

In view of these palpable military conditions, by half-past 4 A. M., on the 21st July, I had prepared and dispatched orders, directing the whole of the Confederate forces within the lines of Bull Run, including the brigade and regiments of Gen. Johnston, which had arrived at that time, to be held in readiness to march at a moment's notice.

At that hour the following was the disposition of our forces:

Ewell's brigade, constituted as on the 18th of July, remained in position at Union Mills Ford, his left extending along Bull Run, in the direction of McLean's Ford, and supported by Holmes' brigade, 2d Tennessee and 1st Arkansas regiments a short distance to the rear—that is, at and near Camp Wigfall.

D. R. Jones' brigade, from Ewell's left, in front of McLean's Ford, and along the stream to Longstreet's position. It was unchanged in organization, and was supported by Early's brigade, also unchanged, placed behind a thicket of young pines, a short distance in the rear of McLean's Ford.

Longstreet's brigade held its former ground at Blackburn's Ford, from Jones' left to Bonham's right, at Mitchell's Ford, and was supported by Jackson's brigade, consisting of Col. James L. Preston's 4th, Harper's 5th, Allen's 2d, the 27th, Lieut.-col. Echoll's, and the 33d, Cumming's Virginia regiments, 2611 strong, which were posted behind the skirting of pines to the rear of Blackburn's and Mitchell's Fords, and in the rear of this support was also Barksdale's 13th regiment Mississippi Volunteers, which had lately arrived from Lynchburg.

Along the edge of the pine thicket, in rear of and equidistant from McLean's and Blackburn's Fords, ready to support either position, I had also placed all of Bee's and Bartow's brigades that had arrived—namely, two companies of the 11th Mississippi, Lieut.-col. Liddell; the 2d Mississippi, Col. Falkner, and the Alabama, with the 7th and 8th Georgia regiments (Col. Gartrell and Lieut.-col. Gardner), in all 2732 bayonets.

Bonham's brigade, as before, held Mitchell's Ford, its right near Longstreet's left, its left extending in the direction of Cocke's right. It was organized as at the end of the 18th of July, with Jackson's brigade, as before said, as a support.

Cocke's brigade, increased by seven companies of the 8th, Hunton's; three companies of the 49th, Smith's Virginia regiments; two companies of cavalry, and a battery under Rogers of four 6-pounders, occupied the line in front and rear of Bull Run, extending from the direction of Bonham's left, and guarding Island, Ball's, and Lewis' Fords, to the right of Evans' demi-brigade, near the Stone Bridge, also under Gen. Cocke's command.

The latter held the Stone Bridge, and its left covered a farm ford about one mile above the bridge.

Stewart's cavalry, some three hundred men of the army of the Shenandoah, guarded the level ground extending in rear from Bonham's left to Cocke's right.

Two companies of Radford's cavalry were held in reserve a short distance in rear of Mitchell's Ford, his left extending in the direction of Stewart's right.

Col. Pendleton's reserve battery of eight pieces was temporarily placed in rear of Bonham's extreme left.

Major Walton's reserve battery of five guns was in position on McLean's farm, in a piece of woods in rear of Bee's right.

Hampton's legion of six companies of infantry, six hundred strong, having arrived that morning by the cars from Richmond, was subsequently, as soon as it arrived, ordered forward to a position in immediate vicinity of the Lewis House, as a support for any troops engaged in that quarter.

The effective force of all arms of the army of the Potomac on that eventful morning, including the garrison of Camp Pickens, did not exceed 21,833 and 29 guns.

The army of the Shenandoah, ready for action on the field, may be set at 6000 men and 20 guns. [That is, when the battle begun: Smith's brigade and Fisher's North Carolina came up later, and made total of army of Shenandoah engaged of all arms, 8334. Hill's Virginia regiment, 550, also arrived, but was posted as reserve to right flank.]

The brigade of Gen. Holmes mustered about 1265 bayonets, 6 guns, and a company of cavalry about ninety strong.

Informed at half-past 5 A. M., by Col. Evans, that the enemy had deployed some 1200 men [these were what Col. Evans saw of Gen. Schenck's brigade of Gen. Tyler's division, and two other heavy brigades, in all over 9000 men and 13 pieces of artillery—Carlisle's and Ayres' batteries—that is, 900 men and two 6-pounders, confronted by 9000 men and 13 pieces of artillery, mostly rifled], with several pieces of artillery in his immediate front. I at once ordered him, as also Gen. Cocke, if attacked, to maintain their position to the last extremity.

In my opinion the most effective method of relieving that flank was by a rapid, determined attack, with my right wing and centre on the enemy's flank and rear at Centreville, with due precautions against the advance of his reserves from the direction of Washington. By such a movement, I confidently expected to achieve a complete victory for my country by 12 o'clock, M.

These new dispositions were submitted to Gen. Johnston, who fully approved them, and the orders for their immediate execution were at once issued.

Brig.-gen. Ewell was directed to begin the movement, to be followed and supported successively by Gens. D. R. Jones, Longstreet, and Bonham respectively, supported by their several appointed reserves.

The cavalry, under Stewart and Radford, were to be held in hand, subject to future orders and ready for employment as might be required by the exigencies of the battle.

About half-past 8 o'clock, A. M., Gen. Johnston and myself transferred our head-quarters to a central position about half a mile in the rear of Mitchell's Ford, whence we might watch the course of events.

Previously, as early as half-past 5, the Federalists in front of Evans' position, Stone Bridge, had opened with a large 30-pounder Parrot rifle gun, and thirty minutes later with a moderate, apparently tentative, fire from a battery of rifle pieces, directed first in front at Evans', and then in the direction of Cocke's position, but without drawing a return fire and discovery of our position, chiefly because in that quarter we had nothing but eight 6-pounder pieces, which could not reach the distant enemy.

As the Federalists had advanced with an extended line of skirmishers in front of Evans, that officer promptly threw forward the two flank companies of the 4th South Carolina regiment, and one company of Wheat's Louisiana battalion, deployed as skirmishers, to cover his small front. An occasional scattering fire resulted, and thus the two armies in that quarter remained for more than an hour, while the main body of the enemy was marching its dubious way through the "big forest" to take our forces in flank and rear.

By half-past 8 A. M., Col. Evans having become satisfied of the counterfeit character of the movement on his front, and persuaded of an attempt to turn his left flank, decided to change his position to meet the enemy, and for this purpose immediately put in motion to his left and rear six companies of Sloan's 4th South Carolina regiment, Wheat's Louisiana battalion, five companies, and two 6-pounders of Latham's battery, leaving four companies of Sloan's regiment under cover as the sole immediate defence of the Stone Bridge, but giving information to Gen. Cocke of his change of position and the reasons that impelled it.

Following a road leading by the Old Pittsylvania (Carter) mansion, Col. Evans formed in line of battle some four hundred yards in rear—as he advanced—of that house, his guns to the front and in position, properly supported, to its immediate right. Finding, however, that the enemy did not appear on that road, which was a branch of one running by Sudley's Springs Ford to Brentsville and Dumfries, he turned abruptly to the left, and marching across the fields for three-quarters of a mile, about half-past 9 A. M., took a position in line of battle; his left, Sloan's companies, resting on the main Brentsville road in a shallow ravine, the Louisiana battalion to the right, in advance some two hundred yards, a rectangular course of wood separating them—one piece of his artillery planted on an eminence some seven hundred yards to the rear of Wheat's battalion, and the other on a ridge near and in rear of Sloan's position, commanding a reach of the road just in front of the line of battle. In this order he awaited the coming of the masses of the enemy now drawing near.

In the mean time, about 7 o'clock, A. M., Jackson's brigade, with Imboden's, and five pieces of Walton's battery, had been sent to take up a position along Bull Run, to guard the interval between Cocke's right and Bonham's left, with orders to support either in case of need—the character and topographical features of the ground having been shown to Gen. Jackson by Capt. D. R. Harris, of the Engineers, of this army corps.

So much of Bee's and Bartow's brigades, now united, as had arrived—some 2800 muskets—had also been sent forward to the support of the position of the Stone Bridge.

The enemy beginning his detour from the turnpike, at a point nearly half-way between Stone Bridge and Centreville, had pursued a tortuous, narrow trace of a rarely-used road, through a dense wood, the greater part of his way, until near the Sudley road. A division under Col. Hunter, of the Federal regular army, of two strong brigades, was in the advance, followed immediately by another division under Col. Heintzelman, of three brigades and seven companies of regular cavalry and twenty-four pieces of artillery—eighteen of which were rifle guns. The column, as it crossed Bull Run, numbered over sixteen thousand men of all arms, by their own accounts.

Burnside's brigade, which here, as at Fairfax Court-house, led the advance, at about forty-five minutes past 9 A. M., debouched from a wood in sight of Evans' position, some five hundred yards distant from Wheat's battalion.

He immediately threw forward his skirmishers in force, and they became engaged with Wheat's command and the 6-pounder gun under Lieut. Leftwich.

The Federalists at once advanced, as they report officially, the 2d Rhode Island regiment, volunteers, with its vaunted battery of six 13-pounder rifle guns. Sloan's companies were then brought into action, having been pushed forward through the woods. The enemy soon, galled and staggered by the fire and pressed by the determined valor with which Wheat handled his battery until he was desperately wounded, hastened up three other regiments of the brigade and two Dahlgren howitzers, making in all quite 3500 bayonets and eight pieces of artillery, opposed to less than 800 men and two 6-pounder guns.

Despite these odds, this intrepid command of but eleven weak companies maintained its front to the enemy for quite an hour, and until Gen. Bee came to their aid with his command. The heroic Bee, with a soldier's eye and recognition of the situation, had previously disposed his command with skill—Imboden's battery having been admirably placed between the two brigades under shelter behind the undulations of a hill about one hundred and fifty yards north of the now famous Henry House, and very near where he subsequently fell mortally wounded, to the great misfortune of his country, but after deeds of deliberate and ever-memorable courage.

Meanwhile, the enemy had pushed forward a battalion of eight companies of regular infantry and one of their best batteries of six pieces (four rifled), supported by four companies of marines, to increase the desperate odds against which Evans and his men had maintained their stand with an almost matchless tenacity.

Gen. Bee now finding Evans sorely pressed under the crushing weight of the masses of the enemy, at the call of Col. Evans threw forward his whole force to his aid across a small stream—Young's branch and valley—and engaged the Federalists with impetuosity; Imboden's battery at the time playing from this well-chosen position with brilliant effect with spherical case, the enemy having first opened on him from a rifled battery, probably Griffin's, with elongated cylindrical shells, which flew a few feet over the heads of our men and exploded in the crest of the hill immediately in rear.

As Bee advanced under a severe fire, he placed the 7th and 8th Georgia regiments, under the chivalrous Bartow, at about 11 A. M., in a wood of second-growth pines, to the right and front of and nearly perpendicular to Evans' line of battle; the 4th Alabama to the left of them, along a fence connecting the position of the Georgia regiments with the rectangular copse in which Sloan's South Carolina companies were engaged, and into which he also threw the 2d Mississippi. A fierce and destructive conflict now ensued; the fire was withering on both sides, while the enemy swept our short, thin lines with their numerous artillery, which, according to their official reports, at this time consisted of at least ten rifled guns and four howitzers. For an hour did these stout-hearted men of the blended command of Bee, Evans, and Bartow breast an unintermitting bullet-storm, animated, surely, by something more than the ordinary courage of even the bravest men under fire. It must have been, indeed, the inspiration of the cause and consciousness of the great stake at issue, which thus nerved and animated one and all to stand unawed and unshrinking in such extremity.

The Federal brigades of Heintzelman's division were now brought into action, led by Ricketts' superb light battery of 6-pounder rifle guns, which, posted on an eminence to the right of the Sudley road, opened fire on Imboden's battery—about this time increased by two rifle pieces of the Washington Artillery, under Lieut. Richardson, and already the mark of two batteries, which divided their fire with Imboden, and two guns, under Lieuts. Richardson and Leftwitch, of Latham's battery, posted as before mentioned.

At this time, confronting the enemy, we had still but Evans' eleven companies and two guns—Bee's and Bartow's four regiments, the two companies 11th Mississippi, under Lieut.-col. Liddell, and the six pieces under Imboden and Richardson. The enemy had two divisions of four strong brigades, including seventeen companies of regular infantry, cavalry, and artillery, four companies of marines, and twenty pieces of artillery. [See official reports of

Cols. Heintzelman, Porter, &c.] Against this odds, scarcely credible, our advance position was still for a while maintained, and the enemy's ranks constantly broken and shattered under the scorching fire of our men; but fresh regiments of the Federalists came upon the field—Sherman's and Keyes' brigades, of Tyler's division—as is stated in their reports, numbering over six thousand bayonets, which had found a passage across the run about eight hundred yards above the Stone Bridge, threatened our right.

Heavy losses had now been sustained on our side, both in numbers and in the personal worth of the slain. The Georgia regiment had suffered heavily, being exposed, as it took and maintained its position, to a fire from the enemy, already posted within a hundred yards of their front and right, sheltered by fences and other cover. It was at this time that Lieut.-col. Gardener was severely wounded, as also several other valuable officers; the adjutant of the regiment, Lieut. Branch, was killed, and the horse of the regretted Bartow was shot under him. The Fourth Alabama also suffered severely from the deadly fire of the thousands of muskets which they so dauntlessly fronted, under the immediate leadership of Bee himself. Its brave colonel, E. J. Jones, was dangerously wounded, and many gallant officers fell, slain or *hors de combat.*

Now, however, with the surging mass of over fourteen thousand Federal infantry pressing on their front, and under the incessant fire of at least twenty pieces of artillery, with the fresh brigades of Sherman and Keyes approaching—the latter already in musket range—our lines gave back, but under orders from Gen. Bee.

The enemy, maintaining the fire, pressed their swelling masses onward as our shattered battalions retired; the slaughter for the moment was deplorable, and has filled many a Southern home with life-long sorrow.

Under this inexorable stress the retreat continued until arrested by the energy and resolution of Gen. Bee, supported by Bartow and Evans, just in the rear of the Robinson House, and Hampton's legion, which had been already advanced, and was in position near it.

Imboden's battery, which had been handled with marked skill, but whose men were almost exhausted, and the two pieces of Walton's battery, under Lieut. Richardson, being threatened by the enemy's infantry on the left and front, were also obliged to fall back. Imboden, leaving a disabled piece on the ground, retired until he met Jackson's brigade, while Richardson joined the main body of his battery near the Lewis House.

As our infantry retired from the extreme front, the two six-pounders of Latham's battery, before mentioned, fell back with excellent judgment to suitable positions in the rear, when an effective fire was maintained upon the still advancing line of the Federalists with damaging effect, until their ammunition was nearly exhausted, when they, too, were withdrawn in the near presence of the enemy, and rejoined their captain.

From the point previously indicated, where Gen. Johnston had established our head-quarters, we heard the continuous roll of musketry and the sustained din of the artillery, which announced the serious outburst of the battle on our left flank, and we anxiously, but confidently, awaited similar sounds of conflict from our front at Centreville, resulting from the prescribed attack in that quarter by our right wing.

At half-past ten in the morning, however, this expectation was dissipated, from Brig.-gen. Ewell informing me, to my profound disappointment, that my orders for his advance had miscarried, but that, in consequence of a communication from Gen. D. R. Jones, he had just thrown his brigade across the stream at Union Mills. But, in my judgment, it was now too late for the effective execution of the contemplated movement, which must have required quite three hours for the troops to get into position for the attack; therefore it became immediately necessary to depend on new combinations and other dispositions suited to the now pressing exigency.

The movement of the right and centre, already begun by Jones and Longstreet, was at once countermanded with the sanction of Gen. Johnston, and we arranged to meet the enemy on the field upon which he had chosen to give us battle. Under these circumstances our reserves, not already in movement, were immediately ordered up to support our left flank, namely: Holmes' two regiments and battery of artillery, under Capt. Lindsey Walker, of six guns, and Early's brigade. Two regiments from Bonham's brigade, with Kemper's four six-pounders, were also called for, and, with the sanction of Gen. Johnston, Gens. Ewell, Jones (D. R.), Longstreet, and Bonham were directed to make a demonstration to their several fronts, to retain and engross the enemy's reserves and forces on their flank, and at and around Centreville. Previously our respective chiefs of staff—Major Rhett and Col. Jordan—had been left at my head-quarters to hasten up, and give directions to any troops that might arrive at Manassas.

These orders having been duly dispatched by staff officers, at 10.30 A. M. Gen. Johnston and myself set out for the immediate field of action, which we reached in the rear of the Robinson and widow Henry's houses, at about 12 meridian, and just as the commands of Bee, Bartow, and Evans had taken shelter in a wooded ravine behind the former, stoutly held at the time by Hampton with his legion, which had made a stand there after having previously been as far forward as the turnpike, where Lieut.-col. Johnston, an officer of brilliant promise, was killed, and other severe losses were sustained.

Before our arrival upon the scene, Gen. Jackson had moved forward with his brigade of five Virginia regiments from his position in reserve, and had judiciously taken post below the brim of the plateau, nearly east of the Henry House, and to the left of the ravine and woods occupied by the mingled remnants of Bee's, Bartow's, and Evans' commands, with Imboden's battery, and two of Standard's pieces placed so as to play upon the oncoming enemy, supported in the immediate rear by Col. J. L. Preston's and Lieut.-col. Echoll's regiments, on the right by Harper's, and on the left by Allen's and Cumming's regiments.

As soon as Gen. Johnston and myself reached the field, we were occupied with the reorganization of the heroic troops, whose previous stand, with scarce a parallel, has nothing more valiant in all the pages of history, and whose losses fitly tell why, at length, their lines had lost their cohesion. It was now that Gen. Johnston impressively and gallantly charged to the front with the colors of the Fourth Alabama regiment by his side, all the field officers of the regiment having been previously disabled. Shortly afterwards I placed S. R. Gist, Adjutant and Inspector-general of South Carolina, a volunteer aid-de-camp of Gen. Bee, in command of this regiment, and who led it again to the front as became its previous behavior, and remained with it for the rest of the day.

As soon as we had thus rallied and disposed our forces, I urged Gen. Johnston to leave the immediate conduct of the field to me, while he, repairing to Portico—the Lewis House—should urge reinforcements forward. At first he was unwilling, but reminded that one of us must do so, and that properly it was his place, he reluctantly, but fortunately, complied; fortunately, because from that position, by his energy and sagacity, his keen perception and anticipation of my needs, he so directed the reserves as to insure the success of the day.

As Gen. Johnston departed for Portico, Col. Bartow reported to me with the remains of the 7th Georgia Volunteers (Gartrell's), which I ordered him to post on the left of Jackson's line, in the edge of the belt of pines bordering the southwestern rim of the plateau on which the battle was now to rage so long and so fiercely.

Col. William Smith's battalion of the Forty-ninth Virginia Volunteers, having also come up by my orders, I placed it on the left of Gartrell's as my extreme left at the time. Repairing then to the right, I placed Hampton's legion, which had suffered greatly, on that flank somewhat to the rear of Harper's regiment, and also the seven companies of the Eighth (Hunton's) Virginia regiment, which, detached from Cocke's brigade, by my orders and those of Gen. Johnston, had opportunely reached the ground. These, with Harper's regiment, constituted a reserve, to protect our right flank from an advance of the enemy from the quarter of the Stone Bridge, and served as a support for the line of battle, which was formed on the right by Bee's and Evans' commands: in the centre by four regiments of Jackson's brigade, with Imboden's four six-pounders, Walton's five guns (two rifled), two guns (one piece rifled) of Stanard's, and two six-pounders of Rogers' batteries, the latter under Lieut. Heaton; and on the left by Gartrell's reduced ranks and Col. Smith's battalion, subsequently reinforced by Falkner's 2d Mississippi regiment, and by another regiment of the army of the Shenandoah, just arrived upon the field—the Sixth (Fisher's) North Carolina. Confronting the enemy at this time my force numbered, at most, not more than six thousand five hundred infantry and artillerists, with but thirteen pieces of artillery, and two companies (Carter's and Hoge's) of Stuart's cavalry.

The enemy's force, now bearing hotly and confidently down on our position, regiment after regiment of the best-equipped men that ever took the field—according to their own official history of the day—was formed of Cols. Hunter's and Heintzelman's divisions, Cols. Sherman's and Keyes' brigades, of Tyler's division, and of the formidable batteries of Ricketts, Griffin, and Arnold, regulars, and 2d Rhode Island and two Dahlgren howitzers—a force of over 20,000 infantry, seven companies of regular cavalry, and twenty-four pieces of improved artillery. At the same time, perilous, heavy reserves of infantry and artillery hung in the distance around the Stone Bridge, Mitchell's, Blackburn's, and Union Mills fords, visibly ready to fall upon us at any moment; and I was also assured of the existence of other heavy corps at and around Centreville and elsewhere, within convenient supporting distances.

Fully conscious of this portentous disparity of force, as I posted the lines for the encounter, I sought to infuse into the hearts of my officers and men the confidence and determined spirit of resistance to this wicked invasion of the homes of a free people, which I felt. I informed them that reinforcements would rapidly come to their support, and we must at all hazards hold our posts until reinforced. I reminded them that we fought for our homes, our firesides, and for the independence of our country. I urged them to the resolution of victory or death on that field. These sentiments were loudly, eagerly cheered wheresoever proclaimed, and I then felt assured of the unconquerable spirit of that army which would enable us to wrench victory from the host then threatening us with destruction.

O my country! I would readily have sacrificed my life, and those of all the brave men around me, to save your honor and to maintain your independence from the degrading yoke which these ruthless invaders had come to impose and render perpetual; and the day's issues have assured me that such emotions must also have animated all under my command.

In the mean time the enemy had seized upon the plateau on which the Robinson and Henry houses are situated—the position first occupied in the morning by Gen. Bee, before advancing to the support of Evans. Ricketts' battery of six rifled guns—the pride of the Federalists, the object of their unstinted expenditure in outfit—and the equally powerful regular light battery of Griffin, were brought forward and placed in immediate action, after having, conjointly with the batteries already mentioned, played from former positions with destructive effect upon our forward battalions.

The topographical features of the plateau, now become the stage of the contending armies, must be described in detail.

A glance at the map will show that it is inclosed on three sides by small watercourses, which empty into Bull Run within a few yards of each other, half a mile to the south of the Stone Bridge. Rising to an elevation of quite one hundred feet above the level of Bull Run at the bridge, it falls off on these sides to the level of the inclosing streams in gentle slopes, but which are furrowed by ravines of irregular direction and length, and shaded with clumps and patches of young pines and oaks. The general direction of the crest of the plateau is oblique to the course of Bull Run in that quarter, and on the Brentsville and turnpike roads, which intersect each other at right angles. Completely surrounding the two houses before mentioned are small open fields, of irregular outline, and exceeding 150 acres in extent. The houses occupied at the time—the one by widow Henry and the other by the free negro Robinson—are small wooden buildings, densely embowered in trees, and environed by a double row of fences on two sides. Around the eastern and southern brow of the plateau an almost unbroken fringe of second-growth pines gave excellent shelter for our marksmen, who availed themseves of it with the most satisfactory skill. To the west, adjoining the fields, a broad belt of oaks extends directly across the crests on both sides of the Sudley road, in which, during the battle, regiments of both armies met and contended for the mastery.

From the open ground of this plateau the view embraces a wide expanse of woods and gently undulating, open country of broad grass and grain fields in all directions, including the scene of Evans' and Bee's recent encounter with the enemy—some twelve hundred yards to the northward.

In reply to the enemy's batteries our own artillery had not been idle or unskilful. The ground occupied by our guns, on a level with that held by the batteries of the enemy, was an open space of limited extent, behind a low undulation, just at the eastern verge of the plateau, some 500 or 600 yards from the Henry House. Here, as before said, some thirteen pieces, mostly 6-pounders, were maintained in action. The several batteries of Imboden, Stanard, Pendleton (Rockbridge artillery), and Alburnis', of the army of the Shenandoah, and five guns of Walton's, and Heaton's section of Rogers' battery, of the army of the Potomac, alternating to some extent with each other, and taking part as needed; all, from the outset, displaying that marvellous capacity of our people as artillerists which has made them, it would appear, at once the terror and admiration of the enemy.

As was soon apparent, the Federalists had suffered severely from our artillery, and from the fire of our musketry on the right, and especially from the left flank, placed under cover, within whose galling range they had been advanced. And we are told in their official reports how regiment after regiment, thrown forward to dislodge us, was broken, never to recover its entire organization on that field.

In the mean time, two companies of Stuart's cavalry (Carter's and Hoge's) made a dashing charge down the Brentsville and Sudley road upon the Fire Zouaves—then the enemy's right on the plateau—which added to their disorder, wrought by our musketry on that flank. But still the press of the enemy was heavy in that quarter of the field, as fresh troops were thrown forward there to outflank us, and some three guns of a battery, in an attempt to obtain a position apparently to enfilade our batteries, were thrown so close to the 33d regiment, Jackson's brigade, that that regiment, springing forward, seized them, but with severe loss, and was subsequently driven back by an overpowering force of Federal musketry.

Now, full 2 o'clock, P. M., I gave the order for the right of my line, except my reserves, to advance to recover the plateau. It was done with uncommon resolution and vigor, and at the same time Jackson's brigade pierced the enemy's centre with the determination of veterans, and the spirit of men who fight for a sacred cause; but it suffered seriously. With equal spirit the other parts of the line made the onset and the Federal lines were broken and swept back at all points, from the open ground of the plateau. Rallying soon, however, as they were strongly reinforced by fresh regiments, the Federalists returned, and by weight of numbers pressed our lines back, recovered their ground and guns, and renewed the offensive.

By this time, between half-past 2 and 3 o'clock, P. M., our reinforcements pushed forward, and, directed by Gen. Johnston to the required quarter, were at hand just as I had ordered forward, to a second effort, for the recovery of the disputed plateau, the whole line, including my reserves, which, at this crisis of the battle, I felt called upon to lead in person. This attack was general, and was shared in by every regiment then in the field, including the 6th (Fisher's) North Carolina regiment, which had just come up and taken position on the immediate left of the 49th Virginia regiment. The whole open ground was again swept clear of the enemy, and the plateau around the Henry and Robinson houses remained finally in our possession, with the greater part of the Ricketts and Griffin batteries, and a flag of the 1st Michigan regiment, captured by the 27th Virginia regiment (Lieut.-col. Echolls), of Jackson's brigade.

This part of the day was rich with deeds of individual coolness and dauntless conduct, as well as well-directed embodied resolution and bravery, but fraught with the loss to the service of the country of lives of inestimable preciousness at this juncture. The brave Bee was mortally wounded at the head of the 4th Alabama and some Mississippians, in an open field near the Henry House, and a few yards distant the promising life of Bartow, while leading the 7th Georgia regiment, was quenched in blood. Col. F. J. Thomas, Acting Chief of Ordnance, of Gen. Johnston's staff, after gallant conduct and most efficient service was also slain. Col. Fisher, 6th North Carolina, likewise fell, after soldierly behavior, at the head of his regiment, with ranks greatly thinned.

Withers' 18th regiment, of Cocke's brigade, had come up in time to follow this charge, and, in conjunction with Hampton's legion, captured several rifle pieces which may have fallen previously in possession of some of our troops; but if so, had been recovered by the enemy. These pieces were immediately turned and effectively served on distant masses of the enemy by the hands of some of our officers.

While the enemy had thus been driven back on our right entirely across the turnpike, and beyond Young's Branch on our left, the woods yet swarmed with them, when our reinforcements opportunely arrived in quick succession, and took position in that portion of the field. Kershaw's 2d and Cash's 8th South Carolina regiments, which had arrived soon after Withers', were led through the oaks just east of the Sudley-Brentsville road, brushing some of the enemy before them and taking an advantageous position along the west of that road, opened with much skill and effect on bodies of the enemy that had been rallied under cover of a strong Federal brigade posted on a plateau in the southwest angle, formed by intersection of the turnpike with the Sudley-Brentsville road. Among the troops thus engaged were the Federal regular infantry.

At the same time, Kemper's battery, passing northward by the Stone Bridge road, took position on the open space—under orders of Col. Kershaw—near where an enemy's battery had been captured, was opened with effective results upon the Federal right, then the mark of Kershaw and Cash's regiments.

Col. Preston's 28th regiment, of Cocke's brigade, had by that time entered the same body of oaks, and encountered some Michigan troops, capturing their brigade commander, Col. Wilcox.

Another important accession to our forces had also occurred about the same time, at 3 o'clock, P. M. Brig.-gen. E. K. Smith, with some 1700 infantry of Elzey's brigade, of the army of the Shenandoah, and Beckham's. battery, came upon the field, from Camp Pickens, Manassas, where they had arrived by railroad, at noon. Directed in person by Gen. Johnston to the left, then so much endangered, on reaching a position in rear of the oak woods, south of the Henry House, and immediately east of the Sudley road, Gen. Smith was disabled by a severe wound, and his valuable services were lost at that critical juncture.

But the command devolved upon a meritorious officer of experience, Col. Elksy, who led his infantry at once somewhat further to the left, in the direction of the Chinn House, across the road, through the oaks skirting the west side of the road, and around which he sent the battery under Lieut. Beckham. This officer took up a most favorable position near the house, whence, with a clear view of the Federal right and centre, filling the open fields to the west of the Brentsville-Sudley road, and gently sloping southward, he opened fire with his battery upon them with a deadly and damaging effect.

Col. Early, who, by some mischance, did not receive orders until 2 o'clock, which had been sent him at noon, came on the ground immediately after Elzey, with Kemper's 7th Virginia, Hay's 7th Louisiana, and Barksdale's 13th Mississippi regiments. The brigade, by the personal direction of Gen. Johnston, was marched by the Hollaham House, across the fields to the left, entirely around the woods which Elzey had passed, and under a severe fire, into a position in line of battle near Chinn's House, outflanking the enemy's right.

At this time, about half-past 3 P. M., the enemy, driven back on their left and centre, and brushed from the woods bordering the Sudley road, south and west of the Henry House, had formed a line of battle of truly formidable proportions, of crescent outline, regaining on their left from the vicinity of Pittsylvania (the old Carter mansion), by Matthew's and in rear of Dugan's across the turnpike near to Chinn's House. The woods and fields were filled with their masses of infantry and their carefully preserved cavalry. It was a truly magnificent, though redoubtable spectacle, as they threw forward in fine style, on the broad, gentle slopes of the ridge occupied by their main lines, a cloud of skirmishers, preparatory for another attack.

But as Early formed his line, and Beckham's pieces playing upon the right of the enemy, Elzey's brigade, Gibbon's 10th Virginia, Lieut-col. Stuart's 1st Maryland and Vaughn's 3d Tennessee regiments, and Cash's 8th and Kershaw's 2d South Carolina, Withers' 18th and Preston's 28th Virginia, advanced in an irregular line almost simultaneously, with great spirit, from their several positions upon the front and left of the enemy in their quarter of the field. At the same time, too, Early resolutely assailed their right flank and rear. Under this continued attack, the enemy was soon forced, first, over the narrow plateau in the southern angle made by the two roads so often mentioned, into a patch of woods on its western slope, then back over Young's branch and the turnpike into the fields of the Dugan farm, and rearward, in extreme disorder, in all available directions towards Bull Run. The rout had now become general and complete.

About the time that Elzey and Early were entering into action, a column of the enemy, Keyes' brigade of Tyler's division, made its way across the turnpike between Bull Run and the Robinson House, under cover of a wood and brows of the ridges, apparently to turn my right, but was easily repulsed by a few shots from Latham's battery, now under and placed in position by Capt. D. B. Harris, of the Virginia engineers, whose services during the day became his character as an able, cool, and skilful officer, and from Albumis' battery, opportunely ordered by Gen. Jackson to a position to the rear of Latham, on a hill commanding the line of approach of the enemy, and supported by portions of regiments collected together by the staff officers of Gen. Johnston and myself.

Early's brigade, meanwhile, joined by the 19th Virginia regiment, Lieut.-col. Strange, of Cocke's brigade, pursued the now panic-stricken, fugitive enemy. Stuart, with his cavalry, and Beckham had also taken up the pursuit along the road by which the enemy had come upon the field that morning; but, soon encumbered by prisoners, who thronged his way, the former was unable to attack the mass of thefast fleeing, frantic Federalists. Withers', R. J. Preston's, Cash's, and Kershaw's regiments, Hampton's legion and Kemper's battery, also pursued along the Warrenton road by the Stone Bridge, the enemy having opportunely opened a way for them through the heavy abatis which my troops had made on the west side of the bridge several days before; but this pursuit was soon recalled, in consequence of a false report which unfortunately reached us, that the enemy's reserves, known to be fresh and of considerable strength, were threatening the position of Union Mills Ford.

Col. Radford, with six companies Virginia cavalry, was ordered by Gen. Johnston to cross Bull Run and attack the enemy from the direction of Lewis' House. Conducted by one of my aids, Col. Chisholm, by the Lewis road, to the immediate vicinity of the Suspension Bridge, he charged a battery with great gallantry, took Col. Corcoran, of the 69th New York Volunteers, prisoner, and captured the Federal colors of that regiment, as well as a number of the enemy. He lost, however, a prominent officer of his regiment, Capt. Weston Radford.

Lieut.-col Munford also led some companies of cavalry in hot pursuit, and rendered material service in the capture of prisoners and of cannon, horse, ammunition, &c., abandoned by the enemy in their flight.

Capt. Lay's company of the Powhatan troops and Unback's

Rangers, Virginia Volunteers, attached to my person, did material service under Capt. Lay, in rallying troops broken for the time by the onset of the enemy's masses.

During the period of the momentous events, fraught with the weal of the country, which were passing on the blood-stained plateau along the Sudley and Warrenton roads, other portions of the line of Bull Run had not been void of action, of moment, and of influence upon the general result.

While Col. Evans and his sturdy band were holding at bay the Federal advance beyond the turnpike, the enemy made repeated demonstrations, with artillery and infantry, upon the line of Cocke's brigade, with the serious intention of forcing the position, as Gen. Schenck admits in his report. They were driven back with severe loss by Latham's (a section), and Rodgers' four 6-pounders, and were so impressed with the strength of that line as to be held in check and inactive, even after it had been stripped of all its troops but one company of the Nineteenth Virginia regiment, under Capt. Duke, a meritorious officer. And it is worthy of notice that, in this encounter of our 6-pounder guns, handled by our volunteer artillerists, they had worsted such a notorious adversary as the Ayers'—formerly Sherman's—battery, which quit the contest under the illusion that it had weightier metal than its own to contend with.

The centre brigades—Bonham's and Longstreet's—of the line of Bull Run, if not closely engaged, were nevertheless exposed for much of the day to an annoying, almost incessant fire of artillery at long range; but by a steady, veteran-like maintenance of their positions, they held virtually paralyzed, all day, two strong brigades of the enemy, with their batteries (four) of rifle guns.

As before said, two regiments of Bonham's brigade, Second and Eighth South Carolina Volunteers, and Kemper's battery, took a distinguished part in the battle. The remainder, Third (Williams'), Seventh (Bacon's) South Carolina Volunteers, Eleventh (Kirkland's) North Carolina regiment, six companies Eighth Louisiana Volunteers, Shield's battery, and one section of Walton's battery, under Lieut. Garnett, whether in holding their post or taking up the pursuit, officers and men discharged their duty with credit and promise.

Longstreet's brigade, pursuant to orders, prescribing his part of the operations of the centre and right wings, was thrown across Bull Run early in the morning, and, under a severe fire of artillery was skilfully disposed for the assault on the enemy's batteries in that quarter, but was withdrawn subsequently, in consequence of the change of plan already mentioned and explained. The troops of this brigade were—First, Major Skinner; Eleventh, Garland's; Twenty-fourth, Lieut.-col. Hairston's; Seventeenth, Corse's, Virginia regiments; Fifth North Carolina, Lieut.-col Jones; and Whitehead's company of Virginia cavalry. Throughout the day these troops evinced the most soldierly spirit.

After the rout, having been ordered by Gen. Johnston in the direction of Centreville in pursuit, these brigades advanced to near to that place, when night and darkness intervening, Gen. Bonham thought it proper to direct his own brigade and that of Gen. Longstreet back to Bull Run.

Gen. D. B. Jones early in the day crossed Bull Run with his brigade, pursuant to orders indicating his part in the projected attack by our right wing and centre on the enemy at Centreville, took up a position on the Union Mills and Centreville road, more than a mile in advance of the run. Ordered back in consequence of the miscarriage of the orders to Gen. Ewell, the retrograde movement was necessarily made under a sharp fire of artillery.

At noon this brigade, in obedience to new instructions, was again thrown across Bull Run to make demonstrations. Unsupported by other troops, the advance was gallantly made until within musket range of the enemy's force—Col. Davis' brigade in position near Rocky Run, and under the concentrated fire of their artillery. In this affair the Fifth, Jenkins' South Carolina, and Capt. Fontaine's company, of the Eighteenth Mississippi regiment, are mentioned by Gen. Jones as having shown conspicuous gallantry, coolness, and discipline under a combined fire of infantry and artillery.

Not only did the return fire of the brigade drive to cover the enemy's infantry, but the movement unquestionably spread through the enemy's ranks a sense of insecurity and danger from an attack by that route on their rear at Centreville, which served to augment the extraordinary panic which we know disbanded the entire Federal arms for the time. This is evident from the fact that Col. Davies, the immediate adversary's commander, in his official report, was induced to magnify one small company of our cavalry which accompanied the brigade, into a force of two thousand men; and Col. Miles, the commander of the Federal reserves at Centreville, says the movement "caused painful apprehensions for the left wing" of the army.

Gen. Ewell, occupying for the time the right of the lines of Bull Run at Union Mills Ford, after the miscarriage of my orders for his advance upon Centreville, in the afternoon was ordered by Gen. Johnston to bring up his brigade into battle, then raging on the left flank. Promptly executed as this movement was, the brigade, after a severe march, reached the field too late to share the glories, as they had the labors, of the day. As the important position at the Union Mills had been left but with a slender guard, Gen. Ewell was at once ordered to retrace his steps and resume his position, to prevent the possibility of its seizure by any force of the enemy in that quarter.

Brig.-gen. Holmes, left with his brigade as a support to the same position in the original plan of battle, had also been called to the left, whither he marched with the utmost speed, but not in time to join actively in the battle.

Walker's rifle guns of the brigade, however, came up in time to be fired with precision and decided execution at the retreating enemy, and Scott's cavalry, joining in the pursuit, assisted in the capture of prisoners and war munitions.

This victory, the details of which I have thus sought to chronicle as fully as were fitting an official report, it remains to record, was dearly won by the death of many officers and men of inestimable value, belonging to all grades of our society.

In the death of Gen. Bernard E. Bee the Confederacy has sustained an irreparable loss, for with great personal bravery and coolness he possessed the qualities of an accomplished soldier and an able, reliable commander.

Cols. Bartow and Fisher, and Lieut.-col. Johnson, of Hampton's legion, in the fearless command of their men, gave earnest of great usefulness to the service had they been spared to complete a career so brilliantly begun. Besides the field-officers already mentioned as having been wounded while in the gallant discharge of their duties, many others also received severe wounds after equally honorable and distinguished conduct, whether in leading their men forward, or in rallying them when overpowered or temporarily shattered by the largely superior force to which we were generally opposed.

The subordinate grades were likewise abundantly conspicuous for zeal and capacity for the leadership of men in arms. To mention all who, fighting well, paid the lavish forfeiture of their lives, or at least crippled, mutilated bodies on the field of Manassas, cannot well be done within the compass of this paper; but a grateful country and mourning friends will not suffer their names and services to be forgotten and pass away unhonored.

Nor are those officers and men who were so fortunate as to escape the thick-flying deadly missiles of the enemy, less worthy of praise for their endurance, firmness, and valor, than their brothers in arms, whose lives were closed or bodies maimed on that memorable day. To mention all who exhibited ability and brilliant courage were impossible in this report; nor do the reports of brigade and other subordinate commanders supply full lists of all actually deserving of distinction. I can only mention those whose conduct came immediately under my notice, or the consequence of whose actions happened to be signally important.

It is fit that I should in this way commend to notice the dauntless conduct and imperturbable coolness of Col. Evans; and well indeed was he supported by Col. Sloan and the officers of the Fourth South Carolina regiment, as also Major Wheat, than whom no one displayed more brilliant courage until carried from the field, shot through the lungs, though happily not mortally stricken. But in the desperate, unequal contest, to which those brave gentlemen were for a time necessarily exposed, the behavior of officers and men generally was worthy of the highest admiration, and assuredly hereafter all those present may proudly say, "We were of that band who fought the first hour of the battle of Manassas." Equal honor and credit must also be awarded in the pages of history to the gallant officers and men who, under Bee and Bartow, subsequently marching to their side, saved them from destruction, and relieved them from the brunt of the enemy's attack.

The conduct of Gen. Jackson also requires mention, as eminently that of an able and fearless soldier and sagacious commander, one fit to lead his brigade; his efficient, prompt, timely arrival before the plateau of the Henry House, and his judicious disposition of his troops contributed much to the success of the day. Although painfully wounded in the hand, he remained on the field to the end of the battle, rendering invaluable assistance. Col. William Smith was as efficient as self-possessed and brave; the influence of his example and his words of encouragement was not confined to his immediate command, the good conduct of which is especially noticeable, inasmuch as it had been embodied but a day or two before the battle.

Cols. Harper, Hunter, and Hampton, commanding regiments of the reserve, attracted my notice by their soldierly ability, as with their gallant commands they restored the fortunes of the day, at a time when the enemy, by a last desperate onset, with heavy odds, had driven our forces from the fiercely contested ground around the Henry and Johnson houses. Veterans could not have behaved better than these well-led regiments.

High praise must also be given to Cols. Cocke, Early, and Rizey, brigade commanders; also to Col. Kershaw, commanding for the time the Second and Eighth South Carolina regiments. Under the instructions of Gen. Johnston, these officers reached the field at an opportune critical moment, and disposed, handled, and fought their respective commands with sagacity, decision, and successful results, which have been described in detail.

Col. J. E. H. Stuart likewise deserves mention for his enterprise and ability as a cavalry commander. Through his judicious reconnoissance of the country on our left flank he acquired information, both of topographical features and the positions of the enemy, of the utmost importance in the subsequent and closing movements of the day on that flank, and his services in the pursuit were highly effective.

Capt. E. P. Alexander, C. S. Engineers, gave me seasonable and material assistance early in the day with his system of signals. Almost the first shot fired by the enemy passed through the tent of his party at the Stone Bridge, where they subsequently maintained their position in the discharge of their duty—the transmission of messages of the enemy's movements—for several hours under fire. Later, Capt. Alexander acted as my aid-de-camp in the transmission of orders and in observation of the enemy.

I was most efficiently served throughout the day by my volunteer aids, Cols. Preston, Manning, Chesnut, Miles, Rice, Heyward, and Chisholm, to whom I tender my thanks for their unflagging, intelligent, and fearless discharge of the laborious, responsible duties intrusted to them. To Lieut. S. W. Ferguson, A. D. C., and Col. Heyward, who were habitually at my side from twelve noon until the close of the battle, my special acknowledgments are due. The horse of the former was killed under him by the same shell that wounded the latter. Both were eminently useful to me, and were distinguished for coolness and courage, until the enemy gave way and fled in wild disorder in every direction, a scene the President of the Confederacy had the satisfaction of witnessing, as he arrived upon the field at that exultant moment.

I also received, from the time I reached the front, such signal service from H. E. Peyton, at the time a private in the Loudon cavalry, that I have called him to my personal staff. Similar services were also rendered me repeatedly during the battle by T. J. Randolph, a volunteer acting aid-de-camp to Col. Cocke.

Capt. Clinton H. Smith, of the general staff, was also present on the field, and rendered efficient service in the transmission of orders.

It must be permitted me here to record my profound sense of my obligations to Gen. Johnston, for his generous permission to carry out my plans, with such modifications as circumstances had required. From his services on the field—as we entered it together—already mentioned, and his subsequent watchful management of the reinforcements as they reached the vicinity of the field, our countrymen may draw the most auspicious auguries.

To Col. Thomas Jordan, my efficient and zealous Assistant Adjutant-general, much credit is due for his able assistance in the organization of the forces under my command, and for the intelligence and promptness with which he has discharged all the laborious and important duties of his office.

Valuable assistance was given to me by Major Cabell, chief officer of the quarter-master's department, in the sphere of his duties—duties environed by far more than the ordinary difficulties and embarrassments attending the operations of a long organized regular establishment.

Col. B. B. Lee, Chief of Subsistence Department, had but just entered upon his duties, but his experience, and long and varied services in his department, made him as efficient as possible.

Capt. W. H. Fowle, whom Col. Lee had relieved, had previously exerted himself to the utmost to carry out orders from these headquarters, to render his department equal to the demands of the service; that it was not entirely so, it is due to justice to say, was certainly not his fault.

Deprived by the sudden severe illness of the medical director, Surgeon Thomas H. Williams, his duties were discharged by Surgeon R. L. Brodie, to my entire satisfaction, and it is proper to say that the entire medical corps of the army, at present embracing gentlemen of distinction in the profession, who had quit lucrative private practice, by their services in the field and subsequently, did honor to their profession.

The vital duties of the ordnance department were effectively discharged under the administration of my Chief of Artillery and Ordnance, Col. S. Jones.

At one time, when reports of evil omen and disaster reached Camp Pickens, with such circumstantiality as to give reasonable grounds of anxiety, its commander, Col. Torrett, the commander of the intrenched batteries, Capt. Sterritt, of the Confederate States Navy, and their officers, made the most efficient possible preparations for the desperate defence of that position in extremity; and in this connection I regret my inability to mention the names of those patriotic gentlemen of Virginia, by the gratuitous labor of whose slaves the intrenched camp at Manassas had been mainly constructed, relieving the troops from that laborious service, and giving opportunity for their military instruction.

Lieut.-col. Thomas H. Williamson, the engineer of these works, assisted by Capt. D. B. Harris, discharged his duties with untiring energy and devotion, as well as satisfactory skill.

Capt. W. H. Stevens, Engineer Confederate Army, served with the advanced forces at Fairfax Court-house for some time before the battle; he laid out the works there in admirable accordance with the purposes for which they were designed, and yet so as to admit of ultimate extension and adaptation to more serious uses as means and part of a system of real defence when determined upon. He has shown himself to be an officer of energy and ability.

Major Thomas G. Rhett, after having discharged for several months the laborious duties of Adjutant-general to the commanding officer of Camp Pickens, was detached to join the army of the Shenandoah, just on the eve of the advance of the enemy; but, volunteering his services, was ordered to assist on the staff of Gen. Bonham, joining that officer at Centreville on the night of the 17th, before the battle of Bull Run, where he rendered valuable services, until the arrival of Gen. Johnston, on the 20th of July, when he was called to the place of Chief of Staff of that officer.

It is also proper to acknowledge the signal services rendered by Col. B. F. Terry and T. Lubbock, of Texas, who had attached themselves to the staff of Gen. Longstreet. These gentlemen made daring and valuable reconnoissances of the enemy's positions, assisted by Capts. Goree and Chichester. They also carried orders to the field, and on the following day, accompanying Capt. Whitehead's troops to take possession of Fairfax Court-house, Col. Terry, with his unerring rifle, severed the halliards, and thus lowered the Federal flag found still floating from the cupola of the court-house there. He also secured a large Federal garrison flag, designed, it is said, to be unfurled over our intrenchments at Manassas.

In connection with the unfortunate casualties of the day—that is, the miscarriage of the orders sent by courier to Gens. Holmes and Ewell to attack the enemy in flank and reverse at Centreville, through which the triumph of our arms was prevented from being still more decisive—I regard it in place to say, a divisional organization, with officers in command of divisions, with appropriate ranks, as in European services, would greatly reduce the risk of such mishaps, and would advantageously simplify the communications of a general in command of a field with his troops.

While glorious for our people, and of crushing effect upon the *morale* of our hitherto confident and overweening adversary, as were the events of the battle of Manassas, the field was only won by stout fighting, and, as before stated, with much loss, as is precisely exhibited in the papers herewith, marked F, G, and H, and being lists of the killed and wounded. The killed outright numbered 269, the wounded 1483—making an aggregate of 1852.

The actual loss of the enemy will never be known; it may now only be conjectured. Their abandoned dead, as they were buried by our people where they fell, unfortunately were not enumerated; but many parts of the field were thick with their corpses, as but few battle-fields have ever been. The official reports of the enemy are studiously silent on this point, but still afford us data for an approximate estimate. Left almost in the dark in respect to the losses of Hunter's and Heintzelman's divisions—first, longest, and most hotly engaged—we are informed that Sherman's brigade—Tyler's division—suffered in killed, wounded, and missing, 609—that is, about eighteen per cent. of the brigade. A regiment of Franklin's brigade—Gorman's—lost twenty-one per cent. Griffin's (battery) loss was thirty per cent., and that of Keyes' brigade, which was so handled by its commander as to be exposed only to occasional volleys from our troops, was at least ten per cent.

To these facts, and the repeated references in the reports of the more reticent commanders to the "murderous" fire to which they were habitually exposed—the "pistol range" volleys and galling musketry, of which they speak as scourging their ranks, and we are warranted in placing the entire loss of the Federalists at over forty-five hundred in killed, wounded, and prisoners. To this may be legitimately added, as a casualty of the battle, the thousands of fugitives from the field, who have never rejoined their regiments, and who are as much lost to the enemy's service as if slain or disabled by wounds. These may not be included under the head or "missing," because, in every instance of such report, we took as many prisoners of those brigades or regiments as are reported "missing."

A list appended exhibits some 1,400 of their wounded and others who fell into our hands and were sent to Richmond. Some were sent to other points, so that the number of prisoners, including wounded who did not die, may be set down at not less than 1,600

Besides these, a considerable number who could not be removed from the field died at several farm-houses and field hospitals, within ten days following the battle.

To serve the future historian of this war, I will note the fact that among the captured Federalists are officers and men of forty-seven regiments of volunteers, besides from some nine different regiments of regular troops, detachments of which were engaged. From their official reports we learn of a regiment of volunteers engaged, six regiments of Miles' division, and the five regiments of Runyon's brigade, from which we have neither sound or wounded prisoners.

Making all allowances for mistakes, we are warranted in saying that the Federal army consisted of at least fifty-five regiments of volunteers, eight companies of regular infantry, four of marines, nine of regular cavalry, and twelve batteries, one hundred and nineteen guns. These regiments at one time, as will appear from a published list appended, marked "K," numbered in the aggregate 54,140, and average 964 each; from an order of the enemy's commander, however, dated July 13th, we learn that 100 men from each regiment were ordered to remain in charge of respective camps—some allowance must further be made for the sick and details, which would reduce the average to eight hundred—adding the regular cavalry, infantry, and artillery present, an estimate of their force may be made.

A paper appended, marked "L," exhibits, in part, the ordnance and supplies captured, including some twenty-eight field-pieces of the best character of arm, with over one hundred rounds of ammunition for each gun, thirty-seven caissons, six forges, four battery wagons, sixty-four artillery horses, completely equipped, five hundred thousand rounds of small-arms ammunition, four thousand five hundred sets of accoutrements, over five hundred muskets, some nine regimental and garrison flags, with a large number of pistols, knapsacks, swords, canteens, blankets, a large store of axes and intrenching tools, wagons, ambulances, horses, camp and garrison equipage, hospital stores, and some subsistence.

Added to these results may rightly be noticed here, that by this battle an invading army superbly equipped, within twenty miles of their base of operations, has been converted into one virtually besieged, and exclusively occupied for months in the construction of a stupendous series of fortifications for the protection of its own capital.

I beg to call attention to the reports of the several subordinate commanders, for reference to the signal parts played by individuals of their respective commands. Contradictory statements, found in these reports, should not excite surprise, when we remember how difficult, if not impossible, it is to reconcile the narrations of bystanders or participants in even the most inconsiderable affair, much less the shifting, thrilling scenes of a battle-field.

Accompanying are maps showing the positions of the armies on the morning of the 21st July, and of three several stages of the battle; also, of the line of Bull Run north of Blackburn's Ford. These maps, from actual surveys made by Capt. D. B. Harrison, assisted by Mr. John Grant, were drawn by the latter with a rare delicacy worthy of high commendation.

In conclusion, it is proper, and, doubtless, expected, that through this report my countrymen should be made acquainted with some of the sufficient causes that prevented the advance of our forces and a prolonged, vigorous pursuit of the enemy to and beyond the Potomac. The War Department has been fully advised long since of all those causes, some of which only are proper to be here communicated. An army which had fought like ours on that day against uncommon odds, under a July sun, most of the time without water and without food, except a hastily-snatched meal at dawn, was not in condition for the toil of an eager, effective pursuit of an enemy immediately after the battle.

On the following day an unusually heavy and unintermitting fall of rain intervened to obstruct our advance with reasonable prospect of fruitful results. Added to this, the want of a cavalry force of sufficient numbers, made an efficient pursuit a military impossibility.

Your obedient servant,

P. G. T. BEAUREGARD,

General Commanding.

To Gen. S. Cooper, Adjutant and Inspector-general, Richmond, Va.

R. H. Chilton,

Adjutant.

EVACUATION OF PENSACOLA NAVY-YARD. FORTS, &c.

BRIGADIER-GENERAL S. M. JONES, COMMANDING.

MOBILE, January 24th, 1862.

SIR: In accordance with your instructions, I have the honor respectfully to tender the following report of my evacuation of the forts, navy-yard, and position at and near Pensacola, Fla.

On being placed in command of that place by Brig.-gen. Samuel Jones, on the 9th of March last, his instructions were to move, as fast as my transportation would allow, the machinery and other valuable property from the navy-yard

This was kept up steadily until the night of the evacuation. On receiving information that the enemy's gunboats had succeeded in passing the forts below New Orleans, with their powerful batteries and splendid equipments, I came to the conclusion, that with my limited means of defence, reduced as I had been, by the withdrawal of nearly all my heavy guns and ammunition, that I could not hold them in check, or make even a respectable show of resistance. I, therefore, determined, upon my own judgment, to commence immediately the removal of the balance of my heavy guns and their ammunition, and dispatched to you for your approval, which was answered by one, advising me to continue doing so. On receipt of Gen. Lee's written instructions on the subject, I pushed on the work with renewed vigor, and night and day kept up the removal of guns and valuable property.

On the afternoon of the 7th instant, I received a dispatch from your Adjutant-general, stating that there were a number of mortar and gun boats off Fort Morgan, and that the fort had fired ten shots at them. Conceiving that the contingency, named in Gen. Lee's instructions, had arrived, viz.: to bring all my available force to this point in the event of an attack, I concluded to promptly leave my position. I, therefore, sent to Montgomery a regiment of unarmed troops. On the next day I ordered the 8th Mississippi regiment, Lieut.-col. Yates, commanding, to proceed at once to this place and report to you, and on the 9th I prepared my plans for generally evacuating.

On the night of the 8th, three companies of cavalry arrived from Montgomery. With these and two companies I already had, I determined to destroy the public property, etc., which I had not been able to remove, and which might prove of benefit to the enemy. As the few troops were so disposed that any reduction in the daytime would attract the notice of the enemy, I merely withdrew the camp and garrison equipage, and sick, in accordance with an order from Gen. Lee to "keep the army mobilized." On the morning of the 9th, all the work of removing sick and baggage having been completed, I published orders that my forces should present themselves to the best advantage to the enemy, and as soon as it was dark they were quietly marched out from their camps and started on the road to Oakfield. Sentinels were posted as usual on the beach, and they were withdrawn one hour after the other troops had left. All these instructions were obeyed to the letter, and much to the credit of the comparatively raw troops under my command. When my infantry were well on the road and out of range of the enemy's guns, the cavalry were assigned their places to commence the necessary destruction, at a signal previously agreed upon, to be given from the cupola of the hospital, and one answering at the navy-yard, Barrancas, and Fort McRae. Precisely at 11 1-2 o'clock, when every thing was perfectly quiet, both on the enemy's side and ours, the most painful duty it ever fell to my lot to perform was accomplished, namely: the signalizing for the destruction of the beautiful place which I had labored so hard night and day for over two months to defend, and which I had fondly hoped could be held from the polluting grasp of our insatiate enemies.

The two blue lights set off by Col. Tattnall and myself at the hospital were promptly answered by similar signals from the other points designated, and scarcely had the signals disappeared ere the public buildings, camp tents, and every other combustible thing from the navy-yard to Fort McRae, was enveloped in a sheet of flames, and in a few moments the flames of the public property could be distinctly seen at Pensacola. The custom-house and commissary storehouses were not destroyed, for fear of endangering private property, a thing I scrupulously avoided. As soon as the enemy could possibly man their guns and load them, they opened upon us with the greatest fury, and seemed to increase his charges as his anger increased. But in spite of the bursting shell, which were thrown with great rapidity, and in every direction, the cavalry proceeded with the greatest coolness to make the work of destruction thorough and complete, and see that all orders were implicitly obeyed. Their orders were to destroy all the camp tents; Forts McRae and Barrancas, as far as possible; the hospital, the houses in the navy-yard, the steamer Fulton, the coal left in the yard; all the machinery for drawing out ships, the trays, shears, in fact every thing which could be made useful to the enemy. The large piles of coal were filled with wood and other combustibles, and loaded shell put all through it, so that when once on fire the enemy would not dare to attempt to extinguish it. Loaded shell were also placed in the houses for the same purpose, and the few small smooth-bore guns, I was compelled to leave, were double-shotted, wedged, and spiked, and carriages chassie burned. The shears in the navy-yard were cut half in two, and the spars and masts of the Fulton were cut to pieces. By the most unremitting labor, I succeeded with my little force and limited transportation in saving all the heavy guns, and nearly all the small-size guns. I took away all the flanking howitzers from Barrancas and the redoubt. In removing the large columbiads from the batteries, which were in full view of the enemy's, I was compelled to resort to Gen. Johnston's plan of replacing them with wooden imitations as they were removed. All the powder and most of the large shot and shell were removed; the small-size shot were buried. I succeeded in getting away all the most valuable machinery, besides large quantities of copper, lead, brass, and iron. Even the gutters, lightning rods, window weights, bells, pipes, and every thing made of these valuable metals were removed, also cordage, blocks, cables, chain-cables, and a large number of very valuable articles of this character, which I cannot here enumerate. All the quarter-master and commissary stores, except such as were not worth the transportation, were sent away. As soon as this was completed, I set hands to work taking up the railroad iron at Pensacola, and others to reeling up the telegraph wires under the protection of a strong guard of cavalry, infantry, and one piece of light artillery.

Having received orders not to destroy any private property, I only destroyed at Pensacola a large oil factory, containing a considerable quantity of rosin, the quarter-master's storehouses, and some small boats, and three small steamers, used as guard-boats and transports. The steamers Mary and Helen were the only private property of their kind burned. The steamboat "Turel," which we had been using as a transport, was sent up the Escambia river, she being of very light draft, well loaded with stores, machinery, etc., with orders to cut down trees, and place every obstruction possible, in the river, behind her. She has arrived safely at a point I deem beyond the enemy's reach, and she has been unloaded of her freight. The casemates and galleys of Fort McRae were filled with old lumber, and many loaded with shell and fired. The galleries and implement rooms, at Barrancas, were similarly dealt with, and the destruction at both places was as complete as it could be without the use of gunpowder; this I did not deem it necessary or proper to use for this purpose. The enemy's furious cannonade only served to make the havoc more complete. There was no damage done by it to man or horse. When it is remembered that all this work has been done by a mere handful of raw troops, with but few arms, and many of them without any arms at all, and this, too, in the very face of a formidable force, I deem it but simple justice to my men to say, that the conduct of each and all of them was worthy of the highest praise. It not unfrequently happened that after standing guard all night, they cheerfully labored all the next day and night. I have not room to make distinctions where all did so well, but I feel constrained to make particular mention of Capt. J. H. Nelson, of the 27th Mississippi regiment, who commanded at Fort McRae, the most exposed and dangerous point; Major Kilpatrick, who commanded at the navy-yard, and Lieut.-col. Conoly, who commanded at Pensacola. These gentlemen deserve the greatest credit for their zeal and watchfulness, in the management of their respective stations. I feel that I am also authorized in saying of the 27th, under Capt. Hays, that during the frequent and terrible alarms, so unavoidable with new troops, it was always cool and ready for serious work. The unwearied exertions, both night and day, of my personal staff officers have received my personal thanks, and I feel called upon to remark that they deserve great credit, as they were so zealous and unremitting in their exertions to assist me in carrying out my orders and of serving the country, that I frequently had to insist on their taking rest for fear that they would completely wear themselves down. On the completion of my work, I proceeded to rejoin my army at Oakfield, six miles north of Pensacola on the railroad, leaving five companies of cavalry in command of Capt. J. T. Myers, an efficient and daring officer, to watch the enemy's movements.

The next morning I proceeded, with the 27th Mississippi regiment, to Mobile, leaving Lieut.-col. Conoly with the 29th Alabama regiment; and Lieut.-col. Tullen, with five companies of Florida volunteers, two of which companies were armed, to guard the railroad, whilst the iron was being removed. I regret to acknowledge the receipt of a telegraphic dispatch from the Hon. Secretary of

War, dated subsequent to my evacuation, directing me not to burn the houses in the navy-yard. I received one from him the day before the evacuation, directing me to spare all private dwellings not useful to the enemy for war purposes, which was done. The first-named dispatch reached me after my arrival in the city.

I am, sir, very respectfully,
Your obedient servant,
THOS. M. JONES,
Acting Brig.-gen. C. S. A.

To Brig.-gen. JOHN H. FORNEY,
Commanding Dep't Ala. and W. Fla.

HEAD-QUARTERS DEP'T ALA. AND W. FLA.,
May 23d, 1862.

I have the honor to transmit, with my approval, the accompanying report of Brig.-gen. T. M. Jones of the evacuation of Pensacola.

I am, sir, very respectfully,
Your obedient servant,
JNO. H. FORNEY,
Brig.-gen. Commanding.

To GEN. S. COOPER, *Adj't and Insp't'r-general, Richmond.*

BOMBARDMENT OF FORT HENRY.

BRIGADIER-GENERAL TILGHMAN, COMMANDING.

RICHMOND, VA., Aug. 9th, 1862.

J. COOPER, *Adjutant and Inspector-general, C. S. A.:*

General:—Inclosed, you will please find a copy of my official report of the bombardment of Fort Henry, on February 6th, 1862, by the Federal fleet, together with accompanying papers.

The original of this report was forwarded from Alton, Illinois, but not having reached your office, I have prepared a copy of the same at the earliest moment practicable, since my release from Fort Warren, Massachusetts.

I remain, respectfully,
Your obedient servant,
LLOYD TILGHMAN,
Brigadier-general C. S. A., Commanding.

Report of Brigadier-general Tilghman on the Bombardment of Fort Henry.

FEBRUARY 12th, 1862.

COL. W. W. MACKALL,
A. A. General, C. S. Army, Bowling Green:

SIR:—My communication of the 7th inst., sent from Fort Henry, having announced the fact of the surrender of that fort to Commodore Foote, of the Federal navy, on the 6th inst., I have now the honor to submit the following report of the details of the action, together with the accompanying papers, marked (A) (B), containing list of officers and men surrendered, together with casualties, &c.

On Monday, February 3d (instant), in company with Major Gilmer, of the engineers, I completed the inspection of the main work, as well as outworks at Fort Heiman, south of Tennessee river, as far as I had been able to perfect them, and also, the main work, intrenched camp, and exterior line of rifle-pits at Fort Henry. At 10 o'clock, A. M., on that morning, the pickets on both sides of Tennessee river, extended well in our front, having reported no appearance of the enemy, I left, in company with Major Gilmer, for Fort Donelson, for the purpose of inspecting, with him, the defences of that place.

Tuesday, the 4th inst., was spent in making a thorough examination of all the defences at Fort Donelson. At noon, heard heavy firing at Fort Henry for half-an-hour. At 4 o'clock, P. M., a courier reached me from Col. Heiman, at Fort Henry, informing me that the enemy were landing in strong force at Bailey's Ferry, three miles below, and on the east bank of the river.

Delaying no longer than was necessary to give all proper orders for the arrangement of matters at Fort Donelson, I left with an escort of Tennessee cavalry, under command of Lieut.-col. Gantt, for Fort Henry, accompanied by Major Gilmer—reaching that place at 11 and a half, P. M. I soon became satisfied that the enemy were really in strong force at Bailey's Ferry, with every indication of reinforcements arriving constantly. Col. Heiman of the 10th Tennessee, commanding with most commendable alacrity and good judgment, had thrown forward, to the outworks covering the Dover road, two pieces of light artillery, supported by a detachment from the 4th Mississippi regiment, under command of Capt. Red. Scouting parties of cavalry, operating on both sides of the river, had been pushed for ward to within a very short distance of the enemy's lines. Without a moment's delay, after reaching the fort, I proceeded to arrange the available force to meet whatever contingency might arise.

The First brigade, under Col. Heiman, was composed of the 10th Tennessee, Lieut.-col. McGavock commanding; 27th Alabama, under Col. Hughes; the 48th Tennessee, under Col. Voorhies; light battery of four pieces, commanded by Capt. Culbertson, and the Tennessee battalion of cavalry, under Lieut.-col. Gantt. Total, officers and men, 1444. The Second brigade, Col. Joseph Drake, 4th Mississippi regiment, commanding, was composed of the 4th Mississippi, under Major Adair; the 15th Arkansas, Col. Gee; the 51st Tennessee, Col. Browder; Alabama battalion, Maj. Garvin; light battery of three pieces, under Capt. Clare, and the Alabama battalion of cavalry, Capt. Milners' company of cavalry, with Capt. Padgett's spy company, a detachment of Rangers, under acting Captain Melton. Total, officers and men, 1215. The heavy artillery, under command of Capt. Taylor, numbering 75, were placed at the guns in Fort Henry. As indicated, some time since, to the general commanding department, I found it impossible to hold the commanding ground, south of the Tennessee river, with the small force of badly armed men at my command, and, notwithstanding the fact, that all my defences were commanded by the high ground on which I had commenced the construction of Fort Heiman, I deemed it proper to trust to the fact that the extremely bad roads leading to that point would prevent the movement of heavy guns by the enemy, by which I might be annoyed; and leaving the Alabama battalion of cavalry and Capt. Padgett's spy company on the western bank of the river, transferred the force encamped on that side to the opposite bank. At the time of receiving the first intimation of the approach of the enemy, the 48th and 51st Tennessee regiments having only just reported, were encamped at Danville, and at the mouth of Sandy, and had to be moved from five to twenty miles, in order to reach Fort

Henry. This movement, together with the transfer of the 27th Alabama and 15th Arkansas regiments from Fort Heiman across the river, was all perfected by 5 o'clock, A. M., on the morning of the 5th. Early on the morning of the 5th the enemy was plainly to be seen at Bailey Ferry, three miles below. The large number of heavy transports reported by our scouts gave evidence of the fact that the enemy were there in force, even at that time, and the arrival every hour of additional boats showed conclusively that I should be engaged with a heavy force by land, whilst the presence of seven gunboats, mounting fifty-four guns, indicated plainly that a joint attack was contemplated by land and water.

On leaving Fort Donelson, I ordered Col. Head to hold his own and Col. Suggs' regiment of Tennessee Volunteers, with two pieces of artillery, ready to move at a moment's warning, with three days' cooked rations, and without camp equipage or wagon train of any kind, except enough to carry the surplus ammunition. On the morning of the 5th I ordered him, in case nothing more had been heard from the country below, on the Cumberland, at the time of the arrival of my messenger, indicating an intention on the part of the enemy to invest Fort Donelson, to move out with the two regiments, and the two pieces of artillery, and take position at the Furnace, half way on the Dover road to Fort Henry,—the force embraced in this order was about seven hundred and fifty men,—to act as circumstances might dictate. Thus matters stood at 9 A. M. on the morning of the 5th.

The wretched military position of Fort Henry, and the small force at my disposal, did not permit me to avail myself of the advantages to be derived from the system of outworks, built with the hope of being reinforced in time, and compelled me to determine to concentrate my efforts by land, within the rifle-pits surrounding the 10th Tennessee and 4th Mississippi regiments, in case I deemed it possible to do more than to operate solely against the attack by the river. Accordingly, my entire command was paraded and placed in the rifle-pits around the above camps, and minute instructions given, not only to brigades, but to regiments and companies, as to the exact ground each was to occupy. Seconded by the able assistance of Major Gilmer, of the engineers, of whose valuable services I thus early take pleasure in speaking, and by Cols. Heiman and Drake, every thing was arranged to make a formidable resistance against any thing like fair odds. It was known to me, on the day before, that the enemy had reconnoitred the roads leading to Fort Donelson, from Bailey's Ferry, by way of Iron Mountain Furnace, and at

10 o'clock, A. M., on the 5th, I sent forward from Fort Henry a strong reconnoitring party of cavalry. They had not advanced more than one-and-a-half miles in the direction of the enemy when they encountered their reconnoitring party. Our cavalry charged them in gallant style, upon which the enemy's cavalry fell back, with a loss of only one man on each side.

Very soon the main body of the Federal advance-guard, composed of a regiment of infantry and a large force of cavalry, was met, upon which our cavalry retreated. On receipt of this news, I moved out in person with five companies of the 10th Tennessee, five companies of the 4th Mississippi, and fifty cavalry, ordering at the same time two additional companies of infantry to support Capt. Red at the outworks. Upon advancing well to the front I found that the enemy had retired. I returned to camp at 5 P. M., leaving Capt. Red reinforced at the outworks. The enemy were again reinforced by the arrival of a large number of transports. At night the pickets from the west bank reported the landing of troops on that side, opposite Bailey's Ferry, their advance pickets having been met one-and-a-half miles from the river. I at once ordered Capt. Hubbard, of the Alabama cavalry, to take fifty men, and, if possible, surprise them. The inclemency of the weather, the rain having commenced to fall in torrents, prevented any thing being accomplished. Early on the morning of the 6th, Capt. Padgett reported the arrival of five additional transports over night, and the landing of a large force on the west bank of the river, at the point indicated above. From that time up to nine o'clock it appeared as though the force on the east bank was again reinforced, which was subsequently proven to be true. The movements of the fleet of gunboats at an early hour prevented any communication, except by a light barge, with the western bank, and by 10 o'clock, A. M., it was plain that the boats intended to engage the fort with their entire forces, aided by an attack on our right and left flanks from the two land forces in overwhelming numbers. To understand properly the difficulties of my position it is right that I should explain fully the unfortunate location of Fort Henry, in reference to resistance by a small force against an attack by land co-operating with the gunboats, as well as its disadvantages in even an engagement with boats alone. The entire fort, together with the intrenched camp spoken of, is enfiladed from three or four points on the opposite shore, whilst three points on the eastern bank completely command them both, all at easy cannon range. At the same time the intrenched camp, arranged as it was in the best possible manner to meet the case, was two-thirds of it completely under the control of the fire of the gunboats. *The history of military engineering records no parallel to this case.* Points within a few miles of it, possessing great advantages and few disadvantages, were totally neglected, and a location fixed upon, without one redeeming feature, or filling one of the many requirements of a site for a work such as Fort Henry. The work itself was well built; it was completed long before I took command, but strengthened greatly by myself in building embrasures and epaulements of sand-bags. An enemy had but to use their most common sense in obtaining the advantage of high water, as was the case, to have complete and entire control of the position. I am guilty of no act of injustice in this frank avowal of the opinions entertained by myself, as well as by all other officers who have become familiar with the location of Fort Henry. Nor do I desire the defects of location to have an undue influence in directing public opinion in relation to the battle of the 6th instant. The fort was built when I took charge, and I had no time to build anew. With this seeming digression, rendered necessary as I believe to a correct understanding of the whole affair, I will proceed with the details of the subsequent movements of the troops under my command. By 10 o'clock, A. M., on the 6th, the movements of the gunboats and land force indicated an immediate engagement, and in such force as gave me no room to change my previously conceived opinions as to what, under such circumstances, should be my course.

The case stood thus: I had at my command a grand total of 2610 men, only one-third of whom had been at all disciplined or well armed. The high water in the river filling the sloughs, gave me but one route on which to retire, if necessary, and that route for some distance, in direction, at right angles to the line of approach of the enemy, and over roads well nigh impassable for artillery, cavalry, or infantry.

The enemy had seven gunboats, with an armament of fifty-four guns, to engage the *eleven* guns at Fort Henry.

Gen. Grant was moving up the east bank of the river from his landing three miles below with a force of twelve thousand men, verified afterwards by his own statement; whilst Gen. Smith, with six thousand men, was moving up the west bank to take a position within four or five hundred yards, which would enable him to enfilade my entire works. The hopes (founded on a knowledge of the fact, that the enemy had reconnoitred on the two previous days thoroughly the several roads leading to Fort Donelson) that a portion only of the land force would co-operate with the gunboats in an attack on the fort, were dispelled, and but little time left me to meet this change in the circumstances which surrounded me. I argued thus: Fort Donelson might possibly be held, *if properly reinforced*, even though Fort Henry should fall, but the *reverse* of this proposition was not true. The force at Fort Henry was necessary to aid Fort Donelson, either in making a successful defence, or in holding it long enough to answer the purposes of a new disposition of the entire army from Bowling Green to Columbus, which would necessarily follow the breaking of our centre, resting on Forts Donelson and Henry. The latter alternative was all that I deemed possible. I knew that reinforcements were difficult to be had, and that unless sent in such force as to make the defence *certain*, which I did not believe practicable, the fate of our right wing at Bowling Green depended upon a concentration of my entire division on Fort Donelson, and the holding of that place as long as possible, trusting that the delay by an action at Fort Henry, would give time for such reinforcement as might reasonably be expected to reach a point sufficiently near Donelson to co-operate with my division by getting to the rear and right flank of the enemy, and in such a position as to control the roads, over which a safe retreat might be effected. I hesitated not a moment. My infantry, artillery, and cavalry, removed of necessity, to avoid the fire of the gunboats, to the outworks, could not meet the enemy there. My only chance was to delay the enemy every moment possible, and retire the command, now outside the main work, towards Fort Donelson, resolving to suffer as little loss as possible. I retained only the heavy artillery company to fight the guns, and gave the order to commence the movement at once. At 10 1-4 o'clock, Lieut. McGavock sent a messenger to me, stating that our pickets reported Gen. Grant approaching rapidly, and within half a mile of the advance work, and movements on the west bank indicated that Gen. Smith was fast approaching also.

The enemy, ignorant of any movement of my main body, but knowing that they could not engage them behind our intrenched camp, until after the fort was reduced, or the gunboats retired, without being themselves exposed to the fire of the latter, took a position north of the forks of the Dover road in a dense wood (my order being to retreat by way of Stewart road), to await the result. At 11 A. M., the flotilla assumed their line of battle. I had no hope of being able successfully to defend the fort against such overwhelming odds, both in point of numbers and in calibre of guns. My object was to save the main body by delaying matters as long as possible, and to this end I bent every effort. At 11.45 A. M., the enemy opened from their gunboats on the fort. I waited a few moments until the effects of the first shots of the enemy were fully appreciated. I then gave the order to return the fire, which was gallantly responded to by the brave little band under my command. The enemy with great deliberation, steadily closed upon the fort, firing very wild until within twelve hundred yards. The cool deliberation of our men told from the first shot fired with tremendous effect. At twenty-five minutes of 1 o clock, P. M., the bursting of our 24-pounder rifle gun disabled every man at the piece.

This great loss was to us in a degree made up by our disabling entirely the Essex gunboat, which immediately floated down stream. Immediately after the loss of this valuable gun, we sustained another loss still greater, in the closing up of the vent of the 10-inch columbiad, rendering that gun perfectly useless, and defying all efforts to reopen it.

The fire on both sides was now perfectly terrific. The enemy's entire force was engaged, doing us but little harm, whilst our shot fell with unerring certainty upon them, and with stunning effect. At this time, a question presented itself to me, with no inconsiderable degree of embarrassment. The moment had arrived when I should join the main body of troops retiring towards Fort Donelson, the safety of which depended upon a protracted defence of the fort. It was equally plain, that the gallant men working the batteries (for the first time under fire), with all their heroism, needed my presence. Col. Heiman, the next in command, had returned to the fort for instructions. The men working the heavy guns were becoming exhausted with the rapid firing. Another gun became useless by an accident, and yet another by the explosion of a shell immediately after striking the muzzle, involving the death of two men and disabling several others. The effect of my absence, at such a critical moment, would have been disastrous. At the earnest solicitations of many of my officers and men, I determined to remain, and ordered Col. Heiman to join his command and keep up the retreat in good order, whilst I would fight the guns as long as one was left, and sacrifice myself to save the main body of my troops. No sooner was this decision made known, than new energy was infused. The enemy closed upon the fort to within six hundred yards, improving very much in their fire, which now began to tell with great effect upon the parapets, whilst the fire from our guns (now reduced to seven) was returned with such deliberation and judgment that we scarcely missed a shot. A second one of the gunboats retired, but I believe was brought into action again. At 1 o'clock 10 minutes, so completely broken down were the men, that but for the fact that *four* only of our guns were then really serviceable—I could not well have worked a greater number. The fire was still continued with great energy and tremendous effect upon the enemy's boats. At 1.30 o'clock, I took charge of one of the 32-pounders to relieve the chief of that piece, who had worked it with great effect from the beginning of the action. I gave the flagship Cincinnati two shots, which had the effect to check a movement intended to enfilade the only gun now left me.

It was now plain to be seen that the enemy were breaching the fort directly in front of our guns, and that I could not much longer sustain their fire without an unjustifiable exposure of the valuable lives of the men who had so nobly seconded me in the unequal struggle. Several of my officers, Major Gilmer among the number, now suggested to me the propriety of taking the subject of a surrender into consideration.

Every moment, I knew, was of vast importance to those retreating on Fort Donelson, and I declined, hoping to find men enough at hand to continue awhile longer the fire now so destructive to the enemy. In this I was disappointed. My next effort was to try the experiment of a flag of truce, which I waved from the parapets myself. This was precisely at 10 minutes before 2 o'clock, P. M. The flag was not noticed, I presume, from the dense smoke that enveloped it, and leaping again into the fort, I continued the fire for five minutes, when, with the advice of my brother officers, I ordered the flag to be lowered, after an engagement of two hours and ten minutes with such an unequal force.

The surrender was made to Flag-officer Foote, represented by Capt. Stemble, commanding gunboat Cincinnati, and was qualified by the single condition that all officers should retain their side arms, that both officers and men should be treated with the highest consideration due prisoners of war, which was promptly and gracefully acceded to by Com. Foote.

The retreat of the main body was effected in good order, though involving the loss of about twenty prisoners, who from sickness and other causes, were unable to encounter the heavy roads. The rear of the army was overtaken at a distance of some three miles from Fort Henry by a body of the enemy's cavalry, but on being engaged by a small body of our men, under Major Garving, were repulsed and retired. This fact alone shows the necessity of the policy pursued by me in protracting the defence of the fort as long as possible—which only could have been done by my consenting to stand by the brave little band. No loss was sustained by our troops in this affair with the enemy. I have understood from the prisoners, that several pieces of artillery also were lost, it being entirely impossible to move them over four or five miles with the indifferent teams attached to them.

The entire absence of transportation rendered any attempt to move the camp equipage of the regiments impossible. This may be regarded as fortunate, as the roads were utterly impassable, not only from the rains, but the backwater of the Tennessee river.

A small amount of quarter-master's and commissary stores, together with what was left of the ordnance stores, were lost to us; also the tents of the Alabama regiment were left on the west bank of the river, the gunboats preventing an opportunity to cross them over. Our casualties may be reported strictly as follows: killed by the enemy, two; wounded severely by the enemy, three (one since dead); wounded slightly by the enemy, two; killed by premature explosion, two; wounded seriously by premature explosion, one; slightly wounded, one; temporarily disabled by explosion of rifle gun, five; making total killed, five; seriously wounded, three; slightly wounded, three; disabled, five; missing, five; total casualties, twenty-one. The total casualties of the enemy were stated, in my presence on the following morning, to be seventy-three, including one officer of Essex killed, and Capt. Porter, commanding Essex, badly scalded.

The enemy report the number of shot that struck their vessels to have been seventy-four, twenty-eight of which struck the flag-ship Cincinnati, so disabling her as to compel her to return to Cairo. The Essex received twenty-two shots, one of which passed, we know, entirely through the ship, opening one of her boilers and taking off the head of Capt. Porter's aid-de-camp. Several shots passed entirely through the Cincinnati, whilst her underworks were completely riddled.

The weak points in all their vessels were known to us, and the cool precision of our firing developed them, showing conclusively that this class of boats, though formidable, cannot stand the test of even the thirty-two pounders, much less the twenty-four calibre rifle shot, or that of the ten-inch columbiad. It should be remembered that these results were principally from no heavier metal than the ordinary thirty-two pounders using solid shot, fired at point blank, giving vessels all the advantages of its peculiar structure, with planes meeting this fire at angles of forty-five degrees. The immense area forming what may be called the roof is in every respect vulnerable to either a plunging fire from even thirty-two pounders or a curved line of fire from heavy guns. In the latter case shells should be used in preference to shot.

Confident of having performed my whole duty to my Government in the defence of Fort Henry, with the totally inadequate means at my disposal, I have but little to add in support of the views before expressed. The reasons for the line of policy pursued by me, are, to my mind, convincing.

Against such overwhelming odds as sixteen thousand well-armed men (exclusive of the force on the gunboats), to two thousand six hundred and ten badly armed in the field, and fifty-four heavy guns against eleven medium ones, in the fort, no tactics or bravery could avail. The rapid movements of the enemy, with every facility at their command, rendered the defence, from the beginning, a hopeless one. I succeeded in doing even more than was to be hoped for at first. I not only saved my entire command, outside the fort, but damaged, materially, the flotilla of the enemy, demonstrating thoroughly a problem of infinite value to us in the future. Had I been reinforced so as to have justified my meeting the enemy at the advanced works, I might have made good the land defence on the east bank. I make no inquiry as to why I was not, for I have entire confidence in the judgment of my commanding general.

The elements even were against us, and had the enemy delayed his attack a few days, with the river rising, one-third of the entire fortification (already affected by it) would have been washed away, whilst the remaining portion of the works would have been untenable by reason of the depth of water over the whole interior portion.

The number of officers surrendered (see paper marked A) was twelve. The number of non-commissioned officers and privates in the fort at the time of the surrender (see paper marked B) was sixty-six, whilst the number in hospital boat (Patton) was (see paper marked C) sixteen.

I take great pleasure in making honorable mention of all the officers and men under my command. To Capt. Taylor of the artillery, and the officers of his corps, Lieuts. Watts and Weller; to Capt. G R. G. Jones, in command of the right battery; to Capts. Miller and Hayden of the engineers; to A. A. A. General McCornico; to Capt. H. L. Jones, Brigade Quarter-master; to Capt. McLaughlin, Quarter-master 10th Tennessee, and to Surgeons Voorhies and Horton, of the 10th Tennessee, the thanks of the whole country are due for their consummate devotion to our high and holy cause. To Sergeants John Jones, Hallum, Cubine, and Selkirk; to Corporals Capass, Cavin, and Kenfro, in charge of guns, as well as to all the men, I feel a large debt is due for their bravery and efficiency, in working the heavy guns so long and so efficiently. Officers and men alike seemed actuated by one spirit, that of devotion to a cause in which was involved "life, liberty, and the pursuit of happiness." Every blow struck was aimed by cool heads, supported by strong arms and honest hearts. I feel that it is a duty I owe to Col. A. Heiman, commanding 10th Tennessee regiment, to give this testimony of my high appreciation of him as a soldier and as a man, due to his gallant regiment, both officers and men. I place them second to no regiment I have seen in the army.

To Capt. Dixon of the engineers, I owe, as does the whole country, my special acknowledgments of his ability and unceasing energies. Under his immediate eye, were all the works proposed by myself at Forts Donelson and Heiman executed, whilst his fruitfulness in resources to meet the many disadvantages of position, alone enabled us to combat its difficulties successfully.

To Lieut. Watts, of the heavy artillery, as acting ordnance officer at Fort Henry, I owe this special notice of the admirable condition of the Ordnance Department at that post. Lieut. Watts is the coolest officer under fire I ever met with.

I take pleasure in acknowledging the marked courtesy and consideration of Flag-officer Foote of the Federal navy, of Capt. Stemble and the other naval officers to myself, officers, and men. Their gallant bearing during the action, gave evidence of a brave, and, therefore, generous foe.

Respectfully, your obedient servant,

(Signed,) LLOYD TILGHMAN,

Brig.-gen. commanding.

(Official,) ED. A. PALFRED,

A. A. General.

A. & I. G. OFFICE, August 29, 1862.

Supplement to the Report of Gen. Tilghman.

RICHMOND, Aug. 9th, 1862.

My attention having been called, since writing the above report, to certain statements made in the somewhat unofficial reports of the battles at Fort Donelson, on the subject of the *condition* of the fortifications at that place, at the time of the arrival of the reinforcements, I deem it highly proper to protect my own, as well as the reputation of the officers and men of my command, and place the facts of the case on record.

Nearly broken down by incessant work from the middle of June, in organizing and perfecting the first Kentucky brigade, and in remodelling the brigade at Hopkinsville, Ky., I was not in the best condition, so late as the *15th of December*, to commence in a new field of operations, and work into perfect shape a *third* brigade, and carry on the system of fortifications on both the Cumberland and Tennessee, necessary for the important line intrusted to my care. The facts of the case are simply these: On reaching Fort Donelson, the middle of December, I found at my disposal, six undisciplined companies of infantry, with an unorganized light battery. Whilst a small water battery of two light guns constituted the available river defence. Four 32-pounders had been rightly placed, but were not available. By the 25th of January, I had prepared the entire batteries (except one piece which arrived too late) for the river defences, built the entire field work with a trace of 2900 feet, and in the most substantial manner, constructed a large amount of abatis, and commenced guarding the approaches by rifle-pits and abatis. This was all done when the reinforcements arrived, and when the total lack of transportation is taken into consideration, as well as the inclemency of the season, and yet find not only the original troops there, but nearly all my reinforcements housed in something like four hundred good cabins, I conceive my time to have been well spent. Whilst this was being done, the strengthening of Fort Henry, the building of all the outworks around it, together with the advanced state of the new works south of Tennessee river,—Fort Heiman, together with its line of rifle-pits and abatis, was all *thoroughly* performed, and satisfy my own mind that officers and men could not have fallen short in their duties to have accomplished so much. The failure of adequate support, doubtless from sufficient cause, cast me on my own resources, and compelled me to assume responsibilities which may have worked a *partial evil*. I aimed at the *general good*, and am the last man to shrink from assuming what is most likely to accomplish such an end. I would further state that I had connected both Forts Henry and Donelson by a line of telegraph from Cumberland City, total length of the line about thirty-five miles, thus placing me in close relations with Bowling Green and Columbus.

(A)

LIST OF COMMISSIONED OFFICERS SURRENDERED AT FORT HENRY, FEBRUARY 6, 1862.

Brigadier-general Lloyd Tilghman, commanding.
Captain H. L. Jones, Quarter-master's Department.
Captain John McLaughlin, Quarter-master's Department.
Captain Joseph A. Miller, Engineer Department.
Captain J. A. Haydon, " "
Captain G. R. G. Jones, Heavy Artillery.
A. A. A. General W. L. McCornico.
Captain Jesse Taylor, Artillery.
Lieutenant W. O. Watts, "
Lieutenant F. J. Weller, "
Surgeon A. H. Voorhies, Medical Department.
Assistant-surgeon W. D. Horton, Medical Department.

(B)

LIST OF NON-COMMISSIONED OFFICERS AND PRIVATES, SURRENDERED AT FORT HENRY, FEBRUARY 6, 1862.

1st Sergeant John Jones, Sergeant H. C. Hallum, Sergeant W. J. B. Cubine, Sergeant W. H. Selkirk.

Corporal N. Capass, wounded; Corporal S. W. Greenleaf.

Privates—Ed. Drake, J. B. White, Thos. Buckingham, Patrick Stout, C. C. Brooks, C. C. Whitford, John Elliott, O. P. Saltsgiver, Alex. Joyce, Thomas Moran, Michael Dassey, L. A. Garvin, A. G. Gibson, S. D. Johnson, John Hardin, Wm. Daniels, William Carter, Thomas Philips, James Campbell, D. H. Hatin, James McHugh, W. H. Rutherford, L. C. Thomason, John Wyall, E. F. Lyle, M. M. Bailey, M. V. Ray, S. R. Myers, B. Sharp, H. Carter, W. J. Miles, C. C. Jones, S. G. Casey, James Mosley, G. W. Cattrell, H. C. Pesk, Fred. Waller, O. F. Wickerson, J. C. Hickey, John Long, R. Garner, T. M. Menitt, J. T. Marshall, J. W. Marshall.

THE BATTLE OF FORT DONELSON.

BRIG.-GEN. FLOYD, COMMANDING.

CAMP, NEAR MURFREESBORO', February 27th, 1862.

GEN. A. S. JOHNSTON:

SIR:—Your order of the 12th of this month, transmitted to me from Bowling Green by telegraph to Cumberland City, reached me the same evening. It directed me to repair at once, with what force I could command, to the support of the garrison at Fort Donelson. I immediately prepared for my departure, and effected it in time to reach Fort Donelson the next morning, 13th, before daylight. Measures had been already taken by Brig.-gen. Pillow, then in command, to render our resistance to the attack of the enemy as effectual as possible. He had, with activity and industry, pushed forward the defensive works towards completion. These defences consisted of an earth-work in Fort Donelson, in which were mounted guns of different calibres to the number of thirteen. A field work, intended for the infantry support, was constructed immediately behind the battery, and upon the summit of the hill in rear. Sweeping away from this field work eastward, to the extent of nearly two miles in its windings, was a line of intrenchments, defended on the outside at some points with abatis. These intrenchments were occupied by the troops already there, and by the addition of those which came upon the field with me. The position of the fort, which was established by the Tennessee authorities, was by no means commanding, nor was the least military significance attached to the position. The intrenchments, afterwards hastily made, in many places were injudiciously constructed, because of the distance they were placed from the brow of the hill, subjecting the men to a heavy fire from the enemy's sharpshooters opposite, as they advanced to or retired from the intrenchments. Soon after my arrival, the intrenchments were fully occupied from one end to the other, and just as the sun rose, the cannonade, from one of the enemy's gunboats, announced the opening of the conflict, which was destined to continue for three days and nights. In a very short time the fire became general along our whole lines, and the enemy, who had already planted batteries at several points around the whole circuit of our intrenchments, as shown by a diagram herewith sent, opened a general and active fire from all arms upon our trenches, which continued until darkness put an end to the conflict. They charged with uncommon spirit at several points along on the line, but most particularly at a point undefended by intrenchments, down a hollow, which separated the right wing, under the command of Brig.-gen. Buckner, from the right of the centre, commanded by Col. Heiman. This charge was prosecuted with uncommon vigor, but was met with a determined spirit of resistance, a cool, deliberate courage, both by the troops of Brig.-gen. Buckner and Col. Heiman, which drove the enemy discomfited, and cut to pieces, back upon the position he had assumed in the morning. Too high praise cannot be bestowed upon the battery of Capt. Porter, for their participation in the rout of the enemy in this assault. My position was immediately in front of the point of attack, and I was thus enabled to witness more distinctly the incidents of it. The enemy continued their fire upon different parts of our intrenchments throughout the night, which deprived our men of any opportunity to sleep. We lay that night upon our arms in the trenches. We confidently expected at the dawn of day a more vigorous attack than ever, but in this we were entirely mistaken. The day advanced, and no preparation seemed to be making for a general onset, but an extremely annoying fire was kept up from the enemy's sharpshooters, throughout the whole length of the intrenchments, from their long range rifles. Whilst this mode of attack was not attended with any considerable loss, it nevertheless confined the men to their trenches, and prevented them from taking their usual rest. So stood the affairs of the field until about 3 o'clock P. M., when the fleet of gunboats, in full force, advanced upon the fort, and opened fire. They advanced in the shape of a crescent, and kept up a constant and incessant fire for one hour and a half, which was replied to with uncommon vigor and spirit by the fort. Once the boats reached a point within a few hundred yards of the fort, at which time it was that three of their boats sustained serious injuries from our batteries, and were compelled to fall back. The line was broken, and the enemy discomfited on the water, giving up the fight entirely, which he soon afterwards renewed. I was satisfied, from the incidents of the last two days, that the enemy did not intend again to give us battle in our trenches. They had been fairly repulsed, with very heavy slaughter, upon every effort to storm our position, and it was but fair to infer that they would not again renew the unavailing attempt at our dislodgement, when certain means to effect the same end without loss were perfectly at their command.

We were aware of the fact, that extremely heavy reinforcements had been continually arriving day and night, for three days and nights, and I had no doubt whatever that their whole available force on the western waters could and would be concentrated here, if it was deemed necessary, to reduce our position. I had already seen the impossibility of holding out for any length of time, with our inadequate number and indefensible position. There was no place within our intrenchments but could be reached by the enemy's artillery from their boats or their batteries. It was but fair to infer, that whilst they kept up a sufficient fire upon our intrenchments to keep our men from sleep and prevent repose, their object was merely to give time to pass a column above us on the river, both on the right and left banks, and thus to cut off all our communication, and to prevent the possibility of egress.

I thus saw clearly that but one course was left, by which a rational hope could be entertained of saving the garrison, or a part of it—that was, to dislodge the enemy from the position on our left, and thus to pass our people into the open country lying southward towards Nashville. I called for a consultation of the officers of divisions and brigades, to take place after dark, when this plan was laid before them, approved, and adopted; and at which time it was determined to move from the trenches at an early hour, on the next morning, and attack the enemy in his position. It was agreed that the attack should commence upon our extreme left, and this duty was assigned to Brig.-gen. Pillow, assisted by Brig.-gen. Johnson, having also under his command, commanders of brigades—Col. Baldwin commanding Mississippi and Tennessee troops, and Col. Wharton and Col. McCausland commanding Virginians. To Brig.-gen. Buckner was assigned the duty of making the attack from near the centre of our lines upon the enemy's forces upon the Wynn's ferry road. The attack on the left was delayed longer than I expected, and consequently the enemy was found in position when our troops advanced. The attack, however, on our part, was extremely spirited, and although the resistance of the enemy was obstinate, and their numbers far exceeded ours, our people succeeded in driving them discomfited and terribly cut to pieces from the entire left. The Kentucky troops under Brig.-gen. Buckner advanced from their position behind the intrenchments up the Wynn's ferry road, but not until the enemy had been driven, in a great measure, from the position he occupied in the morning. I had ordered, on the night before, that the two regiments stationed in Fort Donelson should occupy the trenches vacated by Brig.-gen. Buckner's forces, which, together with the men whom he detached to assist in this purpose, I thought sufficient to hold them. My intention was to hold, with Brig.-gen. Buckner's command, the Wynn's ferry road, and thus to prevent the enemy, during the night, from occupying the position on our left, which he occupied in the morning. I gave him orders upon the field to that effect. Leaving him in position then, I started for the right of our command, to see that all was secure there, my intention being, if things could be held in the condition they then were, to move the whole army, if possible, to the open country, lying southward, beyond the Randolph forge. During my absence, and from some misapprehension, I presume, of the previous order given, Brig.-gen. Pillow ordered Brig.-gen. Buckner to leave his position on the Wynn's ferry road, and to secure his place in his trenches on the right. This movement was nearly executed before I was aware of it. As the enemy were pressing upon the trenches, I deemed that the execution of this last order was all that was left to be done. The enemy, in fact, succeeded in occupying one angle of the trenches on the extreme right of Brig.-gen. Buckner's command, and as the fresh forces of the enemy had begun already to move towards our left, to occupy the position they held in the morning, and as we had no force adequate to oppose their progress, we had to submit to the mortification of seeing the ground which we had won, by such a severe conflict in the morning, reoccupied by the enemy before midnight.

The enemy had been landing reinforcements throughout the day. His numbers had been augmented to eighty-three regiments. Our troops were completely exhausted by four days and nights of continued conflict. To renew it with any hope of successful result was obviously vain, and such I understood to be the unanimous opinion of all the officers present at the council, called to consider what was best to be done. I thought, and so announced, that a desperate onset upon the right of the enemy's forces, on the ground where we had attacked them in the morning, might result in the extricating of a considerable proportion of the command from the position we were in, and this opinion I understood to be concurred in by all who were present; but it was likewise agreed, with the same unanimity, that it would result in the slaughter of nearly all who did not succeed in effecting their escape. The question then arose, whether in point of humanity and a sound military policy, a course should be adopted from which the probabilities were that the larger proportion of the command would be cut to pieces in an unavailing fight against overwhelming numbers. I understood the general sentiment to be adverse to the proposition. I felt that in this contingency, whilst it might be questioned whether I should, as commander of the army, lead it to certain destruction in an unavailing fight, yet, I had a right individually to determine that I would not survive a surrender there. To satisfy both propositions, I agreed to hand over the command to Brig.-gen. Buckner, through Brig.-gen. Pillow, and to make an effort for my own extrication by any and every means that might present themselves to me. I, therefore, directed Col. Forrest, a daring and determined officer, at the head of an efficient regiment of cavalry, to be present for the purpose of accompanying me in what I supposed would be an effort to pass through the enemy's lines. I announced the fact, upon turning the command over to Brig.-gen. Buckner, that I would bring away with me, by any means I could command, my own particular brigade, the propriety of which was acquiesced in on all hands. This, by various modes I succeeded in accomplishing to a great extent, and would have brought off my whole command, in one way or another, if I had had the assistance of the field officers, who were absent from several of the regiments. The command was turned over to Brig.-gen. Buckner, who at once opened negotiations with the enemy, which resulted in the surrender of the place. Thus ended the conflict, running through *four days and four nights;* a large portion of which time it was maintained with the greatest fierceness and obstinacy; in which we, with a force not exceeding 13,000, a large portion of whom were illy armed, succeeded in resisting and driving back with discomfiture, an army consisting of more than 50,000 men. I have no means of accurately estimating the loss of the enemy. From what I saw upon the *battle-field*, from what I witnessed throughout the whole period of the conflict, from what I was able to learn from sources of information, deemed by me worthy of credit, I have no doubt that the enemy's loss in killed and wounded, reached a number beyond 5000 (five thousand). Our own losses were extremely heavy, but for want of exact returns, I am unable to state precise numbers. I think they will not be far from fifteen hundred, killed and wounded. Nothing could exceed the coolness and determined spirit of resistance which animated the men in this long and perilous conflict; nothing could exceed the determined courage which characterized them throughout this struggle, and nothing could be more admirable than the steadiness which they exhibited until nature itself was exhausted, in what they knew to be a desperate fight against a foe very many times their superior in numbers. I cannot particularize in this report to you, the numberless instances of heroic daring, performed by both officers and men, but must content myself for the present, by saying, in my judgment, they all deserve well of the country.

I have the honor to be,
Very respectfully,
Your obedient servant,
JOHN B. FLOYD,
Brig.-gen. commanding.

Supplemental Report of Brigadier-general Floyd.

KNOXVILLE, TENNESSEE, March 20, 1862.

H. P. BREWSTER, A. A. General:

SIR: Your communication of the 16th instant, from Decatur, reached me here to-day, where I came in compliance with an order from Major-gen. Smith, who felt his position endangered from the advance of the enemy.

In that communication you say: "Under date of March the 11th, the Secretary of War says: 'The reports of Gens. Floyd and Pillow are unsatisfactory, and the President directs that both these generals be relieved from command till further orders.' He further directs Gen. Johnston 'in the mean time to request them to add to their reports such statements as they may deem proper on the following points:

'1st. The failure to give timely notice of the insufficiency of the garrison of Fort Donelson to repel attack.

'2d. The failure of any attempt to save the army by evacuating the post when found to be untenable.

'3d. Why they abandoned the command to their inferior officer, instead of executing themselves whatever measure was deemed proper for the entire army.

'4th. What was the precise mode by which each effected his escape from the post, and what dangers were encountered in the retreat.

'5th. Upon what principle a selection was made of particular troops, being certain regiments of the senior general's brigade, to whose use all the transportation on hand was appropriated.

'6th. A particular designation of the regiments saved and the regiments abandoned, which formed part of the senior general's brigade.'

"In obedience to this order, I am directed by Gen. Johnston to request your compliance with the wishes of the President in these particulars, with as little delay as possible, and forward the report to these head-quarters.

"Under the same direction Gen. Johnston has required a report from Col. Forrest, detailing particularly the time and manner of his escape from Fort Donelson, the road he took, the number of enemies he met or saw in making his escape, and the difficulties which existed to prevent the remainder of the army from following the route taken by him in his escape with his command."

I give at once the additional information which seems to be asked for in the communication of the Secretary of War to which you refer.

The first charge is as follows:

"The failure to give timely notice of the insufficiency of the garrison of Fort Donelson to repel attacks."

I presume the general knew, before I was ordered to Fort Donelson, that neither the works nor the troops sent there could withstand the force which he knew the enemy had in hand, and which could be brought speedily to that point. I knew perfectly well that if the whole force under Gen. Johnston's command at Bowling Green had been sent to Fort Donelson, it would prove utterly insufficient to repel the advance of the enemy up the Cumberland river. Gen. Johnston's entire force, including the troops at Donelson, as I understood it, did not exceed thirty thousand (30,000) men. I knew, what I believed everybody else did, for it was made public through the newspapers, that the enemy had in Kentucky alone one hundred and nineteen (119) regiments, and that he had nearly, if not quite, as many at Cairo, St. Louis, and the towns near the mouth of the Cumberland. It was also known that the enemy had unlimited means of transportation for concentrating troops. How then was it possible for Gen. Johnston's whole army to meet that force, which was known to be moving towards the mouths of the Tennessee and Cumberland rivers? The sequel proved that this information was correct, for not only were the troops occupying Kentucky sent up the Cumberland, but large additions were made to them from Missouri and Illinois, as stated by prisoners and by the official reports of their own commanders. I could not, under a sense of duty, call for reinforcements, because the force under Gen. Johnston was not strong enough to afford a sufficient number to hold the place. I considered the place illy chosen, out of position, and entirely indefensible by any reinforcements which could be brought there to its support. It had but thirteen guns, and it turned out that but three of these were effective against iron-clad steamers. I thought the force already there sufficient for sacrifice, as well as enough to hold the place until Bowling Green could be evacuated with its supplies and munitions of war. This I supposed to be the main object of the movement to Donelson, and the only good that could be effected by desperately holding that post with the entirely inadequate means in hand for defence of the Cumberland and Tennessee rivers.

With a less force than fifty thousand (50,000) men, the position at Fort Donelson was, in my judgment, quite untenable, and even with that force it could have been held for only a short time, unless a force of twenty thousand (20,000) men was supporting it at Clarksville, and twenty-five thousand (25,000) more at least had been stationed at Nashville. While these were my own views and opinions, I nevertheless transmitted to Gen. Johnston the exact state of affairs at the fort at every stage of the conflict.

My views and opinions upon the defence of Fort Donelson, and the means of extricating the army from the trap in which necessity had thrown them there, had been set forth in a letter addressed to the general from Clarksville before I received orders to go to Fort Donelson, bearing date 12th of February. I annex a copy of that letter.

CLARKSVILLE, TENN., *Feb.* 12, 1862.

GENERAL JOHNSTON:

SIR:—There is but little known satisfactorily of the enemy or their movements; up to 10 o'clock last night all was quiet as usual at the fort. General Buckner is now there. I have thought the best disposition to make of the troops on this line was to concentrate the main force at Cumberland City—leaving at Fort Donelson enough to make all possible resistance to any attack which may be made *upon the fort*, but no more. The character of the country in the rear and to the left of the fort is such as to make it dangerous to concentrate our whole force there; for, if their gunboats should pass the fort and command the river, our troops would be in danger of being cut off by a force from the Tennessee. In this event, their road would be open to Nashville, without any obstruction whatever. The position at Cumberland City is better; for there the railroad diverges from the river, which would afford some little facility for transportation in case of necessity; and from thence the open country southward towards Nashville is easily reached. Besides, from that point we threaten the flank of any force sent from the Tennessee against the fort. I am making every possible effort to *concentrate* the forces here at Cumberland City. I have been in the greatest dread ever since I reached this place at their scattered condition. The force is inadequate to defend a line of forty miles in length, which can be attacked from three different directions. We can only be formidable by concentration. A strong guard is all that can be left here, and this no longer than your movement can be made. I shall begin to-day, if the engineers report favorably, to blockade the river at the piers of the railroad bridge. I have taken up an idea that a "raft," secured against this bridge, can render the river impassable for the gunboats. If this is possible, it will be an immense relief to the movements above. I am quite sure this blockade can be made at a lower stage of water; but the present stage of water renders this experiment somewhat doubtful, still I will make every exertion to effect the blockade, if possible. I received by telegraph your authority to make any disposition of the troops which in my judgment was best, and acknowledged it by a dispatch immediately. I am acting accordingly.

I am, General, very respectfully,
Your obedient servant,
JOHN B. FLOYD,
Brig-gen. C. S. A.

CHARGE 2D.—"*The failure of any attempt to save the army by evacuating the post when found untenable.*"

I have been unfortunate if I have failed to show in my report of the battle at Fort Donelson that the fight on the 15th of February, outside of our intrenchments, was nothing but an "attempt to save the army by evacuating the fort," which the position and numbers of the enemy had already rendered untenable. In my report of the 27th of February I attempted to explain why we left our intrenchments on the 15th to give battle, and the object I had in view in doing so. I said "I had already seen the impossibility of holding out for any length of time with our inadequate numbers and indefensible position. There was no place in our intrenchments but could be reached by the enemy's artillery from their boats or their batteries. It was but fair to infer that whilst they kept up a sufficient fire upon our intrenchments, to keep our men from sleep and prevent repose, their object was merely to give time to pass a column above us on the river, both on the right and the left banks, and thus to cut off all our communications and to prevent the possibility of egress. I then saw clearly that but one course was left by which a rational hope could be entertained of saving the garrison or a part of it. That was to dislodge the enemy from his position on our left and thus to pass our people into the open country lying southward towards Nashville."

Upon the failure of this enterprise, the causes of which are fully set forth in my report, it obviously became impossible to "save the army by evacuating the post." The "attempt" to save the army had been made. I thought then, and still think, that a more earnest "attempt" could not be made by an equal number of men to accomplish any enterprise by force of arms. To extricate the army, then, involved the necessity of another battle that night, more desperate than that of the morning, because the enemy had been greatly reinforced, and held their former position with fresh troops. There is such a thing as human exhaustion, an end of physical ability in man to march and fight—however little such a contingency may seem possible to those who sleep quietly upon soft beds, who fare sumptuously every day, and have never tried the exposure of protracted battles and hard campaigns. This point had been reached by our men; the conflict, toil, and excitement of unsuspended battle, running through eighty-four hours, was enough to wear out the physical strength of any men; especially so, when the greater part of the time they were exposed to a storm of sleet, snow, and continued frost, and opposed to a force five or six times greater than their own, without shelter or fire. Many of the men had been frost-bitten; and a great many were so overcome by fatigue and want of sleep as to be unable to keep open their eyes, standing on their feet, in the face and under the fire of the enemy.

In fact, the men were totally out of condition to fight. There were but two roads by which it was possible to retire. If they went by the upper road they would certainly have a strong position of the enemy to cut through, besides having to march over the battle-field strewn with corpses; and if they retired by the lower road, they would have to wade through water three feet deep, which latter ordeal the medical director stated would be death to more than half of the command, on account of the severity of the weather and their physical prostration. It was believed in council that the army could not retire without sacrificing three-fourths of it. The consultation which took place among the officers on the night of the 15th was to ascertain whether a further struggle could be maintained, and it was resolved in the negative unconditionally and emphatically. Gen. Buckner, whose immediate command was the largest in the fort, was positive and unequivocal in his opinion that the fight could not be renewed. I confess that I was myself strongly influenced by this opinion of Gen. Buckner; for I have not yet seen an officer in whose superior military ability, clear discriminating judgment, in whose calm unflinching courage and unselfish patriotism I more fully confide than in his. The loss to the Confederacy of so able, brave, and accomplished a soldier is irreparable.

From my own knowledge of the condition of the men, I thought that but few of them were in condition to encounter a night conflict. So the plan of renewing the battle was abandoned; and thus the necessity of surrender was presented. All agreed that the necessity existed. That conclusion having been reached, nothing remained but to consider the manner of it; and that is fully set forth in my former report.

The third charge is, "why they abandoned the command to their inferior officer, instead of executing themselves whatever measure was deemed proper for the entire army."

The "abandonment of command" here imputed, I suppose to mean the act of transferring to Gen. Buckner, who was willing to execute it, the performance of the formalities of surrender. The surrender was a painful and inexorable necessity, which could not be avoided, and not a "measure deemed proper for the entire army." On the contrary, my proposition to take away as large a portion of the forces as possible met, I am sure, with the approbation of the whole council. One of the reasons which induced me to make this transfer to Gen. Buckner was in order that I might be untrammelled in the effort I was determined to make to extricate as many of the command as possible from the fort, to which object I devoted myself during the night of the 15th. So that I accomplished the *fact* of bringing off troops from the position, I thought little of the *manner* of doing so. All possibility of further fighting was over. Not another gun was to be fired; no personal risk was to be incurred; certain and absolute freedom from all personal danger was secured to those who surrendered. Further danger, conflict, and toil could befall those only who should attempt to escape and those I chose to lead.

Nothing was to be done by those who remained but to hoist the white flag and surrender. This I would not do, for the "measure" of surrender had not been thought of by myself or any officer present in the council as one proper for the "entire army." I supposed it to be an unquestionable principle of military action, that in case of disaster it is better to save a part of a command than to lose the whole. The alternative proposition which I adopted in preference to surrendering the "entire army," was to make my way out of the beleaguered camp with such men as were still able to make another struggle, if it could be accomplished; and if it could not be, then to take any consequences that did not involve a surrender.

The fifth charge is, "upon what principle a selection was made of particular troops, being certain regiments of the senior general's brigade, to whose use all the transportation on hand was appropriated."

The answer to this charge leads directly to that of the fourth, and I therefore respond first to this. I presume it is well established that a senior general can select any troops under command for any service or purpose or plan he may choose to execute; and if the means were offered of extricating only a portion of men from a general surrender, I presume the selection of this portion would rest with him rather than with any other person or persons. This would be a sufficient answer to the charge in question, if I chose to rely upon it, which I do not. My real answer I will give fully. It is untrue that "all the transportation on hand was appropriated to certain regiments of the senior general's brigade." It is untrue that a selection was made of "particular troops." I am sure that quite as many men belonging to other brigades were provided with "means of escape," "by the transportation on hand," as were of the senior general's brigade.

Late at night it was ascertained that two steamboats would probably reach the landing before daylight. Then I determined to let Col. Forrest's cavalry proceed on their march by the river road, which was impassable for any thing but cavalry, on account of the backwater and overflow, whilst I would remain behind and endeavor to get away as many men as possible by the boats. The boats came a short time before daylight, when I hastened to the river and began to ferry the men over to the opposite shore as rapidly as possible.

The men were taken on indiscriminately as they came to the boats; but in the first instance more of the "senior general's brigade" were present than of other troops, from this circumstance, namely That when I determined not to surrender, I caused my brigade to be drawn up in line and to await my final preparation for a forward movement. This was promptly done, and as they were nearest the left flank, where the fight would first begin, so likewise were they nearest to the river landing. From this circumstance, it happened that the troops from my immediate command were among the first to enter the boats; but all the men from all portions of the army, who were present and could be gotten on board, were taken indiscriminately as far as I had any knowledge. No man of the army was excluded to make room for my brigade. On the contrary, all who came were taken on board, until some time after daylight, when I received a message from Gen. Buckner that any further delay at the wharf would certainly cause the loss of the boat with all on board. Such was the want of all order and discipline by this time on shore, that a wild rush was made at the boat, which the captain said would swamp her unless he pushed off immediately. This was done, and about sunrise the boat on which I was (the other having gone) left the shore and steered up the river. By this "precise mode" I effected my "escape," and after leaving the wharf, the Department will be pleased to hear, that I encountered no dangers whatever from the enemy.

I had announced in council my determination to take my own brigade and attempt a retreat; and this, I presume, is what is referred to in the charge of "selecting certain regiments of the senior general's brigade." I "selected" this command, because they had been with me in the most trying service for seven months, had been repeatedly under fire, had been exposed to every hardship incident to a campaign, had never on any occasion flinched or faltered, had never uttered a complaint; and I *knew* were to be relied on for any enterprise that could be accomplished. In announcing this intention, it was far from my purpose to exclude any troops who might think proper, or might be physically able, to join me in making the movement.

The sixth charge is, "a particular designation of the regiments saved, and the regiments abandoned, which formed part of the senior general's brigade."

My brigade consisted of the 36th regiment Virginia Volunteers, the 50th regiment Virginia Volunteers, the 51st regiment Virginia Volunteers, the 56th regiment Virginia Volunteers, and the 20th regiment Mississippi Volunteers. No one of these regiments was either wholly saved or wholly left. I could obtain no reports from regiments until I arrived at Murfreesboro'. There our morning reports show the aggregate of each regiment present, respectively, to have been of the 36th regiment Virginia Volunteers, 243; 50th regiment Virginia Volunteers, 285; 51st regiment Virginia Volunteers, 274; 56th regiment Virginia Volunteers, 184: the 20th regiment Mississippi Volunteers handed in no report at Murfreesboro', and what there was of it was ordered away by Gen. Johnston; but I am informed that their morning report will show over three hundred (300) as present. These reports were made before those who had been ferried over the river at Donelson had come up.

A considerable number of men from each of these regiments were "saved," and many of each were left behind. Of my own brigade, a great many who were left effected their escape by every means they could command, and joined their regiments and companies, except the 20th regiment Mississippi Volunteers, which, by Gen. Johnston's order, were detached and sent home to recruit. This regiment, at the last accounts I had of it, immediately after the fight of Fort Donelson, numbered, as already stated, about three hundred (300) men; but I have no accurate information on the subject. The loss I felt most seriously, was that of my three artillery companies of Virginia troops, so remarkable for their efficiency and real gallantry, who had followed me so faithfully throughout my service in Virginia, and who fought so bravely during the whole of the trying conflict at Donelson.

I am, very respectfully,
Your obedient servant,

[Copy.] JOHN B. FLOYD, *Brig.-gen. C. S. A.*
PETER OTEY, *A. A. General.*

Report of Brig.-gen. Pillow.

COLUMBIA, TENNESSEE, February 18, 1862

CAPT. CLARENCE DERRICK,
Assistant Adjutant-general.

On the 9th instant, Gen. A. S. Johnston ordered me to proceed to Fort Donelson and take command of that post. On the 10th instant I arrived at that place. In detailing the operations of the forces under my command at Fort Donelson, it is proper to state the condition of that work, and of the forces constituting the garrison.

When I arrived, I found the work on the river battery unfinished, and wholly too weak to resist the force of heavy artillery. I found a 10-inch columbiad, and a 32-pound rifled gun, which had not been mounted. Deep gloom was hanging over the command, and the troops were greatly depressed and demoralized by the circumstances attending the surrender of Fort Henry, and the manner of retiring from that place. My first attention was given to the necessity of strengthening this work, and mounting the two heavy guns, and the construction of defensive works to protect the rear of the river battery.

I imparted to the work all the energy which it was possible to do, working day and night with the whole command. The battery was without a competent number of artillerists, and those who were there were not well instructed in the use of their guns. To provide for this want, I placed the artillery companies under active course of instruction in the use of their guns. I detailed Capt. Ross, with his company of light artillery, to the command of one of the river batteries. These heavy guns being mounted and provision made for working them, and a proper supply of ammunition having been procured by my orders from Nashville, I felt myself prepared to test the effect of the fire of heavy metal against the enemy's gunboats, though the work stood much in need of more heavy pieces.

The armament of the batteries consisted of eight 32-pounders, three 32-pound carronades, one 8-inch columbiad, and one rifle gun of 32 pounds calibre.

The selection for the site for the work was an unfortunate one. While its command of the river was favorable, the site was commanded by the heights above and below the river, and by a continued range of hills all around the works in its rear. A field work of very contracted dimensions had been constructed for the garrison to protect the battery, but the field works were commanded by the hills already referred to, and lay open to a fire of artillery from every direction except from the hills below. To guard against the effect of fire of artillery from these heights, a line of defensive works, consisting of rifle-pits, and abatis for infantry, detached on our right but continuous on our left, with defences for light artillery, were laid off by Col. Gilmer, engineer of Gen. A. S. Johnston's staff, but on duty with me at the post, around the rear of the battery, and on the heights from which artillery could reach our battery and inner field work, enveloping the inner field work and the town of Dover, where our supplies of commissary and quarter master stores were in depot.

These works, pushed with the utmost possible energy, were not quite complete, nor were my troops all in position, though nearly so, when Brig.-gen. Floyd, my senior officer, reached that station. The works were laid off with great judgment and skill by Major Gilmer, were well executed, and designed for the defence of the rear work—the only objection being to the length of the line, which, however, was unavoidable from the surroundings. The length of the line and the inadequacy of the force for its defence, was a source of embarrassment throughout the struggle which subsequently ensued in defence of the position.

I had placed Brig.-gen. Buckner in command of the right wing, and Gen. B. R. Johnson on the left. By extraordinary efforts we had barely got these works in defensible condition, when the enemy made an advance in force around and against the entire line of outer works.

THE BATTLE OF THE TRENCHES.

The assault was commenced by the enemy's artillery against the centre of our left wing, which was promptly responded to by Capt. Green's battery of field artillery. After several hours of firing between the artillery of the two armies, the enemy's infantry advanced to the conflict, all along the line, which was kept up and increased in violence from one end of the line to the other, for several hours, when, at last, the enemy made a vigorous assault against the right of our left wing—the position assaulted being defended by Col. Heiman's (being a height) brigade, consisted of the 10th Tennessee, under command of Lieut.-col. McGavock, Col. Voorhies', Col. Hughes', and Col. Head's regiments Tennessee Volunteers, and defended by Capt. Maney's field battery.

The assault was vigorously made, and the position vigorously defended, and resulted in the repulse of the enemy here and everywhere around the line. The result of the day's work pretty well tested the strength of our defensive line, and established, beyond question, the gallantry of the entire command, all of which fought gallantly their portion of the line.

The loss sustained by our forces in this engagement was not large, our men being mostly under shelter in the rifle-pits, but we, nevertheless, had quite a number of killed and wounded, but owing to the continued fighting that followed, it was impossible to get any official account of the casualties of the day.

On the same day our battery on the river was engaged with one of the enemy's gunboats, which occasioned quite a lively cannonading for more than an hour, in which the gallant Capt. Dixon, of the engineer corps, was killed instantly at the battery. This officer had been on duty for some time (*months*) at the post, and had shown great energy and professional skill, and, by his gallant bearing on that day, while directing the operations of the day under my orders, had justly earned for himself high distinction. His death was a serious loss to the service, and was a source of no little embarrassment to our operations.

On the 12th we had quiet, but we saw the smoke of a large number of gunboats and steamboats a short distance below; we also received reliable information of the arrival of a large number of new troops, greatly increasing the strength of the enemy's forces, already said to be from 20,000 to 30,000 strong.

BATTLE WITH THE GUNBOATS.

On the 13th, these reinforcements were seen advancing in their position, in the line of investment, and while this was being done, six of the enemy's iron-cased gunboats were seen advancing up the river, five of which were abreast in line of battle, the sixth some distance in the rear. When these gunboats arrived within a mile and a half of our battery, they opened fire on the battery. My orders to the officers, Capt. Shuster and Capt. Standewitz, who commanded the lower battery of light guns, and Capt. Ross, who commanded the lower battery of four guns, were to hold their fire until the enemy's gunboats came within point-blank range of their guns. This they did, though the ordeal of holding their fire, while the enemy's shot and shell fell thick around their position, was a severe restraint to their patriotic impulses; but, nevertheless, our batteries made no response until the enemy's gunboats got within range of their guns. Our entire line of batteries then opened fire. The guns of both were well served. The enemy constantly advancing, delivering direct fire against our batteries from his line of five gunboats, while the sixth boat, moving up in rear of the line, kept the air filled with shells, which fell thick and close around the position of our batteries. The fight continued, the enemy steadily advancing slowly up the river, the shot and shell from 15 heavy rifled guns tearing our parapets and plunging deep in the earth around and over our batteries for nearly two hours, and until his boats had reached within the distance of 150 yards of our batteries.

Having come in such close conflict, I could see distinctly the effect of our shot upon his iron-cased boats. We had given one or two well-directed shots from the heavy guns to one of his boats, when he instantly shrunk back, and drifted helpless below the line. Several shots struck another boat, tearing her iron case, splintering her timbers, and making them crack as if by a stroke of lightning, when she, too, fell back.

Then a third received several severe shocks, making her metal ring and her timbers crack, when the whole line gave way, and fell rapidly back from our fire until they passed out of range. Thus ended the first severe and close conflict of our guns—our heavy guns—with the enemy's gunboats, testing their strength, and the power of our heavy guns to resist them.

The shot from our 32-pounder guns produced but little effect; they struck and rebounded, apparently doing little damage. But I am satisfied, by close observation, that the timbers of the frame-work did not and could not withstand the shock of the 10-inch columbiad or 32-pounder rifled guns. These gunboats never renewed the attack.

I learned from citizens living on the river below, that one of the injured gunboats sunk, and that others had to be towed to Cairo. This information may, or may not, be true, but it is certain that all of the boats were repulsed and driven back, after a most vigorous and determined attack, and that two of the boats were badly damaged, and a third more or less injured.

It is difficult to over-estimate the gallant bearing and heroic conduct of the officers and men of our batteries, who so well and so persistently fought the guns, until the enemy's determined advance brought gunboats and guns into such close and desperate conflict.

Where all did their duty so well, it is impossible to discriminate. The captains already named, and their lieutenants (whose names, for want of official reports, I cannot give), all deserve the highest commendation.

Lieut. George S. Martin, whose company is at Columbus, Ky., but who was ordered to that post by Major-gen. Polk, commanded one of the guns, and particularly attracted my attention by his energy, and the judgment with which he fought his gun.

The wadding of his gun having given out, he pulled off his coat and rammed it down his gun as wadding, and thus kept up the fire until the enemy were finally repulsed.

On the evening of this day, we received information of the arrival of additional reinforcements of infantry, cavalry, and light artillery, by steamboat, all of which were disembarked a short distance below our position.

BATTLE OF DOVER.

On the 14th instant, the enemy were busy throwing his forces of every arm around us, extending his line of investment entirely around our position, and completely enveloping us. On the evening of this day, we ascertained that the enemy had received additional reinforcements. We were now surrounded by an immense force, said, by prisoners whom we had taken, to amount to 52 regiments, and every road and means of possible departure cut off, with the certainty that our sources of supply, by river, would soon be cut off by the enemy's batteries, placed upon the river above us.

At a meeting of general officers, called by Gen. Floyd, it was determined unanimously to give the enemy battle next day, at daylight, so as to cut open a route of exit for the troops to the interior of the country, and thus save our army. We had knowledge that the principal portion of the enemy's forces were massed in encampments in front of the extreme left of our position, commanding the two roads leading to the interior, one of which we must take in retiring from our position. We knew he had massed in encampment another large force on the Wynn's ferry road, opposite the centre of our left wing, while still another was massed nearly in front of the right of our left wing. His fresh arrivals of troops being encamped on the banks of the river two and a half miles below us, from which latter encampment a stream of fresh troops were constantly pouring around us, on his line of investment, and strengthening his several encampments on the extreme right. In each of his encampments, and in each road, he had in position a battery of field artillery and 24-pounder iron guns on siege carriages.

Between these encampments on the road was a thick undergrowth of bush and black jack, making it impossible to advance or manœuvre any considerable body of troops. The plan of attack agreed upon, and directed by Gen. Floyd to be executed, was, that with the main body of the forces defending our left wing I should attack the right wing of the enemy, occupying and resting on the heights reaching to the banks of the river, accompanied by Col. Forrest's brigade of cavalry.

That Gen. Buckner, with the forces under his command, and defending the right of our line, should strike the enemy's encampments and forces on the Wynn's ferry road. That the forces under Col. Heiman should hold his position, and that each command should leave in the trenches troops to hold the trenches. By this order of battle, it was easy to be seen, that if my attack was successful, and the enemy was routed, his retreat would be along his line of investments, towards the Wynn's ferry encampment, and thence towards his reserve at the gunboats below.

In other words, my success would roll the enemy's force in full retreat over upon Gen. Buckner, when, by his attack in flank and rear, we could cut up the enemy and put him completely to rout.

Accordingly, dispositions were made to attack the enemy. At 5 o'clock on the morning of the 15th, I moved out of my position, to engage the enemy. In less than half an hour, our forces were engaged. The enemy was prepared to receive me in advance of his encampment, and he did receive me before I had assumed a line of battle, and while I was moving against them, without any formation for the engagement. For the first half hour of the engagement, I was much embarrassed in getting the command in a position properly to engage the enemy. Having extricated myself from the position and fairly engaged the enemy, we fought him for nearly two hours before I made any decided advance upon him. The loss of both armies on this portion of the field was heavy. The enemy's particularly so, as far as I discovered by riding over the field after the battle. The enemy having been forced to yield this portion of the field, retired to the Wynn's ferry road, Buckner's point of attack. He did not retreat, but fell back, fighting us and contesting every inch of ground.

The fight was hotly contested, and stubborn on both sides, and consumed the day till 12 o'clock, to drive the enemy as far back as the centre, where Gen. Buckner's command was to flank him. While my command was slowly advancing and driving back the enemy, I was expecting to hear Gen. Buckner's command open fire in his rear. I was apprehensive of some misapprehension of orders, and came from the field of battle within the work to ascertain what was the matter. I there found the command of Gen. Buckner massed behind the ridge within the work, taking shelter from the enemy's artillery on the Wynn's ferry road, it having been forced to retire before the battery, as I learned from him. My force was still slowly advancing, driving the enemy forward towards the battery. I directed Gen. Buckner immediately to move his command round the rear of the battery, turning its left, keeping in the hollow, and attack and carry it. Before the movement was executed, my forces forming the attacking party on the right, with Col. Forrest's regiment of cavalry, gallantly charged a large body of infantry, supporting the battery, driving it, and forcing the battery to retire, taking six pieces of artillery, four brass pieces, and two 24-pounder iron pieces.

In pursuing the enemy, falling back from this position, Gen. Buckner's forces became united with mine, and engaged the enemy in a hot contest of nearly an hour, with fresh troops that had now met us. This position of the enemy being carried by our forces, I called off the further pursuit, after seven and a half hours of continuous and bloody conflict. After the troops were called off from the pursuit, orders were immediately given to the different commands to form and retire to the original position in the intrenchments. The operations of the day had forced the enemy around to our right and in front of Gen. Buckner's position in the intrenchments, and when he reached his position, he found the enemy rapidly advancing to take possession of his portion of our works. He had a stubborn conflict, lasting one hour and a half, to regain his position, and the enemy actually got possession of the extreme right of his works, and held them so firmly, that he could not dislodge them. The position thus gained by the enemy was a most important and commanding one, being immediately in front of our river batteries and our field work for its protection.

From it, he could readily turn the intrenched work occupied by Gen. Buckner, and attack in reverse, or he could advance under cover of an intervening ridge directly upon our battery and field work. While the enemy held this position, it was manifest we could not hold the main work or battery.

Such was the condition of the two armies at nightfall, after nine hours of conflict on the 15th inst., in which our loss was severe, leaving not less than 1000 of the enemy dead on the field. We left upon the field all his wounded, because we could not remove them. Such carnage and conflict never perhaps has before occurred on this continent. We took about 300 prisoners, and a large quantity of arms.

We had fought the battle to open our way for our army and to relieve us from an investment which would necessarily reduce us and the position we occupied by famine. We had accomplished our object, but it occupied the whole day, and before we could prepare to leave, after taking in the wounded and the dead, the enemy had thrown around us again, in the night, an immense force of fresh troops, and reoccupied his original position in the line of investment, thus again cutting off our retreat. We had only about 13,000 troops, all told. Of these we had lost a large proportion in the three battles. The command had been in the trenches night and day for five days, exposed to snow, sleet, mud, and ice and water, without shelter, without adequate covering, and without sleep.

In this condition the general officers held a consultation to determine what we should do. Gen. Buckner gave it as his decided opinion, that he could not hold his position half an hour against an assault of the enemy, and said he was satisfied the enemy would attack him at daylight the next morning. The proposition was then made by the undersigned again to fight our way through the enemy's line, and cut our way out. Gen. Buckner said his command was so worn out, and cut to pieces, and so demoralized, that he could not make another fight; that it would cost three-fourths its present numbers to cut its way out; that it was wrong to sacrifice three-fourths to save one-fourth; that no officer had a right to cause such a sacrifice. Gen. Floyd and Major Gilmer I understood to concur in this opinion. I then expressed the opinion that we could hold out another day, and in that time we could get steamboats, and set the command over the river, and probably save a portion of it. To this Gen. Buckner replied that the enemy would certainly attack him in the morning, and that he could not hold his position half an hour. The alternative of these propositions was surrender of the position and command. Gen. Floyd said he would not surrender the command, nor would he surrender himself prisoner. I had taken the same position. Gen. Buckner said he was satisfied nothing else could be done, and that, therefore, he would surrender the command if placed in command. Gen. Floyd said he would turn over the command to me, I passing it to Gen. Buckner, if Gen. Floyd would be permitted to withdraw his command. To this Gen. Buckner consented. Therefore the command was turned over to me, I passing it instantly to Gen. Buckner, saying I would neither surrender the command or myself. I directed Col. Forrest to cut his way out. Under these circumstances Gen. Buckner accepted the command, and sent a flag of truce to the enemy for an armistice of six hours, to negotiate for terms of capitulation. Before this flag and communication was delivered, I retired from the garrison. Before closing my report of the operations of the army at Donelson, I must, in justice to the officers and commands under my immediate command say, that harder fighting or more gallant bearing in officers and men I have never witnessed. In the absence of official reports of brigade and regimental commanders, of which I am deprived by the circumstances detailed in this report, I may not be able to do justice to the different corps. I will say, however, that the forces under my immediate command, during this action, bore themselves with gallantry throughout the long and bloody conflict. I speak with especial commendation of the brigades commanded by Cols.

Baldwin and Wharton, McCausland, Simonton, and Drake, and of Capts. Maney and Green, who fought their guns under the constant and annoying fire of the enemy's sharpshooters, and of the concentrated fire of his field batteries, from which both commands suffered severely. Capt. Maney was himself wounded, so were Capts. Porter and Graves. If I should hereafter receive the reports of regimental and brigade commanders, giving me detailed information of the conduct and bearing of officers and men, I will make a supplemental report. The absence of official reports deprives me of the means of giving lists of the killed and wounded of the different commands. I am satisfied that in such a series of conflicts our loss was heavy. I know the enemy's was, from passing over the field of battle, in the morning immediately after the battle, in company with Gen. Floyd. His loss in killed was terrible, exceeding any thing I had ever seen on a battle-field. Our total force in the field did not exceed 10,000 men, while from what I saw of the enemy's, and from information derived from prisoners of theirs, we are sure he had between thirty and forty thousand men in the field.

I must acknowledge many obligations to Major Gilmer, engineer, for especial and valuable services rendered me in the laying off the works, and the energy displayed by him in directing their construction, and for his counsel and advice. I likewise acknowledge my obligations to Capt. Gus. A. Henry, Jr., my A. A. general, and Col. John C. Burch, my aid-de-camp; to Major Field, to Lieut. Nicholson, to Lieut. Charles F. Masten, and Col. Brandon, my volunteer aid-de-camp; to Major Hays, my assistant commissary, and Major Jones, my assistant quarter-master, for the prompt manner in which they executed my orders under trying circumstances, throughout the long and continued conflicts, and to Major Gilmer, who accompanied me to the field, and was on duty with me during the entire day. Also, to Capt. Parker, of my staff, whom I assigned to the command of Capt. Ross's field battery, with new recruits as gunners; and he fought and served them well. The conduct of these officers, coming under my immediate observation, met my hearty approval and commendation. Col. Brandon was severely wounded early in the action. Col. Baldwin's brigade constituted the front of the attacking force, sustained immediately by Col. Wharton's brigade.

These two brigades deserve especial commendation for the manner in which they sustained the first shock of the battle. I must also acknowledge my obligations to Brig.-gen. B. R. Johnson, who assisted me in the command of the forces with which I attacked the enemy, and who bore himself gallantly throughout the conflict; but having received no official reports from him, I cannot give the detailed operations of his command. I have pleasure in being able to say that Col. Forrest, whose command greatly distinguished its commander, as a bold and judicious officer, and reflected distinguished honor upon itself, passed safely through the enemy's line of investments, and trust it will yet win other honors in the defence of our rights and just cause of our country.

(Official,) GIDEON J. PILLOW, *Brig.-gen. C. S. A.*
JOHN WITHERS, *A. A. General.*
A. & I. G. O., Sept. 17, 1862.

This report was handed to me at Bristol, East Tennessee, by Col. Dobbins, of Mississippi, who was on his way to Richmond, but was detained. I promised Col. Dobbins to deliver it to the adjutant-general at Richmond, but when the matter was mentioned to Hon. J. P. Benjamin, he told me to leave it in the War Office, and to make the above statement. Col. Dobbins handed me the paper on the 28th of February, 1862, and said it had been given to him by Gen. Pillow. E. W. MUNFORD.

Supplemental Report of General Pillow.

HEAD-QUARTERS, THIRD DIVISION,
DECATUR, ALA., March 14, 1862.

COL. W. W. MACKALL, *A. A. General.*

The position we occupied was invested, on the 11th of February, by a force which we estimated at about 20,000 strong. This force had approached us partly by water, but mainly by land from Fort Henry. I considered the force we had sufficient to repulse the assault of this force. We repulsed everywhere a vigorous assault made by our enemies against our position. Fresh troops continued to come every day by water until the 14th. We are satisfied the enemy's forces are not short of 30,000 men. Our impressions of his strength were confirmed by prisoners we had taken on that day.

This evening the enemy landed 13 steamboat loads of fresh troops. It was now manifest that we could not long maintain our position against such overwhelming numbers. I was satisfied the last troops were of Gen. Buell's command. We felt the want of reinforcements, but we did not ask for them, because we knew they were not to be had. I had just come from Bowling Green, and heard that Gen. Johnston could not spare a man from his position. He had, in fact, already so weakened himself, that he could not maintain his position against a vigorous assault. Under these circumstances, deeming it utterly useless to apply for reinforcements, we determined to make the best possible defence we could with the force in hand. Our investment by a force of 30,000 men on the 14th being completed, and the enemy on that evening having received 13 boat-loads of fresh troops, a council of general officers was convened by Gen. Floyd, at which it was determined to give battle at daylight the next day, so as to cut off the investing force, if possible, before the fresh troops were in position. In that council I proposed as a plan of attack, that with the force in the intrenchments of our left wing, and Col. Hanson's regiment, of Gen. Buckner's division, I should attack the enemy's main force, on his right, and, if successful, that would roll the enemy on his line of investments to a point opposite Gen. Buckner's position, where he would attack him in flank and rear, and drive him, with our united commands, back upon his encampments at the river. To this proposition, so far from allowing me to leave Col. Hanson's regiment, Gen. Buckner objected. I waived the point, saying I only asked the assistance of that regiment, because my portion of the labor was, by far, the greatest to be performed, and that upon my success depended the fortunes of the day, and that a very large portion of the troops I had to fight were fresh troops and badly armed.

Gen. Buckner then proposed as a modification of my plan of battle, that he should attack the enemy simultaneously with me, that his attack should be against the position of the Wynn's ferry road, where he had a battery nearly opposite the middle of the left wing, and that he would thus lessen the labors of my command, and strike the enemy in a material point. To this modification I agreed, as an improvement upon my proposed plan. In carrying out this plan, thus agreed upon, it became proper for Col. Heiman's brigade to maintain its position in the line, otherwise the enemy might turn the right of Gen. Buckner's position, take his forces on the right flank, and thus defeat our success. It was arranged accordingly. Gen. Floyd approved this plan of battle, and ordered that it should be carried out next morning by daylight. I then sent for all the commanders of brigades, to explain to them our situation (being invested), our purpose, our plan of battle, and to assign to each brigade its position in my column, all of which was done, and I gave orders to have my whole force under arms, at four and a half o'clock, and to be ready to march out of our works precisely at five o'clock.

At four o'clock I was with my command, all of which were in position, except Col. Davison's brigade, none of which were present. I immediately directed Gen. B. R. Johnson, who was present, and to whose immediate command Col. Davison's brigade belonged, to dispatch officers for that brigade, and to ascertain the causes of delay. He did so. I likewise sent several officers of my staff on the same duty. Both sets of officers made the same report, viz: Col. Davison had failed to give any orders to the colonels of his command, and that Col. D. was sick. It is proper to state he was complaining of being sick when the orders were received. The instructions to the brigade commanders were given about two o'clock that morning. My command was delayed in its advance about half an hour by the necessity of bringing up the brigade.

My column was finally ready and put in motion about 15 minutes after 5 o'clock. I moved with the advance, and directed Gen. B. R. Johnson to bring up the rear. The command of Col. Davison's brigade devolved upon Col. Simonton, which, owing to the reasons already stated, was brought into column in the rear, and into action last, under Gen. Johnson, to whose report, for its good behaviour on the field, I particularly refer, having, in my original report, omitted to state its position on the field. Many of these incidents, not deemed essential to the proper understanding of the main features of the battle of the 12th of February, were omitted in my original report, but are now given as parts of its history. In my original report, I gave the after operations in the battle of the 15th February, and shall now pass over all the events occurring until the council of general officers, held on the night of the 15th. The lodgment of the enemy's force, in the rifle-pits of Gen. Buckner's extreme right, late on the evening of the 15th February, induced Gen. Floyd to call a meeting of general officers at head-quarters that night.

We had fought the battle of the 15th to open the way through the enemy's line of investments, to retire to the interior. The battle had occupied the day. We were until 12 o'clock that night burying the dead. At about 1 o'clock, we had all the commanders of regiments and brigades assembled and given orders to the entire command, to be under arms at 4 o'clock to march out on the road leading towards Charlotte. I had given instruction to Major Hays, my commissary, and Major Jones, my quarter-master, immediately after our evacuation of the place, to burn all the stores. About 3 o'clock (perhaps a little earlier) we received intelligence from the troops in the trenches, that they heard dogs barking around on the outside of our lines, and the enemy, they thought, were reinvesting our position. General Floyd immediately directed me to send out scouts to ascertain the fact. This duty was performed. When the scouts returned, they reported the enemy in large force occupying his original position, and closing up the routes to the interior. Not being satisfied with the truth of the report, I directed Col. Forrest to send out a second set of scouts, and at the same time directed him to send two intelligent men up the bank of the river, to examine a valley of overflown ground, lying to the rear and right of the enemy's position, and if the valley of overflown ground could be crossed by infantry and cavalry, and to ascertain if the enemy's forces reached the river bank. The one set of scouts returned and confirmed the previous reports, viz.: That the woods were full of the enemy, occupying his former position in great numbers. The scouts sent up the river to examine the overflow, reported that the overflown valley was not practicable for infantry, that the soft mud was about half leg deep, that the water was about saddle skirts deep to the horses, and that there was a good deal of drift in the way. We then sent for a citizen, whose name is not remembered, said to know that part of the country well, and asked his opinion. He confirmed the reports of the river scouts.

In addition to the depth of the water, the weather was intensely cold, many of the troops were frost-bitten, and they could not stand a passage through a sheet of water. With these facts before us, Generals Floyd, Buckner, and myself, the two former having remained at my quarters all the intervening time, held a consultation, when Gen. Floyd said: "Well, gentlemen, what is now best to be done?" Neither Gen. Buckner nor myself having answered promptly, Gen. Floyd repeated his inquiry, addressing himself to me by name. My reply was, it was difficult to determine what was best to be done, but that I was in favor of cutting our way out. He then asked Gen. Buckner what he thought we ought to do. Gen. Buckner said his command was so broken down, so cut up, and so demoralized, he could not make another fight, that he thought we would lose three-fourths of the command we had already left if we attempted to cut our way out, and that it was wrong. No officer had a right to sacrifice three-fourths of a command to save the other fourth. That we had fought the enemy from the trenches, we had fought him from his gunboats, and fought our way through his line of investments, that we were again invested with a force of fresh troops, that the army had done all duty and honor required it to do, and more was not possible.

Gen. Floyd then remarked that his opinions coincided with Gen. Buckner. Brig.-gen. B. R. Johnson had previously retired from the council to his quarters in the field, and was not present. In my original report, I stated it was my impression Major Gilmer was consulted, and concurred in the opinions of Gens. Buckner and Floyd; but from subsequent conversations with Major Gilmer, I learn from him he had retired to another room and lain down, and was not present at this part of the conference, and I am therefore satisfied that I was mistaken in the statements in regard to him.

The proposition to cut our way out being thus disposed of, I remarked that we could hold our position another day, and fight the enemy from our trenches; that by night our steamboats that had taken off the prisoners and our own wounded men would return, and that during the night we could set our troops on the right bank of the river, and that we could make our escape by Clarksville, and thus save the army. To this proposition Gen. Buckner said, "Gentlemen, you know the enemy occupy the rifle-pits on my right, and can easily turn my position and attack me in the rear, or move down on the river battery. I am satisfied he will attack me at daylight, and I cannot hold my position half an hour." Regarding Gen. Buckner's reply as settling this proposition in the negative (for I had quite enough to do with my heavy losses of the previous day to defend my own portion of the lines, and I could give him no reinforcements), I then said, "Gentlemen, if we cannot cut out, nor fight on, there is no alternative left us but capitulation, and I am determined that I will never surrender the command, nor surrender myself prisoner; I will die first." Gen. Floyd remarked that such was his determination, and that he would die before he would do either. Thereupon Gen. Buckner remarked that such determinations were personal, and that personal considerations should never influence official action. Gen. Floyd said he acknowledged it was personal with him, but nevertheless it was his determination. Whereupon Gen. Buckner said, that being satisfied nothing else could be done, if he was placed in command, he would surrender the command, and share the fate of the command. Gen. Floyd immediately said, "Gen. Buckner, if I place you in command, will you allow me to draw out my brigade?" Gen. Buckner promptly replied, "Yes, provided you do so before the enemy act upon my communication." Gen. Floyd remarked, "Gen. Pillow, I turn over the command." I replied instantly, "I pass it." Gen. Buckner said,

"I assume it; bring me a bugler, pen, ink, and paper." Gen. Buckner had received pen, ink, and paper, and sat down to the table and commenced writing, when I left and crossed the river, passing outside the garrison before Gen. Buckner proposed his communication to the enemy, and went to Clarksville by land on horseback. I did not know what he had written until I saw the published correspondence with Gen. Grant.

I may be asked if I was in favor of cutting my way out, why, when the command was turned over to me, I did not take it? My reply is, that, though technically speaking, the command devolved on me when turned over by Gen. Floyd, it was turned over to Gen. Buckner in point of fact. All parties so understood it. In proof of this, Gen. Floyd, under his agreement with Gen. Buckner, actually withdrew a large portion of his brigade, by setting them across the river in the steamer Gen. Anderson, that arrived just before daylight. In further proof of this, I embody in this report an order of Gen. Buckner to Gen. B. R. Johnson, after he had assumed command. A copy of order:

HEAD-QUARTERS, DOVER, February 16, 1862.

SIR: The command of the forces in this vicinity has devolved upon me by order of Gen. Floyd. I have sent a flag to Gen. Grant, and during the correspondence, and until further orders, refrain from hostile demonstrations, with a view to prevent a like movement on the enemy's part. You will endeavor to send a flag to the posts in front of your position, notifying them of the fact that I have sent a communication to Gen. Grant from the right of our position, and desire to know his present head-quarters.

Respectfully, your obedient servant,

(Signed) S. B. BUCKNER,
Brig.-gen. C. S. A.

In addition to this, Gen. Floyd was my senior, and of high character and acknowledged ability. Gen. Buckner, though my junior in rank, possesses high reputation as an officer of talents and experience. With the judgment of both against me, if I had acted upon my own conviction, and had failed or involved the command in heavy loss, I was apprehensive it would be regarded as an act of rashness, and bring upon me the censure of the Government, and the condemnation of the country. Besides, without their assistance in command, and with the moral weight of their opinions with the troops against the step, I did not regard it practicable to make a successful effort to cut out. I declined to assume the command when turned over by Gen. Floyd, because it was against my convictions of duty to surrender the command, and under the decision of Gens. Floyd and Buckner (a majority of the council), I could do nothing but surrender it. It is proper to say that the difference of opinion between Gen. Floyd, Gen. Buckner, and myself, upon this branch of the subject, consisted in this, viz.: They thought it would cost three-fourths of the command to cut out. I did not think the loss would be so great. If it had been settled that the sacrifice would be as much as three-fourths, I should have agreed with them that it was wrong to make the attempt. Again: I believe we could have maintained our position another day, and have saved the army by getting back our boats and setting our command across the river; but inasmuch as Gen. Buckner was of opinion that he could not hold his command more than half an hour, and I could not possibly hold my own position of the line, I had no alternative but to submit to the decision of the majority of my brother general officers. While I thus differed with them in opinion, I still think I did right in acquiescing in opinion with them. We all agreed in opinion we could not long maintain the position against such overwhelming numbers of fresh troops. We all agreed the army had performed prodigies of valor, and that, if possible, further sacrifices should be avoided. Men will differ and agree according to their mental organization. I censure not their opinions, nor do I claim merit for my own. The whole matter is submitted to the judgment of the Government.

Since my original report was prepared, I have seen and read the official accounts of Gen. Grant and Com. Foote. From these I learn that the damage done the enemy's gunboats on the 13th, was greater by far than was represented by me in my original report. Four of the enemy's gunboats were badly disabled, receiving over 100 shells from our battery, many of which went entirely through from stem to stern, tearing the frame of the boats and machinery to pieces, and killing and wounding 55 of their crews. Among them was the commander himself. There can, therefore, be no longer any doubt of the vulnerability of these heavy shots; but it required a desperate fight to settle the question, and there is danger that the public mind will run from one extreme to the other, and arrive at a conclusion undervaluing the power of the enemy's gunboats. In estimating the loss inflicted upon the enemy on the 15th February, I saw that the whole field of battle for a mile and a half was covered with his dead and wounded, and believe his loss could not fail short of 5000 men.

I am satisfied from published letters from officers and men of the enemy, and from the acknowledgments of the Northern press, that his loss was much greater than originally estimated in my report. I stated in my original report, that after we had driven the enemy from, and captured his battery on the Wynn's ferry road, and were pursuing him around to our right, and after we had met and overcome a fresh force of the enemy, on the route towards his gunboats, I called off the pursuit, but in the hurry with which that report was prepared, I omitted to state my reasons for so doing. I knew that the enemy had twenty gunboats of fresh troops at his landing, then only about three miles distant; I knew from the great loss my command had sustained during the protracted fight of over seven hours, my command was in no condition to meet a large body of fresh troops, who I had every reason to believe were then rapidly approaching the field. Gen. Buckner's command, so far as labor was concerned, was comparatively fresh, but its disorganization, from being repulsed by the battery, had unfitted it to meet and fight a large body of fresh troops. I therefore called off the pursuit, explaining my reasons to Gen. Floyd, who approved the order. This explanation is now given, as necessary to a proper understanding of the order. It is further proper to say, that from the moment of my arrival at Donelson, I had the whole force engaged night and day in strengthening my position, until the fight commenced, and when the fighting ceased at night it was again at work. I did not, therefore, and could not, get a single morning report of the strength of my command.

The four Virginia regiments did not, I am confident, exceed 350 each for duty. The Texas regiment did not number 300 men. Several Mississippi regiments were equally reduced, while those of Cols. Voorhies, Abernethy, and Hughes (new regiments), were almost disbanded by measles, and did not exceed 200 each for duty. Col. Browden's regiment had but 60 men, and it was by my order placed under Capt. Parker to work artillery. All others were greatly reduced by wastage. The whole force, therefore, was greatly less than could be supposed from the number of nominal regiments. Of this force, Gen. Floyd, under his agreement with Gen. Buckner, before he turned over the command, drew out a large portion of his brigade (how many I do not know) by taking possession of the steamer Anderson, which arrived at Dover just before day, and setting them across the river. A large portion of the cavalry under orders passed out. All of the cavalry was ordered to cut out, and could have gone out but for the timidity of its officers. Several thousand infantry escaped one way or another, many of whom are now at this place, and all others are ordered here as a rendezvous for reorganization. From the list of prisoners published in Northern papers, which I have seen, it required the prisoners of six regiments to make nine hundred men. I do not believe the number of prisoners exceeded that stated by the Northern papers, which is put at 5170 privates.

During the afternoon of the 15th, I had caused the arms lost by the enemy to be gathered up from about half the field of battle, and had hauled and stacked up over 5000 stand of arms, and six pieces of artillery, all of which were lost in the surrender of the place for want of transportation to bring them away.

In regard to the enemy's force with which we were engaged in the battle of Dover, Gen. Grant, in his official report, says that he had taken about fifteen thousand prisoners, that Gens. Floyd and Pillow had escaped with 15,000 men, and that the forces engaged were about equal. While the estimate of prisoners taken, and the number with which Gen. Floyd escaped, is wide of the mark, yet the aggregate of the numbers as given by himself, is 30,000, and his acknowledgments that the forces were about equal, furnishes conclusive evidence that we fought 30,000 men; the same number given by prisoners taken. And agreeing with my original estimate of his strength, Gen. Halleck, in a telegraphic dispatch of 10th February from St. Louis to Gen. McClellan, said "he had invested Fort Donelson with a force of 50,000 men, and he had no doubt all communication and supplies were cut off." This corroborates Grant's statements, for the troops which arrived on the 14th and 15th of February, being 20 steamboat loads, had not reached the battle-field on the morning of the 15th, and it is probable that parts of those that arrived on the evening of the 13th had not reached it.

These sources make it clear, we fought 30,000 of the enemy on the 15th; and that we were reinvested that night with all the enemy's disposable force, including his fresh troops, cannot be doubted. Nothing has occurred to change my original estimate of our loss in the several conflicts with the enemy, at the trenches, with the gunboats, and in the battle of Dover. As to the absence still of regiment and brigade commanders, it is possible that I have not done justice to the officers in my commands. To Brig.-gen. Johnson's report, which is herewith forwarded, I particularly refer for the conduct of officers and commands under his immediate observation during the battle. The forces under my immediate command, in the conflict with the enemy's right, did not exceed 7000, though they never faltered, and drove the enemy from his position, slowly and steadily advancing over one and a half miles, carrying the positions of his first battery, and two of his guns, and of a battery on the Wynn's ferry road, taking four more guns, and afterwards uniting with Gen. Buckner's command, drove the enemy back, sustained by a number of fresh troops.

Yet it is manifest that the fruits of our victory would have been far greater, had Gen. Buckner's column been successful in its assault upon the Wynn's ferry road battery. Equally clear is it, that the enemy, effecting a lodgment in Gen. Buckner's rifle-pits, on his right, brought the command into extreme peril, making it absolutely necessary to take immediate action, in which we were under the necessity of cutting our way out, or holding out another day and throwing the command across the river, or of capitulation. My own position upon these several propositions having been explained more fully and in detail in this, my supplementary report, nothing more remains in the performance of my duty to the Government, but to subscribe myself,

Very respectfully,

Your obedient servant,

(Signed) GID. J. PILLOW,

Brig.-gen. C S. A.

NOTE.—That there may be no doubt of the facts stated in this report, I append the sworn testimony of Col. Burch, Col. Forrest, Majors Henry and Haynes and Nicholson, to which I ask the attention of the Government.

(Signed) GID. J. PILLOW,

Brig.-gen. C. S. A.

NOTE.—My original estimate was, that our loss in killed and wounded was from fifteen hundred to two thousand. We sent up from Dover, 1134 wounded. A Federal surgeon's certificate, which I have seen, says that there were about 400 Confederate prisoners wounded in hospital at Paducah, making 1534 wounded. I was satisfied the killed would increase the number to 2000

Colonel Burch's Statement.

(*Referred to in the foregoing.*)

DECATUR, ALA., March 15th, 1862.

On Saturday evening, February 15th, all of the boats which we had at Donelson were sent up the river with our sick, wounded, and prisoners. After supper, a council of officers was held at Brig.-gen. Pillow's head-quarters. I was not present at this council, but during its session, being in an adjoining room, I learned from some officer that intelligence had been received from scouts on the east side of the river, that fourteen of the enemy's transports were landing reinforcements one and a half or two miles below us, at their usual place of landing. After I had learned this, and during the session of the same council, two couriers came to Brig.-gen. Buckner—one, and perhaps both, sent by Capt. Graves, of the artillery; one stating that a large force was forming in front of our right (Gen. Buckner's) wing; the second stating that large bodies of the enemy were seen moving in front of our right, around towards our left. After the adjournment of this council, about 11 or 12 o'clock, I learned that it had been determined to evacuate the post, cut our way through the right wing of the enemy's investing force, and make our way towards Charlotte, in Dixon county.

Orders were given for the command to be in readiness to march at 4 o'clock, A. M. After this, being in Gen. Pillow's private room, where Gens. Floyd, Pillow, and Buckner all were, two scouts came in, stating that the enemy's camp-fires could be seen at the same places in front of our left that they had occupied Friday. From the remarks of the generals, this information seemed to be confirmatory of information which they had previously received. Major Rice, an intelligent citizen of Dover, was called in and interrogated as to the character of the road to Charlotte. His account of it was decidedly unfavorable. In the course of the conversation which then followed among the generals—Gen. Pillow insisting upon carrying out the previous determination of the council to cut our way out—Brig.-gen. Buckner said that such was the exhausted condition of the men, that, if they should succeed in cutting their way out, it would be at a heavy sacrifice, and, if pursued by the large cavalry force of the enemy, they would be almost entirely cut to pieces. Gen. Floyd concurred with Gen. Buckner. Gen. Pillow said, "Then we can fight them another day in our trenches, and by to-morrow we can have boats enough here to transport our troops across the river, and let them make their escape to Clarksville." Gen. Buckner said—That such was the position of the enemy on his right, and the demoralization of his forces, from exposure and exhaustion, that he could not hold his trenches a half an hour. As an illustration of the correctness of his remark, he said—"You, gentlemen, know that yesterday morning I considered the 2d Kentucky (Hanson's regiment) as good a regiment as there was in the service, yet such was their condition yesterday afternoon that, when I learned the enemy was in their trenches (which were to our extreme right, and detached from the others), before I could rally and form them, I had to take at least twenty men by the shoulders, and put them into line as a nucleus for formation." Gen. Floyd concurred with Gen. Buckner in his opinion as to the impossibility of holding the trenches longer, and asked—"What shall we do?" Gen. Buckner stated that no officer had a right to sacrifice his men, referred to our various successes since Wednesday, at Donelson, and concluded by saying that an officer who had successfully resisted an assault of a much larger force, and was still surrounded by an increased force, could surrender with honor; and that we had accomplished much more than was required by this rule. Gen. Pillow said that he never would surrender. Gen. Floyd said that he would suffer any fate before he would surrender, or fall into the hands of the enemy alive. At the suggestion of some one present, he said that personal considerations influenced him in coming to this determination, and further stated that such considerations should never govern a general officer.

Col. Forrest, of the cavalry, who was present, said he would die before he would surrender; that such of his men as would follow him, he would take out. Gen. Floyd said he would take his chances with Forrest, and asked Gen. Buckner if he would make the surrender? Gen. Buckner asked him if he (Gen. Floyd) would pass the command to him? Gen. Floyd replied in the affirmative. I understood Gen. Pillow as doing the same. "Then," said Gen. Buckner, "I shall propose terms of capitulation," and asked for ink and paper, and directed one of his staff to send for a bugler, and prepare white flags to plant at various points on our works. Preparations were immediately begun to be made by Gen. Floyd and staff, Gen. Pillow and staff, and Col. Forrest, to leave. This was about 3 o'clock, A. M. It was suggested by some one that two boats that were known to be coming down the river might arrive before day, and Gen. Floyd asked, if they came, that he might be permitted to take off on them his troops. Gen. Buckner replied that all might leave who could before his note was sent to Gen. Grant, the Federal commander. Thus ended the conference.

After this I met or called on Gen. Pillow in the passage, and asked him if there was any possibility of a misunderstanding as to his position? He thought not; but I suggested to him the propriety of again seeing Gens. Floyd and Buckner, and see that there was no possibility of his position being misunderstood by them. He said he would, and returned to the room in which the conference was held.

In my statement of what transpired, and of the conversations that were had, I do not pretend to have given the exact language used, and I may be mistaken as to the order of the remarks that I have endeavored to narrate.

(Signed) JOHN C. BURCH,
Aid to Gen. Pillow.

Sworn to and subscribed before me this 15th day of March, 1862.
LEVI SUGANS,
Intendant of the town of Decatur, Ala., and ex officio J. P.

Colonel Forrest's Statement.

(*Referred to in Gen. Pillow's Supplemental Report.*)

MARCH 15, 1862.

Between 1 and 2 o'clock on Sunday morning, February 16th, being sent for, I arrived at Gen. Pillow's head-quarters, and found him, Gen. Floyd, and Gen. Buckner in conversation. Gen. Pillow told me that they had received information that the enemy were again occupying the same ground they had occupied the morning before. I told him I did not believe it, as I had left that part of the field, on our left, late the evening before. He told me he had sent out scouts, who reported large forces of the enemy moving around to our left. He instructed me to go immediately, and send two reliable men to ascertain the condition of a road running near the river bank, and between the enemy's right and the river, and also to ascertain the position of the enemy. I obeyed his instructions, and awaited the return of the scouts. They stated that they saw no enemy, but could see their fires in the same place where they were Friday night; that from their examination, and from information obtained from a citizen living on the road, the water was about to the saddle skirts, and the mud about half leg deep in the bottom where it had been overflowed. The bottom was about a quarter of a mile wide, and the water then about one hundred yards wide. During the conversation that then ensued among the general officers, Gen. Pillow was in favor of trying to cut our way out. Gen. Buckner said that he could not hold his position over half an hour in the morning, and that if he attempted to take his force out, it would be seen by the enemy, who held part of his intrenchments, and be followed and cut to pieces. I told him that I would take my cavalry around them, and he could draw out under cover of them. He said that an attempt to cut our way out would involve a loss of three-fourths of the men. Gen. Floyd said our force was so demoralized as to cause him to agree with Gen. Buckner, as to our probable loss in attempting to cut our way out. I said that I would agree to cut my way through the enemy's lines at any point the general might designate, and stated I could keep back their cavalry, which Gen. Buckner thought would greatly harass our infantry in retreat. Gen. Buckner or Gen. Floyd said that they (the enemy) would bring their artillery to bear on us. I went out of the room, and when I returned Gen. Floyd said he could not and would not surrender himself. I then asked if they were going to surrender the command? Gen. Buckner remarked that they were. I then stated that I had not come out for the purpose of surrendering my command, and would not do it if they would follow me out; that I intended to go out if I saved but one man, and then turning to Gen. Pillow, I asked him what I should do? He replied, "Cut your way out." I immediately left the house and sent for all the officers under my command, and stated to them the facts that had occurred, and stated my determination to leave, and remarked that all who wanted to go could follow me, and those who wished to stay and take the consequences might remain in camp. All of my own regiment, and Capt. Williams, of Helm's Kentucky regiment, said they would go with me if the last man fell. Col. Gaute was sent for and urged to get out his battalion as often as three times, but he and two Kentucky companies (Capt. Wilcox and Capt. Henry) refused to come. I marched out the remainder of my command, with Capt. Porter's artillery horses, and about two hundred men, of different commands, up the river road and across the overflow, which I found to be about saddle-skirt deep. The weather was intensely cold, a great many of the men were already frost-bitten, and it was the opinion of the generals that the infantry could not have passed through the water and have survived it.

(Signed) A. B. FORREST,
Forrest's Regiment Cavalry.

Sworn to and subscribed before me on the 15th day of March, 1862
LEVI SUGANS,
Intendant of town of Decatur, Ala., and ex offi. J. P.

Major Henry's Statement.

(*Referred to in Gen. Pillow's Supplemental Report.*)

DECATUR, ALA., March 13, 1862.

On the morning of the 16th February, 1862, I was present during the council of war held in Brig.-gen. Pillow's head-quarters at Dover, Tennessee, Gens. Floyd, Pillow, Buckner, and Gen. Pillow's staff being present. On account of being very much exhausted from the fight of the 15th inst., I slept the forepart of the night, and came down stairs from my room into Gen. Pillow's about one or two o'clock. At the time I entered Gen. Pillow's room, it had been decided that we should fight our way out, and Gen. Pillow gave me orders to gather up all the papers and books belonging to my department. Whereupon I immediately executed the orders given to me, and then returned to Gen. Pillow's room, when a change of operations had been decided upon, on account of information received from scouts ordered out by Gen. Pillow to ascertain whether the enemy reoccupied the ground they were driven from the day previous. The scouts returned and reported that the enemy had swung entirely around and were in possession of the very same ground. Gen. Pillow being still in doubt, sent a second party of scouts who made a thorough reconnoissance, and reported that the woods were perfectly alive with troops, and that their camp fires were burning in every direction. Gen. Pillow then sent a party of cavalry to inspect a slough that was filled with backwater from the river, to see if infantry could pass. They returned after having made a thorough examination on horseback and on foot, and reported that infantry could not pass, but they thought cavalry could. Communication being thus cut off, Gen. Pillow urged the propriety of making a desperate attempt to cut our way out, whatever might be the consequences, or make a fight in the work and hold our position one more day, by which time we could get steamboats sufficient to put the whole command over the river, and make our escape by the way of Clarksville. Gen. Buckner then said: that in consequence of the worn-out condition and demoralization of the troops under his command, and the occupation of his rifle-pits on the extreme right by the enemy, that he could not hold his position a half hour after being attacked, which he thought would begin about daylight. Gen. Pillow then said: that by the enemy's occupation of the rifle-pits on Gen. Buckner's right, that it was an open gateway to our river battery, and that he thought we ought to cut our way through, carrying with us as many as possible, leaving the killed and wounded on the field. Gen. Buckner then said: that it would cost three-fourths of the command to get the other fourth out, and that he did not think any general had the right to make such a sacrifice of human life. Gen. Floyd agreed with Gen. Buckner on this point. Gen. Pillow then rose up and said: "Gentlemen, as you refuse to make an attempt to cut our way out, and Gen. Buckner says he will not be able to hold his position a half hour after being attacked, there is only one alternative left; that is, capitulation," and then and there remarked that he would not surrender the command or himself, that he would die first. Gen. Floyd then spoke out and said, that he would not surrender the command or himself. Gen. Buckner remarked that, if placed in command, he would surrender the command and share its fate. Gen. Floyd then said: "General Buckner, if I place you in command, will you allow me to get out as much of my brigade as I can?" Gen. Buckner replied, "I will, provided you do so before the enemy receives my proposition for capitulation." Gen. Floyd then turned to Gen. Pillow and said: "I turn the command over, sir." Gen. Pillow replied promptly, "I pass it." Gen. Buckner said: "I assume it; give me pen, ink, and paper, and send for a bugler." Gen. Pillow then started out of the room to make arrangements for his escape, when Col. Forrest said to him: "Gen. Pillow, what shall I do?" Gen. Pillow replied, "Cut your way out, sir;" Forrest said, "I will do it," and left the room.

(Signed) GUS. A. HENRY, Jr.,
Assistant Adj-gen.

To Brig-gen. Pillow.

THE STATE OF ALABAMA, MORGAN COUNTY.

This day personally came before me, Levi Sugans, Intendant of the town of Decatur, County and State aforesaid, Major Gus. A. Henry, Jr., who makes oath in due form of law, that the above statements are true. Sworn to and subscribed before me on the 14th day of March, 1862.

(Signed) GUS. A. HENRY, JR.,
Assistant Adj-gen.

(Signed) LEVI SUGANS,
Intendant.

Major Haynes' Statement.

(*Referred to in Gen. Pillow's Supplemental Report.*)

OFFICE DIVISION COMMISSARY,
DECATUR, ALA., March 13, 1862.

I was present at the council of officers, held at Brig.-gen. Gideon J. Pillow's head-quarters, in the town of Dover, Tenn., on the morning of the 16th February, 1862. Was awoke in my quarters at one o'clock, A. M., by Col. John C. Burch, aid-de-camp, and ordered to report to Gen. Pillow forthwith. I instantly proceeded to head-quarters, where I saw Brig.-gens. Floyd, Pillow, and Buckner, Col. Forrest, Major Henry, Assistant Adj.-generals Gilmer and Jones, and Lieuts. Nicholson and Martin, the two latter volunteer aids to Gen. Pillow. On my entrance in the room, was accosted by Gen. Pillow, and being taken to one side, was informed by him that they had determined to cut their way through the enemy's lines, and retreat from Dover to Nashville, and he desired me to destroy all the commissary stores, and then make my escape across the river. I desired to know at what hour Gen. Pillow wished his order to be executed, when, looking at his watch, he replied at half-past five o'clock. I then retired from the room to inform my assistants of the order, but in one hour, returned to head-quarters.

On re-entering the room, heard Gen. Buckner say, "I cannot hold my position half an hour after the attack," and Gen. Pillow, who was sitting next to Gen. Buckner, and immediately fronting the fireplace, promptly asked, "Why can't you?" at the same time adding, "I think you can hold your position; I think you can, sir." Gen. Buckner retorted, "I know my position; I can only bring to bear against the enemy about four thousand men, while he can oppose me with any given number." Gen. Pillow then said: "Well, gentlemen, what do you intend to do? I am in favor of fighting out." Gen. Floyd then spoke, and asked Gen. Buckner what he had to say, and Gen. Buckner answered quickly, that the attempt to cut a way through the enemy's lines and retreat would cost a sacrifice of three-fourths of the command, and no commander had a right to make such a sacrifice. Gen. Floyd concurring, remarked, "We will have to capitulate; but, gentlemen, I cannot surrender; you know my position with the Federals; it wouldn't do, it wouldn't do;" whereupon Gen. Pillow, addressing Gen. Floyd, said: "I will not surrender myself nor the command; *will die first.*" "Then, I suppose, gentlemen," said Gen. Buckner, "the surrender will devolve upon me?" Gen. Floyd replied, speaking to Gen. Buckner, "General, if you are put in command, will you allow me to take out by the river my brigade?" "Yes, sir," responded Gen. Buckner, "if you move your command before the enemy act upon my communication offering to capitulate." "Then, sir," said Gen. Floyd, "I surrender the command;" and Gen. Pillow, who was next in command, very quickly exclaimed, "I will not accept it; I will never surrender," and while speaking, turned to Gen. Buckner, who remarked, "I will accept and share the fate of my command," and called for pen, ink, paper, and bugler.

After the capitulation was determined upon, Gen. Pillow wished to know if it would be proper for him to make his escape, when Gen. Floyd replied that the question was one for every man to decide for himself, but he would be glad for every one to escape that could. "Then, sir, I shall leave here," replied Gen. Pillow. Col. Forrest, who was in the room, and heard what passed, then spoke: "I think there is more fight in these men than you all suppose, and if you will let me, I will take my command;" Gen. Pillow responding to him, "Yes, sir, take out your command; cut your way out." Gens. Floyd and Buckner assented; Gen. Floyd, by saying, "Yes, take out your command," and Gen. Buckner, by expressing, "I have no objection." The means of getting away was then discussed, and soon thereafter we began to disperse.

While the gentlemen were leaving the room, I approached Gen. Buckner, and wished to know if Gen. Pillow's order, to destroy the commissary stores, should be carried out, and he answered, "Major Haynes, I countermand the order." It may be proper for me to say that I never met Gen. Pillow before the morning of the 9th February, 1862, having been upon Brig.-gen. Charles Clark's staff since my entrance into the service, and only went to Donelson with Gen. Pillow to take temporary charge of the commissariat. Gen. Pillow assigned me to duty on his staff after arriving at Donelson, on the 10th February, 1862.

(Signed) W. H. HAYNES,
Major and Brigade Commissary.

STATE OF ALABAMA, MORGAN COUNTY. SS.

Personally appeared before me, Levi Sugans, Intendant of the town of Decatur, and *ex officio* Justice of the Peace, Major W. H. Haynes, who makes oath that the statements herein made, relating to what was said in the council of officers, on the morning of the 16th February, 1862, are true.

Sworn to and subscribed before me this 14th March, 1862.

(Signed) W. H. HAYNES,
Major and Brigade Commissary.

(Signed) LEVI SUGANS,
Intendant.

Hunter Nicholson's Statement.

(*Referred to in Gen. Pillow's Supplemental Report.*)

I was present at the council of war, held at Brig.-gen. Pillow's head-quarters in Dover, on Saturday night, February 15th, 1862. I came into the room about two o'clock. There were present, Gens. Floyd, Pillow, and Buckner, Major Gilmer, Col. Forrest, and several staff officers, among whom I distinctly remember Major Henry and Col. Burch, of Gen. Pillow's staff.

The generals were discussing the necessity and practicability of marching the forces out of the intrenchments and evacuating the place. Major Rice, a resident of Dover, and an aid-de-camp of Gen. Pillow, was describing the nature of the country and character of the roads over which the army would have to pass. He referred to some citizen, I think a doctor, but do not remember his name, whom he represented as more familiar with the roads. In a little while, or perhaps during the conversation of Major Rice, the gentleman referred to was announced. He gave a description of the roads, which, from my ignorance of the locality, I am unable to repeat. The substance was, however, that though exceedingly difficult, it was possible to pass the road with light baggage trains.

Gen. Pillow asked most of the questions propounded to this gentleman, as also of those to Major Rice. At this point I was called into an adjoining room, where I remained but a few minutes. When I returned, Major Jones, brigade quarter-master, was just entering the room. Gen. Pillow at once approached him, and taking him a little one side, explained to him that it had been determined to evacuate the place, and that he must prepare to burn the quarter-master's stores in his hands. Major Jones inquired at what time. Gen. Pillow replied about daybreak, about half-past five o'clock. Major Jones left very soon, and I did not see him in the room afterwards, that I recollect. In a few minutes Major Haynes, brigade commissary, entered the room, and received similar instructions as to the commissary stores under his charge. About this time a scout was ushered in, who announced that the enemy had reoccupied the lines from which they had been driven during the fight on Saturday. Gen. Pillow doubted if the scout was not mistaken; so another was sent out. About half an hour had elapsed when Major Haynes returned and remained near me in the room during the remainder of the discussion. Just as he entered, Gen. Buckner remarked: "I am confident that the enemy will attack my lines by daylight, and I cannot hold them for half an hour." Gen. Pillow replied quickly: "Why so, why so, general?" Gen. Buckner replied: "Because I can bring into action not over four thousand men, and they demoralized by long and uninterrupted exposure and fighting, while he can bring any number of fresh troops to the attack." Gen. Pillow replied: "I differ with you; I think you can hold your lines; I think you can, sir." Gen. Buckner replied: "I know my position, and I know that the lines cannot be held with my troops in their present condition." Gen. Floyd it was, I think, who then remarked: "Then, gentlemen, a capitulation is all that is left us." To which Gen. Pillow replied: "I do not think so; at any rate we can cut our way out." Gen. Buckner replied: "To cut our way out would cost three-fourths of our men, and I do not think any commander has a right to sacrifice three-fourths of his command to save one-fourth." To which Gen. Floyd replied: "Certainly not."

About this time the second scout sent out returned, and reported the enemy in force occupying the position from which they had been driven. Thereupon two of Col. Forrest's cavalry were sent to examine the backwater, and report if it could be crossed by the army. These scouts returned in a short time, and reported that cavalry could pass, but infantry could not.

Gen. Buckner then asked: "Well, gentlemen, what are we to do?" Gen. Pillow replied: "You understand me, gentlemen, I am for holding out, at least to-day, getting boats, and crossing the command over. As for myself, I will never surrender; I will die first." Gen. Floyd replied: "Nor will I. I cannot and will not surrender; but I must confess personal reasons control me." Gen. Buckner replied: "But such considerations should not control a general's actions." Gen. Floyd replied: "Certainly not; nor would I permit it to cause me to sacrifice the command." Gen. Buckner replied: "Then, I suppose the duty of surrendering the command will devolve on me." Gen. Floyd asked: "How will you proceed?" Gen. Buckner replied: "I will send a flag asking for Gen. Grant's quarters, that I may send a message to him. I will propose an armistice of six hours to arrange terms." A pause here ensued. Then Gen. Buckner asked: "Am I to consider the command as turned over to me?" Gen. Floyd replied: "Certainly; I turn over the command." Gen. Pillow replied, quickly: "I pass it; I will not surrender." Gen. Buckner then called for pen, ink, paper, and a bugler. Gen. Floyd then said: "Well, general, will I be permitted to take my little brigade out if I can?" Gen. Buckner replied: "Certainly, if you can get them out before the terms of capitulation are agreed on." Col. Forrest then asked: "Gentlemen, have I leave to cut my way out with my command?" Gen. Pillow replied: "Yes, sir; cut your way out;" and continuing, "gentlemen, is there any thing wrong in my leaving?" Gen. Floyd replied: "Every man must judge for himself of that." Gen. Pillow replied: "Then I shall leave this place." Here Gen. Pillow left the room; but returning in a short time and taking a seat between Gens. Floyd and Buckner, said: "Gentlemen, in order that we may understand each other, let me state what is my position. I differ with you as to the cost of cutting our way out; but if it was ascertained that it would cost three-fourths of the command, I agree that it would be wrong to sacrifice them for the remaining fourth." Gens. Floyd and Buckner replied: "We understand you, general, and you understand us."

After this I left the room, and soon after, the place.

(Signed,) HUNTER NICHOLSON.

Sworn to and subscribed before me on this 18th day of March, 1862.

(Signed) LEVI SUGANS,

Intendant of the town of Decatur, Ala., and ex-officio J. P.

Response of Brig.-gen. Gid. J. Pillow to the Order of the Secretary of War of March 11, 1862.

To Capt. H. P. Brewster, *A. A. G.:*

Sir: In my supplemental report, which was forwarded through Gen. A. S. Johnston, I have, as I conceived, substantially answered the points as indicated in the order of the Secretary of War as unsatisfactory to the President. But to be more specific, and to reply directly to these points, I beg to say, that:

1. Gen. Floyd reached Fort Donelson early in the morning on the 13th of February, and being my senior officer, assumed the command. Up to that time we had no need of additional forces, for at that time the enemy had only about 20,000 troops, and we had a force fully sufficient to defend the place against that force, and I did not, nor could not, know with what force they meant to invest us. We were attacked by that force, on the 13th, around our whole line, and after three or four hours of vigorous assault, we repulsed his forces everywhere.

After Gen. Floyd's arrival, being second in command, I could not, without a violation of military duty, apply for reinforcements. But I do not seek to shelter myself from responsibility by this consideration. Though the enemy's force greatly exceeded ours, we felt we could hold our position against him, until his large force of fresh troops arrived on the evenings of the 13th, 14th, and 15th. These arrivals, of about 30,000 troops, made it manifest that we could not hold the position long against such overwhelming numbers, particularly as they were then enabled to completely invest us and cut off our communication with the river.

It was then impossible to get reinforcements from Bowling Green or elsewhere in time to relieve us. It required three days, by railroad and river, for the forces which did come to us to get there, owing to the shortness of transportation.

I apprised Gen. Johnston of the arrival of the enemy's large reinforcements, giving him every arrival. But I had just come from Bowling Green, and was of opinion that the force reserved for that position was inadequate for its defence against a large assaulting force, and I knew Gen. Johnston could not give me any reinforcements unless he abandoned the place, a measure which I did not consider it my province to suggest. Knowing this, I felt it my duty to make the best possible defence with the forces we had. We had one additional regiment or battalion there, which Gen. Floyd sent to Cumberland City to protect public stores that had been forwarded to that city. These are the reasons why no application was made for reinforcements.

2. In response to the second point made by the Secretary's order, I have to say that arrangements were all made, orders given the whole command to evacuate the work, and troops were under arms to march out, when information was received that we were reinvested. Up to this time the general officers were all agreed upon the line of action necessary and proper under the circumstances. (See supplemental report.) It was as to the necessity of a change of policy in the new state of the case that the difference of opinion arose among the general officers. I was for cutting our way out. Gens. Floyd and Buckner thought that surrender was a necessity of the position of the army.

In response to the point made by the Secretary's order that it was not satisfactorily explained how a part of the command was withdrawn and the balance surrendered, I have to say:

On the night and evening of the 15th of February, after the battle, in expectation of evacuating the place that night, Gen. Floyd had sent off every steamboat that we had with the prisoners, our sick, and wounded. As matters turned out it was most unfortunate, but I do not perceive how the act could be censured, for it was a measure preparatory to evacuation, and no one could have foreseen the course of events which late that night defeated that measure.

The act, however, was that of my senior officer, and I was not even consulted about its propriety.

When we ascertained, between three and four o'clock that night, that we were reinvested, and the question of our position became one of vital interest to the commanding officers, we had not a single boat, neither skiff, yawl, nor even float, or other ferry boats. There was no means of crossing the river. The river was full, and the weather intensely cold. About daybreak the steamer General Anderson, and one other little boat, came down; one of the boats had on board about 400 raw troops. I had then crossed the river in a small hand flat, about four feet wide by twelve long, which Mr. Rice, a citizen of Dover (acting as my volunteer aid-de-camp), had by some means brought over from the opposite side of the river.

Upon the arrival of these steamers, Gen. Floyd, acting, I presume, under agreement between him and Gen. Buckner, before the command was turned over, crossed over to the opposite shore as many of his troops as he could, until he was directed by Gen. Buckner's staff officer to leave, as the gunboats of the enemy were approaching. This information was given me by Gen. Floyd at Clarksville. My horses were brought across the river on one of the boats that brought over the troops. Myself and staff then made our way to Clarksville by land. These facts explain how a portion of the command were withdrawn when the balance could not be. I, however, had no kind of agency in it.

3. In response to the third point upon which information is called for by the Secretary's order, viz.: Upon what principle the senior officers avoided responsibility by transferring the command, I have only to say that I urged from first to last the duty of cutting through the enemy's lines with the entire command; I was not sustained, but was alone in my position; and with Gen. Buckner's avowal that his troops could not make another fight, and without the assistance of either general in command, and in an enterprise of great difficulty and peril, I could scarcely hope to cut through the enemy's lines unaided. Yet it was against my conviction of duty to surrender.

Under the circumstances in which I was placed, I saw no means of defeating the surrender, and therefore considering myself only technically the recipient of the command; when turned over by Gen. Floyd, I promptly passed, and declined to accept it. It was in this sense that I said in my original report that when the command was turned over to me I passed it. In point of fact, however, the command was turned over by Gen. Floyd to Gen. Buckner.

In proof of which I embody in this report a dispatch from Gen. Floyd, to Gen. A. S. Johnston, on the morning of the 16th February; I also embody an order of Gen. Buckner's, after he had assumed command, to Brig.-gen. B. R. Johnson.

CUMBERLAND CITY, Feb. 16, 1862.

TO GEN. JOHNSTON:

This morning at 2 o'clock, not feeling willing myself to surrender, I turned over the command to Gen. Buckner, who determined to surrender the fort and the army, as any further resistance would only result in the unavailing spilling of blood. I succeeded in saving half of my command by availing myself of two little boats at the wharf—all that could be commanded. The balance of the entire reserve of the army fell into the hands of the enemy. The enemy's force was largely augmented yesterday by the arrival of thirteen transports, and his force could not have been less than fifty thousand. I have attempted to do my duty in this trying and difficult position, and only regret that my exertions have not been more successful.

(Signed) J. B. FLOYD.

Order of Brig-gen. Buckner to Brig-gen. B. R. Johnson.

HEAD-QUARTERS, DOVER, Feb. 16, 1862.

SIR:—The command of the forces in this vicinity has devolved upon me by order of Gen. Floyd. I have sent a flag to Gen. Grant, and during the correspondence, and until further orders, shall refrain from any hostile demonstrations, with a view of preventing a like movement on the enemy's part. You will endeavor to send a flag to the enemy's posts in front of your position, notifying them of the fact that I have sent a communication to Gen. Grant from the right of our position, and desire to know his head-quarters.

Respectfully, your obedient servant,

(Signed) S. B. BUCKNER, *Brig-gen. C. S. A.*

These orders show that all parties knew the command was turned over, not to myself, but to Gen. Buckner. The reason for this was obvious; both Gens. Buckner and Floyd were of opinion that a surrender of the command was a necessity of its position. They had both heard me say that I would die before I would surrender the command.

Gen. Buckner had said, if placed in command, he would make the surrender, and he had agreed with Gen. Floyd, that he might withdraw his brigade. This understanding and agreement, and my position, excluded me from actual command.

Having gone into the council of general officers, and taken part in its deliberations, I felt bound by its decision, although against my conviction of duty. I, therefore, determined not to assume nor accept the command. I still think that in acquiescing in this decision, as a necessity of my position, I acted correctly, although my judgment was wholly against the measure to surrender. I had no agency whatever in withdrawing any portion of the command, except to direct Col. Forrest to cut his way out with his cavalry, all of which I organized into a brigade under him.

5. In response to the 5th and 6th inquiries of the Secretary's orders, I reply, I do not know what regiments of Gen. Floyd's brigade were surrendered, nor which were withdrawn, nor do I know upon what principle the selection was made.

For further information, reference is made to my original and supplemental reports.

Before closing the response to the Hon. Secretary's order, I deem it not improper to say, that the only doubt I felt, in my opinion, I expressed, position assumed, or act I did, was, as to the propriety of retiring from the garrison, when I could not control the fate of the command, whose surrender was not my act, or with my approval. Upon this point, I consulted Gens. Floyd and Buckner.

For these reasons, and knowing that the general officers would not be permitted to accompany the men into captivity, I finally determined to retire, hoping I might be able to render some service to the country.

Very respectfully,

GID. J. PILLOW,

Brig.-Gen. C. S. A

Original Report of Gen. S. B. Buckner, addressed to Col. W. W. Mackall, A. A. G.

HEAD-QUARTERS CUMBERLAND ARMY.
DOVER, TENN., Feb. 18, 1862.

SIR:—It becomes my duty to report that the remains of this army, after winning some brilliant successes, both in repulsing the assaults of the enemy, and in sallying successfully through their lines, has been reduced to the necessity of a surrender.

At the earliest practicable day, I will send a detailed report of its operations. I can only say now, that after the battle of the 15th inst. had been won, and my division of the army was being established in position to cover the retreat of the army, the plan of battle seemed to have been changed, and the troops were ordered back to the trenches. Before my own division returned to their works on the extreme right, the lines were assailed at that point, and my extreme right was occupied by a large force of the enemy. But I successfully repelled their further assaults.

It was the purpose of Gen. Floyd to effect the retreat of the army over the ground which had been won in the morning, and the troops moved from their works with that view; but before any movement for that purpose was organized, a reconnoissance showed that the ground was occupied by the enemy in great strength. Gen. Floyd then determined to retreat across the river, with such force as could escape; but as there were no boats until nearly daylight on the 16th, he left with some regiments of Virginia troops about daylight, and was accompanied by Brig.-gen Pillow.

I was thus left in command of the remnant of the army, which had been placed in movement for a retreat, which was discovered to be impracticable. My men were in a state of complete exhaustion, from extreme suffering, from cold, and fatigue; the supply of ammunition, especially for the artillery, was being rapidly exhausted, the army was to a great extent demoralized by the retrograde movement. On being placed in command, I ordered such troops as could not cross the river to return to their intrenchments, to make at the last moment such resistance as was possible to the overwhelming force of the enemy. But a small portion of the forces had returned to the lines, when I received from Gen. Grant a reply to my proposal to negotiate for terms of surrender. To have refused his terms would, in the condition of the army at that time, have led to the massacre of my troops without any advantage resulting from the sacrifice. I therefore felt it my highest duty to these brave men, whose conduct had been so brilliant, and whose sufferings had been so intense, to accept the ungenerous terms proposed by the Federal commander, who overcame us solely by overwhelming superiority of numbers. This army is, accordingly, prisoners of war; the officers retaining their side-arms and private property, and the soldiers their clothing and blankets. I regret to state, however, that, notwithstanding the earnest efforts of Gen. Grant and many of his officers to prevent it, our camps have been a scene of almost indiscriminate pillage by the Federal troops.

In conclusion, I request, at the earliest time practicable, a Court of inquiry, to examine into the causes of the surrender of this army.

I am, sir, very respectfully,

Your obedient servant,

(Signed) S. B. BUCKNER,

Brig.-gen. C. S. A.

To Col. W. W. Mackall,

A. A. General,

Nashville, Tenn.

Official Report of Operations of Gen. S. B. Buckner's Division in the defence of Fort Donelson, and of the surrender of that post.

RICHMOND, VA., August 11, 1862.

SIR:—I have the honor to make the following report of the operations of that portion of the 2d division of the Central Army of Kentucky, which was detached from Bowling Green and Russellville, Ky., to aid in the defence of Fort Donelson and the village of Dover, on the Cumberland river, Tennessee.

By the courtesy of Brig.-gen. Grant, United States Army, I was permitted to transmit to Clarksville, Tennessee, a brief report of the surrender of Fort Donelson, but, as I now learn, it never reached the head-quarters of Gen. A. S. Johnston, I transmit herewith a copy.

I have been prevented from making an earlier report by the refusal of the Federal authorities, during my imprisonment, either to permit me to make a report or to receive the report of subordinate commanders. Such, indeed, was the discourtesy of the Federal War Department, that, though kept in solitary confinement during my imprisonment, and prevented from holding communications with any of my fellow-prisoners, a request on my part to be informed of the cause of a proceeding so unusual amongst nations pretending to follow the rules of civilized warfare, failed to elicit a response. On the 11th February, ultimo, Brig.-gen. Floyd had resolved to concentrate his division and my own at Cumberland city, with a view of operating from some point of the railway west of that position, in the direction of Fort Donelson or Fort Henry, thus maintaining his communications with Nashville, by the way of Charlotte. I reached Fort Donelson on the night of February 11th, with orders from Gen. Floyd to direct Gen. Pillow to send back at once to Cumberland City the troops which had been designated.

Before leaving Clarksville I had, by authority of Gen. Floyd, ordered Scott's regiment of Louisiana cavalry to operate on the north side of the Cumberland river, in the direction of Fort Donelson, with a view to prevent the establishment of any of the enemy's field batteries which might interfere with our transports. Gen Pillow declined to execute the order of which I was the bearer, until he should have a personal interview with Gen. Floyd. Accordingly, on the morning of the 12th, he left me temporarily in command, and proceeded himself in a steamer to Cumberland city. Before leaving, he informed me that he had directed a reconnoissance to be made by Col. Forrest's cavalry, with instructions in no event to bring on an engagement, should the enemy approach in force.

Gen. Pillow left me under the impression that he did not expect an immediate advance of the enemy, and regarded their approach from the direction of Fort Henry as impracticable. During the morning, Forrest reported the enemy advancing in force with the view of enveloping our line of defence; and for a time he was engaged with his usual gallantry in heavy skirmishing with them, at one time driving one of their battalions back upon their artillery.

About noon Gen. Pillow returned and resumed command; it having been determined to reinforce the garrison with the remaining troops from Cumberland City and Clarksville.

The defences were in a very imperfect condition. The space to be defended by the army was quadrangular in shape, being limited on the north by the Cumberland river, on the east and west by small streams, now converted into deep sloughs by the high water, and on the south by our line of defence. The river line exceeded a mile in length; the line of defence was about two miles and a half long, and its distance from the river varied from one-fourth to three-fourths of a mile. The line of entrenchments consisted of a few logs rolled together and but slightly covered with earth, forming an insufficient protection even against field artillery. No more than one-third of the line was completed on the morning of the 12th. It had been located under the direction of that able engineer officer, Major Gilmer, near the crests of a series of ridges which sloped backwards to the river, and were again commanded in several places by other ridges at a still greater distance from the river. This chain of heights was intersected by deep valleys and ravines, which materially interfered with communications between different parts of the line. Between the village of Dover and the water batteries, a broad and deep valley extending directly back from the river, and flooded by the high water, intersected the quadrangular area occupied by the army, and almost completely isolated the right wing. That part of the line which covered the land-approach to the water batteries, and constituted our right wing, was assigned to me with a portion of my division, consisting of the third or Col. John C. Brown's brigade, which was composed of the 3d Tennessee Volunteers, which was Col. Brown's regiment, 18th Tennessee regiment, Col. Palmer, 32d Tennessee regiment, Col. Cook; half of Col. Baldwin's 2d brigade, temporarily attached to Col. Brown's 2d regiment Kentucky Volunteers, Col. R. W. Hanson; 14th Mississippi Volunteers, Major Doss; 41st Tennessee Volunteers, Col. Farquharson; Porter's battery of six field-pieces; Graves' battery of six field-pieces.

The remaining regiments of Baldwin's brigade, the 26th Tennessee Volunteers, Col. Lillard, and the 26th Mississippi Volunteers, Col. Reynolds, together with the brigade commander, were detached from my command by Brig.-gen. Pillow and assigned a position on the left of the line of entrenchments.

The work on my lines was prosecuted with energy, and was urged forward as rapidly as the limited number of tools would permit; so that by the morning of the 13th my position was in a respectable state of defence.

My disposition of the troops was as follows:

Hanson's regiment on the extreme right; Palmer's regiment, with its reserve, in position to reinforce Hanson; Porter's battery occupying the reserve, in position or reinforce Hanson; Porter's battery occupying the advanced salient, sweeping the road which led to the front, and flanking the intrenchments both to the right and to the left. The reserve of the 14th Mississippi was held as its support. Brown's, Cooks', and Farquharson's regiments were on the left. Graves' battery occupied a position near the extreme left of the intrenchments on the declivity of the hill, whence it swept the valley with its fire and flanked the position of Col. Heiman to the east of the valley.

From three to five companies of each regiment were deployed as skirmishers in the rifle-pits. The other companies of each regiment were massed in columns, sheltered from the enemy's fire behind the irregularities of the ground, and held in convenient positions to reinforce any portion of the line that might be seriously threatened.

No serious demonstration was made on our lines on the 12th.

Early on the morning of the 13th, a column of the enemy's infantry, which was apparently forming to move down the valley between my left and Heiman's right, was driven back by a few well-directed shots from Graves' battery.

About 10 o'clock in the morning the enemy made a vigorous attack upon Hanson's position, but was repulsed with heavy loss. The attack was subsequently renewed by three heavy regiments, but was again repulsed by the 2d Kentucky regiment, aided by a part of the 18th Tennessee. In both these affairs, and also in a third repulse of the enemy from the same position, Porter's battery played a conspicuous part.

About 11 o'clock a strong attack was made on Col. Heiman's position beyond my left. A well-directed fire from Graves' battery upon the flank of the assaulting column materially contributed to repulse the enemy with heavy loss.

The fire of the enemy's artillery and riflemen was incessant throughout the day; but was responded to by a well-directed fire from the intrenchments, which inflicted upon the assailant considerable loss, and almost silenced his fire late in the afternoon. On the preceding night Gen. Floyd had arrived and assumed command of all the troops, and during the morning visited and inspected my lines. My loss during the day was thirty-nine (39) in killed and wounded.

The enemy were comparatively quiet in front of my position during the 14th. On the morning of that day I was summoned to a council of general officers, in which it was decided unanimously, in view of the arrival of heavy reinforcements of the enemy below, to make an immediate attack upon their right, in order to open our communications with Charlotte, in the direction of Nashville. It was urged that this attack should be made at once, before the disembarkation of enemy's reinforcements—supposed to be about fifteen thousand men. I proposed with my division to cover the retreat of the army, should the sortie prove successful. I made the necessary dispositions preparatory to executing the movement, but early in the afternoon the order was countermanded by Gen. Floyd, at the instance, as I afterwards learned of Gen. Pillow, who, after drawing out his troops for the attack, thought it too late for the attempt.

On the night of the 14th it was unanimously decided, in a council of general officers and regimental commanders, to attack the enemy's right at daylight. The object of the attack was to force our way through his lines, recover our communications, and effect our retreat upon Nashville by way of Charlotte, Tenn. This movement had become imperatively necessary in consequence of the vastly superior and constantly increasing force of the enemy, who had already completely enveloped our position. The general plan was for Gen. Pillow to attack his extreme right, and for that portion of my division remaining under my command after being relieved in the rifle-pits by Col. Head's regiment, to make an attack upon the right of the enemy's centre, and, if successful, to take up a position in advance of our works on the Wynn's ferry road, to cover the retreat of the whole army; after which my division was to act as the rear guard.

On Saturday morning, the 15th, a considerable portion of my division was delayed by the non-arrival of Head's regiment at the appointed time, and by the slippery condition of the icy road which forbade a rapid march. My advance regiment, however, the 3d Tennessee, reached a position by daylight in rear of a portion of the intrenchments which had been occupied by Gen. Pillow's troops. As no guards had been left in this portion of the line, and even a battery was left in position without a cannoneer, I deployed the 3d Tennessee in the rifle-pits to cover the formation of my division as it arrived. The regiments were formed, partly in line and partly in column, and covered from the enemy's artillery fire by a slight acclivity in front. In the mean time the attack on the enemy's right was made in the most gallant and determined manner by the division of Gen. Pillow. For the progress of that action, I refer to the reports of Col. Baldwin, Col. Gregg, and their subordinate commanders, which have been transmitted to me, as the senior officer left with the army.

In front of my position the enemy had a heavy battery posted on the Wynn's ferry road, with another battery opposite my left—both sustained by a heavy infantry force.

Major Davidson, acting chief of my artillery, established Graves' battery to the left of the Wynns' ferry road and opened upon the enemy's batteries a destructive fire. I also directed a portion of the artillery to open upon the flank and left rear of the enemy's infantry, who were contesting the advance of Gen. Pillow's division. In view of the heavy duty which I expected my division to undergo in covering the retreat of the army, I thought it unadvisable to attempt an assault at this time in my front until the enemy's batteries were, to some extent, crippled, and their supports shaken by the fire of my artillery. About 9 o'clock, Gen. Pillow urged an advance to relieve his forces. I accordingly sent forward the 14th Mississippi, Major Doss, deployed as skirmishers. At the request of its commander, I assigned the direction of its movements to Major Alexander Cassidy, of my staff. The line of skirmishers was sustained by the 3d and 18th Tennessee. Their line of march unfortunately masked the fire of my artillery upon the Wynn's ferry road, but it continued to play with effect upon the force which was opposing Gen. Pillow's advance. The combined attack compelled the enemy to retire, not, however, without inflicting upon my troops considerable loss. Under a misapprehension of instructions, at a time when my artillery was directed over the heads of the advanced troops upon the enemy's battery, these regiments withdrew without panic, but in some confusion, to the trenches, after the enemy's infantry had been driven a considerable distance from their position.

As the enemy's line of retreat was along the Wynn's ferry road, I now organized an attack further to my right, up a deep valley which led from Heiman's left, in rear of the position occupied by the enemy's batteries.

In order to cover the advance of the infantry column, I directed Capt. Porter, with his artillerists, to serve Green's battery, which was already in position, and, at the same time, sent a request to Col. Heiman to direct Maney's battery to open its fire, while he should deploy a line of skirmishers in advance of his position to cover the right of the valley. Gen. Pillow was at this time, as I afterwards learned, on the heights to my right, occupied by Heiman. Maney's, Porter's, and Graves' batteries now opened a cross fire upon the enemy's battery and position, soon crippling some of his guns and driving their supports, while the 3d, 18th, and 32d Tennessee regiments, under their brigade commander, Col. John C. Brown, moved steadily up the valley, preceded by their skirmishers, who soon became engaged with those of the enemy. This movement, combined with the brisk fire of three batteries, induced a rapid retreat of the enemy, who abandoned a section of his artillery. At the same time my infantry were thus penetrating the enemy's line of retreat, Forrest, with a portion of his cavalry, charged upon their right, while Gen. Pillow's division, under the orders of Gen. B. R. Johnson and Col. Baldwin were pressing their extreme right about half a mile to the left of this position.

In this latter movement, a section of Graves' battery participated, playing with destructive effect upon the enemy's left, while, about the same time, the 2d Kentucky, under Col. Hanson, charged in quick time, as if upon parade, through an open field and under a destructive fire, without firing a gun, upon a superior force of the enemy, who broke and fled in all directions. A large portion of the enemy's right dispersed through the woods and made their way, as was afterwards learned, to Fort Henry.

While this movement was going on, I conducted one piece of artillery, under Capt. Graves, along the Wynn's ferry road, supported by the 14th Mississippi, and sent orders to the residue of Graves' battery and Porter's and Jackson's batteries, and Farquharson's Tennessee regiment to follow the movement with rapidity. I also sent to direct Hanson's regiment to rejoin me. The enemy, in his retreat, had now taken up a strong position on the road beyond the point where it crosses the valley. I directed the position to be attacked by the 3d, 18th, and 32d Tennessee regiments, the first on the left, the others on the right of the road, while Graves' piece took position in the road within two hundred and fifty or three hundred yards of the enemy's guns. These regiments, under the immediate command of Col. Brown, advanced gallantly to the attack, while Graves' piece responded with effect to the enemy's artillery. Notwithstanding their vast superiority in numbers, the enemy were driven, with very heavy loss, from their position, and retreated to the right of the Wynn's ferry road, leaving it entirely open. In this position I awaited the arrival of my artillery and reserves, either to continue the pursuit of the enemy, or to defend the position I now held, in order that the army might pass out on the forge road, which was now completely covered by the position occupied by my division. But Gen. Pillow had prevented my artillery from leaving the intrenchments, and had ordered Farquharson not to join me, and also sent me reiterated orders to return to my intrenchments on the extreme right. I was in the act of returning to the lines when I met Gen. Floyd, who seemed surprised at the order. At his request to know my opinion of the movement, I replied that nothing had occurred to change my views of the necessity of the evacuation of the post, that the road was open, that the first part of our purpose was fully accomplished, and I thought we should at once avail ourselves of the existing opportunity to regain our communications. These seemed to be his own views; for he directed me to halt my troops and remain in position until he should have conversed with Gen. Pillow, who was now within the intrenchments.

After that consultation, he sent me an order to retire within the lines, and to repair as rapidly as possible to my former position on the extreme right, which was in danger of attack. The enemy made no attempt at pursuit. I secured the section of artillery which had been captured, and covered my retrogade movement by Hanson's and Farquharson's regiments. My troops were already much exhausted, but returned as rapidly as possible, a distance of two miles, to their positions. But a small portion of my division had reached their positions, when a division of the enemy, under command of Gen. C. F. Smith, assaulted the extreme right of my position, falling upon Hanson's regiment before it had reached its rifle-pits. This gallant regiment was necessarily thrown back in confusion upon the position of the 18th Tennessee. At this period

I reached that position, and, aided by a number of officers, I succeeded in hastily forming a line behind the crest of a hill which overlooked the detached works which had been seized by the enemy before Hanson had been able to throw his regiment into them. The enemy advanced gallantly upon this new position, but was repulsed with heavy loss. I reinforced this position by other regiments as they successively arrived, and by a section of Graves' battery, while a section of Porter's battery was placed in its former position. During a contest of more than two hours, the enemy threatened my left with a heavy column, and made repeated attempts to storm my line on the right, but the well-directed fire of Porter's and Graves' artillery, and the musketry fire of the infantry, repelled the attempts, and finally drove him to seek shelter behind the works he had taken, and amid the irregularities of the ground. There was probably no period of the action when his force was not from three to five times the strength of mine. Towards the close of the action I was reinforced by the regiments of Cols. Quarles and Sugg and Bailey. Gens. Floyd and Pillow also visited the position about the close of the action.

In a council of general and field officers, held after night, it was unanimously resolved, that if the enemy had not reoccupied, in strength, the position in front of Gen. Pillow, the army should effect its retreat; and orders to assemble the regiments for that purpose were given by Gen. Floyd. But as the enemy had, late in the afternoon, appeared in considerable force on the battle-field of the morning, a reconnoissance was ordered, I think by Gen. Pillow, under the instructions of Gen. Floyd. The report of this reconnoissance, made by Col. Forrest, has been fully stated by Gens. Floyd and Pillow; and from what I have been able to learn since, I am satisfied the information reported was correct. Among other incidents, showing that the enemy had not only reoccupied their former ground, but extended their lines still farther to our left, is the fact that Overton's cavalry, following after Forrest's, was cut off from retreat by an infantry force of the enemy at the point where Forrest had crossed the stream on the river road. When the information of our reinvestment was reported, Gen. Floyd, Gen. Pillow, and myself, were the only members of the council present. Both of these officers have stated the views of the council, but my recollection of some of the incidents narrated differs so materially from that of Gen. Pillow, that, without intending any reflection upon either of those officers, I feel called upon to notice some of the differences of opinion between us. Both officers have correctly stated that I regarded the position of the army as desperate, and that an attempt to extricate it by another battle, in the suffering and exhausted condition of the troops, was almost hopeless.

The troops had been worn down with watching, with labor, with fighting. Many of them were frosted by the intensity of the cold; all of them were suffering and exhausted by their incessant labors. There had been no regular issue of rations for a number of days, and scarcely any means of cooking.

Their ammunition was nearly expended. We were completely invested by a force fully four times the strength of our own. In their exhausted condition, they could not have made a march. An attempt to make a sortie would have been resisted by a superior force of fresh troops; and that attempt would have been the signal for the fall of the water batteries, and the presence of the enemy's gunboats sweeping with their fire, at close range, the positions of our troops; who would have been thus assailed on their front, rear, and right flank, at the same instant. The result would have been a virtual massacre of the troops, more disheartening in its effects than a surrender.

In this opinion Gen. Floyd coincided; and I am certain that both he and I were convinced that Gen. Pillow agreed with us in opinion. General Pillow then asked our opinion as to the practicability of holding our position another day. I replied that my right was already turned, a portion of my intrenchments in the enemy's possession; they were in position successfully to assail my position and the water batteries; and that, with my weakened and exhausted force, I could not successfully resist the assault which would be made at daylight by a vastly superior force. I further remarked, that I understood the principal object of the defence of Donelson to be to cover the movement of Gen. A. S. Johnston's army from Bowling Green to Nashville, and that if that movement was not completed, it was my opinion that we should attempt a further defence, even at the risk of the destruction of our entire force, as the delay even of a few hours might gain the safety of Gen. Johnston's force. Gen. Floyd remarked that Gen. Johnston's army had already reached Nashville.

I then expressed the opinion that it would be wrong to subject the army to a virtual massacre when no good could result from the sacrifice; and that the general officers owed it to their men, when further resistance was unavailing, to obtain the best terms of capitulation possible for them. Gen. Floyd expressed himself in similar terms, and in his opinion I understood Gen. Pillow to acquiesce.

For reasons which he has stated, Gen. Floyd then announced his purpose to leave, with such portion of his division as could be transported, in two small steamers, which were expected about daylight. Gen. Pillow, addressing Gen. Floyd, then remarked that he thought there were no two persons in the Confederacy whom the "Yankees" would prefer to capture than himself and Gen. Floyd, and asked the latter's opinion as to the propriety of his accompanying Gen. Floyd. To this inquiry the latter replied that it was a question for every man to decide for himself. Gen. Pillow then addressed the inquiry to me, to which I remarked that I could only reply as Gen. Floyd had done; that it was a question for every officer to decide for himself, and that in my own case I regarded it as my duty to remain with my men and share their fate, whatever it might be.

Gen. Pillow, however, announced his purpose to leave, when Gen. Floyd directed me to consider myself in command. I remarked that a capitulation would be as bitter to me as it could be to any one, but I regarded it as a necessity of our position, and I could not reconcile it with my sense of duty to separate my fortunes from those of my command.

It is due to Gen. Pillow to state, that some time after the command had been transferred to me, and while preparations were making for his departure, he returned to the room and said to Gen. Floyd and myself, that he wished it understood that he had thought it would have been better to have held the fort another day in order to await the arrival of steamers to transport the troops across the river. I again recapitulated my reasons for thinking it impossible to hold our position; and whatever may have been Gen. Pillow's opinion, he certainly impressed me with the belief that he again acquiesced in the necessity of a surrender.

It was now near daylight of Sunday morning, the 16th. I ordered the troops back to their positions in the intrenchments, and addressed a note, a copy of which is inclosed, to the Federal commander, Brig.-gen. U. S. Grant. His reply is also transmitted. When it was received, but a small portion of the troops had returned to their lines. A portion of my field guns had been spiked when the troops had been withdrawn under Gen. Floyd's order. The gunners had not yet returned to the water batteries. A degree of confusion, amounting almost to a state of disorganization, resulting from the knowledge of our position, pervaded a considerable portion of the troops. A corps of not less than fifteen thousand of the enemy, with fifteen pieces of artillery, were in position to assault the extreme right of the line, which was effectually turned, and the water batteries exposed to assault, without the power of resisting the attack. At the point most strongly threatened I could not have opposed at the time a thousand men. Every road leading from the lines was effectually closed. Even the river road, by which the cavalry had left, and which was impassable by infantry, was closed by a force of the enemy within fifteen minutes after Forrest had passed, and Overton's cavalry was forced to return to the lines. The troops were broken down by unusual privations. Most of them had labored or fought almost incessantly for a week. From Thursday morning until Saturday night they had been almost constantly under fire. From Thursday evening until Sunday morning they had suffered intensely in a heavy snow-storm, and from intense cold, almost without shelter, with insufficient food, and almost without sleep. They had behaved with a gallantry unsurpassed, until the power of further endurance was exhausted. The supply of ammunition was very small. The aggregate of the army, never greater than twelve thousand, was reduced to less than nine thousand men after the departure of Gen. Floyd's brigade. The investing force of the enemy was about fifty thousand strong, and considerably exceeded that force by the following morning. Under these circumstances, no alternative was left me but to accept the terms offered by our ungenerous enemy. A copy of the order of Gen. Grant, fixing the terms of the surrender, is herewith inclosed.

I do not seek to avoid any responsibility which, in the judgment of the President, may attach to my action, which was guided in every instance by a feeling of duty. My chief wish is, that he will find it consistent with the public interest to permit me still to unite my fortunes in the contest for independence with those of the brave men whose gallantry I have witnessed, whose dangers and hardships I have shared, and in common with whom I have endured the privations of imprisonment amongst a vindictive and tyrannical foe. I cannot close this report without calling special attention to the gallant and able conduct of my brigade commanders, Col. John C. Brown, of the 3d Tennessee, and Col. William E. Baldwin, of the 14th Mississippi, and of Col. R. W. Hanson, commanding the 2d Kentucky, detached from Breckinridge's Kentucky brigade. For the operations of Col. Baldwin's troops, I refer to his report, as he was detached from my command during the siege. But he, as well as the other two officers, were conspicuous on every occasion for their gallantry and military judgment, and merit the special approbation of the Government.

Amongst the regimental commanders, Col. J. M. Lillard, and Col. E. C. Cook, merit the highest commendation for their gallant bearing, and the excellent manner in which they handled their regiments; and Major W. L. Doss behaved with marked gallantry. Major George B. Cosby, my chief of staff, deserves the highest commendation for the gallant and intelligent discharge of his duties; and the other members of my staff are entitled to my thanks for their gallantry, and for the efficient discharge of their appropriate duties: Lieut. Charles F. Johnson, aid-de-camp; Lieut. T. J. Clay, acting aid; Major Alexander Cassiday, acting inspector general; Major S. K. Hays, quarter-master; Capt. R. C. Wintersmith, commissary of subsistence; Major Davidson, chief of artillery; Mr. J. N. Gallaher, acting aid; Mr. Moore, acting topographical officer; Mr. J. Walker Taylor, commanding a detachment of guides, and Mr. D. P. Buckner, volunteer aid. Major Barbour, A. D. C. to Brig.-gen. Tilghman, though wounded, remained with me on the 13th. I cannot bestow sufficient praise upon Capt. Porter, and Capt. Rice E. Graves, and their officers and men, for the gallant and efficient handling of their batteries. Artillery was never better served, and artillerists never behaved, under trying circumstances, with greater coolness. Porter's battery, from its more exposed position, lost more than half its gunners; and its intrepid commander was severely wounded late in the afternoon of Saturday, being succeeded in command by the gallant Lieut. Morton.

Capt. Jackson's Virginia battery, though not so frequently engaged, is entitled to notice.

For an understanding of the particular operations of Gen. Pillow's division, I refer you to the reports of his brigade commanders, Col. William E. Baldwin, Col. A. Heiman, Col. John Gregg, and to the reports of their subordinate commanders.

Accompanying this report is a list of the strength of my division, and of its killed and wounded. My aggregate force at the beginning of the contests, which was constantly diminishing, did not exceed 3025 infantry, and two batteries artillery. Two of my regiments, in addition, 844 men, were constantly under the command of Gen. Pillow. The length of my lines exceeded three-fourths of a mile.

I am, sir, very respectfully, your obedient servant,

S. B. BUCKNER, *Brig-gen. C. S. A.*,

Lately commanding 2d Division Central Army of Kentucky.

To: GENERAL S. COOPER,

Adjutant and Inspector General, C. S. A., Richmond, Va.

Correspondence referred to in Gen. Buckner's Report.

HEAD-QUARTERS, FORT DONELSON,
February 16th, 1862.

SIR:—In consideration of all the circumstances governing the present situation of affairs at this station, I propose to the commanding officer of the Federal forces the appointment of commissioners to agree upon terms of capitulation of the forces and post under my command, and in that view suggest an armistice until 12 o'clock to-day.

I am, sir, very respectfully,
Your obedient servant,
(Signed,) S. B. BUCKNER,
Brig.-gen. C. S. A.

To Brig.-gen. U. S. GRANT,
Commanding U. S. Forces near Fort Donelson.

Reply of Gen. Grant to a proposal for an Armistice.

HEAD-QUARTERS ARMY IN THE FIELD,
CAMP NEAR DONELSON, February 16, 1862.

Gen. S. B. BUCKNER,
Confederate Army:

SIR:—Yours of this date, proposing armistice and appointment of commissioners to settle terms of capitulation, is just received.

No terms, except unconditional and immediate surrender, can be accepted. I propose to move immediately upon your works.

I am, sir, very respectfully,
Your obedient servant,
U. S. GRANT,
Brig.-gen.

[Copy.]

Reply of Gen. Buckner to Gen. U. S. Grant.

HEAD-QUARTERS
DOVER, TENN., Feb. 16, 1862.

To Brig-gen. U. S. GRANT, U. S. A.:

SIR:—The distribution of the forces under my command, incident to an unexpected change of commanders, and the overwhelming force under your command, compel me, notwithstanding the brilliant success of the Confederate arms yesterday, to accept the ungenerous and unchivalrous terms which you propose.

I am, sir, your obedient servant,
(Signed) S. B. BUCKNER,
Brig-gen. C. S. A.

Agreement of Gen. Grant to allow officers taken at Donelson to retain their side-arms, &c., &c.,

HEAD-QUARTERS ARMY IN THE FIELD,
FORT DONELSON, Feb. 16, 1862.

Special Order.

All prisoners taken at the surrender of Fort Donelson will be collected as rapidly as practicable near the village of Dover, under their respective company and regimental commanders, or in such manner as may be deemed best by Brig-gen. S. B. Buckner, and will receive two days' rations, preparatory to embarking for Cairo.

Prisoners are to be allowed their clothing, blankets, and such private property as may be carried about the person, and commissioned officers will be allowed their side-arms.

By order U. S. GRANT,
Brig-gen.

Report of Lieut.-col. J. F. Gilmer, Chief Engineer, upon the defence of Forts Henry and Donelson.

ENGINEER'S OFFICE,
DECATUR, ALA., March 17, 1862.

Col. W. W. MACKALL, A. A. General,
Western Department, Decatur, Ala.:

COL.:—In obedience to Gen. Johnston's orders of January 29th, received at Nashville, I proceeded the next day to Fort Donelson and thence to Fort Henry, to inspect the works and direct what was necessary to be done at both.

8

I arrived at Fort Henry the afternoon of the 31st, when I met Brig-gen. Tilghman, commanding the defences on the Tennessee and Cumberland rivers. By the exertions of the commanding general, aided by Lieut. Jos. Dixon, his engineer officer, the main fort (a strong field-work of fine bastion front) had been put in a good condition for defence, and seventeen guns mounted on substantial platforms; twelve of which were so placed as to bear well on the river. These twelve guns were of the following description: One ten-inch columbiad, one rifled gun of 24-pounder calibre (weight of ball 62 lbs.), two 42-pounders, and eight 32-pounders, all arranged to fire through embrasures formed by raising the parapet between the guns with sand-bags, carefully laid.

In addition to placing the main work in good defensive order, I found that extensive lines of infantry cover had been thrown up by the troops forming the garrison, with a view to hold commanding ground that would be dangerous to the fort if possessed by the enemy.

These lines and the main work were on the right hand of the river, and arranged with good defensive relations, making the place capable of offering a strong resistance against a land attack coming from the eastward.

On the left bank of the river there was a number of hills within cannon range, that commanded the river batteries on the right bank.

The necessity of occupying these hills was apparent to me at the time I inspected Fort Henry, early in November last, and on the 21st of that month, Lieut. Dixon, the local engineer, was ordered from Fort Donelson to Fort Henry, to make the necessary surveys, and construct the additional works. He was at the same time informed that a large force of slaves, with troops to protect them, from Alabama, would report to him for the work, which was to be pushed to completion as early as possible.

The surveys were made by the engineer, and plans decided upon without delay, but by some unforeseen cause the negroes were not sent until after the 1st of January last. Much valuable time was thus lost, but under your urgent orders, when informed of the delay, Gen. Tilghman and his engineers pressed these defences forward so rapidly, night and day, that when I reached the fort (31st January last), they were far advanced, requiring only a few days' additional labor to put them in a state of defence. But no guns had been received that could be put in these works, except a few field-pieces; and, notwithstanding every effort had been made to procure them from Richmond, Memphis, and other points, it was apprehended they would not arrive in time to anticipate the attack of the enemy, which, from the full information obtained by Gen. Tilghman, was threatened at an early day either at Fort Henry or Fort Donelson, or possibly on both at the same time. The lines of infantry cover, however, which had been thrown up were capable of making a strong resistance, even without the desired artillery, should the attack be made on that (the left) bank of the river. Experimental firing with the 10-inch columbiad, mounted in main work, showed a defect in the cast-iron carriage and chapis, which threatened to impair the usefulness of this most important gun. With the ordinary charge of sixteen pounds of powder, the recoil was so great as to cause most violent shocks against the rear heuster, threatening each time to dismount the piece. With the aid of an ingenious mechanic, clamps were finally made which served to resist, in some degree, the violence of the recoil. With this exception, the guns bearing on the river were in fair working order.

After the batteries of the main work were mounted, Gen. Tilghman found much difficulty in getting competent artillerists to man them, and he was not supplied with a sufficient number of artillery officers.

Impressed with the great deficiency in the preparations for defending the passage of the river at Fort Henry, the commanding officer expressed to me his fears that it might cause disaster if the place were vigorously attacked by the enemy's gunboats. This he thought his greatest danger.

In conjunction with Gen. Tilghman, I made every effort during the three days I remained at Fort Henry to get all the works and batteries in as good condition for defence as the means at hand would permit. The 3d of February we went over to Fort Donelson to do the same. The works there required additions to prevent the enemy from occupying grounds dangerous to the river batteries and the field-work, which had been constructed for the immdiate defence landward.

It was also important that better protection should be made for the heavy guns (mounted for the defence of the river) by raising the parapet with sand-bags between the guns to give greater protection to the gunners.

The 3d and 4th days of February were devoted to making preparations for this work, and locating lines of infantry cover on the commanding ground around the fort.

In the midst of these labors on the 4th, heavy firing was heard in the direction of Fort Henry, which warned Gen. Tilghman that the enemy had made his attack upon that work. This was soon confirmed by a report from Col. Heiman to the effect that the gunboats had opened fire, and that troops were being landed on the right bank of the river, three and a half to four miles below the fort. The general decided to return to the Tennessee river at once, and expressed, with some anxiety, a wish that I would accompany him. I finally took the responsibility of doing so, with the hope that my professional services might possibly prove useful during the defence. On arriving at Fort Henry, we found the enemy had landed additional troops below, and that every preparation was being made to attack by land and water.

The necessary dispositions for defence were at once entered upon, by making a special organization of the troops, and assigning commands to the officers.

Early the next morning, 5th February, the troops were drawn out under arms, and marched to the respective points each body was to defend—this, with a view to insure order in case it became necessary to form promptly in face of the enemy. The main body of the forces was assigned to the defence of the advanced lines of infantry cover, where they were in a measure beyond the range of shot and shell from the gunboats, and the troops inside of the main fort were to be limited to the men who had received some instructions in the use of heavy guns, and such additional force as could be useful in bringing up full supplies of ammunition. Those assigned to the fort were practised at the battery, under the immediate supervision of the commanding officer, and each one taught, with as much care as possible, his duty in anticipation of the threatened attack.

In such preparations the day was consumed, and it was only at nightfall that the troops were relieved, to seek food and rest; it being quite apparent that the enemy would not attack until next day.

ATTACK ON FORT HENRY, 6TH FEBRUARY, 1862.

During the early part of the day, preparations of the enemy, for an advance with his gunboats, could be observed from the fort—also, the movements of troops at their encampments along the bank of the river below—making it evident that we were to be attacked by land as well as by water.

About half-past 11 o'clock, one of the gunboats had reached the head of the island, about one and a third miles below our batteries, another soon followed, then a third, and a fourth—all coming as nearly abreast as the width of the river would permit. As soon as this line was formed, a rapid fire was opened upon our works (about half-past 12 o'clock), which was returned with spirit by our gunners, who were all at their places, eager for the contest. In a short time after, the rifled cannon burst, killing three of the men at the piece, and disabling a number of others.

The effect of this explosion was very serious upon our artillerists —first, because it made them doubt the strength of these large guns to resist the shock of full charges—and secondly, because much was expected from the long range of rifled cannon against the gunboats. Still, all stood firmly to their work, under a most terrific fire from the advancing foe, whose approach was steady and constant.

From the rear of their lines a fifth gunboat was observed to be firing curvated shot, many of which fell within the work, but to the rear of our guns; many shot and shell were lodged in the parapet, making deep penetrations, but in no case passing through, unless they struck the cheek of an embrasure. One of the 32-pounder guns was struck by a heavy shell passing through the embrasure. All the gunners at this piece were disabled, and the gun rendered unfit for service.

About the same moment, a premature discharge occurred at one of the 42-pounder guns, causing the death of three men, and seriously injuring the chief of the piece and others.

Not many moments later, it was observed that the 10-inch columbiad was silent; the cause of which was at once examined into by Gen. Tilghman, and it was found that the priming wire had been jammed and broken in the vent. A blacksmith (I regret I cannot recall the name of the gallant soldier) was sent for, and he labored with great coolness for a long time, exposed to the warmest fire of the enemy, but in spite of his faithful and earnest efforts, the broken wire remained in the vent, making this important gun unserviceable for the continued contest. By this time the gunboats, by a steady advance, had reached positions not over six or seven hundred yards from the fort. Our artillerists became very much discouraged when they saw the two heavy guns disabled, the enemy's boats apparently uninjured, and still drawing nearer and nearer. Some of them even ceased to work the 32-pounder guns, under the belief that such shot were too light to produce any effect upon the iron-clad sides of the enemy's boats.

Seeing this, Gen. Tilghman did every thing that it was possible to do to encourage and urge his men to further efforts. He assisted to serve one of the pieces himself for at least fifteen minutes; but his men were exhausted, had lost all hope, and there were none others to replace them at the guns. Finally, after the firing had continued about an hour and five minutes, but two guns from our batteries responded to the rapid firing of the enemy, whose shots were telling with effect upon our parapets. It was then suggested to the general that all was lost, unless he could replace the men at the guns by others who were not exhausted. He replied—"I shall not give up the work," and then made an effort to get men from the outer lines to continue the struggle. Failing in this, he sent instructions to the commanders of the troops in the exterior lines to withdraw their forces. As soon as this movement was commenced, confusion among the retiring troops followed—many thinking it intended for a rapid retreat to escape from the enemy's forces, expected to approach from the point of landing below. A few moments later the flag was lowered.

From information received, the strength of the enemy was estimated at nine thousand men. These forces were advancing to cut off the communications with Fort Donelson. Probably the movement would have proved a success, had the garrison remained a few hours longer.

Our force at Fort Henry was about 3200, of which less than 100 were surrendered with the fort.

The fall of Fort Henry, and the power of the enemy to strike at once, with an immense force, at Fort Donelson, made it necessary that the army at Bowling Green should be withdrawn to a point which would secure a prompt passage to the Cumberland river. The vicinity of Nashville seemed the proper position. If the enemy were defeated at Donelson, with prompt reinforcements, there was still a hope that your army might resist the invader, and defend that city; if Donelson fell, it could be promptly passed to the south bank of the river.

DEFENCE OF FORT DONELSON.

The capture of Fort Henry was, for the enemy, a great success, which, it was felt, would embolden him to make an early attack upon Fort Donelson.

To meet this, every effort was made to strengthen the defences. Lines of infantry cover were laid out on commanding grounds around the place, and fatigue parties were daily employed in their construction. To aid the local engineer in the work of defence, I remained at the fort the 7th, 8th, and 9th of February, when Gen. Pillow took command of the whole. At his request, I asked and received authority to remain and aid in the defence.

Immediately on his arrival, the general took active measures to inform himself as to the character of the defences, and had the additional works pressed forward with the greatest activity. Having received reinforcements, and others being expected daily, the lines of infantry cover were extended so as to embrace the town of Dover, where many of our munitions were stored. The time for these works being decided upon, they were at once pressed to completion, and the batteries for the defence of the river strengthened.

By the night of the 12th these were in readiness, and the heavy guns recently received at the fort were mounted. To provide an ample force of artillerists to work the heavy guns, through a long-continued attack, Gen. Pillow detailed Capt. R. R. Ross, and his company of well-drilled men from his battery, to aid in the river defence. The selection of this officer and his command proved most fortunate, as in the obstinate attack that was made by the gunboats they performed noble and effective service.

Brig.-gen Buckner arrived at Fort Donelson on the afternoon of the 12th.

In the mean time, the enemy had landed in large force on the bank of the river below, and other troops were brought over from Fort Henry. The smoke of his gunboats was seen in the distance, warning us that a combined attack was to be expected. Skirmishes were frequent between our pickets and the enemy's forces advancing to meet us.

On the 13th the besiegers opened, with artillery, upon our land defences; and their sharpshooters annoyed our men constantly whenever exposed above the infantry covers, as at the field batteries. One of the gunboats commenced firing upon the river batteries early in the day, throwing shot and shell at long range.

The same morning Gen. Floyd arrived with reinforcements, including three batteries of field-artillery, which were placed in position as promptly as possible. The enemy's fires were kept up throughout the day, and responded to with spirit by our artillery and infantry. In the afternoon an attempt was made to storm the intrenchments on the heights near our centre, but failed—the assailants being handsomely repulsed. One of the guns in the river batteries was struck by a heavy shot from the gunboat, disabling the carriage and killing Lieut. Joseph Dixon, the local engineer officer. Our total loss during the day was considerable, but I am unable to report numbers.

The contest of the day closed. The enemy had gained no footing on our works, or produced any important impression upon them. But our forces were much fatigued, having been under arms all day, and this after three or four days' hard labor upon the intrenchments. To add to their sufferings it turned suddenly cold in the afternoon, and, at dark, commenced snowing and continued the greater part of the night. Inclement as was the weather, it was necessary (to guard against surprise) that the troops should be all night in position along the lines of infantry cover. The next day, the 14th, the besiegers brought up large reinforcements, just landed from numerous transports, and extended their lines, in great strength, towards their right, enveloping our extreme left. They took positions that placed it in their power to plant batteries on the river bank above, and cut off our communications. Such appeared to be their design. In consequence of these movements the firing of the enemy was less frequent than on the previous day.

Early on this afternoon the gunboats were observed to be advancing to attack the river batteries, and at 3 o'clock a vigorous fire was opened from five boats approaching *enchelon*. Our gunners reserved their fire until the gunboats had come within effective range, and then at a signal, every gun was fired—twelve in number. This fire told with great effect, penetrating the iron sides of the boats. The firing now became terrific—the enemy still advancing. In rear of the five boats first engaged, a sixth was reported throwing curvated shot, which passed over our works, exploding in the air just above. After some time, one of the boats was seen to pull back, probably disabled by our shot. The others continued to advance, keeping up a rapid fire.

Our batteries were well served and responded with great effect, disabling, as it was believed, two more of the gunboats. The engagement lasted until ten minutes after 4 o'clock, the gunboats having approached to within three hundred or four hundred yards of our guns, when they withdrew from the contest. Our batteries were uninjured, and not a man in them killed.

The repulse of the gunboats closed the operations of the day, except a few scattering shot along the land defences. It was evident, however, from the movements of numerous bodies of troops around our lines, that the enemy had resolved to invest us, and, when prepared, to attack us in overwhelming numbers, or press us to a capitulation by cutting off supplies and reinforcements.

Gens. Floyd, Pillow, and Buckner, met in council soon after

dark; I was present. After an interchange of views, it was decided to attack the enemy on his extreme right and right-centre, at 5 o'clock in the morning. It was believed that the enemy might be driven back and an opportunity secured to withdraw in safety our forces; that possibly greater advantages might be gained by the attack, which, if well followed up on our part, would result in disaster to the invaders.

This being decided upon, the brigade commanders were at once sent for, and the positions for their respective commands in the order of attack assigned. Brig.-gen. Pillow was to direct the movement against the right of the enemy. Brig.-gen. Buckner, that against his right-centre, advancing along the Wynn's ferry road. A few regiments were to remain to guard the lines.

About 5 o'clock next morning (the 15th) the left wing, under Gen. Pillow, moved to the attack. Brisk fires were opened and kept up by the enemy, and responded to with spirit from our lines, his men generally overshooting, while ours were constantly warned to aim low.

The enemy's fire, after some time, extended towards their extreme right, indicating a design to turn our left. To meet this, a body of troops, under Brig.-gen. B. S. Johnson, made a flank movement and met the foe. After a long struggle, the enemy finally gave way, at first falling back slowly. Our troops pressed forward, and about half-past 9 o'clock, his right wing was in full retreat. Now, the cavalry on our extreme left was brought up and charged with effect on the retreating enemy. Six field-pieces were captured at different points, and, at a later hour of the day, brought within the line of intrenchments. Our success against the right wing was complete.

I now accompanied Gen. Pillow across the field to the point of attack assigned to Gen. Buckner's division. On our arrival there, his division was in rear of the lines of infantry covers, the general and his officers encouraging the troops to renew the attack on the enemy, who still held position in their front. Gen. Buckner stated, that he had, soon after the firing of Gen. Pillow's forces was heard, opened on the enemy with artillery, and followed it up by sending forward two of his best regiments to the assault, that they moved forward over the infantry covers with spirit, and advanced steadily and in order against the enemy. They were soon exposed to heavy fires of small-arms, and of a field-battery planted in their front; and they responded well for some time to the volleys of the besiegers, but finally their ranks were thrown into confusion, and they fell back rapidly in rear of our intrenchments. Gen. Buckner continued to encourage his men, feeling that a little time was necessary to overcome the dispiriting effects of the repulse earlier in the day. In the mean time, the fires of our left wing were heard steadily advancing, driving the enemy back upon his right-centre. This was referred to with encouraging effect upon Gen. Buckner's division. Artillery fires were kept up against the enemy in his front, and soon afterwards he moved forward with his division to renew the attack. The enemy being now pressed in front of his centre by this advance, and on his right flank by the pursuing forces of Gen. Pillow's division, retreated rapidly for some distance towards his left wing; but, receiving heavy reinforcements, the pursuit was checked, and finally the retreating foe made a firm stand, opening from a field-battery, strongly supported by masses of infantry,

About one o'clock an order was given by Gen. Pillow, recalling our forces to the defensive lines. Our forces having returned, they were ordered to the positions they occupied the day previous, involving a march of over a mile for the troops on the extreme right. The enemy at the same time advanced with his reinforcements to attack that flank, and by a prompt movement succeeded in effecting a lodgment within the lines just as our exhausted forces arrived.

A vigorous attempt to dislodge him failed, and at length our men, having suffered much, fell back, leaving him in possession of that portion of our defences. The advantage gained by the enemy placed him in position to assault our right in full force with his fresh troops next morning. Such was the condition of affairs when the darkness of night closed the bloody struggle of the day. In course of the night Gens. Floyd, Pillow, and Buckner met in council. I was not present.

The following morning about 3 o'clock I was told by Gen. Pillow that a surrender had been decided on. He invited me to join himself and staff, as they were not included in the proposed surrender. This I accepted and accompanied him to Clarksville and Nashville, where I had the honor to report to you in person.

From information received, the strength of the enemy at Donelson was estimated to be about fifty thousand. Our effective force was about fifteen thousand.

The surrender at Fort Donelson made Nashville untenable by the forces under your command. Situated in a wide basin, intersected by a navigable river in possession of the invader—approached from all directions by good turnpike-roads, and surrounded by commanding hills, involving works of not less than twenty miles in extent, the city could not be held by a force less than fifty thousand. With all the reinforcements to be hoped for, your army could not be raised to that number before the place would have been attacked by heavy forces of the enemy, both by land and water. The alternative was to withdraw to the interior of the State of Tennessee.

(Signed) J. F. GILMER,
Lieut.-col. and Chief Engineer, Western Department.

Report of G. C. Wharton, commanding First Brigade.

HEAD-QUARTERS 1ST BRIGADE, FLOYD'S DIVISION,
CAMP NEAR MURFREESBORO', TENN., Feb. 22, 1862.

Brig.-gen. JOHN B. FLOYD:

SIR:—I have the honor to submit the following report of the participation of this brigade in the engagement at Fort Donelson:

The advance of the brigade, the 51st regiment Virginia Volunteers, reached Dover, one mile from the fort, about 11 P. M., on Friday, the 7th, and immediately reported to Brig.-gen. B. R. Johnson, who was then in command, and was ordered to encamp near the wharf. About 4 P. M., on the 8th, the 56th regiment Virginia Volunteers arrived, and was ordered to encamp near the 51st. From Saturday to Wednesday following there was skirmishing between our cavalry pickets and the enemy. On Wednesday our pickets were driven in, and the enemy reported advancing in force; the brigade was then ordered to take position on the left of Brig.-gen. Buckner's division, and near the centre of our line of defence. Soon after taking position the enemy commenced to throw shot and shell, which did no execution; Capt. Porter's battery was then ordered to take the position which had been assigned to this brigade, and we were ordered to the support of the left wing, commanded by Brig.-gen. Johnson. We were engaged during the evening and night in constructing breastworks and rifle-pits; during Thursday we were under a heavy fire from the enemy's batteries. There were also frequent engagements with the infantry, in all of which the enemy were repelled.

Thursday night we remained again in the ditches; on Friday there was skirmishing with the infantry and sharpshooters, and occasionally sharp firing from the batteries. On Friday evening oc curred the terrific cannonading between the gunboats and the fort, some of the shells from the boats exploding in and near our lines, but doing no injury. On Saturday morning, at 4 A. M., the brigade was withdrawn from the ditches and placed in line by order of Brig.-gen. Pillow, to make an attack on the enemy's extreme right flank. Col. Baldwin's brigade was placed in advance; this brigade followed next; about 6 o'clock the column was put in motion. We had scarcely passed beyond the line of our defence when the skirmishers of Col. Baldwin's brigade engaged the enemy's pickets. In a few minutes the engagement became general; we were then ordered to deploy and advance, which was done with spirit and promptness. The enemy, after a very obstinate resistance, was forced to retire, but were either rallied or reinforced on the several ridges from which they were again and again driven. Our men, cheering as they charged, pursued them nearly two miles, when orders were received that we should retire to our intrenchments. The brigade was very much exhausted, having been under fire or in the ditches for more than four days. The loss of the 51st was 9 killed, 43 wounded, and 5 missing; of the 56th, 3 men were killed, 37 wounded, and 115 missing. Lieut.-col. J. W. Massie commanded the 51st regiment. His bearing was most chivalric and gallant. Capt. G. W. Davis gallantly led the 56th regiment. Lieut. August Vosberg, attached to the brigade as engineer officer, rendered very efficient service in rallying and leading the men, and throughout the day distinguished himself for gallantry and acts of daring. To mention the many individual instances of heroism and daring would too much lengthen this report; therefore, suffice it to say, that all the officers and men of both regiments behaved with commendable coolness and bravery.

Capt. S. H. Newberry, Lieuts. Henderson and Painter, of the 51st, were wounded; Capt. D. C. Harrison was mortally wounded whilst leading his men to a charge. Lieuts. Ferguson and Haskins were also wounded. A number of improved arms were captured and brought to camp.

On Sunday morning, the 16th, the brigade was ordered from Fort Donelson to Nashville, where valuable service was rendered in guarding and shipping government stores.

Thursday, the 20th, the brigade was ordered to this place, where we are now in camp.

Respectfully submitted,

G. C. WHARTON,
Colonel commanding Brigade.

Report of Colonel John McCausland, commanding Second Brigade.

HEAD-QUARTERS SECOND BRIGADE, FLOYD'S DIVISION,
MURFREESBORO', TENNESSEE, *February* 23.

Brigadier-general JOHN B. FLOYD:

SIR: I have the honor to submit the following report of the action of this brigade, on the 13th, 14th, and 15th of February, 1862, in the engagement near Fort Donelson, between the Confederate States forces and United States forces under Gen. Grant. On the morning of the 13th I received your orders to proceed at once from Cumberland City to Fort Donelson, where we arrived at daylight, and were at once ordered to the trenches. This brigade was posted as a support to Green's battery on the left wing. During the entire day the enemy kept up an incessant fire of shot and shell upon the battery and its support; the men and officers behaved well under the circumstances, and soon became accustomed to the firing. There were five men wounded during the day. On the 14th there was continued skirmishing with artillery and musketry. About 2 o'clock, P. M., the gunboats commenced a heavy bombardment of the fort, the shells passing over and taking the line or works in reverse, and many passing over and through this brigade; however, we suffered no loss, and gathered several large shells (64's, I think). About dark, another battery was posted in front of our position, and during the night it was placed behind a good earthwork, thrown up by the men. About midnight, I received orders to concentrate my brigade near the left wing, which was done promptly, and at daylight of the morning of the 15th, the column under Gen. Pillow sallied from the left and engaged the enemy in a short space of time.

This brigade was a reserve for Col. Baldwin's brigade, but the enemy pressing his right, I at once moved up to his support and engaged the enemy posted in thick undergrowth and a rough and rolling country. I ordered the firing to commence as soon as the enemy was in sight. They were advancing just in front of the 36th Virginia regiment. They, in a short time were checked, and then I ordered a charge upon them; the men came up with a shout and charged the enemy, routed him, and pursued him for two miles, when we were called back by order of Gen. Pillow. The 36th Virginia regiment had 14 killed and 46 wounded. On Sunday morning this brigade was ferried across the river, and are now arriving at this camp. Lieut.-col. Ried was wounded about the close of the action. He and Major Smith behaved gallantly during the day; in fact, men and officers all behaved well. We captured one field-gun and 200 Enfield muskets.

I am, sir, very respectfully,
Your obedient servant,
JOHN McCAUSLAND,
commanding Second Brigade.

Report of Col. W. E. Baldwin, commanding Second Brigade.

FORT WARREN, BOSTON HARBOR,
March 12th, 1862.

Major GEORGE B. CROSBY,
A. A. General:

SIR:—Left by Gen. Buckner at Cumberland City, on the 11th of February. On the night of the 12th instant, I received orders by telegraph from Brig.-gen. Pillow, commanding at Fort Donelson, to hasten to that place with two regiments of my command. The 26th Tennessee, Col. Lillard, and the 26th Mississippi, Col. Reynolds, were immediately embarked and arrived at Dover about 1 o'clock in the morning of Thursday, the 13th. These regiments were at first posted immediately on the left of the centre of our lines of rifle trenches, as a support to one of our batteries. This disposition was changed after daylight the same morning; the 26th Mississippi being placed in the trenches on the *extreme* left, and the 26th Tennessee placed in reserve as a support to the former.

About 9 o'clock, A. M., the enemy commenced a brisk artillery fire, apparently on our whole line. This fire, kept up with but little intermission throughout the entire day, produced but little effect upon the left until late in the evening, when, the enemy having reduced his charges, several of the shells, which had previously passed too high, fell in our midst, mortally wounding one man and slightly wounding two others in Col. Lillard's regiment.

On the 4th the fire was not renewed. About noon, Gen. Pillow directed the left wing to be formed in the open ground to the left and rear of our position in the lines, for the purpose, apparently, of attacking the enemy's right. My command, to which the 20th Mississippi, Major Brown, was temporarily attached, constituted the advance, in the following order: 1st, the 26th Mississippi; 2d, the 26th Tennessee; 3d, the 20th Mississippi.

Formed in column by platoon, we advanced in a road leading from a point about two hundred yards from the left of our trenches, and approaching, nearly perpendicularly, the enemy's right. We had proceeded not more than one-fourth of a mile, when Gen. Pillow ordered a countermarch, saying that it was too late in the day to accomplish any thing; and we returned to our former position in the lines.

Late that night commanders of brigades were summoned to a council at Gen. Pillow's head-quarters, where, after being duly advised of our perilous situation, enveloped by a largely superior force, which was being constantly increased, and our communications already at the mercy of the enemy, it was unanimously determined to endeavor to extricate the army by a bold and vigorous attack on the right of the Federal lines early on the morrow.

The regiments composing our left wing were to form at 4 o'clock, A. M., on the same ground and in the same order as on the previous evening, and to advance, under command of Gen. Pillow, to attack the extreme right of the enemy, supposed to be posted in force at a distance of one and a half or two miles.

This movement was to be supported by our right wing under Gen. Buckner, who was to move from the lines at a later period, follow up the first blow, and, should the combined movement not prove successful in creating a panic in the enemy's ranks, a way might at least be opened by turning his right for the egress of our whole force. In anticipation of thus attempting our escape, the men were directed to take knapsacks, blankets, and all the rations that could be immediately provided.

Precisely at 10 minutes past 4 o'clock on the morning of Saturday, the 15th, Gen. Pillow arrived on the ground, and found my three regiments, which were to constitute the advance, formed and ready to march. Some delay was caused by regiments not arriving promptly, and it was 6 o'clock before the column was put in motion. Marching by the right flank in a narrow and obstructed by-road, the head of the column had advanced not more than one-third of a mile, when, ascending a slight elevation, the advanced guard, composed of a company of the 26th Mississippi deployed, was fired upon by what was supposed at first to be only the enemy's pickets. A second company of the same regiment was immediately thrown forward to support the first; but both were soon driven back by a brisk and well-sustained fire, which indicated the presence of considerable force. Meanwhile the column was formed by company, and the leading regiment deployed into line to the right. This method of forming line of battle was rendered advisable by the peculiar features of the ground, which sloped gently to the right, thickly covered with timber. About ten yards to the left of the road, and running nearly parallel, was a fence, which bounded on that side an open field of some 400 or 500 acres extent. This field afforded no protection to our troops if brought "forward into line," but would expose them, in executing the movement, to a destructive fire, should the enemy have taken advantage of the position.

In executing the deployment, the 26th Mississippi was three times thrown into confusion by the close and rapid fire of the enemy taking the men in flank, and three times were they rallied, finishing the movement some fifty yards to the rear, and a little to the right of the exact point where their line should have been placed. The subsequent conduct of this regiment fully demonstrates the fact that any other than forward movements are extremely dangerous with volunteers, for during the remainder of the day both officers and men behaved with great coolness and gallantry.

The 26th Tennessee was then brought forward, and five companies deployed so as to occupy the space between the fence on the left, and the 26th Mississippi on the right, leaving the remaining five companies in column in the road to strengthen that point, which would evidently become the centre and pivot of operations.

Soon after this disposition was completed, a staff officer having been sent to advise Gen. Pillow that the enemy was before us in force, other regiments were sent forward from the rear of the column to right and left. Col. McCausland, of Virginia, with his command, formed on the right of the 26th Mississippi; the 1st Mississippi, Col. Gregg's Texas, and Lieut.-col. Lyon's 8th Kentucky regiments were formed still farther to our right, the latter regiment thrown back perpendicularly to our line, to prevent the enemy taking advantage of the cover afforded by the slope of the ground to turn our right.

The 20th Mississippi was sent into action, as I have since learned, by direct order of Gen. Pillow, and caused to take position in the field on the left, where they were openly exposed to a destructive fire, which they were not able to return with effect. The regiment was soon recalled, but not before its left wing had suffered heavy loss. Our line advanced some 50 or 100 yards up the slope, and remained stationary for more than an hour, the position of the enemy being so well chosen and covered, that it seemed impossible to gain an inch of ground. A small detachment of Virginia troops on the left of the 26th Tennessee, and in the open field, twice endeavored to gain ground forward to a point where their fire could be effective, but were unable to stand the destructive effect of the minié-balls.

At this juncture the 20th Mississippi again came up across the field, and took possession, slightly covered by an irregularity of the ground.

Observing a regiment or more of our troops posted inactive some 300 or 400 yards still more to our left, where the shallow ravine (which covered our front) spread out and was lost in the plain, I requested the commanding officer to throw forward his left, and advance up the hollow in a direction nearly parallel to our line of battle, and attacking the enemy's right flank. This movement being supported by the whole line—all the regiments on the left throwing forward their left wings—we succeeded in executing a change of front to the right, turning the right of the enemy, and driving him at once from his position.

Up to this time our condition was one of extreme peril, and nothing but the native gallantry of troops, brought forth the first time under heavy fire, and the extraordinary exertions of many of the field and company officers, saved us from being thrown back in confusion into our trenches.

From this time, the enemy were slowly driven from each position, which the ground, favorable for defence, enabled them to take. Two sections of artillery were taken. These, placed to bear on our lines of rifle trenches, were rushed upon in flanks and seized before they could be turned upon us, or be taken from the field. The first section was taken by the 26th Tennessee, the second by the 26th Mississippi. Advancing in a direction nearly parallel to our line of defence, when nearly opposite the centre, our course was for some time impeded by the desperate stand made by the enemy, who was probably reinforced, and occupying ground most favorable for sheltering his troops. Our ammunition had been so rapidly expended as to entirely exhaust the supply of some regiments. Numbers had provided themselves from the cartridge-boxes of the dead and wounded enemy.

Our force had been considerably reduced by casualties, and the numerous attendants who conveyed the wounded from the field. Having no mounted officer to send, I rode up to where Capt. Graves' battery was posted in the trenches, and requested supplies of ammunition and reinforcements, if any could be spared, giving Capt. Graves an intimation as to the relative positions of the forces engaged. Immediately on my return he opened a fire of grape, which so disordered the enemy that we were again enabled to advance, driving him from his camp of the night before.

He took a new position, still further retired, holding it for some time, until Col. Hanson, with the 2d Kentucky regiment, coming to our assistance, poured a fire into the enemy's flank, who immediately fled in confusion.

This completed the rout of the extreme right of the Federal forces. Uncertain as to the movements of our right wing, I paused, to obtain the information necessary to render our future movements effective, and to restore order from the confusion incident to a continuous combat of nearly six hours in the woods.

Here, Gen. B. R. Johnson came up to me for the first time, although I learn that he had, at different times during the morning, directed other portions of the line. He could give no information, but soon after, whilst my attention was directed to the 26th Mississippi and 26th Tennessee, moved off all the other regiments, including the 20th Mississippi. I saw no more of these during the remainder of the day.

After the lapse of an hour, observing troops from the right, returning to their original positions in the lines, I directed the two regiments left with me also to return to the trenches.

Three times during the day I had sent a staff officer to Gen. Pillow, for instructions, advising him of our situation. But no orders or directions were received from him, except to do "the best I could."

Being totally unacquainted with the topographical features of the ground, unadvised as to the movements of the general command, it was impossible for me to do more than simply dislodge the enemy, as from time to time he made a stand before us.

I would beg leave to remark here that the efficiency of the smoothbore musket, and ball and buck-shot cartridges, was fully demonstrated on this occasion, and to recommend that our troops be *impressed* with the advantage of closing rapidly upon the enemy, when our rapid loading and firing proves immensely destructive, and the long-range arms of the enemy lose their superiority.

For lists of killed and wounded, and minor details, recounting the conduct of subaltern officers and men, I beg leave respectfully to refer to reports of regimental commanders, which accompany this report.

Justice requires that I should refer to the coolness and gallantry of Col. Jno. M. Lillard, who, wounded in the early part of the engagement, remained at the head of his command during the whole day. It is difficult to determine which deserves most commendation, this regiment or its commander.

Lieut.-col. Boone and Major Parker, 26th Mississippi, both con ducted themselves as officers and brave men, and this reigiment bore its part well in the conflict.

Major Brown, commanding the 20th Mississippi, is entitled to honorable mention; his left wing thrown, in the early part of the day into an exposed position, by an ill-advised order, held its ground until recalled, and afterwards the whole regiment was among the foremost in every advance. I cannot forbear to mention that Col. McCausland's (—) Virginia, not assigned to my command, voluntarily tendered his co-operation, and was conspicuous for his daring intrepidity. The members of my personal staff deserve especial notice.

Lieut. S. D. Harris, 14th Mississippi, Acting Assistant Adj.-gen., was of great assistance. He merited, and has received my thanks. So, likewise, did Thomas A. Burke, a private in company I, 14th Mississippi, appointed an acting aid-de-camp. T. F. Carrington, a private in company K, 14th Mississippi, also an acting aid-de-camp, was severely, I fear mortally, wounded, in the early part of the action, an accident which deprived me of the services of a valuable aid.

Capt. D. H. Spence, of Murfreesboro, Tenn., volunteer aid, was severely wounded in the head whilst gallantly exposing himself on the top of a fence, and urging "Tennesseans, onward!"

My own regiment, the 14th Mississippi, Major Doss, was sent to Fort Donelson some days in advance of my arrival. The 41st Tennessee, Col. Farquharson, was brought down on the 13th.

Both regiments were posted on the right, and thus temporarily separated from my command.

Neither representations nor solicitations on my part could avail in inducing such change as would reunite these regiments, or place me where I desired to be, under the immediate direction of my proper commander.

The reports of these latter regiments have been made to Col.

John C. Brown, commanding 3d brigade, under whose orders they were temporarily placed.

A condensed statement of killed and wounded is annexed.

Respectfully, your ob't serv't
W. E. BALDWIN,
Col. comd'g. 2d Brigade, Gen. Buckner's Division.

Summary of Killed and Wounded—Saturday, February 15, 1862

OFFICERS.

26th Tennessee—In action, 33; wounded, 7.
26th Mississippi—In action, 39; killed, 1; wounded, 1.
20th Mississippi—In action, 31; killed, 1; wounded, 5.
Staff, 5; wounded, 2.
Total—In action, 108; killed, 2; wounded, 15.

NON-COMMISSIONED OFFICERS AND PRIVATES.

26th Tennessee—In action, 377; killed, 11; wounded, 78.
26th Mississippi—In action, 404; killed, 11; wounded, 68.
20th Mississippi—In action, 469; killed, 18; wounded, 55.
Total in action, 1250; killed, 40; wounded, 201.
Aggregate—In action, 1358; killed, 42; wounded, 216.

Report of Colonel John M. Lillard, of Twenty-sixth Tennessee Regiment in action at Fort Donelson, February, 1862.

To Col. W. E. BALDWIN,
Fourteenth Mississippi, commanding Brigade.

The regiment went into action on Saturday, February 15, 1862, with four hundred, including field and staff, &c. There were eleven killed and eighty-five wounded, many mortally, who have since died. Total killed and wounded, (96) ninety-six.

The enemy were driven back by us, their right wing being driven on their centre and left, making repeated stands, and being repeatedly routed, in which this regiment captured two brass cannon, two flags, the instruments of a band, and several prisoners. Of the conduct of the regiment in action, it is left for the brigade commander to speak.

The killed and wounded are as follows, to wit:

Field and Staff.—John M. Lillard, colonel, wounded slightly in shoulder; Lieut.-col. J. J. O'Dell, wounded slightly in arm; Lieut. J. A. Howell, adjutant, slightly in thigh.

Company A.—Haymond Stephen, wounded in shoulder; H. Sails, in bowels; Newton Deathridge, in side; S. Duckworth, in hip; L. H. Horner, in shoulder; P. J. Cade, in arm; Wash. Deathridge, in arm; W. Rhodes, in side: Ed. Hutson, in side; James Johnson, in hand—Total, 10.

Company B.—Killed, Joshua Collins. Wounded, D. Justice, in thigh; J. Justice, in arm; Sergeant W. M. Bayless, in arm.

Company C.—Killed, John Kenserly. Wounded, Lieut. A. Swaggerly, mortally; Lieut. McNabb, slightly; F. M. Griffin, slightly; George Brotherton, severely; T. T. Bauldwin, severely; A. Gray, in shoulder; J. A. Hicks, in thigh; George McMahan, in shoulder; J. A. Sample, in shoulder; F. M. Jenkin, in hand.

Company D.—Killed, T. D. Nash. Wounded, S. Hamack, R. Stratton, J. Williams, R. Brooks, J. F. Saterfield, J. P. Godwin, H. D. Godwin, A. Hepsher.

Company E.—Killed, Sergeant James Fleming and Joseph Childress. Wounded, F. M. Johns, A. T. Mundy, J. P. Godsey, A. S. Bacon, Corporal Cunningham, D. Moore, and John Mundy.

Company F.—Killed, Private C. Graham. Wounded, Captain H. L. McClinig, mortally; Lieut. Butler, slightly; Sergeant Bruce, slightly; Sergeant McCalluma, slightly; F. Cloud, J. Starke, W. M. Evans, mortally; H. L. Evans, slightly; J. McDade, J. Rothchild, W. Harley, W. Porter, L. La. J. Wright, J. L. Hout.

Company G.—Killed, Corporal Hancock. Wounded, private G. W. Guire, in arm.

Company H.—Killed, George Gross, J. R. Young, and W. Philips. Wounded, B. A. J. Jones, J. Carter, J. W. Kelly, J. M. Myers, S. Brock, and J. W. Davis.

Company I.—Killed, private F. M. Moss. Wounded, Sergeant H. L. White, F. M. Gilleland, H. H. Goin, J. D. Hembree, A. J. Kincade, J. W. Kinkrix, J. R. Kincade, J. R. Kennedy, G. W. Morrison, W. Netherly, J. H. O. Dome, Wm. Worick, A. J. Deathridge, Roland Hatson, John Cutis, A. East.

Company K.—Wounded, L. D. S. Richards, W. Alford, J. Green, Walker McCrony, Ben. Emmet, John George; Richards and Alford, thought mortally.

Respectfully submitted,

JOHN M. LILLARD,

Col. 26th Regiment Tennessee Volunteers.

Report from Major W. M. Brown, Twentieth Missis sippi Volunteers, of the part taken by it in the Battle of Fort Donelson, and all other facts connected with the Investment of the Fort and its Surrender.

RICHMOND, VA., April 12, 1862.

To Gen. G. W. RANDOLPH,
Secretary of War, C. S. A.:

I am directed by his Excellency, President Davis, to make your department a report of the part taken by the 20th Mississippi regiment in the engagement with the enemy at Fort Donelson, February 13th, 14th, and 15th, 1862; also, all the other facts concerning the investment and subsequent surrender of that post.

The regiment was assigned to the command of Brig.-gen. John B. Floyd, in Western Virginia, during the past summer, and went to Kentucky, and from thence to Fort Donelson, as part of his immediate command, arriving at that place at daylight on the 13th of February.

By sunrise, we were ordered into position as a reserve, immediately in rear of a point which was said to be our centre. During the day, heavy cannonading was kept up on both sides, mostly of shells and shrapnel, which resulted in killing one man and wounding three or four slightly. At night, we bivouacked in position until 12 o'clock, when an order came from Gen. Pillow to relieve the 7th Texas regiment, commanded by Gen. George John Gregg, then in the trenches. At that time, brisk firing was going on, supposed to be induced by the enemy's scouts and sharpshooters. The breastworks were thought insufficient from the test of the preceding days, so the remainder of the night was occupied in strengthening them, and cleaning out the trenches, now partially filled with water and snow.

The next day (Friday) was spent in occasional engagements with the enemy's sharpshooters. The fort was actively engaged in repelling an attack of the gunboats of the enemy. My position did not afford me a view of the proceedings, which have been fully reported by others. About 10 o'clock, I received an order to form our regiment on the extreme left in an open field, for the purpose of making a sortie on the enemy, which formation was executed in a very short time. By order of Gen. Pillow, the 20th Mississippi was attached to the brigade of Col. W. C. Baldwin, 14th Mississippi regiment, for this occasion. Before the order to advance had been given, a few guns of the enemy were heard, and by the time we had advanced one hundred yards, a private of company D was shot down, showing that the enemy was close at hand. We continued the march for two hundred yards more, when the order to halt was given, said to come from Gen. Floyd, with the explanation that we did not have time to accomplish what he wanted, and the order to countermarch being given, we did so in proper order, and we took our position in the trenches.

About 10 o'clock on that night (Friday) I received an order to form again as on the preceding evening, which was executed promptly, and by direction of Gen. Pillow, was again under the command of Col. W. E. Baldwin, 14th Mississippi regiment, acting brigadier. I made a report to him of the casualties of that day, while in captivity, but as he has been prohibited from making a statement to the War Department of this government, as likewise Gen. Buckner, I hereby substantially append the same of that day's proceedings, which was confined particularly to the 20th Mississippi regiment. Being the only field-officer in command, who was present, I was greatly assisted by Capt. H. Coutey, and Capt. C. K. Massey, company D, who were selected voluntarily by the officers of the regiment to assist in field duty, there being some difficulty as to seniority of captains. Adj. J. M. Cooper was also very efficient, and tendered valuable assistance.

Assistant-surgeon T. B. Elken was present, and rendered every assistance in his power to the wounded.

CASUALTIES OF THE SEVERAL COMPANIES.

Company A, Capt. H. Coutey, Lieut. R. M. Wilson.

Killed, private H. N. Vowel—1.

Wounded, Lieut. R. M. Wilson, privates J. Jamaison, Davy Morgan, J. R. Gumm, W. M. Brown—5.

Surrendered—51.

Company B, Capt. W. A. Rover, Lieuts. T. B. Sykes, Murf, and Robert.

Killed, Sergeant Dan. Howard, privates Dick Cooper, Tom Carroll, Rufus Gore, John Dabbs, James Whalen, John C. Pollack, D. A. Kyle, W. M. Langston—9.

Wounded, mortally, J. McEwen (since dead); mortally, J. K. Famier (dead).

Seriously and slight, H. Y. Bresly, L. C. Steward, Henry Catley, S. F. Williams, J. R. Seely, J. P. Willis, W. T. Porter, Sam. M. Johnson, B. W. McCullen, J. A. Wamble, J. H. Wore; missing, Edward Brown, John Lynch, G. C. Robinson—11.

Company B, surrendered—34 aggregate.

Company C, Capt. J. Z. George, Lieuts. J. M. Liddle, T. W. Keyes, and Stoddard, 69 privates—73 aggregate.

Wounded, D. L. Jackson—1.

Surrendered—66.

Company D, Capt. C. K. Massey, Lieuts. J. C. Williams, Datson, and McClelland, 54 privates—58 aggregate.

Killed, Sergeant W. H. Horden—1.

Surrendered—54.

Company E, Lieut. W. S. Champlin, commanding, 1 commissioned officer, 41 privates—42 aggregate.

Killed, private J. P. Wattlebaum—1.

Wounded, Lieut. J. S. Champlin, Sergeant W. K. Washington, Corporal J. P. Yates, privates Y. J. Bell, W. T. Bandy, H. Frederick, W. O. Fink, J. Germain, R. McCarty, W. M. Redman, F. C. Seely, H. F. Zenan—12.

Surrendered—35.

Company F, Capt. H. B. Graham, Lieuts. O. R. Eastland and L. E. R. Sterling.

Wounded, Lieut. O. R. Eastland, badly, Lieut. E. R. Sterling, Sergeant Odom, Corporal Fleming, private Welch—5.

Surrendered—54.

Company G, Lieut. W. R. Nelson commanding, 34 privates—35 aggregate.

Killed, privates G. White, C. Nabers, E. Wallace—3.

Wounded, Sergeant M. Maken, privates J. Starke, Early J. Finder, W. Wingo, J. M. Cully, J. Bevel—7.

Surrendered—31.

Company H, 1st Lieut. R. W. Paine commanding, Lieuts. J. S. Barbee and Harrison.

Killed, Lieut. R. W. Paine, private Dan. A. Davis—2.

Wounded, Lieut. J. H. Barbee, privates M. Davis, James M. Wilson, John H. Faulkner, James M. Finny—5.

Surrendered—43.

Company I, Capt. W. M. Chatfield, Lieut. Williams, 34 privates—36 aggregate.

Wounded, D. W. Thompson—1.

Surrendered—52.

Company K, D. T. Patterson, Lieuts. Oldham and Conway.

Killed, private T. H. Perry—1.

Wounded, W. Dioyne, badly; T. Rooke, badly; slightly, D. C. Patterson, Sergeant J. Dodd, privates R. H. Fox, W. C. Copshow, L. O. Young, James Gensel, W. S. Sandrod, Pat. Horn, Pyshus Stephens.

Surrendered—59.

RECAPITULATION:

Aggregate engaged—500.

Killed—20.

Wounded—58.

Surrendered—454. That being the number returned by the commanding officer of companies on Sunday, February 16, 1862, the day we were surrendered; afterwards many of them reported that they had known several to escape.

On the morning of Saturday, the 15th February, when marched out to attack the enemy, we were third in the order of advance. The enemy's pickets and sharpshooters commenced firing upon us soon after the order to advance, and by the time we had gained three hundred yards we were under a brisk fire, which came from a hill in front, covered with timber. By order from Gen. Pillow, the regiment was formed on the left of the road perpendicular to the road in the woods, immediately behind a fence, with an open field in front.

Subsequently I received an order from the same source to wheel the regiment to the right, through the field behind the line of fence, parallel to the road. This movement subjected us to a cross fire, and very much exposed us to the enemy on both sides under cover of the woods.

I had this fact represented to Gen. Pillow, who ordered me back to my first position.

At this time the five left companies were actually engaged on the hill, and not hearing the command, did not obey with promptness. The destruction at this time in their ranks demonstrated the fierceness of the conflict, and their unflinching bravery. I would mention especially Lieut. R. W. Paine, of company "H," who fell at this time, a martyr to his country's cause. There also was wounded, Capt. D. F. Patterson, company "K," Lieut. J. R. Eastland, company

"F," was badly, perhaps mortally wounded. He refused to be carried from the field, and exclaimed, "*Never mind me, boys; fight on, fight on.*" Lieut. J. W. Barbee, company "H," was wounded, and forced to retire.

Capt. W. A. Rover, commanding company "B," Lieut. W. R. Nelson, commanding company "G," Lieuts. S. B. Sykes, Conway, Murf, Roberts, W. S. Chaplin, commanding company "E," and Lieut. Harrison, are all deserving of honorable mention, for their conduct at this place.

To enumerate all the officers and privates who were deserving of notice for their gallantry throughout the day would to return a list of all who were on the field, and I would refer you to the foregoing list; but as fortune had thrown the left of the regiment in a more fiercely contested place, of which the suffering truly indicated, it is but justice to give these companies some especial notice.

On several other occasions during the day we were ordered to advance, and charge through the woods, part of the time under the eye and immediate direction of Gen. B. R. Johnson, on the extreme left, until the enemy were instantly driven off. Our movements under that officer seemed to take the enemy by their flank and rear. We opposed several of their lines of reserve, which retired with but little resistance, at 12 o'clock. I was instructed by Gen. Johnson to remain with the brigade of Col. Joseph Drake, of 4th Mississippi, then on my left. The regiment on my right very soon commenced retiring to the intrenchments; I did not learn by whose order, or for what purpose. In two or three hours a heavy column of the enemy attacked us in front, which was repulsed with little or no loss to us. They then endeavored to flank our right, and thereby cut us off from the breastwork, now about three-fourths of a mile distant. Col. Drake being so informed, gave the order to move, by the right flank, and continue the firing, which was executed.

By this time many companies were without ammunition; such was the case of many of Col. Drake's command. On this account, we retired to the trenches in proper order. When called upon the field, this regiment had been withont sleep for four nights, during which time they were marching, working, and watching in the trenches, encountering a severe snow-storm, without tents or cooking utensils. Notwithstanding all these privations and sufferings, every order was obeyed with the greatest alacrity. Every man seemed to feel that much depended upon himself.

At 1 o'clock on Saturday night I was sent for to report to Gen. J. B. Floyd, which I did promptly, and received notice from him that the place was to be surrendered, but that he would not surrender himself, and would cut his way out with his immediate command. To carry out this determination, he ordered me to form my regiment on the left of our line, as on the previous morning, with the Virginia regiment. While executing this order, anaid-de-camp of Gen. Buckner brought an order countermanding this arrangement, and directing me to the steamboat landing to embark on one or two boats then momentarily expected.

I went immediately to Gen. Floyd so as better to understand the movement, and from him learned the authenticity of the instructions, and also that we would embark; according to the rank of commanding officers, Col. Wharton's brigade and McCausland's brigade would precede mine in order. I was further directed to place a strong guard around the steamboat landing to prevent stragglers from going aboard. The boats being detained until nearly daylight, and the news of a surrender spreading through the camp, caused many to flock to the river, almost panic-stricken and frantic, to make good their escape by getting on board. In all this confusion I am proud to say, the 20th *Mississippi regiment* stood like a *stonewall*, which, as the necessity had required it, I had thrown in a *semi-circle* around the landing, to protect Gen. Floyd, and his Virginia regiments while embarking, and when the last hope had vanished of getting on board, according to the orders and promises of Gen. Floyd, and we realized the sad fate that we *had been surrendered*, the regiment stacked arms in good order, without the least intimidation, but full of regret. I am not able to state why we were not taken aboard the boat. There was about two hundred men and officers between my regiment and the boat. When Gen. Floyd was on board, I sent my adjutant to say we were ready to go aboard. I did not get a satisfactory answer, but learned that the general was fighting off the men in my front, who I thought belonged to one of the Virginia regiments, commanded by Major Thomas Smith, who has since informed me that some did not go. There seemed to be room enough for us all, and if he wanted them out of the way, I could have cleared the banks in a moment's time. When the boat left there did not seem to be fifty men on board (seen on deck). It is, perhaps, unbecoming in me to say whose fault it was that my regiment was not embarked, but I certainly owe it to myself to show that it was not mine.

While this excitement was going on, Gen. Buckner sent for me, and informed me that unless the steamboat left the landing immediately, he would throw a bomb-shell into it; that he had sent word to the boat to that effect.

He made some further remarks of an explanatory character, among others that we were in danger of being shelled by the gun-boats of the enemy, as he had surrendered the place, and the gun-boats were, or might be, at the fort. That his honor as an officer, and the honor and good faith of the Confederacy, required that at daylight he should turn over every thing under his command, agreeable to the terms of capitulation with Gen. Grant, of the Federal army. I returned to the boat to make every effort to get aboard, but it had shoved off, and was making up the river, with very few persons aboard. If I have been at fault, and caused the unnecessary imprisonment of my regiment, I am deserving the *eternal infamy of my fellow-soldiers;* but on the contrary, there is not an officer or private of the regiment, who witnessed the proceedings, who does not freely and cheerfully exonerate me from any blame whatsoever.

During the summer and fall campaign in Western Virginia, Kentucky, and Tennessee, this regiment has done credit to themselves and their State, for the arduous service they performed at Sewall's Mountain, Cotton Hill, and Fort Donelson. Their manly endurance of privations, prompt obedience to orders, and their eagerness for the fray, was *never* excelled by veteran soldiers of any army, and has entitled the 20th Mississippi to a prominent place in the history of this revolution.

In obedience to my instructions to furnish the department whatever information I may have of the battle of Donelson, I hereby append an unofficial statement which I have in my possession, made by "W. E. Baldwin, captain infantry, C. S. A., colonel 14th Mississippi Volunteers, commanding 2d brigade, 2d division (Gen. Buckner), Central Army, Ky.," from October 30, 1860.

To supply an anticipated omission in the future history of our country, it may not be improper here to state, that this brigade was composed of the following regiments:

14th Mississippi, commanded by Major W. T. Doss; 26th Tennessee, commanded by Col. J. M. Lillard; 26th Mississippi, commanded by Col. A. E. Reynolds; and 41st Tennessee, commanded by Col. R. Farquharson, was temporarily divided in the line around Fort Donelson; the 14th Mississippi and the 41st Tennessee being posted in the right wing, under Gen. Buckner's immediate supervision.

The 26th Tennessee and the 26th Mississippi were posted under my own command on the extreme left. These regiments, with the 20th Mississippi, under Major W. N. Brown, which was added to the command, constituted the advance in our attack on the enemy's right at 6 o'clock on the morning of February 15th, 1862.

They all behaved with great gallantry in a six hours' combat, which resulted in the total defeat of the enemy's right; whereby a way was opened for a retreat of the army. The opportunity not having been seized, and the enemy, 60,000 strong, having completely enveloped our little force, numbering, before the losses occasioned by four days' constant engagements, about 12,000 officers and men. The senior generals, Floyd and Pillow, relinquished the command to Gen. Buckner, and made their escape; the former taking with him about 1500 troops of his immediate command, only leaving Major Brown, with the 20th Mississippi, who, like veterans, were silently and steadily, though sullenly, guarding the embarkation of troops, while their chief was seeking safety.

The command was immediately surrendered on the morning of the 16th February, by Gen. Buckner, who shared the fate of his command.

It is unbecoming in soldiers to criticise the conduct of superiors, but when, after rejecting the councils of *juniors*, the condition of affairs is placed beyond the power of human means to retrieve, the *senior* endeavors to escape responsibility by throwing the same upon the *former*, *comment is unnecessary*.

After surrendering, the force was taken on transports, the rank and file separated from the officers. Most of the officers were confined in Camp Chase, near Columbus, Ohio. On the 4th of March, the field officers, fifty in number, were brought from that place to this (Fort Warren), where we have since been waiting with patience for the time to come when we can again strike for our homes and our country's independence.

FORT WARREN, March 19th, 1862.

It may not be improper here for me to state, that should any arrangement be established with the Federal government for the exchange of prisoners of war, that in consideration of services rendered by this regiment, and the further fact, it is mustered *for the war*, I should request it be placed first on the list to be exchanged.

Respectfully submitted,

W. M. BROWN,

Major 20th Mississippi regiment

Report of the Third Brigade—Colonel John C. Brown.

To Major G. B. Cosby,

A. A. General, Second Division, Central Army, Kentucky.

Sir: I have the honor to report that the 3d, 18th, and 32d Tennessee regiments, composing the 3d brigade of your division, arrived at Fort Donelson on the 9th and 10th days of February, and were assigned position by Brig.-gen. Pillow, then in command on the right of the line of defences—the extreme right being occupied by the 2d Kentucky regiment. I commenced at once the construction of rifle-pits and forming abatis by felling timber, but the supply of tools was wholly inadequate, and before the works were scarcely half completed, the enemy appeared in our front on Wednesday, the 12th, about noon. After this, the incessant fire from the enemy's sharpshooters rendered labor on our works almost impossible during the day, and large fatigue parties were necessary during the entire nights of Wednesday, Thursday, and Friday, although the weather was intensely cold. On Thursday, the 13th, the 14th Mississippi, commanded by Major W. L. Doss, and the 41st Tennessee, commanded by Col. R. Farquharson, were temporarily attached to my brigade. The centre of my portion of the line, being the most elevated and commanding point, was defended by Capt. Porter's light battery of six guns, while Capt. Graves' battery was posted near the left, commanding a long wide valley, separating my left from Col. Heiman's right. The position was an admirable one to support my left and Col. Heiman's right, while it also commanded the hills immediately in front. About 11 o'clock on Thursday I discovered the enemy moving in considerable force upon Col. Heiman's centre, and before the column came within range of Col. Heiman, and indeed before it could be seen from Col. Heiman's position, I directed Capt. Graves to open fire from all his guns, which he did with such spirit and fatal precision, that in less than fifteen minutes the whole column staggered and took shelter, in confusion and disorder, beyond the summit of the hill still further to our left, when Col. Heiman opened fire upon it, and drove it beyond range of both his and my guns. Later in the day the enemy planted one section of a battery on a hill, almost in front of Capt. Graves, and opened an enfilading fire upon the left of my line, and at the same time a cross fire upon Col. Heiman. Capt. Graves, handling his favorite rifle piece with the same fearless coolness that characterized his conduct during the entire week, in less than ten minutes knocked one of the enemy's guns from its carriage, and almost at the same moment the gallant Porter disabled and silenced the other, while the supporting infantry retreated precipitately before the storm of grape and canister poured into their ranks from both batteries. Nearly one-half of my command was constantly deployed in the rifle-pits, while the residue was held under arms and in position as a reserve; but on Thursday, Col. Hanson, on the extreme right, being attacked by a large force, I sent, by Gen. Buckner's orders, the 18th Tennessee to his support, which remained with him until Friday night. On Saturday morning I had orders to move my command towards the left, so soon as Col. Head should relieve my men in the rifle-pits. He was late in reporting, and without waiting longer I put the column in motion, directing the men in the rifle-pits to follow us, so soon as relieved, which they did very promptly, but in some disorder. My whole command was provided with three days' cooked rations, and marched with their knapsacks, the purpose being to turn the enemy's right wing, and march out on the Wynn's ferry road, to fall back upon Nashville. Arriving at the point where the Wynn's ferry road crosses the intrenchments, the 3d Tennessee was deployed in the rifle-pits, while the remaining regiments were held in reserve. The enemy had already been attacked on his right by our left wing, and we were awaiting the proper moment of co-operation, and by Gen. Buckner's directions I sent the 14th Mississippi to the front as skirmishers, the enemy occupying a hill in considerable force not far distant. The 3d and 18th Tennessee regiments (the former commanded by Lieut.-col. Thomas M. Gordon, and the latter by Col. J. B. Palmer), were sent forward in quick succession to support the 14th Mississippi. As they advanced over the abatis and through comparatively open ground, and especially on reaching the summit of the hill, they were met by a murderous fire. Some confusion ensued, but they returned a steady fire until the enemy retired under cover of dense timber and undergrowth, withdrawing his battery, which had been pouring a heavy fire into our reserves. Further pursuit being impracticable in that direction, and companies having become separated and somewhat intermixed, on account of the obstacles over which they had marched, the command retired within the intrenchments, and immediately re-formed to renew the attack still further to the right, whither the enemy were retiring. And about twelve o'clock, under the direction of Brig.-gen. Buckner, I led the 3d and 18th Tennessee, as well as the 32d Tennessee (Col. Ed. C. Cook), across an open field on the right of the Wynn's ferry road, under the fire of a battery posted on that road. As we appeared upon the summit of the hill, the force supporting the battery retreated about 300 or 400 yards still further to our right and further from our lines, leaving one section of the battery, which fell into our hands. The hill to which the enemy retreated was so densely covered with trees and undergrowth that our skirmishers could not ascertain his position and numbers, but we were led to suppose that his battery at that point was supported by a force not exceeding one thousand men; but it was afterwards ascertained that his strength was nearly seven thousand, while there were five regiments within supporting distance.

Acting upon the first and only information we could then obtain, a charge was ordered, and the whole command moved forward with spirit and animation, but when within about 100 yards of the enemy, who was upon higher ground, we were met by a fire of grape and musketry that was terrific, but fortunately passing above our heads. We halted and opened a fire of musketry upon them, which, although continuing only a few minutes, killed and wounded not less than 800 of the enemy. Lieut.-col. Gordon of the 3d, having been wounded, ordered the regiment to fall back under cover of the hill. I rallied it at about 100 yards, and placed it in command of Col. Cheairs. The 18th and 32d fell back a short distance, and just then being reinforced by the 14th Mississippi, we were renewing the attack, when the enemy left the field, leaving his dead and wounded. While we were engaged, the gallant Graves came in full speed to our assistance, with a part of his battery, and maintained his position until the enemy retired. Our loss in this engagement did not exceed fifty in killed and wounded. But the brave and accomplished Lieut.-col. Moore, of the 32d Tennessee regiment, fell mortally wounded, while aiding his no less worthy commander in cheering his men to the charge. Just as the enemy left the field, entirely opening the Wynn's ferry road, my command was ordered by Brig.-gen. Pillow, repeated by Brig.-gen. Floyd, to return at once to its position on the right of our line of defences. My men had scarcely deployed in the rifle-pits, when I was ordered to reinforce Col. Hanson on the extreme right, whose works had been stormed and taken by the enemy before he had reoccupied them. An obstinate fire was maintained until dark, but we held the ground to which Col. Hanson had retired, although opposed by a superior force of fresh troops. Capts. Porter and Graves did efficient service in their engagement with their batteries—indeed, they excited the admiration of the whole command, by an exhibition of coolness and bravery, under a heavy fire (from which they had no protection), which could not be excelled. Capt. Porter fell, dangerously wounded by a minié ball through his thigh, while working one of his guns—his gunners being, nearly all of them, disabled or killed. The command then devolved upon Lieut. Morton, a beardless youth, who stepped forward like an old veteran, and nobly did he emulate the example of his brave captain.

Fatigue parties were employed until 2 o'clock Sunday morning strengthening our position, when an order reached me, to spike the guns on my line and march my command towards the left as on Saturday morning. The order was instantly executed, but before the column had proceeded one mile I was directed to countermarch and reoccupy the works, and display flags of truce from the front of our works. At 9 o'clock the same morning the command was surrendered.

My command was so much worn and exhausted from incessant labor and watching during the entire week—exposure to intense cold, as well as from the fatigues of the battle on the preceding day, as to be wholly unable to meet any spirited attack from the enemy on Sunday morning. Our ammunition, both for artillery and small-arms, was well-nigh exhausted.

It might do injustice to others to particularize many instances of daring and bravery among officers and men. With but few exceptions, they all deserve the highest praise for the determined and gallant spirit with which they bore themselves under their first exposure to fire—

My killed amount to - - - - - 38
My wounded amount to - - - - 244

For details, reference is made to the report of regimental commanders, marked respectively A. B. C. D. and E.

I have the honor to be, sir,

Very respectfully, your obedient servant,

JOHN C. BROWN,

Col. 3d Tennessee regiment, commanding 3d brigade.

February 16, 1862.

Report of Major N. F. Cheairs, commanding Third Tennessee Regiment.

FORT WARREN, BOSTON HARBOR,
MASSACHUSETTS, March 10, 1862.

To Col. JOHN C. BROWN, *commanding Third Brigade, Second Division Central Army of Kentucky, C. S. A.*

The 3d Tennessee regiment of volunteers arrived at Fort Donelson on the night of the 8th of February, 1862, with an aggregate, reported for duty, of seven hundred and fifty men. On the day after reaching Donelson the whole regiment was employed in the preparation of works of defence—rifle-pits, trenches, &c., at which both men and officers continued night and day, until the evening of the 12th, at which time a skirmish took place with the Federals about a mile or a mile and a half in advance of our trenches, by a company of the 18th Tennessee regiment, who had been sent out on picket duty. Immediately after the return of said company to the trenches, Gen. Buckner's division, which occupied the right of the whole line of our defence, was arranged in order of battle for the general engagement which ensued. The 3d Tennessee regiment occupied the fourth position from the right, and five companies were deployed in the rifle-pits, and five held in reserve, commanded by myself, with orders to sustain the companies deployed in the pits, under the command of Lieut.-col. S. M. Gordon, and to support Porter's artillery on my right, as circumstances might require. Such was the position held by the 3d Tennessee regiment until the morning of the 15th February. At about four o'clock of said morning, the 3d Tennessee regiment was ordered to be put in motion and march in the direction of our left wing, with knapsacks, haversacks, and three days' rations, with whatever else that could be conveniently carried. This order was immediately executed, and the regiment marched out beyond and to the right of Dover, where it was halted and ordered to deploy as skirmishers in the rifle-pits, and to the left of the 14th Mississippi and 18th Tennessee, at about half-past eight or nine o'clock in the morning. The 14th Mississippi and 3d Tennessee were ordered by Col. Brown (Gen. Buckner also being present) to attack one of the enemy's batteries, located some three or four hundred yards in front of our trenches, and, from their position, were firing heavily upon us. This battery was supported by several regiments of infantry. We succeeded (after a hot contest of about three-quarters of an hour) in driving the enemy back, and occupied their position until ordered back to the trenches by Major Cassaday, of Gen. Buckner's staff. The 3d, 18th, and 32d Tennessee regiments were ordered across the trenches to attack another one of the enemy's batteries, supported by a heavy column of infantry, located on or near the Wynn's ferry road, and much farther from our works. The 3d Tennessee was on the left, the 18th in the centre, and the 32d on the right, in the arrangement for the attack. The trenches were soon crossed, and the battalions formed in double column, and marched in the direction of the battery. When within about one hundred and fifty yards of it, it opened upon us with grape and canister, and seconded by the infantry. Lieut.-col. Gordon being in command of the 3d regiment, ordered it to lay down. In a few seconds he was wounded, and by some unfortunate order being given just at that time, which the regiment took for retreat, and thereupon did retreat some hundred or hundred and fifty yards, when they were rallied by Col. Brown, and reformed in line of battle. Gen. Buckner being present, and discovering the enemy had also fallen back, ordered me, as next in command to Lieut.-col. Gordon (he having retired from the field), to take the 3d Tennessee regiment back to the trenches, which order I obeyed. On arriving at the trenches, I met with Gen. Pillow, who ordered me (after ascertaining that I was in command) to take the 3d Tennessee regiment back to the position we had occupied on the right wing, and the one we had left at about four o'clock in the morning. I immediately formed the regiment and executed the order. A few minutes after reaching our original position, an attack was made upon Col. Hanson, the 2d Kentucky regiment's trenches, by the enemy in strong force. Col. Hanson not having more than one or two companies in position, fell back upon the 18th Tennessee (Col. Palmer), and I was ordered to bring up the 3d Tennessee to support the 2d Kentucky and 18th Tennessee, which order was executed at the shortest possible notice, and, in justice to the officers and soldiers, must say that they bore themselves most gallantly, notwithstanding they were completely, or nearly so, worn down by incessant fighting and fatigue duty. For eight consecutive days we succeeded in driving back the enemy, although they had fresh and we had exhausted troops. Lieut.-col. Gordon was in command of the regiment from the time we arrived at Donelson, on the night of the 8th, until about one o'clock, P. M., on the 15th, when he was wounded and retired from the field. I was then in command until the surrender, which was at six o'clock, Sunday morning, February 16th, 1862.

For a detailed account of the killed and wounded of the 3d Tennessee regiment, during the entire fight at Donelson, I refer you to the subjoined paper, marked A.

Killed, twelve; wounded, seventy-six.

The foregoing report of the conduct and actions of the 3d Tennessee regiment, and of its casualties at Fort Donelson, I have the honor to submit to you.

Very respectfully,

N. F. CHEAIRS,

Major Commanding 3d Tennessee Regiment.

Report of Colonel Joseph B. Palmer, commanding 18th Tennessee regiment.

FORT WARREN, BOSTON HARBOR,
MASSACHUSETTS, March 7th, 1862.

To Col. JOHN C. BROWN, *commanding Third Brigade, Second Division, Central army of Kentucky, C. S. A.*

The 18th regiment of Tennessee volunteers arrived at Fort Donelson on the 8th of February, 1862, with an aggregate reported for duty of six hundred and eighty-five (685), and these encamped mainly without tents or other protection from the weather, and with scarcely any cooking utensils, until the surrender of the forces at that point on the 16th day of the same month.

On the day after reaching Donelson, the whole regiment was employed in the preparation of works of defence—rifle-pits, trenches, etc., at which both men and officers continued without relief or rest, night and day, until the 12th. Early in the forenoon of that day, pursuant to orders from brigade head-quarters, I ordered out company C, commanded by Capt. W. R. Butler, on picket service, with the usual instructions. They went in the direction of the enemy's lines, about one and a half miles, and took position, when suddenly they discovered several thousand Federal troops advancing towards our encampment. Capt. Butler, thus finding his position greatly exposed, conducted a prudent and skilful retreat, gradually falling back, so as to keep the enemy under constant observation—finally fired upon them and came within my encampment, submitting a report of this intelligence, which I immediately communicated to you and Gen. Buckner in person. Gen. Buckner's division, which occupied the right of the whole line of our defence, was therefore arranged in order of battle for the general engagement which ensued. The 2d Kentucky (Col. Hanson's) was first, and my regiment second on the right. I deployed companies A, B, and G, (Capts. Rushing, Joyner, and McWhirter,) in the rifle-pits immediately in my front, placing them in command of Major S. W. Davis. The other companies were formed in double column first in rear of the former, in charge of myself and Lieut.-col. A. G. Carden, with orders from Gen. Buckner to sustain the line covered by my deployment—to support Porter's artillery on my left, or reinforce Col. Hanson on my right, as circumstances might require. Such was the position held by me until the morning of the 15th February. I had occasion, however, on the 13th, to dispatch companies E and K (Capts. Lorre and Bandy) to reinforce Col. Hanson, upon whom the enemy was opening a considerable fire, but, after a very spirited engagement, the attack was repulsed. I had occasion also on the 14th to send the balance of my reserve (Capts. Webb, Wood, Putnam, Butler, and Lieut. John's companies) to reinforce the right, where it was expected the enemy would on that day make a desperate attack, simultaneously with a fire on the fort from their gunboats. But owing probably to a failure of success in the latter, no further than the general fire was made upon us at that time. On Saturday morning, 15th February, at about two and a half or three o'clock, I received orders from brigade head-quarters to put my whole command in motion, and to march in the direction of our left wing, with knapsacks, haversacks provided with three days' rations, and whatever else men and officers could carry—sending all my wagons, .except enough for the transportation of ordnance stores across Cumberland river. I proceeded immediately to execute this order, and marched out beyond and to the right of Dover, where I was ordered to halt and take position in a general line of battle, on the right of the 3d Tennessee regiment. Very soon afterwards the 14th Mississippi and 3d Tennesse were ordered by Col. Brown (Gen. Buckner also being present) to attack one of the enemy's batteries, just in our front, and about three hundred yards beyond the trenches, which, from their position, were firing heavily upon us. This battery was supported by several regiments of infantry, which, in connection with it, turned a terrible fire on the two regiments just named, against which they fought gallantly and bravely, thus making a severe engagement, which, having continued for some considerable time, I was ordered across the trenches to their support, and reached there just about the time the enemy abandoned their position and yielded the ground. Under the order of Major Cassaday, I returned to my former position, in connection with the other two regiments, in the general line of battle. The 3d Tennessee, 32d and 18th Tennessee, were then ordered across the trenches to attack another one of the enemy's batteries, located on or near the Wynn's ferry road, and much further beyond our works. Col. Cook's regiment was on the right, my own in the centre, and Col. Brown's on the left, in the arrangement for this attack. The trenches were soon crossed, the battalions formed in double column, and we marched on to the supposed position of the battery, Col. Cook being in advance of my regiment, with skirmishers in his front. We found some, I may say much, embarrassment in having insufficient information in regard to the enemy's location, as we could only judge in reference to that by the smoke and reports of pieces lately heard and seen in that direction. We found also very considerable difficulty in marching in the requisite order, owing to the timber and denseness of the undergrowth, on which the snow was thickly depositing and melting somewhat rapidly.

We advanced forward, however, in quick time, until, nearing the enemy, we halted for the purpose of gaining, if possible, some more definite idea of his position, the skirmishers having rallied on their battalion without (as I learned from Col. Cook) being able to furnish very definite information. Col. Cook and myself advanced a few paces beyond our commands, for the purpose of taking such observations as would enable us to direct the movements of our regiments to the best possible advantage. We discovered portions of the enemy's baggage at the distance of about one hundred yards, just over the point of a hill in our front. Being thus better satisfied of their position, and that an engagement must immediately occur, we accordingly deployed as rapidly as possible in line of battle, my right resting on Col. Cook's left, and the 3d Tennessee on my left. The enemy opened a terrific fire upon us about the time, or before we had fairly executed the deployment. The force here against us consisted of one battery, supported by six infantry regiments, all of which ultimately engaged in the fight. I ordered my entire command to fire and load kneeling, as in that position the main body of the enemy's fire would and did pass over us.

The officers and men under me, on this occasion, evinced great coolness, bravery, and determination for success in this most unequal contest. They directed their fire with unusual accuracy, which told desperately and rapidly upon the enemy, who, under its terrible effect and force, gave ground, while we advanced upon them about twenty paces. A further advance would have lost, on our part, an advantage in position, by which we had been very considerably benefited. And although the enemy continued their retreat until they had gone beyond the reach of our guns, it was not deemed consistent with the orders for the movements of our whole army on that day, as made known on the previous night from Gens. Floyd, Pillow, and Buckner to myself and other commanders of regiments, to pursue the several forces any further in that direction. Besides this, many of my arms (flint-lock muskets), by coming in contact with the melting snow, had become too inefficient for further use until they could be dried and put in proper order. My ordnance-wagons were more than a half mile distant, and the men only had a few rounds of ammunition each remaining in their boxes. I marched my regiment, therefore, back to a better position, a distance of, say one hundred and fifty paces, ordered the men to put their pieces in order, by drying them as rapidly as possible, sent for an additional supply of ammunition, made details to have my wounded taken from the field and properly cared for, and threw out a small number of skirmishers in connection with Col. Cook, to notice the movements and position of the enemy, who reported that he had gone back beyond the Wynn's ferry road, and could not be seen at all from the position of our late engagement.

I was informed on the afternoon of the 14th of February, and again, at a late hour of that night, by Gen. Buckner and Col. Brown, that, for the reasons given at the time (not material here to recite), the generals in command had determined to evacuate Donelson and move the whole of our troops to Nashville, or in that direction, and orders were given me, by Col. Brown, to prepare my command accordingly, with rations, &c., for the march. I was further informed that, to execute this purpose, our whole army would, at an early hour on the morning of the 15th, move upon the right wing of the Federal lines, cut our way through, and march out in the direction stated. The whole of the enemy's right having been driven back, thus, I was informed, removing all further difficulty in the way of executing our purpose. I was every moment expecting to receive orders to march my regiment, together with the balance of our troops, in the direction of Nashville. But, before I could get all of my dead and wounded from the field, and have them provided for and disposed of, an order came to me, said at the time to come from Gen. Pillow, to move my command immediately back to the position from which I started on that morning, and which I had been holding for several days. I accordingly returned to my trenches. In a very few minutes after I reached my position, and before Col. Hanson (just to my right) had gained his trenches, several Federal regiments, under command of Gen. C. F. Smith, commenced their attack, and took possession of a part of Col. Hanson's unoccupied works. Unable, under these circumstances and against such remarkable odds, to drive back the attacking regiments, Col. Hanson immediately fell back, with his command, on my line, where, reinforced by the 14th Mississippi, the 3d, 41st, 49th Tennessee, and parts of other commands, a long and desperate struggle ensued, closing at sunset with a decided and brilliant victory to our arms—the fight having lasted for at least two hours. The losses of the enemy, in all the engagements above referred to, as ascertained by subsequent visits to their grounds, were, indeed, very great, exceeding ours, both in killed and wounded, I must say, in any moderate estimate, at least *seven* to one.

Besides the conflicts, already named in this report, the Federal forces made several attempts upon my works, but were in every instance gallantly met, and signally repulsed.

On the night of the 15th, the whole of my command, except the detail made to continue the work of strengthening and extending our breast-works, stood to their arms, constantly expecting a renewal of engagements, until about 2 o'clock of the following morning. At this hour I received orders from brigade head-quarters to move my regiment as rapidly as possible to Dover, a distance of one and a half miles, where, I was informed, further orders would be given me. It was, however, well understood among all parties that the object of the march was to evacute our entire position. I reached Dover some time before daylight, and reported to Gens. Floyd, Pillow, and Buckner, all of whom were still there, and who ordered me to halt and await further directions. A messenger from Col. Brown's head-quarters soon came, ordering me back to my trenches, and, on returning to my quarters, found that Gen. Buckner's whole command had been surrendered. This was my first notice of that fact, and was thus received on Sunday morning at half-past 5 o'clock.

Throughout the period covered by this report, the men and officers of my command underwent an astonishing amount of hard labor and toil—suffering greatly from the want of rest, from terrible exposure and fatigue, and in the absence of nearly all the comforts even of camp life. But every demand upon their strength and energy was promptly met. Every order was unhesitatingly obeyed, and every hardship and suffering bravely and patiently endured, evincing a glorious spirit of self-sacrifice and determination, now mentioned alike in simple justice to them and with the utmost pride and satisfaction to myself. On the field my entire field and staff, company officers and men (with scarcely a noticeable exception), bore themselves nobly and gallantly, displaying, on every occasion, a dauntless courage and patriotism, alike deserving the praises of their chivalrous State, and the approval of a glorious country.

Many officers and men of my command are justly entitled to the merit of personal honor and distinction. Lieut. W. W. Smith, of company C, shot, and killed instantly on the field, fell covered with glory in the gallant discharge of his duties, as did the other lamented dead and wounded of my regiment. With a very grateful recollection of my whole command for their soldierly and manly demeanor throughout our whole campaign, I cannot close this report without submitting with it acknowledgements for valuable services and kind offices done me by Lieuts. Nat. Gooch, of company C, and John M. Douglass, of company G, who are also very justly entitled to all I have heretofore stated on behalf of other officers.

Owing to the sudden and unexpected separation from my company officers, I am unable to submit, with this report, the names of the killed and wounded of my regiment, and can, therefore, only state them in the aggregate:

There were killed on the field	4
Mortally wounded	6
(Supposed) not mortally	38
Missing	4
Total	52

The foregoing report of the conduct and action of my regiment, and of its casulties at Fort Donelson, I have on this day the honor to submit to you. Very respectfully,

JOSEPH B. PALMER.

Col. commanding 18*th Tennessee regiment.*

Report of Col. Edward C. Cook, commanding Thirty-Second Tennessee Regiment.

FORT DONELSON, STEWART CO., TENN.,
February 16th, 1862.

Col. JOHN C. BROWN,
Col. commanding Third Brigade, Second Division,
Central Army, Kentucky:

The 32d Tennessee regiment reached Fort Donelson on the night of the 10th inst., with five hundred and fifty-five men, rank and file, many of the regiment having been left sick at Russellville, Kentucky, many at Bowling Green, Kentucky, and some on furlough sick at home. We were placed on the left of Gen. Buckner's division. The entire regiment was employed making intrenchments till the same were finished. The enemy began to fire upon us with artillery and sharpshooters as early as Tuesday evening the 11th.

The weather was extremely cold, and being kept continually at labor and on duty, we suffered much from exposure. The regiment, although held in readiness at every moment, was not engaged in actual fight until Saturday the 15th. On Friday night we were ordered to have cooked rations for three days, and with knapsacks packed, to be ready to march at 4 o'clock next morning. I then learned that it had been determined by the generals in council at that hour, to march to the extreme left of our intrenchments, attack the enemy's right wing and turn it, and if we succeeded, to march for Nashville. The next morning at 4 o'clock, our brigade marched to the left of our intrenchments. Just as we were appproaching the extreme left of our intrenchments, Gen. Buckner 'ordered me to place my regiment in column of division under cover of the hill in the rear of Green's battery, and to sustain it. We remained here until about 10 o'clock A. M., when Gen. Pillow ordered me to move my regiment to the right, and to cross the intrenchments and attack a battery of the enemy, which was then firing at us, and seemed to be situated some eight hundred yards from our intrenchments. Just as we were marching across the intrenchments, Gen. Buckner and Col. Brown came up, and upon learning the order Gen. Pillow had given, Gen. Buckner ordered me to proceed to attack the battery, and ordered Col. Palmer, with his regiment, to sustain me. I forwarded the regiment, crossed the intrenchments, threw out two companies as skirmishers, and moved forward the regiment in the direction of the enemy's battery. The skirmishers very soon engaged the enemy's skirmishers, drove them back, killing some, taking five prisoners, and capturing some five minnie muskets.

We moved forward through woods with thick undergrowth, the bushes were covered with snow which was melting slowly, and it was very difficult to move forward. We had advanced within seventy-five or a hundred yards of the enemy, and he had opened fire upon us with his battery, when Col. Brown rode up and ordered me to move my regiment to the right and attack the battery at this point. The bushes were very thick, and we could with great difficulty move forward. Our skirmishers fired upon the enemy, and rallied upon the battalion. I immediately ordered the regiment to kneel and fire, and to load and fire kneeling. The fire began. Col. Palmer, on my left immediately opened fire from his regiment. The firing was kept up rapidly. The regiment all the while slowly, but gradually, moved forward. We were protected by cover of the timber and hill from the enemy's shot. Lieut.-col. W. P. Moore fell very early in the action, wounded in the right knee, and was carried from the field to the hospital. This left me with no field officer to aid me, Major Brownlow having been left sick at Russellville—Adjutant Jones being on duty part of the day, but was not with the regiment in the engagement. I soon discovered many of the muskets failed to fire, the priming being wet (the most of the regiment being armed with inferior flint-lock muskets). After a while the left wing of the regiment began to fall back slowly, and then the right wing, in good order; and being satisfied the condition of many of the guns, in order to do execution, must be wiped and dried, and knowing that the regiment, after falling back a short distance, would be entirely protected from the enemy's shot, I determined to let them fall back. After they fell back about one hundred yards I halted the regiment, and ordered the men to wipe and dry their guns. Upon inquiry as to why they fell back, the officers informed me they heard an order "to fall back," and believed it came from proper authority. After the guns were cleaned, I threw out two companies of skirmishers, who proceeded as far as the "Wynn's ferry road," in which was placed the enemy's battery, when we attacked, and the skirmishers returned and reported that the enemy had retired beyond the road, and could not be seen. After waiting some time and receiving no orders, Col. Palmer and I, after consultation, determined to march our regiments back to the intrenchments where we had crossed, and where my regiment had left their knapsacks. When we reached the intrenchments, Major Cosby gave me an order from Gen. Buckner to march my regiment immediately back to the intrenchments we had left in the morning. At this moment we felt satisfied that the Wynn's ferry road was clear, and the way to Nashville open. "That fortune had smiled upon us, and that we ought to prove to her we were worthy of her favors." We marched rapidly back to our intrenchments and took position in them. In a few minutes the enemy appeared in large force in front of us, and threatened to attack us until night came on. Early at night I received orders to have three days' cooked rations prepared, and with knapsacks packed to be ready to march at four o'clock next morning. At the appointed hour we marched out for Dover, and before we reached Dover we were ordered to return to our intrenchments, and learned that capitulation for a surrender was going on. It gives me pleasure to state that the officers and privates of the regiment, although jaded from labor and exposure, at all times exhibited great willingness to obey, and anxiety to promptly execute all orders. In battle they behaved coolly and courageously, and not one of the regiment ever left the line or his post of duty. The morale of the regiment was not corrupted or destroyed, and even after it was known we were surrendered, we had not a single straggler from the regiment.

During the engagement on the 15th, we lost in killed and had wounded in company A, commanded by Capt. Willis Worley, one killed, three wounded, whose names I cannot give, as I have no report from company A. I hereto attach a list of the other companies of the regiment, giving the names, number engaged, and the killed, wounded, and missing. At the earliest moment it can be obtained, I will forward a list of company A, to be made a part of the exhibit hereto.

Our gallant Col. Moore died from the wound he received. The regiment, as well as all who knew him, deeply mourn his death.

The surgeon, James F. Grant, Quarter-master John T. Shephard, Commissary E. Shields Wilson, Quarter-master Sergeant James P. Campbell, were all at their post and did their full duty. Capt. John D. Clark, a drill master, was on duty during the entire week, and in the engagement of the 15th. Capt. D. C. Sims, a drill master, assigned to my regiment, was on duty a portion of the week, but not in the engagement of the 15th, being reported sick.

RECAPITULATION.

Number of regiment, rank and file, at Fort Donelson, -	555
" " at Donelson, not engaged on Saturday,	21
" " " engaged on Saturday, -	534

Number of regiment,	killed,	- - - - -	3
" "	wounded and surrendered,	- -	15
" "	" and not surrendered,	-	21
" "	missing,	- - - -	1
" "	escaped,	- - - -	1
" "	wounded,	- - - -	36
" "	surrendered,	- - - -	528

Respectfully,

ED. C. COOK,
Colonel 32d Tennessee Regiment.

FORT WARREN, *July* 30, 1862.

Report of Major W. L. Doss, commanding 14th Mississippi regiment.

To Col. JOHN C. BROWN, *commanding 1st brigade,*
Gen. Buckner's division:

SIR: I have the honor to report the following operations of the 14th regiment Mississippi Volunteers, during the engagement at Fort Donelson, ending on the 15th February, 1862.

On the morning of the 15th of February, at 3 o'clock, A. M., I received orders to have my regiment in readiness to move in two hours. About daylight we took up line of march in the direction of our left wing. It was with great difficulty that we progressed, owing to the country, which was hilly or mountainous, and covered with snow and ice.

During our march shells were constantly falling around us, without doing us any damage, until we halted in rear of the intrenchments, where I formed the regiment in close column by company. We were protected to some extent from the shells of the enemy by forming on the hill-side, which was thickly set with undergrowth. At this place Capt. J. L. Crigler, of company "G," was severely wounded in the right arm, by the explosion of a shell, and was unable to proceed farther with his company.

I received orders to deploy two companies as skirmishers, and soon after the battalion was ordered to dislodge a battery in position, apparently about four hundred yards to our front. The regiment moved off by the right-flank, until it reached our intrenchments, when it advanced in line of battle. We very soon came to a small field, containing about ten or fifteen acres, where our march was somewhat impeded by an abatis made by the enemy. At this point we were fired upon by their skirmishers. I ordered the battalion not to return the fire. The right wing of the battalion was faced to the right, and marched up the hill some distance under a heavy fire; then faced to the front, and ordered to open fire upon the enemy. In the meantime the left wing had marched through a gap in the abatis, faced to the right and rejoined the four right companies, when a general engagement ensued. At this point Capt. F. M. Rogers, of Company "E." fell, gallantly cheering his men on. The engagement at this point continued for about an hour or more; the men displaying great coolness and bravery, and the officers great gallantry. The regiment suffered severely at this point, and was ordered to retreat by Major Cassady, who had been appointed by Gen. Buckner to assist me (Col. Baldwin being in command of a brigade on the extreme left). After falling back some two hundred yards, I endeavored to rally the regiment on the 18th Tennessee regiment, but Major Cassaday insisted and gave the order to the regiment to fall back to the intrenchments, which was done. After remaining there about one hour, we were again ordered out by Gen. Buckner to support a section of Capt. Graves' battery. We marched down the Wynn's ferry road about one mile, and halted on the top of a hill by Gen. Buckner, when the enemy's battery opened a galling fire of shot and shell upon us. It was soon ascertained that Capt. Graves' battery could do but little good there, and was ordered back (I think by Gen. Pillow), whereupon my regiment was ordered to take its original position on the right. Upon our arrival there we found that the enemy were in possession of the intrenchments on the extreme right, which had been occupied by the 2d Kentucky regiment, and which was then engaged with the enemy to regain their original position.

My regiment was immediately ordered to their support, and on arriving there we found the enemy advancing upon us in considerable numbers, when we were ordered to open fire upon them, which was kept up from about 3 o'clock until about dark, when the enemy retired. The men slept upon their arms during the night. About 1 o'clock I received your order to have my regiment ready to march in an hour, which order was countermanded about daylight.

Respectfully submitted,

W. L. DOSS,

Major commanding 14th regiment Mississippi Volunteers.

LIST OF KILLED, WOUNDED, AND MISSING OF THE FOURTEENTH MISSISSIPPI REGIMENT.

Co. A— *Wounded.*—T. A. Miller, G. J. Everett, J. P. Watts, G. M. Hill, Wm. Rogers.

Co. B—*Wounded.*—H. S. Jack, C. C. McCracken.

Co. C—*Killed.*—J. J. Clark, J. G. Watt, G. T. James, R. M. Bell. *Wounded.*—J. E. Davis, J. F. Merchant, J. H. Montgomery, W. H. Petty, Lieut. F. Duquercron, L. L. Cooper, W. H. Peebles, W. H. Hogan, Joe White, T. T. Wetherly, Willis Cooke, Wm. H. Pierce, Corporal McNatt, J. W. Hardy.

Co. D—*Killed.*—Amos Carter. *Wounded.*—N. Harris, Lieut. Wm. M. McGowen, T. King, C. Hodgers, J. Carter, C. D. Brashier, R. Herring.

Co. E—*Killed.*—Capt. F. M. Rogers, Private Elliott. *Wounded.* Sergeant J. G. Crump, Sergeant Nabers, Privates Clarke, Nash, Nash, Hamack, Bickerstaff, Simms, Green. *Missing.*—Carter, Allison.

Co. F—*Killed.*—Dudley Truman, N. B. Holmes. *Wounded.*—Lieut. Stephens, Private S. Boggett, J. G. Moore, J. P. Webb, N. Moore, Tom Moore, Tom Crow, Joe Ingram, James La, John Woodall, John Kirpkatrick. Three missing, names not given.

Co. G—*Killed.*—L. Murphy, Sergent J. L. Perkins. *Wounded.* Capt. J. L. Craigler, J. S. Tucker, T. Donoho, J. T. Peters, J. E. Reeves, A. J. Rolling, J. M. Rollins, P. W. Selby, B. L. Smith, James Stallings, W. H. Ward.

Co. H — *Killed.* — Sergeant B. F. Bearman, Private McInis. *Wounded.*—Washington Jones, J. N. Alexander, W. T. Fisher, R. L. Hill, James Horden, J. D. Addy, R. L. Mayes, Corporal Barnes, Jos. Fairchild, G. M. Marcy, Capt. S. J. Gohlson. *Missing.*—Robt. West, Wm. West, H. Coats, Wm. McDowell.

Co. I—*Killed.*—J. J. Johnson, J. L. Sadler, Patrick Barrow. *Wounded.*—James Brock, James West, W. L. Stewart, W. Kendal, W. Moss, J. T. Johnson, Joel Butler, William Beales, James Tyrone.

Co. K—*Killed.*—J. F. Williams. *Wounded*—H. C. Howard, A. Kirk, — Sappington, — Witherspoon, — McCowan, R. Reagh. *Missing.*—Buckingham.

Total—killed, 17; wounded, 84; missing, 9.

W. L. DOSS,

Major commanding 14th regiment Mississippi Vols.

Report of Col. Robert Farquharson, commanding Forty-First regiment Tennessee Volunteers.

In obedience to an order from Gen. Pillow, the regiment arrived at Fort Donelson about ten o'clock, A. M., Thursday, February 13th, 1862.

Field Officers, Commissioned and Non-Commissioned, Staff Officers.—Robert Farquharson, Col.; Robt. G. McClure, Lieut.-col.; Thomas G. Miller, Major; Jake Anthony, Lieut. and Adj.; Albert G. Clopton, Surgeon; Wm. B. Smith, Assistant Surgeon; Edward A. Norton, Acting Assistant Surgeon; John K. Farris, Hospital Steward and Acting Assistant Surgeon; Thomas B. McNaughton, Commissary of Subsistence; John Gordon, Acting Commissary of Subsistence; W. E. Barringer, 1st Lieut. and drill instructor; Wm. G. Reed, 1st Lieut. and drill instructor; John L. Dusenbury, Sergeant Major; Erwin P. Jett, Quarter-master Sergeant; Albert Frierson, Ordnance Sergeant.

Companies.—A.—W. W. James, Capt. 1 1st Lieut., 2 2d Lieuts., 3 sergeants, 4 corporals, 65 privates; aggregate 76.

B.—Wm. L. Brown, Capt. 2 2d Lieuts., 4 sergeants, 3 corporals, 48 privates; aggregate 58.

C.—J. D. Scott, Capt. 1 1st Lieut., 1 2d Lieut., 4 sergeants, 2 corporals, 44 privates; aggregate 53.

D.—J. H. George, Capt. 1 2d Lieut., 4 sergeants, 1 corporal, 53 privates; aggregate 60.

E.—Lieut. Fondvill, commanding. 1 1st Leiut., 1 2d Lieut., 2 sergeants, 4 corporals, 33 privates; aggregate 41.

F.—A. S. Boone, Capt. 2 2d Lieuts., 4 sergeants, 1 corporal, 59 privates; aggregate 67.

G.—C. H. Bean, Capt. 1 1st Lieut., 2 2d Lieuts., 2 sergeants, 2 corporals, 41 privates; aggregate 49.

H.—J. C. Osburn, Capt. 4 sergeants, 3 corporals, 46 privates; aggregate 54.

I.—A. M. Kieth, Capt. 1 1st Lieut., 2 2d Lieuts, 4 sergeants, 2 corporals, 44 privates; aggregate 54.

K.—J. A. Moore, Capt. 1 1st Lieut., 2 2d Lieuts., 3 sergeants, 4 corporals, 37 privates; aggregate 48—560.

Field officers, commissioned and non-commissioned, staff, &c., &c., 15.

Aggregate, 575.

Remarks and Casualties.—Thomas B. McNaughton, Commissary of Subsistence, killed February 13th, 1862. John K. Wiley, private, company C, killed February 15th, 1862.

Mark Collier, private, company A, slightly wounded February 13th, 1862.

H. M. Carter, private, company A, wounded February 14th, 1862.

George W. Alexander, private, company A, sick and missing; A. P. Blackwell, private, company A, sick and missing; L. M. Ruse, private, company A, sick and missing; J. M. Johnson, private, company A, sick and missing; Young Taylor, private, company A, sick and missing; N. B. Reese, private, company A, missing; N. S. Ruse, private, company A, missing; Mark Redd, private, company A, missing; H. D. Hoots, 1st sergeant, company A, missing; G. W. Lane, private, company A, missing; Joseph Pamplin, private, company A, missing; J. D. Cook, private, company A, missing; George Blackwell, private, company B, sick and missing; Nicholas Burns, private, company B, missing; John W. Formwalt, private, company C, missing; Jessie C. Franklin, 1st sergeant, company D, missing; James J. Alexander, private, company D, sick and missing; John W. Wicks, private, company D, missing; James Hill, private, company E, wounded; George J. Hamby, private, company E, wounded; E. L. Brobston, private, company E, missing; H. W. Smiley, private, company E, missing; R. M. Drumgoole, private, company F, wounded; George Gregory, private, company F, wounded; H. A. Wilson, private, company F, sick and missing; Charles Driver, private, company I, missing; William Driver, private, company I, missing; Peter Williams, private, company I, missing; E. M. Patterson, private, company K, missing; W. W. Koonce, private, company K, sick and missing.

RECAPIULATION.

Went into the fight with 575 aggregate.

Killed.—T. B. McNaughton, commissary, and J. K. Wiley, private, company C.

Wounded, six.—Mark Collier, company A; H. M. Carter, company A; James Hill, company E; George B. Hamby, company E; R. M. Drumgoole, company F; George Gregory, company F.

Missing, 26.—Non-commissioned officers and privates.

The regiment executed all the orders given to it, and, as far as I know, each man did his duty.

R. FARQUHARSON,

Col. 41st regiment Tennessee Volunteers.

Report of Col. A. Heiman, commanding Brigade

RICHMOND, August 9th, 1862.

MAJOR G. B. COSBY, *A. A. General.*

SIR:—My imprisonment since the surrender of the troops at Fort Donelson, prevented me from reporting the operations of the Brigade under my command during the action at Fort Donelson before now. In the absence of Gen. Pillow, who commanded the Division to which my Brigade was attached, it becomes my duty, and I have the honor to submit to you the following report:

After the battle of Fort Henry, on the 6th of February last, I was directed by Gen. Tilghman, then in command of the defences of the Tennessee and Cumberland rivers, to retreat with the garrison of the Fort by the upper road to Fort Donelson. The garrison consisted, besides the company of artillery which was surrendered with the Fort, of two Brigades the first commanded by myself, and the second by Col. Drake, consisting of an aggregate of about 2,600 men. After a very tedious march, we reached Fort Donelson at 12 o'clock at night, where Col. Head, of the 30th Tennessee, was in command during the absence of Gen. Tilghman. Expecting the arrival of Gen. B. R. Johnson and other general officers in a few days, I did not assume command, which would have been my duty, being next in command to Gen. Tilghman.

Gen. Johnson arrived on the 8th, Gen. Pillow on the 9th, Gen. Buckner on the 12th, and Gen. Floyd on the 13th of February.

The Brigade assigned to my command consisted of the 10th Tennessee, Lieut.-col. McGavock, 42d Tennessee, Col. Quarles, 48th Tennessee, Col. Voorhies, 53d Tennessee, Col. Abernathy, 27th Alabama, Col. Hughes, and Capt. Maney's Light Battery, amounting in all to an aggregate of about sixteen hundred (1600) men.

This Brigade formed the right of Gen. Pillow's Division, and was in line on the left of the Division of Ger. Buckner, who commanded the right wing.

The ground I occupied in line of defence was a hill somewhat in the shape of a V, with the apex at the angle, which was the advance point as well as the centre of my command, and nearly the centre of the whole line of defence. From this point the ground descended abruptly on each side to a valley. The valley on my right was about five hundred yards in width, and divided my command from Gen. Buckner's left wing. The one on my left was about half that width, and run between my left wing and the Brigade commanded by Col. Drake. These two valleys united about a half a mile in the rear. The ground in front of my line (2600 feet in length) was sloping down to a ravine, and was heavily timbered.

We commenced to dig rifle pits and felling abatis on the 11th, and continued this work during the following night, under the directions of Major Gilmer and Lieut. Morris, Engineers, the latter belonging to Gen. Tilghman's staff. The pits were occupied by Lieut.-col. McGavock's Regiment on the right, Col. Voorhies' Regiment on the left, Cols. Abernathy's and Hughes' Regiments and Maney's Battery in the centre. Col. Quarles' Regiment I held in reserve, but several of his companies also had to occupy the pits, the other Regiments not being sufficient to cover the whole line. Col. Head, 30th Tennessee Regiment, occupied the valley between my command and Col. Drake's Brigade. I was afterwards informed that this Regiment also was placed under my command, but the Col. not having reported to me, I did not know it.

In the meantime the enemy commenced forming his line of investment, and his pickets were seen in every direction. Early on the morning of the 12th he had two batteries placed in range of my position, one on my left and front, and the other on the other side of the valley on my right. Both were in the edge of the woods and under cover, while Capt. Maney's Battery on the summit of the hill was entirely exposed, not only to the enemy's artillery, but also to their sharpshooters. No time could yet have been spared to protect his guns by a parapet, besides we were ill provided with tools for that purpose. However, our battery had some advantage over the battery on my left in altitude, and had also a full range of a large and nearly level field to the left, which the enemy had to cross to attack Col. Drake's position, or my own from that direction. In that respect and some other points the position of my battery was superb. The enemy's battery on my right had only range of part of my right wing, but was in a better position to operate on Gen. Buckner's left wing. Both batteries opened fire at 7 o'clock in the morning, and kept it up until 5 o'clock in the evening, firing at any position on our line within their range. Their fire was returned by Maney's Battery, Graves' Battery of Col. Brown's command, and a battery at Col. Drake's position. The enemy's guns were nearly all rifled, which gave them a great advantage in range and otherwise. However, with the exception of the loss of two artillery horses, my command met with no other serious casualties on that day. At night I strengthened my pickets and directed Lieut.-col. McGavock to throw a strong picket across the valley on my right. There were no rifle-pits or any other defences in that valley, although a road leading from Dover to Paris landing on the Tennessee river runs through it. Col. Cook, of Col. Brown's Brigade, co-operated with Lieut.-col. McGavock in guarding this point afterwards. Strong parties were kept at work during the whole night in improving the rifle-pits and felling abatis.

Daylight next morning (13th) showed that the enemy was not idle either. During the night he placed another battery in position on my left, and the one on my right he had considerably advanced, to get a better range on my right and centre, and on Capt. Graves' battery. He had also thrown across the main valley two lines of infantry (advance and rear), about three-quarters of a mile from our line, and the firing of all his batteries was resumed early in the morning, and was promptly answered by our batteries. One of our gunners had both his hands shot off while in the act of inserting the friction primer.

At about 11 o'clock my pickets came in, informing me of the advance of a large column of the enemy. Having myself been convinced of that fact, and finding that they were deploying their columns in the woods in front of my right and centre, I directed Capt. Maney to shell the woods, and use grape and canister when they came within the proper range, which was promptly executed. Capt. Graves seeing the enemy advancing upon my line, with excellent judgment, opened his battery upon them across the valley. In the meantime, their sharpshooters had approached my line through the woods, fired their minié rifles from behind the trees, killing and wounding Maney's gunners in quick succession. First Lieut. Burns was one of the first who fell. Second Lieut. Massey was also mortally wounded, but the gallant Maney, with the balance of his men, stood by their guns like true heroes, and kept firing into their lines, which steadily advanced within forty yards of our rifle-pits, determined to force my right wing and centre. Now the firing commenced from the whole line of rifle-pits in quick succession. This constant roar of musketry, from both lines, was kept up for about fifteen minutes, when the enemy were repulsed, but they were rallied, and vigorously attacked us the second and third times, but with the same result, and they finally retired. They could not stand our galling fire. The dry leaves on the ground were set on fire by our batteries, and I regret to state that several of their wounded perished in the flames. The pickets I sent out after their retreat, brought in about sixty muskets and other equipments they had left behind. I learned from two prisoners who were brought in, that the attack was made by the 17th, 48th, and 49th Illinois regiments, and have since learned from their own report that they lost in that attack forty killed and two hundred wounded. Our loss I cannot accurately state, nor am I able to give the names of killed and wounded, as subsequent events prevented me from getting reports of the different commanders; but I am sure that my loss is not over ten killed and about thirty wounded, nearly all belonging to Capt. Maney's artillery and Col. Abernathy's regiment, which was at that time under the command of Lieut.-col. Winston. The firing from their batteries continued all day. Late in the evening, Gen. Pillow reinforced me with a section of a light battery under Capt. Parker. The night was unusually cold and disagreeable. Snow and sleet fell during the whole night; nevertheless, we constructed a formidable parapet in front of the battery, in which I was actively assisted by Major Grace, of the 10th Tennessee. This hard and most unpleasant labor was chiefly performed by Col. Quarles' regiment. It was a horrible night, and the troops suffered dreadfully, being without blankets.

Next day (14th), finding the enemy again in line across the valley, and believing that he would attempt to force my line on my right, I directed Capt. Maney to move a section of his battery down the hill in range of the valley. The advance of the enemy towards this direction would then have been checked by Graves' and Maney's batteries, and the fires of McGavock's and Cook's regiments, from the right and left; but no demonstration was made in that direction, although I considered it the weakest point in our line.

During the whole day my command was exposed to a cross fire of the enemy's batteries, and were much annoyed by their sharpshooters. At 11 o'clock at night I was summoned to attend a consultation of general officers at Gen. Floyd's head-quarters.

The general opinion prevailed that the place could not be held against at least treble the number of our forces, besides their gunboats, and that they could cut off our communication at any time and force a surrender, therefore it was agreed to attack the enemy's right wing in force at 4 o'clock in the morning, and then to act according to circumstances, either to continue the fight or to cut through their lines and retreat towards Nashville.

Gen. Buckner was to move a little later and attack the enemy's flank at the moment he was to give way to our forces in his front. I was directed to hold my position. Col. Bailey was to remain in the fort (near the river), and Head's regiment was to occupy the vacated rifle-pits of Gen. Buckner's command. I doubted very much that these positions, isolated as they were from each other, could be held if attacked, and I stated my fears to Gen. Floyd, who replied, if pressed, to fall back on the fort, or act as circumstances would dictate. At the appointed hour on the 15th, the different brigades moved to their assigned positions.

Major Rice, aid-de-camp to Gen. Pillow, brought an order to me from Gen. Buckner, to send a regiment forward, and hold the Wynn's ferry road until the arrival of Gen. Buckner's division. This duty I assigned to Col. Quarles' regiment, who returned after the fulfilment of this order. Major Cunningham, Chief of Artillery, directed by Gen. Floyd, reported to me that two light batteries were at my disposal. Having more guns than I could use to an advantage, and not a sufficient number of gunners to work them, I respectfully declined the offer, but requested him to send me efficient gunners for at least one battery. This was done. Major Cunningham came with them and remained with me for some time. During the day my guns were used to the best advantage, and at one time with excellent effect against the enemy's cavalry, who immediately after were pursued by Forrest's cavalry.

About noon I was directed by an aid-de-camp of Gen. Buckner to guard the fire of my battery, as he intended to send a column to charge one of the enemy's batteries. Seeing these regiments pass my left in the open field, and being aware that my left wing could not be attacked at that time, I sent two regiments from my left (Col. Voorhies and Col. Hughes) to their support, but before they could reach the ground, the three attacking regiments were withdrawn. The battery was not taken, and my regiments returned. Early in the evening the different troops were ordered back to their respective rifle-pits, but the fighting continued at different points until night. At 2 o'clock in the morning of the 16th, Lieut. Morman, aid-de-camp to Gen. Johnson, brought the order to vacate the rifle-pits without the least noise, and to follow the movement of the troops on my left, stating at the same time that it was the intention to fight through their lines before the break of day. All the forces were concentrated near Dover, under the command of Gen. Johnson. In the meantime white flags were placed on the works of our former lines, and by the time the sun rose above the horizon, our forces were surrendered.

Much credit is due to Capts. Manpy and Parker, of the artillery, for their gallant conduct during the action, as well as to many other officers and men, whom, in the absence of reports from their respective commanders, I am unable to particularize, but it gives me great pleasure to state, that with very few exceptions, they all have done their duty like brave and gallant soldiers.

To Capt. Leslie Ellis, Acting Assistant-adjutant General, and my aid-de-camp, Capt. Bolen, I am particularly indebted for their untiring exertions in assisting me in the performance of my duties.

Very respectfully, your obedient servant,

A. HEIMAN, *Colonel commanding brigade.*

Report of the 42d Tennessee regiment, at the Battle of Fort Donelson, ending February 16, 1862.

COLUMBIAN HOTEL, RICHMOND, VA.,
August 11, 1862.

To Brig.-gen. BUCKNER:

SIR: The 42d Tennessee regiment, Col. Quarles, was quartered at Clarksville, Tenn., and on Wednesday, the 12th of February, received orders from Brig.-gen. Pillow to proceed to Fort Donelson, where we arrived next morning on a transport under a heavy fire. The companies were formed on the boat and marched off in regular order, and in passing through the village of Dover, we had two or three men wounded, one mortally, by the enemy's shells. We were consigned to Col. Heiman's brigade, where a hot fire was then being carried on. Three companies were thrown into the trenches on the flank of Col. Abernathy's regiment; the balance were retained as a support. Soon after our arrival the firing ceased, and the enemy withdrew. In the course of the evening the whole regiment was thrown into the trenches, where they remained until Saturday morning, with but little skirmishing, when the regiment was ordered about half a mile to the left and again placed in the trenches. Here it was not designated to what brigade the regiment belonged. A heavy conflict was here being waged in our front about 10 o'clock, A. M. I believe it was your brigade engaged, and it was here the coolness and daring of Col. Quarles first became conspicuous. The regiment on his flank began to leave the trenches under a heavy fire from the enemy's batteries. Col. Quarles rallied the stragglers and returned them to the trenches. The regiment remained here until about 4 o'clock, P. M., when we were ordered to the extreme right, where the enemy were reported to have taken some of our trenches.

Cold and benumbed as were the troops, they double-quicked for one and a half miles through the mud, slush, ice, and snow, formed in front of the enemy, and with a brisk fire of some twenty minutes caused the enemy to retire.

I believe you were present, and know with what gallantry it was done. Before closing my report, I will call your attention to the cool, gallant conduct of Col. Quarles. He was always at the head of his regiment, and set a gallant example for his officers and men.

The loss of the regiment was eleven wounded, four mortally. The number engaged, four hundred and ninety-eight, rank and file.

The above report is respectfully submitted.

T. McGINNIS, *Acting Adj. 42d Tenn. regiment.*

Report of Colonel John W. Head.

CHATTANOOGA, TENNESSEE, *August* 23, 1862.

To S. COOPER,

Adj.-Gen. Confederate States:

SIR: The surrender of Fort Donelson having prevented me from making a regular report, by the advice of Gen. Buckner I respectfully submit the following to you:

In the organization of the troops at Fort Donelson by Gen. Pillow, after the fall of Fort Henry, the 49th regiment of Tennessee volunteers, commanded by Col. Bailey, the 50th commanded by Col. Sugg, and the 30th commanded by myself, were placed under my command as a brigade, and ordered to garrison the fort. On Wednesday, the 12th day of February, two of the enemy's gunboats ascended the river and opened a fire upon the river batteries and fort. This was continued but a short time, and resulted in no injury to us.

On Wednesday evening the 30th regiment was ordered by Gen. Pillow to take position in the outer line of defence between the right of the brigade commanded by Col. Drake and the left of the brigade commanded by Col. Heiman.

The enemy were encamped, in force, in front of the position. I accompanied the regiment, leaving the fort garrisoned by the 49th and 50th, under the immediate command of Col. Bailey. The men were immediately put to work preparing rifle-pits for their protection. The pits were completed by Thursday morning.

We were fired upon occasionally during the fight on Thursday, but the enemy not being in range of our guns, it was not returned by us.

During the bombardment of the fort and river batteries on Friday by the enemy from their boats, our position was in range of their fire. The officers and men, however, behaved with coolness and gallantry.

About two o'clock on Saturday morning, I received orders to report my regiment to Gen. Buckner on the right wing. This I did without delay. I was ordered by Gen. Buckner to occupy with my regiment the line of defence before held by his command, and if attacked and overpowed, to fall back into the fort.

The trenches to be held covered a distance of about three-quarters of a mile. The regiment numbered about four hundred and fifty men fit for duty. The companies of Capts. Carson and Sample were placed in the pits on the extreme right, before held by the regiment of Col. Hanson; the company of Capt. Martin was held as a reserve. The three companies were placed under Major Turner, with instruction to report the first appearance of the enemy. The balance of the regiment was disposed of along the pits occupied by the remainder of Gen. Buckner's forces. During the morning a brisk fire was kept up with the enemy's sharpshooters, resulting in a few casualties on both sides.

About two o'clock, P. M., the forces of Gen. Buckner commenced arriving at their encampments from the conflict with the enemy on their right wing, my regiment still occupying the pits. About four o'clock, P. M., and before the regiment of Col. Hanson could be arranged in the pits, the enemy in heavy force attacked the three companies under Major Turner on the extreme right. They held their position with great gallantry, pouring a destructive fire into the ranks of the enemy, until he passed between the pits and overpowered them. They then fell back across a ravine on the next hill, and in connection with other forces resumed the fight. I immediately reported the facts to Gen. Buckner, who ordered out a part of his command to sustain us. Seeing that the soldiers of Gen. Buckner's command were greatly exhausted from the severe conflict they had been engaged in with the enemy in the forenoon, and that a bold and desperate effort was being made to force us back, I ordered the 49th and the right wing of the 50th regiments from the fort to sustain us. This I was forced to do without consultation with or orders from Gen. Buckner, in consequence of his position rallying and bringing his men into the engagement. The left wing of the 50th was left in the fort, under Lieut.-col. Lockhart, with orders to report promptly the first demonstration against the fort, I also ordered the companies of Capts. Jones and Lovell, of the 30th, from their position in the trenches, it being out of the range of the enemy to sustain their comrades on the right. The remainder of the 30th were in position and engaged in the fight.

Lieut.-col. Robb, of the 49th, was mortally wounded while aiding in bringing the regiment into the fight. He was an officer of high moral worth, beloved by his command, and acted with commendable courage. His death was a serious loss to the service. Cols. Bailey and Sugg gallantly led their commands into the action. Their men fought with great coolness and courage, and contributed very materially in repulsing the enemy. Indeed all the officers and men under my command, although imperfectly drilled, discharged their duty, and are entitled to the thanks of the country. They suffered much from exposure in the sleet and snow, for want of sleep and food, but they bore it without a murmur. Lieut.-col. Murphy, of the 30th, was confined during the greater part of the week to his bed from sickness, but, when able, was with the command and rendered efficient service.

Company A, of the 30th, commanded by Capt. Bidwell, was in charge of one of the river batteries, and both officers and men won for themselves the praise of all who witnessed their heroic conduct. During the engagement I also ordered two of the heavy guns in the fort to open upon the enemy. About eleven o'clock Saturday night, I received orders to march my brigade into Dover immediately, to join the army in the evacuation of the place. By two o'clock, A. M., I was in Dover with my command, but was then ordered back to camps, information having been received that the place was surrounded. I was also advised that a surrender was determined upon, and that the command had been transferred to Gen. Buckner. I was suffering from exposure, and threatened with pneumonia.

When it was known that a surrender was determined upon, the surgeon of the 30th advised me that if I was taken prisoner in my condition it might cost me my life. I called upon Gen. Buckner, stated the facts to him, and asked his advice as to the propriety of my escaping. He replied that it was a matter that I must determine for myself; that he felt it his duty to remain and share the fate of his men. Feeling that I could be of no service to my command or to the country by a surrender, I left the encampment and made my escape up the river. On my return I reported myself to Gen. A. S. Johnston, at Murfreesboro', for duty. He assigned me none. I was unwilling to retain my commission under the circumstances, and tendered my resignation, the acceptance of which was, as I was advised, recommended by Gen. Johnston.

JOHN W. HEAD,
Colonel Commanding Brigade.

Report of Col. Roger W. Hanson, commanding Second Kentucky regiment.

RICHMOND, VA., Aug. 8th, 1862.

To Major G. B. COSBY, *A. A. General.*

On the —— day of February, in pursuance of orders, I proceeded with my regiment upon the cars from Russellville, Kentucky, to Clarksville, Tennessee. When I arrived there, I was ordered by Gen. Pillow to embark immediately for Fort Donelson, I arrived there that night. Gen. Bushrod Johnson accompanied us, and when we arrived, he took command. Gen. Pillow arrived on the ——, and soon after his arrival he placed the troops in the position afterwards held by them. I was assigned to the extreme right of the line, extending to the right of Col. Palmer's regiment, to a slough formed by the high state of water in the river. The position was about half a mile in length, and was a protection in front and to the right of the original line of defence marked out for the Fort. I was directed to construct rifle-pits, which I did, locating them more than a hundred yards apart, at points best commanding the approaches to the position. They were made in a day and a night, and were necessarily very imperfect. I was directed to give up my tools to be used upon other parts of the defences. On Wednesday the 12th February, the enemy made his appearance in large force, pressing around in our front, with the evident intention of investing our position. Nothing was done to oppose or prevent his progress, and the following morning found his lines extending from the point of their disembarking to a point on the river above our position. On Thursday morning, the enemy made three several attacks upon my position—in all of which they were repulsed with but slight loss upon our part and very heavy upon theirs. In resisting these attacks, I was greatly assisted by Porter's battery upon the left—it always fired at the *right time* and to the *right place.* On Thursday night I was reinforced by Capt. Jackson's Virginia artillery—

four pieces. Although the night was cold and inclement, and the men much exhausted from the day's fighting and several days of hard work, we succeeded in getting these pieces in good position and well protected. On Friday I was reinforced also by Col. Palmer's regiment. We remained under arms and in ranks all day Friday, expecting the attack to be renewed. The firing of the sharpshooters was incessant from Thursday morning until the surrender, disturbing and almost destroying the repose of my command.

On Saturday morning I was conducted by yourself to the position assigned us, as a reserved regiment and a supporting force for Graves' artillery. I was directed not to leave my trenches until I was relieved by a Tennessee regiment from the Fort. The failure of this regiment to arrive as soon as contemplated, delayed me in reaching the point assigned me. A small detachment of Tennesseeans arrived, and I placed them in the trenches, and immediately thereafter moved rapidly to the battle field.

I remained in rear or near Graves' battery, under the immediate supervision of Gen. Buckner, until about noon, when Col. Baldwin, of Mississippi, announced to me that he was out of ammunition, and stated that unless he could get ammunition and reinforcements, there was great danger of losing the ground which had been won. I had near by a wagon of ammunition, and with the perseverance of Quarter-master Estep and Lieut. Semple, the ammunition was soon supplied. Previous to this period, some one, mounted, and purporting to be a staff officer, approached the regiment and ordered off two of the left companies to reinforce Col. Baldwin's command. These two companies, supposing it to be the order of Gen. Pillow or Buckner, moved off at a double quick, and were soon engaged with the enemy, and against greatly superior numbers.

Col. McCausland, of Virginia, arrived, and said that unless they were reinforced, the enemy would retake what they had gained; that after four hours of hard fighting, the enemy were bringing forward new troops, and in overwhelming numbers. I examined the state of the contest. I saw Col. Forrest make two gallant but unsuccessful charges. I saw that the enemy were gradually driving us back. My men were eager for the fight. I felt confident I could dislodge the enemy and drive them from their position. I sent for Gen. Buckner; he had gone to the right, and was conducting another movement. There was no time for delay. I concluded to take the responsibility and make the effort.

I marched the regiment by the front across the abatis, a distance of more than a quarter of a mile. When I reached the little ravine where Forrest was with his cavalry, I halted the regiment, and was joined by the two detached companies. In front of us was an open space, which had formerly been occupied as a camp. This space was about two hundred yards in width. Beyond this space, in the timber and thick under-growth, the enemy were posted. I directed the regiment, when the command was given, to march at quick time across this space, and not to fire a gun until they reached the woods in which the enemy were posted. The order was admirably executed, and although we lost fifty men in killed and wounded, in crossing this space, not a gun was fired until the woods were reached. The enemy stood their ground until we were within forty yards of them, when they fled in great confusion, under a most destructive fire. This was not, strictly speaking, a charge bayonets, but it would have been one if the enemy had not fled.

Graves' battery was then moved up, and my regiment moved forward several hundred yards. While Graves was moving up his ammunition, and other preparations were being made to hold this position, the order came from Gen. Pillow to return to the trenches. Up to this period the success was complete.

When I returned to my position, and before the companies had reached the trenches, the enemy attacked in large force and took them. I fell back to the original line of defence, and being reinforced by several regiments, this position was retrieved; Gen. Buckner, at this point, being present and in command. This position was a stronger one than the one lost, and every effort was made that night to construct defences, but the men were so exhausted, from labor and loss of sleep, that it was utterly impossible. I will take the liberty to add, that up to the time when we were ordered back to the trenches, our success was complete and our escape secure.

It is also my opinion that the exhaustion of the men from loss of sleep and labor, together with the demoralization caused by the loss of our trenches on the right, rendered the surrender unavoidable. The officers and men of my regiment acted with great gallantry. The list of the killed and wounded I have heretofore furnished.

ROGER W. HANSON,
Col. Second Kentucky Regiment.

Report of Colonel John Gregg, commanding 7th regiment Texas Volunteers.

RICHMOND, VA., August 8, 1862.

Major GEORGE COSBY, *A. A. General, Richmond:*

MAJOR: In the absence of any one who was in command of the brigade or division of which my regiment was a part at the time of the battle of Fort Donelson, I make my report of the action of the regiment to Gen. S. B. Buckner. I hope this will be considered proper, as it is the only method by which I can give to the brave men under my command the tribute which I think due to their behavior in that battle.

The regiment was assigned its place in the line designated as our line of defence. On Wednesday the 12th February, cleared away the timber in our front and completed the digging of our rifle-pits during the day and at night. The enemy began to cannonade our intrenchments at 9 o'clock, A. M., on Thursday, and kept it up until 4 o'clock, P. M., during a greater part of the time making an enfilading fire with shells, which was well directed, and by which Lieut. E. B. Rosson, of company A, was killed, and Thomas Jordan, a private in company G, was slightly wounded. On Friday we were not engaged. But on Saturday morning about half an hour before sunrise, we set out with other regiments to make the sortie upon the enemy's right wing. After filing around the base of the hill, upon which the enemy were drawn up, we came to our position, at the distance of half a mile, upon the right of our line. I caused the regiment to front and advance up the hill side, under a fire from the enemy's skirmishers. Just before reaching the crest of the hill, their line drawn up behind it delivered fire, and a most galling one it was. Here fell Lieut.-col. J. M. Clough, Capt. Wm. B. Hill, of company H, and Lieut. J. W. Nowlin, of company A, neither of whom spoke after being shot; and here also quite a number of our non-commissioned officers and privates were killed and wounded. But our line continued to advance, pouring a most destructive fire into the enemy's ranks. In about half an hour their line broke and we pursued them to the next ridge, upon which a fresh line was drawn up. I caused the regiment to continue our forward movement and to keep up a continuous fire, and in a short time the second line broke and fled, leaving in our hands the six-pounder, with ammunition and horses. We continued to press them, until a third force was seen drawn up in a ravine near a clearing, and upon this we pressed and continued to fire, until it also broke and fled. And although the slaughter of the enemy had before been very great, their difficulty in getting through the felled timber caused our fire to be much more destructive upon them at this place. For more than the distance of a mile through the woods, the earth was strewed with the killed and wounded of the enemy. George Blain, a private in company G, captured and brought to me Major Post, of the 8th Illinois infantry, and there were other prisoners taken. But all this was not done without severe loss to ourselves. Of the three hundred and fifty or sixty officers and men, whom I led into the fight, twenty were killed on the field, and thirty-four were disabled by wounds. I must acknowledge the very efficient assistance of Major Granbury in the management of the regiment throughout the entire day. Where all behaved with such coolness and courage, it is hardly admissable to name particular individuals; but the conspicuous gallantry of Lieut.-col. Clough, of Capt. Hill, and Lieuts. Rosson and Nowlin, will ever be thought of with admiration by those who witnessed, and cherished as a glorious memory by their friends.

Submitted respectfully. JOHN GREGG,

Col. 7th regiment Texas Infantry.

Summary of Killed and Wounded in the Second Division, Central Army of Kentucky, in the engagements at Fort Donelson, Tennessee.

In the 3d Brigade, Col. Jno. C. Brown, commanding:

38 killed, 246 wounded ....aggregate		284
2d Kentucky regiment..........................	(about)	80
Issaquena battery..............................	(")	3
Porter's "	(")	25
		392

In the two regiments of the 2d Brigade, (Col. Baldwin), detached, and under the command of Gen. Pillow:

26th Tennessee,.............	11 killed,	78 wounded.	
26th Mississippi,............	11 "	68 "	
Staff and other officers,.......	2 "	15 "	aggregate, 165
Total.........................			557

The proximate aggregate strength of the various regiments was as follows:

3rd Tennessee	750	
17th Tennessee	625	
32nd Tennessee	400	
14th Mississippi	650	
41st Tennessee	400	
2nd Kentucky	600	
		3,025*

Detached, and under command of Gen. Pillow:

26th Tennessee	401	
26th Mississippi	443	
		844

Aggregate strength of Buckner's division, under his own command, exclusive of two batteries of artillery, 3,025.

Aggregate detached under Gen. Pillow, 844.

Aggregate infantry of Buckner's division under him and Gen. Pillow, 3,869

Estimate of Killed and Wounded in those portions of Gen. Pillow's command, reporting their operations at Fort Donelson, Tennessee, through Gen. S. B. Buckner.

	Killed	Wounded
Col. Heiman's brigade	10 killed,	30 wounded.
Col. Gregg's regiment	20 "	34 "
Major Brown's regiment	18 "	55 "
	48	119

Aggregate 167.

* This should be 3,425 if the returns are correct. [Clerk.

REPORT OF THE OPERATIONS OF THE ARMY IN NEW MEXICO.

BRIG.-GEN. W. U. SIBLEY, COMMANDING.

HEAD-QUARTERS, ARMY OF NEW MEXICO,
FORT BLISS, TEXAS, May 4, 1862.

General S. COOPER,
Adjutant and Inspector-general,
Richmond, Va.:

GENERAL:—I have the honor to report, for the information of the Secretary of War, the operations of this army during the months of February, March, and April, ultimo.

This report is made to cover the whole campaign, for the reason that the special reports of the various commanders, herewith inclosed, enter sufficiently into detail to elucidate the various actions in which the troops were engaged during the campaign.

It is due to the brave soldiers I have had the honor to command, to promise that from its first inception, the "Sibley brigade" has encountered difficulties in its organization, and opposition and distaste to the service required at its hands, which no other troops have met with.

From misunderstandings, accidents, deficiency of arms, &c., instead of reaching the field of its operations early in September, as was anticipated, I found myself, at this point, as late as the middle of January, 1862, with only two regiments and a half, poorly armed, thinly clad, and almost destitute of blankets. The ranks were becoming daily thinned with those two terrible scourges to an army, small pox and pneumonia. Not a dollar of quarter-master's funds was on hand, or had ever been to supply the daily and pressing necessities of the service, and the small means of this sparse section had been long consumed by the force under the command of Lieut.-col. Baylor, so that the credit of the government was not as available a resource as it might otherwise have been.

Having established a general hospital at Dona Ana, I determined to move forward with the force at hand. Accordingly, during the first week in January, the advance was put in march for old Fort Thorn. Thence on the 7th of February, the movement was continued to a point seven miles below Fort Craig, when the Santa Fe papers boasted we were to be met and overwhelmed by Canby's entire army. On the 16th of February, a reconnoissance in force, was pushed to within a mile of the fort, and battle offered in the open plain. The challenge was disregarded, and only noticed by the sending out of a few well-mounted men to watch our movements. The forces of the enemy were kept well concealed in the "bosque" (or grove) above the fort and within its walls.

The reconnoissance proved the futility of assaulting the fort in front, with our light mettle, and that our only hope of success was to force the enemy to an open field fight. It was accordingly determined by a partial retrograde movement to cross the Rio Grande to the east bank, turn the fort, and force a battle for the recrossing. To do this, involved first, the hazardous necessity of crossing a treacherous stream in full view of the fort; second, to make a "dry camp" immediately opposite, and remote from the fort only a mile and a half, and the next day to fight our first battle. The enemy seemed to have been so confounded by the boldness and eccentricity of these movements, that the first was accomplished without molestation, save a demonstration on the afternoon of the 20th, as we were forming our camp, by the crossing of some 2500 infantry and cavalry, with the purpose, apparently, of making an assault upon our lines. Here, the spirit and courage of our men were evidenced by the alacrity shown in getting into line to confront the enemy. A few rounds from our well-directed guns, under the management of Capt. Teel, Lieuts. Riley and Woods, checked his advance, and drove him to the cover of his sand-revolted mud walls.

It is proper to state here, that these operations, approved by me, were conducted by Col. Thomas Green, of the 5th regiment; the state of my health having confined me to the ambulance for several days previous.

On the morning of the 21st, considering that the impending battle must decide the question at issue, though still very weak, I took the saddle at early dawn, to direct, in person, the movement. Green's regiment, with the battalion of the 7th, under Lieut.-col. Sutton, and Capt. Teel's battery, were ordered to make a strong threatening demonstration on the fort; whilst Scurry, with the 4th, well flanked by Pyron's command on the left, should feel his way cautiously to the river.

This movement was unfortunately delayed by the loss, during the night, by careless hurding, of a hundred mules of the baggage train of the 4th regiment. Rather than the plan should be defeated, a number of wagons were abandoned, containing the entire kits, blankets, books, and papers of this regiment; and meanwhile, what was left of the trains was kept in motion over the sand-hills, which the enemy had deemed impossible.

On reaching the river bottom at Valverde, it was ascertained that the enemy, anticipating our movement, had thrown a large force of infantry and cavalry up the river to dispute the water with us. Pyron immediately engaged him with his small force of 250 men, and gallantly held his ground against overwhelming odds, until the arrival of Scurry with the 4th regiment and Lieut. Riley's battery of light howitzers. At 12 M., the action becoming warm, and the enemy evidently receiving large reinforcements, I ordered Green's regiment, with Teel's battery, to the front.

These, in the course of an hour, gallantly entered into action, and the battle became general. Subsequently, Lieut.-col. Sutton, with his battalion, was ordered forward from the rear, and did right good service, leading his men even to the cannon's mouth. At one and a half P. M., having become completely exhausted, and finding myself no longer able to keep the saddle, I sent my aids and other staff officers to report to Col. Greene. His official report attests the gallantry of their bearing and his final success, resulting in the capture of their battery and driving the enemy in disorder from the field, and thus evidencing his own intrepidity and the indomitable courage of all engaged.

From information derived from reliable sources, the forces opposed to us could not have been less than 5,000 men, with a reserve of 3,000 at the fort. Ours did not exceed 1,750 on the field, viz.: the 4th regiment, 600, 5th 600, 7th 300, and Pyron's command, (of 2d mounted rifles,) 250. This signal victory should have resulted in the capture of the fort, as fresh troops had been brought forward to pursue and follow the discomfited column of the enemy. A flag of truce was opportunely dispatched by the Federal commander before he reached the gates of his fort, and which was for two hours supposed by our troops to be a proposition to surrender.

This flag had for its object, the burying of the dead and removal of their wounded; and I regret to state here, for the sake of old associations, that under this flag, and another sent next day, the enemy, availing himself of our generosity and confidence in his honor, not only loaded his wagons with arms picked up on the battle-field, but sent a force up, and actually succeeded in recovering from the river one 24-pounder, which had been left in our hands. Even a guidon and a flag, taken in the same way, under the cover of night and a white flag, were boastingly pointed to, in an interview under a flag of truce between one of my aids and the Federal commander at the fort, as trophies of the fight.

The burying of the dead and care of the wounded occasioned a delay of two days on the field, thus leaving us with but five days' scant rations. In this dilemma the question arose whether to assault the fort in this crippled condition, or move rapidly forward up the river where supplies of breadstuffs and meat could be procured. The latter course, in a council of war, was adopted. Depositing our sick at Locorro, 30 miles above Fort Craig, the march was uninterruptedly made to Albuquerque, where, notwithstanding the destruction by the enemy of large supplies by fire, ample subsistence was secured. A very considerable quantity of supplies and ammunition was also obtained at Cubero, a temporary post 60 miles west of Albuquerque. Other supplies were also taken at Santa Fe, and upon the whole we had a sufficiency for some three months.

It is due to the 4th regiment to mention at this place an action of devotion and self-sacrifice worthy of high praise, and more commendable because they are Texans.

In the action at Valverde, many of their horses were killed, thus leaving them half foot, half mounted. The proposition being made to them to dismount, the whole regiment, without a dissenting voice, a cavalry regiment which had proudly flaunted its banner before the enemy on the 20th, took the line of march on the 24th, a strong and reliable regiment of infantry.

Having secured all the available stores in and about Albuquerque, and dispatched Major Pyron with his command to Santa Fe to secure such as might be found there, I determined to make a strong demonstration on Fort Union.

With this view, Col. Scurry, with the 4th, and the battalion of Col. Stute's regiment under Major Jordan, were pushed forward in the direction of Galestio, whilst Col. Green, with his regiment, (5th,) being somewhat badly crippled in transportation, was held for a few days in hand to check any movement from Fort Craig.

Meanwhile, the enemy, having received reinforcements at Fort Union of 950 men from Pipe's Peak, on or about the 12th of March, took the initiative and commenced a rapid march on Santa Fe.

Major Pyron, reinforced by four companies of the 5th regiment, under Major Shropshire, receiving notice of this movement, advanced at once to meet him, on the high road between Santa Fe and Union. On the 26th of March a sharp skirmish ensued, described in detail by that officer, wherein many acts of daring heroism were enacted. The company of "brigades," (Independent Volunteers), under the command of Capt. John Phillips, is said to have done good service. One of their number, Mr. Thomas Cator, was killed, and two wounded. On this occasion, as on every previous one, this company showed a devotedness to the cause which has elevated them and inspired confidence throughout the army. Col. Scurry reached the scene of action at daylight next morning, and the next day fought the battle of Glorietta, driving the enemy from the field with great loss.

His report is respectfully referred to for the details of this glorious action. Pending this action, I was on my rout to Santa Fe, in rear of Green's regiment, which had meanwhile been put in march for that place, where, on my arrival, I found the whole exultant army assembled. The sick and wounded had been comfortably quartered and attended; the loss of clothing and transportation had been made up from the enemy's stores and confiscations; and indeed every thing done which should have been done.

Many friends were found in Santa Fe who had been in durance. Among the rest, Gen. Wm. Pelham, who had but recently been released from a dungeon in Fort Union.

After the occupancy of the capitol of the Territory for nearly a month from the time of our first advance upon it, the forage and supplies obtainable there having become exhausted, it was determined to occupy with the whole army the village of Murzana, intermediate between Fort Union, Albuquerque, and Fort Craig, and securing, as a line of communication, the road to Fort Stanton.

This plan was disconcerted, however, by the rapid and continuous expresses from Albuquerque, urging the necessity of reinforcements to hold the place (the depot of all our supplies) against the advancing forces of Canby from Craig.

The entire force was accordingly moved by forced marches in the direction of Albuquerque, arriving too late to encounter the enemy, but time enough to secure our limited supplies from the contingency of capture.

In our straightened circumstances, the question now arose, in my mind, whether to evacuate the country or take the desperate chances of fighting the enemy in his stronghold, Union, for scant rations at the best.

The course adopted was deemed the wisest.

On the morning of the 12th of April, the evacuation commenced by the crossing of Scurry's 4th regiment, the battalion of Stute's regiment, Pyron's command, and a part of the artillery, by ferry and ford, to the west bank of the river. Green's regiment was ordered to follow, but finding the ford to be difficult, he encamped for the night on the east bank, hoping to be able, on the ensuing morning, to find a better ford lower down the river. Accordingly, on the next day that officer proceeded with his regiment as low down as Peratto, opposite Los Lunal, the point at which I had halted the balance of the army to await his arrival. In the meantime, Canby, having formed a junction with a large force from Fort Union, debouched through a canon after nightfall to the neighborhood of the river, taking a commanding position in close proximity to Green's camp, and in the morning opened a furious but harmless cannonade.

On being notified of the critical situation of this detached portion of the army, the whole disposable force at Los Lunal, reserving a sufficient guard for the train, was dispatched to its relief. The passage of the river by this force and the artillery was successfully effected, under the direction of Col. Scurry.

Following shortly after with a portion of my staff to assume the immediate command, and having crossed the river, I was notified by several officers, who had preceded me some hundred yards, of the rapid approach of a large number of the enemy's cavalry. Finding myself completely cut off, I had no other alternative than to recross the river amid a shower of balls. The day was occupied at Peratto in ineffectual firing on both sides. After nightfall I gave orders for the recrossing of the whole army to the west bank of the river, which was effected without interruption or casualty, and on the next morning the march down the river was resumed. The enemy followed on the opposite bank, and both armies encamped in full view of each other, the river alone intervening.

The transportation and artillery had by this time become such an incumbrance on the heavy, sandy road, without forage or grass, that the abandonment of one or the other became inevitable. My original plan had been to push on by the river route, in advance of the enemy, having the start of him two whole days from Albuquerque to Fort Craig, attack the weak garrison, and demolish the fort.

This plan was defeated by Col. Green not finding a crossing of the river at a convenient point.

Col. Green, and Col. Scurry, with several other practical officers, here came forward and proposed, in order to avoid the contingency of another general action in our then crippled condition, that a route through the mountains, avoiding Fort Craig, and striking the river below that point, should be pursued, they undertaking with their respective commands to push the artillery through at all hazards and at any expenditure of toil and labor. Major Coopwood, who had familiarized himself with the country, undertook the difficult and responsible task of guiding the army through this mountainous, trackless waste.

The arguments presented in favor of this course were potent. Besides having the advantage of grass and a firm road, with very little difference in distance, the enemy would be completely mystified, as afterwards proved to be the case. Accordingly, all the wagons which could possibly be dispensed with were ordered to be abandoned on the ground, seven days' provisions to be packed on mules, and the entire force put in march after night-fall. The route was a difficult and most hazardous one, both in respect to its practicability and supply of water. The successful accomplishment of the march not only proved the sagacity of our guide, but the pledge of Col. Scurry that the guns should be put over every obstacle, however formidable, by his regiment, was nobly fulfilled. Not a murmur escaped the lips of these brave boys. Descents into and ascents out of the deepest canons, which a single horseman would have sought for miles to avoid, were undertaken and accomplished, with a cheerfulness and ability which were the admiration and praise of the whole army. Thus, in ten days, with seven days' rations, a point on the river, where supplies had been ordered forward, was reached. The river, which was rising rapidly, was safely crossed to the east bank, under the direction of Col. Green, and, at this moment, I am happy to repeat, the whole force is comfortably quartered in the villages extending from Dona Ana to this place.

My chief regret, in making this retrogade movement, was the necessity of leaving hospitals at Santa Fe, Albuquerque, and Socorro. Everything, however, was provided for the comfort of the sick, and sufficient funds, in Confederate paper, provided them to meet every want, if it be negotiated. It has been almost impossible to procure specie upon any terms. One thousand dollars is all I have been able to procure for the use of the hospitals and for secret service. The ricos, or wealthy citizens of New Mexico, had been completely drained by the Federal powers, and adhering to them, becoming absolute followers of their army, for dear life and their invested dollars. Politically, they have no distinct sentiment or opinion on the vital question at issue. Power and interest alone control the expression of their sympathies. Two noble and notable exceptions to this rule were found in the brothers Raphael and Manuel Armijo, the wealthiest and most respectable native merchants of New Mexico. The latter had been pressed into the militia, and was compulsorily present in the action at Valverde. On our arrival at Albuquerque, they came forward, boldly, and protested their sympathy with our cause, placing their stores, containing goods amounting to $200,000, at the disposal of my troops.

When the necessity for evacuating the country became inevitable, these two gentlemen abandoned luxurious homes and well filled storehouses, to join their fate to the Southern Confederacy. I trust they will not be forgotten in the final settlement.

In concluding this report, already extended beyond my anticipations, it is proper that I should express the conviction, determined by some experience, that, except for its political geographical position, the Territory of New Mexico is not worth a quarter of the blood and treasure expended in its conquest. As a field of military operations, it possesses not a single element, except in the multiplicity of its defensible positions. The indispensable element, food, cannot be relied on. During the last year, and, pending the recent operations, hundreds of thousands of sheep have been driven off by the Navajoes. Indeed, such were the complaints of the people in this respect, that I had determined, as good policy, to encourage private enterprises against that tribe and the Apaches, and to legalize the enslaving of them.

As for the results of the campaign, I have only to say that we have beaten the enemy in every encounter, and against large odds; that, from being the worst armed, my forces are now the best armed in the country. We reached this point last winter in rags, and blanketless. The army is now well clad, and well supplied in other respects. The entire campaign has been prosecuted without a dollar in the quarter-master's department, Capt. Harrison not having yet reached this place. But, sir, I cannot speak encouragingly for the future. My troops have manifested a dogged, irreconcilable detestation of the country and the people. They have endured much, suffered much, and cheerfully; but the prevailing discontent, backed up by the distinguished valor displayed on every field, entitles them to marked consideration and indulgence.

These considerations, in connection with the scant supply of provisions, and the disposition of our own citizens in this section, to depreciate our currency, may determine me, without waiting for instructions, to move by slow marches down the country, both for the purpose of remounting and recruiting our thinned ranks.

Trusting that the management of this more than difficult campaign intrusted to me by the Government may prove satisfactory to the President,

I have the honor, General, to be,
Your obedient servant,
H. F. SIBLEY,
Brig.-gen. Commanding.

Dispatches from Capt. Tom P. Ochiltree, Assistant Adjutant General, Army of New Mexico.

SAN ANTONIO, April 27th, 1862.

TO COMMANDING OFFICER, C. S. A., *New Orleans, La.:*

I addressed a letter to you from Mesilla, Arizona, asking that an inclosed dispatch be telegraphed to his Excellency, President Davis; for fear that it did not reach its destination, I write again from this place.

In the event of both dispatches reaching New Orleans simultaneously, I would respectfully ask that this one should be sent and the former one retained, as this is more correct in details, etc.

I have the honor to be, very respectfully,
TOM P. OCHILTREE,
Assistant Adj.-gen., Army of New Mexico.

SAN ANTONIO, TEXAS, April 27th, 1862.

HIS EXCELLENCY, PRESIDENT DAVIS:

I have the honor to inform your Excellency of another glorious victory achieved by the Confederate army of New Mexico.

On the 27th March, Liet.-col. Scurry, with 1000 men from the 2d, 4th, 5th, and 7th Texas mounted volunteers, met, attacked, whipped, and routed 2000 Federals, 23 miles east of Santa Fe.

Our loss was 33 killed and 35 wounded—among the killed was Major Ragnet, and Capt. Buckholt, of the 4th, and Major Shropshire, of the 5th Texas mounted volunteers; Lieut.-col. Scurry, commanding, was twice slightly wounded, and Major Pyron, commanding battalion 2d T. M. R., had his horse blown from under him by a shell.

The enemy's loss was over 700 killed and wounded—500 being left on the field. Their rout was complete, and they were scattered from the battle-field to Fort Union.

The Confederate flag flies over Santa Fe and Albuquerque. At the latter place, the flag was made of a captured United States flag, raised, upon a United States flag-staff, the salute fired by a captured United States battery, and Dixie played by a captured United States band.

The Federal force defeated at Glorietta, consisted of 1600 Pike's Peak volunteers, and 600 regulars, under command of Col. Slough. I have the honor to inform your Excellency that I will wait upon you with important dispatches in a few days.

Very respectfully,

TOM P. OCHILTREE,

Assistant Adj.-gen., Army of New Mexico.

Report of the Battle of Glorietta, Colonel Scurry, commanding.

SANTA FE, NEW MEXICO, March 31, 1862.

To Major A. M. JACKSON,

A. A. General, Army New Mexico.

MAJOR: Late on the afternoon of the 26th, while encamped at Galistoe, an express from Major Pyron arrived with the information that the major was engaged in a sharp conflict with a greatly superior force of the enemy, about sixteen miles distant, and urging me to hasten to his relief. The critical condition of Major Pyron and his gallant comrades was made known to the command, and in ten minutes the column was formed, and the order to march given. Our baggage train was sent forward under a guard of one hundred men, under the command of Lieut. Taylor, of the 7th regiment, to a point some six miles in the rear of Major Pyron's position; the main command marching directly across the mountains to the scene of conflict. It is due to the brave men making this cold night march to state, that where the road over the mountain was too steep for the horses to drag the artillery, they were unharnessed, and the men cheerfully pulled it over the difficulties of the way by hand. About three o'clock in the morning we reached Major Pyron's encampment at Johnson's ranche in *cañon* Cito. There had been an agreed cessation of hostilities until eight o'clock the next morning. Too much praise cannot be bestowed upon the courage of the officers and men engaged in the affair of the 26th. As soon as daylight enabled me, I made a thorough examination of the ground, and so formed the troops as to command every approach to the position we occupied, which was naturally a very strong one. The disposition of the troops was soon completed, and by 8 o'clock were ready to receive the expected attack. In this position we remained until the next morning. The enemy still not making their appearance, I concluded to march forward and attack them. Leaving a small wagon guard, I marched in their direction with portions of nine companies of the 4th regiment, under their respective officers (Capts. Hampton, Lesseure, Foard, Crosson, Geiseher, Alexander, Buckholt, Odell, and Lieut. Holland, of company B, Capt. Scarborough being unwell), four companies of the 7th, under Capts. Hoffman, Gardner, Wiggins, and Adair, four companies of the 5th regiment, under Capts. Shannon and Ragsdale and Lieuts. Oaks and Scott; three pieces of artillery under Lieut. Bradford, together with Capt. Phillips' company of independent volunteers. From details and other causes they were reduced, until, all combined, they did not number over six hundred men fit for duty. At about six miles from our camp the advance guard gave notice that the enemy were near, in force. I hastened in front to examine their position, and found they were about one mile west of "Pigeon's Ranche," in *canon Glorietta.*

The mounted men who were marching in front were ordered to retire slowly to the rear, dismount, and come into the action on foot. The artillery was pushed forward to a slight elevation in the *canon*, and immediately to open fire. The infantry were rapidly deployed into line, extending across the canon from a fence on our left up into the pine forest on our right.

About the time these dispositions were made, the enemy rapidly advanced in separate columns, both upon our right and left. I dispatched Major Pyron to the right to check them in that direction, and placing the centre in command of Major Ragnet, I hastened with the remainder of the command to the left.

A large body of infantry, availing themselves of a gulch that ran up the centre of an inclosed field to our left, were moving under its cover past our left flank to the rear of our position.

Crossing the fence on foot, we advanced over the clearing some two hundred yards under a heavy fire from the foe, and dashed into the gulch in their midst, pistol and knife in hand. For a few moments a most desperate and deadly hand to hand conflict raged along the gulch, when they broke before the steady courage of our men, and fled in the wildest disorder and confusion.

Major Pyron was equally successful, and Major Ragnet with his force charged rapidly down the centre. Lieut. Bradford, of the artillery, had been wounded and borne from the field. There being no other officer of the artillery present, three guns constituting our battery had been hastily withdrawn before I was aware of it

Sending to the rear to have two of the guns brought back to the field, a pause was made to reunite our forces, which had become somewhat scattered in the last rencountre. When we were ready to advance, the enemy had taken cover, and it was impossible to tell whether their main body was stationed behind a long adobe wall that ran nearly across the canon, or had taken position behind a large ledge of rocks in the rear. Private W. D. Kirk, of Capt. Phillips' company, had taken charge of one of the guns, and Sergeant Patrick, of the artillery, another, and brought them to the ground. While trying by the fire of these two guns to ascertain the locality of the enemy, Major Shropshire was sent to the right with orders to move up among the pines until he should find the enemy, when he was to attack them on that flank. Major Ragnet, with similar orders, was dispatched to the left. I informed these gallant officers that as soon as the sound of their guns was heard I would charge in front with the remainder of the command. Sending Major Pyron to the assistance of Major Ragnet, and leaving instructions for the centre to charge as the fire opened on the right, I passed in that direction to learn the cause of delay in making the assault. I found that the gallant Major Shropshire had been killed. I took command of the right and immediately attacked the enemy, who were at the ranche. Majors Ragnet and Pyron opened a galling fire upon their left from the rock on the mountain side, and the centre charging down the road, the foe were driven from the ranche to the ledge of rocks before alluded to, where they made their final and most desperate stand. At this point three batteries of eight guns opened a furious fire of grape, canister, and shell upon our advancing troops.

Our brave soldiers, heedless of the storm, pressed on, determined, if possible, to take their battery. A heavy body of infantry, twice our number, interposed to save their guns. Here the conflict was terrible. Our men and officers, alike inspired with the unalterable determination to overcome every obstacle to the attainment of their object, dashed among them. The right and centre had united on the left. The intrepid Ragnet, and the cool, calm, courageous Pyron, had pushed forward among the rocks, until the muzzle of the opposing forces' guns passed each other. Inch by inch was the ground disputed, until the artillery of the enemy had time to escape with a number of their wagons. The infantry also broke ranks and fled from the field. So precipitate was their flight, that they cut loose their teams and set fire to two of their wagons. The pursuit was kept up until forced to halt from the extreme exhaustion of the men, who had been engaged for six hours in the hardest contested fight it had ever been my lot to witness. The enemy is now known to have numbered fourteen hundred men, Pike's Peak miners and regulars, the flower of the United States army.

During the action, a part of the army succeeded in reaching our rear, surprising the wagon guard, and burning our wagons, taking at the same time some sixteen prisoners. About this time a party of prisoners, whom I had sent to the rear, reached there, and informed them how the fight was going in front, whereupon they beat a hasty retreat, not, however, until the perpetration of two acts which the most barbarous savage of the plains would blush to own. One was the shooting and dangerously wounding the Rev. L. H. Jones, chaplain of the 4th regiment, with a white flag in his hand; the other an order that the prisoners they had taken be shot in case they were attacked on their retreat. These instances go to prove that they have lost all sense of humanity, in the insane hatred they bear to the citizens of the Confederacy, who have the manliness to arm in defence of their country's independence.

We remained upon the battle-field during the day of the 29th, to bury our dead and provide for the comfort of the wounded, and then marched to Santa Fe to procure supplies and transportation to replace that destroyed by the enemy.

Our loss was thirty-six (36) killed and sixty (60) wounded. Of the killed, 24 were of the 4th regiment, 1 of the 5th regiment, 8 of the 7th regiment, and 1 of the artillery.

That of the enemy greatly exceeded this number, 44 of their dead being counted where the battle first opened. Their killed must have exceeded considerably over 100.

The country has to mourn the loss of four as brave and chivalrous officers as ever graced the ranks of any army. The gallant

Major Shropshire fell early, pressing upon the foe and cheering his men on. The brave and chivalrous Major Ragnet, who fell mortally wounded while engaged in the last and most desperate conflict of the day. He survived long enough to know and rejoice at our victory, and then died with loving messages upon his expiring lips. The brave, gallant Capt. Buckholt, and Lieut. Mills, conducted themselves with distinguished gallantry throughout the fight, and fell near its close. Of the living, it is only necessary to say all behaved with distinguished courage and daring.

This battle proves conclusively that few mistakes were made in the selection of the officers in this command. They were ever in the front, leading their men into the hottest of the fray. It is not too much to say, that even in the midst of this heroic band, among whom instances of individual daring and personal prowess were constantly occurring, Major Pyron was distinguished by the calm intrepidity of his bearing. It is due to Adjutant Ellsbury R. Lane, to bear testimony to the courage and activity he displayed in the discharge of his official duties, and to acknowledge my obligations for the manner in which he carried out my orders.

I have the honor to be, very respectfully,

Your obedient servant,

W. R. SCURRY,

Colonel commanding A. N. M.

Report of the Battle of Valverde, Colonel Greene, commanding.

CAMP VALVERDE, February 22, 1862.

Major A. M. JACKSON,

A. A. General, Army of N. M.:

SIR:—I have the honor of submitting to you the following report of the battle of Valverde, fought on yesterday, by a part of the brigade of Gen. Sibley, under my command. While in the act of turning Fort Craig, on the east side of the Rio Grande, Major Pyron, with 200 men, was sent to reconnoitre early in the morning of the 21st the route around the Mesa, north of the fort, and secure a footing on the river above. Whilst Major Pyron was approaching the river with his command, the enemy appeared in considerable numbers between his command and the river, on the north of the Mesa, and opened on him about 8 o'clock, a heavy fire of artillery and small-arms being between him and the water. The gallant Pyron, with his brave little force, kept up the unequal contest for an hour or two, until the arrival of Lieut.-col. Scurry, with a part of his regiment and Lieut. Riley's howitzer battery. Scurry took position on the right of Pyron, and both kept up the contest and maintained their position behind a low line of sand-hill. About this time, one section of Capt. Teel's battery came up, and took position, and replied to the fire of the enemy. At 12 o'clock, while under the orders of the general I was threatening the fort on the south side of the Mesa, I received his orders to move up with all my disposable force to the support of Lieut.-col. Scurry and Major Pyron, after leaving a sufficient force to protect the train which was then moving from our late camp around the Mesa to the battle-ground, and which was stretched out for several miles. Our train was threatened by a considerable body of troops of the enemy who made their appearance on the Mesa. Detaching Lieut.-col. Sutton's command, and a detachment from my own regiment to protect the train, I moved up with as much speed as practicable, with eight companies of my regiment, sending forward Major Lockridge with the two companies of lancers under Capts. Lang and McCowan. My companies were placed in the line of battle between Pyron, on the left, and Scurry, on the right, except three, which were sent by me under Lieut.-col. McNeill, to drive the enemy from the north point of the Mesa, where they were annoying our left, and threatening our train.

After these dispositions, I moved up to the line of battle myself, and, by the orders of the general, took command of the forces present. The enemy during the day, and with little intermission, kept up a brisk cannonade upon us, to which our 6-pounders, under Capt. Teel, replied with effect. The enemy repeatedly advanced with their skirmishers to near our lines, killing many of our horses tied in the rear. About 3 o'clock, P. M., a most galling fire was opened upon Lieut.-col. Scurry's command, on our right, by three or four hundred of the enemy's riflemen. Capt. Lang, of the 5th regiment, with about forty of his lancers, made at this time one of the most gallant and furious charges on these light troops of the enemy ever witnessed in the annals of battles. His little troop was decimated, and the gallant captain and Lieut. Bass severely wounded—the latter in seven places. The enemy were repulsed by this gallant charge, and our right was for some time unmolested.

Large bodies of the enemy's infantry having crossed the river about half-past 3 o'clock, P. M., bringing over with them six pieces of splendid artillery, took position in front of us, on the bank of the river, at a distance of six hundred yards. In addition to this body of troops, two 24-pound howitzers were placed on our left flank by the enemy. These were supported by a regiment of infantry and a regiment of cavalry. The heaviest fire of the whole day was opened about this time on our left, which was under the command of the gallant Lockridge. Our brave men on that part of the line maintained the unequal fight with desperate courage, though overwhelmingly outnumbered. Lieut.-col. Sutton, now coming up with a part of his battalion, took position on our left.

The enemy, now being on our side of the river, opened upon us a tremendous fire of round shot, grape, and shell. Their force in numbers was vastly superior to ours, but having the most unbounded confidence in the courage of our troops, I ordered a charge on their battery and infantry of regulars in front, and at the same time, Major Ragnet, of the 4th, with four companies of the same, and Capt. Ragsdale's company of the 5th, was directed by me to charge as cavalry upon the infantry and Mexican cavalry and the two 24-pound howitzers on our flank.

Our dismounted troops in front were composed of parts of the 4th and 5th regiments T. M. V., and parts of Lieut.-col. Sutton's and most of Pyron's battalions, Teel's, Riley's, and Wood's batteries of artillery, numbering about 750 on the ground. Major Ragnet's cavalry numbered about 250, making about 1000 men in the charge.

At the command to charge, our men leaped over the sand-bank, which had served as a good covering to them, and dashed over the open plain, thinly interspersed with cotton-wood trees, upon the battery and infantry of the enemy in front, composed of United States regulars and Denver City Volunteers, and in a most desperate charge and hand-to-hand conflict completely overwhelmed them, killing most of their gunners around their cannon, and driving the infantry into the river. Never were double-barrelled shot-guns and rifles used to better effect. A large number of the enemy were killed in the river with shot-guns and six-shooters in their flight.

Whilst we were occupied with the enemy in front, Major Ragnet made a gallant and most timely charge upon the infantry and cavalry of the enemy on our left flank. This charge was made against ten times the number of Ragnet's force, and although we suffered severely and were compelled to fall back, he effected the object of his mission and occupied the attention of our powerful enemy on the left, while our dismounted men were advancing upon those in front and running them into the river.

So soon as the enemy had fled in disorder from our terrible fire in front, we turned upon his infantry and cavalry and twenty-four pounders on our left flank, just engaged by Major Ragnet. We charged them as we had those in front, but they were not made of as good stuff as the regulars, and a few fires upon them with their own artillery and Teel's guns—a few volleys of small arms, and the old Texas war shout, completely dispersed them. They fled from the field, both cavalry and infantry, in the utmost disorder, many of them dropping their guns to lighten their heels, and stopping only under the walls of the fort. Our victory was complete. The enemy must have been 3,000 strong, while our force actually engaged did not exceed 600. Six splendid pieces of artillery, and their entire equipage, fell into our hands, also many fine small arms.

This splendid victory was not achieved without severe loss to us.

Major Lockridge, of the 5th, fell at the mouth of the enemy's guns, gallantly leading our brave troops to the assault.

Lieut.-col. Sutton, of the 7th, fell mortally wounded at the head of his battalion, while assaulting the enemy's battery.

Several of our officers were desperately wounded, some of them, no doubt, mortally. Among them are the gallant Capt. Lang, of the lancers, and Lieut. Bass, both of company B, and Lieut. Hubbard, of company A, 5th regiment.

Capt. Heurel, of the 4th, fell in the gallant cavalry charge of Major Ragnet. He was one of the most distinguished of the heroes of the day. Like the gallant Lang, of the 5th, he could not appreciate odds in a battle.

I cannot say enough in praise of the gallantry of our surviving officers and men. It would be invidious to mention names. Were I to do so, the rolls of Capts., Lieuts., and men, would have to be here inserted. I will only mention the principal field and staff in the engagement. The cheering voice of Lieut.-col. Scurry was heard where the bullets fell thickest on the field. Lieut.-col. McNeil, and the gallant Major Pyron, who has been before mentioned, displayed the most undaunted courage. Major Ragnet, of the 4th, though wounded, remained at his post, and retired not until the field was won. These were the field officers present, as I have just stated. The Capts., Lieuts., and men in the action, displayed so much gallantry that it would be invidious to make distinctions. They fought with equal valor, and are entitled to equal credit with the field and staff here mentioned.

I will not close this report without a just meed of praise to the general staff, who served me as aides-de-camp during the day. Colonel W. L. Robards was in the dashing charge of the gallant Lang, and wounded in several places.

Capt. Tom P. Ochiltree, aid-de-camp to Gen. Sibley, was exceedingly useful to me on the field, and active during the whole engagement. He assisted me, in the most critical moment, to cheer our men to the assault. He deserves the highest praise for his undaunted chivalry and coolness, and I recommend him to the Gen. for promotion.

Capt. Dwyer was also very useful, gallant, and active during the whole action.

I cannot close without the mention of Capt. Frazier, of the Arazona Volunteers. To him, more than all others, we are indebted for the successful turning of Fort Craig. He led us over the high ground around the Mesa to the east of the fort, where we at all times had the advantage of the enemy, in case he had attacked us in the act of turning the fort.

I will personalize only further by the mention of my own regimental staff.

Sergeant-major C. B. Sheppard shouldered his gun and fought gallantly in the ranks of Capt. McPhail's company in the charge Lieut. Joseph D. Sayers, adjutant of the 5th, during the whole day, reminded me of a hero of the days of chivalry. He is a gallant, daring, and dashing soldier, and he is as cool in a storm of grape, shell, canister, and musketery as a veteran. I recommend him, through the Gen., to the President for promotion.

Our killed and wounded are as follows:

Second Regiment Texas Mounted Volunteers, Major Pyron's command—Killed 4, wounded 17, missing 1.

Teel's Battery—Killed 2, wounded 4.

Fourth Regiment Texas Mounted Volunteers, Lieut.-col. Scurry's command—Killed 8, wounded 36.

Fifth Regiment Texas Mounted Volunteers, Col. Green's regiment—Killed 20, wounded 67.

Seventh Regiment Texas Mounted Volunteers, Lieut.-Col. Sutton's command—Killed 2, wounded 26.

Total killed 36, wounded 159, missing 1.

Since which time Lieut.-Colonel Sutton, of the seventh, and two privates of the fifth, and two of Teel's battery have died from wounds received in battle.

The enemy's loss was far greater than ours. The precise number cannot be ascertained by us, as many were killed in the river, and as the enemy's white flag, asking permission to gather up their dead and wounded, came almost before the sound of the last cannon had ceased to reverberate in the hills. It is confidently asserted and believed, by many of our officers and men, that the enemy, under the flag of truce, picked up many small arms, and carried them off with the dead wagons; that they also carried off their two twenty-four pound howitzers, which were left by them in the river. It is certain that, during the cessation of hostilities, they picked up a company flag and guidon of my regiment, left on the field during our charge, while they were gathering up their wounded and dead; and, it is said, these are considered by them as trophies. I do not believe the commanding officer of the enemy is aware of these facts, as he would not have spoken of stolen flags as trophies.

I think, from the best information in my possession, that the enemy's loss must have been, in killed and wounded, at least three hundred and fifty or four hundred. Among their killed were several gallant officers.

The gallant McRea fell at his guns. Several other Capts. and Lieuts. were killed. Capt. Rosell, of the 10th U. S. infantry, and several privates of the 5th and 10th infantry and Denver City Volunteers were taken prisoners.

Respectfully submitted,

THOMAS GREEN, *Col. 3d Reg. T. M. V.*

Report of Col. W. R. Scurry.

VALVERDE, NEW MEXICO, Feb. 22d, 1862.

A. M. JACKSON, *A. A. G. Army of New Mexico:*

MAJOR:—Early on the morning of yesterday, while the army was encamped on the east side of the Rio Grande, opposite Fort Craig, I received orders to march with my command, (4th Regiment T. M. V.) and take possession at as early an hour as practicable of some point on the river above Fort Craig, at which water might be obtained. By eight o'clock the regiment took up the line of march, accompanied by Capt. George Frazier, of Major Pyron's battalion (with his company), acting as guide for the command. Supposing that we were the advance of the army, to prevent surprise, I ordered Major Ragnet to take the advance, with four companies and Capt. Frazier's company, throwing out at the same time front and flank patrols. In a short time I learned that Major Pyron, with one hundred and eighty men, was in our advance. Aware of the great vigilance of that active officer, I recalled Major Ragnet and re-united the regiment. A report was received from Major Pyron that the road was clear of the enemy, and the river in sight. But in a short time a second message was received, through Capt. John Phillips, from the Major, informing me that large masses of the enemy were in his front and threatening an attack. As his force was but small, I was fearful that he would be overpowered before we could reach him, and accordingly pushed forward, guided by Capt. Phillips, as rapidly as our horses could carry us, to his relief, and found him gallantly maintaining a most unequal contest against vastly superior numbers. Dismounting my command, we formed on his right and joined in the conflict. For near two hours we held our position in front of an enemy now known to be near five thousand strong, while our own forces were not over seven hundred in number. Immediately, upon reaching the field, Capt. Frazier joined the command to which he belonged, where he did good service during the remainder of the day.

Upon opening fire with the Light Howitzer battery, under Lieut. John Riley, it was found to be ineffectual against the heavier metal of the enemy. It was therefore ordered to cease firing and be withdrawn under cover.

At about one o'clock, Capt. Teel, with two guns of his battery, reached the ground. Being placed in position on our right, he opened a galling fire upon the left flank of the enemy, whereupon the enemy commenced a furious cannonade upon him from their entire battery, consisting of eight guns. So heavy was their fire that the Capt. soon found himself with but five men to work the two guns. A bomb exploding under his pieces had set the grass on fire; still this gallant officer held his position and continued his firing upon the enemy, himself seizing the rammer and assisting to load the piece.

Seeing his situation, I ordered Lieut. Riley, with his command, to join him, and assist in the efficient working of his guns. During the balance of the day, this brave little band performed the duty assigned them. Judging by the heavy firing on the left that Major Pyron was hard pressed, Capt. Teel, with more of his guns, which had just reached the ground, was dispatched to his relief. Major Ragnet, with four companies of the regiment, was ordered to maintain our position there. I remained on the right with the balance of my command and two pieces of Teel's battery, under Lieut. J.

H. McGinness, to hold in check the enemy, who were moving in large force in that direction, to turn our flank. About this time Major Lockridge, of the 5th regiment, arrived on the field and reported himself, with a portion of that command. He was ordered to join our troops on the left. During all this time the fire of the enemy had been extremely heavy, while, owing to the shorter range of most of our guns, our fire was reserved until they should approach sufficiently near our position to come within range of our arms, when they were invariably repulsed with loss. Soon after the arrival of Major Lockridge, Col. Green reached the field and assumed command. At about three o'clock in the afternoon, in extending our line to prevent the enemy ftom turning our right, I found myself with only two companies (Capt. Hardeman's and Crosson's), opposed to a force numbering some four hundred men, the other four companies being several hundred yards to my left. It was here that that daring charge was made by Capt. Lang, of the 5th regiment, with a small body of lancers. But desperate courage was ineffectual against great odds and superior arms; and this company then sustained the greatest loss of life of any company of the brigade. This charge, otherwise unfortunate, had the effect of bringing the enemy within range of our guns, when the two pieces of Capt. Teel's battery and the small-arms of Capts. Hardeman's and Crosson's companies opened an effective fire upon them, before which they rapidly retreated with considerable loss. Just before sunset, Lieut. Thos. P. Ochiltree, of Gen. Sibley's staff, brought an order to prepare for a charge all along the line.

All prepared for its prompt execution, and when the words "Up, boys, and at them!" was given, straight at their battery of six guns, supported by columns of infantry and cavalry, some seven hundred yards in front of our position, went our brave volunteers, unmindful of the driving storm of grape and canister and musket balls sent hurling around them. With yells and ringing shouts they dashed on and on, until the guns were won and the enemy in full retreat before them. After carrying the battery, their guns were turned upon themselves, Capts. Hardeman and Walker manning those on the right. Lieut. Ragnet, of Riley's battery, being on the ground, I placed one gun in his charge, manning it with such of the men as were nearest. The rammer being gone, a flag-staff was used in its stead. Capt. Teel, coming up, an effective fire was kept up as long as the enemy was in reach. In the meantime, a most timely and gallant charge was made by Major Ragnet from our left, thus effecting a favorable diversion at the moment of our charge upon their battery. This charge by Major Ragnet and his command was characterized by desperate valor.

In the last brilliant and successful charge which decided the fortunes of the day, there were six companies of the 4th regiment, T. M. V., under their respective Capts., (Hardeman, Crosson, Lesner, Foard, Hampton and Nunn.) Besides those I saw Capts. Shropshire, Killsough and McPhail, of the 5th regiment, and Capt. Walker, of Major Pyron's battalion.

The brave and lamented Major Lockridge, of the 5th regiment, fell almost at the muzzle of the enemy's guns.

Major Pyron was also in the thickest of the fray, and contributed much by his example to the success of the charge, as did also Lieut. Ochiltree, of the General's staff.

There were others there whom I now regret my inability to name. Where all, both officers and men, behaved so well, it is impossible to say who is the most deserving of praise. The enemy retired across the river and were in full retreat, when Major Ragnet, Capts. Shannon, Adair, Alexander, Buckholdt, and Lieut. Shurmond, reached the field with their companies mounted. I asked and obtained permission from Col. Green to cross the river with these companies to pursue the flying foe.

When the head of the column reached the opposite shore, we were ordered to return. Night closed in on the hard-won field of Valverde. This brilliant victory, which, next to heaven, we owe to the heroic endurance and unfaltering courage of our volunteer soldiers, was not won without loss. Of the regiment which I have the honor to command, there were eight killed and fifty-six wounded, two of which were mortal. It affords me great pleasure to be able to bear testimony to the calm, cool, and discriminating courage of Col. Thomas Green during the fight. Major Pyron, also, deserves great credit for his soldierly bearing from the commencement to the close of the battle. Of the general's staff, Major Jackson was early on the ground, as was also Major Brownrigg, Capt. Dwyer and Lieut. Ochiltree, actively engaged in the discharge of the duties assigned them. Each of these gentlemen exhibited that high courage which I hope will ever distinguish the officers of the army. To Majors Jackson and Brownrigg I am under obligations for valuable aid in the early part of the action. It is due to the Adj. of this regiment, Ellsbury R. Lane, that I should not close this report without stating that he was actively and bravely engaged in the discharge of his duties, on horseback, until his horse failed, when, taking a gun, he entered the ranks of Capt. Hampton's company, and did duty as a private during the remainder of the day.

I have the honor to be,
Very respectfully,
Your obedient servant,
W. R. SCURRY,
Lieut. Col. Commanding 4th Regt. T. M. V.

Report of Major Henry W. Ragnet.

CAMP VALVERDE, ARMY NEW MEXICO,
February 23, 1862.

To A. M. JACKSON,
A. A. Gen., Army New Mexico:

MAJOR: About sunrise on the 21st instant, whilst in camp opposite Fort Craig, I was ordered by Lieut.-col. Scurry to take four companies of the 4th Texas mounted volunteers, to which would be added Capt. Frazier's company from Major Pyron's battalion, and march as an advance to the river at the best point for approaching it above the fort, supposed to be about six miles distant. After marching about three miles I was ordered to halt and join Lieut.-col. Scurry, who was approaching with other companies of the regiment and Lieut. Riley's artillery.

Our course was then changed for a nearer point on the river. After a half hour's march, whilst descending a canon, the rapid advance of the head of our column gave notice that we were approaching the enemy. And emerging into the valley, the firing of skirmishers told that Major Pyron, who had been marching on our left flank, was already engaged with the enemy. A half mile gallop brought us within range of the enemy's artillery, when Lieut.-col. Scurry ordered us to dismount and advance, when we were soon within range of their small arms, and took position on the right of Major Pyron, behind a low bank, about 9 A. M. After we had taken this position about half an hour, the enemy moved up on our right with the evident intention of flanking us, which at the time would have been fatal; when Lieut.-col. Scurry, dividing the command, assigned that position to me, and moved up to the position occupied by him during the day, and checked their advance.

The troops at this time with me were Major Pyron, with his battalion of one hundred and eighty men, under Capts. Walker, Stafford, and Frazier, Lieuts. Nicholson and Jett, four companies of the 4th regiment, under Capts. Scarborough, Buckholt, Harvell, and Alexander. About noon, one piece of Capt. Teel's battery, under Lieut. Bradford, was added to my position, which did good service until the heavier metal of the enemy silenced it. Soon after the arrival of this gun, Major Lockridge arrived with three companies of the 5th regiment Texas mounted volunteers, under Capts. Shropshire, Campbell, and Ragsdale, and Major Pyron and Lieut. Bradford's commands were withdrawn to the right. Major Lockridge called my attention to the gun, which had been partly disabled and silenced on our left at the foot of the Mesa, where it had been placed in an endeavor to disable the enemy's battery on the west bank of the river. I ordered company B, 4th regiment, Capt. Scarborough, to the rescue, and with part of that company under their captain and Sergeant Nelson, of company H, 4th regiment, Capt. Alexander, and some of that company, I succeeded in drawing the gun by hand from its perilous position, amid the hottest cannonading on that part of the field, losing only one man killed and a few wounded.

The horses of this gun had nearly all been killed by the enemy's artillery. This gun was then used by three of Lieut. Riley's company, assisted by a few others, until I ordered the fire discontinued, for want of gunners, leaving it double shotted to await an anticipated charge of the enemy. The enemy threatened us in such great numbers, and their fire was so heavy, that Major Lockridge and myself each sent messengers to Col. Green for reinforcements, failing to get which, Major Lockridge deemed it prudent to fall back to a sand-bank, about one hundred yards in our rear, which was done by companies, after the artillery and the wounded had been removed. This gave us a better position, as the ground was somewhat broken in front.

The section of Teel's artillery was now withdrawn to the right, leaving only one howitzer under Lieut. Wood, who had arrived at our new position. Lieut.-col. Sutton now arrived on the field, approaching in our rear, when a messenger was dispatched, asking that he be ordered to remain by us.

He soon marched up to the right, and then returned. Major Lockridge now told me that we were to move up and join the forces on the right, for a charge, that he would cover any movement to get my horses which were on the left and rear. Ordering the companies of the 4th regiment to horse, I soon marched up on the right, in the rear of the rest of the command, dismounted, and ordering the companies then with me, under Capts. Buckholt, Harvell, and Alexander, of the 4th, and Capt. Ragsdale, of the 5th, into line to advance.

Col. Green rode up and ordered me to reserve my command for a charge as cavalry. No sooner were we mounted, than an order came by Major Pyron to move down to the left, and menace the enemy now flanking us in large force. Marching down to within six hundred yards, I dismounted my command under cover, when I was joined by Capt. Scarborough, of the 4th, and received an order through Capt. Dwyer to charge the enemy.

Aligning in single rank, I charged to within about one hundred yards of the enemy's lines, composed of infantry, supported by cavalry on each flank and in the rear, and by artillery on their right, when, looking back, I saw great confusion from the wounded and falling horses, for we had aligned and advanced under the heavy fire of their infantry and artillery. I thought we could not break their lines, and ordered my command to fall back, and rally at the sand-bank which we had left on our rear and left. When I had arrived at the sand-bank, I found that most of my command had passed it for some others still on their left, and that the position was untenable, as the enemy's artillery now raked it. I ordered those there to follow those yet in advance, and, rallying, we could return. Finding Lieut. Wood with one howitzer, uselessly exposed under the enemy's fire, I ordered him to a position between the enemy and the train, to protect it as well as he could, and, ordering such of my command as I met to join in the action on the right, I galloped down, then too late, however, to participate in that brilliant charge which gave us the victory.

A few moments after reaching the river bank, Lieut.-col. Scurry asked permission of Col. Green to cross and pursue the enemy with some fresh companies that had just come up, which permission being granted, I joined with my command, who were present, and, as the head of our column gained the opposite shore, we were ordered back. Shortly after the arrival of the flag of truce, ended the battle of Valverde, after sunset. During the entire day, my position on the left was under a constant fire of the enemy's heaviest artillery, and their small arms, whose longer range enabled them to keep out of our small arm range. When they threatened an advance, and would reach our aim, they were repulsed.

The gallant Major Lockridge, of the 5th, whilst in command of the left, won the admiration of all who saw him, and whose regrets are now mingled with those of his other friends at his death. The brave Harvell, of this command, who fell in the charge he had so impatiently waited for, added another to the list of our gallant dead at Valverde. For the officers and privates whom I had the honor to command on that day, I can well say that they have never faltered in their dangerous duty; and for those, less than two hundred, whom I led to the charge, against more than eight times their numbers, together with artillery, the recital of the act is their praise. This charge, though at the cost of nearly one-fifth the men and horses in killed and wounded, succeeded in checking the flank movement of the enemy, in time to enable the charge which won the day to be made.

Very respectfully,

Your obedient servant,

HENRY W. RAGNET.

Major 4th regiment T. M. V.

Report of Major C. S. Pyron.

SOCORO, NEW MEXICO,
February 27, 1862.

Major A. M. JACKSON,

Assistant Adjutant-general, Army of New Mexico:

MAJOR: On the morning of the 21st instant, I left our camp opposite Fort Craig, with one hundred and eighty men of my command, under Capts. Walker and Stafford, Lieut. Nicholson, of Capt. Crosswood Spy's company, and Lieut. Jett, company B, 2d regiment mounted volunteers, to reconnoitre the road leading to the river near Valverde. Upon reaching the river, I could see the water with none of the enemy intervening. I immediately dispatched a note to the general commanding, stating the road was clear and the water in sight, and proceeded leisurely to the river to water our horses, they having been over twenty-four hours without water.

When I reached the woods I discovered a body of cavalry, which I supposed to be about four companies, and immediately gave chase, they withdrawing to my left. I followed, until reaching the bank of a slough in the bottom, when I found myself in front of a large force of all arms. Immediately my men were formed along the bank, when the action commenced, and for over one hour, by the courage and determination of the men, I was enabled to maintain the position in the unequal struggle, when I was relieved by the 4th regiment Texas mounted volunteers, under the command of Lieut.-col. W. R. Scurry.

For near two hours, our joint commands held opposition against odds of three to one, checking every attempt to outflank us, and checking every effort to drive us back. The arrival of Teel's battery of artillery was the first reinforcements we received, but it was soon followed by Major Lockridge's battalion of the 5th regiment Texas mounted volunteers, and, at about 1 o'clock, Col. Green reached the field and took command.

Late in the afternoon, a general charge was made along our line, by which a battery of artillery, consisting of six guns, was taken, and their left driven back.

Following rapidly up our successes, the enemy were driven back at all points, and the field of Valverde was won.

It is proper to state that all the officers and men of my command behaved in the most gallant manner, and, where all were equally brave, it would be invidious to particularize. It is sufficient to say that it was a day on which deeds of personal valor were continually occurring.

I cannot consent to close this report without bearing my testimony to the gallant bearing and personal valor of Cols. Green, Scurry, and Sutton, and Majors Ragnet and Lockridge, and others equally courageous.

I have the honor to be, sir,

Yours most respectfully,

C. S. PYRON,

Major 2d Texas Mounted Rangers.

R. J. O. GRADY,

Sergeant-major and Acting Adjutant.

Report of Captain Powhatan Jordan.

IN CAMP NEAR SOCORO, N. M.,
February 27, 1862.

Gen. H. F. SIBLEY, *C. S. A.:*

GENERAL: I have the honor to report the first battalion of 7th regiment Texas mounted volunteers in the battle of Valverde, N. M., on the 21st of February. The first battalion 7th regiment, under command of Lieut.-col. J. S. Sutton, with companies C and H, of the 5th regiment, were detailed, as a guard for the transportation, on the morning of the 21st. Before the train had gotten fairly out of camp, we were apprised of the fight having commenced at Valverde crossing of the Rio Grande by hearing the sullen roar of cannon.

The train being in danger of attack, we were kept in position as the guard, and all thought, for a time, the 7th would have no share in the conflict, but, in about two hours after the commencement of the battle, an officer appeared with the order for us to move on to the battle-field.

Col. Sutton detached, from his command, companies A and F, of the 7th, and company C, of the 5th, to remain, and then gave the order to forward, when the remainder of his command, consisting of companies B, F, and I, of the 7th, and F, of the 5th, moved on to the scene of action. We went in a gallop and were met on the field by Major Lockridge, who ordered us to take position on the left. We were here held for some hour or more, running the gauntlet by countermarch under a most galling and destructive fire from their batteries. While in this position, we lost two men and some three horses killed. The battle having now continued several hours, the charge was ordered, and the 7th was most gallantly led in the charge by Lieut.-col. Sutton, who fell mortally wounded when within twenty paces of the enemy's battery.

The battle was now soon ended, and victory was ours, though purchased, by the 7th, with the death of the heroic Sutton.

The 7th done its duty bravely, nobly, all acting gallantly. To make mention of individuals would be unjust. They all shared equally the dangers of the field, and all deserve equal praise.

To Capt. Prigin and his company, H, of the 6th, who acted with our command, we must give great credit for their coolness and gallantry, and wish himself and company to share with us whatever credit may fall to our command.

Accompanying is the list of killed and wounded, together with the horses killed in the battle, as furnished me by captains of companies.

I have the honor to be, very respectfully,

Your obedient servant,

POWHATAN JORDAN,

Capt. comd'g 1st bat. 7th reg't T. M. V., Army N. M.

Report of Capt. T. T. Teel.

CAMP LOCKRIDGE, N. M.,
February 27th, 1862.

Major A. M. JACKSON,
Assistant Adj.-gen. C. S. A.:

SIR:—I have the honor to report to the general commanding the army of New Mexico the operations of the light battery, which I had the honor to command, in the battle of Valverde, N. M., on the 21st day of February, 1862.

I received orders on the morning of the 21st, at camp, five miles below the battle ground, and opposite Fort Craig, to detach one section of the battery under Lieut. Bradford, to march in the front of the column and head of the train to Valverde, and place the other section and remain myself in rear with the 2d regiment of Sibley's brigade, which orders were executed.

About an hour after the head of the column had moved, I received intelligence that a large body of the enemy's cavalry, infantry, and artillery had taken up the line of march for Valverde.

I then placed the section of the battery in command of Lieuts. Bennett and McGinness, and went to the head of the column; before reaching the head of the train, I heard the firing of the advance at Valverde.

I found Lieut. Bradford, with his section, at the head of the train, and ordered the pieces to the place of firing at a gallop, and in a few minutes it was placed in battery, about the centre of Lieut.-col. Scurry's regiment, and commenced firing upon the battery of the enemy and his line in a few minutes. I lost one man killed, and two wounded, which left but five cannoniers to man the two pieces. I then kept up the fire alternately with the pieces. Finding it impossible to use the pieces with steady and effective fire, I called upon Lieut.-col. Scurry for men to fill up the detachments of the guns, which were immediately sent from Lieut. Riley's company of howitzers. After sustaining the action for some time, the enemy changed his front. I then placed the section in another position.

Lieuts. Bennett and McGuinness, having by this time reached our line, I ordered them to place their section in battery, which they did, and opened upon the enemy with good effect.

From the great length of the enemy's line, and his superior number, I found it necessary to detach the pieces. Lieut. Bradford was sent to the extreme left flank with his piece, to support Majors Lockridge and Pyron's commands, which had been engaged with the enemy for more than an hour. Lieut. McGuinness, with his gun, on the right of Major Lockridge's battalion. Lieut. Bennett, at the centre of the right flank, and the other piece at the extreme right flank. Lieut. Riley, with his battery of howitzers, with the left wing, and Lieut. Woods, with his battery of howitzers, on the right wing. The different pieces and howitzers changed positions, however, during the action, as circumstances required, and were used with effect whenever the enemy presented a front, or his battery in view.

Having received orders that our troops were about to charge the enemy, I placed the guns in battery upon the extreme right flank as a reserve, in case the charge was unsuccessful, so that I could open the line of the enemy with raking shots, or engage his battery until our troops would prevent my firing by their closing with the enemy. The charge was made by our line, and in eight minutes his battery captured and his troops completely routed. Lieut. Ochiltree, aid-de-camp, rode back and ordered the guns forward, which order was executed, and soon the enemy's guns, as well as ours, were opened on his retreating forces. Firing was kept up from our guns until the enemy's rear was out of range of them; I then ordered the firing to cease.

I lost four men killed, including two which died the day after the battle, and six wounded; twenty-five horses killed and wounded, one gun partially disabled, and eight sets of harness rendered unserviceable. I refer, with great pleasure, to the gallant conduct of Lieuts. Bennett, McGuinness, and Bradford, of my company, as well as Lieuts. Riley, Woods, Ragnet, and Falcrod, of the batteries of howitzers, also of the non-commissioned officers and privates of all the batteries.

I cannot close my report without bearing testimony to the bravery and coolness of the officers under whom I acted during this sanguinary and well contested battle. Col. Green, and especially Lieut.-col. Scurry, who so promptly manned my guns from his regiment (the 1st), and who was present with my guns under the heavy fire in the morning, and whose voice was heard above the din of battle, and smoke, and flame, and death, encouraging the men to stand by their posts. Also the lamented Lockridge; Major Jackson, Assistant Adj.-gen.; Major Brownrigg, Brigade Commissary; Lieut.-col. McNiel, and Lieut. Ochiltree, aid-de-camp, who were rallying the men to the charge, and were in the line leading on the troops; also Capt. Dwyer, of the staff, Col. Roberts, and Major Ragent. Also the deep obligations I am under to Lieut.-col. Scurry, and Capt. Scarborough and his company, who hauled out a disabled piece by hand under a hot fire; to Capts. Campbell, McPhail, and Kelloe, and their respective companies, for the promptness and willingness with which they replaced the killed and wounded at my guns; many of their comrades having been killed and wounded while aiding in manning the battery during the action.

Very respectfully, your obedient servant,

T. T. TEEL, *Capt. Artillery.*

REPORT OF THE EVACUATION OF COLUMBUS.

L. POLK MAJOR-GENERAL, COMMANDING.

HEAD-QUARTERS, 1ST GRAND DIVISION, ARMY OF THE MISSISSIPPI,
HUMBOLT, March 18, 1862.

To Col. THOMAS JORDAN, *A. G. A.*,
Jackson, Tenn.

On the day of the evacuation of Columbus, I telegraphed Gen. Beauregard. It was accomplished, and I avail myself of the first leisure I have had to submit my official report. Upon receipt of instructions from the War Department, through Gen. Beauregard, "to evacuate Columbus, and select a defensive position below," I proceeded to arrange and organize a plan for the accomplishment of that object, and to execute it with as much celerity as the safety of my command and the security of the public property at risk would allow. The position below offering most advantages for defensive works, and which it was agreed to adopt, was that embracing Island No. 10, the main land in Madrid Bend, on the Tennessee shore, and New Madrid. At the two latter places, works had been thrown up during the last autumn, and measures were already in progress for increasing their strength, by the construction of heavy batteries. On the the 25th of February, I issued orders for the removal of the sick, as a preparatory step. Orders were also issued by me for the removal of the commissary and quarter-master's stores, then the ordnance stores of every description, and then the heavy guns. These orders were executed promptly and in the most satisfactory manner.

To Brig.-gen. McCown was assigned the command of the River defences, at the position chosen. His division was ordered thither on the 27th. A sufficient number of guns having been placed in battery to make that position secure, all the rest of the troops, excepting the cavalry, moved on the 1st. Gen. Stuart's brigade going by steamer to New Madrid, the remainder marching by land to Union City under Gen. Cheatham. I remained with my staff and the cavalry, to supervise the completion of the work, until the following day. The last shipment of articles of special value being made, the quarters and other buildings erected by our troops were consigned to the flames by the cavalry, and at 3 P. M., myself and staff followed our retiring column.

The enemy's cavalry—the first of his forces to arrive after the evacuation—reached Columbus in the afternoon next day, 24 hours after the last of our troops had left. In five days we moved the accumulations of six months, taking with us all our commissary and quarter-master's stores—an amount sufficient to supply my whole command for eight months; all our powder and other ammunition and ordnance stores, excepting a few shot and gun carriages, and every heavy gun in the fort. Two 32-pounders, in a remote outwork, were the only valuable guns left, and these, with three or four small and indifferent carronades similarly situated, were spiked and rendered useless.

The whole number of pieces of artillery composing our armament was one hundred and forty.

Respectfully, your obedient servant,

L. POLK,

Major-Gen. Commanding.

REPORTS OF THE BATTLE OF SHILOH.

G. T. BEAUREGARD, GENERAL COMMANDING.

HEAD-QUARTERS ARMY OF THE MISSISSIPPI,
CORINTH, MISS., April 11th, 1862.

TO GENERAL S. COOPER, *Adjutant and Inspector-gen., Richmond:*

GENERAL:—On the 2d ultimo, having ascertained conclusively, from the movements of the enemy on the Tennessee road, and from reliable sources of information, that his aim was to cut off my communications in west Tennessee with the eastern and southern States, by operating from the Tennessee river, between Crump's landing and Eastport, as a base, I determined to foil his designs by concentrating all my available forces at and around Corinth.

Meanwhile, having called on the governors of the States of Tennessee, Mississippi, Alabama, and Louisiana, to furnish additional troops, some of them, chiefly regiments from Louisiana, soon reached this vicinity, and with two regiments of Gen. Polk's command from Columbus, and a fine corps of troops from Mobile and Pensacola, under Major-gen. Bragg, constituted the army of the Mississippi. At the same time, Gen. Johnston being at Murfreesboro', on the march to form a junction of his forces with mine, was called on to send at least a brigade by railroad, so that we might fall on and crush the enemy, should he attempt an advance from under his gunboats.

The call on Gen. Johnston was promptly complied with. His entire force was also hastened in this direction, and by the 1st of April our united forces were concentrated along the Mobile and Ohio railroad, from Bethel to Corinth, and on the Memphis and Charleston railroad, from Corinth to Iuka.

It was then determined to assume the defensive, and strike a sudden blow at the enemy, in position under Gen. Grant, on the west bank of the Tennessee river, at Pittsburg, and in the direction of Savannah, before he was reinforced by the army under Gen. Buell, (then known to be advancing for that purpose), by making rapid marches from Nashville *via* Columbia. About the same time Gen. Johnston was advised that such an operation conformed to the expectations of the President.

By a rapid and vigorous attack on Gen. Grant, it was expected he would be beaten back into his transports, and the river so captured in time to enable us to profit by the victory, and remove to the rear all the stores and munitions that would fall into our hands in such an event. It was never contemplated, however, to retain the position thus gained and abandon Corinth, the strategic point of the campaign.

Want of general officers, needful for the proper organization of divisions and brigades of an army brought thus suddenly together, and other difficulties in the way of an effective organization, delayed the movements until the night of the 2d instant, when it was heard from a reliable quarter that the junction of the enemy's armies was near at hand. It was then, at a very late hour, determined that the attack should be attempted at once, incomplete and imperfect as were our preparations for such a grave and momentous adventure. Accordingly that night, at one o'clock A. M., the preliminary orders to the commanders of the corps were issued for the movement.

On the following morning, the detailed orders of movement, a copy of which is herewith, marked "A," were issued, and the movement, after some delay, commenced, the troops being in admirable spirits. It was expected we should be able to reach the enemy's lines in time to attack him on the 5th instant. The men, however, for the most part, were unused to marching, the roads narrow, and traversing a densely wooded country, became almost impassable after a severe rain storm on the 4th, which drenched the troops in bivouac, hence our forces did not reach the intersection of the road from Pittsburg and Hamburg, in the immediate vicinity of the enemy, until late Saturday afternoon.

It was then decided that the attack should be made on the next morning at the earliest hour practicable, in accordance with the orders of the movement.

That is, in three lines of battle, the first and second extending from Owl creek on the left to Lick creek on the right, a distance of about three miles, supported by the third and the reserve. The first line, under Major-gen. Hardee, was constituted of his corps, augmented on his right by Gladden's brigade, of Major-gen. Bragg's corps, deployed in line of battle, with their respective artillery following immediately by the main road to Pittsburg, and the cavalry in rear, on the wings. The second line, composed of the other troops of Bragg's corps, followed the first at the distance of five hundred yards, in the same order as the first. The army corps under Gen. Polk followed the second line at the distance of about eight hundred yards, in lines of brigades, deployed with their batteries in rear of each brigade, moving by the Pittsburg road, the left wing suported by cavalry. The reserve, under Brig.-gen. Breckinridge, following closely on the third line, in the same order, its right wing supported by cavalry.

These two corps constituted the reserve, and were to support the front lines of battle by being deployed, when required, on the right and left of the Pittsburgh road, or otherwise act according to the exigencies of the battle.

At 5 A. M., on the 6th instant, a reconnoitering party of the enemy having become engaged with the advanced pickets, the commander of the forces gave orders to begin the movement and attack as determined upon, except that Fabrie's brigade of Breckinridge's division, and detached to support the left of Bragg's corps and line of battle when menaced by the enemy, and the other two brigades were directed to advance by the road to Hamburgh to support Bragg's right, and at the same time Maney's regiment of Polk's corps was advanced by the same road to reinforce the regiment of cavalry and battery of four pieces, already thrown forward to watch and guard Greer's, Tanner's, and Borland's fords, on Lick creek.

Thirty minutes after 5 o'clock, A. M., our lines and columns were in motion, all animated evidently by a promising spirit. The first line was engaged at once, but advanced steadily, following in due order, with equal resolution and steadiness, by the other lines, which were brought up successively into action, with rare skill, judgment, and gallantry, by the several commanders, as the enemy made a stand with his masses rallied for the struggle for his encampment. Like an Alpine avalanche our troops moved forward, despite the determined resistance of the enemy, until after 6 o'clock P. M., when we were in possession of all his encampments between Owl and Lick creek but one, nearly all his field artillery, about thirty flags, colors, and standards, over three thousand prisoners, including a division commander (Gen. Prentiss), and several brigade commanders, thousands of small arms, an immense supply of subsistence, forage, and munitions of war.

All the substantial fruits of a complete victory. Such, indeed, as rarely have followed the most successful battles, for never was an army so well provided as that of the enemy.

The remnant of his army had been driven in utter disorder to the immediate vicinity of Pittsburg, under the shelter of the heavy guns of his iron-clad gunboats, and we remained undisputed masters of his well-selected position and admirably provisioned cantonments, after over twelve hours of obstinate conflict with his forces, who had been beaten from them and the contiguous covert, but only by a sustained onset of all the men we could bring together into action.

Our loss was heavy, as will appear from the accompanying returns marked "B."

Our commander-in-chief, General A. S. Johnston, fell mortally wounded, and died on the field at 2.30 P.M., after having shown the highest qualities of a commander, and a personal intrepidity that inspired all around him, and gave resistless impulses to his columns at critical moments.

The chief command then devolved on me, though at the time I was greatly prostrated, and suffering from the prolonged sickness with which I had been afflicted since early in February.

The responsibility was one which, in my physical condition, I would have gladly avoided, though cast upon me when our forces were successfully pushing the enemy back upon the Tennessee river, and, though supported on the immediate field by such corps commanders as Major-gens. Polk, Bragg, and Hardee, and Brig.-gen. Breckinridge, commanding the reserve.

It was after 6 o'clock P.M., as before said, when the enemy's last position was carried, and his forces finally broke and sought refuge behind a commanding eminence, covering the Pittsburg landing, not more than half a mile distant, and under the guns of their gunboats, which opened on our eager columns a fierce and annoying fire, with shot and shell of the heaviest description. Darkness was close at hand; officers and men were exhausted by a combat of over twelve hours without food, and jaded by the march of the preceding day through mud and water. It was, therefore, impossible to collect the rich and opportune stores of war, scattered broadcast in the field before us, left in our possession, and impracticable to make any effective dispositions for their removal to the rear.

I accordingly established my head-quarters at the church of Shiloh, in the enemy's encampments, with Major-gen. Bragg, and directed our troops to sleep on their arms, in such positions in advance and rear as corps commanders should determine, hoping from news received by a special dispatch, that delays had been encountered by Gen. Buell in his march from Columbia, and that his main force, therefore, could not reach the field of battle in time to save Gen. Grant's scattered fugitive forces from capture or destruction on the following day.

During the night the rain fell in torrents, adding to the discomforts and harrassing condition of our men; the enemy, moreover, had broken their rest by a discharge, at measured intervals, of heavy shells, thrown from the gunboats; therefore, on the following morning, the troops under my command were not in condition to cope with an equal force of fresh troops, armed and equipped like our adversary, in the immediate possession of his depots, and sheltered by such an auxiliary as the enemy's gunboats.

About 6 o'clock on the morning of the 7th of April, however, a hot fire of musketry and artillery opened from the enemy's quarter on our advanced line, assured us of the junction of his forces, and soon the battle raged with a fury which satisfied me I was attacked by a largely superior force. But from the outset our troops, notwithstanding our fatigue and losses from the battle of the day before, exhibited the most cheering veteran-like steadiness. On the right and centre the enemy was repulsed in every attempt he made with his heavy columns in that quarter of the field. On the left, however, and nearest to the points of arrival of his reinforcements, he drove forward line after line of his fresh troops, which were met by a courage and resolution of which our country may be proudly hopeful. Again and again our troops were brought to the charge, invariably to win the position already in issue; invariably to drive back this foe. But hour by hour, thus opposed to an enemy constantly reinforced, our ranks were perceptibly thinned under the increasing withering fire of the enemy, and at 12 meridian, eighteen hours of hard fighting had sensibly exhausted a large number, my last reserves had necessarily been disposed of, and the enemy was evidently receiving fresh reinforcements after each repulse. Accordingly, after 1 P. M., I determined to withdraw from so unequal a conflict, securing such of the results of the victory of the day before as was then practicable.

Officers of my staff were immediately dispatched with the necessary orders to make the best disposition for a deliberate, orderly withdrawal from the field, and to collect and post a reserve to meet the enemy, should he attempt to push after us. In this connection I will particularly mention my Adjutant-general, Col. Jordan, who was of much assistance to me on this occasion, as he had already been on the field of battle, on that and the preceding day.

About 2 o'clock P. M., the lines in advance, which had repulsed the enemy in their last fierce assault on our left and centre, received the orders to retire. This was done with uncommon steadiness, and the enemy made no attempt to follow.

The lines of troops established to cover this movement had been disposed on a favorable ridge, commanding the ground of Shiloh church; from this position our artillery played upon the woods beyond for a while, but upon no visible enemy, and without a reply. Soon satisfied that no serious pursuit was or would be attempted, this last line was withdrawn, and never did troops leave battle-field in better order; even the stragglers fell into the ranks and marched off with those who had stood more steadily to their colors. A second strong position was taken up about a mile in rear, where the approach of the enemy was waited for more than one hour, but no effort to follow was made, and only a small detachment of horsemen could be seen at a distance from this last position, merely observing our movements.

Arranging through my staff officers for the completion of the movements thus begun, Brig.-gen. Breckinridge was left with his command as a rear guard, to hold the ground we had occupied the night preceding the first battle, just in front of the intersection of the Pittsburg and Hamburg roads, about four miles from the former place, while the rest of the army passed in the rear, in excellent order.

On the following day, Gen. Breckinridge fell back about three miles to Meckey's, which position we continue to hold, with our cavalry thrown considerably forward, in immediate proximity to the battle-field.

Unfortunately, towards night on the 7th instant, it began to rain heavily; this continued throughout the night. The roads became almost impassable in many places, and much hardship and suffering here ensued, before all the regiments reached their encampments.

But despite the heavy losses and casualties of the two eventful days of the 6th and 7th of April, this army is more confident of ultimate success than before its encounter with the enemy.

To Major-gens. Polk, Bragg, and Hardee, commanding corps, and to Brig.-gen. Breckinridge, commanding the reserve, the country is greatly indebted for the zeal, intelligence, and energy with which all orders were executed; for the foresight and military ability they displayed, in the absence of instruction in the many exigencies of the battle, on a field so densely wooded and broken, and for their fearless deportment as they repeatedly led their commands personally to the onset upon their powerful adversary. It was under these circumstances that Gen. Bragg had two horses shot under him, that Major-gen. Hardee was slightly wounded, his coat cut with balls, and his horse disabled, and that Major-gen. Breckinridge was twice struck with spent balls.

For the services of their gallant subordinate commanders, and their officers under them, as well as for the details of the battle-field, I must refer to the reports of corps divisions, and brigade commanders, which shall be forwarded as soon as received.

To give more in detail the operations of the two battles resulting from the movement on Pittsburg than now attempted, must have delayed this report for weeks, and interfered with the important duties of my position; but I may be permitted to say, that, not only did the obstinate conflict of Sunday leave the Confederates masters of the battle-field and our adversaries beaten, but we left that field on the next day, only after eight hours' successive battle with a superior army of fresh troops, whom we had repulsed in every attack upon our lines, so repulsed and crippled, indeed, as to leave it unable to take the field for the campaign for which it was collected and equipped at such enormous expense and with such profusion of all the appliances of war. These successful results were not achieved, however, as before said, without severe loss; a loss not to be measured by the number of the slain or wounded, but by the high social and personal position of so large a number of those who were killed or disabled, including the commander of the forces, whose high qualities will be greatly missed in the momentous campaign impending.

I deeply regret to record, also, the death of the Hon. George Johnson, Provisional Governor of Kentucky, who went into action with the Kentucky troops, and continually inspired them by his words and example. Having his horse shot under him Sunday, he entered the ranks of a Kentucky regiment on Monday, and fell mortally wounded towards the close of the day. Not his State alone, but the whole Confederacy, will mourn the death of this brave, upright, and noble man.

Another gallant and able soldier and Captain was lost to the service of the country, when Brig.-gen. Gladding, commanding first brigade, Withers' division, second army corps, died from a severe wound, received on the 6th instant, after having been conspicuous to his whole command and army for courage and capacity.

Major-gen. Cheatham, commanding first division first corps, was slightly wounded, and had three horses shot under him.

Brig.-gen. Clark, commanding second division of the first corps, received a severe wound, also, on the first day, which will deprive the army of his valuable services for some time.

Brig.-gen. Hindman, engaged in the onset of the battle, was conspicuous for a cool courage in finding his men, even in the thickest of the fray, until his horse was shot under him, and he was so severely injured by the fall, that the army was deprived the following day of his chivalric example.

Brig.-gens. B. R. Johnson and Bowen, most meritorious officers, were also severely wounded in the first combat, but it is hoped will soon be able to return to duty with their brigades.

To mention the many field-officers who died or were wounded, while gallantly leading their commands into action, and the many instances of brilliant individnal courage displayed by officers and men in the twenty hours of battle, is impossible at this time; but their names will be made known to their countrymen.

The immediate staff of the lamented Commander-in-chief, who accompanied him to the field, rendered efficient service, and either by his side, or in carrying his orders, shared his exposure to the casualties of a well contested battle-field. I beg to commend their names to the notice of the War Department, namely: of Capts. H. P. Brewster and A. Wickliffe, of the Adjutant and Inspector-general's Department; Capt. Theo. O'Hara, Acting Inspector-general; Lieut.-gen. Baylor, and Thomas M. Jack, aides-de-camp; volunteer aides-de-camp, Col. Wm. Preston, Major D. M. Hayden, E. W. Munford, and Calhoun Benham; Major Albert J. Smith and Captain Quarter-master's Department.

To these gentlemen was assigned the last sad duty of accompanying the remains of their lamented chief from the field, except Capts. Brewster and Wickliffe, who remained and rendered valuable services as staff officers on the 7th of April.

Gen. Isham G. Harris, of Tennessee, went into the field with Gen. Johnston; was by his side when he was shot, aided him from his horse, and received him in his arms when he died. Subsequently the Governor joined my staff, and remained with me throughout the next day, except when carrying orders, or employed in encouraging the troops of his own State, to whom he gave a conspicuous example of coolness, zeal, and intrepidity.

I am also under many obligations to my own general, personal, and volunteer staff, many of whom have been so long associated with me. I append a list of those present on the field on both days, and whose duties carried them constantly under fire, namely: Col. Tho. Jordon, Capt. Clifton H. Smith, and Lieut. John M. Otey,

Adjutant-general's Department; Major George W. Brent, Acting Inspector-general; Col. R. B. Lee, Chief of Subsistence, whose horse was wounded; Lieut.-col. S. W. Ferguson, and Lieut. A. R. Chesolm, aides-de-camp; volunteer aides-de-camp; Col. Jacob Thompson, Major Numa Augustin, Major H. E. Peyton, Capt. Albert Ferry, B. B. Waddell. Capt. W. W. Porter, of Major-gen. Crittenden's staff, also reported for duty, and shared the duties of my volunteer staff on Monday.

Brig.-gen. Frudeau, of Louisiana volunteers, also, for part of the first conflict, was with me as volunteer aid.

Capt. E. H. Cummins, signal officer, also was actively employed as a staff officer both days. Nor must I fail to mention that private W. E. Goolsby, 11th regiment Virginia volunteers, orderly to my head-quarters since last June, repeatedly employed to carry my verbal orders to the field, discharged the duty with great zeal and intelligence.

Other members of my staff were necessarily absent from the immediate field of battle, entrusted with respective duties at their head-quarters, viz: Major Eugene E. McLean, Chief Quarter-master; Capt. E. Deslaude, Quarter-master's Department. Lieut.-col. Furguson, A. D. C., early on Monday, was assigned to command and direct the movements of a brigade of the second corps.

Lieut.-col. Gilmer, Chief Engineer, after having performed the important and varied duties of his place, with distinction to himself and material benefit to the country, was wounded late on Monday. I trust, however, I shall not long be deprived of his essential services.

Capt. Lockett, Engineer Corps, Chief Assistant to Col. Gilmer, after having been employed in the duties of his corps on Sunday, was placed by me, on Monday, in command of a battalion without field officers. Capt. Fremeaux, Provisional Engineer, and Lieuts. Steel and Helm, also rendered material and even dangerous service in the line of their duty. Major-gen. (now general) Braxton Bragg, in addition to his duties as chief of staff, as has been before stated, commanded his corps, much the largest in the field, on both days, with signal capacity and soldiership.

Surgeon Foard, Medical Director, Surgeon R. L. Burdle, and Surgeon D. W. Tandal, Medical Director of the Western Department, with Gen. Johnston, were present in the discharge of their arduous and high duties, which they performed with honor to their profession. Capt. Thomas Saunders, Messrs. Scales and Medcalf, and Mr. Tully of New Orleans, were of material aid on both days, ready to give news of the enemy's positions and movements, regardless of exposure.

While thus partially making mention of some of those who rendered brilliant, gallant, or meritorious service to the field, I have aimed merely to notice those whose position would most probably exclude their services from the reports of corps, or subordinate commanders.

From this agreeable duty, I turn to one in the highest degree unpleasant; one due, however, to the brave men under me. As a contrast, to the behavior of most of the army who fought so heroically, I allude to the fact, that some officers, non-commissioned officers, and men, abandoned their colors on the first day, to pillage the captured encampments; others retired shamefully from the field on both days, while the thunder of cannon and the roar and rattle of musketry told them that their brothers were being slaughtered by the fresh legions of the enemy. I have ordered the names of the most conspicuous of these cowards and laggards to be published in orders.

It remains to state that our loss in the two days in killed outright, was 1,728, wounded, 8,012, missing, 957; making an aggregate of casualties 10,699. This sad list tells in simple language of the stout fight made by our countrymen, in front of the rude log chapel at Shiloh; especially when it is known that on Monday, from exhaustion and other causes, not twenty thousand men on our side could be brought into action.

Of the losses of the enemy I have no exact knowledge. Their newspaper report is very heavy. Unquestionably it was greater, even in proportion, than our own on both days, for it was apparent to all that their dead left on the field outnumbered ours two to one. Their casualties, therefore, cannot have fallen many short of 20,000 in killed, wounded, prisoners, and missing.

Through information derived from many sources, including the newspapers of the enemy, we engaged on Sunday the divisions of Gen. Prentiss, Sherman, Hurlbert, McClernand and Smith, of 9,000 men each, or at least 45,000 men. This force was reinforced Sunday night by the divisions of Gens. Nelson, McCook, Crittenden and Thomas, of Major-gen. Buell's army, some 25,000 strong, including all arms; also Gen. L. Wallace's division of Gen. Grant's army, making at least 33,000 fresh troops, which added to the remnant of Gen. Grant's forces on Monday morning, amounting to 20,000, made an aggregate force of at least 53,000 men arrayed against us on that day.

In connection with the results of the battle, I should state that most of our men who had inferior arms, exchanged them for the superior arms of the enemy; also, that most of the property, public and personal, of the camps, from which the enemy were driven on Sunday, was rendered useless, or greatly damaged, except some of the tents.

With this are transmitted certain papers, to wit:

Order of movements, marked A.

A list of the killed and wounded, marked B.

A list of captured flags, marked C.

A map of the field of battle, marked D.

All of which is respectfully submitted through my volunteer aid-de-camp, Col. Jacob Thompson, of Mississippi, who has the flags in charge; also the standards and colors captured from the enemy.

I have the honor to be, General,
Your obedient servant,
G. T. BEAUREGARD, *General Commanding.*

(A.)

SPECIAL ORDERS AS TO MOVEMENT OF TROOPS.

HEAD-QUARTERS ARMY OF THE MISSISSIPPI,
CORINTH, MISS., April 3d, 1862.

TO GENERAL S. COOPER,
Adjutant and Inspector-general, Richmond:

Special Orders, No. 8.

I. In the impending movements, the corps of this army will march, assemble, and take order of battle in the following manner, it being presumed that the enemy is in position about a mile in advance of Shiloh Church, with the right resting on Owl creek and his left on Lick creek:

1. The *third corps*, under Major-gen. Hardee, will advance as soon as practicable on the Ridge road from Corinth to what is called the Bark road, passing about half a mile northwest of the workhouse. The head of the column will bivouac, if possible, at Meckey's house, at the intersection of the road from Monterey to Savannah.

The *cavalry*, thrown well forward during the march, will recon noitre and prevent surprise, will halt in front of the Meckey House on the Bark road.

2. *Major Waddell*, A. D. C. to Gen. Beauregard, with two good guides, will report for service to Major-gen. Hardee.

3. At three o'clock, A. M., to-morrow, the third corps, with the left in front, will continue to advance by the Bark road until within sight of the enemy's out-posts, on advanced positions, when it will be deployed in line of battle, according to the nature of the ground, its left resting on Owl creek, its right towards Lick creek, supported on that flank by half of its cavalry. The left flank being supported by the other half. The interval between the extreme right of this corps and Lick creek, will be filled with a brigade or division, according to the extent of the ground, from the second corps. These troops, during the battle, will also be under the command of Major-gen. Hardee.

He will make the proper disposition of the artillery along the line of battle, remembering that the rifle-guns are of long ranges, and should be placed in very commanding positions in rear of the infantry, to fire mainly on the reserves and second line of the enemy, but occasionally will be divided on his batteries and heads of columns.

II. The *second corps*, under Major-gen. Braxton Bragg, will assemble at Monterey, and move thence as early as practicable; the right wing with left in front, by the road from Monterey to Savannah; the head of the column to reach the vicinity of Meckey's house, at the intersection of the Bark road, before sunset. The cavalry with this wing will take position on the road to Savannah, beyond Meckey's, as far as Owl creek, having advanced guards and pickets with the front. The left wing of this corpse will advance at the same time, also left in front, by the road from Monterey to Purdy; the head of the column to reach by night the intersection of that road with the Bark road. This wing will continue the movement in the morning as soon as the rear of the third corpse shall have passed the Purdy road, which it will then follow.

The second corps will form the second line of battle, about one thousand yards in rear of first line. It will be formed, if practicable, with regiments in double columns at half distance, disposed as advantageously as the nature of the ground will admit, and with a view to facility of development. The artillery placed as may seem best to Major-gen. Bragg.

III. The *first corps*, under Major-gen. Polk, with the exception of the detached divisions at Bethel, will take up its line of march by Ridge road, hence to Pittsburg, half an hour after the rear of the third corpse shall have passed Corinth, and will bivouac to-night in the rear of that corps, and to-morrow will follow the movements of that corps, with the same interval of time as to-day. When the head of column shall have reached the vicinity of the Meckey House, it will be halted in column, or massed on the line of the Bark road, according to the nature of the ground, as a reserve. Meanwhile, one regiment of its cavalry will be placed in observation on the road from Johnston's House to Stantonville. Another regiment or battalion of cavalry will be posted in the same manner on the road from Monterey to Purdy, with the rear resting on or about the intersection of that road with the Bark road, having advanced guards and pickets in the direction of Purdy.

The forces at Bethel and Purdy will defend their positions as already instructed, if attacked, otherwise they will assemble on Purdy, and thence advance, with advanced guards, flankers, and all other prescribed military precautions, by the road thence to Monterey, forming a junction with the rest of the first corps at the intersection of that road with the Bark road leading to Corinth.

IV. The *reserve* of the forces will be concentrated, by the shortest and best routes, at Monterey as soon as the rear of the second corps shall have moved out of that place. Its commander will take up the best position whence to advance as required, either in the direction of Meckey's or of Pratt's House, on the direct road to Pittsburg, if that road is found practicable, or in the direction of the Ridge road to Hamburg, throwing all its cavalry on the latter road, as far as its intersection with the one to Pittsburg passing through Grierford or Lick creek.

This cavalry will throw well forward advanced guards and videttes towards Grierfield, and in the direction of Hamburg, and during the impending battle, when called to the field of combat, will move by the Grierfield road.

A regiment of the infantry reserve will be thrown forward to the intersection of the Grand Hill road to Hamburg, as a support to the cavalry.

The *reserve* will be formed of Breckenridge's, Bowens, and Salhem's brigades, as now organized, the whole under Brig.-gen. Breckinridge.

V. Gen. Bragg will detach the 51st and 52d regiments of Tennessee Volunteers, Blount's Alabama, and Desha's Arkansas battalions, and Bain's battery from his corps, which, with two of Carroll's regiments, now en route for the head-quarters, will form a garrison for the post and depot at Corinth.

VI. Strong guards will be left on the railroad bridges between Iuka and Corinth, to be furnished in due proportion from the com mands of Iuka, Burnsville, and Corinth.

VII. Proper guards will be left at the camps of the several regiments of the forces on the field. Corps commanders will determine the force of the guards.

VIII. Wharton's regiment of Texas cavalry will be ordered forward at once to scout on the road from Monterey to Savannah, between Meckey's and its intersection with the Pittsburg Purdy road. It will annoy and harass any force of the enemy coming that way to assail Cheatham's division at Purdy.

IX. The chief engineer of the forces will take all due measures and precautions, and give requisite orders for the repairs of all the bridges, causeways, and roads on which our army may move in the execution of their orders.

X. The troops, individually so intelligent, and with such a grand interest involved in the issne, are urgently enjoined to be obedient and observant of the orders of their superiors in the hour of battle. Their officers must constantly keep them in hand, and prevent the waste of ammunition by heedless firing. The fire should be slow, always, at a *distant mark.* It is expected that much and effective work will be done with the bayonet.

By command of Gen. A. S. JOHNSTON:

THOMAS JORDAN,

A. A. General.

(B.)

KILLED, WOUNDED, AND MISSING IN THE BATTLE OF SHILOH. GENERAL BEAUREGARD COMMANDING.

1*st Corps*—Major-gen. Polk; 1st division, Brig.-gen. Clark; 1st brigade, Col. R. M. Russell; killed, 97; wounded, 512.

2d brigade, Brig.-gen. A. P. Stewart; killed, 93; wounded, 421; missing, 3.

2d division, Major-gen. Cheatham; 1st brigade, Brig.-gen. B. R. Johnson; killed, 120; wounded, 607; missing, 13.

2d brigade, Col. W. H. Stephens; killed, 75; wounded, 413; missing, 3.

Total—Killed, 385; wounded, 1,953; missing, 19.

2*d Corps*—Gen. Bragg; 1st division, Brig.-gen. Ruggles; 1st brigade, Col. Gibson; killed, 95; wounded, 488; missing, 90.

2d brigade, Brig.-gen. Anderson; killed, 67; wounded, 313; missing, 50.

3d brigade, Col. Pond; killed, 89; wounded, 336; missing, 167.

2d division, Brig.-gen. Withers; 1st brigade, Brig.-gen. Gladden; killed, 129; wounded, 597; missing, 103.

2d brigade, Brig.-gen Chalmers; killed, 82; wounded, 343; missing, 29.

3d brigade, Brig.-gen. Jackson; killed, 91; wounded, 364; missing, 194.

Total—Killed, 553; wounded, 2,441; missing, 634.

3*d* *Corps*—Maj.-gen. Hardee, 1st brigade, Brig.-gen. Hindman; killed, 109; wounded, 546; missing, 38.

2d brigade, Brig.-gen. Cleburn; killed, 188; wounded, 790; missing, 65.

3d brigade, Brig.-gen. Wood; killed, 107; wounded. 600; missing, 38.

Total—Killed, 404; wounded, 1,936; missing, 141.

Reserve—Major-gen. Breckinridge, 1st Kentucky brigade; Col. Trabue; killed, 151; wounded, 557; missing, 92.

2d brigade, Brig.-gen. Bowen; killed, 98; wounded, 498; missing, 28.

3d brigade, Col. Statham; killed, 137; wounded, 627; missing, 45.

Total—Killed, 386; wounded, 1,682; missing, 165.

RECAPITULATION:

Killed	1,728
Wounded	8,012
Missing	959
Total	10,699

(C.)

LIST OF FLAGS CAPTURED AT THE BATTLE OF SHILOH, NEAR THE TENNESSEE RIVER, APRIL 6, 1862.

HEAD-QUARTERS, ARMY OF THE MISSISSIPPI,
CORINTH, MISS. April 23, 1862.

Five (5) blue silk Regimental Colors.
Twenty (20) Federal Flags.
One (1) Garrison Flag.
Two (2) Guidons.

THOMAS JORDAN, *A. A. General.*

(E.)

Field Return of the Army of the Mississippi, before and after the Battle of Shiloh, fought April 6th and 7th.

Head-quarters Army of the Mississippi,
Corinth, Miss, April 21st, 1862.

	Effective total before battle.	Effective total after battle.
First Army Corps, Major-gen. L. Polk,........	9,136	6,779
Second Army Corps, Gen. B. Bragg,..........	13,589	9,961
Third Army Corps, Major-gen. W. J. Hardee,..	6,789	4,609
Reserve, Brig.-gen. John C. Breckinridge,.....	6,439	4,206
Total infantry and artillery,..................	35,953	25,555
Cavalry, Brig.-gen. F. Gardner,..............	4,382	4,081
Grand total,.............................	40,355	29,636

Difference 10,699, casualties in battle of Shiloh.

The battle-field being so thickly wooded that the cavalry was useless and could not operate at all.

Respectfully submitted and forwarded,

G. T. BEAUREGARD,
General Commanding A. M.

Letter of General Braxton Bragg.

Head-quarters Department No. 2,
Mobile, Ala., July 25, 1862.

Gen. S. Cooper, *Adj't and Insp'r-general, C. S. A., Richmond.*

Sir:—Herewith I have the honor to forward my official report, as commander of the second corps Army Mississippi, of the battle of "Shiloh." The great delay, somewhat unusual with me in official matters, has resulted from a combination of unavoidable circumstances. Wishing to make it complete, the reports of all subordinates were desired; but, at last, several are wanting. My own time has been so much occupied, too, that it is not rendered as soon, nor is it as complete, as I could have desired.

I am, sir, very respectfully,
Your obedient servant,
BRAXTON BRAGG,
General Commanding.

Report of General Braxton Bragg.

HEAD-QUARTERS SECOND CORPS, A. M.,
CORINTH, MISS., April 30, 1862.

Brig.-gen. THOMAS JORDAN, *Chief of Staff.*

GENERAL:—In submitting a report of the operations of my command, the second army corps, in the action of Shiloh, on the 6th and 7th of April, it is proper that the narrative of events on the field be preceded by a sketch of the march from here. But few regiments of my command had ever made a day's march. A very large proportion of the rank and file had never performed a day's labor. Our organization had been most hasty, with great deficiency in commanders, and was, therefore, very imperfect. The equipment was lamentably defective for field service, and our transportation, hastily impressed in the country, was deficient in quantity and very inferior in quality. With all these drawbacks, the troops marched, late on the afternoon of the 3d, a day later than intended, in high spirits, and eager for the contest.

The road to Monterey, eleven miles, was found very bad, requiring us until eleven o'clock on the 4th, to concentrate at that place, where one of my brigades joined the column. Moving from there, the command bivouacked for the night near the Meckey House, immediately in rear of Major-gen. Hardee's corps, Major-gen. Polk's being just in our rear.

Our advance cavalry had encountered the enemy during the day, and captured several prisoners, being compelled, however, to retire. A reconnoissance, in some force, from the enemy made its appearance during the evening in front of Gen. Hardee's corps, and was promptly driven back.

The commanders of divisions and brigades were assembled at night, the order was read to them, and the topography of the enemy's position was explained as far as understood by us. Orders were then given for the troops to march at three o'clock A. M., so as to attack the enemy early on the 5th. About two A. M. a drenching rain storm commenced, to which the troops were exposed without tents, and continued until daylight, rendering it so dark, and filling the creeks and ravines to such an extent as to make it impracticable to move at night. Orders were immediately sent out to suspend the movement until the first dawn of day. Continued firing, by volleys and single shots, was kept up all night and until seven A. M. next morning, by the undisciplined troops of our front, in violation of positive orders. Under such circumstances, little or no rest could be obtained by our men, and it was seven o'clock in the morning before the road was clear, so as to put my command in motion, though it had been in ranks and ready from three A. M., in the wet and cold, and suffering from inaction. At this juncture the commanding general arrived at our position. My column, at last fairly in motion, moved on without delay, until arriving near where the Pittsburg road leaves the Bark road, when a message from Major-gen. Hardee announced the enemy in his front, and that he had developed his line. As promptly as my troops could be brought up in a narrow road, much encumbered with artillery and baggage wagons, they were formed according to order of battle, about eight hundred yards in rear of Hardee's line, my centre resting on the Pittsburg road, my right brigade, Gladden's, of Wither's division, thrown forward to the right of the first, Major-gen. Hardee's force not being sufficient for the ground to be covered.

In this position we remained anxiously awaiting the approach of our reserve, to advance upon the enemy, now but a short distance in our front. The condition of the roads, and other untoward circumstances, delayed them until late in the afternoon, rendering it necessary to defer the attack until next morning. The night was occupied by myself and a portion of my staff in efforts to bring forward provisions for a portion of the troops then suffering from their improvidence. Having been ordered to march with five days' rations, they were found hungry and destitute at the end of three days. This is one of the evils of raw troops, imperfectly organized, and badly commanded; a tribute, it seems, we must continue to pay to universal suffrage, the bane of our military organization. In this condition we passed the night, and at dawn of day prepared to move. The enemy did not give us time to discuss the question of attack, for soon after dawn he commenced a rapid musketry fire on our pickets. The order was immediately given by the commanding general, and our lines advanced. Such was the ardor of our troops that it was with great difficulty they could be restrained from closing up, and mingling with the first line. Within less than a mile, the enemy was encountered in force at the encampments of his advanced positions, but our first line brushed him away, leaving the rear nothing to do but to press on in pursuit. In about one mile more, we encountered him in strong force along almost the entire line. His batteries were posted on eminences, with strong infantry supports. Finding the first line was now unequal to the work before it, being weakened by extention, and necessarily broken by the nature of the ground, I ordered my whole force to move up steadily and promptly to its support.

The order was hardly necessary, for subordinate commanders, far beyond the reach of my voice and eye in the broken country occupied by us, had promptly acted on the necessity as it arose, and by the time the order could be conveyed, the whole line was developed and actively engaged.

From this time, about seven and a half o'clock, until night, the battle raged with little intermission. All parts of our line were not constantly engaged, but there was no time without heavy firing in some portion of it.

My position for several hours was opposite my left-centre (Ruggles' division), immediately in rear of Hindman's brigade, Hardee's corps. In moving over the difficult and broken ground, the right brigade of Ruggles' division, Col. Gibson commanding, bearing to the right, became separated from the two left brigades, leaving a broad interval. Three regiments of Major-gen. Polk's command opportunely came up and filled this interval. Finding no superior officer with them, I took the liberty of directing their movements in support of Hindman, then as before, ardently pressing forward, and engaging the enemy at every point.

On the ground which had come under my immediate observation, we had already captured three large encampments and three batteries of artillery. It was now about ten and a half o'clock.

Our right flank, according to the order of battle, had pressed forward ardently, under the immediate direction of the commanding general, and swept all before it. Batteries, encampmants, storehouses, munitions in rich profusion, were ours: and the enemy fighting hard and causing us to pay dearly for our successes, was falling back rapidly at every point. His left, however, opposite our right, was his strongest ground and position, and was disputed with obstinacy. It was during this severe struggle that my command suffered an irreparable loss in the fall of Brig.-gen. Gladden, commanding 1st brigade, Withers' division, mortally, and Col. D. W. Adams, Louisiana regular infantry (his successor), severely wounded. Nothing daunted, however, by these losses, this noble division, under its gallant leader, Withers, pressed on with the other troops in its vicinity, and carried all before them. Their progress, however, under the obstinate resistance made, was not so rapid as was desired, in proportion to that of the left, where the enemy was less strong; so that, instead of driving him, as we intended, down the river, leaving the left open for him to pass, we had really enveloped him on all sides, and were pressing him back upon the landing at Pittsburg.

Meeting at about 10 and a half o'clock, upon the left-centre with Major-gen. Polk, my senior, I promptly yielded to him the important command at that point, and moved towards the right, in the direction in which Brig.-gen. Hindman, of Hardee's line, had just led his division.

Here we met the most obstinate resistance of the day, the enemy being strongly posted with infantry and artillery on an eminence immediately behind a dense thicket. Hindman's command was gallantly led to the attack, but recoiled under a murderous fire. The noble and gallant leader fell severely wounded, and was borne from the field he had illustrated with a heroism rarely equalled.

The command soon returned to its work, but was unequal to the heavy task. Leaving them to hold their position, I moved further to the right, and brought up the first brigade (Gibson of Ruggles' division), which was in rear of its true position, and threw them forward to attack this same point. A very heavy fire soon opened, and after a short conflict, this command fell back in considerable disorder. Rallying the different regiments by means of my staff officers and escort, they were twice more moved to the attack, only to be driven back by the enemy's sharpshooters occupying the thick cover. This result was due entirely to want of proper handling.

Finding that nothing could be done here, after hours of severe exertion and heavy losses, and learning the fall of our commander, who was leading in person on the extreme right, the troops were so posted as to hold this position, and leaving a competent staff officer to direct them in my name, I moved rapidly to the extreme right. Here I found a strong force, consisting of three parts, without a common head; Brig.-gen. Breckinridge with his reserve division pressing the enemy; Brig.-gen. Withers, with his splendid division, greatly exhausted, and taking a temporary rest, and Major-gen. Cheatham, with his division of Major-gen. Polk's command, to their left and rear. These troops were soon put in motion, responding with great alacrity to the command of "forward, let every order be forward." It was now probably past 4 o'clock, the descending sun warning us to press our advantage, and finish the work before night should compel us to desist.

Fairly in motion, these commands again, with a common head and a common purpose, swept all before them. Neither battery, nor battalion could withstand their onslaught. Passing through camp after camp, rich in military spoils of every kind, the enemy was driven headlong from every position, and thrown in confused masses upon the river bank, behind his heavy artillery, and under cover of his gunboats at the landing. He had left nearly the whole of his light artillery in our hands, and some three thousand or more prisoners, who were cut off from their retreat by the closing in of our troops on the left, under Major-gen. Polk, with a portion of his reserve corps, and Brig.-gen. Ruggles, with Anderson's and Pond's brigades of his division.

The prisoners were dispatched to the rear under a proper guard, all else being left on the field, that we might press our advantage. The enemy had fallen back in much confusion, and was crowded in unorganized masses on the river bank, vainly striving to cross. They were covered by a battery of heavy guns well served, and their two gunboats, which now poured a heavy fire upon our supposed positions, for we were entirely hid by the forest. Their fire, though terrific in sound, and producing some consternation at first, did us no damage, as the shells all passed over, and exploded far beyond our positions.

As soon as our troops could be again formed and put in motion, the order was given to move forward at all points, and sweep the enemy from the field. The sun was about disappearing, so that little time was left us to finish the glorious work of the day; a day unsurpassed in the history of warfare for its daring deeds, brilliant achievements, and heavy sacrifices.

Our troops, greatly exhausted by twelve hours' incessant fighting, without food, mostly responded to the order with alacrity, and the movement commenced with every prospect of success, though a heavy battery in our front, and the gunboats on our right, seemed determined to dispute every inch of ground.

Just at this time, an order was received from the commanding general, to withdraw the forces beyond the enemy's fire. As this was communicated in many instances direct to brigade commanders, the troops were soon in motion, and the action ceased. The different commands mixed and scattered, bivouacked at points most convenient to their positions, and beyond the range of the enemy's guns. All firing, except a half hour shot from the gunboats, ceased and the whole night was passed by our exhausted men in quiet. Such as had not sought shelter in the camps of the enemy, were again drenched before morning by one of those heavy rain storms which seemed to be our portion for this expedition.

Such was the nature of the ground over which we had fought, and the heavy resistance we had met, that the commands of the whole army were very much shattered. In a dark or stormy night, commanders found it impossible to find and assemble their troops; each body or fragment bivouacking when night overtook them.

In this condition, morning found us confronting a large and fresh army, which had arrived during the night, and for the first time the enemy advanced to meet us. He was received by our whole line with a firm and bold front, and the battle again raged.

From this hour until 2 P. M., the action continued with great obstinacy and varying success. Our troops exhausted by days of incessant fatigue, hunger, and want of rest, and ranks thinned by killed, wounded, and stragglers, amounting in the whole, to nearly half our force, fought bravely, but with the want of that animation and spirit which characterized them the preceding day. Many instances of daring and desperate valor, deserving of better success, failed for want of numbers.

My personal services were confined during this day to the extreme left of our line, where my whole time was incessantly occupied. The troops in my front consisted of Ruggles' division, Col. Wobue's brigade of Breckinridge's reserve, and other detachments of different corps, all operating to the left of Shiloh church. This force advanced in the early morning, and pressed the enemy back for nearly a mile, securing for our left flank an eminence in an open field near Owl creek, which we held till near the close of the conflict, against every effort the enemy could make. For this gallant and obstinate defence of our left flank, which the enemy constantly endeavored to force, we were indebted to Col. Wobue's small brigade in support of Capt. Burn's battery. Against overwhelming numbers, this gallant command maintained its position from the commencement of the action, until about twelve o'clock, when our forces on the left falling back, it was left entirely without support, far in front of our whole army. Safety required it to retire. During this time, the right and centre were actively engaged. Withers' division, in conjunction with portions of Hardee's and Breckinridge's commands, obstinately disputed every effort of the enemy. But his overwhelming numbers, a very large portion being perfectly fresh troops, the prostration of our men, and the exhaustion of our ammunition,—not a battalion being supplied,—rendered our position most perilous, and the commanding general ordered a retrograde movement to commence on the right. This was gradually extended to the left, now held by Ketchum's battery. The troops fell back generally in perfect order, and formed in line of battle on a ridge about half a mile in the rear. Ketchum retiring slowly as the rear guard of the whole army.

The enemy evinced no disposition to pursue. After some half hour our troops were again put in motion and moved about a mile further, where line was formed, and final arrangements were made for the march of our camp to Corinth, the enemy making not the slightest demonstration upon us.

This orderly movement, under the circumstances, was as creditable to the troops as any part of the brilliant advances they had made.

A "Field Return" of the force carried into action, marked "A," and a return of killed, wounded, and missing, marked "B," and the reports of division commanders, marked "C" and "D," accompanied by those of subordinate commanders, are herewith forwarded. Of the missing, a few are ascertained to have fallen into the hands of the enemy, mostly wounded. The others were, no doubt, left dead on the field.

The heavy loss sustained by the command will best indicate the obstinacy the resistance met, and the determination with which it was overcome.

For the part performed by the different portions of the corps, reference is made to the reports of subordinate commanders.

The division of Brig.-gen. J. M. Withers was gallantly led by that officer from the first gun to the close of the action, and performed service rarely suppassed by any troops on the field.

Brig.-gen. A. H. Gladden, first brigade of this division, fell early in the action, mortally wounded, whilst gallantly leading his men in a successful charge. No better soldier lived—no truer man or nobler patriot ever shed his blood in a just cause.

Later in the day, Col. D. W. Adams, Louisiana infantry, who had succeeded to this splendid brigade, was desperately wounded whilst gallantly leading it; and later still, Col. Z. C. Deas, 22d Alabama Volunteers, fell pierced by several balls.

Brig.-gen. James R. Chalmers, at the head of his gallant Mississippians, filled, he could not have exceeded, the measure of my expectations. Never were troops and commanders more worthy of each other and of their State.

Brig.-gen. J. K. Jackson did good service with his Alabama brigade on the first day; but becoming much broken, it was not unitedly in action thereafter.

The excellent regiment of Col. Jos. Wheeler, however, joined, and did noble service with Gladden's brigade.

Brig.-gen. D. Ruggles, commanding second division, was conspicuous throughout both days, for the gallantry with which he led his troops. Brig.-gen. Patton Anderson, commanding a brigade of this division, was also among the foremost where the fighting was hardest, and never failed to overcome whatever resistance was opposed to him. With a brigade composed almost entirely of raw troops, his personal gallantry and soldierly bearing supplied the place of instruction and discipline.

It would be a pleasing duty to record the deeds of many other noble soldiers of inferior grade, but as subordinate commanders have done so in their reports, a repetition is unnecessary. I shall be pardoned for making an exception in the case of Capt. R. W. Smith, commanding a company of Alabama cavalry, which served as my personal escort during the action. For personal gallantry and intelligent execution of orders, frequently under the heaviest fire, his example has rarely been equalled. To him, his officers, and his men, I feel a deep personal as well as official obligation.

By the officers of my staff I was most faithfully, laboriously, and gallantly served throughout both days, as well as on the marches before and after the action. A record of their names is an acknowledgment but justly due.

Major Geo. G. Garner, As't. Adj.-gen. (horse wounded on Sunday.)
Capt. H. W. Walter, Assistant Adj.-gen.
Capt. G. B. Cook, " "
1st Lieut. Tonson Ellis, Regular Aid.
" F. S. Parker, " "
Lieut.-col. F. Gardner, C. S. A.
" W. K. Beard, Florida Volunteers (wounded on Monday), Acting Inspector gen.
Major J. H. Hallenquist, P. A., Chief of Artillery.
Capt. W. O. Williams, P. A., Assistant to Chief of Artillery.
" S. H. Lockett, C. S. Engineers.
" H. Oladnoski, C. S. A., Chief of Ordnance.
Major J. J. Walker, P. A., Chief of Subsistence.
" L. F. Johnston, P. A., Chief Quarter-master.
" O. P. Chaffee, P. A., Assistant Quarter-master.
Surgeon A. I. Foard, C. S. A., Medical Director.
" J. C. Nott, P. A., Medical Inspector.

Doctor Robert O. Butler, of Louisiana Volunteers, for the occasion rendered excellent service in our field hospitals.

Lieut.-col. David Urquhart, Aid to the Governor of Louisiana, served me with great intelligence and efficiency as Volunteer Aid.

Several other officers, during the engagement, temporarily separated from their own commands, did me the favor to act on my staff, and served me efficiently. Privates H. Montague and M. Shehan, Louisiana infantry, and private John Williams, 10th Regiment Mississippi Volunteers, orderlies in attendance on myself and staff, though humble in position, rendered services so useful and gallant that their names are fully entitled to a mention in this report. They encountered the same dangers, and, when necessary, performed nearly the same duties as officers of my staff, without the same incentives. In rallying troops, bringing up stragglers and enforcing orders against refugees, they were especially active, energetic, and efficient.

It may not be amiss to refer briefly to the causes it is believed operated to prevent the complete overthrow of the enemy, which we were so near accomplishing, and which would have changed the entire complexion of the war.

The want of proper organization and discipline, and the inferiority in many cases of our officers to the men they were expected to command, left as often without system or order, and the large proportion of stragglers resulting, weakened our forces, and kept the superior and staff officers constantly engaged in the duties of file-closers. Especially was this the case after the occupation of the enemy's camps, the spoils of which served to delay, and greatly to demoralize our men. But no one cause, probably, contributed so greatly to our loss of time, which was the loss of success, as the fall of the commanding general. At the moment of this irreparable disaster, the plan of battle was being rapidly and successfully executed under his immediate eye and lead on the right. For want of a common superior to the different commands on that part of the field, great delay occurred after this misfortune, and that delay prevented the consummation of the work so gallantly and successfully begun and carried on, until the approach of night induced our new commander to recall the exhausted troops for rest and recuperation, before a crowning effort on the next morning. The arrival during the night of a large and fresh army to reinforce the enemy, equal in numbers at least to our own, frustrated all his well-grounded expectations, and after a long and bloody contest with superior forces, compelled us to retire from the field, leaving our killed, many of our wounded, and nearly all the trophies of the previous day's victories.

In this result we have a valuable lesson, by which we should profit—never on a battle-field to lose a moment's time; but, leaving the killed, wounded and spoils to those whose special business it is to care for them, to press on with every available man, giving a panic-stricken and retreating foe no time to rally, and reaping all the benefits of a success never complete, until every enemy is killed, wounded, or captured. No course so certain as this to afford succor to the wounded and security to the trophies.

I am, sir, very respectfully,
Your obedient servant,
BRAXTON BRAGG, *General Commanding.*

P. S. The transmission of this report has been delayed from time to time, that those from subordinate commanders with a complete and perfect list of killed, wounded, and missing might accompany it. In this hope I am yet disappointed to a certain extent.

(A.)

Field Return, showing the Number of Killed, Wounded, and Missing, and the Aggregate Strength of each Division, 2d Corps, Army of the Mississippi, April 6th, 1862.

Withers' Division; killed, 293; wounded, 1334; missing, 253; total, 1880; aggregate strength, 6482.

Ruggles' Division; killed, 240; wounded, 1103; missing, 269; total, 1612; aggregate strength, 6484.

Grand total; killed, 533; wounded, 2437; missing, 522; total, 4492; aggregate strength, 12,966.

Report of Brig.-gen. Withers.

Head-quarters Withers' Division,
Camp near Tupelo, June 20th, 1862.

Major:—I have the honor to report that before daylight, on Saturday morning, the 5th of April, this division was reported ready to march, and that immediately after the rear of the advanced command was in motion, it moved forward in the following order:

1st—Gladden's brigade.
2d—Chalmer's brigade.
3d—Jackson's brigade.

Arriving near the proposed line of battle, by order of Gen. Bragg, Gladden's brigade was thrown forward to the right of Gen. Hardee's advanced or attacking lines. Jackson's brigade was then positioned about 300 yards to the rear of Gladden's, its left resting on the Bark road. Chalmers' was formed on the right of Jackson's, its right resting on a creek, tributary to Lick creek, being in echelon to, and on, Gladden's right. Clanton's cavalry having reported for duty with the division, was placed in the rear of Chalmers, with a strong picket on the right and front. Thus, the division bivouacked for the night.

The attacking line being put in motion early on the morning of the 6th, this command was ordered forward, retaining its relative position. With the advance it was soon perceptible that there was a gradual but steady inclination to the left, thus increasing the distance to, and exposing our flank on, Lick creek. To remedy this, Col. Clanton was directed to sweep down Lick creek with his cavalry, and to protect our right from surprise.

By this time, our attacking line was warmly engaged with the enemy, and steadily driving them back. Learning that the enemy were in force in front of Gen. Chalmers, whose brigade extended to the right of our attacking line, he was ordered forward to attack them. This he did promptly, gallantly, and successfully. Moving forward, we passed the first camp, from which the enemy had been driven, and came up with Gladden's brigade, formed in square, and under command of Col. D. W. Adams, 1st Louisiana infantry, Gen. Gladden having been dangerously, and, as the result unfortunately proved, mortally wounded. In the meantime, Chalmers' brigade had moved steadily onward, and after a short but hot contest, drove the enemy from their second camp. Having thus become too much separated from the remainder of the command, Gen. Chalmers was ordered to resume his position on Jackson's right. Here some delay occurred in moving forward, the movements of the enemy being concealed; and a report being brought in that they were forming in line of battle some distance on our right, Gen. A. S. Johnston, who was present, immediately ordered the division to move to the right. This movement was promptly and rapidly performed, over ground that was rough, broken, and heavily timbered. Having led the command about one-half or three-fourths of a mile to the right, it was halted, until the cavalry should ascertain whether the enemy still outflanked us. Satisfied that there was no enemy on our right, the order was given to advance. The nature of the ground, over which we had to pass, rendered it most difficult for the artillery to keep up with the eager and rapid movements of the infantry. With such batteries, however, as Robertson's, Grady's, and Gage's, there could be no failure. Gen. Jackson, descending rapidly the hill on which his brigade had rested, found the enemy in strong force on the opposite slope. He promptly engaged, and, after a sharp but warm contest, drove them from their position. Col. Moore, of the 2d Texas, here displayed great gallantry. In quick pursuit, we passed an extensive camp, beyond which, and on the opposite side skirting the wood, the enemy, occupying some houses, had formed a second line. From this position they were also quickly driven, but soon formed a third line, on a ridge running nearly parallel with the Hamburg and Pittsburg road.

Gen. Jackson was ordered to move forward a short distance, and rest his command in a ravine, until the artillery could be brought up. This was quickly done, and it opened immediately, with telling effect, on the enemy. Gen. Chalmers, in the meantime, advanced rapidly upon the enemy, in strong force, beyond an old field, concealed and protected by a worm fence and thick undergrowth. After a short conflict, they were dislodged, and driven from their position, and Chalmers halted his command for a supply of ammunition.

These movements caused the brigades to be too widely separated, being at right angles, Jackson's facing north, and Chalmers' east. Chalmers was, therefore, ordered to move his command to its position on Jackson's right. Satisfied by the report of the energetic and indefatigable Clanton, that there was no enemy on our right, and being convinced, by the heavy and continuous firing, that they were in force on our left, the division was ordered to wheel on a movable pivot to the left. This movement, which was in accordance with the general plan of battle, as explained by the commanding general to the division and brigade commanders, soon developed the enemy in strong force, who stubbornly contested our advance, but were driven before the cool and steady Jackson, and the gallant and impetuous Chalmers. Reinforcements were now called for on our left, where heavy firing still continued; but this division being hotly engaged throughout the lines, Col. Rich, of the 1st Missouri, whose regiment was in our rear, having become detached from Gen. Brown's brigade, was ordered to the support. He moved off immediately at double-quick, and dashed into the fight with good effect. An order for reinforcements was now received from Gen. Bragg. As the entire line was now warmly engaged, with no support, Gen. Breckenridge, who had just had a sharp conflict with, and driven the enemy before him, was called on to render the desired assistance. This was done without other delay than that necessary to furnish his troops with ammunition.

This division still continued fiercely engaged, until Chalmers, having routed the forces before him, began to sweep down on the left flank of the heavy force in front of Jackson; at the same time that Gladden's brigade, now under command of Col. Deas, of the 22d Alabama, the bold and impetuous Adams having been dangerously wounded in the head, whilst gallantly leading his command, began to press him on his right. Thus positioned, the enemy surrendered, and were marched out on the Hamburg road, through Jackson's brigade, and placed by me in charge of Col. Shorter, with his regiment, the 18th Alabama, and marched to Corinth. The enemy captured proved to be the command of Gen. Prentiss.

This division was then advanced to the Pittsburg edge of the field, in which the enemy had stacked their arms, and halted for a supply of ammunition. Most of the regiments were supplied from the camps of the enemy. The order was now given by Gen. Bragg, who was present on the right during the fierce fight, which ended in the capture of Prentiss, to "Sweep every thing forward." This division was moved promptly forward, although some regiments had not succeeded in getting a supply of ammunition, and had just entered a steep and precipitous ravine, when the enemy opened a terrific fire upon it. Staff officers were immediately dispatched, to bring up all the reinforcements to be found, and the order was given to brigade commanders to charge the batteries. These orders were being obeyed, when, to my astonishment, a large portion of the command was observed to move rapidly by the left flank, from under the fire of the enemy. Orders were immediately sent to arrest the commanding officers, and for the troops to be promptly placed in a position for charging the batteries.

Information was soon brought, however, that it was by Gen. Beauregard's orders, delivered thus directly to brigade commanders, that the troops were being rapidly led from under the fire of the enemy's gunboats. Thus ended the fight on Sunday, and thus was this command disorganized, an evil sorely felt during the next day.

Receiving at this time an order from Gen. Bragg, to take command of all the troops on the right, and it being now near dark, the order was given to fall back about half a mile, and bivouack for the night. Chalmers' brigade resting in rear nearest the enemy, and the remainder of the troops at the second of the camps from the one last captured, under command of Col. Wheeler, 19th Alabama. Here we met Col. Hardee, with Col. Martin's 1st Confederate regiment.

At 4 o'clock, Monday morning, the troops were put in motion to form line of battle, on the road leading from this camp diagonally to the left and rear, to a road branching off to the right, from the Bark and Pittsburg roads, and nearly a mile distant from the camp. Chalmers' brigade was to form the rear guard until this otherwise fragmentary command could be worked into some shape, the order being given to force all stragglers into ranks. The head of this line had but just reached the point at which it was to halt, when an order was received from Gen. Bragg to move my command to the assistance of Gen. Anderson, who was hotly pressed by the enemy. With receipt of this order came a message from Gen. Chalmers, that he had already had one fierce engagement with the enemy, and was then in the second. Every available man was immediately marched back, and line of battle formed near the position occupied by us through the night, Chalmer's brigade being on the right, the 19th and 21st Alabama, and the 2d Texas, on the left, Col. Moore, of the 2d Texas, being in command of the left. Robertson's battery was placed in position at the edge of an old field, with instructions to sweep the enemy from our front, and also to aid some command on the left (believed to be Anderson's) which seemed to be warmly engaged. The reserve consisted of the "Crescent La.," Col. Martin's Confederate regiment, and Maney's 1st Tenn., with whatever other troops, from time to time, could be picked up.

At this time an order was received from Gen. Beauregard to charge the enemy, in conjunction with Gen. Breckinridge. The charge was made by us, but Gen. Breckinridge was neither there nor subsequently in that portion of the field. The enemy proved to be in such numbers that it became necessary to bring our entire force into action, and the fight continued with sullen desperation for several hours, and with alternate success. Between half-past two and three o'clock, finding that the enemy were content to hold their position and not advance on us, our line of the morning was resumed, the left under the command of the gallant Col. Maney, of the 1st Tennessee regiment. Shortly after this an order was received from Gen. Bragg to withdraw the troops in good order, and form line of battle on the crest of the hill on the right branch of the Bark road. This was done, and the command slowly and in good order retired through two of the enemy's camps, not a gun being fired, and formed line of battle as ordered; the advanced line under

Col. Wheeler; the reserve under Col. Martin, with Col. Moore, of the 2d Texas, to support a battery, commanding a road running to our right and rear. The cavalry was thrown to our front. Thus we remained until dark, the entire army, with the exception of the cavalry, having retired from the field, when we received an order from Gen. Bragg, that, holding the command in readiness to form line of battle at any moment, we would fall back to Meckey's. This order was obeyed; Chalmers' worn brigade and the Crescent regiment were permitted to pass on to the rear, and the remainder of the troops marched to within about a mile of Meckey's, where they were placed under the command of Col. Wheeler, who, throughout the fight, had proved himself worthy of all trust and confidence—a gallant commander and an accomplished soldier—and there bivouacked for the night. After eleven o'clock at night we arrived at Meckey's, where we found that Gen. Breckinridge was in command of what has been called the rear guard. With him, Col. Wheeler, with his regiment, the 19th Alabama, was left on Tuesday morning, and the remainder of the command marched back to Corinth.

Though temporarily detached, the reports from Gladden's brigade were forwarded to division head-quarters. From these and the proximity of the brigade during the fight, abundant evidences of the ability and gallantry of its commanders are furnished. The true and tried Gladden fell early on the morning of the 6th, the fearless Adams about half-past eleven o'clock. From that hour, during that and the next day, the brigade was ably commanded by Col. Deas, of the 22d Alabama, who, though without a staff officer to aid him, proved himself equal to the occasion, and worthy of the gallant command to which he had succeeded, and which, although severely wounded, he continued to hold through the fight.

The division entered the fight sixty-four hundred and eighty-two strong, and came out with an aggregate loss of nineteen hundred and eighteen, apportioned among the several brigades as follows:

	killed	wounded	missing
Gladden's—	129 killed;	597 wounded;	103 missing.
Chalmer's—	82 "	343 "	— "
Jackson's—	86 "	365 "	213 "

thus furnishing stern but sad evidence of the manner in which the command discharged its duty.

In the fight on Sunday, Capt. D. E. Huger, Assistant-adj.-gen., Provisional Army; Lieut. B. M. Thomas, C. S. A., Acting Inspector Gen.; Lieut D. F. Withers, A. D. C.; and volunteer aids, R. W. Withers, S B. Howe, William Williamson, and L. E. Smith, discharged the duties of their respective positions with active zeal and gallantry. Through the fight on Monday, Capt. Huger, Lieut. Thomas, and Volunteer-aid R. W. Withers, were all the staff present on the right, the others having become separated Sunday evening, and each more than sustained the reputation gained the day before. Major Reynolds, of the 2d Texas, volunteered as a staff officer when the division commander was temporarily alone, and performed gallant and efficient service.

To Mr. Lafayette Veal, a noble and patriotic citizen of Tennessee, this command and the country are indebted for laborious and indispensable services, in guiding our right under constant fire down Lick creek and the Tennessee river to within half a mile of Pittsburg.

Brigade and regimental reports were duly forwarded, and the causes which have delayed the handing in of this report are known to the commanding general.

I am, major,
Very respectfully,
Your obedient servant,
J. M. WITHERS,
Brigadier General, commanding Division.

Major GEO. G. GARNER,
Assistant Adjutant General.

Report of Col. J. Q. Loomis, commanding First Brigade.

CAMP NEAR CORINTH, MISS.,
April 13th, 1862,

D. E. HUGER,
Captain and Assistant Adjutant General:

SIR:—Herewith I have the honor to transmit such of the reports as I have been able to procure from the regimental commanders.

To attempt a report of the brigade would be a difficult work upon my part. The officers who commanded during the engagement are either killed or wounded; and those upon whom the labor should more properly devolve, and who could more properly speak of the action of the brigade, are absent.

We engaged the enemy at seven and a half o'clock A. M., on the 6th instant, under command of Gen. Gladden, and in a short time, while leading a charge upon the enemy's lines and battery, that gallant officer received a wound, of which he has since died. In his death, our country has sustained a serious loss. He was one of nature's noblemen; a good soldier, an accomplished gentleman, and a true patriot. Long will his name live in the memory of those whom he so gallantly led against our enemy's forces. About this time, too, Major Armstead, of the 22d Alabama regiment, fell, a true patriot and brave soldier, in the full discharge of the duties of his position. While we pause to drop a tear of sorrow upon his grave, let us be encouraged to emulate his brave deeds.

After Gen. Gladden was wounded, the command devolved upon Col. Adams, of the 1st Louisiana infantry, who continued in charge, doing deeds of noble daring, until about 2 o'clock, P. M., when he fell severely wounded. Colonel Deas, of the 22d Alabama, then took command for the rest of the day, receiving several wounds, but still remaining upon the field, deporting himself as a true soldier, exposing himself to the fire of the enemy, and winning the hearts of the whole brigade. On Monday, the brigade becoming disunited, attached themselves to different commands, but continued on the field until ordered to retire.

So far as came under my observation, the officers deported themselves as *men*, fighting nobly for all that is most dear, "life, liberty, and the pursuit of happiness." The undersigned hopes that in a short time, those who commanded the brigade may return to their wonted health, and be prepared to make a report that will do full and ample justice to a command that bore itself so gallantly on the field.

Very respectfully, your most obedient servant,

J. Q. LOOMIS,

Colonel commanding 1st Brigade, Withers' Division.

Report of Col. Daniel W. Adams.

CORINTH, MISS., May 20, 1862.

D. E. HUGER,

A. A. G., General Withers' Division:

SIR:—As the Col. of the first regiment of Louisiana infantry in the early part of the day, in the battle of Shiloh, on the 6th of

April, 1862, in command of my regiment, and subsequently in command of the brigade to which it was attached, it was my duty to have reported to you before this, but I have been delayed, by the effects of the very severe wound I received, until the present moment.

As you are aware, Gen. Gladden's brigade, to which my regiment belonged and constituted the right, were attached, on the evening of the 5th April, to Gen. Hardee's division, and was placed on the right, and in that position went into the battle on the morning of the 6th. As we approached the enemy, we found immediately in front of us the encampments of several regiments and the head-quarters of Gen. Prentiss, who was in command of that division of their army. Their line of battle, composed of infantry, supported by artillery, was formed just outside of their encampments, with detachments of sharpshooters in the thick woods and bushes on our right. When we reached a position of about two hundred yards of the enemy's lines, near the hour of half-past eight o'clock A. M., they opened a very heavy fire upon us with the rifled muskets, followed very soon thereafter with the fire of their artillery. In a very short time after the engagement commenced, Gen. Gladden, who was gallantly commanding in the advance of the brigade, received a very severe wound—which afterwards proved mortal—from a cannon shot, and having to be taken from the field, relinquished the command of the brigade in my favor. Finding that the enemy were then pouring a most destructive fire upon us, I ordered a rapid advance of the brigade, to drive them from their cover and position; but, as we advanced, the fire became so very severe, that I found the whole brigade began to falter, and finally to fall back. Fearing the worst consequences, I rode to the color-bearer of the first regiment, Louisiana infantry, the command of which I had turned over to Major Farrar, and seizing the battle-flag, placed myself in front of the brigade and called upon them to follow me, which they did with great alacrity; and leading them close to the enemy's lines, I ordered a charge, which was promptly and effectively executed. The enemy was driven from their position and retreated very rapidly. Following them, we took possession of the encampment and of Gen. Prentiss' head-quarters, and some of the privates of the Louisiana regiment seized and secured seven stand of colors. During our advance and the charge, Captain Robertson's battery of artillery, attached to the brigade, opened on the enemy with great power and effect, and greatly aided in accomplishing the enemy's defeat. Shortly after we had driven the enemy from this encampment and taken possession, I formed the line of battle on the other side of it, for a further advance. The enemy reappeared at a distance of some three or four hundred yards, and apparently, as reported to me, largely reinforced, formed the line of battle, and commenced advancing on us, opening at the same time with their artillery. I immediately ordered Capt. Robertson's battery up, which was rapidly placed in position and returned the enemy's fire with such promptness and great effect, that it drove them from their guns and caused them to abandon their battery, which we afterwards took possession of. About this time Gen. Hardee and staff passed, and the Gen. instructed me to throw out some companies in advance as skirmishers, to see if the enemy were really in front of us, in large force, and to avoid collision with our friends; which I did, and found that the representations were correct, and that the enemy was being reinforced and advancing on our posititon. At this time, I received an order from Gen. Bragg to advance with the brigade, and would have done so immediately, but found that many of the men in the command, had nearly exhausted their ammunition. As soon as this deficiency was supplied, I ordered an advance, when the divisions of Gens. Cheatham and Breckinridge coming up to my right and left, and advancing, a portion of their forces were so interposed between my command and the enemy's, that when within range, I received a message so requesting me, and was constrained to halt and remain in that position for over an hour.

During this time, the enemy opened upon us again with their artillery, when I directed Capt. Robertson to return their fire, which he did with great effect. Capt. ——— battery of artillery, also came up and rendered valuable services and assistance. Awaiting a change of position that could allow me to advance, and riding down the line of the brigade, about the hour of half-past two o'clock, I received a very severe wound from a rifle ball in the head, which caused me to be taken form the field, and I had to relinquish the command to Col. Zack Deas, of the 22d Alabama regiment.

During the time that I was in command of the first Louisiana regiment, and the brigade, the officers and men generally acted with great gallantry and courage, and the brigade is entitled to credit for having carried one of the enemy's strongest positions.

Very respectfully,

(Signed) DANIEL W. ADAMS,

Col. 1st Regiment Louisiana Infantry.

Report of Col. Z. C. Deas.

MOBILE, April 25th, 1862

To D. E. HUGER,
Captain and A. A. General, Corinth, Miss.:

CAPTAIN:—I have the honor to report that, on the morning of the 6th April, this brigade, composed of the 1st Louisiana infantry, Col. D. W. Adams, 21st Alabama, Lieut.-col. S. W. Cayce, 22d Alabama, Col. Z. C. Deas, 25th Alabama, Col. J. Q. Loomis, 26th Alabama, Col. Coltart, and Robertson's battery, Capt. Robertson, under command of Brig.-gen. Gladden, moved out of camp, marching in line of battle, and shortly after 7 o'clock, came upon the enemy, when the engagement commenced. One of their batteries was playing upon us with effect, but in a short time Robertson's battery was brought on our side, which soon silenced theirs. We then charged, driving the enemy flying through their camp. In this charge several colors were captured.

Just before this charge was made, Gen. Gladden, while gloriously sustaining the reputation won in Mexico, at the head of the immortal Palmetto regiment, received a wound from a cannon ball, which proved fatal.

Beyond this camp, the brigade now under command of Col. Adams, was halted, and after a time, a battery stationed near their next camp opened upon us, which was responded to by Robertson's, and after a sharp contest, silenced.

Orders were now received to move forward in support of Gen. Chalmers, and while here, the gallant Adams, when encouraging his men by his reckless daring and apparent contempt of the missiles of death flying thick around him, received a severe wound in the head.

The command of the brigade now devolved upon me, without instructions, without a staff officer, or even one of my own regiment mounted to assist me. I moved forward to aid where I could, and before proceeding far, came up with Gen. Breckinridge, who was warmly engaged on my right. I immediately advanced to his assistance. The fire here was very severe, and I sent back for the 26th Alabama to come up (which they failed to do), and also for a battery, which was brought up promptly, and with this assistance, after a hard and long continued struggle, we succeeded in driving the enemy back. At this point Gen. Bragg came up and ordered me to change direction. Obliquing to the left, in a short time I came upon the enemy again drawn up some distance in front of another camp, and after a short but very sharp engagement, drove them before me, pursuing them to their camp, where I assisted in capturing a large number.

Here, in the hot pursuit, the 21st and 25th Alabama became separated from me in the woods, and before I had time to find them, I received an order from Gen. Withers to form on the extreme left, where I remained until night came on, and then attempted to get back to the camp I had left, but got into a different one. My men being now completely exhausted, and not having had anything to eat since morning, I encamped here for the night.

On inspection I found I had under my command only the 1st Louisiana infantry and the 22d Alabama, numbering respectively 101 and 123 men, with about an average of fifteen rounds of ammunition, although both regiments had replenished during the day.

At daylight on the morning of the 7th, I sent Capt. R. I. Hill to hunt for Gen. Withers' division, and also to get information. He soon returned, and reported that the enemy were advancing. I immediately marched over and formed on the left of a division commanded by Col. Russell. Under his orders we advanced, but perceiving the enemy's skirmishers on our left and rear, fell back to our first position. While here, the enemy opened upon us with artillery, when we moved beyond the crest of a hill, and I placed my command in support of a battery, where I remained until I received orders from Gen. Bragg to attack a force on my left. While marching to this attack, I was joined by the 4th Kentucky, and with these fragments of regiments, numbering together less than five hundred, I attacked two brigades, but after continuing this unequal contest for nearly half an hour, and nearly one-half of my command had been killed or wounded, I gave the order to fall back, which was done in good order. I now formed and moved forward again, with the remnant of my brigade (now reduced to about sixty men), in the last attack under Gen. Beauregard. Here my second horse was killed, and I, having been wounded some time previously, was unable to march.

The indomitable courage and perseverance of the officers and men of this brigade, the willingness and gallantry with which they advanced to the attack when called upon, after having endured almost superhuman fatigues in the desperate and long continued struggles of Sunday and Monday, are deserving of the highest encomiums. Where so many acted nobly it might appear invidious to particularize; but impartiality compels me to record as first in the fight, the 1st Louisiana infantry and 22d Alabama.

I wish here to call the attention of my superiors to such field officers as especially distinguished themselves, under my immediate supervision, for their coolness and gallant bearing under the hottest fire: Lieut.-col. F. C. Marrast, 22d Alabama, Major F. H. Farrar, 1st Louisiana infantry, and Major George D. Johnston, 25th Alabama, and also to Adjutants Kent, 1st Louisiana, Stout, 25th Alabama, Travis, 22d Alabama, and Sergeant-major Nott, 22d Alabama, acting as aids, for their gallantry and bravery in extending my orders. This report is written without having received any of the regimental reports, and without being able to consult with any of the officers, which will account for my not mentioning all the officers of this brigade who distinguished themselves on the field of Shiloh. For this information I beg respectfully to refer to the regimental reports, and also to refer to document *A* for the killed, wounded, and missing.

I am, captain, very respectfully,
Your obedient servant,
Z. C. DEAS,
Col. commanding 1*st Brigade, Withers' Division.*

Report of Col. Deas, of the operations of the 22d Alabama regiment.

HEAD-QUARTERS 22D ALABAMA REGIMENT, P. A.,
CORINTH, MISS., April 11th, 1862.

GENERAL:—I have the honor to report that on the morning of 6th instant, about 6 o'clock, under orders of Gen. Gladden, I moved my regiment out of camp, numbering 404 rifles and 31 officers, and forming a part of Gen. Gladden's brigade. Marching in line of battle, at about 7 o'clock we came upon the enemy, drawn up in front of their camp, where they opened fire upon us, with their infantry and a battery of artillery, to which we responded. Robertson's battery was brought into action, which soon silenced theirs, and shortly afterwards the enemy wavered, and we charged over their dismantled guns, driving them through their camp, where we halted to reform, and after a short time they again opened upon us with another battery, which was silenced by our batteries. We then moved forward a few hundred yards, and halted in support. Here Col. Adams, who was in command (Gen. Gladden having been very seriously wounded by a cannon ball in the first engagement), was seriously wounded, and the command of the brigade devolving upon me, Lieut.-Col. Marrast took command of my regiment, and will finish this report. Major R. B. Armistead was mortally wounded in the first engagement, but he fell where every brave soldier should be found to fall—in the front rank, doing his whole duty, and urging his men on to victory. In him his country has lost a most intelligent and gallant officer.

Very respectfully,

Your obedient servant,

Z. C. DEAS,

Colonel Commanding.

Report of Lieut.-col. S. W. Cayce.

HEAD-QUARTERS 21ST REGIMENT, ALA. VOL'S.,
CORINTH, MISS., April 13th, 1862.

To Lieut. J. STOUT,
Acting Assistant Adjutant General:

SIR:—I have the honor to submit annexed a tabular statement of the loss sustained by my command, (21st Alabama Volunteers,) in the late battle near Monterey, on the 6th and 7th inst., amounting in the aggregate to 198 killed, wounded, and missing.

Called suddenly from the rank of lieutenant to the command of the regiment, having only been placed in charge by Gen. Gladden, on the 5th inst., I would especially express my sense of the great assistance rendered me by Major Stewart, and senior Capt. John F. Jenett, acting as field officers, who, throughout the whole fight, fully sustained themselves as brave and gallant officers. In point of fact, late Sunday evening (when I had the misfortune to have my horse shot, bruising my foot much, and causing me to fall into the hands of the enemy, from whom, however, I was fortunately soon rescued), and Monday morning, the regiment was under the Major's command.

When all did so well, it would seem invidious to make any distinctions; nevertheless, I would mention Lieut. Parker, acting Adjutant; Capts. Chamberlain and Stewart, Lieuts. Rogers, Williams, and Savage, as particularly active in the discharge of their several duties.

The men, as a general thing, behaved with great steadiness, though exposed at times to a perfect hurricane of shot and shell. No less than five men having fallen as color bearers. The movements of the command having all been by brigade; ordered by brigade commandants, and executed under their supervision, I do not deem it necessary to rehearse them.

I am, sir, very respectfully,
Your obedient servant,
S. W. CAYCE.
Lieut.-col. commanding 21st Alabama Volunteers.

Col. Loomis, *commanding 1st Brigade:*

The undersigned having tendered his resignation, the acceptance of which, however, was not received until after the fight, and having been in command as stated in the report of Lieut.-col. Cayce, does hereby respectfully concur in said report, and endorses its recommendations.

F. STEWART,
Late Major 21st Alabama Volunteers.

Report of Lieutenant-colonel J. C. Marrast.

Head-quartes 22d Alabama regiment, P. A.,
Corinth, Miss., April 12, 1862.

General: I have the honor to report, that about 11 and a halt o'clock a. m., Sunday, April 6th, the command of this regiment devolved upon me, in consequence of the wounding of the gallant Col. Adams, 1st Louisiana regiment, and the succession of Col. Deas to the command of the Gladden brigade. Col. Adams fell at half-past 11 o'clock, whilst the two regiments were under cover, the enemy firing upon us with artillery and infantry. We advanced from that position through one of the enemy's camps into a hollow, from which point we discovered the enemy in houses on the hill beyond. Col. Deas ordered me to send two companies to dislodge them, whereupon, Capt. Weedon, in command of his company, A, and Capt. Nott, of company B, gallantly charged the enemy, and driving him before them. The regiment then closed upon the houses, and occupied them as a cover, for about one hour, and did the enemy much damage, who was throwing a heavy fire of artillery and infantry upon us. Our loss in this engagement was very severe. We then charged upon the enemy's position, driving him before us about four or five hundred yards, when he made another stand, pouring into us a heavy fire. We were then halted in support of our artillery, and kept as much as possible under cover, but our loss in this affair also, was considerable. Capt. A. L. Gaines, of company C, was here killed, gallantly leading his company. From this position, the enemy were finally driven back, and retreated beyond their camps, when the regiment was halted and ordered into camp for the night. On the morning of the 7th April (Monday), at daylight, I formed my regiment, numbering 1 field and 18 company officers, and 124 non-commissioned officers and privates. This regiment, together with the 1st Louisiana, under command of Col. Deas, was ordered to march, and form on the extreme left of the line of battle, then being formed, in which position it remained one hour. Orders being received to advance, the regiment moved forward about three hundred yards, in the direction of a point occupied by the enemy's batteries, then playing, without effect, upon us. We then halted in a hollow, under cover. From this position, I threw out a skirmishing party of twenty men, under command of Capt. Hart, of company K. A few minutes thereafter, we were ordered to fall back, the skirmishers not hearing the call to return, Lieut. Wood, of company I, with two men, were ordered up the slope of the hill to warn them, which party has not since been heard from, and are supposed to be prisoners. Capt. Hart's party returned to the command all safe, and reported not having seen them. The regiment was then, with the 1st Louisiana, placed under cover, in support of two of our batteries, where we lay for about two hours, when the whole fell back a distance, perhaps half a mile; when, the new line of battle being formed, my regiment again regained its position on the extreme left, and advanced towards the enemy's position, some three hundred yards, when, under cover of the timber, we engaged the enemy, for perhaps twenty-five minutes, having been left with the 1st Louisiana infantry, isolated and alone, the main line having fallen back to near the original place of formation. In this affair, our loss being severe, we were ordered by Col. Deas to fall back to our position in the line, which was done in good order. Very soon thereafter, the second advance upon the enemy's position was attempted, and after advancing about two hundred yards, were halted. Placing my men under cover of the timber, we opened fire upon the enemy, which was sustained for only a few minutes. Meeting with a very heavy fire from the enemy, our entire line at this time wavered and fell back again to the original position. Our lines being reformed, my regiment in its position on the left, we again advanced towards the enemy, some one to two hundred yards, and very soon fell back again under order. At this time Col. Deas was compelled, from loss of blood from wounds received hours before, to retire from the field, from which time my regiment was represented in every movement made towards the enemy, and never retired without an order, and did not leave the field until the horses and gunners were removed from the two pieces of Capt. Ketchum's battery, which had to be abandoned. Being informed by the officer in command of the battery, that he had been deserted by the troops left for his support, I felt it my duty to volunteer the services of my regiment for his support. When my command left this position, not a man of our army was in front of us.

I beg to mention the following officers, non-commissioned officers, and privates, who were particularly conspicuous for soldierly bearing and bravery, throughout the action of two days:

Capt. John Weedon, of company A.
Lieut. J. M. Whitney, of company A.
Corporal Alexander Inman, of company A, killed.
Corporal S. V. Cain, of company A, wounded.
Corporal W. Sumner, of company A.
Private J. L. Penesy, of company A.
Private J. J. Faught, of company A.
Capt. J. Deas Nott, of company B.
Private Bartlett Anderson, of company B, wounded.
Private H. C. McMillan, of company B.
Capt. A. L. Gaines, of company C, killed.
Private Frank Allen, of company C.
Private Wm. West, of company H.
Capt. A. P. Love, of company I, wounded.
First Sergeant S. J. Skinner, of company I.
Capt. J. R. Northcutt, of company E, wounded.
Sergeant R. J. Moore, of company E, wounded.
Corporal James M. Tedder, of company E, wounded.
Capt. B. R. Hart, of Company K.
Second Lieutenant R. L. Marick, of company K, wounded.
Private Aaron Coffey, of company K.
Private Monroe Brown, of company K.
Capt. E. H. Armistead, of company D.

Capt. R. J. Hill, A. Q. M., wounded.
Adjutant E. F. Travis, wounded.
Sergt.-major H. J. Nott.
Quartermaster-sergt. C. J. Michailoffsky.

Very respectfully,
Your obedient servant,
J. C. MARRAST,
Lieut-col. Commanding.

Report of Col. J. Q. Loomis.

CORINTH, MISS., 13th April, 1862.

A. A. A. GENERAL:

SIR:—I have the honor to submit the annexed report of the losses sustained by the 25th Alabama regiment, in the battle of the 6th and 7th instant. Owing to the prevalence of the measles and mumps, I was able to take but three hundred and five (305) men in the action; of this number —— were lost in killed and wounded.

This regiment formed a part of the 1st brigade of Wither's division, under command of Gen. Gladden. This report not being intended as an eulogy on the regiment, I will only say it did its duty, fighting side by side with the other regiments of the brigade, charging promptly when ordered, and in good order, and only falling back when commanded. With the brigade, it was engaged in every charge and attack on the 6th, and on the 7th, the brigade being disorganized, the regiment fell in with a Missouri regiment, and fought until the conclusion of the engagement.

I remained in command of the regiment until 4 o'clock on the 6th, assisted greatly by my major, Geo. D. Johnston, and Adjutant Stout, whose coolness and intrepidity upon the field is worthy of all praise. About 4 o'clock, I received a wound upon the head from a musket ball, doing very slight external injury, but producing a concussion of the brain, and rendering me unfit for commanding during the rest of the engagement.

Major Johnston then took command, and led the regiment gallantly through the fight.

Three stands of colors were captured from the enemy—one was presented by Major Johnston to Gen. Hardee, upon the field, the other two were thoughtlessly torn up by the men, and taken as mementoes of the battle. The officers, most of them, bore themselves gallantly upon the field.

Capt. Costello, Lieuts. Smith and Slaughter, deserve especial mention. Sergeant Scofield captured two flags. Private Vaun was the first at a battery, and took the color-bearer's horse. Numbers of such instances might be mentioned, if necessary, but all did well —a noble rivalry existed of who should do the most, and the whole brigade acquitted themselves as men should who were fighting for their homes and firesides.

I am, sir, very respectfully,
Your ob't serv't,
J. Q. LOOMIS,
Colonel 25th Regiment, Ala., P. A.

Report of Lieutenant-Colonel William D. Chadwick.

HEAD-QUARTERS 26TH ALABAMA REGIMENT,
April 12, 1862.

TO MAJOR C. D. ANDERSON,
A. A. Gen. 1st Brigade, Wither's Division, Army of the Miss.:

SIR: In the absence of the colonel commanding, it becomes my duty to report the action of this regiment in the battle of the 6th and 7th instant. Our position was on the left of Gladden's brigade, joining the right of Gen. Hardee's command. The regiment entered the engagement exceedingly wearied and without breakfast. I was ordered, on leaving the city the 3d instant, to bring up the rear of the brigade and take charge of the baggage train. The miserable condition of the roads caused an almost incessant bogging of the overloaded wagons. It was, therefore, late at night when we reached Monterey, where we were joined by Col. Coltart, who for the first time took command. We were scarcely quiet in our bivouac when we were disturbed by a heavy shower. The following night was spent in the same manner, and with less rest. On the 5th we reached our line of battle, in front of the enemy's camp. After having rested in place a few hours, we were ordered on picket duty. The night was spent without sleep. Returning to the line of battle a little after daylight, we were ordered forward without a moment's halt. On reaching the scene of action, the regiment was momentarily thrown in rear of our brigade by the troops on our left precipitately rushing in before us while we were crossing a marsh. A perplexing confusion ensued, which it was evident could only be remedied by moving up on the right of our own brigade; which was done, without an order from Gen. Gladden, as we were unable to obtain one. We occupied the only available space in the line, and in a few moments were hotly engaged, contributing a full share to the driving back of the enemy. When the charge was made upon the line and into the camp of the enemy, the 26th was among the first to penetrate them. Passing through the camp, we were halted in rear of the tents, along a line of tents immediately beneath the path of a terrific cannonading between our own and the enemy's batteries. There Major Gwyne was wounded by an exploding shell. After remaining in this position for nearly an hour, and having regained our proper position in our own brigade, we were ordered forward and again engaged the enemy, about five hundred yards in advance of the position first mentioned. The conflict was severe for a short time, when the enemy, falling back, moved to our left. The regiment made a corresponding movement to prevent his flanking us. Here we were exposed to a heavy fire from the enemy's batteries and small arms without being able to return it, owing to the position of one of our own batteries, which had fallen back from the high ground in advance of us, and taken position immediately in our front. After remaining fifteen or twenty minutes in this position, we again moved to the right, and advancing to the margin of an open field, found ourselves again in the midst of a severe conflict. Here Col. Coltart was wounded and the regiment suffered seriously. The colonel being compelled to retire, and Major Gwyne having been disabled, I was left without the aid of any field officer. Our firing was continued briskly until the colonel returned, having had his wound dressed. He was able to remain but a few moments. Seeing the exhausted condition of the regiment, he ordered, or rather advised me, to withdraw it from the field. I resolved, however, to continue as long as the remainder of the command was able to contribute any thing to what I regarded as an approaching triumph. The enemy's fire having ceased for a time, the regiment was ordered to rest in place for a few minutes, after which I determined to advance. Just at this time, however, I was officially informed that Gen. Shaffer's brigade was to come by the road which lay beyond the open field, immediately in my front and parallel with its eastern margin. I at once determined to report this to Col. Deas, then in command of our brigade, and with his concurrence to remain in the position until Shaffer's brigade should approach, and then move in co-operation with it. I was ordered by Col. Deas to do so. Watching the road narrowly,

I discovered a column of at least two regiments approaching by the designated road. On viewing them minutely, aided by Major Mumford, of Gen. Johnston's staff, I found them to be Federal troops. They halted immediately in my front, advanced to the fence and some houses, and opened a severe fire upon us. Feeling assured that the regiments of our brigade on our right had advanced, or would do so, I resolved to charge the enemy and drive them from the fence and houses just mentioned, provided I could get any support on my left that would prevent their flanking me. The gallant Col. Forrest offered his support. The charge was made, and the enemy driven from the position. The position of the cavalry, however, on my left in a tangled wood, prevented their rendering the assistance which they would otherwise have done. The regiment on my right did not fire a gun while I remained in the position. We, however, maintained it long enough to fire about ten rounds, suffering at the same time the most terrific fire from the enemy in our front and from both flanks of his column. He also turned his artillery upon the houses about which we were sheltered. Having only about two hundred men left, and seeing that they must all be sacrificed if I remained, without gaining any material advantage, I withdrew them to a road in rear of the field and awaited orders, the men being quite exhausted. Finding no one to whom I could report, I then moved back to the enemy's camp near where we had entered it in the forenoon. This was about 4 o'clock P. M. Col. Coltart was able to join us at that place, and ordered the regiment a few hundred yards further back, where we spent the night.

Monday morning, April 7, Col. Coltart's condition compelled him to leave the regiment for Corinth. The regiments of our brigade having been scattered, I was ordered by Gen. Withers to report to Brig.-gen. Chalmers. We went into battle in his brigade. Attacks of sickness, extreme exhaustion, and in some cases a want of moral courage, had reduced our number to less than one hundred and fifty men. With these we went into battle, but with very little efficiency, owing to the physical exhaustion of the men and the condition of our arms.

After retiring from the last engagement of the day previous, I had ordered the men to load their pieces which had been discharged, and the unexpected rain of the previous night had wet the loads, so that many of them could not be fired. I had not a ball-screw in the regiment, and could not extract them. Owing to these circumstances, my men were exceedingly dispirited, though they obeyed every order, and the most of them did the best they could. After engaging the enemy twice, I reported the condition of my men and arms to Gen. Withers, who ordered me to retire with them, and remove the impediments of the guns as best I could. I ordered the guns unbreeched and cleaned, which was promptly done, and I reported for orders. By this time, however, the firing had ceased along the whole line, or nearly so, and our forces were being withdrawn. I was ordered into a line of battle fronting the enemy's camp, where I remained until the troops moved towards Corinth, and was among the regiments that brought up the rear of the column.

The commissioned officers of my regiment, with two or three exceptions, behaved themselves in a manner worthy of themselves and the glorious cause which they defended. The non-commissioned officers and privates of the regiment, with an exception of a number for whose whereabouts I am not able to account, fought bravely to the last.

We went into the action of the 6th with 440 men.

Enclosed document A reports the number of killed and wounded.

Enclosed document B reports the number of guns lost and taken, with the circumstances attending.

WM. D. CHADWICK,
Lieut.-Col. commanding 26th Alabama regiment.

Report of the Action of the Second Brigade, Brigadier-gen. James R. Chalmers, commanding.

HEAD-QUARTERS, SECOND BRIGADE, SECOND CORPS,
ARMY OF THE MISSISSIPPI,

CORINTH, MISSISSIPPI, April 12, 1862.

CAPTAIN:—I respectfully submit the following report of the action of the troops under my command, in the late engagement with the enemy near Pittsburgh, on the Tennessee river:

On the morning of the 4th instant, while in command of the advanced forces, at Monterey, Tennessee, I received orders to hold my command ready to march at a moment's notice; and, on the morning of the 5th, we crossed Lick creek, and moved as far as Meckey's, on what is known as the Bark road, leading from the direction of Corinth to the Tennessee river. In obedience to orders, my brigade was under arms and ready to march at two o'clock of the following morning, and stood from that time until daylight, in a hard drenching rain, as the orders to march had been countermanded, on account of the darkness and extreme bad weather. At dawn, the first brigade of this division, under the command of Brig.-gen. Gladden, filed past me, and we, falling into its rear, moved forward until our march was arrested by the column of Major-gen. Hardee, the rear of which had not got in motion when we reached its encampment. After some delay, we moved on to a position about two miles in front of the enemy's line. On reaching the ground, I found our line of battle deployed, and Gen. Gladden's brigade, which it was at first intended should be held in reserve in the second line on my right, was deployed into line of battle and thrown forward into the first line of battle, on the right of Major-gen. Hardee's command, to fill the interval between his right and Lick creek; and there being still another vacancy between the right of Gen. Gladden's brigade and the creek, my brigade was extended in *echelon* in the rear of and to the right of Gen. Gladden, and held in line by battalions at half distance doubled on the centre. Upon an examination of the country, it appeard to me that our progress would be much retarded if we attempted to move by battalion in double column on the centre, and upon the suggestion being made to Brig.-gen. Withers and Major-gen. Bragg, it was ordered that the supporting line should move by the right of companies to the front. In this order we commenced the march early on the morning of the 6th. The space between Owl and Lick creeks was about a half mile narrower where we first deployed our line of battle than it was in front of the enemy's line, and as the space between Gen. Gladden's left and Lick creek increased as we advanced, it became necessary that my brigade should move up into the front line, on the right of Gen. Gladden, which was done, and being now in the front line, skirmishers from each regiment were at once thrown forward. In obedience to orders from Gen. Withers, the right of this brigade was advanced by a gradual left wheel, so that when we first encountered the enemy we were marching in a north-east direction, and met him in line of battle in front of his first encampment on our right.

When we arrived in sight, our line of battle was formed, and the brigade moved steadily forward in the following order: The 10th Mississippi regiment, in command of Col. R. A. Smith on the right; the 7th Mississippi regiment, Lieut.-col. H. Mayson, commanding, second; the 9th Mississippi regiment, Lieut.-col. W. A. Rankin, third;

the 5th Mississippi, Col. A. E. Fant, fourth; 52d Tennessee, Col. B. J. Lea, on the left, and Gage's battery, light artillery, in the rear. When within about one hundred and fifty yards of the enemy, the line was halted, and a heavy firing ensued, in which a number of our men were killed and wounded, and Col. Lea and Major Randle, of the 52d Tennessee regiment, lost their horses. After several rounds were discharged, the order to charge bayonets was given, and the 10th Mississippi regiment, about three hundred and sixty strong, led by its gallant colonel, dashed up the hill, and put to flight the 18th Wisconsin regiment, numbering nearly a thousand men. The order to charge having been given from the right flank, where I was then stationed, was not heard down the line, and, consequently, the 10th Mississippi moved alone in the first charge, though it was quickly followed by the 9th and 7th Mississippi, when the whole line of the enemy broke and fled, pursued by these three regiments, through their camps and across a ravine, about a half a mile, to the opposite hill, where they were halted by command of Gen. Johnson. The 5th Mississippi and 52d Tennessee, having been left behind in the charge, were moved up to their positions, and the 5th Mississippi was now placed next to the 10th Mississippi. The enemy was reinforced, and drew up in our front, supported by a battery of artillery and some cavalry. We were about to engage them again, when we were ordered by Gen. Johnston to fall back, which was done. The enemy supposing that we were in retreat, fired several volleys of musketry at us, whereupon, we faced about, returned their fire, and they ceased firing. Being commanded to remain here until we should receive further orders, we rested about half an hour, when a guide, Mr. Lafayette Veal, was sent to conduct us still further to the right, where we learned that the enemy were attempting to turn our flank. Moving by the right flank, we filed to the right, directly south, until we recrossed the ravine behind us, and when we reached the summit of the opposite hill we moved in a south-east direction, until our right rested upon the edge of Lick creek bottom. Here, again, we were ordered to rest, which we did for some half hour. When we again started forward, a few skirmishers of the enemy, having secretly advanced close to our left, fired upon the 52d Tennessee regiment, which broke and fled in most shameful confusion. After repeated efforts to rally it, this regiment was ordered out of the lines, where it remained during the balance of the engagement, with the exception of two companies, Capts. J. A. Russell and A. A. Wilson, who, with their commands, fought gallantly in the ranks of the 5th

Mississippi regiment. When the orders were received from Gen. Withers to move on, skirmishers were thrown out in front of the whole line, and placed in command of Major F. E. Whitfield, of the 9th Mississippi regiment, who led them with great coolness and with marked ability and skill. Our orders were to swing around, with our right resting on the creek bottom, and to drive the enemy before us towards Pittsburgh, and we accordingly moved forward, advancing most rapidly on the right, and gradually wheeling the whole line.

In this order we were marching, when our skirmishers developed the enemy concealed behind a fence, in thick undergrowth, with an open field or orchard in his front. The width of this orchard was about 350 or 400 yards, and behind it was a very steep and perfectly abrupt hill, at the foot of which ran a small branch. At the base of this hill ran the Hamburg and Pittsburg road, skirting the orchard at its base, and then turning to the right, running along side of it, the orchard running to the right of the road. The ground from the branch to the fence, where the enemy was concealed, was a gradual ascent, and our line was in full view of the enemy from the time it crossed the stream.

The 9th Mississippi was now on the left, and there was a space of about thirty yards between its left and the Hamburg and Pittsburg road. As soon as I discovered the position of the enemy, I ordered up Gage's battery, which, until now, had not been engaged, and put it in position on the hill above the branch. My line moved on across the orchard in most splendid style and perfect order, and, to my great surprise, not a shot was fired until we came within about forty yards of the fence. Then a heavy fire was opened on us in front, and at the same time a column was seen coming, at double-quick, down the Hamburg and Pittsburg road, with the evident intention of getting in our rear and cutting off the whole brigade. As soon as this column was fairly in sight, coming over the opposite hill, Gage's battery opened a well-directed fire on its head, and it was scattered in confusion, and at the same moment our infantry made a charge in front, and, after a hard fight, drove the enemy from his concealment, though we suffered heavily in killed and wounded.

After this fight, our ammunition was exhausted, and the wagons being some distance behind, we lost some time before it was replenished. As soon, however, as the ammunition could be distributed, we moved on with the right resting on the edge of the Tennessee river bottom, with the same orders as before. When we had gone about a quarter of a mile, we again encountered the enemy, in a very strong position on a hill, with a deep ravine in his front, and a very stubborn fight ensued, in which we lost many gallant men, among them the Rev. M. L. Weller, Chaplain of the 9th Mississippi regiment—a pure man, an ardent patriot, and a true Christian—and Capts. R. J. Armstrong and L. C. K. Bostick, of the 5th Mississippi regiment, who fell gallantly leading on their respective companies. Here again Gage's battery did good service, though it was some time before it could be brought into position, owing to the rough nature of the ground, and the want of roads; and I here take occasion to say, that I cannot speak too highly of the energy, skill, and labor displayed by the men of this battery throughout the day, in cutting their way through a thickly wooded country, over ravines and hills almost impassable to ordinary wagons. After about an hour's hard fighting, the enemy again retreated, leaving many of his dead on the field.

About this time, the gunboats from the river began to throw their shells amongst us, and we pressed rapidly forward in line of battle towards the centre, where the battle seemed to be raging fiercely. We were soon met by an officer, stating that he belonged to Gen. Crittenden's staff, and that he had been hotly engaged with the enemy, and needed assistance. As near as I could judge of the position of affairs, our troops were then in a line of battle running from south to north, and facing east or a little north of east. My line was running from east to west, and facing north. Moving at a double-quick over several ravines and hills, we came upon the enemy, and attacked him on his flank. This was the fourth fight in which my brigade had been engaged during the day, and after a severe firing of some duration, finding the enemy stubbornly resisting, I rode back for Gen. Jackson's brigade, which was lying down for reserve in my rear and to my left. I did not see Gen. Jackson, but finding Col. Wheeler, called upon him to take up the fight, which he did with promptness and vigor. I sent a staff officer to command my brigade to lie down and rest until they received further orders, and then followed up Gen. Jackson's brigade myself, until I came upon Major-gen. Bragg, commanding in the thickest of the fight, to whom I reported my action. I had been there but a few moments, however, when some of our troops were driven back in confusion, and Gen. Bragg called out to "bring up Chalmer's brigade."

I rode back immediately to where I had ordered my men to halt, and found that they had not understood the orders, and had pressed on after the retreating foe. Riding rapidly after them, I reached them just after the enemy had raised the white flag, and a number of the enemy had surrendered to the 9th Mississippi, which was then some distance in advance of the other Confederate troops.

Col. Shaw, of the 14th Iowa regiment, and a senior Captain, commanding some companies of the 28th Illinois regiment, surrendered to Major F. E. Whitfield, and the Col. of the 18th Missouri, with a portion of his command, surrendered to Lieut. Donald McKenzie, company K, 9th Mississippi regiment.

About a quarter of an hour after the surrender, some of our troops, supposed to be of Gen. Polk's division, made their appearance on the opposite side of the surrendered camps, and were with great difficulty prevented from firing upon the prisoners. The cavalry very soon arrived, and the prisoners were turned over to them, and were carried to the rear. It was then about four o'clock in the evening, and after distributing ammunition, we received orders from Gen. Bragg to drive the enemy into the river. My brigade, together with that of Brig.-gen. Jackson, filed to the right, and formed facing the river, and endeavored to press forward to the water's edge, but, in attempting to mount the last ridge, we were met by a fire from a whole line of batteries, protected by infantry, and assisted by shells from the gunboats. Our men struggled vainly to ascend the hill, which was very steep, making charge after charge without success, but continued the fight until night closed the hostilities on both sides.

During this engagement, Gage's battery was brought up to our assistance, but suffered so severely that it was soon compelled to retire. This was the sixth fight in which we had been engaged during the day, and my men were too much exhausted to storm the batteries on the hill; but they were brought off in good order, formed in line of battle, and slept on the battle-field, where I remained with them.

Early on the following morning I received notice that the enemy was advancing, and was ordered by Gen. Withers to fall back about a half mile, and form on the right of Gen. Jackson's brigade, and follow him over to the left, where it was supposed the fight would be. We fell back and waited for Gen. Jackson to file past to the left, intending to follow him as directed, but before we could get away the enemy came charging rapidly upon us, and the fight of the second day commenced. We waited quietly until the enemy advanced within easy range, when we opened fire upon him and he fled. We then attempted to move by the left flank, so as to follow Gen. Jackson, when we were again attacked, and a fight of about one hour and a half ensued, from which we retired, after having exhausted our ammunition. During this engagement Major F. E. Whitfield was severely wounded in the hip, and brought to the rear

Our ammunition wagons not being at hand, we fell back to the first camp that we had taken from the enemy, where we found an abundant supply of the appropriate calibre. I sent a staff-officer to Gen. Withers, about an hour before for assistance, and reinforcements now arrived, under my gallant commander (Brig.-gen. Withers), who, it gives me pleasure to testify, was always found at the right place, at the right time, guiding and supporting whatever portion of his division needed assistance. I formed the reinforcements, consisting of the Crescent regiment, Louisiana volunteers, a Tennessee regiment, under Lieut.-col. Venable, and an Alabama regiment, Lieut.-col. Chadwick, into line, and moved them forward to meet the enemy, after having turned over the command of my own brigade to Col. R. A. Smith, of the 10th Mississippi regiment, with instructions to hold himself a thousand yards in the rear, in reserve. The reinforcements skirmished awhile with the enemy, but when the first serious charge was made upon them, they broke, and Col. Smith was compelled to bring my brigade again to the front. The fight raged fiercely for some time, and my men were compelled to retire in some confusion, being overwhelmed by the superior number of the enemy. After retreating about three hundred yards, they were rallied and drawn up in line at the foot of a hill. The enemy pursued slowly, until he came within range of our fire, when he was boldly met, and, in turn, driven back until we had again occupied the ground we had previously left. Here the enemy was reinforced and the fight renewed, and we were gradually being driven back down the hill again, when Col. Preston Smith arrived, with the 154th regiment Tennessee volunteers and Blythe's Mississippi volunteers, who came gallantly to our assistance and took position on our right. Believing that one bold charge might change the fortunes of the day, I called upon my brigade to make one more effort, but they seemed too much exhausted to make the attempt, and no appeal seemed to rouse them. As a last resort, I seized the battle flag from the color-bearer of the 9th Mississippi regiment, and called on them to follow. With a wild shout the whole brigade rallied to the charge, and we drove the enemy back and re-occupied our first position of the morning, which we held until the order to retreat was received, when we fell back in good order, the enemy not daring to pursue. Col. Wheeler, of the 19th Alabama regiment volunteers, was with a small remnant of his regiment at this time fighting with a small remnant of the Mississippians, on foot himself, and bearing the colors of his command. In this last charge, so gallantly made, the 9th Mississippi sustained a heavy loss in the fall of her brave commander, Lieut.-col. Wm. A. Rankin, who fell mortally wounded, after having led his men fearlessly throughout the whole of the first and second day. Most of my command behaved well. Col. R. A. Smith, of the 10th Mississippi regiment, was particularly distinguished for his bold daring, and his clarion voice could be heard above the din of battle, cheering on his men. Major F. E. Whitfield, of the 9th Mississippi regiment, led the skirmishers during Sunday, and deserves great credit for his courage and coolness. He was wounded in the hip early on Monday morning, and taken from the field. Col. Fant and Major Stennis, of the 5th Mississippi regiment, and Lieut.-col. Mayson, commanding the 7th Mississippi, were all conspicuous in the thickest of the fight. All the Mississippians, both officers and men, with a few exceptions elsewhere reported, behaved well. The 52d Tennessee (except two companies, under Capts. J. A. Russell and A. N. Wilson, who fought with the 5th Mississippi,) behaved badly. Gage's battery did manful service on the 6th, but on the 7th was not in the fight. I cannot conclude without mentioning the signal service rendered me by the gentlemen of my staff. To Capt. Henry Craft, Assistant Adj.-gen., I am greatly indebted for the order and system established in a new brigade, composed very largely of troops never before placed in brigade, and having but little knowledge of their respective duties. On the field he rendered all the service required of him, and had his horse slightly wounded when bearing an order. First Lieut. Geo. T. Banks, aid-de-camp, was always at his post, and in a most fearless manner discharged all the duties of his hazardous position. First Lieut. W. T. Stricklin, Adjutant of the 3d Mississippi regiment, who made his escape from Fort Donelson after its surrender, being ordered to report to me for duty, was placed on my staff as Acting-Inspector-gen., and bore himself gallantly during the fight. Capt. B. S. Crump, A. C. S., Capt. Jas. Barr, and Lieut. M. M. Shelley, both of the late 10th Mississippi regiment, rendered me efficient service as volunteer aids. Wm. A. Rains, Sergeant-major, and Fleming Thompson, private in company "K," both of the 9th Mississippi regiment, two brave Mississippi boys of but 17 years of age, accompanied me on horseback, and in the absence of staff-officers bore orders under the heaviest of the fire. Sergeant-major Rains deserves especial notice for having carried an order with promptness and decision, on Sunday evening, when we were attacking the batteries, under the heaviest fire that occurred during the whole engagement. I must also acknowledge the valuable assistance rendered by our guide, Mr. Lafayette Veal, of McNairy county, Tenn., who remained with us closely, and was ever ready to give any information and aid in his power. Without him our movements would have been comparatively in the dark, and much retarded, whilst with his guidance we were enabled to move rapidly towards our desired end. Col. Clanton's 1st regiment of Alabama cavalry held themselves on our right, to support us, and though they rendered no especial service, their presence may have protected our flank from an attack, and I cannot conclude without mentioning Col. Clanton himself, who remained almost all the time with my brigade, and though constantly exposed to the most dangerous fire, exhibited the most fearless and exemplary courage, cheering on those who seemed inclined to falter or grow weary, and with a detachment of his cavalry supplying us with ammunition when our wagons could not reach us. It is impossible to say with accuracy how many prisoners we took, as they were turned over to the cavalry as fast as they surrendered, singly and in squads, and once in a large body, without being counted. The number cannot fall short of sixteen hundred. We went into the fight two thousand and thirty-nine (2,039) strong; of these, about four hundred were of the 52d Tennessee regiment, three hundred of whom were not engaged in the fight, leaving us only seventeen hundred and thirty-nine (1739) men. Of these we had eighty-two (82) killed, and three hundred and forty-three (343) wounded, a return of which has been heretofore made, giving the names of the killed and wounded, and the character of the wounds.

I have the honor to be,
Very respectfully, captain,
Your obedient servant,
JAS. R. CHALMERS,
Brigadier General, com'g. 2d Brigade,
Withers' Division, 2d Corps,
Army of the Mississippi.

Report of Brig.-gen. John K. Jackson, commanding Third Brigade, Withers' Division.

HEAD-QUARTERS THIRD BRIGADE,
WITHERS' DIVISION, SECOND ARMY CORPS, A. M.,
CORINTH, MISS., April 26th, 1862.

Capt. D. E. HUGER,
A. A. General:

CAPTAIN:—I have the honor to report, that after a fatiguing march, and great exposure to bad weather, the 3d brigade of Withers' division, second army corps, army of Mississippi, arrived at the place of rendezvous near the battle field of Shiloh, at about 12 o'clock, on Saturday, 5th April, inst. The brigade was composed of the 2d Texas regiment of infantry, Col. J. C. Moore; the 19th Alabama regiment, Col. Joseph Wheeler; the 18th Alabama regiment, Col. Eli S. Shorter; the 17th Alabama regiment, Lieut.-col. K. C. Favis, and Capt. J. P. Girardey's battery of light artillery, in the aggregate, 2208. The brigade was ordered to take position in the second line on the left of Gen. Chalmers' brigade, whose right rested on Lick creek swamp.

The regiments were first drawn up in line of battle, in the order to form right to left, in which they are above named, with the battery on the extreme left. The infantry were then broken by the right of companies to the front, and ordered to hold themselves in readiness to move at a moment's notice. My brigade remained in this position during the remainder of Saturday, and thus bivouacked on Saturday night.

On Sunday morning, 6th, the order was given for an advance. The infantry and artillery commenced the movement about daylight, moving by right of companies to the front, through the forest, with a view to a rapid formation at any moment, by company into line. The order received and extended was, that the second line should follow up the advance of the first line at the distance of about 1000 yards in its rear, and support it as occasion required; at the same time, bearing off well to the right, and resting upon the left of Gen. Chalmers' brigade, gradually sweeping round by a protracted wheel of the whole line to the left. The march being rapid, by the eagerness of the men to press upon the enemy, which they were urged to do fiercely and furiously. I found that the first line was soon warmly engaged; that solid shot and shells from a battery of the enemy, passing over the first line, and occasionally wounding one of my men. Advancing rapidly, I found that the engagement was between Gen. Gladden's brigade and the enemy, and that the latter had been driven from their camps. Following on, I came up with Gen. Gladden's brigade, just beyond this camp, formed in squares. Just here, heavy firing was heard to the left, and, by order of Gen. Johnston, my brigade was moved in that direction, by the left flank, up a ravine. Before proceeding far, another order was received to change direction and move to the right, as the enemy were deployed there. During this time, Capt. Girardey used his battery, with effect, upon a battery of the enemy, which was playing on us from the brow of the hill opposite.

Moving off, perhaps half a mile to the right, I took position again on the left of Gen. Chalmers'. A camp of the enemy being just opposite to my centre, and separated from it by a deep and almost impassable ravine. The enemy was drawn up in line at the edge of the wood, which skirted his camp. Throwing forward two companies deployed as skirmishers, a sharp fire was provoked from the enemy, and returned with spirit. Girardey's battery was placed in position, on the edge of the hill overlooking the enemy and his camp. By a well-directed fire of shells and solid shot, he caused the enemy to waver, and the infantry who had advanced to the bottom of the ravine, were ordered to charge. They did this with a cheer; the enemy fell back, and the camp was ours. The enemy formed again in the skirt of wood on the opposite side of their camp ground, and poured a hot fire into my line. Ordered to advance, they did so at a double-quick, charged through the camp, and again drove the enemy from his position, who rallied on the next ridge, prepared to meet us, as we ascended from an almost impassable ravine and morass, by which we were separated from them. Planting sections of Capt. Girardey's battery in favorable position, I directed him to open fire upon the enemy. This order was promptly executed, and, after a spirited cannonade, well responded to, the enemy began to waver, and the infantry again charged with a like successful result.

At this point, Gen. Breckinridge rode up, and requested me to come to his relief. Upon inquiring of him, I learned that the point at which he required relief was in the direction of my advance, according to Gen. Withers' orders. I assured Gen. Breckinridge that I would be there as soon as the enemy, who continued to oppose me with a stubborn resistance, could be driven before me. For a mile and a half or more, this fighting was uninterrupted, save when the enemy were retiring to reform. By this time, gradually swinging or wheeling round, my brigade was moving towards the front, occupied at daylight in the morning, having completely outflanked the enemy, and driving him back without pause. Drawn up now behind the rails of a worm fence on the opposite side of a field, he hoped to stay our progress by a murderous fire, as my men crossed the open space. But the effect was fruitless of the desired result, and our advance was unchecked. The engagement in the wood beyond the field was the hottest of the day, and while progressing, Gen. Chalmers rode up to me, and informed me that he had turned over that fight to my brigade, and that his was resting. One of my regiments, returning for want of ammunition, was rallied, and sent back into the contest, with orders to use the bayonet. Immediately afterwards, Gen. Gladden's brigade was ordered to my support, but before becoming actively engaged, the enemy displayed a white flag. An officer of the Texas regiment was sent to receive the surrender, which he did, along with several of the swords of the officers.

Cavalry being sent around to our right, took charge of the prisoners (about 1500 in number) and carried them to the rear. Col. Shorter, with his regiment, was ordered to carry these prisoners to Corinth, which was done. My brigade was ordered to change direction again, face towards Pittsburg, when the enemy appeared to have made his last stand, and to advance upon him. Gen. Chalmers' brigade being again on my right and extending to the swamp of the Tennessee river. Without ammunition, and with only their bayonets to rely on, steadily my men advanced, under a heavy fire from light batteries, siege pieces, and gunboats. Passing through the ravine, they arrived near the crest of the opposite hill, upon which the enemy's batteries were; but could not be urged further without support. Sheltering themselves against the precipitous sides of the ravine, they remained under this fire for some time. Finding an advance, without support, impracticable, remaining there under fire useless, and believing that any further forward movement should be made simultaneously along our whole line, I proceeded to obtain orders from Gen. Withers; but before seeing him, was ordered by a staff officer to retire. This order was announced to me as coming from Gen. Beauregard, and was promptly communicated to my command.

In the darkness of the night, which had then fallen upon us, my regiments became separated from each other. Col. Favis, with the

17th Alabama, falling back to the line occupied by us in the morning. Col. Moore, with the Texas, and Col. Wheeler, with the 19th Alabama, taking a different position, and the battery, with which I remained, falling back to Shiloh Church. Col. Shorter, with the 18th Alabama, had taken the prisoners to Corinth. Thus closed Sunday, 6th April, upon my brigade.

On Monday morning, my battery was early sent into action, but as I saw no more of it until after the order to retire, I refer to the accompanying report of the Capt., Girardey. So, also as to the regiments, I refer to the reports of their respective commanders.

Finding myself without a command, after diligent search for them, I was requested by some staff officer, not now recollected, to take command of three new regiments near the road below Shiloh Church, to rally all stragglers upon them, and be ready to move up at any moment. This was done as far as possible, it being very difficult to make men reform, after they have lost their pride sufficiently to obtain their consent to fly. Two lines, at different points, were thus formed, but never required for action, as the enemy did not pursue. Returning, I found Col. Favis' 17th Alabama, commanded by Gen. Breckinridge, and used by him to stop stragglers, and form another line at the place of our halt on Saturday. Passing on to Monterey, where I consulted with Gen. Chalmers as to the disposition of some prisoners and as to his remaining there. I arrived at Corinth at 11 1-2 P. M., Monday night.

One stand of colors captured by Col. Wheeler's 19th Alabama, two by Lieut.-col. Favis, 17th Alabama, and three by Capt. Girardey's company, have been returned.

Where all the officers of my command, with a few rare exceptions, conducted themselves so well, I could not mention any particularly without doing the injustice of silence to others. To the officers of my staff, I am indebted for their courage, accuracy, and activity.

I am, captain, your obedient servant,

JOHN K. JACKSON,

Brig.-gen., commanding 3d Brigade,
Withers' Division, 2d Army Corps, A. M.

Report of Col. John C. Moore, of the Second Regiment Texas infantry, in action of the 6th of April.

HEAD-QUARTERS 2D REGIMENT, TEXAS INFANTRY,
CAMP NEAR CORINTH, MISS., April 19th, 1862.

Capt. J. B. CUMMINGS,
A. A. General, 3d Brigade, Withers' Division:

SIR:—I have the honor to make the following report of the part taken by the 2d regiment Texas infantry, in the battle of Shiloh, on the 6th instant.

In justice to my regiment, permit me to say that no other regiment entered the fight on that day under more unfavorable circumstances than the 2d Texas. Leaving Houston, Texas, on the 12th March, we arrived here on the 1st April, after a long and exhausting march. Remaining in camp but one day, we left on the 3d for the field of Shiloh. Not having received the provisions ordered for the regiment, we left with a short two and a half days' rations. By Saturday morning our provisions were all exhausted, yet the men moved forward with light hearts and buoyant spirits without a murmur of complaint. By this time many who had left camp with worn out shoes became totally barefooted, and many of the men, as well as some of the officers, returned to camp, after the battle, in their bare feet.

Early on the morning of the 6th, while the regiment acted as a support to Gen. Hardee's division, we lost one man killed, and two or three wounded. At about half-past 8 o'clock we moved to the right, and took position in the front line of battle, on the left of Gen. Chalmers' brigade. This brought us near a small stream, which I was told was known as Lick creek. Soon after we took position, the enemy deployed as skirmishers, opened fire on our line, wounding two or three of our men, and also mortally wounding Capt. Brooks, who was carried to the rear, and died on the 8th. The enemy being concealed behind trees and logs, Capt. Smith was ordered to deploy his company as skirmishers, cover our front, and ascertain the exact position of the enemy; at the same time Capt. Girardey's battery was thrown forward, and by firing into the woods, seemed to disperse the enemy's forces. Being now ordered to advance, we proceeded some two or three hundred yards to the brow of a hill, where the enemy appeared in considerable force, within range of our guns, but on the opposite side of a narrow bottom of low land. Opening fire, we advanced to the foot of the hill, when we gave the command "double-quick," which being done, the right of the regiment passing through an open field under a fire, we reached the brow of the opposite hill and halted. We were now near the enemy's camp, and under the fire of a large force, at a short distance in front, sheltering themselves in houses, which were in front of their camp. Seeing the right of our regiment suffering severely, and the advantage of the enemy in their sheltered position, we again gave the order "charge," which was well done, driving the enemy before us from their camps, killing and wounding a considerable number, and taking six prisoners. On reaching the road, passing though the encampment, we were fired on by a large force to our right, from behind or through openings, from a collection of farm houses. As the enemy seemed intending to turn our right flank, we fell back some fifty yards, protected from their fire by rising ground in front. Here we changed direction to the right, and again charged the enemy, driving them from the houses across a ravine and over the opposite hill. On reaching the ravine we halted; Capt. Girardey's battery having opened a fire from the hill in our rear, the shots passing over our heads. While in this position, Gen. Chalmers' forces were engaging the enemy on our right. They were exposed to a galling fire from a large force, and though fighting like heroes, seemed at last to be giving back, and Capt. Girardey's battery suffering severely at the same time, Adj. Mangum (a brave and efficient officer,) was ordered to request the battery to cease firing, that we might advance to the assistance of the Mississippians, without being exposed to the fire of our own guns. The space between the right of Col. Wheeler's regiment and the left of Gen. Chalmers' brigade being sufficient for a line of only three companies, we ordered forward Capts. Smith, McGinnis, and Christian, with their companies. They advanced at a double-quick, and after a short but severe engagement routed the enemy, being supported by the other companies of the regiment close in the rear of the line. As we passed over the ground in front, the number of dead and wounded showed that our balls had done fearful execution in the ranks of the enemy.

The line being now reformed, after crossing a deep ravine, we were ordered to sweep around by a slow wheel to the westward, and proceed to where we now heard a heavy fire of artillery and musketry. After proceeding in the direction for perhaps half a mile, we came up to a force covering our entire front, and to the right and left as far as we could see through the woods. In this position, the right of our regiment rested in a deep ravine, the left on a high hill, exposed to a very heavy fire, which passed over or through the ranks of our friends in front. Here we halted and ordered the men to lie down, but remained in this position but a few minutes, amidst a perfect shower of balls, wounding several of the men, though prostrate on the ground. The left wing being now thrown into some confusion under a fire which they could not return, it fell back some fifty yards and reformed. The command "forward," was given immediately, and on coming up again to the first position it was found that the right wing had advanced as the left fell back. Being but a short distance in the rear, the left advanced at double-quick and soon joined the other, in certainly one of the most brilliant actions of the day. We think we may be permitted to say that the regiment had already done noble work, yet this last and closing action of the day may be remembered with pride by the officers and men of the 2d Texas infantry. They charged the camp with a shout, in the face of the enemy's artillery and musketry, and though they met an obstinate resistance, they soon drove the enemy from their encampment into the roads beyond, taking some five or six prisoners on the ground. On reaching the north-western side of the encampment, where we were still engaging the enemy, a Federal officer (a Colonel) came dashing up near our lines, and cried out, "boys, for God's sake stop firing, you are killing your friends!" The boys, not being deceived, ordered him to halt as he dashed off; but, declining to accept the invitation, he soon fell dead with his horse. At this place our men also shot an officer who was driving off at a furious rate in a buggy. On being shot, he sprang to his feet, and fell backwards from his buggy. We now observed the enemy in full force, formed in line to the left and front of us, and suppposing from their position that it was their intention to try to turn our left flank and cut us off from our forces on that side, the interval on the left being at that time very considerable, we fell back about one hundred yards to the left and rear, still keeping up a fire at long range. While the line was thus being formed, the cry "white flag" was raised, the command "cease firing" given, and in a few minutes an officer, unknown to us, rode up and said that a force of one thousand of the enemy wished to surrender to the Texas regiment. At this time a regiment of cavalry passed between us and the prisoners, and before we could get further information on the subject, they were in the hands of other parties. This caused our men much regret, as they had just had an obstinate contest with these very men, and we feel certain it was their Colonel who was shot from his horse, as he rode directly from their position in approaching ours. Capt. Ashbel Smith was wounded severely in the arm at this camp. He had borne himself with great gallantry during the day, and we thus lost for the present the services of a brave and excellent officer.

From this point we marched to the eastward, towards the Tennessee river. As we were about marching, a shell from the enemy fell and exploded in our ranks, mortally wounding two men of Capt. Orien's company. After advancing about half a mile we came to a deep ravine, and found ourselves in front of a heavy battery of the enemy, at the distance of four or five hundred yards to our front. They opened on us a fire of shot and shell, which did but little damage, as the balls generally passed over our heads and across the ravine. After having kept up this fire for a considerable time, they then changed the position of some of their guns, placing them so as to bring on us a raking fire up the ravine from our right. Seeing this state of things, we made a rapid retreat from our unpleasant position, and proceeded back to the camp last taken, having been told that we would here receive further orders. It was dark when we reached the camp, and after waiting an hour or so, we bivouacked near the encampment, in a drenching rain.

First Lieut. Dan Gallaher was sent to look for ammunition soon after we took this camp. He did not return, and is supposed to have been taken prisoner. After having passed the night in the rain, and having had our sleep occasionally disturbed by the bursting of a shell in our vicinity, we proceeded early the next morning about half a mile and joined Col. Wheeler's regiment.

Here we received orders from Gen. Withers to march again to meet the enemy. After marching some two miles we halted near the enemy's lines, and having been placed in command of a brigade, we turned over that of the regiment to Lieut.-col. W. P. Rogers.

Lieut.-col. Rogers and Major Runnels, of this regiment, did their duty nobly on the 6th, and we doubt not their coolness and courage attracted the attention of the general commanding. The company officers, so far as we could observe, with one exception (Lieut. Foster, now under arrest), performed their respective parts bravely, so much so, indeed, that it seems to me, if I should mention favorably only a portion of them, I would be doing injustice to the others. Accompanying this report, I have the honor to submit a list of the killed, wounded, and missing, on the 6th. This report is much longer than I intended it to be when I commenced, but I trust you will at least excuse this, perhaps its least fault. I am, captain,

Very respectfully, your obedient servant,

JOHN C. MOORE, *Col. 2d regiment Texas Infantry.*

P. S.—I have omitted to state that at the last camp taken by our regiment, we captured two pieces of artillery, having shot the horses, and the cannoniers making their escape on foot. We were thus unable to bring them off the field.

JOHN C. MOORE,
Col. 2d regiment Texas Infantry.

Report of Col. S. C. Moore, of the 2d regiment Texas Infantry, in the action of the 7th instant.

CAMP NEAR CORINTH, MISS.,
April 21, 1862.

A. A. G., Withers' Division:

SIR: I have the honor to report that, on arriving near the enemy's lines on Monday, the 7th instant, I was placed, by Gen. Withers, in command of a brigade, composed of the 2d Texas, 19th and 21st Alabama.

Up to this date I have received no reports from the commanders of regiments. Being only nominally in command of an irregular organization, reports of the action may have been made to other commanders.

Before advancing, an officer and staff rode up and inquired for Gen. Withers. The general not being present just then, the officer gave orders to throw forward two companies as skirmishers, cover our front, learn the position of the enemy, and then fall back. On asking from whom I received this order, I was answered, "Gen. Hardee." The order was given, but before executed was countermanded by the same authority. The brigade then moved forward under the personal direction of Gen. Hardee and staff, with a careful warning that Gen. Breckinridge was in our front engaging the enemy.

After advancing some two hundred yards, a large force was seen in our front and to the right, but in a thick wood. This force was still believed to be our friends, and the caution again and again given not to fire, as they were Breckinridge's men. The left wing of the brigade passing through an open field was now considerably in advance of the right, which passed through a thicket of low small brushwood. We soon learned that a truly sad mistake had been made respecting the force in front; for, permitting us to come up near their lines, where they had a deadly cross-fire on our left wing, still in an open field, the enemy, from the shelter in the woods, now poured into the whole line a most murderous fire. So sudden was the shock, and so unexpected was the character of our supposed friends, that the whole line soon gave way from right to left in utter confusion. The regiments became so scattered and mixed, that all efforts to reform them became fruitless. Many of the officers, however, succeeded in gathering squads, and joined other commands during the battle.

I have included in my report of the 6th the entire number of killed, wounded, and missing of the 2d regiment Texas infanty.

I am, sir, very respectfully,

Your obedient servant,

JOHN C. MOORE,

Col. 2d regiment Texas Volunteers.

Special Report of Col. J. C. Moore.

HEAD-QUARTERS THIRD BRIGADE, WITHERS' DIVISION.
CAMP NEAR CORINTH, MISS., April 25, 1862.

Capt. D. E. HUGER,
A. A. G., Withers' Division:

SIR:—Having heard that the 2d regiment Texas infantry, of which I am proud to have the honor of being colonel, has been spoken of as having acted badly on the field of battle, on the morning of the 7th inst., I feel it my duty, in justice to the regiment, to make the following "special report" for the information of the general commanding the 2d corps, army of the Mississippi.

As stated in my former report, I was not in command of my regiment on that day; having been placed by Gen. Withers in command of a brigade, composed of the 19th and 21st Alabama, and 2d Texas. Having formed the brigade in line of battle as ordered, the 21st Alabama on the right, the 2d Texas in the centre, and the 19th Alabama on the left, a general officer and staff rode up and inquired for Gen. Withers, who had just left our position. He ordered me to throw forward skirmishers, cover our front, feel the position of the enemy, and then fall back. On asking from whom

18

I received the order, I was answered, "Gen. Hardee." The order was immediately given for deploying the skirmishers, but before it could be executed it was countermanded, and the brigade, except the 19th Alabama, who acted as a support, advanced under the personal direction of Gen. Hardee and staff, who generally gave orders directly, and not through myself as commander of the brigade.

I beg permission to state here, that Gen. Bragg, who did me the honor to recommend me for promotion, perhaps feels (as I am told) some little doubt of the propriety of the recommendation, since hearing the remarks referred to at the beginning of this report. If, as commander of the brigade, I had taken upon myself the responsibility of advancing upon the enemy without first feeling his position with skirmishers, then I might justly be held responsible for the result. But such was not the case.

Before the advance was ordered, we were told that the brigade was to act as a support to Gen. Breckinridge, who was engaging the enemy in front, and while advancing, we were warned again and again, by one or more staff officers, not to fire on our friends in front. The greater part of the 2d Texas passed over an open field, and the enemy allowed them to approach near their lines before firing. Even after the enemy opened fire, the officers of the 2d Texas report the order was still given not to fire on our friends, and in one instance, after a private returned the fire of the enemy, a staff officer rode up and drew his pistol, threatening to "blow off the man's head if he fired again." Major Runnels reports, that while the order not to fire was being repeated to the regiment, he saw that the force in front were not friends, and ordered the men to fire and charge them; but just at that time a most galling fire was poured into the regiment, and the cry "fall back," being heard in a voice unfamiliar to him, he countermanded the order, but it was too late to be effective. The men fell back in great confusion, with the result detailed in my former report. I doubt not that our failure to drive back the enemy at this time and place, may be attributed wholly to the mistake regarding the character of the force in front, the multiplicity of the commands, and the consequent confusion of the men, not knowing whom to obey.

I am, sir, very respectfully,

Your obedient servant,

JOHN C. MOORE,

Colonel 2d Texas, commanding Brigade.

Report of Col. Joseph Wheeler.

HEAD-QUARTERS 19TH REGIMENT ALABAMA VOLUNTEERS,
CAMP THREE MILES FROM THE FIELD OF SHILOH,
April 12th, 1862.

To Capt. JOSEPH B. CUMMING,
Assistant Adj.-gen. Third Brigade, Withers' Division:

CAPTAIN:—In compliance with General Order No. —, from head-quarters of this army, I have the honor to state that on the morning of the 6th instant, the 19th regiment Alabama volunteers formed a part of Gen. Jackson's brigade, the second from the right of the second line of battle. When the first line opened the engagement, a few of our men were wounded by the scattering shots of the enemy. We were then ordered forward, and entered the most advanced Federal camps behind the first line. We were then directed to move about a mile to the right and front, where we formed in first line of battle, in which we continued during the remainder of the day. Gen. A. S. Johnston ordered the regiment, with his own lips, to charge the camps of the 59th Illinois regiment, to do which it was necessary to pass down a deep ravine, and mount a steep hill on the other side. This duty was performed by the regiment under a heavy fire from a screened foe, with rapidity, regularity, and cool gallantry. But little resistance was offered after reaching the camps, as the enemy fled before us to the crest of another ravine back of, and about two hundred yards from, their camp. After forming line in the face of the enemy, we were ordered to lie down while the artillery was placed in position to our rear, and fired over our heads sufficiently to shake their line. The regiment then moved forward rapidly, driving the enemy before it, and dislodging him from every place he attempted to make a stand, taking several prisoners, and killing and wounding large numbers. It was now about three o'clock in the afternoon. The regiment had been marching and fighting since half past six A. M., had been through three of the enemy's camps, and in three distinct engagements. The enemy being now driven from all their positions on our right, we were ordered to march to the left and centre, to where a heavy fire was going on. The regiment changed front, forward on the tenth company, and marched rapidly by the right of companies to the front, some one and a half or two miles in the direction indicated, coming upon the left of Gen. Chalmers' brigade. The regiment, while marching through a burning wood, encountered a heavy fire from the enemy, who were drawn up in front of and to the right of a large camp, which fire the regiment returned with effect. I was here met by Gen. Chalmers, who told me his brigade was worn out and overpowered by superior numbers, and said the troops must move to his assistance. The regiment then moved quickly to and in advance of his left, and dislodged the enemy from a strong position they had taken in large force, screened by a ridge and house. We advanced about two hundred yards, the enemy having retreated a short distance to another hill, where they were reinforced, and, in a great measure, secured from our fire. The regiment here exhibited an example of cool, heroic courage, which would do credit to soldiers of long experience in battle. Subjected as they were to a deadly fire of artillery and a cross fire of infantry, they stood their ground with firmness, and delivered their fire rapidly, but with cool deliberation and good effect. During this fire, Gen. Chalmers' brigade having retired from our view, finding it necessary to move to the right in order to support Col. Moore, who had just come up with his regiment (the 2d Texas), we were met by a new and warm fire, which was vigorously returned. At this moment the enemy raised a white flag, which caused us to slacken our fire, but as a large force of theirs to the left of our front continued a heavy fire, probably not knowing that their commander had surrendered, I moved the regiment a few yards obliquely to the rear, to secure a more favorable position. His fire was soon silenced. Our cavalry moved up, and conducted the prisoners, amounting to about three thousand men, out before us. The regiment was then ordered to take charge of these prisoners, and started with them to the rear, but was halted and formed in line, with orders to charge the enemy to the river. But after passing through the deep ravine below the lowest camps, we were halted within about four hundred yards of the river, and remained ready to move forward for about half an hour, when night came on, and we were ordered to the rear, and were assigned to bivouac by Gen. Withers. During all this movement, the regiment was under a heavy fire from their gunboats and other artillery.

The regiment slept on their arms during the night. Early next morning, Gen. Hardee came up with a body of troops and directed me to join him. After moving back a short distance, we were met by Gen. Withers, who took immediate command of a brigade, of which the 19th regiment formed a part, and ordered us to move forward to support Gen. Breckinridge. On reaching the ground we were placed on Gen. Hardee's left, and by his order the regiment was deployed as skirmishers before his entire command. After being again assembled, the regiment advanced and engaged the enemy. About 11 o'clock Gen. Chalmer's brigade came to our assistance, and we remained attached to his brigade, continually engaging the enemy, until we were ordered to retire in the evening, when we followed his brigade a short distance to the rear. Gen. Withers here directed me to form a brigade by joining my regiment to some other troops which he placed under my command.

After the remainder of the army had passed to the rear of this brigade, the final order was given for the brigade to retire.

This is a brief and necessarily imperfect report of the action of the regiment during the time called for by your order.

Too high praise cannot be accredited to the company officers and men for their conduct during the entire engagement. Exposed as they had been for two nights previously to drenching rains, without tents, and with little covering, they were of course somewhat jaded; but at the first sound of the enemy's guns they moved forward with a cheerful alacrity and good order, that showed clearly that it was such music as they loved. Under fire almost incessantly the first day, they moved from one position to another, as they were ordered, not only with firmness but with enthusiasm. On Monday some of the officers and men were so exhausted as to be unable longer to endure the fatigues of the march and battle. The remainder evinced the most untiring endurance and excellent courage. The list of casualties herewith presented, amounting to thirty-three and a third per cent. of the aggregate strength of the regiment (both officers and men) on the 6th instant, testifies with sufficient eloquence to the patriotic devotion of the 19th Alabama regiment. One stand of the enemy's colors was taken by the regiment, which has been previously forwarded. The gallantry and heroic courage of the field and staff, Lieut.-col. E. D. Tracy and Major McSpadden, and Adj. Walker, was conspicuous. Adj. Walker was wounded on the 6th, and retired from the field. Lieut.-col. Tracy had his horse shot from under him on Monday, and during the entire two days exhibited marked coolness and noble bearing. He, together with Major McSpadden, remained with the regiment from the beginning of the engagement Sunday morning, until its termination Monday evening. Lieuts. Palmer, Hagood, Barry, Neighbors, Hods, Anderson, and B. F. Porter, and Serg.-major P. L. Griffitts, also remained with the regiment during the entire two days, and displayed commendabl fortitude and manly courage.

I am, captain,
Very respectfully,
Your obedient servant,
JOSEPH WHEELER,
Colonel commanding 19th regiment Alabama Volunteers.

Report of Captain Girardey.

CAMP JACKSON, NEAR CORINTH, MISS.,
April 12, 1862.

To Capt. Jos. B. CUMMINGS, *A. A. A. General,*
3d brigade, C. S. A., of the Miss. Withers' division:

CAPTAIN: I have the honor to report, that on Sunday morning, the 6th inst., the battery under my command became engaged for the first time, about 9 o'clock, with a battery of the enemy, which I observed to be contending with one of our own batteries. The battery of the enemy, being thus exposed to two fires, was soon silenced. In this engagement, we sustained no loss, notwithstanding the enemy's fire was skilfully directed towards us. The enemy's battery was posted in rear of a camp that was located about the centre of the first line of their camps. One of my cannoniers, after the engagement, went to where the battery was stationed and returned with their colors, which I forwarded to Gen. Withers, commanding 2d division.

After leaving this camp, I received orders to take position in front of the brigade on a hill facing the camp of the enemy. In placing the battery in position, I observed some of the enemy's skirmishers stationed behind trees, in a deep ravine on the left and front of the hill. This fact was clearly established, as I was fired at by several, and immediately Lieut. A. Speliers, of my company, shot one of them with a Yankee rifle that was taken from the enemy by one of my cannoniers. I reported the same to the general commanding the brigade, and asked for skirmishers to encounter the enemy (while placing my guns in a position to fire down the ravine), which request was complied with In this engagement Lieuts. Barnes and Speliers' sections were brought into action, the other could not be placed in an advantageous position; we first fired some canister upon the enemy in the ravine, and then shelled their camp, we, consequently, sustained no loss in this engagement. From this place, we pushed forward on the enemy's camp, from which they had retreated and formed on a ridge to the right, where they were screened by a dense growth of bushes; I placed four pieces of my battery fronting the enemy at a distance of about one hundred yards, and two pieces flanking them on the right. We commenced firing with canister, which we continued to use with terrible effect, they resisting us with desperate valor. In this engagement, Lieut. J. J. Jacobus fell mortally wounded, while gallantly commanding his section. Gunner A. Roesel was killed while aiming his gun; both were shot through the forehead by rifle or musket balls. Lieut. C. Speath was wounded in the right arm. John Halbert shot through both arms. J. T. Nethercus shot through the neck. Tho's J. Murphy and S. A. Ingolls in the hip—all bravely engaged at their posts. Our loss in this engagement would have been greater, had it not been for the brave charge made by the regiments, under our gallant commander, Brig.-gen. Jackson.

In three subsequent engagements, during the day, we sustained no loss, excepting two horses wounded. A limber from one of my pieces being broken, I took *one* from the broken battery captured (in the morning's engagement), of the enemy and attached it to my gun. Also replenished my stock of ammunition from that of the enemy; (the Yankee ammunition is in capital order, especially the friction tubes, which are superior to ours; they were of good service in our subsequent engagement). On Monday morning, the 7th instant, my battery being separated from the brigade, I proceeded forward, towards the enemy's line. Approaching Brig.-gen. Claiborn's command, I discovered the enemy's line in the woods beyond an open field. They attempted to form in the rear of Gen. Claiborn's command, who was stationed on my right. I took position directly in front of the enemy and engaged them for a few minutes, when they shifted their position, fronting Gen. Claiborn's command. I then changed front to the left, to support Gen. Claiborn, whose forces had made no demonstration to prevent the enemy's position.

The enemy's battery opened a heavy fire upon us, killing two of my horses and disabling several, also wounding two of my cannoniers (P. C. Buckley by a shell, and B. Wolfe by a musket ball), flesh wounds, both in action at their posts. Having expended the ammunition of two pieces engaged, the caissons of same being detained in passing a branch of a ravine, I ordered them to fall back, and withdrew the three that were in charge of Lieuts. Barnes and Speliers, to form on the right (during the movement, the infantry engaged the enemy), they having lost several horses, were compelled to leave one of their pieces. I returned to get my piece—in passing the enemy's camp, near the open field, I perceived the enemy moving towards our left, and I immediately engaged them, and was joined by Capt. Robinson's battery (without any support of infantry near) in the midst of a heavy and fierce fire of the enemy's battery. I received orders to cease firing. Our brigade (3d), just then passing, I joined and followed them in accordance to orders, under the impression to make an attack upon some other point. I was then called on to detail my cannoniers to man a battery in Gen. Breckinridge's command, to which I complied. We arrived in camp on Tuesday, the 8th inst., and on the 9th received orders to return to Monterey. It was impossible for the entire battery to proceed forward, on account of the used up and worn out condition of our horses, also much of our harness being broken and unserviceable. One section is now, and since that time, on duty at Monterey.

I omitted to state, that at the place of engagement where Lieut. Jacobus fell, Corporal Hughes captured a banner, and private Hill a marker's flag, which I forwarded to Gen. Withers. I also forwarded nine (9) muskets to the ordnance depot. Corporal J. Van Dohlen, of my company, during the entire actions of both days, gave evidence of distinguished courage and bravery. In conclusion, allow me to state that the entire command, throughout the action, fought with cool and determined bravery, and I trust contributed much towards our successful efforts on the battle-field.

I remain, captain, with high consideration,

Very respectfully, your ob't servant,

J. P. GIRARDEY,

Captain commanding Washington Light Artillery,
Georgia Volunteers.

P. S.—Wm. H. Pool was wounded in the breast by a musket ball. Wm. H. Stanley, shoulder dislocated—fell from horse, while on his march on the field, on the 6th inst.

Report of Brig.-gen. Ruggles, commanding Division.

HEAD-QUARTERS RUGGLES' DIVISION, 2D CORPS, A. M.,
CORINTH, MISS., April 25, 1862.

To Major G. G. GARNER,
Assistant Adjutant-general:

SIR:—I have the honor to submit the following report of the services of my division at the battle of Shiloh, Tennessee, on the 6th and 7th instants:

On Sunday morning, the 6th instant, at daybreak, the three brigades composing my division occupied the position in line of battle, in double column at half distance, which had been, under the orders of the previous day indicated, extending from the Bark road on the right, towards Owl creek on the left, a distance of some two miles. Major-gen. Hardee's advance, extending from the Bark road a short distance towards my left, constituted my first line.

About sunrise I sent orders to the commanders of brigades to advance, with deploying intervals, taking the first as the brigade of direction.

Soon afterwards, receiving orders from Major.-gen. Bragg, I directed Col. R. L. Gibson's first brigade to march by the right flank across the Bark road, and then advance in support of the first line, as previously ordered.

I then made dispositions as rapidly as possible, to insure conformity on the part of the other brigades of my division with this change of plan.

The commander of the 3d brigade, Col. Preston Pond, had been already directed to throw one regiment of infantry and a section of Capt. Ketchum's guns into position on the Owl creek road, and prevent his turning our left flank.

Four companies of cavalry, under Capts. J. T. Jenkins (commanding), A. Tomlenson, J. J. Cox, and J. Robins, covered our right and left flank.

Returning from a rapid supervision along the line, when approaching the Bark road, the enemy opened fire from point to point in rapid succession, driving back some troops of the first line.

The Washington Artillery, under Capt. Hodgson, was then brought forward, and two howitzers and two rifled guns, commanded by Lieut. Slocumb, with two guns under Major Hoop, were put in position on the crest of a ridge near an almost impenetrable, boggy thicket, ranging along our front, and opened a destructive fire in response to the enemy's batteries, then sweeping our lines at short range. I also sent orders to Brig.-gen. Anderson to advance rapidly with his second brigade, and as soon as he came up I directed a charge against the enemy, in which some of the 6th Mississippi and 2d Tennessee joined. At the same time I directed other troops to move rapidly by the right, to turn the enemy's position beyond the swamp, and that the field artillery follow as soon as masked by the movement of the infantry. Under these movements, vigorously executed, after a spirited contest, the enemy's whole line gave way, and our advance took possession of the camp and batteries against which the charge was made. I sent, then, orders to Col. Pond to advance rapidly the 3d brigade, swinging to the right, meeting the development of the enemy's line of fire, sweeping the camp on the left, and to prevent surprise on his left flank.

Subsequently, I sent orders to Col. Looney's 38th regiment, Tennessee, and the section of Ketchum's battery then on the Owl creek road, to conform to these movements. In the mean time the first brigade (Gibson's) united with Brig.-gen. Hindman's advance, after having driven the enemy from their camp on our right, engaged in repeated charges against the enemy's new line, now held on the margin of an open field swept by his fire.

The enemy's camps on our left being apparently cleared, I endeavored to concentrate forces on his right flank in this new position, and directed Capt. Hodgson's battery into action there. The fire of this battery and a charge from the 2d brigade put the enemy to flight. Even after having been driven back from this position, the enemy rallied and disputed the ground with remarkable tenacity for some two or three hours against our forces in front and his right flank, where cavalry, infantry, and artillery mingled in the conflict.

As the enemy finally gave way, I directed the movement of the 2d brigade towards the right along the crest of the ridge, following the line of the enemy's continued resistance, and sent a section of Ketchum's battery into action, on a road leading towards Pittsburg, in a position overlooking the broken slope below, to reply to batteries nearly in front, and in the forest to the right, with which the enemy swept a large circuit around, sending also Col. Smith's Louisiana Crescent regiment (3d brigade) to support this battery, then harassed by skirmishers, and to seize the opportunity to charge the enemy's position. I then put a section of guns in position on the road leading along the ridge still farther to the right, which was forced soon to retire under the concentrated fire of the enemy's artillery. Discovering the enemy in considerable numbers moving through the forest on the lower margin of the open field in front, I obtained Trabue's and Standford's light batteries, and brought them into action and directed their fire on masses of the enemy then pressing forward towards our right, engaged in a fierce contest with our forces then advancing against him in that direction. For a brief period the enemy apparently gained ground, and when the conflict was at its height these batteries opened upon his concentrated forces, producing immediate commotion, and soon resulted in the precipitate retreat of the enemy from the contest.

At this moment the 2d brigade and the Crescent regiment pressed forward and cut off a considerable portion of the enemy, who surrendered.

Subsequently, while advancing towards the river, I received instructions from Gen. Bragg to carry forward all the troops I could find, and while assembling a considerable force ready for immediate action, I received from Col. Augustin notice of Gen. Beauregard's orders to withdraw from the further pursuit; and finding soon afterwards that the forces were falling back, I retired with them, just as night set in, to the open field in rear; and as I received no further orders, I directed Gen. Anderson and Col. Gibson to hold their troops in readiness, with their arms cleaned and cartridges supplied, for service the next morning.

For the movement of the 3d brigade during the day, sweeping the left around towards the enemy's centre, and the position held during the night, reference is made to the report of Col. Pond, the brigade commander.

On the morning of the 7th, about 6 o'clock, a message from Col. Pond gave notice that the enemy were in his front in force, and that he would endeavor to hold him in check until he should receive reinforcements. My 1st and 2d brigades moved immediately to the field, and joined Col. Pond in his position.

Some time afterwards, Col. Pond's brigade was ordered to the right, and Col. Gibson's then occupied the left, with a part of which, and some two companies of cavalry, we made the attempt to charge the enemy's right flank and silence a battery there, in which we only partially succeeded, with Col. Fagan's 1st Arkansas regiment, from the exhausted condition of the infantry, and fruitless attempt of the cavalry.

We succeeded, however, after having silenced and dislodged the battery, in maintaining a position well advanced upon the enemy's flank, until recalled and moved to the centre and left of our line, where the conflict raged most fiercely for some hours with varying fortune, until on the approach of night our troops were withdrawn from the field.

In falling back, I commanded the artillery, infantry, and cavalry, constituting the second line, or rear guard, of the movement.

In these successive conflicts, covering a period of nearly two days, the troops of my division displayed almost uniformly great bravery and personal gallantry, worthy of veterans in the cause.

The regiments were remarkable for their steadiness in action, the maintenance of their organization in the field, and their good conduct generally from the beginning to the end of these battles.

In consequence of the hurried nature of my report, I shall not enter into details touching the personal conduct of many officers and men distinguished for their gallantry, or the special and signal services of regiments. Commending, however, the reports of brigade, regimental, and independent company commanders, in all particulars, to special consideration.

It gives me pleasure to acknowledge the services on the field, promptly and gallantly rendered, of Capt. Roy M. Hooe, Assistant Adj.-gen, and 1st Lieut. M. B. Ruggles, aid-de-camp, throughout the successive conflicts; of Lieut. L. D. Sandidge, Acting Assistant Inspector-gen., the greater part of both days; of Major John Claiborne, chief quarter-master, a part of the day; of Surgeon F. W. Hartford, chief surgeon, slightly wounded, who rendered important services in the field until the wounded required his professional services; of Major E. S. Ruggles, volunteer aid-de-camp, until disabled in the left arm by the explosion of a shell near the close of the first day; of Capt. G. M. Beck, volunteer aid-de-camp, and of Col. S. S. Heard, Louisiana volunteers, who volunteered and rendered important services on the field both days, and Dr. P. S. Sandidge, who volunteered professionally, and although partially disabled by being thrown against a tree, accompanied me to the end of the contest. Major Hollinquist, chief of artillery, rendered me important services during a part of the second day.

I have to regret the loss of Lieut. Benjamin King, Acting Assistant-gen, killed during the first day, and of private Munsel W. Chapman, of the 7th Louisiana volunteers, my secretary, towards the close of the second day, and of corporal Adam Cleniger, and private John Stemaker, of Capt. Cox's cavalry, who were killed while serving as couriers under my immediate orders.

I am, sir, very respectfully,
Your obedient servant,
DANIEL RUGGLES,
Brigadier-general C. S. A., Comd'g Division.

Report of Col. Randall Lee Gibson, Commanding First Brigade, Ruggles' Division.

HEAD-QUARTERS, FIRST BRIGADE, RUGGLES' DIVISION,
CORINTH, MISS., April 12, 1862.

Capt. R. M. HOOE,
Assistant Adjutant-general:

SIR:—I have the honor to submit the following report of the part taken by the 1st brigade, Ruggles' division: composed of the 19th regiment Louisiana volunteers, Col. B. L. Hodge; 1st Arkansas regiment, Col. James Fagan; 13th regiment Louisiana volunteers, Major A. P. Avegno, commanding; and the 4th regiment Louisiana volunteers, Col. H. W. Allen, in the action of the 6th and 7th instant. At daybreak on the morning of the 6th, the brigade was posted on the right of Ruggles' division and held in double column at half distance, by command of Brigadier-gen. Ruggles; the right resting on the old Ridge road. Its position was afterwards changed further to the right; the left brought up to the old Ridge road by order of Major-gen. Bragg. I was then ordered to march rapidly by the right flank to the support of Brig.-gen. Hindman. In the execution of this order, we passed within reach of a battery of the enemy on our left, from the fire of which several casualties resulted. Proceeding again by the left flank, in line of battle, we marched through the enemy's camp, and up to the battery, which was taken at the instant by the first line. It was at this point that we first opened fire on the enemy.

I was then commanded by Major-gen. Bragg to attack the enemy in a position to the front and right. The brigade moved forward in fine style, marching through an open field under a heavy fire, and half way up an elevation covered with an almost impenetrable thicket, upon which the enemy was posted. On the left, a battery opened, that raked our flank, while a steady fire of musketry extended along the entire front. Under this combined fire, our lines were broken and the troops fell back. But they were soon rallied and advanced to the contest. Four times the position was charged; four times the assault proved unavailing. The strong and almost inaccessible position of the enemy; his infantry well covered in ambush, and his artillery skilfully posted and efficiently served, was found to be impregnable to infantry alone. We were repulsed. Our men, however, bore their repulse with steadiness.

When a larger force of infantry and artillery was moved to flank this position on the right, a part of the brigade formed on the left of the assaulting line, and a part held a position to the rear in the old field near by. The enemy was driven from his position. From this, his retreat became precipitate, and in obedience to orders, we moved with the main body of the army towards the river.

I was again commanded by Brig.-gen. Ruggles to retire my command from the fire of the gunboats. In this movement, considerable disorder ensued, owing to the fact that all the troops were closely massed near the river. My whole command was kept together for the night, except the 19th regiment Lousiana Volunteers, Col. B. L. Hodge, who, in spite of my exertions and his own, did not succeed in reporting to me until after the battle of the 7th.

We had hardly taken position in line of battle under the immediate supervision of Brig.-gen. Ruggles, early on the morning of the 7th instant, when I was ordered to advance a certain distance and then oblique to the right. An abrupt descent of fifty or sixty feet, perhaps more, from a ridge to a swamp, added very much to the fatigue of the men, and disturbed very decidedly the regularity and rapidity of this movement.

At the command, however, to charge a battery, on the right flank of which we were marching, they advanced with enthusiasm and captured a field battery from the enemy under a galling fire. Finding that a battery was playing upon us from the right, while the enemy was attempting to throw forward a heavy force on our left, with a view of assailing our own battery to our rear and circumventing my entire command, I withdrew the brigade into a ravine and threw forward a portion of the troops to my left, whose steady fire drove back the advancing lines. I also sent forward officers to bring down the battery we had captured, from the summit of the hill upon which our flag was posted, with a view of opening its guns on the enemy, but the want of ammunition prevented this.

At about this moment I was ordered to proceed in all haste to the position assigned me in the morning, near which the battle was now hotly contested. The rout we were obliged to take was, at times, very abrupt, thickly covered with undergrowth, and filled with swampy bottoms. My men were considerably jaded and scattered in the rapid march, but just so soon as they could be formed in line and replenished with ammunition, they were hurried into the fight. Under the inspiration of the presence of our superior officers, Gens. Beauregard and Ruggles, men already sinking with fatigue or wounds, rallied again and entered the lines. It was impossible to preserve much order in this movement. Col. Fagan, 1st Arkansas, led his regiment to the charge. Major Avegno, the 13th regiment Louisiana Volunteers, Lieut.-col. Hunter,—Col. Allen having been wounded the day previous,—rallied the 4th regiment Louisiana Volunteers. The regiments were somewhat mixed, but altogether the brigade moved forward. We continued the conflict until the forces generally retired, and at the last position near the hospital, it was gratifying to see so many officers and men of the brigade formed in line ready to meet the enemy. Under orders from Major-gen. Bragg, I moved to the rear and encamped at Monterey. Such was the part, briefly stated, borne by the 1st brigade in the engagements of the 6th and 7th inst. It is not my duty to laud either the officers or the men. A report annexed will show the loss it sustained in killed, wounded, and missing. That regiments thrown together for the first time should have moved throughout the battle with precision and celerity, was scarcely to be expected. But that their disposition was good, cannot be questioned. A loss of nearly one-third of the command in killed, wounded, and missing, of itself, proclaims the steadfast valor of the men. The names of the brave dead will be treasured in the hearts of their countrymen. Their gallant deeds shall immortalize the last scene of Confederate triumph, and inspire their surviving comrades with the desire to emulate their examples.

Lieut.-col. Thompson, Capts. Gibson, McMahon, and several other officers of the 1st Arkansas, and Capt. Hilliard, of the 4th regiment Louisiana Volunteers, fell at the head of their men on the first day, as patriots fall for country and firesides. They were noble soldiers. On the second day the gallant Capt. Tooraen was killed urging forward his men. Major A. P. Avegno was dangerously wounded rallying his command on the second day. Col. Hodge, 19th, Col. H. W. Allen, 4th regiment Louisiana Volunteers, and Col. Fagan, 1st Arkansas, were everywhere. So likewise were

Lieut.-col. S. E. Hunter, 4th regiment Louisiana, and Capt. Dubroca, 13th regiment Louisiana Volunteers, while in command of their respective regiments. Many of the companies of the different regiments were left without officers. In the capture of the battery on the second day, the officers and men discovered the qualities of true and heroic soldiers. It was in the first charge on the 6th, that Lieut. Ben. King was mortally wounded. Although recently promoted to the staff of Brig.-gen. Ruggles, he was acting as my aid, and up to the moment that he received his mortal wound, bore himself with great coolness and gallantry. He had long been associated with me, and his loss deprived his country of one of its most accomplished, brave, and devoted officers. He fell in the discharge of his duty, and was borne from the field without a word but of good cheer to those near him. Among the living, where all acted well, it would perhaps be invidious to mention any who may have rendered themselves more conspicuous than others.

Mr. Robert Pugh, as my aid on the 6th, rendered valuable services, and Lieut. H. H. Bein, A. A. A. G., also during the same day, was of very great assistance to me.

The loss of so many brave officers and true men, together with the hardships endured in falling back to this point, had at first a depressing effect on the command, but it is rallying very fast, and will again move forward with resolution to meet our defeated foe.

I have the honor to remain, captain,

Your obedient servant,

RANDALL LEE GIBSON,

Col. commanding 1st Brigade, Ruggles' Division.

Report of Col. B. L. Hodge.

HEAD-QUARTERS OF 19TH REGIMENT LA. VOLS.
Corinth, Miss.

To Col. R. L. GIBSON,
Commanding 1st Brigade, Ruggles' Division:

SIR:—In pursuance with your orders, I have the honor to submit herewith a brief report of the part taken by my regiment in the engagements with the enemy, on the 6th and 7th inst., at Shiloh church.

My regiment being on the right of the 1st brigade of the division commanded by Brig.-gen. Ruggles, was bivouacked on the night of the 5th inst. immediately to the right of the "Bark," or "Old Bark road," as I understood the road to be called that led to the enemy's encampment. At half-past 5 o'clock A. M., on the morning of the 6th, we commenced the march, and in accordance with your orders, I conducted the regiment so as to leave space for the 1st Arkansas regiment, Col. Fagan, which was immediately on our left, to deploy into line.

Advancing to the front in conformity with these instructions, my command soon crossed over to the right of the road, when Gen. Bragg himself, in person, ordered me so to conduct my regiment forward, that when formed into line of battle the said road should be immediately on my right.

Having repassed to the left of the road, I continued to move forward rapidly, until we came in sight of the enemy's camp, when, by your order through Mr. Pugh, I halted the regiment, having previously deployed them into line. At this time my regiment was in the woods, the 1st Arkansas on my left, in a field. Immediately after our line halted, a battery of the enemy, posted on an eminence to the left and rear of their front line of camps, opened on us with shot and shell. Although exposed to this fire for fully half an hour, only two of my men were wounded; the guns of the enemy at this point being served with little effect, except upon the tree tops around us. This battery having been captured by the troops of some other command, and our brigade having been moved forward a short distance beyond the outer line of the enemy's camps, my regiment upon the verge of an old field, we for the first time engaged the enemy. Seeing that the distance was too great for our arms to do execution, we ceased firing after two or three rounds. The enemy again noticed our appearance by a few shell, but with even less effect than before.

From this point we moved about half a mile to the right, and a little in advance. Passing through a wheat field, we crossed a road leading in the direction of Hamburg. At this time the 1st Arkansas and my regiment were well together in line, as I could see while passing through the field. Just after crossing the road, my regiment entered a small farm, a log cabin near the centre, our line extending across the field. We had advanced midway the little farm, which is about one hundred and fifty yards in width, when the enemy, lying in ambush about eighty or one hundred yards beyond the outer fence, and directly in our front, opened fire upon our entire line. Although the fire was not expected at the moment, the advance of the regiment was not checked in the slightest degree, but moving forward steadily to the fence, the men commenced to deliver their fire at will. Owing to the impenetrable undergrowth between the enemy's position and ours, I was unable to see him; and from the manner of the men looking through the bushes as if hunting an object for their aim, it was apparent that they, too, were unable to descry the concealed foe, and were only firing at the flash of the enemy's pieces. Seeing that my men were being rapidly shot down, and having no reason to believe that we were inflicting equal injury upon the enemy, I gave the order to cease firing and charge bayonets. Officers and men alike obeyed the order promptly. So dense and impenetrable became the thicket of undergrowth, that after my men had boldly forced their way twenty or thirty steps into it, and it seeming impossible to make further progress, I again gave the order to commence firing. The regiment now gradually fell back to the fence. Finding that the enemy were now opening a cross fire upon us from our left, and seeing a large number of my small command killed and wounded, I deemed it my duty to order the regiment to fall back to the other side of the little farm, which was accordingly done in good order. In this unequal contest, unequal on account of the enemy's local position, the regiment sustained heavy loss. In this one action, out of little less than three hundred, we had lost, in killed and wounded, between forty and fifty as brave and gallant men as ever risked their lives in the defence of a righteous cause.

Adjutant J. P. Harris, Lieut. Clark, of company I, Lieut. Spears, company C, here fell severely wounded. As of others, so I have the pleasure of bearing testimony of these, they did their duty well and nobly.

Having fallen back beyond the small farm, I halted the regiment and waited in the hope that the enemy would leave his covert and give us a fair fight. But he too fully appreciated his great advantage of position to give it up. Remaining in this position a short time, having no order from you or our division commander, I received an order from Gen. Bragg, transmitted through one of his staff, to advance again and attack the same position from which we had just withdrawn. Of course the order was obeyed without delay, but I requested the officer to say to the general that I thought it impossible to force the enemy from this strong position by a charge from the front, but that a light battery playing on one flank, and a simultaneous charge of infantry on the other, the position could be carried with but small loss. Again we advanced into the little farm, and again, when midway the clearing, the enemy opened fire upon us. Again we pressed on to the outer fence directly in front of his ambuscade. Here we remained exposed to his merciless fire for over half an hour, without the power to inflict any apparent injury upon the hidden foe. In justice to my command, again I ordered them to fall back, which was done in as good order as before. In this second attack, we had lost, in killed and wounded, fifteen men of desperate courage and unflinching bravery. Among them, Lieut. Leverett, of company D, mortally wounded, Lieut. Maples, company B, slightly wounded. It would, under the circumstances, have been madness to have kept my command there longer. I may be permitted to add, sir, that this formidable position of the enemy, after having withstood the repeated attacks of various regiments, was only carried at last by a charge upon the right flank, supported by a battery on the left.

After the enemy were driven from this stronghold, we, with several brigades, moved towards the river. It was then nigh sunset. In accordance with your order, we commenced falling back about dusk, and being separated from the brigade, I conducted the regiment to the camp of the enemy, where I had established a temporary hospital during the day. I was in the saddle till a late hour of the night, endeavoring to find your head-quarters. But being unable to do so, I concluded to let my men sleep in the tents where they were, having learned that we were a short distance to the right of the second brigade, Gen. Anderson, and immediately with Capt. Girardey's battery, which had been on my right most of the day.

Early Monday morning, I had my regiment in motion to join you, and was moving with Capt. Girardey's battery towards the left, where I expected to join the brigade, when I was ordered by Gen. Withers to send my regiment under my lieutenant-colonel to support Brig.-gen. Chalmers on the right. At the same time Gen. Withers assigned me to the command of the Crescent regiment, Col. Smith, and a battery, 5th company Washington artillery, as a brigade to support the line in front, which was at that time engaging the enemy a little beyond the outer line of the enemy's camp, and a short distance to the right of where Gen. Beauregard had his head-quarters Sunday night. Having marched forward about four or five hundred yards, our line halted, to await the issue of the conflict going on in front of us. A short time elapsed, when the line in front of us gave way, and we engaged the enemy. Just at this time I had the misfortune to be thrown from my horse, and being badly bruised and stunned, was borne from the field.

In conclusion, sir, I desire to do simple justice to my regiment, by stating the fact that the officers and men did their whole duty—nothing more, nothing less.

Of the part taken by my regiment in the engagement on Monday I am not now able to furnish a report, owing to the sickness of my lieutenant-colonel, who commanded, not being able to render me a statement. His verbal report shows my regiment actively engaged all day. So soon as he renders me his report, I will immediately transmit it to you, to form a conclusion to this report, and to show how my regiment was engaged while I was assigned to another command.

I have the honor, colonel, to be,
With distinguished regard,
Your obedient servant,
B. L. HODGE,
Col. 19th Regiment La. Vols.

Report of Colonel James T. Fagan.

HEAD-QUARTERS 1ST ARKANSAS REGIMENT,
NEAR CORINTH, MISSISSIPPI,
April 9, 1862.

Colonel R. L. GIBSON,
Commanding 1st brigade, Ruggles' Division:

COLONEL: I beg leave to submit the following report of the part taken and the loss sustained by my regiment in the battles of the 6th and 7th instant. Under the circumstances, it must necessarily be meagre and imperfect. Were it at my command, I should use no gloss and finish of language on the occasion. A simple reference to the list of casualties will tell, in terms too plain to be misunderstood, the story of our loss and sufferings, and the degree of daring that was exhibited throughout those two memorable days. It is impossible, also, to give any detailed account of the movements and manœuvres of the regiment. The extent and nature of the ground over which it marched precludes this. A brief report of the most important engagements with the enemy is all that I can render.

Where a command behaved as well, generally, as did the 1st Arkansas regiment, it is hard to discriminate or designate any individual instances of bravery. Officers and men did their duty well, and conducted themselves as men should who fight for all that is near and dear to them. Against odds, and at great disadvantage, they fought, time and again, bravely, desperately, defiantly; and where they could not by heroic daring force their way, they crimsoned the ground with their life-blood.

On the 6th instant, my regiment was the right centre regiment of the 1st brigade, and held this position during the day. The first casualties that befell it were on the morning of that day, whilst the regiment was filing through the margin of an old field, in full view, and at a short distance from the camps of the enemy, and a strong battery posted near them. Here Capt. Wm. A. Crawford, of company E, was seriously wounded by a bomb bursting right under him, and at the same time several of my men of companies A, E, F, near and around him. I felt the loss of Capt. Crawford very much, thus early in the day, for I knew well his coolness and decision, and what his presence was worth to his command. It was an hour and more after this, before we had the first real engagement with the enemy. It occurred in an old field to the right of the first, where the regiment engaged a force of the enemy's infantry supported by a battery of artillery. It lasted only a few minutes; the enemy retired. Our loss at this point was several in killed and wounded. The manner in which my men sustained themselves in this, the first engagement, was gratifying, and fully justified my expectations, and fortified the belief of what they would do when the time should come which "tried men's souls."

It was not long before that time arrived; it was about noon, the turning point of the day and the turning point of the battle. Upon the edge of a wheat-field, to the right of the field last mentioned, the regiment, with the whole brigade, was drawn up in line of battle, and, marching directly to the front across the field, entered a dense thicket of undergrowth, which led down to a ravine and to a hill beyond. Here we engaged the enemy, three different times, and braved a perfect rain of bullets, shot and shell. Exposed, facing great odds, with the enemy in front and on the flank, the regiment endured a murderous fire until endurance ceased to be a virtue. Three different times did we go into that "valley of death," and as often were forced back by overwhelming numbers, intrenched in a strong position. That all was done that could possibly be done, the heaps of killed and wounded left there give ample evidence. On the right of the regiment, dauntlessly leading the advance, fell Lieut.-col. John B. Thompson, mortally wounded, pierced with seven balls. His loss no one can feel so sensibly as myself. Like Havelock, he united the graces of religion to the valor of the soldier. Here fell

Capt. J. T. Gibson, of company H, and Capt. Jesse T. McMahan, of company C, mortally wounded, whilst cheering their men and leading them on the charge. Major J. W. Colquitt was here severely wounded, and Capt. Jas. Newton, of company A, dangerously. Lieut. L. C. Bartlett, of company C, was killed, and several other commissioned officers wounded—all gallantly leading that forlorn hope. It was late in the afternoon when the enemy were repulsed, and were followed up in the direction of the river. That night we slept in the enemy's tents, worn with fatigue, decimated in numbers, but elated that such a hard fought day had such a glorious close.

About 7 o'clock A. M., on Monday, the 7th inst., the regiment marched from the tents it had occupied during the night, being on this day on the right of the 1st brigade. Marching towards the left, orders were received to charge a battery of artillery some distance off and to the left. The order was executed, and one field-piece taken, but abandoned again under a brisk fire from the enemy, who were concealed in numbers in the woods beyond. Under this fire, several of my men were wounded; none seriously. Retiring into a ravine, the regiment was withdrawn from its exposed position and left that portion of the field. An hour or so later, it was marched towards the right, where every inch of ground was being hotly contested, and here the regiment engaged the enemy for some time in the most desperate and determined style, moving steadily on against the ranks in front of them, and when broken and temporarily thrown into disorder by the tremendous numbers before them, they only retired to rally again and come on with renewed eagerness to the charge. They rallied around their colors and pressed on, time and again, until they were forced to retire by the overwhelming pressure against them. Here we suffered severely, losing several commissioned officers in killed and wounded, and leaving many brave men who had ever been foremost in the fray dead or dying.

After this, little occurred that is worthy of mention. The regiment soon after left the field under orders, and encamped that night at Monterey, in the quarters occupied by it previously to going out to fight. Night closed upon us tired and foot sore, but not dispirited.

I have thus given, colonel, a summary account of the part that my regiment took in the fight on each day. It only remains for me to add the list of casualties. As before said, these speak with an eloquence more powerful than words.

Capt. A. J. Morgan, of Arkansas, kindly volunteered as my aid, and rendered valuable services during the engagement.

I remain, colonel,

With much respect, very truly,

JAMES F. FAGAN,

Col. commanding 1st Arkansas regiment.

Report of Capt. E. M. Dubroca.

Col. R. L. Gibson,

Sir:—I respectfully submit to you the report of the part taken by the 13th regiment Louisiana Volunteers, in the battles of the 6th and 7th instant. Being totally unacquainted with the ground, and at that time not dreaming that the command of the regiment would devolve upon me, I had not taken minute notice of the different movements of the regiment, and am afraid my report will be a very imperfect one. I shall refrain from naming any of my fellow officers for their gallant deeds on the battle-field, as my attention was principally occupied in attending to my own company, until late in the engagement of the 7th. On the morning of the 6th, the regiment, commanded by Major Avegno, was led into action about 7 o'clock A. M. We first encountered the enemy in one of their camps, which I suppose was the first of their camps, still occupied by the enemy. There we were formed in line of battle. On our right was the 1st Arkansas, and on our left the 4th Louisiana. We marched through an open field, under a deadly fire of shell, grape, and musketry, and formed in line on the edge of the enemy's camp. Our loss in crossing the field was very heavy. Capt. Cassard, of company H, was wounded in the leg, and retired from the field. Capt. O'Leary, of company A, received a slight wound in the shoulder, but still retained his command. We were ordered to the right, to charge the enemy, who were laying in ambush at the foot of a hill, entirely hidden from us by a dense undergrowth, which screened their position. We were first apprised of their proximity by a shower of musketry sweeping through our ranks. Bravely did our gallant little band stand its ground, and return the enemy's fire. But "there is a time when endurance ceases to be a virtue." Overwhelmed by numbers, we were forced to fall back, and reform anew, and a second and a third time we returned to the charge, leaving on the field some of our brave soldiers. Capt. Campbell, of company B, being wounded in the arm, his company was left in charge of his orderly-sergeant, two of his lieutenants being sick, and one on detached service. Major Avegno, being afflicted with a severe cold, and unable to speak, transferred the command to Capt. O'Leary, of company A. Nothing of importance transpired that night. We occupied the enemy's tents.

On Monday, the 7th, at 7 o'clock, A. M. the order was given to "Fall in to face the enemy again." Although worn out by fatigue, and after an almost sleepless night, cheerfully and gladly did the 13th obey the order. We were ordered to charge a battery, in position on a hill at some distance. It was not long before I could see our brave boys cheering and following the flying Yankees, who left two pieces of artillery behind them, although it was not our good fortune to hold them long. The order to fall back to a neighboring ravine was given, then again we had a glimpse of the Yankees, and fired a few volleys at them. Lieut. Daly was wounded in the head by a piece of shell, and was taken to a hospital close by, occupied by some of the enemy's wounded. We were then ordered to the position we occupied in the morning, and after forming in line of battle, we charged on the enemy in an open field. Our loss in wounded was very heavy. Capt. O'Leary, of company A, received a second wound in the thigh, and then gave up the command of the regiment to me. With some few of our men and about two hundred men from different regiments, we made a last and desperate charge, in which Major Avegno was wounded in the leg. The order to retreat was then given.

All of which I respectfully submit,

E. M. DUBROCA,

Captain 13th Reg't Louisiana Vols.

Report of the 4th Louisiana Regiment, in the Battle of Shiloh, on the 6th and 7th instant, H. W. Allen, Colonel commanding.

CAMP NEAR CORINTH, MISS., April 10, 1862.

COLONEL:—On the morning of the 6th, the 4th Louisiana went into the engagement with about 575 men, rank and file. All the commissioned officers were present, and participated in the engagement, except Lieuts. Turnbull, Blum, and Lemmon, absent on sick furlough. While drawn up in line of battle and awaiting orders, a Tennessee regiment, immediately in our rear, fired into us by mistake, killing and wounding a large number of my men. This was a terrible blow to the regiment, far more terrible than any inflicted by the enemy. It almost demoralized the regiment, who, from that moment, seemed to dread their friends much more than their enemies. At the command to advance, we charged up the hill into an almost impenetrable thicket.

The enemy opened a deadly fire, which was quickly returned. During the engagement, Col. Fagan, of the 1st Arkansas, sent word to Capt. Favrot, of the Delta rifles, "for God's sake to cease firing, that we were killing his men, and he was killing ours." Capt. Favrot, being on the extreme right, gave the order to cease firing. While in this position, a murderous fire was poured into us from the masked batteries of grape and canister, and also from the rifle-pits.

The regiment retired—formed again, and again charged. Here fell many of my bravest and best men, in the thick brushwood, without ever seeing the enemy. The young, but gallant Capt. J. T. Hilliard, commanding Company I, Hunter rifles, was killed here. Here fell Capts. Taylor and Pennington, and Lieuts. Holmes and Aillet and Landry; Capt. Taylor being most fearfully wounded. In this position we remained, firing volley after volley, until the enemy had ceased his firing.

By order of Gen. Bragg, I took position on the hill, and at a later hour, marched the regiment to the last scene of action, and remained till ordered to retire to camp.

MONDAY THE 7TH.

Having suffered from loss of blood and intense pain, I placed the regiment under the command of Lieut.-col. S. E. Hunter, and rode over to the hospital to get relief. After having my wound dressed, I was about lying down, in order to take a little rest, when a general stampede began of wagons, ambulances, and men. I mounted my horse immediately, and rode after the disgraceful refugees. I succeeded in putting a stop to the stampede, and placed cavalry in the rear, with orders to cut down all who attempted to pass. Here I met an aid of Gen. Bragg, who ordered me to rally all the stragglers, and form them in line. This I did. After forming a battalion, Lieut.-col. Barrow, commanding the 11th Louisiana, came to me with the remnant of his regiment, and placed himself and regiment under my command. This force, together with the remnants of two Alabama and one Tennessee regiment, made a large body of men, who stood firm in front of the hospitals, ready to receive the advancing columns of the enemy.

While rallying the stragglers, I came across two batteries that had lost all their commissioned officers. These I took possession of, sent for ammunition, supplied them with men from my command, and sent one of them to Gen. Beauregard. This battery fired the last shots against the enemy. The other battery, and the forces under my command, held their position, in the very face of the enemy, until ordered to be retired by command of Gen. Bragg.

The regiment went into action on the morning of the 7th, under command of Lieut.-col. Hunter. The officers and men fought the whole day under his command, and behaved, as I am informed, with much gallantry, under the most trying circumstances.

On this day fell Capt. C. E. Tooraen, of the West Feliciana rifles, fighting at the head of his company. He was the bravest of the brave, and in his death our country has sustained a serious loss. I cannot particularize the daring acts of officers and men. The whole regiment acted throughout the whole engagements of the 6th and 7th (with a few exceptions) with great gallantry.

I cannot close this report without honorable mention of my regimental color-bearer, Benjamin W. Clarke, and the color-guard, D. B. Gorham, T. H. Corcoran, and R. Turner. For two long days, amid shot and shell, and a hail-storm of balls, they held the flag firm and erect, and brought it back torn into tatters by the bullets of the enemy. The loss of the regiment is as follows, viz:

Killed—Two (2) officers—Capts. Tooraen and Hilliard. Twenty-two (22) men.

Wounded—Twelve (12) officers—Capts. Pennington and Taylor, Lieuts. Holmes, Adams, Aillet, Landry, and Smith, Capt. Wingfield, Lieuts. Latil, Carter, Amacker, Barton, Skolfield. One hundred and fifty-one (151) men.

Missing—One officer—Lieut. Jenkins. Twenty-one (21) men.

Total loss—Two hundred and nine (209).

H. W. ALLEN,

Colonel commanding 4th Louisiana regiment.

Report of General Patton Anderson.

HEAD-QUARTERS 2D BRIGADE RUGGLES' DIVISION,
2D ARMY CORPS, ARMY OF THE MISSISSIPPI,
CORINTH, MISS., April 17, 1862.

To Captain R. M. HOOE,
A. A. General.
Division Head-quarters:

CAPTAIN:—I have the honor to make the following report of the part taken by my brigade in the actions of the 6th and 7th of April, at Shiloh, near the Tennessee river.

On the night of the 4th, in his tent, near Meckey's house, Gen. Bragg developed to the division and brigade commanders the plan of the proposed attack upon the enemy's forces, encamped at and around Shiloh Church. By this plan, Ruggles' division was to form on the left of the second line of battle, its left resting upon Owl creek and its right on or near the Bark road. My brigade (the 2d) was to compose the reserve of this division, and occupy a position several hundred yards in rear of its centre, for the purpose of supporting the right or left, as occasion might require. A sufficient interval was to be left between the 1st and 3d brigades to admit of my deploying forward into line, should such a movement be found necessary.

The furious storm which raged during the greater portion of the night of the 4th, prevented the movement of the army from its bivouac at Meckey's, until some time beyond the hour designated by Gen. Bragg, although my brigade was ready to march at 3 o'clock, A. M., of the 5th, and was so reported at the division head-quarters. At about 3 o'clock, P. M., of the 5th, my command took its position in the column on the Bark road, marching left in front, in the direction of Shiloh. The roads were much blocked up by the trains of wagons and artillery attached to the corps in front. In order to reach my position in the designated line of battle at the hour indicated in the plan, I left the main road, taking a course through the woods parallel to the road, passing other trains and brigades, till the way was found open, only a short distance at the point at which I was to file off to the left, and form line at right angles, or nearly so, with the Bark road, on which the column was moving. This point was reached by the head of my column at about 4 P. M., on the 5th instant, Col. Pond, commanding the 3d brigade, Ruggles' division, having preceded me in the direction of Owl creek. After leaving the Bark road, and following Col. Pond's command about half a mile, I found his rear halted and his line being formed. Meeting Gen. Bragg at this point, he gave me some directions as to the formation, rectifying in some measure the line formed by Col. Pond. Soon after this, I met Brig.-gen. Ruggles, commanding the division, who substantially reiterated Gen. Bragg's instructions, which I was in the act of carrying out. I formed the brigade two hundred and seventy yards in rear of the division, in column at half distance, doubled on the centre, my right and left respectively half masked by the left and right of the 1st and 3d brigades. After posting an adequate guard, arms were stacked, and the troops bivouacked on the lines. The night was clear, the air cool and bracing, quite in contrast with the previous one.

At 4 A. M., on the 6th inst., the men were aroused without fife or drum, and silently, but promptly, resumed their arms, ready for the order to move forward. This order was soon received, and obeyed with alacrity. At this time, the second line of battle (of which my brigade composed a reserve on the left) was supposed to be about 1000 yards in rear of the 1st, or Gen. Hardee's line. We had not moved forward over half this distance, however, when I discovered that we were approaching within two or three hundred yards of it, having taken the step and direction from the 1st brigade (Col. Gibson's) on my right. I also discovered at this time that the right of Col. Pond's (the 3d brigade) had not yet taken up the line of march. A few moments previous, I had received an order from Gen. Bragg, through one of his staff, to close the interval in front of me, by forming on Col. Gibson's left. This had been executed before we halted a moment to allow Gen. Hardee's line to regain its proper interval. Both lines were soon in motion again, and before proceeding far, a few scattering musket shots were heard, apparently about half a mile to our right, and after a short interval, one or two volleys succeeded, the sound coming in the same direction. Occasional reports were now heard along our right and centre, and seemed to be gradually extending towards our left. At this time my brigade was marching in line of battle, in the following order, from right to left, viz.: The 17th regiment of Louisiana Volunteers, aggregate 326, commanded by Lieut.-col. Charles Jones; the Confederate Guards Response battalion, aggregate 169, commanded by Major F. H. Clack; the Florida battalion, about 250 aggregate, commanded by Major S. A. McDowell; the 9th Texas infantry, 226 aggregate, commanded by Col. W. A. Stanley; and the 20th regiment Louisiana Volunteers, 507 aggregate, commanded by Col. Auguste Reichard. The 5th company Washington Artillery, 155 men, commanded by Capt. W. Irving Hodgson, following the centre as nearly as the nature of the ground would permit, ready to occupy an interval either between the Florida battalion and the 9th Texas, or between the 9th Texas and 20th Louisiana, as necessity or convenience might require; the whole composing a force of 1634 men. The engagement had now fairly commenced on the right, and that portion of Major-gen. Hardee's line, to which we were now moving up, by order of Gen. Bragg, was sharply engaging the enemy's skirmishers. The face of the country at this point, consisting of alternate hills and boggy ravines, overgrown with heavy timber and thick underbrush, presented features remarkably favorable for the operations of skilful skirmishers. Our impetuous volunteers charged them, however, wherever they appeared, and drove them from their cover back to their lines near the first camp met with on the Bark road, leading towards Pittsburg. Here the enemy, having greatly the advantage of position for both his infantry and artillery, made a more creditable stand. A battery of his field pieces was in position on the height of a domineering hill, from four to six hundred yards in front of our lines, commanding his camp and the approaches to it. Immediately in our front, and between us and this battery, ran a boggy ravine, the narrow swamp of which was thickly overgrown with various species of shrubs, saplings, and vines, so densely interwoven as to sometimes require the use of a knife to enable the footman to pass. Over this the enemy's battery had a full field to fire upon our whole lines. As we descended the declivity, terminating in the swamp, and on the opposite skirts of the swamp, his infantry had all the advantages presented by such shelter on one side and obstacles on the other. This ravine and its accompanying obstacles could be avoided on the right, but my position in the line required a dislodgment of the enemy from his cover, before taking a movement in that direction, lest he should fall upon my flank and rear, before I could make the circuit of the swamp and hill, to reach him where he was.

The most favorable position attainable by our field pieces was selected, and Capt. Hodgson was directed to open fire upon the enemy's battery, (now playing vigorously upon us,) with solid shot and shrapnel, and when occasion offered, without danger to our own troops, to use canister upon his infantry. This order was obeyed with alacrity. Taking advantage of this diversion in our favor, the infantry was directed to pass through the swamp, and drive the enemy before it, until Capt. Hodgson could either silence his battery, or an opportunity presented of taking it with the bayonet. The movement was made with spirit and vigor. As my left reached the thicket at the ravine, a regiment on our left and front, which had been unable to cross the branch, came back in some confusion, breaking the lines of the 20th Louisiana, and causing similar confusion in its ranks. Both were soon, however, reformed, and the 20th Louisiana (Col. Reichard) regained its proper position in line, and forced its way across the swamp under a heavy fire from the enemy. At this time the most of my right, the 17th Lousiana, the Confederate Guards, and the Florida battalion, had crossed the branch and made a charge up a hill into the edge of the enemy's camp, but his battery was playing upon them with such vigor that they fell back, in order, a short distance, to a point where they were sheltered by the brow of the hill. The perceptibly diminishing fire from the enemy's battery was soon, by Capt. Hodgson's superior practice, entirely silenced. Our infantry, which, in the meantime had crossed the boggy ravine, pressed up the hill on the other side, driving the enemy from his camp, and reaching the battery in time to pour several rounds into the ranks of the fleeing cannoniers and their supports, both right and left. The action now became general, as was evidenced by the unremitting roll of small arms and artillery along the whole line.

In the attack upon the camp first alluded to, and the taking of the battery, my command had assumed a position in the front line, availing itself, for this purpose, of an interval nearly in front of us, in our first line of battle. After passing their first battery, and being driven through their second and third camps into the fourth, the enemy made a more obstinate resistance, being favored in this by the nature of the ground. Once, and again, our volunteers nobly responded to the order to dislodge him. The odds in numbers were in his favor, as well as the advantage in position, but as comrade after comrade fell by his side, each Confederate seemed to be inspired with fresh courage and determination to win the fight, or lose his life. At one time the lines upon my right wavered, and seemed to give way for a moment, but a wave of the hat to my own brigade, (the voice could not be heard) seemed well understood, and the command "forward," which it implied, was most gallantly executed. Again the lines of the enemy gave way, but a battery to our left and front now disclosed itself in heavy fire upon our centre and right. About this time each command in the brigade lost several gallant officers and many not less gallant men. I dispatched an aid, Lieut. Davidson, to the rear to order up a battery, and withdrew the infantry a short distance to better shelter. The artillery gained a favorable position in a few minutes, perhaps before Lieut. Davidson had had time to deliver my order, and promptly opened fire upon its antagonist. The infantry was brought up again on the right of the battery, at supporting distance, held its fire till a favorable moment arrived, when a few well directed volleys, followed by a shout and a charge to the front, caused the enemy again to give way in some confusion, leaving his battery behind.

It is entirely out of my power to give a circumstantial account of all the operations of the command during the remainder of this day's work. Our movements were all onward. Meeting one of Gen. Bragg's aids about this time, I remarked to him, that "from the position originally assigned me, that of a reserve, I had worked my way into the front line." In a few moments he passed again and said, "no difference, the general desires you to go wherever the fight is thickest." The enemy's fire in front and to our left was now evidently diminishing. Not so, however, on our right. I therefore determined to swing around on my right, and endeavor to press the enemy's right centre back upon his right, where Gen. Hardee's invincible columns were driving him towards the river. One of his batteries lay immediately in our front, concealed by undergrowth and a sharp ravine. In approaching it, I met Col. Smith, of the Crescent regiment, who had become detached from his brigade, and now proposed to unite with mine, to which I gladly consented, and directed him to form on my left. After consulting together for a few moments, and making some inquiry of Gen. Gardner, who was passing at the moment, and who had reconnoitered the ground in the vicinity of the battery which lay in our front, and which, by this time, was getting our range pretty well. I determined to move around my right a short distance, letting Col. Smith go to the left, and, from the position thus gained, to make a simultaneous movement upon the infantry supporting the battery, while a section of our own field pieces engaged them in front.

In moving forward through the thick underbrush before alluded to, I met a portion of a Louisiana regiment (13th, I think), returning, and their officers informed me that I could not get through the brush. I pushed forward, however, and had crossed the ravine and commenced the ascent of the opposite slope, when a galling fire from infantry, and canister from howitzers, swept through my ranks with deadly effect. The thicket was so dense that it was impossible for a company officer to be seen at platoon distance. The enemy's canister was particularly well-directed, and the range, being that of musketry, was well calculated to test the pluck of the sternest. So far as I was able to observe, however, there was no consternation or dismay in our ranks. The 20th Louisiana suffered most, its gallant colonel having his horse shot, and many of its rank and file meeting soldiers' deaths. They fell back, fighting as they retired, to a point from fifty to a hundred yards in the rear, where the brow of a hill afforded shelter from the canister. A hurried reconnoisance revealed a point from which the enemy could be more advantageously assailed. Lieut. Davidson, of my staff, was dispatched to Gen. Ruggles, not far off, with a request that he would send up a few pieces of artillery to a position indicated, whence a vigorous fire, I felt confident, would soon silence the battery, which was the main obstacle to our onward movement. Changing my position somewhat to suit the circumstances (several officers of the 20th Louisiana having reported to me their men were unable to make another charge, by reason of the complete state of exhaustion they were in), I determined to make another effort to dislodge the enemy from his position, with what of my command was left. Gen. Ruggles had now placed our battery in position. Col. Smith, of the Crescent regiment, had driven the enemy's sharpshooters from the cover of a log cabin and a few cotton bales on the extreme left and near the road, and the enemy was being sorely pressed upon the extreme right by our columns upon that flank, and I felt the importance of pressing forward at this point. The troops, too, seemed to be inspired with the same feeling. Our battery opened rapidly, but every shot told. To the command "forward," the infantry responded with a shout, and in less than five minutes after our artillery commenced playing, and before the infantry had advanced within shot range of the enemy's lines, we had the satisfaction of seeing his proud banner lowered, and a white one hoisted in its stead. Our troops on the right had been engaging a portion of his lines, unseen by us on account of an intervening hill, and when the white flag was run up, they reached it first. The sun was now near the western horizon; the battle around us had ceased to rage. I met Gen. Ruggles, who directed me to take a road, which was not far to my left, and to move down in the direction of the river. I had not proceeded far when, overtaking me, he ordered a halt till some artillery could be taken to the front, when he would give me further directions. Soon after halting, several brigades, composing portions of Gens. Polk and Hardee's commands, filed across the road in front of me, and moved off to the left, at a right angle to the road, and commenced forming line of battle in an open field and woods beyond. Several batteries passed down the road in the direction of Pittsburg. One soon returned, and filed off into the field where the infantry was forming. The enemy's gunboats now opened fire. Gen. Ruggles directed me to move forward a short distance, and by inclining to the right to gain a little hollow, which would probably afford better protection for my men against shell than the position I then occupied. I gained the hollow and called a halt, ordering the men to take cover behind the hill, and near a little ravine which traversed the hollow. We occupied this position some ten or fifteen minutes, when one of Gen. Ruggles' staff directed me to retire to the enemy's camp, beyond the range of his floating guns. In filing off from this position several men were killed and many wounded by the exploding shells of the enemy. It was now twilight. As soon as we had placed a hill between us and the gunboats, the troops moved slowly and apparently with reluctance from the direction of the river. It was eight o'clock at night before we had reached a bivouac near Gen. Bragg's head-quarters, and in the darkness of the night the 20th Louisiana and portions of the 17th Louisiana and Confederate Guards, got separated from that portion of the command in which I was, and encamped on other ground. By the assistance of my staff, the whereabouts of the whole command was ascertained before we slept. I reported in person to Gen. Ruggles, who gave some directions in regard to collecting the stragglers, and requested that I should report to him again if any thing of importance occurred during the night. I retired to the bivouac, which was in an open field and apple orchard, near the Big spring. I had purposely avoided the enemy's tents, fearing the effect their rich spoils might produce upon hungry and exhausted troops. Before twelve o'clock one of those terrific rain storms, to which we had so frequently been exposed of late, set in with pitiless vehemence, which was scarcely abated till dawn of day. With my saddle for a seat, and a blanket thrown over my head, I sat all night at the root of an apple tree. My staff and troops cheerfully partook of the same fare.

Soon after daylight on Monday morning, the 7th, I received orders from both Gens. Bragg and Ruggles, through their staff officers, to hold myself in readiness to move out and meet the enemy. I hastened to make preparations accordingly. The command was marched off from its bivouac by the right flank, in the direction of

20

Pittsburg, and after proceeding about a half of a mile, was formed in line of battle on the right of some Tennessee troops, believed to belong to Gen. Cheatham's command. Some delay was had at this point by the constant delay of troops in fragments of brigades, regiments, and companies. A portion of the 20th Louisiana, the Confederate Guards battalion, and 9th Texas regiment, had become detached from my immediate command, by permitting other troops to cut them out on the march, and in falling into line. A line of battle was, however, formed, and a forward movement commenced. By this time our skirmishers on the right had engaged those of the enemy, but no general action had begun.

Our advance movement had not continued far, however, till the enemy's lines were disclosed in front. Our troops went into action with a spirit and alacrity scarcely to be expected after the fatigues and hardships of the previous days and nights. The enemy was evidently in large force, and his troops were fresh. The first onset was maintained with spirit by both armies, and for nearly an hour the conflict raged in this part of the field with doubtful results. Several times we pressed forward against the superior numbers of the enemy's fresh columns, but he stubbornly maintained his position. Our officers and men seemed resolved to drive him back, and summoning every thing for another struggle, we led the columns up with a volley and a shout from the whole line, which proved irresistible, and sent him flying back to his second line, which was strongly posted some two hundred yards in the rear. About this time Col. Campbell, commanding a Tennessee regiment (number not remembered), attached himself to my brigade, and fought gallantly during the day. I received an order about the same time to support a column then hotly engaged some half mile to my right, but before reaching the position, our column had fallen back to better ground, and I was directed to support a battery on our left in conjunction with Col. Trabue's Kentucky command. I filed off to the left, crossing a camp and the avenue under a heavy fire, and reached a ravine on Col. Trabue's right, with my right resting upon the border of the avenue. The enemy's battery was in position some four hundred yards to our front, and ours was about the same distance to my left, in a favorable position to silence it. Sharpshooters had been thrown forward, and taken position behind a line of logs that had been rolled out to one side of the avenue, and were now picking off my men as they stood waiting for our battery to accomplish its work. I ordered forward a detachment of skirmishers to dislodge the enemy's sharpshooters, who were posted behind the breastwork of logs before alluded to. They accomplished their work in handsome style, and held the position from which they annoyed the cannoniers, who were playing upon our battery on the left. Observing this advantage, I rode over to the battery to see the commanding officer of the infantry, posted on my left, and between me and the battery, to ascertain if he could spare me a force sufficient to enable me to charge and take the enemy's pieces. I first met Major Monroe, of the 4th Kentucky, who referred me to Gen. Trabue, to whom I was soon introduced. Hurriedly explaining to him my strength and position, and urging the importance of taking the battery in question, adding my conviction that it could be done, he readily consented to furnish me two regiments for that purpose, and directed an officer near by to accompany me to where the regiments were posted. I had not proceeded, however, beyond his sight, when he called to me, and approaching, said: "Upon reflection, I think I had better not let those regiments leave their present position, since I am directed to support this battery, if attacked." I returned to my command, and found that the enemy had discovered my position, obtained the range, and was shelling us at a rapid rate. Not having the force to take his battery, and being unable to obtain assistance in that part of the field, I withdrew to a position a short distance in the rear, and behind the brow of the next hill. Here I found Gen. Cheatham, with a portion of his command, who had fallen back from a point farther to the left. I formed on his right, and the enemy now appearing on the left, we encountered him again, and pushed him back a short distance to where more favorable ground enabled him to stand. We were in an open plain with a few scattering trees, but not enough to afford material shelter. The opposing forces were strongly posted in superior numbers in a dense wood, affording excellent cover. Our troops stood and saw their comrades fall about them, but returned the fire with spirit for a length of time, till some detached commands on the extreme left gave way, when the whole line retired behind the brow of a hill, some hundred and fifty to two hundred yards in the rear. Here they rallied and formed again. Gen. Cheatham was particularly active in effecting the re-formation, urging his troops to make a stand, and assuring them of their ability to repulse the enemy. Lieut. Sandidge, also of Gen. Ruggles' staff, did gallant service in the same way. I take pleasure in referring to a circumstance which came under my own observation, as none of his immediate superiors were present to record it. When one of Gen. Cheatham's regiments had been appealed to in vain to make a charge on the advancing foe, Lieut. Sandidge, seizing its colors, and holding them high over head, calling upon the regiment to follow him, he spurred his horse to the front, and charged over the brow of the hill amidst a shower of leaden hail from the enemy. The effect was electrical. The regiment moved gallantly to the support of its colors, but superior numbers soon pressed it back to its original position. Col. Stanley, of the 9th Texas, did the same thing with the same result.

Large numbers of stragglers could now be seen in all directions, making their way to the rear. Officers of several regiments reported to me that their commands were out of ammunition, and that the ammunition wagons had all retired to the rear. I detailed a non-commissioned officer and two men from the Florida battalion to go in search of ammunition. He soon returned, having succeeded in finding a few boxes in a camp near by—whether left there by our wagons or by the enemy, I am unable to say. While the ammunition was being distributed, one of Gen. Beauregard's staff came by and directed us to retire in order, in the direction of our hospital. On reaching the brow of the next hill, in an open space, I halted the brigade and faced about, hoping with the assistance or two pieces of artillery, which I observed near by, that a check would be given to the enemy's advance, if indeed he could not be driven back. He had halted, evidently, in doubt whether to advance or not. I rode up to an officer who appeared to have charge of the pieces alluded to, and requested him to open fire upon a line which I pointed out. He informed me that he was out of ammunition, had no horses to draw off his pieces, and had just received orders to spike them and leave them on the ground. The enemy's lines were still at a halt. I moved on up the road till I met an officer, who told me it was Gen. Bragg's order, that the infantry should form on a certain ridge, which was pointed out. I formed there, but was soon directed by Col. Jordan, of Gen. Beauregard's staff, to fall back to another hill, which he designated, and there form at right angles with the road. I did as directed, and waited some time for further orders, or for the enemy to advance. A staff officer from Gen. Beauregard then came, and ordered the infantry to retire to Monterey, parallel with a road a short distance to my left. At a fork of the road, a portion of the command took the road to Meckey's. The balance proceeded to Monterey under their respective officers. I went to Meckey's, as did a portion of my staff, where I met Gen. Ruggles, and reported to him for further instructions. He directed me to proceed the next morning with my command to Corinth, and there resume our camps, the tents of which had been left standing when we started for Shiloh.

It is not proper that I should close this report without bringing to the notice of the general commanding the names of such officers as made themselves conspicuous for their gallantry and efficiency in the field. Lieut.-col. Charles Jones, commanding the 17th regiment Louisiana volunteers, was wounded early in the action, and retired from the field. Major F. H. Clack, commanding Confederate Guards battalion, was ever where the conflict raged hottest, holding his command well in hand, cheering, encouraging and stimulating the men to deeds of valor and renown. Major Clack had two horses shot under him. Major McDowell, commanding the Florida battalion, was borne wounded from the field, before the action had fairly begun. The command devolved upon Capt. Poole, who bore himself most gallantly throughout the two days' conflict. The skill with which he handled his command reflected the highest credit upon him as an officer, while the desperation with which his troops fought brings new lustre to the arms of the State they represented, and paints imperishable fame upon the colors they so proudly bore. Col. Stanley, of the 9th Texas regiment, has already been incidentally alluded to. The language of eulogy could scarcely do more than simple justice to the courage and determination of this officer and his valorous Texans. Ever in the thickest of the fight, they were always ready to respond to any demand upon their courage and endurance. Col. Reichard, commanding the 20th Louisiana regiment, deserves the highest commendation and praise for his indefatigable valor, in leading his command wherever the foe was strongest. Col. Reichard's skill and efficiency as an officer are only excelled by his intrepidity and valor. Lieut.-col. Boyd, of the same regiment, did his whole duty, regardless of a painful wound in the arm, which he received in the first day's engagement. Major Von Zinker, also, performed well his part, having three horses shot under him during the conflict. Capt. W. Irving Hodgson, commanding the 5th company, Washington Artillery, added fresh lustre to the fame of this already renowned corps. It was his fine practice from the brow of the hill overlooking the enemy's first camp, that enabled our infantry to rout them in the outset, thus giving confidence to our troops, which was never afterwards once shaken. Although the nature of the ground over which my infantry fought was such as frequently to preclude the use of artillery, yet Capt. Hodgson was not idle. I could hear of his battery, whenever artillery was needed. On several occasions, I witnessed the effect which his canister and round shot produced upon the enemy's masses, and once saw his cannoniers stand to their pieces under a deadly fire, when there was no support at hand, and when to have retired would have left that part of the field to the enemy. When a full history of the battles of Shiloh shall have been written, the heroic deeds of the Washington Artillery will illustrate one of its brighest pages, and the names of Hodgson and Slocomb will be held in grateful remembrance by a free people, long after the sod has grown green upon the bloody hills of Shiloh!

Many other names deserve to be recorded as bright ornaments to the roll of the brave who fought at Shiloh, but the limits of my report, already too extended, forbid it. Where all behaved so well, I would prefer not to omit a name from the list, but such a course is impracticble at this time. I take pleasure in referring to the reports of the regimental commanders for more minute detail in relation to the battle; and for the names of many subalterns, non-commissioned officers, and privates, who deserve notice and commendation for gallant conduct on the field.

I beg leave to be permitted, in this connection, to record the names of my staff officers, to whom I am greatly indebted for their very active assistance throughout the battle. Capt. Wm. G. Barth, A. A. G. and Chief of Staff, rendered invaluable service in transmitting orders and making perilous reconnoissances. I was deprived of his services during a portion of the time, by his horse being killed under him, the place of which he found it difficult to supply. Lieut. Wm M. Davidson, aid-de-camp, was constantly by my side, except when absent by my orders, all of which he delivered with promptitude and intelligence. While engaged in this, and passing from one portion of the field to another, he made many narrow escapes, having frequently to pass under most galling fires to reach his point of destination. Lieut. John W. Janes, 5th Georgia regiment, acting aid-de-camp, also rendered useful service early in the action of the sixth (6th), but getting cut off during the day, by some means, from the command, I saw nothing more of him till late in the evening, when he rejoined me, and remained with me till we withdrew from the field. Capt. Henry D. Bulkley, acting brigade commissary, also served on my personal staff on the occasion, and did good service till a minnie ball deprived him of his horse. As soon as he was able to supply himself again, he rejoined me and gave me his ready assistance. Lieut. Wm. McR. Jordan, 1st Florida regiment, temporarily attached as an acting aid-de-camp, was always at his post, ready to perform any service required of him. A spent ball striking him in the loin, compelled him to retire for a while from the field, but he soon returned, having received no other injury than a severe contusion, which, though painful, did not disable him. Capt. John T. Sibley, brigade quarter-master, deserves the highest praise for his activity and promptitude in keeping up our supply of ammunition during the day's fight. He was ever present, ready to respond to any call for this indispensable want of the soldier on the battle-field. He was equally efficient in bringing off from the field all the ammunition not consumed, as well as his wagons, ambulances, mules, or other means of transportation, returning to Corinth without the loss of any. Surgeon C. B. Gamble, Brigade Medical Director, was indefatigable in his labors throughout both days of the battle; rendering, cheerfully and promptly, his professional services whenever and wherever needed. These were not pretermitted during the night of the 6th and 7th, after others, exhausted by the fatigues of the battle-field, had sought early repose. In the discharge of his duty, while endeavoring to alleviate the pains of our wounded, and to bring away as many of them as could be safely removed, he fell into the hands of the enemy after our rear guard had retired. Our army can illy spare, at this time, one whose private worth is so inestimable, and whose professional skill is invaluable.

For a detailed statement of the killed, wounded, and missing of my command, I refer to the reports and lists transmitted, by which it will appear, that I took into the field an aggregate of 1,636. The casualties were 434, a loss of a little over 26 per cent. Among 14 mounted officers, including my staff, eleven horses were killed under their riders.

Very respectfully,

Your obedient servant,

PATTON ANDERSON,

Brigadier-general, Com'g 2d Brigade,

Ruggles' Division 2d Corps,

Army of the Mississippi.

Report of Col. W. A. Stanley.

HEAD-QUARTERS 9TH REGIMENT TEXAS INFANTRY,

CORINTH, MISS., April 15, 1862.

To Gen. P. ANDERSON,

Commanding 2d Brigade, Gen. Ruggles' Division:

SIR:—I have the honor herewith to report the proceedings of my regiment in the battle of Shiloh, on the 6th and 7th of April,

1862. On the morning of the 6th, we advanced in line of battle under a heavy fire of artillery and musketry from the enemy's first encampment. Being ordered to charge the enemy with our bayonets, we made two successive attempts, but finding, as well as our comrades in arms on our right and left, it almost impossible to withstand the heavy fire directed at our ranks, we were compelled to withdraw for a short time, with considerable loss. Being then ordered, we proceeded immediately to the support of the Washington Artillery, which, from their battery's well directed fire, soon silenced the battery of the enemy. After which we immediately charged, routing the enemy from their first encampment, and continued a forward double-quick march until we passed through two other encampments of the enemy, where we found our troops again heavily engaged with a second battery and its supports, to the galling fire of which my regiment was openly exposed. At this point my horse was shot from under me, and several of my bravest men were killed and wounded. We nevertheless succeeded in driving the enemy from their battery, killing a number and pursuing the remainder a considerable distance beyond. At this point, the supply of ammunition in the cartridge-boxes of my men being exhausted, I was compelled to resort to my ammunition wagon, a short distance off, for a fresh supply. In the meantime, firing continued incessantly on our right. We were then ordered to join the command in that direction, who were reported to have the enemy badly routed, and driving them towards their gunboats. After proceeding some distance, we found ourselves in the range of shell and shot fired from the boats and vicinity. At this point, night put a close to the action for the day of the 6th. We retired from this point to form our encampment for the night, our troops being more or less scattered, some having been completely exhausted from the fatigues of the day. We formed them in two groups, leaving one to encamp on the battle-field, the other near the general hospital.

On the morning of the 7th, I again formed my regiment, and proceeded to the battle-field. After arriving there, the enemy again opened fire on our left. We were ordered to the support of a battery stationed to defend that point, but our support not being required at the time we reached the battery, two companies of my regiment were deployed as skirmishers, while the remainder stood in line of battle in a hollow at a distance of two hundred yards from the breastworks of the enemy, our skirmishers returning and reporting the enemy advancing towards the breastworks. At this moment the skirmishers of the enemy appeared at the breastworks, when we were ordered to charge them, which we did successfully, although under a heavy fire of both musketry and artillery, only one man being wounded in the charge. After their guns were silenced at this point, we were ordered to the right, where a heavy fire of small arms had commenced. On reaching the scene of action at this point, the enemy seemed to have been routed, having ceased firing.

After being halted and formed in line of battle, firing again commenced on our left. We were ordered again to that point, and there became engaged with a strong force of the enemy's line. We advanced, and sustained our position for some time after the troops on our right and left had given way, but my regiment being small, and losing two among our bravest officers, Capt. J. J. Dickson, of company "I," and Lieut. Hamil, of company "F," they being killed at this point, with several of my men, I was compelled to fall back, though still keeping up our fire. We again rallied and formed in line, making a desperate struggle, causing the enemy to fall back for a short distance. The enemy then making a move towards our right flank, we fell back in line, taking advantage of the cover of some rising ground to secure them, and there remained, the enemy retiring towards the woods on our right. We were then withdrawn from the field.

The number taken into action was two hundred and twenty-six (226), including officers and enlisted men.

The number killed in action, three (3) commissioned officers and eleven (11) enlisted. Wounded, two (2) commissioned and forty (40) enlisted. Missing, eleven (11) enlisted.

To the best of my recollection, the foregoing is a correct report of the proceedings of my regiment on the 6th and 7th instant.

Very respectfully,
Your obedient servant,
W. A. STANLEY,
Colonel Commanding.

Report of Col. S. S. Heard.

HEAD-QUARTERS 17TH LOUISIANA VOLUNTEERS,
April 15th, 1862.

To W. G. BARTH,
A. A. G. General, 2d Brigade, Ruggles' Division:

SIR:—The reason why Capt. D. W. Self, company B, did not

appear on the field of battle at Shiloh until the morning of the 7th instant was this: That officer was confined to his bed by a severe attack of pneumonia when the regiment left Corinth, on the 3d inst. He (Capt. Self), feeling himself able on the evening of the 6th to join his regiment, left Corinth and joined the regiment late Sunday evening, after the action of the 6th had closed.

I am, general, very respectfully,

Your obedient servant,

S. S. HEARD,

Colonel commanding 17th La. Volunteers.

Report of Lieutenant-Colonel Charles Jones.

HEAD-QUARTERS 17TH REGIMENT LOUISIANA VOLUNTEERS,
CAMP CORINTH, April 11, 1862.

To W. G. BARTH,
Captain and Assistant Adjutant-general, C. S. Forces:

SIR: I have the honor to submit the following report of the part taken by the 17th regiment Louisiana volunteers, in the action of the 6th and 7th instant, near the Tennessee river.

We were brought into action on the morning of the 6th, occupying the extreme right of the brigade, until we were exposed to the enemy's artillery, where we remained for some time, until we were ordered, with a portion of the line on our right and left, to take a battery immediately in our front. A Tennessee regiment, the 22d, I think, was in front of us. We were delayed a moment by this regiment, when I gave the order to charge. When we reached the top of the hill, the enemy poured into us a murderous fire. The Tennessee regiment before referred to, retired by a flank through our lines, cutting their way through the centre of our fourth company, separating our right from our left, and throwing us into some confusion. We did not retire, however, until we had poured several volleys into the enemy. We lost several killed and wounded in this charge. We retired to the foot of the hill to re-form for a second attack. The right wing also retired further to the right, having been cut off from the colors by the Tennessee regiment. They charged the second time with, I think, the 20th Louisiana, on the enemy's left line of support, when the battery was secured. I charged with the left wing on the enemy's right, around the left of the hill, when I received a destructive flank fire from another of the enemy's batteries, as well as from his small arms. From this position we were compelled to fall back to our first. It was in this second charge that Capt. R. H. Curry, of company C, and Capt. W. A. Maddux, of company I, both fell severely wounded.

It was now my object to unite the two wings which were acting separately, the right under command of Capt. Rogers, of company A. I found this impossible; and, with the left, which was much the larger portion, and to which the colors were attached, I advanced, by the left flank, to take a position about 200 yards in front. In accomplishing this, we had to cross a ravine, where we were exposed to a raking fire of shot and shell, as well as from small arms. It was in passing this ravine that my sergeant-major, Thuron Stone, who had been of great service to me thus far in the action, fell at my side leading the column. He was shot through the thigh, though not dangerously. On reaching the hill, 1st Lieut. T. O. Hines, of company K, had his left arm carried away by a cannon ball. Immediately after, I received a very severe shock and bruise by being thrown from my horse. He was frightened by the bursting of a bomb. Having recovered from my fall and secured my horse, I hurried on to the action. I could not find my left wing, which I afterwards learned behaved gallantly, under command of Capt. Otterson, of company H. I found a portion of the right wing joined with the Confederate Guard and a portion of the 11th Louisiana. We charged upon a line of the enemy, and drove them from the field. We remained in this position for a considerable time, when Gen. Anderson arrived with the 20th Louisiana, and ordered the line forward. At this moment I was wounded in the arm by a minié ball, and retired. After having my wound dressed, I immediately returned to the field in search of my command. I fell in with Gen. Ruggles, and reported myself to him. He invited me to remain with him, as the action was drawing to a close. The enemy having retired and left us in possession of the field, and being unable to find more than about fifty of my command, I, with my adjutant, who had received a slight wound, retired with this small force to the ambulance depot to assist the wounded, and remain during the night. Our wounded suffered greatly, having nothing to protect them from the rain, which fell in torrents a greater portion of the night. Many of them lay that night in pools of water two or three inches deep. On the morning of the 7th I sent my adjutant on to form the regiment, or such portions of it as he could find near the Big Spring. When I came up with my small command, I found that my adjutant had joined some other brigade with what number he could find. I, with what few men I had managed to gather together (about 200 in all), composed of stragglers from different regiments, with the aid of Capt. Self, of company B, who had now for the first time appeared upon the field, and some other officers, managed to form a line, and keep it in place, until ordered by Gen. Ruggles to advance. The general, at this instant, rode in front of the lines, and seizing the flag from the hands of the color-bearer, gallantly led them to the charge. In this charge he was assisted by Col. S. S. Heard. Capt. Self, of company B, fell severely wounded. Our forces now began to retire from the field.

The officers and soldiers under my command, so far as came under my observation, behaved with much gallantry. They went into action on the second day, however, with much less alacrity than on the day previous, which I attributed to the fatigue and exposure of the previous day and night.

With great respect,

Your obedient servant,

CHARLES JONES,

Lieut.-col. commanding 17th regiment Louisiana Volunteers.

Report of Major Franklin H. Clack.

HEAD-QUARTERS CONFEDERATE GUARDS RESPONSE BATTALION,
CAMP NEAR CORINTH, MISSISSIPPI,
April 10th, 1862.

To Brig.-gen. PATTON ANDERSON,
Commanding 2d Brigade, Ruggles' Division, 2d Grand Division, Army of the Miss., Camp near Corinth, Miss.:

SIR:—I have the honor to report, that in obedience to your orders about 5 o'clock A. M. of the 6th instant, I drew up my command in column at half distance on the left of the 17th regiment Louisiana volunteers, which occupied the right of your brigade, at a point distant, as I was informed, about three miles from the enemy's nearest camp, and between Owl creek and Bark road, in McNairy county, Tenn. The position assigned the brigade at first, that of a reserve, to support the 1st and 2d brigades of Gen. Ruggles' division, having been changed, I formed my battalion in line of battle, under your orders, in the same relative position as at first, in the brigade, which at that time formed the left of Gen. Hardee's line. On arriving at the ridge nearest the enemy's first camp, owing to some accident, the 17th regiment Louisiana volunteers became for a time separated from my right, and the 1st Florida and the 9th Texas remained in their position on my left. The order was then given to advance, and I took up a position in a hollow immediately below a hill, on which was a camp of the enemy, and on the slope beyond which they had a battery in position. The charge was made by my battalion, supported on my right by a portion of a regiment which I was informed constituted a part of Gen. Polk's command. The enemy were being driven back with much effort, and stubbornly resisting, when some one in the force on the right gave the order to fall back, and, simultaneously, that force came rushing back, bearing my own men with them. I drew off my force to the hollow, from which we had charged. The second charge was successful, and we pursued the enemy through that and another camp, and were brought to a stand by discovering a considerable force of the enemy posted in a thick wood on a slope to our left. Having been separated from you, I consulted with Lieut.-col. Jones, of the 17th Louisiana, who, I found, had joined me on my left, and with Gen. Russell, and we deemed it advisable to pause. You then placed the brigade in line, and, if I am not mistaken in localities, led us to the successful attack of a camp on the left of our line. From this time, sir, until the close of the day, I am unable to describe the various localities in which you led us to the attack. We made several other successful charges, being ordered from one part of the field to others, where our services were most needed. Having bivouacked that night in a camp of the enemy, on the succeeding morning, at 5 A. M., in obedience to your orders, I formed my line, and we were placed as a reserve. Being ordered to the left, in advance, with the artillery on our left, the enemy were discovered in position, in our front, protected by log breastworks; the order was given to charge, which was executed, and the enemy driven from their position. It was then discovered that they had a camp on the hill behind their breastworks, and after our flag had been planted in their camp, a battery, placed on a slope about 500 yards to our left, opened on us, and you ordered us to fall back to the ravine, whence we had charged. The enemy still having our range, you ordered a further retiring beyond range. From this, to our final actions with the brigade, my ignorance of the geographical details of the localities of the battle-ground, and the numerous charges and changes made in our position, prevent my giving any specific details of operations, except that I remember we were kept busy in moving and in attack. Having arrived at that camp of the enemy on the left of the large parade ground, you ordered an advance, to dislodge the enemy occupying a wood skirting the rear of this camp. I understood we were ordered to support an attack, to be made by quite a large force on our right, which I did not perceive, however. Having advanced, and engaged the enemy, it becoming apparent they were in great force, you ordered us to fall back. From this time I lost sight of you, and my command became somewhat scattered. I succeeded, however, in rallying them on the brow of the hill overlooking the enemy's camps, and under the personal instructions of Gen. Beauregard, formed line of battle, incorporating in my command some fragments of the 9th Texas and 1st Florida. After futile endeavors on the part of several officers, myself among the number, to rally a sufficent number to renew the attack, I awaited orders. None came, and perceiving the two lines that were drawn up, ostensibly to support the advance of which we formed the right, diminishing by stragglers, and finally filing off, I drew off my command, flanking and filing to the right, immediately after troops on my left; some few in number had broken from the line and filed to the left. Not having received any specific instructions, or orders, I led my command to my last encampment at this place. I regret, sir, that the irregular course of the engagement of the 6th and 7th instant renders it difficult for me to be specific, a difficulty made almost absolute by the rapidity with which you changed the positions of your brigade, and the many points you were called on to attack, for while your command was intended as a reserve, I believe it never once occupied that position, or that of a support, or any other force than that of an attacking force. I cannot close this feeble report, sir, without calling your attention to a matter which my sense of duty impels me to mention, the strong immediate necessity for the strictest moral and severe discipline. Had we but had this discipline, there would not now be an enemy's foot pressing the soil in the vicinity of our late battle. I am convinced that nothing but the daring courage exhibited by a large portion of our force enabled us to sustain ourselves. Deeming it a duty, also, to suggest any thing that, in my opinion, may tend to correct what I regard an evil, I must say that the volunteering system, as far as my experience goes, is an evil, the greater, in an inverse ratio, as is the term of service short. Be assured, general, that we never can cope successfully with our foe unless we discipline our forces, and that the discipline necessary should be perfect. Our military organization can never be obtained under the volunteer system. We must have recourse to drafting or conscript. The scenes, sir, we both witnessed on the 6th and 7th instant, when stragglers would fall from their own lines, and retiring under cover of another line, fire recklessly to the front, must convince you of the justness of my remarks. Not in this alone, but the disorders resulting from want of proper discipline were numberless; the most fatal to the consummation of a success so gallantly begun, being the lawless spirit of plunder and pillage so recklessly indulged in. While our foe throws down all the barriers of constitutional liberty in his career of oppression and invasion, we are fatally lacking in the most important element of resistance, not that I would imitate his example, but our laws are amply sufficient to correct the evil, did we but enforce them.

I regret to be compelled to report quite a severe loss in my command. It is as follows: five killed on the field, five mortally wounded, one dangerously wounded, twenty severely wounded, fourteen slightly wounded, and one missing; total casualties, forty-five. My actual force in the field, was one hundred and forty-four muskets, and nine officers. To the gallant bearing of my officers, I cannot bear too high a tribute; ever present until disabled, they rendered most efficient service.

To Assistant Quarter-master Lieut. Monheimer, is due great credit for the efficient manner in which he kept the battalion supplied with ammunition and took off the wounded. In the death of 1st Lieut. Macbeth, of company B, I lost a most valuable officer, and his country a noble and brave son.

Capt. Macmurdo, after conducting his company through both days, with singular coolness and bravery, was disabled in the last charge by a severe contusion in the breast by a spent ball. Capt. Fowler and Lieuts. Hyatt and Hardie were severely wounded while gallantly discharging their duty. Adjutant Price and Lieuts. Bouner and Browne rendered very efficient service. From the report of Capt. Macmurdo, of company A, I desire to call your attention to the gallant bearing of privates Harris and North, of his company, who, after the color-sergeant was wounded, bore the flag of the battalion gallantly in the front until severely wounded. Lieut. Price, in command of company B., mentions, with much approbation, the brave conduct of color-sergeant Doyle and private Cuff, of that company.

In conclusion, sir, when I reflect, that this command had never been under fire before, that they were called out to meet the enemy after a most fatiguing march, and that they were moved from one portion of the field to another very rapidly during both days, I will not be thought to express myself too strongly, when I say that they did their duty, as officers and men, gallantly, and I may well say efficiently.

I have the honor to be, very respectfully,
Your obedient servant,
FRANKIN H. CLACK,
Major Confederate Guards Response Battalion.

Report of Col. Augustus Reichard, commanding Twentieth regiment Louisiana Volunteers.

HEAD-QUARTERS, 20TH REGIMENT LOUISIANA VOLUNTEERS,
CAMP NEAR CORINTH, April 11, 1862.

Capt. W. G. BOOTH,
A. A. A. General 2d Brigade:

SIR:—I beg leave to submit the following report in relation to the participation of my regiment in the battle of Shiloh, on the 6th and 7th instants:

I took into the field three field, five staff, and twenty-seven company officers, with 472 rank and file, with whom, according to the disposition made, I occupied the extreme left of the brigade, somewhat in rear of the right of Col. Pond's brigade.

Soon after the commencement of the battle, the brigade moved forward, and, as we approached the enemy, I was ordered to file off by the left, in the execution of which movement, the regiment passing through a dense undergrowth, in which it was impossible to see five paces ahead, I suddenly was informed that we were separated from the balance of the brigade. Just at the moment, when I was retracing my steps to rejoin the brigade, a Tennessee regiment, in full retreat, broke right through my line, causing much disorder. The regiment, however, soon rallied, regained its position, and gallantly fought during the whole day, side by side with the other regiments of the brigade. At the last charge, towards evening, when my regiment was severely cut up by a cross fire from rifle-pits and a battery, pouring fourth a hail storm of canister, my regiment was separated from the rest of the brigade, and, as night set in, I led the remnants of the regiment to our hospital, where we bivouacked.

The next morning, having collected many of my men who had

been scattered about, I put the regiment in movement, and, adding whatever stragglers I could gather on the road, reported to Gen. Beauregard for orders. He ordered me to reinforce Gen. Breckinridge, who found himself hard pressed on our left; and, after reporting to him, took immediate part in the fight that was going on before us. The enemy having fallen back, Gen. Breckinridge ordered me to go to the support of a battery which had taken position to our right beyond an open field, sweeping an open passage, leading, I suppose, to the river. The enemy in front having been dislodged, and there being no further necessity to remain with the battery, I moved towards the left where the fight was hardest. On the way I met Gen. Breckinridge, and, asking for further orders, he directed me to join Gen. Cheatham's brigade, but, in case I should not be able to find him, to join any other brigade where I could make myself most useful. Not finding Gen. Cheatham's brigade, and meeting my own commander, Gen. J. Patton Anderson, I of course joined his brigade, and kept up fighting under his command until the order for retreat was issued.

My regiment fought this their first battle with the utmost bravery, and where, with very few exceptions, almost every one faithfully performed his duty, it is almost out of place to make distinctions. I cannot, however, omit to mention 1st Lieut. Bishop, of company A, who, throughout both days, made himself conspicuous for his gallantry, and the cool, collected manner in which he was unremittedly occupied to keep his company well in hand. Lieut.-col. Boyd was slightly wounded early in the first day's fight, but remained at his post until that evening. Major Von Zinker bravely led several attacks with the colors in his hand, but was disabled early on the second day by the fall of his horse, which was killed under him. The color-bearer, Sergeant Hoffmann, paid, with his life, the gallant manner in which he carried the colors always into the thickest of the fight.

The annexed statement, A, gives a revised account of the killed, wounded, and missing.

I remain, sir, your most obedient servant,

AUGUSTUS REICHARD,

Col. commanding 20th regiment La. Vols.

Report of Capt. W. G. Poole.

HEAD-QUARTERS, FLORIDA BATTALION,
April 12th, 1862.

To Gen. PATTON ANDERSON,
Brig.-gen., commanding 2d Brigade, Ruggles' Division:

GENERAL:—In accordance with your circular of the 11th of this month, I have the honor to make the following report:

In the first place, it becomes a painful duty to record the fall of Major McDonald, being seriously wounded early in the action of the 6th, whereupon the command immediately devolved upon me.

Pressing forward, we gained the valley opposite and close to the first camp of the enemy, and in the first charge lost several of my command in killed and wounded. I then joined the brigade at the second camp, and was ordered forward to support a portion of our advance columns. The advance having fallen back, placed us in front, where for some time we were exposed to a galling fire from the enemy. It was at this time that our battalion suffered most. 1st Lieut. L. M. Anderson, of company A (commanding), was shot in the forehead and instantly killed, and the company being without a commander, I ordered 2d Lieut. Stevens, of company B, to the command. In a very few minutes he was also severely wounded. I then ordered 1st Lieut. Turner, of company C, to take command. Capt. Means and 1st Lieut. Miller, of company B, and 2d Lieut. Turner, of company C, and Lieut. Hull, commanding company I, (since dead), were wounded. Several non-commissioned officers and privates were also killed and wounded while under this fire. I then withdrew the battalion (by order) to the protection of a section of the Washington Artillery battery. Forming with the brigade, we again advanced and assisted in routing a portion of the enemy's forces that had taken position in an encampment on our left. My command then, with a portion of the brigade, proceeded forward as far as within range of the heavy guns on the Tennessee river, where we were for some time exposed to the enemy's shells. One or two of my command were either killed or mortally wounded while under this fire. We then fell back to the enemy's camp, and bivouacked during the night. On the morning of the 7th, being too hoarse to take command of the battalion, I turned it over to Capt. W. C. Bird, of company C.

Accompanying this report will be found a list of the killed, wounded, and missing of each company—all of which is most respectfully submitted.

W. G. POOLE,
Senior Captain, commanding Florida Battalion.

Report of Captain Hodgson.

HEAD-QUARTERS 5TH COMPANY,
BATTALION WASHINGTON ARTILLERY.

CAMP MOORE, CORINTH, MISS., April 9, 1862.

To Brig.-gen. PATTON ANDERSON,
Commanding 2d brigade, Ruggles' Division, Army Miss.:

GENERAL: In accordance with "usage," I hereby report to you, the "action" of my battery in the battle of the 6th and 7th inst.

My battery, consisting of 2 6-pounder smooth bore guns, 2 6-pounder rifled guns, and 2 12-pounder howitzers—total, 6 pieces fully equipped, with ammunition, horses, and men, entered the field just in the rear of the 20th Louisiana regiment (the right regiment of your brigade), on Sunday morning, the 6th inst., on the hill, overlooking, from the south-west, the encampment of the enemy, immediately to the front of it, and to the northeast, being the first camp attacked and taken by an army.

At 7 o'clock A. M., we opened fire on their camp, with our full battery of six guns, firing shell and spherical case shot, soon silencing one of their batteries, and filling the enemy with consternation. After firing some forty (40) rounds thus, we were directed by Gen. Ruggles to shell a camp immediately upon the left of the one just mentioned, and in which there was a battery, from which the shot and shell were thrown on all sides of us. With two howitzers, and two rifled guns, under Lieuts. Slocumb and Vaughn, assisted by two pieces from Capt. Sharp's battery, we soon silenced their guns, and had the extreme gratification of seeing our brave and gallant troops charge through these two camps, running the enemy before them at the point of the bayonet.

At this point, I lost your command, and, on the order of Gen. Ruggles, to go where I heard the most firing, I passed over the first camp captured, through a third, and on to a fourth, in which your troops were doing sad havoc to the enemy. I formed in battery on your extreme left, in the avenue of the camp, and commenced firing with canister from four (4) guns, into the tents of the enemy, only some 50 yards off. It was at this point I suffered most. The skirmishers of the enemy, lying in their tents, only a stone's throw from us, cut holes through their tents near the ground, and with "white powder" or some preparation which discharged their arms without report, played a deadly fire in among my cannoniers, killing three men, wounding 7 or 8, besides killing some of my most valuable horses, mine among the rest. As soon as we were well formed in battery, and got well to work, we saw them creeping from their tents and making for the woods, and immediately afterwards saw your column charge the whole of them in ambush, and put them to flight.

A visit through that portion of their camp, at a subsequent hour, satisfied me, from the number of the dead and the nature of their wounds, that my battery had done its duty. Losing you again, at this point, on account of the heavy brushwood through which you charged, I was requested by Gen. Trudeau to plant two guns further down the avenue, say about two hundred yards off, to shell a fifth camp, further on, which I did, and after firing a dozen or more shell, had the satisfaction of seeing the cavalry charge the camp, putting the enemy to flight, killing many, and capturing many wounded prisoners.

Being again without a commanding-general, and not knowing your exact position, I received and executed orders from Gen. Hardee, and his aid, Col. Kearney, also, from Col. Chisholm, of Gen. Beauregard's staff, and, in fact, from other aids, whose names I do not know, going to points threatened and exposed, and where firing was continual, rendering cheerfully all the assistance I could with my battery, and reduced in men and horses, all fatigued and hungry.

At about 2 o'clock P. M., at the instance of Gen. Hardee, I opened from the 5th camp we had entered, fired upon a sixth camp, due north—silencing the battery and driving the enemy from their tents;—said portion of the army of the enemy were charged, and their battery captured, afterwards lost again, by the Guard Orleans and other troops on our left, under Col. Preston Pond, Jr. This was about the last firing of my battery on the sixth instant. Taking the main road to Pittsburg landing, we followed on the heels of our men, after a retreating and badly whipped army, until within three-fourths of a mile of the Tennessee river, when the enemy began to shell the woods from their gunboats. Gen. Ruggles ordered us back to the enemy's camp, where we bivouacked for the night.

I received orders, on the morning of the 7th, at about 5 and a half o'clock, to follow your command with my battery, and at 6 o'clock, being ready to move, could not ascertain your position—so took position on the extreme right of our army, supported by the Crescent regiment, of Col. Pond's brigade in our rear, and an Arkansas regiment on my front, and I think the 21st Tennessee regiment on my left flank, all under Gen. Hardee, or, in fact, *he* seemed to be the master spirit, giving all orders and seeing that they were properly executed. At about 9 o'clock, Gen. Breckinridge's command on our extreme front had pushed the enemy up and on to within several hundred yards of our front, when we opened fire with shell and shot with our full battery. After firing some 70 rounds, we took position further on, just on the edge of the open space ahead, and with our full battery, assisted by two pieces of McClung's battery, we poured some 60 rounds into the enemy, who continued to advance upon us until within some 20 yards of us, when Col. Marshall J. Smith, of the Crescent regiment, gallantly came to our rescue—charging the enemy at the point of the bayonet, putting them to flight and saving our three extreme right pieces, which would have been captured but for them.

It was at this point I again met with severe losses. Lieut. Slocumb, Serg't Green, several privates, and many horses fell at this point, either killed or badly wounded.

After the enemy had retreated well in the woods, I had my guns limbered and taken from the field. My men broken down, my horses nearly all slain, ammunition out, and sponges all broken and gone, I was in the act of making repairs, and preparing for another attack, when I was ordered by Gen. Beauregard to retire, in order, to Monterey, which I did that evening—and afterwards to this point, arriving last evening, with my battery all complete, with the exception of three caissons, a battery wagon, and forge, which I had to abandon on the road for want of fresh horses to draw them in.

At the request of Gen. Beauregard, I detailed from my command twelve men under a non-commissioned officer, to remain and act with Capt. Byrne's (or Burns') battery on a prominent hill on the Pea Ridge road, overlooking the battle-field, to cover the retirement of our army. They all came in to-day, safe and sound.

We captured two stand of United States colors, which were handed over to Gen. Beauregard. We also captured several U. S. horses and mules, some of which we have now, others we have lost.

I cannot close this report without again calling to your favorable notice the names of my Lieuts. Slocumb, Vaughn, and Chalaron, for their coolness and bravery on the field was daring and gallant, and worthy your consideration.

I have the honor to be,

Yours very truly,

W. IRVING HODGSON,

Captain.

Supplementary Report of Capt. Hodgson.

HEAD-QUARTERS 5TH COMPANY,
BATTALION WASHINGTON ARTILLERY,
CAMP MOORE, CORINTH, MISS., April 11th, 1862.

To Capt. G. W. BARTH,
Acting Assistant Adjutant-general:

CAPTAIN:—I herewith tender to you a supplemental report, in regard to matters connected with the battle of the 6th and 7th instant. My battery fired, during said actions, from the six guns, seven hundred and twenty-three rounds, mostly from the smooth-bore guns and howitzers, a large proportion of which was canister. Some of our ammunition chests being repacked from a captured caisson, and other canister borrowed from Capt. Robertson's battery, which he kindly loaned.

The badly torn wheels and carriages of my battery from minié balls, will convince any one of the close proximity to the enemy in which we were. I had twenty-eight (28) horses slain in the battery, exclusive of officers' horses.

I cannot refrain from applauding to you the gallant actions of Sergeants Bartley, Blair, and Smith, Corporals O'Brien, Higgins, Davidson, Biggs, Spearing, and Holmes, also of privates Boyden, Duggan, Murphy, Bayne, Leckie, Shotwell, Jones, Salter, Mathis, Scott, Fahnestock, Levy, Tomlin, Johnson, Teixas, Wing, and Hartnett, all of whom, with the young men killed, were at their posts during the action, and behaved most gallantly. Many of them, for the first time under fire, conducted themselves as veterans.

I have the honor to be,

Yours very truly,

W. IRVING HODGSON,

Captain.

Capt. Hodgson's Report referring to Reports of the 9th and 11th instant.

HEAD-QUARTERS 5TH COMPANY,
BATTALION WASHINGTON ARTILLERY,
Camp Moore, Corinth, Miss, April 12th, 1862.

TO CAPT. WM. G. BARTH,
Acting Assistant Adj.-general:

CAPTAIN:—Referring to my reports of the battle of the 6th and 7th instant, under dates of the 9th and 11th instant, I have had conversations with the "chiefs of sections" of my battery on the subject, and ascertain that there are so many of the "rank and file" that behaved gallantly on those occasions, that it would make too long a list, and be too invidious, to mention names.

You will therefore please erase those portions of my reports which refer to that subject, beginning with A. Gordon Bakewell, and ending with privates Wing and Hartnett.

By so doing, you will much oblige,
Yours very truly,
W. IRVING HODGSON, *Captain.*

Report of Col. P. Pond, Jr., commanding Third Brigade.

HEAD-QUARTERS 3D BRIGADE,
1ST DIVISION, A. M.

Capt. R. MASON HOOE:

SIR:—I have the honor to submit, through you, to Brig.-gen. Ruggles, commanding 1st division, 2d G. D. A. M., the following reports of the movements of the third brigade of his division, on Sunday and Monday, the 6th and 7th of April, 1862:

On the morning of the 6th, at daylight, the brigade was formed in the order of battle with columns doubled on the center at battalion distance, the right resting on the left of Gen. Anderson's brigade, with the left extended towards Owl creek, and covering the left of Gen. Hardee's line, about five hundred yards to the rear.

At about eight o'clock an order was received from Gen. Ruggles to throw one regiment with one section of guns to the left towards Owl creek. In compliance with this order, Col. Looney's regiment, 38th Tennessee, and one section of Capt. Ketchum's battery, were thrown about three-quarters of a mile to the left, and the position assigned to them, covered on the front and flank with cavalry skirmishers. These dispositions were not quite completed, when an order was received from Gen. Ruggles to advance the whole of his line. The brigade moved forward, in double columns, over very difficult ground, endeavoring to preserve the proper interval between itself and Gen. Anderson's brigade, and, at the same time, to guard the flank of the line on Owl creek. After advancing some six hundred yards, the brigade was halted near some small houses, with a large field on the left, and also with a similar field in front. Enemy's skirmishers being seen towards Owl creek, Col. Looney's regiment, with a section of Capt. Ketchum's battery, were again sent to the left to the distance of three-quarters of a mile and posted to command the Owl creek road. Information being received from Col. Looney that the enemy were ambushed in his front, the Crescent regiment, under Col. M. J. Smith, was detached to report to Col. Looney, and to support him. Shortly after, an order came from Gen. Hardee for the left to advance. In response to this order, the 16th and 18th Louisiana Volunteers, and a battalion Orleans Guards, advanced until they reached the line occupied by the second brigade, commanded by Gen. Anderson, which brigade was engaging the enemy in one of his camps, and which he was stubbornly contesting.

This camp having been carried, the whole line advanced through a narrow strip of woods and across a wide field until we reached the main and last camp of the enemy, which was not occupied—this camp having, apparently, been abandoned without a contest, as there were no evidences of any struggle having taken place there. As we approached this camp, a few of the enemy were seen on our left, who fired a few shots at us, but who were soon dispersed by one shot from Capt. Ketchum's battery. When we entered the edge of the field in which this main camp was situated, we perceived the enemy in full retreat. The left of the brigade was immediately thrown forward, and the whole put in motion, at double-quick, to cut him off; and the movement would, without doubt, have been successful, but when nearly across the field a dreadful fire was received from our own forces on the right, killing and wounding several of the 18th regiment Louisiana Volunteers, under the command of Col. Monton. Not knowing at first from whence the fire was directed, and fearing that I might have passed some of the enemy's forces, the brigade was halted and thrown back about one hundred yards to the edge of the woods. Wher our troops on the right advanced across the opening, this brigade advanced on the same line, passed through the main camp, and through a very deep ravine beyond it. At this time we were moving a little in advance of the front line, which was commanded by Gen. Hardee. Upon reaching the crest of the hill the command encountered a heavy fire of grape at a distance of about four hundred yards. The brigade was thrown back under the cover of the hill, and Capt. Ketchum's battery placed in position on the hills to the rear to silence the enemy's battery and disorganize its infantry supports. While waiting for Capt. Ketchum's battery to get into position, I reconnoitered and discovered the enemy posted in considerable numbers in a camp some two or three hundred yards to our front and left, and in a similar camp immediately to my front and right, from which the fire of the battery had been received and was still continued. At this time, about 4 P. M., Col. Ferguson brought peremptory orders to me to charge the battery with my brigade. Col. Ferguson was informed that there was a battery immediately in front, and said he would inform Gen. Hardee, and report to me. Immediately after Col. Ferguson left me, the Washington Artillery was placed in battery to the right of the enemy's main camp, and made an effort to silence the enemy's battery in my front, but failed to do so. By orders, said by Col. Ferguson to be the orders of Gen. Hardee, my brigade was filed left in front up a deep ravine in a direction flanking the enemy's battery, and, while the head of column was some three hundred yards in front of the battery, by the direction of Col. Ferguson, speaking as for Gen. Hardee, I ordered the charge. This brought my troops under the fire of the enemy's battery and three of his regiments in an oblique column, instead of line of battle, and the fire became so destructive that the troops recoiled under it.

The 18th Louisiana regiment suffered severely in this charge, also the Orleans Guards; the 16th Louisiana, less than either, being on the right, and, consequently, in what might be called the rear of the column. As my troops were advancing to this charge, we again received a severe fire from our own troops on the right, which, added to the fire of the enemy, almost disorganized the command. In order to reform, we were compelled to fall back about one hundred and fifty yards to the enemy's main camp, where we were rejoined by Col. Looney, with his regiment, he having received orders to leave his position on Owl creek road, and unite with the brigade.

The camp on my right was subsequently abandoned by the

enemy and occupied by our troops—the enemy withdrawing his battery. I heard sharp firing from my right on that camp in which the 38th Tennessee was engaged before it united with the brigade. The camp to my left continued to be occupied in considerable force, and as the duty of guarding the left was placed in my hands, and being separated about a quarter of a mile from the forces immediately on my right, I felt that any rash or inconsiderate advance or engagement of our troops might result in the exposure of my left and rear, and, therefore, made no attack on it. The charge made on the enemy's battery, by which the 18th regiment suffered so severely, was not in accordance with my judgment. I did it reluctantly, and in obedience to peremptory orders. If left to myself, I had the means of taking it, and would have taken it in twenty minutes after my battery had been brought into action. There was a wide gap between my left and Owl creek. I was alone with my brigade, without any thing to support my own rear on the left of the general line, and, therefore, felt it my duty to take every step with extreme caution, and to keep my force in hand to hold Owl creek against any and every contingency. In this I was acting in strict accordance with the plan of battle communicated to me by Gen. Bragg, on the evening of the 5th instant, and to this plan I rigidly adhered, no advice having reached me of change of plan. At night, after the battle ceased, acting in obedience to orders received through the day from a great variety of sources, I formed my infantry line considerably in advance of our general front. I immediately fell back to this line, resting my right on the main camp of the enemy, and extending my left to Owl creek, establishing police guards round each regiment, with picket in rear and front, and to the left across Owl creek. My ranks were then opened, and the men caused to lie down on their arms. There was some picket firing during the night, but nothing important developed itself. I would mention that on Sunday evening, just after the firing ceased, I heard cheering on the river below me, evidently proceeding from a large force, to which my men responded, thinking it to be from their friends, and, when the cheering ceased, a band played the air of "Hail Columbia" from a boat that was ascending the river.

My bivouac on Sunday night was within a mile of the river, and within four hundred yards of the enemy's lines. During the night our main line was thrown back about three-quarters of a mile without the movement being communicated to me. On Monday morning, at daylight, a sharp skirmish took place between pickets and was immediately followed by a sharp engagement between my lines and those of the enemy. A battery was also opened against my right at a range of about four hundred yards.

At this time I discovered that our main line had fallen back, and that my brigade was alone in the presence of the enemy, who was in strong force. I regarded the position as perilous, and should, no doubt, have been cut off or cut to pieces, but for the cool, intrepid, and gallant conduct of Capt. Ketchum, who brought his battery into position on my right, and maintained a spirited and effective fire against the enemy within infantry range, while my regiments were withdrawn under the lead of their respective commanders. I cannot speak too highly of the coolness and intrepidity of Col. Monton, Major Gober, Col. Looney, and Capt. Morton, manifested by the orderly manner in which they withdrew their respective commands over the most difficult ground, and united themselves, without disaster, with the main line. The infantry movement left Capt. Ketchum's battery exposed, but, as the whole was in great peril, I thought it better to sacrifice the pieces than the regiments, if any thing had to be lost. Capt. Ketchum, however, withdrew, covered by the regiment of Texas Rangers, exhibiting throughout the whole a degree of skill and courage, which mark him as an artillery officer of the highest merit. In fact, the safety of my command is due to him. Upon reaching the main line, the left of which was at the enemy's first camp on the Savannah road, I was ordered by Gen. Ruggles to form on the extreme left, and rest my left on Owl creek. While proceeding to execute this order, I was ordered to move by the rear of the main line to support the extreme right of Gen. Hardee's line. I was again ordered by Gen. Beauregard to advance and occupy the crest of a ridge in the edge of an old field. My line was just formed in this position, when Gen. Polk ordered me forward to support his line. While moving to the support of Gen. Polk, an order reached me from Gen. Beauregard to report to him, with my command, at his head-quarters. This was on the extreme left, where my brigade became engaged in the fight which continued until the contest between the armies finally ceased. As Gen. Ruggles was present at this point, no report of particulars is necessary.

My command was kept once in hand through the occurrences ot both days, and brought off the field in as good order as it entered it under my immediate command. Col. Monton was wounded in the fight at the church, and Major —— was wounded in the knee, in the charge on the enemy's battery.

The Crescent regiment was not seen by me during the engagement, but I received information, from various sources, that it was in the fight on the right, and served with marked gallantry and effect.

Very respectfully,

P. POND, Jr.,
Colonel commanding Brigade.

Report of Casualties in Third Brigade, First Division.

16th Louisiana Volunteers—Killed, 14; seriously wounded, 13; slightly wounded, 31; mortally wounded, 5; missing, 27. Total, 90. See report.

38th Tennessee—Killed, 7; seriously wounded, 17; slightly wounded, 26; missing, 15. Total, 65. See report.

Orleans Guards—Killed, 17; slightly wounded, 55; missing, 18. Total 90. See report.

Ketchum's Battery—Killed, 1; slightly wounded, 13. Total, 14. Sick 23.

18th Regiment Louisiana—Killed, 13; slightly wounded, 80; missing, 118. Total, 211.

Crescent—Killed, 23; slightly wounded, 84; missing, 20. Total, 127.

Grand total, 597.

This is only a rough report. I will cause others to be made in accordance with general orders. Those reported as missing are occasionally coming in.

P. POND, Jr.,
Colonel commanding 3d Brigade.

I must call attention to the case of that gallant officer and soldier, Capt. Walter Crain, whose battery has been taken from him. I saw him fighting gallantly in the ranks with his rifle, and, in the engagement of Monday, he received a severe wound. If gallantry would entitle an officer to his command, none deserve it more than Capt. Crain.

Report of Col. Alfred Monton.

Camp near Corinth, April 12, 1862.

To Lieut. O. O. Cobb,
A. A. A. G., C. S. Forces:

Sir:—Herewith I respectfully submit a report of the part taken by the 18th Louisiana volunteers, in the engagements of the 6th and and 7th instant.

Leaving this camp at about 3 P. M., on the 3d, I reached the line of battle on the 5th, at about 5 P. M. Early on the 6th, I was ordered to take position, facing the enemy in an eligible location, and await the arrival of the balance of the brigade. I advanced opposite to the enemy's camp, and halted in a field about 400 yards distant therefrom. My skirmishers ascended the slope of the hill, and exchanged shots with the enemy for about fifteen minutes, when the latter withdrew. I then pushed forward, and perceived about 500 of the enemy in retreat. Anxious to intercept them, I rushed on at double-quick, but unfortunately, our troops on the right, mistook us for the enemy, owing, I presume, to the blue uniform of a large number of my men, and opened on us with cannon and musket. This impeded my progress and brought me to a halt, until a staff officer signalled to our troops to cease firing. On the cessation of the firing, I moved on to the camp and captured 29 prisoners, who were placed in charge of Lieut. W. Prescott, company K, who transferred them to Col. Eli S. Shorter, 18th Alabama, on receipt. But for this unfortunate occurrence, the probability is, I would have captured the whole number of the enemy that was fleeing. Here one man was killed, and Capt. Huntington, company H, and three privates, were wounded by the fire of our friends. Thence we moved onward to a deep ravine under cover from the enemy's shells. Notwithstanding, company F had one private killed and another wounded.

Thence, about 4 P. M., I moved by the left flank through the continuation of the same ravine, with the view of charging the battery which had been continuously firing on us. Before reaching a proper position, and while directly in front of the battery, distant from it about six or seven hundred yards, I received peremptory orders to move up the hill and charge the battery. The order was instantly obeyed. About four hundred yards from the battery, my line became entirely uncovered, and thence my regiment rushed forward alone at double-quick, towards the battery, being all the time exposed to an incessant fire, both from the battery and its supports. At about sixty or seventy yards from the battery, which then commenced moving from its position and began to retreat, the enemy had opposed to my regiment, then numbering about five hundred, three regiments of infantry, two of which kept up an incessant cross fire on my troops, and the third, as soon as unmasked by the battery, also opened upon us. Thus exposed, my men falling at every step, being unsupported, and unable to accomplish the capture of the battery, or the repulse of the enemy, I was compelled to retire, leaving my dead and wounded on the field. Here two hundred and seven officers and men fell either dead or wounded, and Lieut.-col. Roman and I had our horses shot under us. I must add, that, in my opinion, the order to charge the battery was prematurely given; that is, before our troops had taken proper position to act effectually and support one another, otherwise, I am inclined to believe the battery would have been captured.

After rallying the regiment, I moved off to the left, and took posstion opposite the enemy's lines, distant about three hundred yards, which were covered by infantry and artillery. Throwing out pickets to protect my line, I bivouacked for the night. By this time, my men were completely exhausted, as they had neither slept nor eaten since the evening of the 4th, and had been continually on the march. On the night of the 6th, it rained almost constantly, and being without cover, by the morning of the 7th they were thoroughly drenched and worn out from lack of food and rest. At about half-past 6 on the 7th, the enemy, in large force, opened on us with cannon and musket. My troops being in full view from the battery, I fell back under cover from their shells. While in this position, orders were received at about 8 A. M. to move to the right of the line. From this hour, until about half-past 1 P. M., we were constantly marching and countermarching; the "Orleans Guards" in the meantime, having been attached to my command. About 2 P. M., we were ordered to move on the enemy, which was done without energy or life, by the troops, twice in succession, notwithstanding the noble and daring efforts of Gens. Beauregard and Bragg to lead them on in the face of the enemy. The fact is, the men were completely exhausted from inanition and physical fatigue; many dropping in the attempt to move ownward. Here I was wounded in the face, and three privates remained on the field, either killed or wounded. I was then compelled by reason of my wound to abandon the field.

Thence, by order, my troops fell back, about half past 3 P. M., to a line a little beyond Shiloh church, and about half-past 4 P. M., they moved by the left flank to the rear, and reached Corinth on the 8th, at about 3 P. M., as I have been informed by the lieut.-col. then in command.

A complete field return has already been forwarded, and I beg leave to call attention to the number of killed and wounded officers. Allow me to add further, that my report of this morning, exhibits only ten officers for duty, viz.: One captain, four first lieutenants, and five second lieutenants.

Very respectfully,
Your obedient servant,
ALFRED MONTON,
Col. 18th regiment Louisiana Volunteers.

Report of Col. E. S. Shorter.

HEAD-QUARTERS, CAMP OF THE 3D BRIGADE,
WITHERS' DIVISION, 2D CORPS, A. M.,
NEAR CORINTH, April 9th, 1862.

Capt. J. B. CUMMING,
Assistant Adjutant-general:

SIR:—Inclosed, I have the honor to submit to you a report of the casualties that occurred to my regiment in the great historic battle at Shiloh Church, on Sunday, the 6th instant. The number of non-commissioned officers and privates, actually engaged in the first battle, was only four hundred and thirteen. During this long continued fight of about one hour and upwards, my men nearly exhausted the fifty rounds of cartridges that had previously been distributed to them. A considerable number of the men had none whatever left. By order of Gen. Jackson, after the enemy had been routed, and we were advancing, I sent back to the ammunition train and procured a new supply. The regiment was actively engaged in all the battles during that day in which the brigade participated. Our loss was very heavy, to wit: twenty killed, eighty wounded, and twenty missing. Most of those classed among the missing, doubtless were taken prisoners by the enemy, as they were with Dr. Barnett, our surgeon, who was captured on Monday, while attending to the wounded. It is reported to me on good authority, that the enemy fired on Dr. Barnett and his party, while under the yellow flag, and when the surgeon was actually engaged in dressing the wounds of one of the enemy.

The officers (with but one exception) and the men of the regi ment conducted themselves throughout the several engagements with much gallantry and spirit. Lieut. Rogers, who was in com mand of company B, abandoned his company twice, and wholly dis appeared from the field. He is here now in arrest, and proper charges will be filed against him. Lieut.-col. Holtzclaw was dangerously wounded in the first engagement, while he was gallantly discharging his duty.

Respectfully, &c.,

ELI S. SHORTER,

Colonel 18th Alabama Regiment.

Report of Colonel R. F. Looney.

REGIMENTAL HEAD-QUARTERS, 38TH TENN. REGIMENT,
CAMP NEAR CORINTH, MISS., April 26, 1862.

To Brigadier-General RUGGLES,
Commanding Division:

GENERAL: I have the honor to report the service rendered by the 38th Tennessee regiment, in the battle of Shiloh, on the 6th and 7th of April.

Early on the morning of the 6th, we were ordered to move rapidly to the left as far as Owl creek, which position was promptly taken by the Crescent and 38th Tennessee regiments and Capt. Ketchum's battery. This position was held until about 11 o'clock A. M., when we were ordered to move to the right. Under this order, at a double-quick, I moved my command in the neighborhood of, and to the right of, Shiloh church, and in front of a battery which was playing upon us. We advanced as we received orders, firing upon the enemy as we advanced. Shortly we approached a camp of the enemy, only an open field intervening. To the right, and in advance of the camp, we discovered the enemy in considerable force. We poured upon him a destructive fire, which caused him soon to begin to retire. Near the camp was a battery, all the while playing upon our forces. I received an order to charge the battery and camp under cover of the woods to the right, from Major-gen. Polk, through his son, Capt. Polk. I quickly examined the route as ordered, and saw the camp and battery could be reached, and the order carried out in effect, with but little more risk by moving rapidly through the open field. I ordered the charge, which was promptly and successfully executed, as to the camp and battery, and I suppose at least one thousand prisoners. After I reached the camp, some cavalry and Col. Cummins' Tennesee regiment came up. We were soon moved farther to the left. Night approached, and we lay down without fire and in the rain, about six hundred yards from the camp of the 77th Illinois, I think. On the morning of the 7th, at daylight, the 3d brigade of your division was drawn up in line of battle. Almost instantly we were fired upon by a battery brought up in the night, within a very short distance, and supported by a large force. I immediately ordered my regiment to fire, and three rounds were delivered at the enemy, with what effect I am unable to say.

About this time our own battery in our rear opened, leaving us exposed to the shells of friend and foe, which caused us to take position to the rear of our guns. We were moved quickly from one point to another, to the support of brigade commanders unknown, until about 11 o'clock A. M.

A short time after this, we were ordered to Shiloh church, in the direction of Pittsburg and near a camp occupied by the enemy. After having been held by Gen. Beauregard for about fifteen minutes, I received an order from him through Gov. Harris, of Tennessee, to charge the camp and the enemy. My regiment was in the centre. There were, I suppose, two regiments on my right and three on the left. We drove the enemy far beyond his camp, my regiment being far in advance of any other troops, when we were ordered to retire.

Three times did they charge the enemy and drive him from his position at every point. I delivered the last volley at the enemy on Monday, and when we were withdrawn from this part of the field, I found the army drawn up in beautiful order to retire.

For a list of the killed, wounded, and missing of my regiment, I refer to a report heretofore furnished.

I deem it but just and proper that I should make mention of the gallant bearing of the officers and men of my command.

Capt. John C. Carter deserves the highest praise for his great coolness and high courage displayed throughout the entire engagement. At one time he took the flag, and urging his men forward, rendered me great assistance in moving forward the entire regiment. Capts. Cotler, Hardy, Umphleet, Thrasher, and Mayfield, for their gallant bearing, are entitled to great credit. They discharged their whole duty.

Capt. Abington was with his company throughout the first day of the battle, and conducted himself handsomely, but, being in delicate health, was not able to be with his company on the 7th.

Lieuts. Koen, March, Green, Hutchinson, Pugh, Chilcut, Ketchum,

Loving, Jones, Wait, and Briggs, were at all times at their posts, and their gallantry was worthy of the cause for which they struggled.

With but few exceptions, the men did their duty and fought bravely.

To Adj. Sanford I am greatly indebted for assistance rendered me throughout the entire engagement, and for his gallant bearing and high courage too many praises cannot be given.

Lieut. Haller, though feeble from ill health, was with his company and at his post all the while, and on Monday, in the absence of his captain, gallantly led his men through the fight.

Respectfully submitted.

R. F. LOONEY,
Colonel 38th Tennessee Regiment.

Report of Major Daniel Gober, Commanding 16th regiment Louisiana Volunteers.

HEAD-QUARTERS 16TH LOUISIANA REGIMENT,
CAMP NEAR CORINTH, MISS.,
April 26, 1862.

To Brig.-gen. RUGGLES,
Commanding Division:

GENERAL: I respectfully submit the following report of the operations of the 16th regiment Louisiana volunteers, in the action at Shiloh, on the 6th and 7th inst., the command of which regiment had devolved upon me, in consequence of the absence, on duty, of Lieut.-col. Mason, and the assignment to Col. Preston Pond, Jr., of the command of the 3d brigade, Gen. Ruggles' division.

The extraordinary degree of sickness prevalent in camp, and the absence of company B, left for guard duty at Corinth, had diminished the effective force of the regiment, upon entering the engagement, to 330 rank and file.

The participation of the regiment in the action of Sunday the 6th, though it was frequently exposed to the fire of the enemy during the morning, and was subjected to occasional losses in consequence of its exposure, was not perhaps sufficiently important to justify a special notice of its movements until in the afternoon, when a portion of the brigade, including the 16th regiment, was ordered to charge one or more of the enemy's batteries, the position and strength of which were evidently unknown or gravely misapprehended. The accomplishment of this order proved to be impracticable, and the effort to execute it resulted in our repulse, with considerable loss of killed and wounded. Early in the morning of the 7th, the battle was renewed by the opening of one of the enemy's batteries upon us from a concealed point in the woods near the grounds upon which the regiment had bivouacked during the previous night.

Having retired to a more favorable position, where line of battle was formed, the regiment, in conjunction with the balance of the brigade, was immediately moved forward to meet the advancing columns of the enemy. Becoming thus engaged, at an early hour in the morning of the 7th, the regiment continued in action and efficient service until the cessation of hostilities in the afternoon—the locality of its operations varying but little during the day.

The withdrawal of our forces having been ordered at 4 o'clock in the afternoon, the regiment, in exhausted and reduced condition, rejoined the brigade from which it had been temporarily separated, and fell back in the direction of Monterey.

For the casualties of the regiment, reference is made to the report of the killed, wounded, and missing, rendered in conformity with order No. —.

DANIEL GOBER,
Major commanding 16th La. Volunteers.

Report of Captain W. H. Ketchum.

CORINTH, MISSISSIPPI,
April 15th, 1862.

COLONEL:—On Friday, 4th instant, we took up our line of march from Monterey, proceeding on the Savannah road, joining our brigade (Col. Pond's) from whom we had been detached for several days. Nothing of interest occuring this day, we encamped about five miles out. The next morning, taking our regular position in line, we advanced until about 5 P. M., forming in line of battle on the extreme left, my battery masked by Capt. Jenkins' and Capt. Robins' cavalry companies. There having been some skirmishing in advance and on our right this day, and the enemy's camps not being more than a mile in our front, distinctly hearing the tattoo from their different camps, I deemed it prudent to keep my horses in harness all night. At 6 o'clock the next morning (Sunday, 6th) the battle commenced, and we marched steadily to the front in line of battle, holding different positions as ordered, when an order reached me to place my battery in position, commanding the approach from Owl creek, where it was thought the enemy would attempt to get through on our flank. In this position I was supported by the 38th Tennessee and Crescent regiments. After remaining here in position for some little time, two sections of my battery were ordered to join Col. Pond immediately, who was in advance and on the right. I took charge of this battery of four pieces, leaving the 3d section, 2 pieces, with Lieut. Bond. On arriving where Col. Pond was with the balance of his brigade, we commenced an advance movement again through the woods, swamps, and old fields, without any regard to roads.

The fighting from 6 A. M. up to this time had been very severe on our right. And until now in an open field we had not experienced the whistling of the enemy's balls. And finding the enemy firing at us from a log-house, with a camp in rear, we fired our first round, which was a shell from a howitzer, at the house, throwing it immediately in the house. This was about 10 A. M. The enemy leaving, we continued advancing through their deserted camps, until arriving at a camp where they were drawn up in line of battle, Col. Pond ordered me to advance, and shell them out. Moving up my four pieces, I opened on them with spherical case and shell, gradually advancing on the camp by half battery. In a short time, the enemy left their camp in double-quick for the woods on their right. At this moment, an aid from Gen. Hardee rode up, ordering me with my battery to the left, where he reported the enemy in force. On arriving at an eminence on the road commanding a camp on the right of the one we had just shelled, we found the enemy in large force, and the woods in the gorge below, between my battery and the camp, filled with sharpshooters. Some Texas rangers, who directed me, lost four or five of their men from these sharpshooters, while pointing out the enemy's position. I opened fire on the camp, advising the rangers to dismount and enter the woods as skirmishers, which they nobly did, while we effectually shelled the camp. I think this was Col. Wharton's regiment. They supported us gallantly in all our engagements with the enemy the balance of the day. Col. Pond's fine brigade was badly cut up in a charge on a battery in one of these camps, which

I have always thought might have been avoided, had my battery not been withdrawn from the advance I was making on this camp. This same evening, we engaged one of the enemy's batteries, and silenced them after about one and a half hours' firing. Night coming on, we placed our pieces in battery on their parade ground, adjoining a house on the right of their camp, where a number of our dead and wounded lay. This was at the instance of Col. Ferguson, of Gen. Beauregard's staff. On our left in the woods was our infantry support, Col. Pond's command. A continual firing from the gunboats was kept up all night. Daylight in the morning found our teams hitched up, our men chilled through by the cold rain, sleeping without tents or much covering, still most manfully and cheerfully did they man their pieces, to reply to a battery which opened on us. In this position we fought them a half hour, and finding they had our range, and our situation being too much exposed, losing some of our horses, I retired about one hundred yards, to a position which I desired the evening previous. Here we opened our pieces upon them rapidly, and having good command of their battery, succeeded in silencing them in a little more than a half hour's firing, and then opened on a body of infantry which appeared near the position occupied by Col. Pond the evening previous. During this engagement, Col. Wharton's rangers remained on our right in line of battle, witnessing the duello, and ready to charge any effort of the enemy to take my battery. At this time an order came from Col. Pond for me to fall back immediately, he being some distance in our rear. Limbering up, we retired, coming again into battery wherever we could be of service, engaging batteries and bodies of infantry at different points. And while engaged with a battery, we found Lieut. Bond with his section doing good execution a short distance to our right. We now came under Gen. Bragg's immediate orders, and our infantry were being hard pressed by the enemy. Advancing the battery in a gallop on a road bringing us on the enemy's left, we came into battery, discharging canister from our six pieces at a distance of forty or fifty yards, checking his advance, and driving them back in the thicket, our troops rallying again. We remained in this position, using canister freely, until recalled by Gen. Bragg to some other position. We were joined here by an officer with one piece and three or four cannoniers, who asked permission to join my battery, so that we had seven pieces in position. In this fight we lost one man and several wounded. One of our pieces got disabled here. The splinter bar broken, and the piece up to the hubs in mud, it was impossible to get it out. The firing from this time up to the close of the fight was unusually severe from musketry, and also artillery, in which we were constantly engaged, Gen. Bragg remaining with the battery up to the last moment of the fight, and after our infantry had withdrawn from the field, he ordered me to withdraw by sections, in good order, covering the retreat, and taking position for any advance of the enemy. We encamped on the road that night, and made Corinth next evening, 8th instant, as ordered.

My first section, commanded by First Lieut. Garrity, was managed with remarkable coolness and ability, prompt in executing all orders, and firing with marked precision. The gunner to his howitzer, Corporal Ingalls, did great credit to himself in this respect. His pieces are brought back in good order. Second Lieut. Bond, 3d section, behaved gallantly when with me on Monday, which was our most severe fighting, and when detached from me on Sunday and part of Monday, the most flattering account of his section is given by those whom he was with. His guns are back in good order. Third Lieut. Carroll, 2d section, also behaved gallantly, cheering his men through the thickest of the fight. His section lost one piece and two caissons, which was unavoidable.

To mention cases of individual merit might be most appropriately made, and could not be done without naming the whole command, with two or three exceptions. My loss in killed, 1; wounded, 12. Horses, 15.

Very respectfully,
Your obedient servant,
WM. H. KETCHUM,
Captain Alabama State Artillery, company A.

To the unremitting attention of our surgeon, Dr. John P. Barnes, who was with us on the field, and untiring in his attentions to the wounded, I shall ever feel grateful, and cannot say too much in his praise.

Very respectfully,
Your obedient servant,
WM. H. KETCHUM,
Captain Alabama State Artillery.

Report of Col. Marshall J. Smith.

HEAD-QUARTERS CRESCENT REGIMENT,
THIRD BRIGADE, RUGGLES' DIVISION,
Camp McPheeters', April 14, 1862.

To Col. PRESTON POND, Jr.,
Commanding 3d Brigade, Ruggles' Division, &c.:

COLONEL: I submit, herewith, a report of the operations of my regiment on the 6th and 7th instant, in the battle of Shiloh, near Pittsburg.

In obedience to your order, on the morning of the 6th, I took position with my regiment on the right of Col. Looney's 38th Tennessee regiment, the left of the latter resting on Owl creek, to guard the road leading to the enemy's camp, and to prevent their turning our left, supported by two pieces from Ketchum's battery, commanded by Lieut. Philip Bond. We remained in this position until about 1 1-2 o'clock, P. M., when we received orders through Col. Beard, aid to Gen. Bragg, to come immediately to the front. We moved both regiments by the right flank rapidly forward, and to the right. My own, throwing off their blankets and all incumbrances, to facilitate their movements, passed through the enemy's camps, which appeared to have been the scene of severe conflict, towards the heavy firing in front, passing by the position occupied by Gen. Beauregard, who ordered us to "go forward and drive the enemy into Tennessee." Advancing about three hundred yards further, through open woods, raked by shell from the enemy's batteries, we came up with Gens. Polk, Ruggles, and Anderson. The enemy's battery, sustained by sharpshooters, occupied a hill to the right of an open field, which contained a house, a cotton pen, some cotton bales, &c., behind which the sharpshooters were posted in considerable force. After consultation, Gen. Polk directed Gen. Anderson to the right, and Looney's and my regiment to the left. I found the fire so heavy from the battery and sharpshooters, that in my judgment, it became prudent to drive them from this stronghold, before feeling to the left, which we did by a charge, driving them towards their battery and from the thicket in front of it. The two pieces of Ketchum's battery came up and were assigned position by me. Lieut. Bond promptly responded to the heavy fire from the enemy's battery, and by his coolness and precision, in a short time succeeded in silencing them. I then filed my regiment around to the right through a heavy thicket, passing between two of our regiments, of what State, I am unable to say, and advancing under the orders of Gen. Polk, took position in front of the enemy, who, retreating, had taken position behind fences and houses, to secure themselves from the fire of our forces, who were pressing them from the front. Our flank fire caused them to break and run to their quarters, where we opened a heavy fire upon them, and filing again to a more advanced position, surrounded them, when the surrender of a large number took place. I myself received the swords of many of them, among whom were Col. Morton, 23d Mo., and Capt. McMichael, Acting Adj.-gen. to Gen. Smith. Gen. Prentiss surrendered on the same spot, some fifteen minutes after, not to me, because I was engaged in preventing the escape of those already prisoners, but, I am told, to some private of Col. Freeman's Tennessee regiment! That my regiment was in advance of the others at the surrender, and that I was ordered to receive the surrender by Gen. Polk, there is no room for doubt. A flag was surrendered at the same time, but being engaged in advancing on the enemy, I lost sight of it. We also captured at this place a fine bronze 18-pound howitzer. In the several charges incident to the final surrender of this camp, we had several brave men killed, and many wounded. The enemy again formed line of battle in the woods between the camp and Pittsburg, and we formed behind the batteries placed to oppose them, and after being shelled for some little time, the enemy broke, retreating towards Pittsburg. It is reported that the white flag was raised at this time, which was not so, as the stars and stripes were plainly visible. After their retreat, the gunboats opened a most destructive fire, which we endured for some time, not being able to reply, and under orders, we retired in good order from the point gained, and took up our quarters for the night in one of the enemy's encampments. I received orders from Gen. Beauregard to be prepared for action at 6 o'clock A. M. the next morning, the 7th inst., and to move towards the Bark road. When near Gen. Beauregard's head-quarters, I received orders to move to the support of Gen. Chalmers, who was then engaged with the enemy. We were formed in line by Gen. Withers, to move forward to the support of the advanced line, with the 19th Louisiana on our right. As the army advanced, the forces in front of us retired, and the Washington Artillery, Capt. Hodgson, forming his battery in front of us, we supported him. This battery gallantly maintained their position, dealing destruction upon the foe, until the artillery on their left retired, leaving them alone. At this moment the enemy advanced in heavy force, and the artillery properly fearing such odds, limbered up and filed off to our left. We then advanced, covering the movement of the artillery, saving several of their pieces, and driving the enemy before us. Here fell Capts. Graham and Campbell, two of my best and most gallant officers, and in this same charge fell, killed and wounded, most of the gallant spirits whose loss we now deplore.

The enemy being again reinforced, after having been driven back, in order to prevent being flanked, we were forced to retire to the ravine. The 1st Missouri, lying under the brow of the hill, sent a volley into the enemy, which threw them into confusion, and my regiment, rallying again, charged the enemy. Here my color sergeant, Shilling, with three of the color guard, were shot down, and the flag was handed to Sergeant Lyons, of the Twiggs Guards, who bore it faithfully and fearlessly over the hill. This time, with another regiment on our left, we drove the enemy into a wheat field, and back to the undergrowth, when finding them supported by two regiments in ambush, we retired in good order to the ravine. Four times thus, we drove the enemy back, every time coming upon us with fresh troops. At about 3 o'clock, when the troops were ordered to retire, we did so by the orders of Gens. Hardee and Withers, being held, with other regiments, under command of Col. Wheeler of the Alabama regiment, to protect the withdrawal of the other troops of our army, until between five and six o'clock, P. M., when we proceeded to a point about three and a half miles from Monterey, where we encamped during the night, returning the next morning to this camp. My men were exhausted, and were absolutely sinking on the way from the effects of fatigue, want of food, sleep, and rest. We left the field of battle a half mile in advance of the point where we commenced the fight, and within that space lay those brave men who had fallen dead and wounded, numbering one hundred and seven, a detailed report of which is annexed.

Lieut.-col. McPheeter's, Major Basworth, Capts. Hardenburg (Commissary), and Gribble (Quarter-master), and Adjutant Venables, behaved gallantly.

Among the line officers, I have great satisfaction in mentioning the following as distinguished for coolness, bravery, and the faithful discharge of their duty:

Company A, Lieuts. Stephens, Handy, and Le Gay, the last two wounded.

Company B, Capt. Haynes, Lieuts. Claiborne and Howell.

Company C, Lieut. Bullitt, who supplied the place of the lamented Graham, after he fell, offering to carry the colors himself.

Company D, Lieuts. Kleslier and Forstall.

Company E, Lieuts. Airey and Holmes.

Company F, Capt. Austin, and Lieut. Guillett, the latter exhibiting a courage bordering on impetuosity.

Company G, Capt. Helm, and Lieuts. Mullen, Shepperd, and Enderly; Lieuts. Fisher and Perry being wounded early in the action.

Company I, Capt. Knight, who, though wounded, I found a difficulty in keeping from the field. Lieut. Field, who, supplying his place, conducted himself with coolness and bravery. Lieut. Seaman.

Company K, Lieut. McDougall, supplying the place of the gallant Campbell. Lieuts. Garrison and Collie.

Company L, Capt. Davidson was cool and collected. On Monday I was deprived of his valuable services. Lieut. Lewis well filled the post. Lieut. Fellows was seriously wounded.

In regared to the conduct of the privates, there are many that acted with great gallantry and coolness. There are but two, and that particularly on account of their youth, whom I will mention: Paul Le Moncier, company B, and James Hanafy, company H.

MARSHALL J. SMITH,
Colonel Crescent Regiment.

Captain Jenkins' Consolidated Report of Casualties of 1st Battalion Alabama Cavalry.

CAMP CAVALRY BATTALION,
NEAR CORINTH, MISS., April 18th, 1862.

To R. M. HOOE, *A. A. G.:*

A. A. GENERAL: Herewith inclosed, you find report of all of the captains of my battalion 1st Alabama cavalry.

Below, number of casualties:

Capt. Jenkins' company, no casualties; Capt. Cox's company, 2 men killed, 1 horse killed, 2 wounded; Capt. Robins' company, 3 men wounded, 2 horses killed, 2 wounded; Capt. Tomlinson's company, 3 men wounded, 4 horses killed, 5 wounded. Total, 2 men killed, 6 wounded, 7 horses killed, 9 wounded. None missing.

I have the honor to remain, sir,
Your obedient servant,
T. F. JENKINS,
Senior Captain, commanding 1st Battalion Alabama Cavalry.

Report of the action and part taken by Capt. Jenkins, commanding the 1st Battalion Alabama Cavalry, in the engagements of the 6th and 7th instant.

CAMP CAVALRY BATTALION, CAVALRY BRIGADE,
NEAR CORINTH, MISS., April 18, 1862.

To Brig.-gen. RUGGLES:

GENERAL: I herewith submit a report of the part taken by my company in the action of the 6th and 7th inst. On the first day of the action, my company was attached as support to a section of Capt. Ketchum's battery on the left flank of Brig.-gen. Ruggles' division. In the afternoon of the same day, when the battery was ordered forward, my company, by order of Gen. Beauregard, dismounted to fight on foot. I advanced with the 27th regiment Tennessee, but did not have the gratification of exchanging shots with the enemy before their final retreat to the gunboats. Nothing of note occurred in the action of the 6th inst.

On the morning of the 7th, I was ordered to the extreme left as flankers and skirmishers, and was advancing in that position when Major-gen. Bragg ordered me to join Col. Brewers' battalion in the charge upon one of the enemy's batterys on the left—but being ordered to retire before reaching the battery, did not succeed in its capture. The remainder of the day, we remained in rear of Gen. Ruggles' division, as support to Capt. Ketchum's battery. 2d Lieut. McIntosh was attached as commander of Gen. Ruggles' body-guard on both days of the action. Nothing occurred deserving particular note. Number of men engaged on the 6th, 52; on the 7th, 47. No casualties.

T. F. JENKINS,
Commanding Battalion of Cavalry.

Capt. Tomlinson's report of the Battles of the 6th and 7th of April.

CAMP NEAR CORINTH, MISS.,
April 18, 1862.

My company of Alabama mounted volunteers was under command of Brig.-gen. Ruggles on the 6th and 7th instant, at Shiloh church.

Seven of my men, with a corporal, were detained as couriers, under the immediate command of Lieut. S. McIntosh. From the time the battle began to 12 o'clock, M., my command was with Gen. Ruggles on the battle-field, and from that time until 4 o'clock I was engaged in watching the movements of the enemy on our left wing. The remainder of the day and also the night was under the command of Capt. Cox.

Monday morning I was ordered by Brig.-gen. Ruggles to form line of battle with a Tennessee battalion on the left. Soon orders came to assist in a charge with said battalion and Texas Rangers. The charge, from some cause, was not made, and we fell back, where my command remained, until ordered by Gen. Bragg to hasten to Corinth to overtake and aid the escort with the prisoners.

I went on the field with three commissioned officers, six non-commissioned officers, and forty-eight privates. In the evening, private George W. McCurdy was shot by the enemy through the right hand with a musket ball. Same evening, corporal W. D. King was slightly wounded in the right arm. In the morning, sergeant John J. Cochran was thrown from his horse and his left shoulder was dislocated. None missing.

I had four horses killed and five wounded. I captured two muskets and three horses, all of which I now have, and lost five of Colt's pistols.

Respectfully submitted,

A. TOMLINSON,

Captain Mathew's Rangers.

Report of Captain Cox, of the action and part taken by his command in the battles of the 6th and 7th of April.

CAMP CAVALRY BATTALION, NEAR CORINTH, MISS.,
April 18th, 1862.

CAPTAIN:—The cavalry company, Prattsville dragoons, of Capt. Jenkins' cavalry battalion, carried to the battle of Shiloh, on the 6th April, four commissioned officers, four sergeants, four corporals, one bugler, and thirty-three privates. The company, with Capt. Tomlinson's company, was ordered to advance with the right wing of Gen. Ruggles' division. After entering the first camp of the enemy,

Capt. Tomlinson was ordered to reconnoitre the woods on the left of that division. My own was ordered to remain with Gen. Ruggles, which was used during the day of the 6th as couriers and rallying troops. In the evening of the 6th, I was ordered by Gen. Ruggles to carry an order to the Texas Rangers to charge the enemy, and my company to charge with them. We started for that purpose in columns of fours. The front columns of the Texas Rangers met the infantry of the enemy, and an order was given to retire; the cause I do not know, but think the position of the enemy was such the charge could not be made.

Monday morning, the 7th, was ordered with Gen. Ruggles; remained with him until ordered by the General to go with Capt. Jenkins' company, and support a section of Ketchum's battery. Went for that purpose, but found the section retiring to take its former position. Was next ordered by Capt. Jenkins to go with his company and the Texas Rangers to charge the enemy's left flank. In the evening of the 7th, took position in the rear, as ordered, until relieved by Gen. Bragg, as a part of his body-guard.

On the 6th, private John Stracker was killed while we were with Gen. Ruggles.

On the morning of the 7th, Corporal Adam Clanigen was killed; one horse killed, and two others had their legs broken. Took off of the field one horse, two muskets, one Sharpe's rifle, and six guns of different makes, which have been turned over to the Quarter-master and Ordnance Master.

Very respectfully,

Your obedient servant,

J. J. COX.

Captain Prattsville Dragoons.

Report of Captain Robins of the action and part taken by his command in the engagements of the 6th and 7th of April.

NEAR CORINTH, MISS., April 18th, 1862.

On Sunday, the 6th of April, fifteen men of my command were detailed to act as couriers. Ten of them acted as couriers for Gen. Ruggles, and five for Gen. Pond. The balance of my command masked Ketchum's battery until it went into action. My command was then ordered by Gen. Beauregard to bring up stragglers, which was executed, until the enemy began the retreat. I was then ordered by Gen. Beauregard to report to Gen. Ruggles. After reporting to Gen. Ruggles, he put several hundred prisoners in my charge, which he had captured. I guarded them during the night, and on Monday took them to Corinth, Miss., and put them on the cars. My men behaved well, and were willing and ready to obey any order that was given them. Three of my men were wounded, two horses killed, and two horses wounded. Two sabres and one Colt's navy pistol lost. Total number of men engaged, 73.

J. ROBINS,
Commanding Cavalry.

REPORT OF THE EVACUATION OF JACKSONVILLE.

COL. W. G. DILWORTH, COMMANDING.

HEAD-QUARTERS DISTRICT E. AND M. FLORIDA,
TALLAHASSEE, FLA. April 15, 1862.

To Capt. T. A. WASHINGTON,
Assistant Adj.-gen., Pocataligo, S. C.:

CAPTAIN:—I have the honor to report to the commanding general the evacuation of Jacksonville by the enemy which was done on the 9th instant.

When the enemy first occupied Jacksonville, and while all the Federal troops were retreating in confusion and disorder, I, as Col. 3d M. F. V., ordered a part of my regiment to advance in the direction of Jacksonville, and took position within ten miles of the city, with only two hundred and fifty effective men. Soon I had eight companies of my regiment with me. After making a thorough reconnoisance of the city, I became convinced that I could not attack the city without heavy loss, and could be driven out by the enemy's gunboats.

I then determined to commence a system of annoyance by attacking their pickets, foraging parties, &c. I made a successful attack on the pickets near the city of Jacksonville, killing four and taking three prisoners, when I was ordered to take command of the district. Col. Davis was then ordered to the command of the forces near Jacksonville, and has most successfully carried on the system which I commenced, and which has resulted in their evacuation of the place. Col. Davis I regard as an efficient officer, and commend him to your favorable consideration.

I have further to report, that after the evacuation, the enemy returned with a flag of truce, and were permitted to land fifty-two negroes, which were taken in charge by the commander of the post.

I inclose a list of prisoners taken near Jacksonville, and ask instructions as to what disposition will be made of them.

I also ask permission to exchange three of them for three of ours, which were taken at Santa Rosa, near Pensacola, and are here on parole. This exchange could be made at Fernandina.

I inclose reports of Col. Davis, reporting the capture of three prisoners.

I have the honor to subscribe myself,

Your obedient servant,

W. G. DILWORTH,

Colonel commanding.

List of Prisoners recently captured in this Department, E. and M. Florida, now in confinement in these Head-quarters, Tallahassee, April 15, 1862.

Corporal John E. Austin,	company H.,	4th	N. H.	Regiment.
Private Sol. C. Burnford,	"	"	"	
" Levi Martin,	"	"	"	
" W. C. Woodworth,	"	"	"	
" Chas. A. McQuestrel,	"	"	"	
" Geo. E. Cotton,	company D,	"	"	
" Jas. S. Thompson,	"	"	"	
1st Sergeant Richard Webster,	company I,	9th	Maine	Regiment.
Corporal James W. Bowman,	"	"	"	
Private Isaac Whitner,	"	"	"	
" John E. Kent,	"	"	"	
" Andrew B. Merrell,	"	"	"	
" Wesley Adams,	"	"	"	

Report of Col. W. S. Dilworth.

HEAD-QUARTERS PROVISIONAL FORCES,
EAST AND MIDDLE FLORIDA,
Tallahassee, April 13th, 1862.

To Major-gen. PEMBERTON,
Commanding Department So. Ca. and Geo:

SIR:—I have the honor to inform you that six Federal prisoners were brought into our lines near Jacksonville, on the 11th instant, and were, on yesterday, lodged in the jail of this city. Their names are as follows:

Age—45	Ord. Serg't Richard Webster,	company	I,	9th	Maine	reg.
" 28	Corp'l James W. Bowman,	"	"	"	"	"
" 31	Private Isaac Whitner,	"	"	"	"	"
" 17	" John E. Kent,	"	"	"	"	"
" 24	" Andrew B. Merrell,	"	"	"	"	"
" 20	" Wesley Adams,	"	"	"	"	"

I have the honor to be, general,
Your obedient servant,
W. S. DILWORTH,
Col. commanding.

J. L. CROSS, *A. A. A.-gen.*

Report of Col. W. G. Dilworth.

HEAD-QUARTERS DISTRICT E. AND M. FLA.,
Tallahassee, Fla., April 15th, 1862.

To Capt. T. A. WASHINGTON,
Captain and A. A.-general, Pocotaligo, S. C.:

CAPTAIN:—I have the honor to report to the general commanding this department, that the 1st cavalry regiment Florida volunteers have not yet started for Tennessee, and inclose herewith report of Col. Davis as to the condition of horses, etc., etc. I also inclose the order of Brig.-gen. J. W. Trapier, delaying the removal of this regiment, for reasons specified in the order. I respectfully ask for instructions on the subject of the removal of this regiment to Tennessee. I was ordered to take command of this district on the 1st inst., and am not responsible for the non-removal of Col. Davis' regiment of cavalry.

Will the General commanding be pleased to instruct me on this subject at his earliest convenience.

I have the honor to subscribe myself,

Your obedient servant,

W. G. DILWORTH,

Col. commanding.

(Copy.)

Order to Col. Davies.

HEAD-QUARTERS PROVISIONAL FORCES,
DEPARTMENT EAST AND MIDDLE FLORIDA,
TALLAHASSEE, March 25th, 1862.

SPECIAL ORDER, No. 118.

* * * * * * * *

Col. Wm. G. M. Davis, 1st Florida cavalry, will proceed to camp Langford, with his whole command, and relieve Col. Dilworth, 3d R. F. V., in command of all the forces in that portion of the state, provided Col. Hopkins, 4th R. F. V., is not present.

As soon as the arms now *en route* for Lake City shall have arrived at that point, Col. Davis will, with his regiment, proceed immediately to Tennessee, and report for duty to Gen. A. S. Johnston, C. S. A.

* * * * * * * *

By order of GEN. TRAPIER.

R. H. ANDERSON, *Major and A. A.-general.*

(A true copy) J. O. A. GERRY.

Letter from Colonel Davis, First Cavalry, with regard to condition of Horses, &c., &c.

CAMP LANGFORD, April 8th, 1862.

CAPTAIN:—Soon after my arrival at this post, I caused an examination to be made of the condition of the horses of the 1st regiment Florida cavalry, with a view to ascertain their fitness to be marched to Tennessee. I regret to say, that owing to hard service, want of all food for days at a time, and an entire absence of long forage for nearly two months, all the horses, with but few exceptions, are so much reduced as to be entirely unfit for any service which would require that they should be used continually for three days. I can use them for scouting within a distance of forty or fifty miles, where they are not ridden more than twenty or thirty miles a day, and often rested. Many of them could not do any duty, they are so much reduced. There are at least two hundred that ought to be condemned, or put into some wild pasture. I think if two-thirds were sent to Paine's prairie and put to pasture, the other third would be fit for such service as would be required of them here. The placing of the broken down horses in pasture would in six weeks put them all in good condition that are capable of being made serviceable. A number of the horses have died, some have been abandoned on the various marches. From this statement, the Colonel will perceive that the regiment is entirely unfit to proceed to Tennessee as a cavalry corps. If the government will mount it in Tennessee, the men are well instructed and could render service. The horses as they are would not be worth what it would cost the government to feed them on the road, and the pay allowed for their use. As we have a complete new cavalry equipment, and have good men, who have learned the drill, it would be a matter of regret that the regiment should not be employed as cavalry. I am using about two hundred and fifty men as scouts, who are mounted on the best horses. You are aware that there are two hundred and fifty horses at Camp "Mary Davis," belong ing to three companies now on duty here dismounted. These horses are all in good order, and capable of any service. Two hundred of the horses here could be put in good condition if not used for one month, and would be fit for service in Tennessee. If we condemned all the rest, we should lack, to mount the command, about four hundred horses. The dismissal of the horses would be a great hardship upon the men, unless compensation was made by the Government. They have been rendered unserviceable by reason of the inability of the government to furnish forage, and by exposure to the weather. The officers have become security for the men, who bought the horses on credit, and the pay now due would not indemnify them. I do not, therefore, recommend the condemnation of the horses, unless some compensation is made the men. I have the honor to request that the Colonel commanding will make such communication on the subject to the department as he may deem proper, that I may receive instructions.

I have the honor, &c.,

Your obedient servant,

W. G. M. DAVIS.

(A Copy.)

Report of Col. W. G. M. Davis.

HEAD-QUARTERS PROVISIONAL FORCES,
EAST FLORIDA,
Camp Langford, April 12th, 1862.

To Capt. J. S. CROSS,
Acting Assistant Adjutant-general,
Department East and Middle Florida:

CAPTAIN: I have the honor to report, for the information of the Colonel commanding the department, that Capt. Wm. M. Footman, company F, 1st Florida cavalry, in charge of a detachment of forty men, same corps, sent by me to watch the movements of the enemy near Fernandina, and to repel any effort made to leave the island of Amelia for the main land, in such small parties as he might be able to cope with. In the execution of such orders he encountered two men on the railroad, who had landed from a hand car, and made them prisoners without resistance. In a short time afterwards he found a party of five men at the house of Judge O'Neal. One of the party offering resistance, was killed, and the rest then made prisoners. The whole of the prisoners were sent here by Capt. Footman, and I have sent them by the train to-day, under a guard of five men, to be delivered to you at Tallahassee. I desire particularly to commend the conduct of Capt. Footman, who has on this occasion, as he has at all times, proved himself a zealous, intelligent, and efficient officer. I am about to increase Capt. Footman's force to one hundred men. He will be assisted by parties of citizens, should he at any time need them, and I look for good news from him before long. He will alarm the enemy and keep them confined to the island.

I remain, very respectfully,
Your obedient servant,
W. G. M. DAVIS,
Colonel commanding regiment.

(A Copy.)

Report of A. A. A.-gen. E. E. Whitner.

ADJUTANT'S OFFICE, PROV. FORCE, EAST FLA.,
CAMP LANGFORD, April 8th, 1862.

To Capt. J. S. CROSS,
Acting Assistant Adj.-gen,
Department East and Middle Florida:

I have the honor to inform you that two men belonging to the Federal army were sent to this camp yesterday by Capt. Hughes, 1st Florida cavalry, who is guarding the country between this post and Jacksonville, in charge of Lieut. Hughes. The men were met by a sergeant of Capt. Hughes' command, on the Rings road. They were entirely without arms, and did not seem to desire to shun the sergeant, but waited for him to come up, when they inquired the way to the plank road. The sergeant conducted them to the road at the point where Capt. Hughes was bivouacked. Upon being questioned, the men said they desired to get into our lines in order to be sent home on parole of honor.

I have the honor to be,
Your obedient servant,
E. E. WHITNER,
A. A. A.-general, East Florida.

REPORT OF THE BOMBARDMENT OF FORTS JACKSON AND ST. PHILIP, AND THE FALL OF NEW ORLEANS.

HEAD-QUARTERS DEPARTMENT NO. 1,
JACKSON, MISS., May 27, 1862.

Gen. S. COOPER,
Adjutant and Inspector-general, Richmond, Va.:

SIR:—Herewith, I have the honor to inclose my report of event attendant upon the fall of New Orleans. Also, the reports of Gen. Smith and Gen. Duncan—accompanying the latter, are a diagram o Forts Jackson and St. Philip—the report of Lieut.-col. Higgins and

Capt. Squires, and a report of the killed and wounded at these points.

Respectfully, your obedient servant,

M. LOVELL,

Major-gen. commanding.

Report of Major-gen. Lovell, commanding.

HEAD-QUARTERS DEPARTMENT NO. 1,
VICKSBURG, 22d May, 1862.

Gen. S. COOPER,
Adjutant and Inspector-general, Richmond, Va.:

SIR:—Herewith, I have the honor to transmit the reports of Brig.-gens. Duncan and Smith, with the accompanying documents, of the operations preceding and attendant upon the fall of New Orleans.

The department is fully aware, from my official correspondence and telegraphic dispatches, of the exact nature of the defences erected for the protection of that city. Consisting in general terms of an exterior line of forts and earthworks, intended to prevent the entrance of the armed vessels of the enemy, and an interior line in the immediate vicinity of the city, which was constructed almost entirely with reference to repelling any attack made by land with infantry. Where this line crossed the river below the city, it was intended to have a battery of twelve 32 and ten 42-pounders, which it was considered would enable us to drive back any small number of ships that might succeed in passing the obstructions at the forts, under the fire of their guns. But, whether sufficient or not, no more were to be had, and subsequently, at the earnest request of the naval authorities, I transferred the 42-pounders to the steamers "Carondelet" and "Bienville," for service on Lake Ponchartrain, in connection with Forts Pike and Macomb. Immediately after I assumed command of the department, finding that there were no guns of the heaviest calibre, I applied to Richmond, Pensacola, and other points, for some 10-inch columbiads and sea coast mortars, which I considered necessary to the defence of the lower river, but none could be spared; the general impression being that New Orleans would not be attacked by the river, and I was therefore compelled to make the best possible defence with the guns at my disposal. Twelve 42-pounders were sent to Forts Jackson and St. Philip, together with a large additional quantity of powder, and being convinced that with the guns of inferior calibre mounted there we could not hinder steamers from passing, unless they could be detained for some time under the fire of the works, I pushed forward rapidly the construction of a raft, which offered a complete obstruction to the passage of vessels up the river, except through a small opening, and then only one at a time. The forts had seventy-five or eighty guns that could be brought successively to bear upon the river, were manned by garrisons of well trained artillerists, affording a double relief to each gun, and commanded by officers who had no superiors in any service. Under these circumstances, although I feared the high water in the Spring, with the accompanying drift, would carry away the raft, yet every confidence was felt that the river would remain closed until such time as the iron-clad steamers, "Mississippi" and "Louisiana," could be finished, which I was confidently informed would not be later than the 1st of February. The first raft constructed was not carried away by the high water and drift until the latter part of February. But with funds placed at my disposal by the citizens of New Orleans, another was placed in position in March, by the energetic labors of Col. Higgins and others, and the position was again temporarily secure. No heavy guns had yet been received, although strenuous applications were made by me to get some from Pensacola, when that place was abandoned. The general impression of all those to whom I applied was, that the largest guns should be placed above New Orleans, not below, although I had notified the department on the 22d March, that in my judgment the fleet only awaited the arrival of the mortar vessels to attempt to pass up the river from below. By means, however, of an energetic and persevering officer, Major W. P. Duncan, Commissary of Subsistence, three 10-inch columbiads and five mortars were finally procured and brought over just in time to be put up as the firing commenced. Thinking that the enemy's troops at Isle Breton were intended to land at Quarantine and act in rear of Fort St. Philip, I ordered Col. Sysmauski's regiment of ninety day's men, armed with shot guns, to that point as a protection. I had likewise organized two companies of sharpshooters and swamp hunters, under Capts. Mullen and Lartique, which were sent down for operation upon the enemy's vessels from the banks of the river, but the high water, keeping the men day and night nearly waist deep in water, soon compelled them to abandon their positions. I will here state that every Confederate soldier in New Orleans, with the exception of one company, had been ordered to Corinth to join Gen. Beauregard, in March, and the city was only garrisoned by about 3,000 ninety day troops, —called out by the Governor, at my request,—of whom about 1,200 had muskets, and the remainder shot guns of an indifferent description.

The river rose rapidly in April, and soon drove out Sysmauski's regiment, which was removed to the west bank, about six miles above Fort Jackson. The whole country became one vast sheet of water, which rose in the forts and covered places heretofore safe from its encroachments. Under the tremendous pressure of this current and a storm of wind and rain, the second raft was broken away in the night of Friday, the 11th of April, two days before the enemy first opened fire. The fourteen vessels of Montgomery river defence expedition had been ordered by the department, when completed, to be sent up to Memphis and Fort Pillow, but believing the danger of attack to be greater from below, I detained six of them at New Orleans, of which change the department was fully advised. At my suggestion, Gov. Moore had also fitted up two steamers, which were sent to the forts below the city. A large number of fire-rafts were also constructed and steered down, and two small steamers were employed for the special purpose of towing these rafts into position where they could be most effective, so as to leave the armed vessels free to operate against the enemy. I telegraphed Gen. Beauregard to send down the iron-clad ram Manassas, and when the Secretary of the Navy ordered the steamer Louisiana to be sent also up the river, I protested through the War Department, being satisfied that we required more heavy guns below. She was eventually permitted to go down the river on Sunday, the 20th of April, but not in a condition to use her motive power with effect.

It was hoped that, notwithstanding this, she would be able to assume a position below Fort St. Philip, discovering the location of the mortar boats, and being herself proof against direct fire, dislodge the enemy with her guns, which were of very heavy calibre. Knowing, also, that the incessant bombardment kept Gen. Duncan closely confined to Fort Jackson, so that he could give no orders to the river defence steamers, I placed the whole under the control of Capt. Mitchell, the armed steamers as well as the tugs intended to tow down the fire-rafts. I will here state, that the river defence fleet proved a failure, for the very reasons set forth in my letter to the department of the 15th of April. Unable to govern themselves, and unwilling to be governed by others, their almost total want of system, vigilance, and discipline, rendered them useless and helpless, when the enemy finally dashed upon them suddenly in a dark night.

I regret very much that the department did not think it advisable to grant my request to place some competent head in charge of these steamers. Learning, subsequently, that the Louisiana was anchored above the forts and that the fire-rafts were not sent down, I telegraphed Capt. Mitchell, requesting him to attend to it, and afterwards called upon Commodore Whittle and entreated him to order the steamer to take the desired position below the forts. This he declined to do, but telegraphed Capt. Mitchell, telling him "to strain a point to place the vessel there, if in his judgment it was advisable." No change, however, was made, and in the night of the 23d March, I went down myself in a steamboat to urge Capt. Mitchell to have the Louisiana anchored in the position indicated, also to ascertain why the fire-rafts were not sent down. A few moments after the attack commenced, and the enemy succeeded in passing with fourteen ships, as described in Gen. Duncan's report, and the battle of New Orleans, as against ships of war, was over. I returned at once to the city, narrowly escaping capture, and giving orders to Gen. Smith, in command of the interior lines, to prepare to make all possible resistance to the enemy's fleet at the earth-work batteries below the town, instructed Col. Lovell to have several steamers ready to remove, as far as possible, the commissary and ordnance stores, being satisfied that the low developments at Chalmette could offer no protracted resistance to a powerful fleet, whose guns, owing to the high water, looked down upon the surface of the country, and could sweep away any number of infantry by an enfilading fire. These lines, as before remarked, were intended mainly to repel a land attack, but in a high stage of water were utterly untenable by infantry against guns afloat. It having been reported to me that a sufficient number of desperately bold men could easily be got together to board the enemy's vessels and carry them by assault, I authorized Major James to seize such steamers as might be necessary for his purpose, and to attempt it. He called for one thousand men by public advertisement, but being able to find but about a hundred who would undertake it, he abandoned the project. On the morning of the 25th, the enemy's fleet advanced upon the batteries and opened fire, which was returned with spirit by the troops as long as their powder lasted, but with little apparent effect upon the enemy. The powder intended for this battery of 32-pounders, had been transferred by me to the steamer Louisiana a few days before, under the supposition that it would render much better service from her heavy rifles and shell guns than with a battery of light 32's. For the operations at these works, you are respectfully referred to Gen. Smith's report. The greater portion of the ordnance stores, provisions, and quarantine property, were sent from the city by rail or steamer, and a portion of the volunteers also took the cars for Camp Moore, seventy-eight miles distant on the Jackson railroad. The greater part of the ninety days' troops disbanded and returned to their homes. There were two or three regiments and smaller bodies of men raised for Confederate service, in the city at the time, but being entirely without arms of any kind, they could be of no service, and were also ordered to Camp Moore. I adopted this course, recognizing the perfect absurdity of confronting more than a hundred guns afloat, of the largest calibre, well manned and served, and looking down upon the city, with less than three thousand militia, mostly armed with indifferent shot guns. It would, in my judgment, have been a wanton and criminal waste of the blood of women and children, without the possibility of any good result, for the enemy had only to anchor one of his ships at Kenner to command the Jackson railroad, and he could have reduced the city to ashes at his leisure, *without our being able to make any resistance whatever.*

Why he did he not occupy Kenner and cut off all exit from the the city immediately, I do not understand. Presuming that he would do so, as a matter of course, I had requested Capts. Poindexter and Gwathney, of the Navy, to have all the steamers ready in Lake Pontchartrain, to carry the troops over to Madisonville, whence they could reach Camp Moore. A portion of them were taken over by this route. Knowing that the enemy would at once seize the Opelousas railroad, and thus cut off the troops occupying the works on the coast of west Louisiana, I sent orders to the different commanding officers at Ports Livingston, Guiorr, Quitman, Berwick and Chene, to destroy their guns, and taking their small arms, provisions and ammunition, to rejoin me at Camp Moore. Major Joy brought away the troops at the two latter forts, in a very creditable manner, but those at the other works became demoralized, disbanded, and returned to New Orleans. I gave verbal instructions to Col. Fuller, to have the garrison of Forts Pike and Macomb, battery Bienvenu and Tower Dupre, ready to move at a moment's notice, as their posts were dependent on the city for provisions, and frequently for water. It was understood that the naval steamers, in connection with other vessels in the lake, should bring away these garrisons when called upon to do so, and after my arrival at Camp Moore, orders were given on the 26th, to go for them, as I had been informed that Forts Jackson and St. Philip had been surrendered. Finding that this report was untrue, I immediately countermanded the orders, giving instructions that they should be held until further notice, but before either could reach Madisonville, it was reported that the whole command was already at Covington. I advised Capt. Poindexter to make his way to Mobile, with his armed steamers, but he concluded to destroy them. We, however, procured from them some of the guns and ordnance stores, which I ordered immediately to Vicksburgh, to be put in position there.

On the 25th, Capt. Bayley, of the Federal Navy, demanded the surrender of the city, and that the flags should be taken down, and the United States flag put up on the Mint, Custom-house, and other public buildings. To this demand I returned an unqualified refusal, declaiming that I would not surrender the city or any portion of my command, but added, that feeling unwilling to subject the city to bombardment, and recognizing the utter impossibility of removing the women and children, I should withdraw my troops and turn it over to the civil authorities. This I did in compliance with the openly expressed opinion of all the prominent citizens around me—that it would be a useless waste of blood, without being productive of any beneficial results to the cause, for the troops to remain. Capt. Bayley then returned to his ship, under escort through the city, at his own request, of two officers of my staff, Col. Lovell and Major James, and I then advised the Mayor not to surrender the city, nor to allow the flags to be taken down by any of our people, but to leave it to the enemy to take them down himself. This advice was followed by the city authorities; but the idea being held out, in their subsequent correspondence with the Federal officers, that they were placed in a defenceless condition, by the withdrawal of the troops, but for which a different course might have been pursued, I promptly telegraphed to Major James, of my staff, then in the city, offering to return at once with my whole command, if the citizens felt disposed to resist to the last extremity, and remain with them to the end. I had deliberately made up my mind, that although such a step would be entirely indefensible, in a military point of view, yet if the people of New Orleans were desirous of signalizing their patriotism and devotion to the cause by the bombardment and burning of their city, I would return with my troops and not leave as long as one brick remained upon another. The only palliation for such an act would be that it would give unmistakable evidence to the world that our people were in deadly earnest. This determination, plainly expressed in my dispatches to Major James (herewith transmitted, marked A), was read by him to the Mayor, and also to the city council, in presence of one or more prominent citizens. The opinion was generally and freely expressed by the Mayor and others, that the troops ought not to return. (See report of Major James, hereunto appended, marked B.) I went to the city myself, however, on the night of the 28th of April, and in order that there might be no mistake, made the same proposition in person to the Mayor. He said he did not think it advisable for the troops to return—that such a step would only be followed by a useless sacrifice of life, without any corresponding benefit, and urged decidedly that it be not done. I, however, addressed him a letter (herewith appended, marked C,) declaring my willingness to return and share a bombardment with them, and waited until the night of the 29th for an answer, but receiving none in writing, returned to Camp Moore. The same proposition was made by me, in the course of the day, to several prominent citizens, but was invariably discountenanced by them.

For a week after the withdrawal of the troops, I had a number of officers in the city, and kept trains running regularly, which brought out a large amount of government property and stores, as well as those of the State of Louisiana. Nearly every thing was brought away, except the heavy guns and some property which persons in their fright had destroyed, and every thing might have been saved, had not persons refused to work for my officers, fearing that they might be subjected to punishment by the enemy. Many, also, refused to work for Confederate money, which occasioned some delay and difficulty in the removal of stores. I feel gratified, however, in being able to state that we brought away all the troops that would leave, and, including the property of the State, a greater amount in value than belonged to the government. What we failed to bring was from inability to get transportation. In this duty I was mainly assisted by Col. Lovell, Major James, Major Ball, Capt. Venables, and Lieut. McDonald, to whom the government is greatly indebted for the safety of much valuable property. It was a source of great distress to me, to see the result of months of toil and labor swept away in a few hours, but it was, in my opinion, mainly attributable to the following causes, which I could not by any possibility control.

1st. The want of a sufficient number of guns of heavy calibre, which every exertion was made to procure, without success.

2d. The failure, through inefficiency and want of energy of those who had charge of the construction of the iron-clad steamers Louisiana and Mississippi, to have them completed in the time specified, so as to supply the place of obstructions; and, finally, the declension of the officers in charge of the Louisiana to allow her (though not entirely ready) to be placed as a battery in the position indicated by Gen. Duncan and myself. On these last points I could only advise and suggest, as they appertained to a separate and independent department, over which I had no control whatever. (See letter of Major James, hereunto appended, marked D). Opened fire on the 13th of April, which was kept up, at intervals, for five days, when the mortars opened, and, from that time, with but a single interruption of a few hours, a bombardment was kept up for seven days and nights, which, for great rapidity and accuracy of range, has no parallel. More than twenty-five thousand shells were thrown, of which not less than one-third fell within the limits of Fort Jackson, yet the garrison held out, although wet, without change of clothing, and exhausted for want of rest and regular food, with a heroic endurance which is beyond all praise. That the enemy succeeded in passing a large portion of his fleet by the forts on a dark night, under a heavy fire, is due to no fault of the garrison of the forts. They did their whole duty, nobly and heroically, and had they been seconded, as they should have been by the defences afloat, we should not have to record the fall of New Orleans.

To the officers of my staff, who underwent months of severe and arduous labor, collecting supplies, creating resources, with the most limited means, and preparing all sorts of materials and munitions of war by ingenious makeshifts, I return my thanks. Left in the city with a small force of badly armed militia, all opportunity for distinction or glory was cut off, yet they never flagged in their zeal and devotion to the cause. When the country knows all that was done, and under what disadvantages it was accomplished, I feel confident that their verdict will do ample justice to those who shared equally in the labors of preparation, while they were denied the glory of taking part in the defence. The battle for the defence of New Orleans was fought and lost at Forts Jackson and St. Philip.

The extraordinary and remarkable conduct of the garrisons of these forts, in breaking out in open mutiny, after covering themselves with glory by their heroic defence, is one of those strange anomalies for which I do not pretend to account. The facts are recorded and speak for themseves. The causes will, probably, never be known in full.

For the detailed accounts of the bombardment of the forts, and the engagements at the time of the passage of the fleets by them and the batteries at Chalmette, you are respectfully referred to the accompanying reports of Gens. Duncan and Smith. There were no batteries except at these two points, for the reason that no guns could be procured to place in them. I had frequent occasion to regret that it was found impossible to give me control of the defences afloat as well as here. A single controlling head might have made all the resources more available and efficient in working out the desired result.

Very respectfully, your obedient servant,

M. LOVELL,
Major-gen. Commanding.

(A.)

CAMP MOORE, April 28, 1862.

Major JAMES, *New Orleans:*

If the people are willing to stand the result, I will bring 4,500 men down, as soon as I can give them arms and powder, and stay as long as a brick remains. It is their interest I am endeavoring to consult, not the safety of my men. I having nothing but infantry and two batteries of field artillery, which would be of no use against ships. I will come down myself if they wish it, and bring the men along as fast as ready. They are newly raised regiments, and are being now armed and equipped as you know. Can begin to bring them down to-morrow, if that is the desire of the citizens. Shall I come down myself to-night? Will do so if I can be of any assistance, and leave Gen. Smith to complete the organization, and bring down the five regiments when ready. The citizens must decide as to the consequences. I will come if it is wished, cheerfully.

M. LOVELL,
Major-gen. Commanding.

CAMP MOORE, April 28th, 1862.

Major JAMES, *New Orleans:*

I shall start down myself with an aid now, and am perfectly ready, if it is the desire of the city, to hold it to the end. It is for them to say, not me.

M. LOVELL,
Major-gen. Commanding.

(B.)

Gen. M. Lovell:

Sir:—I have the honor to report, that while I was in the city of New Orleans, on the 27th of April, executing your orders to assist in removing the Government and State property, and while the negotiations were going on between the city authorities and the Federal officers for the surrender, I was informed that the nature of the replies to the naval commander was such as to throw some censure upon yourself, for leaving them, as the mayor styled it, without military protection.

I deemed it my duty to advise you of this immediately, the result of which was the inclosed dispatches from you, offering to return with your troops, and afford them all the protection in your power, but that the responsibility of any results that might ensue must rest upon the citizens themselves. I read your dispatches to the City Council, which was then in session, in presence of Mr. Pierre Soulé, who happened to be there at the time. That gentleman, who seemed to speak for the mayor and Council, most emphatically declared that you ought not to return with your troops, as did also the mayor and members of the Council. Several of them, however, declared that they would be glad to have you return alone, and see matters for yourself, to which effect I telegraphed you. You came to the city that evening, with a single aid-de-camp, and went with me to the mayor's house, where you, in my presence, told him that the citizens should have no cause to say that they were obliged to submit for want of military protection; that you were ready and willing to bring your whole command into the city within 24 hours, and undergo a bombardment with them, if that was their desire. That you had withdrawn, to enable the citizens to decide the matter for themselves, as it was they, and not you, who had their families and property at stake. In reply, the mayor earnestly declined your offer, stating that you had done all in your power, and that it would be a useless waste of life to bring the troops into the city. He also urged you, by all means, to retire from the city for your own safety, and subsequently asked me to persuade you to leave as soon as possible, as he would be hung, if the United States authorities found you were at his house.

Very respectfully,

your obedient servant,

L. L. JAMES,

Volunteer Aid-de-camp.

HEAD-QUARTERS DEP'T NO. 1, NEW ORLEANS.

Hon. JOHN T. MONROE,
Mayor of New Orleans:

SIR:—When the enemy, having succeeded in passing our defences on the river with his fleet, anchored abreast the city, it was apparent that the infantry troops under my command could offer no effectual resistance, and their presence would only serve as a pretext and justification for them to open their guns upon a city crowded with women and children, whom it was impossible to remove. Under these circumstances, I determined at once to withdraw my troops, and leave it to the citizens themselves to agree upon the course of action to be pursued, in relation to the welfare of their families and property. I now beg leave to say, that if it is the determination of the people of the city to hold it at any and all hazards, I will return with my troops, and share the danger with them. That my return will be followed by bombardment, is, in my opinion, certain, but if that is the conclusion come to, I will afford all the protection in my power.

Very respectfully,

M. LOVELL,
Major-gen. commanding.

(D.)

CAMP MOORE, April 30, 1862.

To Gen. M. LOVELL,
Commanding Department No. 1:

GENERAL:—At your request, upon my return from Forts Jackson and St. Philip, I accompanied you to call upon Com. Whittle, of the navy, at his head-quarters in New Orleans, for the purpose of getting that officer, if possible, to place the iron-clad gunboat "Louisiana" in a position below Forts Jackson and St. Philip, from which she could enfilade the position of the enemy's mortar fleet, and drive them from it, thereby relieving the forts, for a time at least, from the heavy bombardment then going on, which would allow Brig.-gen. Duncan to make such repairs as were necessary, and what was equally necessary, give the garrison some rest. The position designated for the vessel to be placed in was in an eddy upon the Fort St. Philip side of the river, and under the protection of the guns of both forts, and entirely out of the line of the bombardment; and, it would require a change of position of the mortar fleet to enable them to strike the vessel with shell, if she could have been struck at all. All these facts were fully explained by yourself to Com. Whittle, and he was requested, by you, by all means, to place the vessel in said position, even if she was lost, as the maintaining the position then held by your troops in the forts, without this assistance, was merely a question of time. To this earnest appeal, upon your part, Com. Whittle telegraphed to Commander Mitchell, of the fleet stationed just above the forts, "to strain a point, *if in his judgment it was necessary*, to comply with your request, and place the Louisiana in the position before spoken of." As the result shows, the request of Com. Whittle to Commander Mitchell was not complied with.

I make this statement *voluntarily*, in order that, if ever the question of the defences of New Orleans should arise, that you can have every evidence to show that it was not certainly the want of proper exertions on the part of the land forces which caused the fall of New Orleans.

Very respectfully, your obedient servant,

L. L. JAMES,

Volunteer Aid-de-camp.

Report of Brig.-gen. J. K. Duncan, commanding Coast Defences.

NEW ORLEANS, LA., April 30, 1862.

Major J. G. PICKETT,

Ass't Adj't-general, Department No. 1, Camp Moore, La.:

I have the honor to submit the following report of the bombardment of Forts Jackson and St. Philip, La., from the 16th to the 24th of April, 1862.

About the 27th of March, I was informed by Lieut.-col. E. Higgins, commanding Forts Jackson and St. Philip, composing a part of the coast defences under my command, that the enemy's fleet was crossing the bars, and entering the Mississippi river in force. In consequence, I repaired at once to that post, to assume the general command of the threatened attack upon New Orleans, which I had always anticipated would be made from that quarter. Upon my arrival, I found that Fort Jackson was suffering severely from transpiration and backwater, occasioned by the excessive rise in the river, and the continued prevalence of strong easterly winds. Notwithstanding every effort which could be made, the water kept daily increasing upon us, partly owing to the sinking of the entire site, and to the natural lowness of the country around it, until the parade-plain and casemates were very generally submerged to the depth of from three to eighteen inches. It was with the utmost difficulty, and only then by isolating the magazines, and by pumping day and night, that the water could be kept out of them.

As the officers and men were all obliged to live in these open and submerged casemates, they were greatly exposed to discomfort and sickness, as their clothing and feet were always wet. The most of their clothing and blankets, besides, were lost by the fire hereinafter mentioned. Fort St. Philip, from the same causes, was in a similar condition, but to a lesser extent.

No attention having been previously paid to the repeated requisitions for guns of heavy calibre for these forts, it became necessary, in their present condition, to bring in and mount, and to build the platforms for the three 10-inch and three 8-inch columbiads, the rifled 42-pounder, and the five 10-inch sea coast mortars, recently obtained from Pensacola on the evacuation of that place, together with the two rifled 7-inch guns, temporarily borrowed from the naval authorities in New Orleans. It was also found necessary to prepare the old water battery to the rear of and below Fort Jackson, which had never been completed, for the reception of a portion of these guns, as well as to construct mortar proof magazines and shell rooms within the same.

In consequence also of the character of the expected attack by heavy mortars, it was deemed advisable to cover all the main magazines at both forts with sand bags to a considerable depth, to protect them against a vertical fire.

After great exertions, cheerfully made by both officers and men, and by working the garrisons by reliefs night and day, this work was all accomplished by 13th of April. No sooner had the two rifled 7-inch navy guns been placed in position, however, than orders arrived to dismount one of them immediately, and to send the same to the city at once, to be placed on board of the iron-clad steamer Louisiana. I strongly remonstrated against this removal, by telegraph, but was informed in reply that the orders were imperative, and that the gun must be sent without fail. It was accordingly sent, but with great difficulty, owing to the overflow and the other causes stated. The garrisons of both forts were greatly fatigued and worn out by these labors, performed as they were under pressure, and within sight of the enemy, and owing to the many discomforts and disadvantages we were laboring under, in consequence of high water. In the mean time, I had called upon the general commanding the department, for two regiments, to be stationed at the quarantine buildings, six miles above the forts, to act as a reserve force, and to co-operate with the forts, in case of a combined land and water attack. I also asked for Capt. W. G. Mullen's company of scouts and sharpshooters, to be stationed in the woods below Fort Jackson, on the right bank of the river, for the purpose of picking off the officers and men from the enemy's vessels, when assuming their several positions of attack. Capt. Mullen's company, of about 125 men, was sent down as requested, and stationed in part in the point of woods below Fort Jackson, and the remainder on the Fort St. Philip side, opposite the raft obstructing the river. The Chalmette regiment, consisting of about 500 men, Col. Sysmauskie commanding, was sent to the quarantine. A part of it was stationed there, and company detachments were placed at the head of the several canals, leading from the river into the back bays of the same, to guard against a land force being thrown in launches above us.

Four steamers of the river fleet, protected, and to a certain extent made shot-proof with cotton bulk-heads, and prepared with iron prows to act as rams, viz: the Warrior, Stonewall Jackson, Defiance, and Resolute, commanded by Capts. Stephenson, Philips, McCoy, and Hooper, respectively, were sent down to report to and co-operate with me. The steamers Governor Moore and General Quitman, prepared as those before mentioned, and commanded by Capts. B. Kennon and A. Grant, were sent down in like manner to co-operate with the forts, and ram such vessels of the enemy as might succeed in passing. The naval authorities also sent down the C. S. steam ram Manassa, Capt. Warly, C. S. navy, commanding. She was stationed a short distance above Fort Jackson, with her steam up constantly, to act against the enemy as occasion might offer. Subsequently, also, Capt. F. B. Renshaw, C. S. Navy, arrived in command of the C. S. steamer Jackson. The raft of logs and chains, which had formerly been placed across the river, having proven a failure, upon the rise in the stream and the constant velocity of the drift-bearing current, a new obstruction had been placed across the river, opposite Fort Jackson, by Lieut.-col. E. Higgins, prior to his assumption of the command of the forts. This consisted of a line of schooners anchored at intervals, with bows up stream, and thoroughly chained together amidships, as well as stern and stem. The rigging, ratlines, and cable, were left to trail astern of these schooners, as an additional impediment, to tangle in the propeller wheels of the enemy. This schooner raft was seriously damaged by the wind storm on the 10th and 11th of April, which parted the chains, scattered the schooners, and materially affected its character and effectiveness as an obstruction.

In addition to the wind, the raft was also much damaged by allowing some of the fire barges to get loose and drift against it, through the carelessness of those having them in charge. A large number of these fire barges were tied to the banks above both forts, ready at all times to be towed into the current and against the enemy, for the double purpose of firing his ships, and to light up the river by night to insure the accuracy of our fire. My instructions to the river fleet, under Capt. Stephenson, (see attached document A,) were, to be in the stream above the raft, with such boats as had stern guns, in order to assist the forts with their fire, in case the enemy should attempt the passage, as well as to turn in and ram, at all hazards, all such vessels as might succeed in getting above the raft. He was also required to take entire control of the fire-barges, (see attached document B,) to reconnoitre the enemy above the head of the passes, and to keep a watch boat below every night, near the point of woods, to signal the approach of the enemy. The accompanying diagram will illustrate all the points referred to in this report.

The same instructions were given to Capts. Kennon and Grant, and, upon his arrival, Capt. Renshaw was duly informed of the arrangements made, in which he promised heartily to co-operate. While the enemy remained at the Head of the Passes, twenty-two and a half miles below the forts, and, subsequently, when he came up to the Jump, or Wilder's Bayou, the boats of the river fleet took turns in running down and watching his movements. For a few nights, also, at this time, one of them was kept below as a guard boat. We had telegraphic communication, besides, down to within half a mile of the Jumps, nine miles below the forts, which, together with scouts operating in the bays to the east and west of the river, in skiffs and perogues, kept us duly posted, meanwhile, of the enemy's movements below as far down as the South-west Pass. The enemy was not, meanwhile, idle in the interim. His large vessels were worked over the South-west bar, after failing to make an entrance at Pass a l'Outre, and the mortar fleet was brought up as far as the S. W. Pilot Station, where the mortars were scaled and afterwards tested. From seven to thirteen steam sloops of war and gunboats were constantly kept at the Head of the Passes or at the Jump, to cover his operations below, and to prevent our observing his movements by way of the river. By gradual and regular approaches, he carefully closed up the forts, day by day, and opened the attack as hereinafter detailed.

April 9. One of our reconnoitring steamers was chased and followed up by two of the enemy's gunboats as far as the point of woods below Fort Jackson, but were soon forced to retire by a few shots from our batteries. This was his first reconnoissance, and our fire was not returned.

April 13. Several of the hostile gunboats again came up to make observations. They would occasionally show themselves, singly or in pairs, above the point of woods, and exchange a few shots with the forts, and then retire again behind the point. Our sharpshooters obtained a few shots on this occasion, but with very partial result, owing to the lowness of the surrounding country and the extreme rise in the river. Many of the men were up to their waists in water, and, in consequence, sickness prevailed among them, and unfitted them for duty.

The enemy spent the principal part of the day in firing grape and canister, and in shelling the woods to drive them out. This was repeated the following day, the enemy not coming within range or sight of the forts, but confining himself to shelling the woods below. The sharpshooters were all driven out by this second day's firing. Our telegraphic communication below was also broken up, as the wires were removed and many of the posts cut and torn down by the enemy.

There being no other point, above or below, where the sharpshooters could profitably act in that capacity, and as many of them were unfit for duty from exposure, I deemed it advisable to dispense with their services and send them to the city, which was accordingly done.

It being of the highest importance, however, to keep up the telegraphic communication below, Lieut. T. J. Royster's company, sappers and miners, 22d regiment Louisiana volunteers, volunteered his services with fifteen men of his company, to act as sharpshooters in perogues, and cover the operator in repairing the line and re-establishing the connection with the forts above, as well as to annoy the enemy. This also failed, from the great difficulty of managing the perogues effectively in the dense undergrowth of the swampy woods below, and the telegraph and the sharpshooters had to be abandoned in consequence.

April 15. The enemy brought up his whole fleet, extending the same from the Head of the Passes to the Point of Woods below the forts. Orders were repeatedly given to Capt. Stephenson, of the river fleet, to cause the fire-barges to be sent down nightly upon the enemy; but every attempt seemed to prove a perfect abortion, the barges being cut adrift too soon, so that they drifted against the banks directly under the forts, firing our wharves and lighting us up, but obscuring the position of the enemy. In consequence, I turned the control of them, as well as the boats employed to tow them into the stream, over to Capt. Renshaw, the senior naval officer present. I also directed Capts. Kennon and Grant to report to him for orders, as I found great difficulty in communicating with or controlling the vessels afloat, and directed Capt. Stephenson, with his four boats, to co-operate with Capt. Renshaw in every possible way. These boats of the river fleet, it seemed, could not be turned over directly to the immediate command of naval officers, owing to certain conditions imposed by the Navy Department.

April 16. From half-past seven o'clock A. M., the enemy's gunboats came round the point repeatedly for observation, but were invariably forced to retire by our fire. In the mean time, he was locating the position of the mortar flotilla, composed of twenty-one schooners, each mounting one 13-inch mortar and other guns, close against the bank on the Fort Jackson side, and behind the point of woods. At half-past four o'clock P. M., the enemy ran out a gunboat and fired upon the fort, under cover of which two mortar boats were brought out into the stream. These boats opened fire upon Fort Jackson at five P. M., which was continued for an hour and a half, the enemy, under our fire, retiring behind the point of woods.

One fire-barge sent down successfully against the enemy at four o'clock A. M., which drifted in among his vessels and was fired upon by them, creating considerable movement and perturbation. During the day, Capts. Renshaw, Kennon, Seant, Stephenson, and Hooper, passed in turns with their boats below the raft, now very much disconnected and scattered, and exchanged a few shots with the hostile gunboats and mortar-boats.

Two more abortive attempts were made to send down fire-barges against the enemy during the night.

April 18. At 9 o'clock A. M., the enemy opened upon Fort Jackson with his entire mortar-fleet of twenty-one vessels, and with rifled guns from his gunboats. Fifteen of them were concealed behind the point of woods, and the other six hauled out in the stream at an angle with them (see diagram), just at the extreme range of our heaviest guns. Our fire disabled one gunboat and one mortar-boat, causing those in the stream to retire behind the cover of the woods. Generally our shots fell short for lack of elevation, and in consequence of the inferiority of our powder compared to that of the enemy. Even our nearest gun—a 10-inch sea-coast mortar—would not reach his boats with the heaviest charges. The enemy ceased firing at seven o'clock P. M., having fired this day 2,997 mortar shells.

The quarters in the bastions were fired and burned down early in the day, as well as the quarters immediately without the fort. The citadel was set on fire and extinguished several times during the first part of the day, but later it became impossible to put out the flames, so that when the enemy ceased firing, it was one burning mass, greatly endangering the magazines, which, at the time, were reported to be on fire. Many of the men, and most of the officers, lost their bedding and clothing by these fires, which greatly added to the discomforts of the overflow. The mortar fire was accurate and terrible, many of the shells falling everywhere within the fort, and disabling some of our best guns. I endeavored to get the naval forces to carry down fire-barges against the enemy so as to disperse it, but they were all let go above the raft, and with such a lack of judgment, that they only lodged under the forts, and did not reach the enemy.

(See attached document C.)

None of the boats acted as a guard-boat below the raft at night, so that in consequence, the enemy sent up two launches to examine the character of the raft obstructing the river.

April 19th. The mortar fleet again opened at 6 and a half o'clock A. M., and the fire was constantly kept up throughout the day. Gunboats constantly came above the point during the day to engage the forts, but were as constantly driven back by our fire. One of them we crippled, which was towed behind the point of woods. The enemy's fire was excellent, a large proportion of his shells falling within Fort Jackson. The terre-plein, parade-plain, parapets, and platforms were very much cut up, as well as much damage done to the casemates. The magazines were considerably threatened, and one shell passed through into the casemates containing fixed ammunition. One 10-inch and one 8-inch columbiad, one 32 and one 24-pounder, and one 10-inch siege mortar, disabled in the main work. Also, two 32-pounders in the water battery.

Bombardment continued very regularly and accurately all night. Failures again made in sending down fire barges.

April 20. Some rain in the morning. Bombardment constant throughout the day with occasional shots from the gunboats around the point. Wind very high. No fire-barges sent down to light up the river or distract the attention of the enemy at night. In consequence, between 11 and 12 o'clock P. M., under cover of the heaviest shelling during the bombardment thus far, one of the enemy's gunboats came up in the darkness and attempted to cut the chains of the raft and drag off the schooners. A heavy fire was opened upon her, which caused her to retire, but not until she had partially accomplished her purpose. The raft after this could not be regarded as an obstruction. The fire continued uninterruptedly all night.

April 21st. Firing continued all day and all night without interruption. Several guns disabled. Disabled guns were repaired, as far as practicable, as often as accidents happened to them or their platforms. Fort Jackson by this time was in need of extensive repairs almost everywhere, and it was with extreme pleasure that we learned of the arrival, during the night, of the iron-clad steamer Louisiana, under the cover of whose heavy guns we expected to make the necessary repairs.

April 22d. By the direction of the major-general commanding the department, every thing afloat, including the towboats, and the entire control of the fire-barges, was turned over to Capt. John K. Mitchell, C. S. Navy, commanding the C. S. Naval Forces, Lower Mississippi river. I also gave Capt. Mitchell one hundred and fifty of our best men from Forts Jackson and St. Philip, under Lieuts. Dixon and Gandy, and Capt. Ryan, to serve a portion of the guns of the Louisiana, and to act as sharpshooters on the same vessel. In an interview with Capt. Mitchell, on the morning of this date, I learned that the motive power of the Louisiana was not likely to be completed within any reasonable time, and that in consequence it was not within the range of probabilities that she could be regarded as an aggressive steamer, or that she could be brought into the pending action in that character. As an iron-clad, invulnerable floating-battery, with sixteen guns of the heaviest calibre, however, she was then as complete as she would ever be. Fort Jackson had already undergone, and was still subjected to, a terrible fire of 13-inch mortar shells, which it was necessary to relieve at once, to prevent the disabling of all the best guns at that fort. And although Fort St. Philip partially opened out the point of woods concealing the enemy, and gallantly attempted to dislodge him or draw his fire, he nevertheless doggedly persisted in his one main object, of battering Fort Jackson. Under these circumstances I considered that the Louisiana could only be regarded as a battery, and that her best possible position would be below the raft, close in on the Fort St. Philip's shore, where her fire could dislodge the mortar boats from behind the point of woods, and give sufficient respite to Fort Jackson to repair in extenso. This position (X on the accompanying diagram), would give us three direct and cross-fires upon the enemy's approaches, and at the same time insure the Louisiana from a direct assault, as she would be immediately under the guns of both forts. Accordingly, I earnestly and strongly urged these views upon Capt. Mitchell, in a letter of this date (copy lost), but without avail, as will be seen by his reply attached as document D.

Being so deeply impressed myself with the importance of this position for the Louisiana, and of the necessity of prompt action, in order to insure the success of the impending struggle, I again urged this subject upon Capt. Mitchell during the latter part of the same day, as absolutely indispensable and imperative to the safety of New Orleans, and to the control of the lower Mississippi. My efforts were ineffectual to get him to move the boat from her original position above the forts. His reply is attached as document E, in which he is sustained by all the naval officers present having the command of vessels. I also addressed him two other notes through the day, the one in regard to sending fire-barges against the enemy, and the other relative to keeping a vigilant look out from all his vessels, and asking for co-operation, should the enemy attempt to pass during the night. (See attached document F.)

Bombardment continued during the day and night, being at times very heavy. During the day our fire was principally confined to shelling the point of woods from both forts, and with apparently good results, as the mortar-fire was slackened towards evening. The casemates were very much cut up by the enemy's fire, which was increased at night. There was little or no success in sending down fire-barges, as usual, owing in part to the condition of the towboats Mosher, Music, and Belle Algerine, in charge of the same, explained by attached document G. This does not excuse the neglect, however, as there were six boats of the river fleet available for this service, independent of those alluded to, and fire-barges were plentiful.

April 23d. The day broke warm, clear, and cloudless. No immediate relief being looked for from our fleet, the entire command was turned out to repair damages under a very heavy fire of the enemy.

The bombardment continued, without intermission, throughout the day, but slackened off about 12 o'clock M., at which hour there was every indication of an exhaustion on the part of the mortar flotilla. Hence it became evident that the tactics of the enemy would necessarily be changed into an attack with broadsides by his larger vessels. In consequence, these views were laid before Capt. Mitchell, and he was again urged to place the Louisiana at the point before mentioned, below the raft and near the Fort St. Philip bank of the river, to meet the emergency. (See attached document H.) Capt. Mitchell's reply is attached in documents E, I, J, and K, wherein he positively declines again to assume the only position which offered us every possible chance of success, and Capts. McIntosh, Huger, and Warly sustain Capt. Mitchell in his views of the case. Just before sundown, under a very heavy mortar fire, the enemy sent up a small boat, and a series of white flags were planted on the Fort St. Philip bank of the river, commencing about 380 yards above the lone tree upon that shore. (See diagram.) This confirmed my previous views of an early and different attack from the usual mortar bombardment, especially as I presumed that these flags indicated the positions to be taken up by the several vessels in their new line of operation. As nothing was to be expected from the Louisiana, after the correspondence during the day, I could only inform Capt. Mitchell of this new movement of the enemy (see attached document L), and particularly impress upon him the necessity of keeping the river well lit up with fire-barges, to act as an impediment to the enemy, and assist the accuracy of our fire in a night attack. Lieut. Shyrock, C. S. N., Capt. Mitchell's aid, came on shore about 9 o'clock, P. M., to inform me that the Louisiana would be ready for service by the next evening—the evening of the 24th.

I informed him that time was every thing to us, and that to-morrow would, in all probability, prove too late. Lieut.-col. Higgins warmly seconded my opinion, and warned Lieut. Shyrock that the final battle was imminent within a few hours.

In regard to lighting the river, Lieut. Shyrock stated that fire-barges would be regularly sent down throughout the night, every two hours; and as none had been sent up to that hour (9½ o'clock, P. M.), he left, informing me that this matter would be attended to as soon as he arrived on board.

To my utter surprise, not one single fire-barge was sent down the river, notwithstanding, at any hour of this night. It was impossible for us to send them down, as every thing afloat had been turned over to Capt. Mitchell, by order of the Major-gen. commanding, and the fire-barges, and the boats to tow them into the stream, were exclusively under his control. In consequence of this criminal neglect, the river remained in complete darkness throughout the entire night. The bombardment continued all night, and grew furious towards morning.

April 24th. At 3½ o clock, A. M., the larger vessels of the enemy were observed to be in motion, and, as we presumed, to take up the positions indicated by the small flags planted by them on the previous evening. I then made my last and final appeal to Capt. Mitchell, a copy of which is attached as document M.

The Louisiana was still in her old position above Fort St. Philip, surrounded by her tenders, on board of which was the majority of her cannoniers and crew,—and the other boats of the fleet were generally at anchor above her, excepting the Jackson, Capt. Renshaw, C. S. N., commanding, which had been sent the day before, at my suggestion, to prevent the landing of forces through the canals above. The McRae lay near and above the Louisiana, and the steam-ram Manassa, with her tender, remained in her constant position above Fort Jackson, both with steam up, and ready for immediate action. The enemy evidently anticipated a strong demonstration to be made against him with fire-barges. Finding upon his approach, however, that no such demonstration was made, and that the only resistance offered to his passage was the expected fire of the forts—the broken and scattered raft being then no obstacle—I am satisfied that he was suddenly inspired, for the first time, to run the gauntlet at all hazards, although not a part of his original design. Be this as it may, a rapid rush was made by him, in columns of twos in echelon, so as not to interfere with each other's broadsides. The mortar fire was furiously increased upon Fort Jackson, and in dashing by, each of the vessels delivered broadside after broadside of shot, shell, grape, canister, and spherical case, to drive the men from our guns.

Both the officers and men stood up manfully under this galling and fearful hail, and the batteries of both forts were promptly opened at their longest range, with shot, shell, hot shot, and a little grape, and most gallantly and rapidly fought, until the enemy succeeded in getting above and beyond our range.

The absence of light on the river, together with the smoke of the guns, made the obscurity so dense that scarcely a vessel was visible, and in consequence, the gunners were obliged to govern their firing entirely by the flashes of the enemy's guns. I am fully satisfied that the enemy's dash was successful, mainly owing to the cover of darkness, as a frigate and several gunboats were forced to retire as day was breaking. Similar results had attended every previous attempt made by the enemy to pass or to reconnoitre, when we had sufficient light to fire with accuracy and effect. The passage was of short duration, having been accomplished between 3½ A. M. and daylight, under a very rapid and heavy pressure of steam. Of the part taken in this action by the Louisiana, Manassa, and the other vessels composing the co-operating naval forces, I cannot speak with any degree of certainty, excepting that the Louisiana is reported to have fired but twelve shots during the engagement. But to the heroic and gallant manner in which Capt. Huger handled and fought the McRae, we can all bear evidence. The Defiance, Capt. McCoy, commanding, was the only vessel saved out of the river fleet.

Shortly after daylight, the Manassa was observed drifting down by the forts. She had been abandoned and fired, and was evidently in a sinking condition.

The McRae was considerably cut up in this action by shot and grape.

The Resolute was run on shore about a mile above the forts, where she hoisted a white flag, but, by the prompt action of the McRae, she was prevented from falling into the hands of the enemy. She was subsequently wrecked and burned. The Warrior was run ashore and fired on the point just above Fort St. Philip.

Nothing was known by us of the movements of the Stonewall Jackson, the Governor Moore, or the General Quitman. The steamers Mosher, Music, and Belle Algerine, in charge of the fire-barges, were all destroyed. So was also the Star. The heroic courage displayed by the officers and men at both forts was deserving of a better success, especially after the fortitude which they constantly exhibited through the long tedium of a protracted bombardment, unsurpassed for its terrible accuracy, constancy, and fury.

Thirteen of the enemy's vessels, out of twenty-three, succeeded in getting by, viz.: the Hartford, Pensacola, Richmond, Brooklyn, Mississippi, Oneida, Iroquois, Cayuga, Wissahickon, Sciota, Kinco, Kallahdin and Pinola. In addition to the foregoing, and to Verona, and such other vessels as were sunk, there were six gunboats and one frigate engaged in this action, besides the mortar flotilla. Heavy chains were flaked along the sides of the most of these vessels as an iron-proof protection. The extent of the damage which was done to the enemy, we had no means of ascertaining. The vessels which passed all came to an anchor at or below quarantine, six miles above the forts, where they remained until about 10 o'clock A. M., when they all passed slowly up the river, with the exception of two gunboats left at the quarantine as a guard.

Shortly after the fleet above got under weigh, a gunboat from below made her appearance with a flag of truce, and verbally demanded the surrender of the forts, in the name of Commander D. D. Porter, U. S. Navy, commanding the mortar flotilla, under the penalty of reopening the bombardment, which had ceased shortly after the passage, in case of refusal. The demand was rejected, and the bombardment was reopened about 12 o'clock M. It continued until near sundown, when it ceased altogether. The entire mortar fleet, and all the other vessels excepting six gunboats, then got under weigh and passed down the river and out of sight, under full steam and sail. A vigilant look out was kept up above and below during the night, but all remained quiet. So long as the mortar fleet remained below, the position wherein the Louisiana could render the greatest assistance to the forts was the one below Fort St. Philip hereinbefore mentioned, where the fire from her batteries could dislodge the enemy from behind the point of woods.

After the mortar fleet had left, however, and when the enemy had got in force above the forts, the question was materially changed, in consequence of the fact that all of our heavy guns at both forts had been mounted to bear upon the lower approaches, and not on those above.

The most effective position which the Louisiana could then take as a battery, was in the bight above Fort Jackson, where her guns could protect our rear, and sweep the long reach of river above, towards the quarantine. This would still insure her safety, as she would be under the guns of both forts. This is evident by a reference to the point (XX) on the diagram.

In several personal interviews, and by correspondence with Capt. Mitchell on this date, (see attached documents N, O, P, Q, and R,) I requested him, during the morning of the 24th, while the mortar fleet was below, to place the Louisiana below the raft and dislodge it; and later in the day, when the mortar fire was nearly exhausted, to place her in the position (XX) above Fort Jackson, to assist in repelling an attack from the vessels above.

During the day she was in an unfit condition to assume either position, for the reasons given by Capt. Mitchell in his letters to me. The intoxicated volunteers referred to were none of my men, nor did they get their liquor at the forts, as there was none on hand there during the bombardment, excepting the small supplies of hospital stores in the medical department.

April 25th. No attack attempted during the day by the enemy, either from above or below. The gunboats from the quarantine and from the point of woods below occasionally showed themselves for observation, but without firing. During the day all the principal guns that would admit of it at both forts were prepared at once so as to traverse in a full circle, and bear above or below as necessity might require. Some of the 24-pounder barbette guns at Fort Jackson were also replaced by guns of heavier calibre, to bear on the river above.

Permission was granted by the enemy to the Confederate States Steamer McRae to proceed to New Orleans, under a flag of truce, with the wounded. Availing ourselves of the offer of Capt. Mitchell, the seriously wounded of both forts were sent on board of her. As it was late when the wounded were all gotten on board, the McRae did not get off until the next morning. Still failed during the day in getting Capt. Mitchell to place the Louisiana in the bight above Fort Jackson, where she could act against the enemy from above. One of the raft schooners was burned during the night to light the river, and all remained quiet.

April 26th. A gunboat with a white flag dropped down from the quarantine to escort the McRae on her mission. The McRae did not again return to the forts. Four of the enemy's steamers were in sight at the quarantine at dawn. A gunboat occasionally showed herself below to reconnoitre. In the direction of Bird Island, and back of the salt works, a large steam frigate and an ordinary river steamer appeared in sight, the latter working her way up the bay behind Fort St. Philip, apparently towards the quarantine. During the day, Capt. Mitchell communicated with the enemy above, under a flag of truce, and learned that the city had surrendered, and that the Confederate States steam ram Mississippi had been burned by our authorities. The wreck of the floating dock or battery drifted by the forts about 4 o'clock P. M.

The Louisiana was not placed in the position required of her during the day, Capt. Mitchell promising to put her there the next day, the 27th. Another raft-schooner burned for light, and all quiet during the night. No shots exchanged during the day.

April 27. At daylight, the steamer which had been observed the day before, working her way up in the back bays, was in view, immediately in the rear of Fort St. Philip, and near the mouth of the Fort Bayou. A frigate and five other vessels were also in sight towards Bird Island, one of which was seen working her way up the bay. From ten to thirteen launches were visible near the boat back of Fort St. Philip, by means of which troops were being landed at the quarantine above us. About 12 o'clock M., one of the enemy's gunboats from below made her appearance, under a flag of truce, bearing a written demand for the surrender of the forts, signed by commander David D. Porter, U. S. N., commanding mortar flotilla. (See attached document S.) The forts refused to surrender. (See attached document T.) About 4 o'clock P. M., the French man-of-war Milan, Capt. Clouet commanding, passed up to the city, after asking and obtaining permission to do so. The position of the Louisiana still remained unchanged.

So far, throughout the entire bombardment and final action, the spirit of the troops was cheerful, confident, and courageous. They were mostly foreign enlistments, without any great interests at stake in the ultimate success of the revolution. A reaction set in among them during the lull of the 25th, 26th, and 27th, when there was no other excitement to arouse them than the fatigue duty of repairing our damages, and when the rumor was current that the city had surrendered, and was in the hands of the enemy. No reply had been received from the city to my dispatches, sent by couriers, on the 24th and 25th, by means of which I could reassure them. They were still obedient, but not buoyant and cheerful. In consequence, I endeavored to revive their courage and patriotism, by publishing an order to both garrisons, attached hereto as document U. I regret to state that it did not produce the desired effect. Every thing remained quiet, however, until midnight, when the garrison at Fort Jackson revolted en mass, seized upon the guard and posterns, reversed the field-pieces commanding the gates, and commenced to spike the guns, while many of the men were leaving the fort in the mean time, under arms. All this occurred as suddenly as it was unexpected.

The men were mostly drawn up under arms, and positively refused to fight any longer, besides endeavoring by force to bring over the St. Mary's cannoniers, and such other few men as remained true to their cause and country. The mutineers stated that the officers intended to hold out as long as possible, or while the provisions lasted, and then blow up the forts, and every thing in them; that the city had surrendered, and that there was no further use in fighting; that the enemy were about to attack by land and water, on three sides at once, and that a longer defence would only prove a butchery. Every endeavor was made by the officers to repress the revolt, and to bring the men to reason and order, but without avail. Officers upon the ramparts were fired upon by the mutineers, in attempting to put a stop to the spiking of the guns.

I am greatly indebted to the Rev. Father Nachon, for his efforts to quell the mutineers, through some of whom he learned that the revolt had been discussed among them for two days, and yet there was no one man true enough to communicate the fact to his officers. Signals also were said to have been passed between the forts during the night, and while the mutiny was at its height. Being so general among the men, the officers were helpless and powerless to act.

Under these circumstances, there was but one course left, viz.: to let those men go who wished to leave the fort, in order to see the number left, and to ascertain what reliance could be placed upon them. About one-half of the garrison left immediately, including men from every company, excepting the St. Mary's cannoniers, volunteers and regulars, non-commissioned officers and privates, and among them many of the very men who had stood last and best to their guns throughout the protracted bombardment and the final action when the enemy passed. It was soon evident that there was no fight in the men remaining behind, that they were completely demoralized, and that no faith or reliance could be placed in the broken detachments of companies left in the fort.

In the mean time, we were totally ignorant of the condition of affairs in Fort St. Philip, and as all of our small boats had been carried away by the mutineers, we could not communicate with that fort till the next morning. As the next attack upon the forts was likely to be a combined operation by land and water, and as Fort St. Philip was the point most threatened, from the nature of the country around it, and from the character of the work itself, with narrow and shallow ditches, and but little relief to the main work, it was self-evident that no reduction could be made in its garrison to strengthen that of Fort Jackson, even if all the men there remained true. In fact, two additional regiments had been asked for at quarantine, in anticipation of such an attack, to act as a reserve to strengthen the garrisons of both forts. With the enemy above and below us, it will be apparent at once, to any one at all familiar with the surrounding country, that there was no chance of destroying the public property, blowing up the forts, and escaping with the remaining troops. Under all these humiliating circumstances, there seemed to be but one course open to us, viz.: to await the approach of daylight, communicate then with the gunboats of the mortar flotilla below, under a flag of truce, and negotiate for a surrender under the terms offered us by Commander Porter, on the 26th inst., and which had previously been declined.

April 28th. A small boat was procured, and Lieut. Morse, Post-adjutant, sent over to convey the condition of affairs to Fort St Philip, as well as to Capt. Mitchell, on the Louisiana. Capt Mitchell and Lieut. Shyrock, C. S. N., came on shore and discussed the whole question; after which they left, remarking that they would go on board, and endeavor to attack the enemy above at the quarantine, notwithstanding that reasons had been given, from time to time, for not moving this vessel into her proper position, only a few hundred yards distant. Capts. Squires and Bond, Louisiana artillery, and Lieut. Dixon, commanding the company of C. S. regular recruits, came on shore shortly afterwards from Fort St. Philip, and concurred with us, that, under the circumstances, we could do nothing else than surrender, as they were not at all confident of the garrison there, after the unlooked for revolt at Fort Jackson, although none of their men had left, or openly revolted.

For these reasons, a flag of truce was sent down to communicate with the enemy below, and to carry a written offer of surrender under the terms offered on the 26th instant. (See attached Document V.) This communication brought up the Harriet Lane and three other gunboats opposite the fort, with white flags at the fore, white flags being displayed from the yards of the flag-masts at both forts, while the confederate flags waved at the mast-heads. While negotiations were pending on the Harriet Lane, it was reported that the the steamer Louisiana, with her guns protruding, and on fire, was drifting down the river towards the fleet. As the wreck, in descending, kept close into the Fort St. Philip shore, the chances were taken by the enemy without changing the position of his boats.

The guns of the Louisiana were discharged at random as she floated down, and the boat finally blew up near Fort St. Philip, scattering its fragments everywhere within and around the fort, killing one of our men and wounding three or four others.

Capt. McIntosh, C. S. N., who had been severely wounded in the discharge of his duty on the night of the enemy's passage, and who was then lying in a tent at that fort, was nearly killed also. As far as I could learn, however, the Louisiana was fired prior to the time that the enemy's boats, with white flags, came to an anchor abreast of the forts to negotiate. She was fired in her first and original position, without any change of any kind since her arrival at the forts.

The terms of capitulation are attached hereto as Document W, in addition to which Commander Porter verbally agreed not to haul down the Confederate flag or hoist the Federal, until the officers should get away from the forts.

The officers of Fort Jackson and the St. Mary's cannoniers left about 4 o'clock P. M., for the city, on board of the U. S. gunboat Kennebec, and arrived on the morning of the 29th in New Orleans. The officers of Fort St. Philip were sent up the next day, and all the men subsequently, within a few days, as transportation could be furnished, excepting the men who revolted on the night of the 27th, many of whom enlisted with the enemy. Upon my arrival in the city, I found the enemy's vessels were lying off the town, and that no flag, excepting that of the State of Louisiana, on the City Hall, was visible upon the shore. I also learned that flag officer Farragut had directed it to be hauled down, and the U. S. flag hoisted in its stead, upon the penalty of shelling the city within forty-eight hours, if the demand was not complied with, and that he had warned the city authorities to remove the women and children within the time specified.

I therefore deemed it my duty to call at once upon the mayor at the City Hall, and inform him of the fate of the forts below, which I did accordingly. Learning there, from one of his aids, that the major-general commanding the department was still in the city, I called upon him in person, and verbally reported the main incidents of the bombardment, the passage of the enemy, and the capitulation of the forts.

I have the honor to inclose herewith the report of Lieut.-col. E. Higgins, twenty-second regiment Louisiana volunteers, commanding Forts Jackson and St. Philip, and those of the different company and battery commanders, together with the surgeon's reports of the killed and wounded. The report of Colonel Sysmauski, commanding the Chalmette regiment at quarantine, has not been received by me, so that I am unable to report upon his operations.

I fully indorse the just praise bestowed in the inclosed reports upon the officers at both forts, and warmly return them my thanks. They all distinguished themselves by cool courage, skill, and patriotism throughout the entire bombardment, and by the patient fortitude with which they bore the several trying ordeals of water, fire, and the energetic fury of the enemy's protracted and continuous fire.

I must also bear testimony to the cheerful courage and prompt and willing obedience with which the men performed their duties throughout the bombardment, and up to the sad night when they took the rash and disgraceful step of rising against their officers, breaking through all discipline, and leading to such disastrous and fatal consequences. I can charitably account for it only on the grounds of great reaction after the intense physical strain of many weary days and nights of terrible fire, during which they were necessarily subjected to every privation from circumstances beyond our control, but which they had not the moral courage to share and sustain with their officers, all of whom were subjected to the same hardships in every particular.

To Lieut.-col. Higgins, commanding the forts, my thanks are especially due, for his indefatigable labors in preparing his heavy batteries, preparatory to the attack, almost in the face of the enemy, and for the quiet, skilful and judicious manner in which he caused them to be fought. He was present everywhere, and did his whole duty well and thoroughly. Capt. M. T. Squires, Louisiana regiment of artillery, as senior officer in charge of Fort St. Philip, under orders of Lieut.-col. Higgins, commanding, fully sustained every anticipation entertained of his gallantry, skill, and efficiency.

During the first day's bombardment, when Capt. Anderson was wounded, my aid-de-camp, Lieut. William M. Bridges, Louisiana artillery, volunteered to command the ten-inch columbiads on the main work, and I return him my thanks for the gallant and efficient manner in which he fought them during the rest of the action.

I take great pleasure in making personal mention of my volunteer aids, Capt. Wm. Y. Seymour and Capt. Y. R. Smith, for the valuable assistance which they rendered me at all times. My thanks are also due to Doctors Bradbury and Foster, who volunteered their services to assist Assistant Surgeons L. Burk and C. D. Lewis, at Forts Jackson and St. Philip respectively, and most efficiently did they aid in this department. Doctor Bradbury remained at Fort Jackson until its fall, and was parolled. Doctor Foster, at my request, accompanied the wounded soldiers to the city on the C. S. steamer McRae.

Messrs. Fulda, Stickney, and Sergeant Y. R. Poindexter, 4th Mississippi volunteers, telegraphic operators, rendered the most valuable services in keeping open our communication above and below, under the most dangerous and difficult circumstances. Although we have failed in our mission of keeping the enemy's fleet from passing the forts, and have been subjected to the deep humiliation of surrendering the charge intrusted to our keeping to the enemies of our country, I must nevertheless state, in common justice to myself and those under my command, that to the very best of our ability, with the means at our disposal, our whole duty was performed faithfully, honestly, and fearlessly. If all had to be gone through with again, under similar events and circumstances, I know that we should be forced to the same results and consequences.

Great as the disaster is, it is but the sheer result of that lack of cheerful and hearty co-operation from the defences afloat, which we had every right to expect, and to the criminal negligence of not lighting up the river at night, when the danger was imminent, and the movements of the enemy absolutely known, almost to the hour of the final attack. Except for the cover afforded by the obscurity of the darkness, I shall always remain satisfied that the enemy would never have succeeded in passing Forts Jackson and St. Philip.

I am, very respectfully,
Your obedient servant,
J. K. DUNCAN,
Brig.-gen., late commanding Coast Defences.

NEW ORLEANS, LA., May 13, 1862.

Major J. G. PICKETT,
Assistant Adjutant-general, Department No. 1,
CAMP MOORE, LA.:

MAJOR:—In addition to the foregoing report, I wish to add, that upon the arrival of the paroled enlisted men from Forts Jackson and St. Philip in this city, I endeavored, to the best of my ability, to see that they were properly cared for, until such time as they could be sent out of town. As far as it could be done, they were paid in part for the time due, and arrangements were also made through the city safety committee to have them boarded and lodged temporarily, all with the view of preventing them from going over to the enemy through distress and starvation. In this I was very much assisted by Capt. M. T. Squires and 1st Lieut. L. B. Taylor, Louisiana regiment of artillery. Notwithstanding that they were thus amply provided for, scores of them have been daily going over to the enemy and enlisting since, until now there are but a very few left from either fort not in the ranks of the enemy. Although I really did think, at the time of the surrender, that some few of the men were loyal, the facts which have since come to light have perfectly satisfied me that nearly every man in both forts was thoroughly implicated and concerned in the revolt on the night of the 27th of April, with the exception of the company of St. Mary's cannoniers, composed mostly of planters.

Very respectfully, your obedient servant,

J. K. DUNCAN,

Brig.-gen., late commanding Coast Defences.

(Document A.)

FORTS JACKSON AND ST. PHILIP, LA.,
April 6th, 1862.

To Capt. STEVENSON,
Commanding River Fleet, present:

CAPTAIN:—Keep your boats in constant readiness at all times for the enemy's approach. Should he attack, all your fleet must be kept above the raft, and such of your boats as have stern guns should lay in the middle of the stream above the raft, and without the field of our fire, and use these guns against the enemy.

Should any boat of the enemy by any means get above the raft, you must instantly ram it with determination and vigor, at all risks and at every sacrifice. All signal mast-head lights should be kept extinguished at night, or never hoisted. Trusting to your known energy, and to the great expectations anticipated of the river fleet by your friends, I have every confidence that your whole duty will be thoroughly performed.

Very respectfully,
Your obedient servant,
(Signed) J. K. DUNCAN, *Brig.-gen.*

(Document B.)

HEAD-QUARTERS FORTS JACKSON AND ST. PHILIP,
April 9th, 1862.

To Capt. JNO. A. STEPHENSON,
Commanding River Fleet, present:

CAPTAIN:—Keep one of your boats constantly below, night and day, opposite the wooded point, where you can watch the movements of the enemy. Signal us his approach, and the number of vessels seen coming up, and give me a copy of the signals for our government at the forts.

I wish you to take the entire control of the fire-rafts, and you will be assisted therein by the steamers Star, Algerine, and such other boats as I can procure from the city for the purpose.

Your own knowledge of the river and the currents will enable you to set them adrift at such time as your judgment warrants.

Very respectfully,
Your obedient servant,
J. K. DUNCAN,
Brigadier-general, com'g. Coast Defences.

(Document C.)

JACKSON, April 18th, 1862.

To Col. HIGGINS:

DEAR SIR:—Yours just received. The fire-barge was sent down, as I supposed, by your order. Capt. Grant accompanied me to select a proper place to let her go. She was fired by my order, but was not aware that she was too close to the fort, but the *eddy* current, after firing, probably brought her into too close proximity to the fort. I regret the affair was an abortion.

Respectfully,
(Signed) T. B. RENSHAW, C. S. N.

(Document C.)

C. S. STEAMER LOUISIANA, OFF FORT JACKSON,
April 22d, 1862.

To Gen. J. K. DUNCAN,
Commanding Coast Defences, Fort Jackson:

GENERAL:—I have the honor to acknowledge the receipt of yours of this date, asking me to place the Louisiana in position below the raft, this evening, if possible.

This vessel was hurried away from New Orleans before the steam power and batteries were ready for service.

Without a crew, and in many respects very incomplete, and this condition of things is but partially remedied now, she is not yet prepared to offer battle to the enemy; but, should he attempt to pass the forts, we will do all we can to prevent it, and it was for this purpose *only* that she was placed in position where necessity might force her into action, inadequately prepared as she is at this moment.

We have now at work, on board, about fifty mechanics, as well as her own crew and those from other vessels, doing work essential to the preparation of the vessel for battle. Under these circumstances, it would, in my estimation, be hazarding too much to place her under the fire of the enemy.

Every effort is being made to prepare her for the relief of Fort Jackson—the condition of which is fully felt by me; and the very moment I can venture to face our enemy with any reasonable chance of success, be assured, general, I will do it, and trust that the result will show you that I am now pursuing the right course.

I am, very respectfully,

Your obedient servant,

(Signed) JNO. K. MITCHELL,

Commanding C. S. Naval Forces, Lower Miss.

P. S.—The Jackson, with launch No. 3, will go up to the Quarantine this afternoon, to watch the enemy, as suggested in your note this morning.

Respectfully, etc.,

(Signed) J. K. M.

(Document E.)

C. S. Steamer Louisiana, near Fort Jackson,
April 23d, 1862.

To Gen. J. K. Duncan,
Commanding Coast Defences, Fort Jackson:

General:—On the receipt, last night, of your second communication of yesterday's date, asking me to place this vessel under the fire of the enemy, I consulted the commanding officers of the C. S. Naval vessels present on the subject, and herewith annex a copy of their opinion, sustaining my own views on the subject.

I feel the importance of affording relief to your command as soon as possible; but, general, at the same time, I feel, and I *know*, the importance to the safety of Forts Jackson and St. Philip, and the city of New Orleans, of having this vessel in proper condition before seeking an encounter with the enemy. If he seeks one, or attempts the passage of the forts before this vessel is ready, I shall meet him, however unprepared I may be.

We have an additional force of mechanics from the city this morning, and I hope, that by to-morrow night, the motive power of the Louisiana will be ready, and in the mean time, her battery will be in place, and other preparations will be completed, so as to enable her to act against the enemy. When ready, you will be immediately advised.

I have the honor to be, very respectfully,

Your obedient servant,

(Signed) JNO. K. MITCHELL,

Commanding C. S. Naval Forces, Lower Miss.

(Document E.)

C. S. STEAMER LOUISIANA, NEAR FORT JACKSON,
April 22, 1862.

Two communications having this day been received from Brig.-gen. Duncan (herewith attached, marked No. 1 and 3, and also the answer of Commander J. K. Mitchell, No. 1, marked No. 2), requesting that the Louisiana be placed in position below the raft in the river, near Fort Jackson, a consultation was held by Commander J. K. Mitchell, with Commander McIntosh and Lieuts. Commanding Huger and Warly, who fully sustained the views of Commander Mitchell, as expressed in his reply (marked No. 2) declining to comply with the request of Brig.-gen. Duncan.

(Signed) C. F. McINTOSH, *Com'd'g C. S. N.*
(Signed) T. B. HUGER, *Lieut. Com'd'g.*
(Signed) N. S. WARLY, *Lieut. Com'd'g.*
(Signed) GEORGE S. SHYROCK,
Lieut. C. S. N., aid to commanding officer.

(Document F.)

C. S. STEAMER LOUISIANA, FORT JACKSON,
April 22, 1862.

Gen. J. K. DUNCAN,
Commanding Coast Defences at Fort Jackson:

GENERAL:—Your two notes of this date have been received. A fire has been ordered to be built below St. Philip, as you requested, except that it will be on the beach; and a raft will be kept ready to fire, and turn adrift, as you requested, near Fort Jackson, in the event of the apprehended attack being made by the enemy to-night. I shall also direct a vigilant look out to be kept by all the vessels, and to co-operate with you to prevent the passage of the forts at every hazard.

Your request respecting the report of the bad condition of the engines of the Mosher will claim my attention as soon as possible.

I have the honor to be, very respectfully,

Your obedient servant,

(Signed) JOHN K. MITCHELL,

Commanding C. S. Naval Forces, Lower Mississippi.

(Document G.)

C. S. Steamer Louisiana, off Fort Jackson,
April 22, 1862.

To Lieut. commanding Huger, Assistant Engineer ———, Assistant Engineer ———, *C. S. Steamer McRae, off Fort Jackson:*

Gentlemen:—The steamers Mosher and Belle Algerine having been represented as being unfit for service, you will please to examine them carefully, without delay, and report to me in duplicate their condition. In the performance of this duty, please state the cause of any damage you may discover, with such recommendations as, in your judgment, you may deem proper.

I am, very respectfully,

Your obedient servant,

JOHN K. MITCHELL,

Commanding C. S. Naval Forces, Lower Mississippi river.

Capt. Huger will fill up the blanks with the names of the two engineers he thinks most suitable for the service, belonging to the McRae.

C. S. Steamer Louisiana, April 22, 1862.

Samuel Brock,
Senior Engineer, McRae:

Sir: In obedience to your order, we have held a survey upon the steamer Belle Algerine and the tug Mosher. The latter has, we think, loosened the after-bearing of her shaft. This we can, I think, obviate in a few hours. The Belle Algerine leaks badly in the bows from two holes knocked in her, the Capt. reports, while working in the raft, and, also, while landing guns at Fort St. Philip.

This we can also remedy, and are now doing so. I trust by to-night both vessels will be serviceable.

Very respectfully, your obedient servant,
(Signed) T. B. HUGER,
Commanding McRae.

To JOHN K. DUNCAN,
Commanding Coast Defences:

GENERAL: Above you will see the report on the vessels reported to you as unfit for service. I send it for your information.

Respectfully, your obedient servant,
JOHN K. MITCHELL,
Commanding C. S. Naval Forces

(Document H.)

FORT JACKSON, LA., April 23, 1862.

Capt. J. K. MITCHELL,
Commanding Naval Forces Lower Mississippi river:

CAPTAIN: I am of the opinion that the mortar practice of the enemy against Fort Jackson must be nearly exhausted, and that there is every indication that the enemy, as the next plan of attack, is about to move his large vessels to the point of woods, and open upon us with his broadsides. One of the large vessels has already been brought up and placed in position. Should the above prove to be the case, it is imperatively and absolutely necessary that the batteries of the Louisiana should be brought into action, as well as those of Forts Jackson and St. Philip.

A proper position for the Louisiana would be on the Fort St. Philip side, a short distance below the raft and close to the shore, which will give us three direct and cross fires upon the point of attack.

Earnestly calling your attention to this subject, and, as you can see from your position the movements of the enemy, and can, consequently, know when to act,

I remain, very respectfully,
Your obedient servant,
J. K. DUNCAN,
Brig.-gen. commanding Coast Defences.

(Document I.)

C. S. STEAMER LOUISIANA,
NEAR FORT JACKSON, April 23d, 1862.

To Brig.-gen. J. K. DUNCAN,
Commanding Coast Defences, Fort Jackson:

GENERAL: I am in receipt of your letter of this date, in which you express your belief that the enemy is about to change his place of attack, and open the broadside of his larger ships on the forts, and in which you make certain suggestions as to the position to be taken by this ship.

By reference to a letter of mine to you of yesterday's date, and of (No. 1) of this date, you will be apprised of the condition of this ship. Should an attack be made as anticipated, I shall be governed by circumstances, and do all I can against the enemy.

I have the honor to be, very respectfully,
Your obedient servant,
JOHN K. MITCHELL,
Commanding C. S. Naval Forces Lower Mississippi.

(Document J.)

C. S. STEAMER LOUISIANA,
OFF FORT JACKSON, April 23d, 1862.

To Gen. J. K. DUNCAN,
Commanding Coast Defences, Fort Jackson:

SIR: I inclose herewith a copy of a communication received on the 21st inst., from Capt. Stevenson, from which you will perceive that, notwithstanding Gen. Lovell's order to him, this letter so qualifies my authority as to relieve me from all responsibility as to the movements of the vessels of the river fleet under his command.

I have the honor to be,
Very respectfully,
Your obedient servant,
(Signed,) JOHN K. MITCHELL,
Commanding C. S. Naval Forces Lower Mississippi.

(Document K.)

RIVER DEFENCE, C. S. GUNBOAT WARRIOR,
FORT JACKSON, April 21st, 1862.

Commander J. K. MITCHELL, *Confederate States Navy:*

SIR:—I am in receipt of an order from Major-gen. M. Lovell, dated 20th instant, in which I am directed to place myself and my whole command at this point under your orders. Every officer and man on the river defence expedition, joined it with the condition that it was to be independent of the navy, and that it would not be governed by the regulations of the navy, or be commanded by naval officers. In the face of the enemy I will not say more. I will co-operate with you, and do nothing without your approbation, and will endeavor to carry out your wishes to the best of my ability, but in my own way, as to the details, and the handling of my boats. But I expect the vessels under my charge to remain as separate command. All orders for their movements, addressed to me, will be promptly executed if practicable, and I undertake to be responsible for their efficiency when required. I suppose this is all that is intended by the order of Major-gen. Lovell, or that will be expected from me by you.

Respectfully yours, &c.,
JOHN A. STEVENSON,
Senior Captain commanding River Fleet at Fort Jackson.

Our signals should be made to assimilate at once. Capt. Renshaw and myself could arrange this if you wish, as no doubt but you are greatly fatigued, and still much to do and arrange. Any thing I can do, rely on it being done promptly and cheerfully.

Yours, &c.,
(Signed) J. A. S.

(Document L.)

FORT JACKSON, LOUISIANA, April 23d, 1862.

Capt. J. K. MITCHELL,
Commanding Naval Forces Lower Mississippi River:

CAPTAIN:—The enemy has just sent up a small boat, and planted a series of white flags on the Fort St. Philip side, commencing about 350 yards above the lone tree. It is the probable position of his ships in the new line of attack, which, in my opinion, he contemplates for attacking Fort Jackson with his large vessels. As you may not have seen this operation, I furnish you with the information. Please keep the river well lit up with fire-rafts to-night, as the attack may be made at any time.

Very respectfully,
Your obedient servant,
(Signed) J. K. DUNCAN,
Brig.-general commanding Coast Defences

(Document M.)

FORT JACKSON, LOUISIANA, 3½ o'clock A. M.,
April 24th, 1862.

Capt. J. K. MITCHELL,
Commanding Naval Forces Lower Mississippi River:

CAPTAIN:—As I anticipated, and informed you yesterday, the enemy are taking up their position at the present moment, with their large ships on the Fort St. Philip shore, to operate against Fort Jackson. They are placing themselves boldly, with their lights at their mast-heads. You are assuming a fearful responsibility if you do not come at once to our assistance with the Louisiana and the fleet. I can say no more.

Very respectfully,
Your obedient servant,
J. K. DUNCAN,
Brigadier-general.

(Document N.)

C. S. GUNBOAT LOUISIANA,
NEAR FORT ST. PHILIP,
April 24th, 1862.

To Brig.-gen. J. K. DUNCAN,
Commanding Coast Defences, Fort Jackson:

GENERAL:—On returning to the Louisiana, I find that we have no tender on whose steam-power we can rely, aad many of the volunteer troops on board of the W. Burton are intoxicated. Under these circumstances, as well as the exhausted condition of our own crew, and excessive difficulty in handling the vessel, will prevent our taking the position, at least to-day, that I proposed, and was arranged between us this forenoon.

I will, however, as you suggested in your communication, take up a position above, to protect the approaches in that direction.

Having no adequate motive power of our own, it will be an easy matter for the enemy's vessels that have it, to take up such a position that our guns cannot reach him for want of elevation, or be brought to bear upon him. I will, however, do all I can to keep him back from above.

The McRae has lost her 9-inch gun: of course, we cannot expect much assistance from her.

I have the honor to be,
Very respectfully,
Your obedient servant,
J. K. MITCHELL,
Commanding C. S. Naval Forces Lower Miss.

(Document O.)

C. S. STEAMER LOUISIANA,
FORT ST. PHILIP, April 24th, 1862.

To Gen. J. K. DUNCAN,
Commanding Coast Defences, Fort Jackson:

GENERAL:—Your 2d and 3d notes, of this date, are at hand. We are in a helpless condition, for the want of tug-boats. The W. Burton is crippled, and the Landis also, and the gunboat Defiance will not do any thing for us. If she comes within my reach, I will deprive her captain of his command, by force, if necessary.

The anchor we have down cannot purchase, and we are afraid to ship it, to move about three hundred yards higher up, where we can be better secured.

We shall probably remain where we are, and do all we can to defeat the enemy, should he attack us again.

It will be out of our power, I am afraid, to light up the bank below St. Philip to-night, or to set adrift fire-boats, as none are at hand, and they have all disappeared, apparently.

I have the honor to be,
Very respectfully,
Your obedient servant,
JNO. K. MITCHELL,
Commanding C. S. Naval Forces Lower Miss.

(Document P.)

FORT JACKSON, LOUISIANA,
April 24th, 1862.

To Capt. J. K. MITCHELL,
Commanding C. S. Naval Forces Lower Miss.:

CAPTAIN:—From all we can see and learn, the enemy, with the exception of one or two gunboats has passed up the river, so that there will be no use in changing your present position to one further above. I regret to learn the condition of the volunteer troops on board the W. Burton. This, together with the exhausted condition of your crew, will prevent your taking up the position below, which was agreed upon this morning, for the present. You may be able to take it up, however, when your crew recover from their fatigue, and when you are able to quell the irregularities of the volunteers.

Very respectfully,
Your obedient servant.
J. K. DUNCAN,
Commanding Coast Defences.

(Document Q.)

FORT JACKSON, LOUISIANA,
April 24th, 1862.

To Capt. J. K. MITCHELL,
Commanding C. S. Naval Forces Lower Mississippi.:

CAPTAIN: As I have no boats of any kind, I must ask of you to light up the river with fire-barges to-night, if it possibly lies in your power. The absence of light greatly impairs the accuracy and effectiveness of our fire upon the enemy.

Very respectfully,
Your obedient servant,
J. K. DUNCAN, *Brig.-gen.*,
Commanding Coast Defences.

(Document R.)

FORT JACKSON, April 24th, 1862.

To Capt. J. K. MITCHELL,
Commanding C. S. Naval Forces Lower Miss.:

CAPTAIN: The lower schooner will be lighted by firing her from a row-boat from Fort St. Philip at early dusk. As this light dies away the next one above will be fired, and so on, all night.

Unless you can better yourself materially, I would not advise any movement on your part from your present position, owing to all the adverse circumstances mentioned in your letter.

In regard to the Defiance, the authority over her which I formerly had has been transferred to you; but we will freely lend you any assistance which you may require in deposing her commander, or in exercising your authority over her.

Keep a vigilant look out for another attack to-night, when we will mutually support each other, and do all that we possibly can.

Capt. Squires has been directed by Col. Higgins to furnish you such assistance as you may require.

Very respectfully,
Your obedient servant,
J. K. DUNCAN, *Brig.-gen.*,
Commanding Coast Defence.

(Document S.)

MISSISSIPPI RIVER, April 26th, 1862,
U. S. Steamer Harriet Lane.

To Col. EDWARD HIGGINS,
Commanding Confederate Forces.
In Forts Jackson and St. Philip:

SIR: When I last demanded the surrender of Forts Jackson and St. Philip, I had no positive assurance of the success of our vessels in passing safely the batteries on the river. Since then I have received communications from Flag-officer Farragut, who is now in possession of New Orleans. Our troops are or will be in possession of the prominent points on the river, and a sufficient force has been posted outside of the bayous to cut off all communications and prevent supplies. No man could consider it dishonorable to surrender, especially under these circumstances, when no advantages can arise by longer holding out, and by yielding gracefully he can save the further effusion of blood.

You have defended the forts gallantly, and no more can be asked of you. I feel authorized to offer you terms sufficiently honorable to relieve you from any feeling of humiliation. The officers will be permitted to retire on parole with their side arms, not to serve again until regularly exchanged. All private property will be respected. Only the arms and munitions will be surrendered to the U. S. Government, and the vessels lying near the forts. No damage must be done to the defences. The soldiers also will be parolled, and be permitted to return to their homes, giving up their arms.

I am aware that you can hold out some little time longer, and am also aware of the exact condition, as reported to us by a deserter, which convinces me that you will only be inflicting on yourself and those under you unnecessary discomforts without any good result arising from so doing.

Your port has long been closed to the world, by which serious injury has been experienced by many loyal citizens. I trust that you will not lend yourself to the further injury of their interests, where it can only entail calamity and bloodshed, without any possible hope of success or relief to your forts.

Your surrender is a mere question of time, which you know is not of any extent, and I therefore urge you to meet my present proposition. By doing so you can put an end to a state of affairs which will only inflict injury upon all those under you, who have strong claims upon your consideration.

I remain, very respectfully,
Your obedient servant,
(Signed) DAVID R. PORTER,
Commanding Mortar Fleet.

(Document T.)

HEAD-QUARTERS FORTS JACKSON AND ST. PHILIP,
April 27th, 1862.

To Commodore D. R. PORTER,
U. S. Navy, commanding Mortar Fleet:

SIR:—Your letter of the 26th instant, demanding the surrender of these forts, has been received.

In reply thereto, I have to state that no official information has been received by me, from our own authorities, that the city of New Orleans has been surrendered to the forces of Flag-officer Farrigut, and until such information is received, no proposition for a surrender can for a moment be entertained here.

Very respectfully,

Your obedient servant,

EDWARD HIGGINS,

Lieut.-col. commanding.

(Document U.)

FORT JACKSON, LA., April 27th, 1862.

SOLDIERS OF FORTS JACKSON AND ST. PHILIP:

You have nobly, gallantly, and heroically sustained, with courage and fortitude, the terrible ordeals of fire, water, and a hail of shot and shell, wholly unsurpassed during the present war. But more remains to be done. The safety of New Orleans and the cause of the Southern Confederacy—our homes, familes, and every thing dear to man—yet depend upon our exertions.

We are just as capable of repelling the enemy to-day as we were before the bombardment. Twice has the enemy demanded your surrender, and twice has he been refused.

Your officers have every confidence in your courage and patriotism, and feel every assurance that you will cheerfully and with alacrity obey all orders, and do your whole duty as men, and as becomes the well-tried garrisons of Forts Jackson and St. Philip. Be vigilant, therefore, and stand by your guns, and all will yet be well.

(Signed) J. K. DUNCAN,

Brig.-gen., commanding Coast Defences.

(Document V.)

HEAD-QUARTERS, FORTS JACKSON AND ST. PHILIP,

April 28th, 1862.

To Commodore DAVID R. PORTER,

United States Navy,

Commanding Mortar Feet:

SIR:—Upon mature deliberation, it has been decided to accept the terms of surrender of these forts, under the conditions offered by you in your letter of the 26th instant, viz.: that the officers and men shall be parolled—officers retiring with their side-arms. We have no control over the vessels afloat.

Very respectfully,
Your obedient servant,
EDWARD HIGGINS,
Lieut.-col. commanding.

(Document W.)

UNITED STATES STEAMER HARRIET LANE,
FORTS JACKSON AND ST. PHILIP,
Mississippi River, April 28, 1862.

By articles of capitulation, entered into this the twenty-eighth day of April, one thousand eight hundred and sixty-two, between David D. Porter, Commander U. S. Navy, commanding U. S. Mortar Flotilla, of the one part, and Brig.-gen. J. K. Duncan, commanding the coast defences, and Lieut.-col. Edward Higgins, commanding Forts Jackson and St. Philip, of the other part, it is mutually agreed:

1st. That Brig.-gen Duncan and Lieut.-col. Higgins shall surrender to the Mortar Flotilla Forts Jackson and St. Philip, the arms, munitions of war, and all the appurtenances thereunto belonging, together with all public property that may be under their charge.

2d. It is agreed by Commander David D. Porter, commanding the Mortar Flotilla, that Brig.-gen. Duncan and Lieut.-col. Higgins, together with the officers under their command, shall be respected. Furthermore, that they shall give their parole of honor not to serve in arms against the goverment of the United States, until they are regularly exchanged.

3d. It is further agreed by the Commander David D. Porter, commanding the Mortar Flotilla, on the part of the United States Government, that the non-commissioned officers, privates, and musicians, shall be permitted to retire on parole, their commanding and other officers becoming responsible for them, and that they shall deliver up their arms and accoutrements in their present condition, provided that no expenses accruing from the transportation of the men shall be defrayed by the Government of the United States.

4th. On the signing of these articles by the contracting parties, the fort shall be formally taken possession of by the U. S. naval forces composing the mortar flotilla. The Confederate flag shall be lowered, and the flag of the United States hoisted on the flag-staffs of Forts Jackson and St. Philip.

In agreement of the above, we, the undersigned, do hereunto set our hands and seals.

DAVID D. PORTER,
Commander Mortar Flotilla.
W. B. RENSHAW,
Commander U. S. N.
W. W. WAINRIGHT,
Lieut. commanding U. S. steamer Harriet Lane.
J. K. DUNCAN,
Brig.-gen. commanding Coast Defences.
EDWARD HIGGINS,
Lieut.-col. C. S. A., commanding Forts Jackson and St. Philip.

Witnessed by
Ed. T. Nichols,
Lieut. commanding U. S. gunboat Winona.
C. H. Russell,
Lieut. commanding U. S. gunboat Kennebeck.

Report of Lieut.-col. Ed. Higgins.

Head-quarters Forts Jackson and St. Philip,
April 27, 1862.

Lieut. W. M. Bridges,
A. A. A.-gen., 2d Brigade, Department No. 1, *N. O.:*

Sir:—I have the honor to report that on Friday, the 18th inst., the naval force of the U. S., which has been for some weeks in the river, making preparation for an attack on these forts, commenced the bombardment of Fort Jackson.

Fire from their mortar fleet was opened at 9 o'lock A. M. The force employed by the enemy against us consisted of twenty-one mortar vessels and a fleet of about twenty-one steam vessels of war, carrying more than two hundred guns of the heaviest calibre. The mortar vessels, when they opened fire, were all concealed from our view save six, which took position in sight of the forts, and within our longest range. These we soon forced to retire. They joined the rest of their fleet behind the point of woods, and, concealed from view, renewed their fire.

Orders had been issued to the officers and men of my command to retire to the casemates of the forts the moment the bombardment commenced. The order being obeyed, nothing was left for us to do but receive the furious storm of shell which was hailed upon us. Our citadel was soon destroyed by fire. All the buildings around and in connection with the fort shared the same fate.

From Friday morning until the following Thursday, we sustained this terrible battering. Several times during the bombardment the enemy's gunboats attempted to pass up the river, under cover of their mortar fire, and on each occasion our batteries were promptly manned, and the enemy's advance gallantly repelled.

At half past three A. M., on Thursday, it was observed that the mortar fire was increased to an intensity of fury which had not been previously reached. At the same time a movement was observed in the steam fleet below. Our batteries were instantly in readiness, and were at once engaged in a most terrific conflict with the enemy's fleet of fourteen steamships, which, dashing by the fort in the darkness of the night, pouring in their broadsides of shot, shell, grape, canister, and shrapnel, succeeded in getting beyond our range and in our rear. During the forenoon a demand was made by Commodore Porter, commanding the mortar fleet, for a surrender of the forts. This proposition was promptly refused, and the bombardment was again commenced and continued until four P. M., when all firing ceased.

I inclose you the reports of company and battery commanders, also the surgeon's report of killed and wounded. I fully indorse the encomiums of the company commanders upon the officers under their command, and feel myself bound to record my high admiration of the coolness, courage, and fortitude of all the officers of both forts.

Capt. J. B. Anderson, company "G," Louisiana artillery, was wounded early in the conflict, while heroically fighting his guns. Notwithstanding his severe wound, he rendered the most gallant and efficient service to the last.

Capt. W. B. Robertson, who commanded a detached work called the water battery, remained with his command during the whole of the protracted ordeal, without cover of any kind, although suffering from severe physical disease, and scarcely able, at times, to walk around his battery. He was most ably and gallantly assisted by Capt. R. J. Bruce, Louisiana artillery.

First Lieut. Eugene W. Baylor, who was in command of the 42 pounder barbette battery, and First Lieut. Richard Agar, of the same battery, did all that gallant officers and men could do.

The officers stationed at the heaviest batteries, on the river front, were, the greater part of the time, fatigued as they were, obliged to be constantly with their detachments at their guns to prevent surprise. Lieuts. A. N. Ogden, Bevuet Kennedy, and William T. Mumford, of the Louisiana artillery, particularly distinguished themselves in this service.

Although not under my immediate command, I cannot omit to mention the devoted conduct of your aid-de-camp, Lieut. Wm. M. Bridges, who, upon the disability of Capt. Anderson, immediately volunteered his services, and took charge of the two 10-inch columbiads, and fought them night and day with ceaseless energy.

Lieut. J. U. Gains, in command of the 32-pounder battery, on the river front, assisted by Lieut. E. D. Woodlief, Capt. S. Jones, company "I," Louisiana volunteers, Capt. F. Peter, company "I," 22d regiment, Louisiana volunteers, fought their batteries gallantly and well. Lieut. Thomas K. Pierson, 23d Louisiana volunteers, was killed in the thickest of the fight, while gallantly fighting his guns.

The St. Mary's Cannoniers, Capt. S. O. Comay, have my warmest gratitude and admiration for their whole conduct, both in face of the enemy, and in the severe and arduous fatigue duties, which they discharged, always and at all times, with alacrity and energy. They are an honor to the country, and well may their friends and relations be proud of them.

The report of Capt. M. T. Squires, who was the senior officer at Fort St. Philip, is inclosed, with the reports of the other officers. Capt. Squires fought the batteries of Fort St. Philip most gallantly. He was in charge of that fort during the whole bombardment. The severe work at Fort Jackson required my constant presence there. I had every confidence in the coolness, courage, and skill of Capt. Squires and his officers, and most satisfactorily did they discharge their duties. I refer you to his report for the mention of the individual conduct of his officers.

The floating battery "Louisiana," the steam ram Manassas, and the Confederate steamer McRae, together with a number of vessels which had been fitted up by the Confederate and State Governments, were in the river above the forts at the time the enemy dashed by. I am unable to state what assistance, if any, was rendered by the greater portion of these. At daylight I observed the McRae gallantly fighting, at terrible odds, contending, at close quarters, with two of the enemy's powerful ships. Her gallant commander, Lieut. Thomas B. Huger, fell, during the conflict, severely, but, I trust, not mortally wounded.

The Manassas I observed under weigh, apparently in pursuit of one of the vessels of the enemy, but I soon lost sight of her.

I would here observe, that I think an investigation should be demanded into the conduct of the authorities afloat, whose neglect of our urgent entreaties to light up the river during this sad night contributed so much to the success of our enemies.

My adjutant, Lieut. C. N. Morse, was indefatigable in the discharge of his important duties, which required his constant presence near my person, and has my sincere thanks.

Surgeon Sommerville Burke, C. S. A., and Dr. Bradbury (who kindly volunteered his services when he became aware of the attack on the forts), were unremitting in their attention to the wounded, fearlessly exposing themselves, at all times, in the discharge of their duties.

Lieut. Charles Warmes, ordnance officer, distinguished himself by the self-sacrificing attention to arduous and important duties. Day and night he was at his post, and, by his great exertions, our magazine was saved from being flooded, the water having risen considerably above the floor.

Lieuts. Mann and Royster, of Capt. Ryan's company, rendered fearless and efficient service.

Capt. Ryan was with a detachment of his company, on board the "Louisiana," during a portion of the bombardment, and in the fight of Thursday morning. At all times his services were most promptly rendered.

Mr. James Ward rendered me the most important services during the bombardment. In charge of the firemen, he made almost superhuman exertions during the burning of the citadel. He has my warmest gratitude.

I have the honor to remain,

Very respectfully, your obedient servant,

ED. HIGGINS,

Lieut.-Col. C. S. A., commanding Forts Jackson and St. Philip.

Supplemental Report of Lieut.-col. Higgins.

NEW ORLEANS, April 30th, 1862.

To Lieut. WM. M. BRIDGES,
Aid-de-camp and A. A. A.-gen., 2d Brigade:

SIR:—I have the honor to report, that on the morning of the 27th April, 1862, a formal demand for the surrender of Forts Jackson and St. Philip was made by Com. David D. Porter, commanding U. S. mortar fleet.

The terms which were offered were of the most liberal nature; but so strong was I in the belief that we could resist successfully any attack which could be made upon us, either by land or water, that the terms were at once refused. Our fort was still strong. Our damage had been, to some extent, repaired. Our men had behaved well, and all was hope and confidence with the officers, when, suddenly, at midnight, I was aroused by the report that the garrison had revolted, had seized the guard, and were spiking the guns. Word was sent us, through the sergeants of companies, that the men would fight no longer. The company officers were immediately dispatched to their commands, but were driven back. Officers were fired upon when they appeared in sight upon the parapet. Signals were exchanged by the mutineers with Fort St. Philip. The mutiny was complete, and a general massacre of the officers, and a disgraceful surrender of the fort, appeared inevitable.

By great exertion, we succeeded, with your influence, in preventing this disgraceful blot upon our country, and were fortunate in keeping the passion of the men in check, until we could effect an honorable surrender of the forts, which was done by us, jointly, on the morning of the 28th inst.

As the facts and documents relating to this matter are in your possession, it is unnecessary for me to dwell longer on this humiliating and unhappy affair. I wish to place on record here the noble conduct of Capt. Comay's company, the St. Mary's cannoniers—who alone stood true as steel, when every other company in Fort Jackson basely dishonored their country.

I have the honor to remain, very respectfully,
Your obedient servant,
ED. HIGGINS, *Lieut.-col. C. S. A.*,
Late commander Forts Jackson and St. Philip.

Report of Captain M. T. Squires.

FORT ST. PHILIP, April 27th, 1862.

Lieut. CHARLES N. MORSE,

Post-adjutant, Fort Jackson, Louisiana:

SIR:—I have the honor respectfully to submit the following report:

Early on the morning of Friday, the 18th instant, perceiving by the movements of the enemy, that they were about taking up their position, the heavy guns were ordered to open upon them, to annoy them in the execution of their purpose as much as possible; but the distance being great, and the range extreme, with but very little success, the enemy taking little or no notice of our fire, only answering by a few rifle shells, at long invervals. The 13-inch mortar after the 13th round became useless, the bed giving way under it, breaking in two, and the mortar coming upon the ground. The enemy retired from our sight at 8 o'clock P. M., and nothing more was heard of him that night.

At an early hour of the morning of the 19th instant, the enemy again took up a position identical with that of the previous, excepting that no mortar boats were on this shore, all keeping close behind the point of woods, and opening fire upon Fort Jackson, which was allowed to continue without interruption from this side. Fearing the effect, and having ascertained the exact range and distances, determined to open upon them, and draw off some of the fire to this side, if possible. It was immediately done, and with partial success, three of the mortar boats opening upon us with but little effect.

On the 20th, 21st, and 22d, the fire of the enemy still continued from their mortar boats, with an occasional shot from the gunboats. The only damage done, during these days, was the damaging the platform of the 24-pounder gun in salient near main magazine, the shell passing under, and throwing it up, but not rendering it useless. Our fire was slow and deliberate, with no visible results more than the driving back of two of the mortar boats, which were partially exposed around the wooded point. The fire of the enemy, although warm, well-directed, and sustained, was, for the most part, either short or very much over. Up to this time, the only guns used were the columbiad battery in the main work, and the 13-inch mortar, disabled on the first day. In the lower water battery, one 8-inch columbiad and one 7-inch rifle gun, worked by Capt. R. C. Bond's company; four 10-inch sea coast mortars, by Capt. J. H. Lamon's company. On the 23d, the enemy still kept up a regular fire, to which we did not reply all day. At 3 1–2 o'clock of the morning of the 24th, the men were ready, and standing at their guns, having received information that there was a movement by the enemy. No vessels were to be seen, and the first notice of an enemy nearing us was the reply to the shots from Fort Jackson, and the gunners were ordered to fire by the flashes of the enemy's guns, which was done, but the fire was entirely too high, and passed over them. Immediately after this, a vessel came in sight, and they followed each other in rapid succession, seemingly in pairs, one of the two keeping back far enough to enable her to deliver her fire from her broadsides. The fire from our guns was rapid, and from the little that could be seen and heard, was accurate, but after the first discharge, the smoke almost hid them from sight, and we were again compelled to judge by the flashes of their guns. As to the effect of the fire, it is impossible to state what it was, as the darkness, aided by the smoke, rendered seeing out of the question. A three masted propeller ran ashore during, the engagement, above the upper water-battery, and remaining there several minutes with a fire-barge alongside, her rigging had caught fire, but was immediately extinguished. We were not able to open upon her, as one of the columbiads had been previously dismounted, and the other could not be brought to bear, besides, their hands were full with other vessels coming up, and the 24-pounder in the salient of the upper water-battery, bearing directly upon her, had been broken in too near the trunnions. The vessels passed close under our guns, taking advantage of the eddy, which runs up with considerable force, and it was found impossible to get more than one or two shots at any one vessel, they passed with such rapidity.

All our guns were worked with courage, energy and skill, excepting the upper water battery, where some confusion arose, caused by the men not being so thoroughly drilled as they should have been. Company C, of the Confederate Recruits, Lieut. J. K. Dixon, were fully prepared to work the guns of this battery, and would have done so with effect, but were two days before ordered on board the floating battery "Louisiana," and their place was supplied by Capt. Assanheimer's Company B, 24th regiment Louisiana Volunteers, who had only been drilled a few times, and Capt. Massicott's company D, Chalmette regiment, who were raw undrilled, perfectly ignorant even of the use of the shot guns with which they were armed, and had never been drilled at artillery. As soon as it was seen that the guns did not open, Lieut. A. J. Quigly, with such men as could be gathered, was sent to attend to them, which was done, so far as they were concerned, to the satisfaction of that officer. The company of Confederate recruits, under Lieuts. Dixon and Blow, were detailed to report to Capt. Mitchell, C. S. Navy, for duty on board the "Louisiana," as per instructions dated headquarters Forts Jackson and St. Philip, April 21st, 1862, where they remained until the evening of the 24th instant. Capt. Lartigue's company did good service as scouts and sharpshooters, many of them being out at all times. On the night of the 23d, seven of them were sent to ascertain the movements of the enemy, and all returned without accomplishing any thing. Two other scouts, one from company K, and the other of company F, were out on the same mission, and had it not been from the failure of the rockets, which by an accident became wet, would have signalled their approach much sooner. As it was, the only intimation I received was the firing of one of their muskets. The following is the number of projectiles used, &c.: six hundred and seventy-five (675) 8-inch solid shot, one hundred and seventy-one (171) 8-inch shells, thirteen 13-inch from columbiad battery, &c., in main work; one hundred and forty-two 10-inch mortar shells from lower mortar battery, four hundred and seventy shot, shell, and grape, lower water battery; one hundred and twenty shot, grape, and canister, from upper water battery. Capt. R. C. Bond, assisted by 1st Lieuts. Carleton Hunt and Wm. E. Ellis, and his company K, Capt. J. H. Lamon, with the assistance of 1st Lieut. H. W. Fowler, with his company C, in the lower battery, manning the 42 and 32-pounders respectively; Lieuts. Lewis B. Taylor and W. B. Jones, with company F, at the columbiad battery, and Lieut. A. J. Quigly, with supernumeraries of company F, taken from main work to man guns of upper water battery, behaved with gallantry, energy, coolness, and bravery, worthy of imitation; and all, both officers and men, deserve the highest praise that could be given to anyone, for the honorable part they performed during the whole time since the commencement of this trying conflict. Capt. Chas. Assanheimer's company B, did their best, both his officers and men. Individual acts of heroism are numerous, but where all did so well, it would appear invidious to mention names. Suffice it to say, that were every thing to be done again, or any thing else required to be performed, one could ask no other privilege than to have the same men to do it—

feeling satisfied it would be as well carried out as possible. The injury to the fort was slight. Of the guns, one banded 7-inch rifle was bursted by the explosion of a shell in its bore near the muzzle, and one 24-pounder gun was broken in two about 14 inches in front of the trunnions, by being struck by a solid shot. An 8-inch columbiad was dismounted, but only temporarily useless, the gun being uninjured and soon remounted. The platform of one 24-pounder gun was undermined by a shell, but not rendered entirely useless. One of the uprights of a 42-pounder gun-carriage was partially shot away, but can still be of service.

With many thanks to all officers and men for their assistance and efficient aid, and humbly bowing before the will of Almighty God,

I am, very respectfully,
Your obedient servant,
(Signed) M. T. SQUIRES,
Captain Louisiana Artillery.

List of Killed and Wounded during the Eight Days Bombardment of Fort Jackson.

To Lieut.-col. Ed. Higgins,
Commanding Forts Jackson and St. Philip:

April 18. Private Helzel, company D, 1st artillery, contusion, leg.
" " Fogorty, " " "
" Capt. J. B. Anderson, co. B, " wound in hand.
" Private Tymon, co. E, " in back.
" " Friedman, " " in hand.
" " Shields, " " killed.
" " O'Brien, St. M. 22d La., wound'd in ankle, slightly.
Wounded 6........................Killed 1.

April 19. Private Clark, company B, 1st artillery, killed.
" " Tho's. McCarty, " E, " wounded in arm.
" " Reims, co. St. M. C., wounded in hand and arm.
" " F. F. Heyle " killed.
Wounded 2........................Killed 2.

April 20. Corp. Morris, company B, 1st artillery, killed,
" Private Ashton, " D, " w'd in breast and arm
" " Sumkel, " E, " on toe.
Wounded 2........................Killed 1.

April 21. Private Reed, company H, 1st artillery, wounded on foot.
Wounded 1.

April 22. Private Londenstein, co. Yagers, 22d La. vols., wounded on shoulder.
" " Kelley, St. M. C., 22d La. vols., wounded on foot.
Wounded 2.

April 23. Private Kergan, co. A, 22d La. vols., wounded in back.
Wounded 1.

April 24. Private Robert Collier, co. D, 1st art., wounded in face.
" " Stephen Welsh " B, " killed.
" " Michael Burke, " " " "
" " Williams, " D, " wounded in knee.
" " Albion Gooch, " " " killed.
" Sergeant Williams, " E, " wounded in eye.
" " Lynch, " " " " in stomach
" Private Johnson, " " " " in arm.
" Sergeant Jackson, " H, " " "
" Corporal Smith, " " " killed.
" Private M. Sullivan, " " " w'd in arm and leg.
" Sergeant Gusman, co. A G. 22d La. vols., " "
" Lieut. Pierson, " " " killed.
" Private Shultz, " " " w'd in hip, dead.
" " J. Benson, " " " killed.
" " T. Kroupe, St. M. 23d vols., thigh amputated.
" " Wagner, " " wounded in arm.
" " Alberts, " " " in hand.
" " Z. Drozer, Yagers, 22d La. vols., w'd in hand & face.
" " F. Bradieaux, St. M. C., wounded on nose.
" " A. Haydel, " " in both legs.
" " A. Whaley, " arm amputated, dead.
" " E. Hoydel, " killed.
" Lieut. Godeaux, " wounded in hand.
" Private J. Duffy, 1st art., fractured upper maxillary.
" " F. Kroupe, St. M. 23d La. vols., wounded on head.
" Corporal H. Weigand, Yagers, 22d La. vols., on head.
" Private John Shin, A. G., 22d La. vols., bruised.
" " James O'Neil, co. H, 1st art., wounded in hand.
" Corporal J. Harmon, St. M., 23d La. vols., w'd in breast.
Wounded 21 ....Killed 9.

Total wounded 33......Total Killed 9.

(Signed) SOMERVILLE BURKE,
Assistant Surgeon, C. S. A.

List of Killed and Wounded in Fort St. Philip,

FORT ST. PHILIP, April 26th, 1862,

To Lieut. CHARLES W. MORSE,

Post Adjutant, Fort Jackson:

SIR: I have to report two killed and four wounded at Fort St. Philip, viz:

Company D, Chalmette regiment............1 killed.
" " " " ....2 wounded.
" F, 1st La. artillery................1 killed.
" K, " " ....2 wounded.

Very respectfully,

(Signed) CHARLES D. LEWIS.

Assistant Surgeon, C. S. A.

Report of Brigadier-general M. L. Smith.

CAMP MOORE, TANGIPAHOA, LA.,
May 6th, 1862.

To Major J. G. PICKET,

Assistant Adjutant-general:

MAJOR: I herewith submit a report of the operations of the troops under my command at the Chalmette and McGee lines, on the approach of the enemy's vessels from Forts Jackson and St. Philip to the city of New Orleans. These interior lines of defence are constructed with special reference to an attack by land, but, terminating them on the river banks, were two batteries calculated for twelve and twenty guns respectively, and at the time of the action containing five and nine. Ten 42-pounders, intended for this battery, were turned over to the navy for the defence of New Orleans by water. This has been considered as depending upon the forts mentioned, which are well constructed, permanent works, rather well armed, and far stronger than any other that could be hastily erected. With this view, all the available material, both of guns and ammunition, had been concentrated there prior to the bombardment, and during its continuance was being added to in such quantities daily as the means of the department admitted of, it being evident that the decisive struggle was there to be made. As soon, therefore, as it became certain that the large vessels of the enemy had succeeded in passing, there no longer existed a chance of preventing them from reaching New Orleans, and the short resistance made by the few guns mounted in the two batteries of the interior lines was made through a sense of duty, but without any expectation of success, the enemy numbering as many vessels, less one, as we had guns.

On the side of the river, where I was in person during the action, were stationed three companies of Lieut.-col. Pinckney's battalion of sharpshooters. With the five guns on the other side, were Capt. Patton's company of the 22d Louisiana volunteers, one company from Fort Pike, under Lieut. Butter, one company, Beauregard battery, besides two battalions of infantry collected in camp for instruction, as well as to guard the line in case of the enemy's landing and attacking by land—all under immediate command of Gen. Buisson.

The enemy's vessels had approached to within about the fourth of a mile before we opened on them, the first gun being from Pinckney's battery, and immediately followed by several from the battery on the opposide side, and as promptly replied to from the enemy's vessels. The engagement lasted until every round of ammunition on hand was fired, both officers and men displaying a coolness and intrepidity that was gratifying, especially as regards the men, who then for the first time in their lives discharged a heavy gun. The firing on our side was spirited, perhaps a little uncertain; on the enemy's, heavy and well directed.

During the engagement their vessels gradually lessened the distance, until near enough to open with grape and canister.

The ammunition being expended, and every sense of duty satisfied, permission was given to Col. Pinckney to withdraw his command along the line of field works affording shelter, which was done deliberately, officers and men retiring together. The casualties were one killed and one wounded. The battery on the Chalmette side seemed well served, and no doubt was so, judging from the character of the officers present.

The enemy, steaming up between us and the city, prevented the retreat of the troops to that point. They were accordingly directed to gain the Opelousas railroad and reach Camp Moore via Lafourche, or such route as might be found best. Lieut.-col. Pinckney has already reported with his command, but somewhat reduced in numbers.

In concluding this report, I wish particularly to call attention to the admirable assistance rendered by Lieuts. McDonald and B. M. Harrod, on engineer duty, both before and after the action. Their conduct could not have been better. Lieut. Frost, on special duty, was also of material assistance, but in carrying out some instructions, was accidently absent during the engagement.

Having received no report from Gen. Buisson concerning the operations on his side of the river, I am unable to refer to them more particularly.

Respectfully submitted.

M. L. SMITH,
Brig.-gen. commanding 3rd Brigade.

REPORT OF THE AFFAIR AT SOUTH MILLS.

REPORT OF MAJOR-GEN. HUGER.

HEAD-QUARTERS DEPARTMENT OF NORFOLK,
NORFOLK, VA., April 28, 1862.

Gen. R. E. LEE,
Commanding, etc.:

GENERAL:—I have received through Brig.-gen. Blanchard, commanding 3d brigade, the reports of Col. A. R. Wright, and Col. Ferebee, commanding the drafted North Carolina militia, and Lieut. D. A. French, who succeeded to the command of the battery after the death of its gallant captain, McComas. I would forward these reports to you at once, but there are some discrepancies and omissions in them which I desire first to have corrected, and will therefore try to make a brief statement from these reports, to give you and the War Department information concerning this severe and well-fought action, which was successful, inasmuch as the enemy failed to accomplish his object, and was obliged to retire to his vessels with great loss.

I send herewith a sketch of the country between South Mills and Elizabeth City, showing the position of the battle.

All the forces under the command of Col. Wright were the 3d regiment Georgia volunteers, some drafted militia, under Col. Ferebee, of North Carolina, (Col. Ferebee omits to state in his report how many he had on duty,) McComas' battery of arttllery, 11 rified pieces and 3 bronze 6-pounders, and one company of cavalry—Capt. Gillette's Southampton company. On Friday, the 18th, I had ordered forward the 32d N. C. regiment, (Col. Brabbles,) and the 1st Louisiana regiment, (Col. Vincent's,) but they did not arrive until after the battle.

On Friday, the 18th, Col. Wright occupied South Mills with three companies of his regiment, 160 strong, and the drafted North Corolina militia. Two companies at the intrenchments at Richardson's Mills, 125 effectives, and five companies, about 300 men, and McComas' battery of artillery at Elizabeth City. On Friday evening, anticipating the enemy's advance, and in compliance with my instructions to concentrate his forces at or near South Mills, he ordered the companies at Elizabeth City to retire nine miles to Richardson's Mills. From some cause not yet explained, these companies did not leave Elizabeth City until after day-light on Saturday morning. The cavalry companies from Camden court-house reported at 8 1-2 o'clock on the 19th, the enemy approaching, having then passed the court-house. Col. Wright moved forward with his three companies, and at 9 1-2 was met by Capt. McComas, with his battery. After advancing three miles from South Mills, the road emerged from the woods, and the fields on the right and left extended 160 to 180 yards to thick woods and swamp. On the edge of the woods on both sides of the road, and perpendicular to it, was a small ditch, the earth from which was thrown up on the south side in a ridge, upon which was a heavy rail fence. From this point the road led through a narrow lane (Sawyer's lane) for one mile, with cleared land on both sides of it. Here he determined to make his stand. About three hundred yards from the woods ran a deep, wide ditch, parallel with the one first mentioned, and extending to the woods on either side of the road, and a short distance beyond it were dwellings and out-houses which would give cover to the enemy. Col. Wright therefore ordered them burnt. The large ditch in his front he filled with fence rails and set them on fire, his object being to have this ditch so hot by the time the enemy came up they could not occupy it. (A). This ditch is marked on sketch as "roasted ditch."

Two pieces of artillery (the road was too narrow for more) were placed in the road just where it emerged from the woods, which commanded the road with the range of the guns. He also threw down the fence for 300 yards in front of the guns, and tossed the rails into the road to destroy the effect of the enemy's ricochet firing, and to deprive him of the cover of the fences. The fences on the sides of the woods were taken down and laid in heaps on the embankment in front of his men. All these arrangements were made, and it was 11 o'clock before he was joined by Lieut.-col. Reed and the seven companies from below. Two of these, under Major Lee, were placed at River bridge, with one piece of McComas' artillery, with directions to destroy it and stop the enemy there if he should attempt to get into our rear by coming up the west side of the river. Lieut.-col. Read and three companies 3d Georgia, (and by Col. Ferebee's report, the North Carolina militia,) were placed about a mile in the rear at the meeting of an old road, to protect that passage and serve as a reserve. The remaining five companies were deployed in open order across the road on the right and left of the artillery, protected by the ditch and fence rails on the banks. The smoke from the burning buildings and fences was rolled towards the enemy, thus masking the position. At fifteen minutes before 12 o'clock the front of a heavy column of the enemy was seen passing through the smoke, and Capt. McComas opened a destructive fire on them, which checked their advance for half an hour, when they again approached under the fire of a 12-pounder, but soon retired entirely out of sight in considerable confusion. Up to three o'clock thrice had the heavy columns of the enemy been beaten back by the heavy fire of Capt. McComas' artillery, and our only casualties one man wounded and one wheel injured.

At 15 minutes after 3 P. M., the enemy again advanced and deployed two regiments to their right, our left. Three regiments, after advancing towards us, were driven back by the well-directed fire of Capt. McComas' artillery, and Capts. Nesbitt's and Musgrove's companies. Capt. McWhirter's fire also caused the Zouaves on our right to retire, and this attack ceased by 25 minutes before 4. Our loss up to this time was very slight, while that of the enemy was very severe, as we could plainly see them fall, and they had raised the hospital flag on a building in rear of their line. They soon advanced again, two regiments skirting the woods on our left, and approached near enough to engage the skirmishers. One company from the right was moved over, and Col. Reed ordered to send one company from the reserve. The enemy deployed in the open field, and bore down rapidly, but the heavy fire of musketry caused them to waver, and they fled back to the fence. Three regiments and a field piece were in the centre, and the 9th New York regiment on the right. The fire was now brisk from one end of the line to the other, and the enemy were held in check, when, just at this moment, Capt. McComas was killed by a minié ball, and his men, who, for four hours, had fought with most indomitable courage, became panic-stricken, and left the field, taking their pieces with them. Col. Wright succeeded in rallying them and getting two pieces and a few men in position, and the enemy had advanced so close that canister was fired on them with effect, and they again fell back. The ammunition in the limber boxes was exhausted, and during the temporary absence of Col. Wright, the artillery left the field. The enemy made a charge upon our line, but the steady fire, at close distance, (Col. Wright estimates it at 50 yards,) caused them to break in confusion, and they fell back.

Taking advantage of their confusion, Col. Wright now fell back in good order to intrenchments on Joy's creek, about two miles in his rear, and called in Lieut.-col. Read's and Major Lee's commands, and there awaited the enemy, who, it appears, were so badly injured, that they made no advance, but at about 8 P. M. began to retreat to their boats. At this time I am informed that several companies of the 32d North Carolina regiment joined Col. Wright, who, during the night retired from this position to the N. W. Lock. Col. Wright states his loss at six killed, nineteen wounded, and three taken prisoners. The enemy's loss he estimates as very large, as high as 300. Col. Wright states that the regiments opposed to him were the 9th, 21st and 89th New York, and the 21st Massachusetts, 6th New Hampshire, and 51st Pennsylvania regiments, (we have prisoners or wounded of five of these regiments,) the whole commanded by Brig.-gen. Reno.

Among the killed he is grieved to announce the loss of Capt. McComas, an estimable gentleman, and brave and skilful officer, whose conduct throughout the action elicited the highest praise. All the command engaged behaved in the most gallant manner, standing firmly against overwhelming odds, until ordered to fall back to our intrenchments. They maintained their position over five hours, and killed and disabled more of the enemy than we had in action. On returning to the field next day, we recovered 1100 pounds powder, and the arms, accoutrements, tools, etc., left by the enemy. I have already reported his leaving such wounded as he could not remove, and I have sent them to Fortress Monroe on parole. Some ten or twelve stragglers were taken on the 20th, and held as prisoners of war. I will forward the original reports as soon as they are corrected, and meanwhile submit this as a summary.

Very respectfully,

Your obedient servant,

BEN. HUGER,

Major.-gen., commanding.

REPORT OF OPERATIONS ON TENNESSEE RIVER AND AT BRIDGEPORT.

BRIG.-GEN. LEADBETTER, COMMANDING.

HEAD-QUARTERS 1ST BRIGADE, EAST TENN.,
CHATTANOOGA, May 5, 1862.

To Major H. L. CLAY,
Assistant Adjutant-general:

MAJOR:—I have the honor to report that the enemy, eleven or twelve hundred strong, advanced against Bridgeport on the 29th ult. My command, guarding the bridges at that place, consisted of 450 infantry of the newly raised regiments, the Georgia 39th and 43d, with 150 cavalry employed only as scouts. The infantry was posted on the heights in advance of the West bridge, about 500 yards distant, leaving a rear guard of 50 men near the bridge end and on either side of it, covered by musketry breastworks. Two iron six-pounders, old guns, had been placed in the position last named, but were withdrawn as soon as the enemy's advance had developed itself as an attack.

You are aware that a defence of the place by a small force was very difficult. The two bridges, with the high railroad embankment between them, were a mile and a quarter long, extending in one straight line towards the heights before mentioned, and these heights were of far too great extent to be properly occupied and held by our forces. The enemy could advance in any direction on our front and flanks, and cut off our troops from the bridge, or else drive them to a disastrous retreat, under a fire destructive to their only avenue of escape. To have placed our men at the bridge end and along the river bank, would have been to subject them to a plunging fire from the heights, together with the disadvantages before mentioned. On the island, or at the east shore of the river, they would have occupied low ground and been unable to protect the West bridge against surprise and destruction. Finding, at 5 P. M., that the enemy were near at hand, the two guns were removed on a platform car, and immediately after, the troops were defiled across, the rear guard only remaining. At this time I crossed at the east end of the West bridge, in order to see that every thing was prepared for blowing up a span; and while examining the magazine within the bridge, the enemy opened fire, apparently with a rifled gun and howitzer. Ascending to the roadway, I found the rear guard crossing the bridge at double-quick, and at the same time observed some ten or twelve of our scouts at six or eight hundred yards south-west of the bridge end, hastening to cross. After waiting a reasonable time, and finding that they had apparently decided not to move, I ordered the fuse to be shortened and fired. This was done by Lieut. Margraves, of the sappers and miners, assisted by one man of his company. The charge which was exploded, consisted of two hundred pounds of powder in one mass, but from the difficulty of confining it, the effect was not such as had been hoped for, and the span did not fall. I determined, therefore, to carry out the spirit of your instructions, and to burn the East bridge. With the assistance of Capt. Kane, of the artillery, and Lieut. Margraves, it was soon in flames and impassable to the enemy. During the retreat of the rear guard and the burning of the bridge, the enemy kept up a warm fire of shells along the line of the track, but fortunately with little effect. Only two of our infantry were hit and slightly wounded by fragments. Finding that the enemy was advancing his guns upon the island, and directing his fire towards our encampment, which had never been removed to the west bank, the tents were ordered to be struck and be prepared to move. This was an immediate necessity, and regarding the position there untenable, I determined to evacuate it. As the receipt of supplies depended on the integrity of the railroad track to Chattanooga, and the road at several points touches the river bank, it would have been easy for the enemy to cross above us, destroy the track or bridges, or else plant his guns on the opposite side so as to command the road, closing it to the passage of trains. We would thus have been compelled to retire, perhaps across the mountain eastward, leaving the road to Chattanooga open. I preferred to retire to Chattanooga, disembarrassing ourselves of sick, wounded, and baggage, and then returning to a favorable point on the road, hold the enemy under observation, always hoping for reinforcements. If he advanced, it was reasonably expected it would be with his whole force of 5,000 men. Being unable to find the telegraph or the operator, removed from Bridgeport in the retreat, and esteeming it my duty to communicate to you, at the earliest practicable moment, this movement of the enemy, I came up on the train of that evening, bringing up the sick, some men unfortunately wounded by railroad accident, and about half of the command. A train was sent down for the remainder as soon as possible, and it brought up also the baggage.

Before the attack, two old iron 6-pounders of Kane's battery had been planted on the east bank, in the only place available, but very difficult of access, and were abandoned under the enemy's fire and the heat of the burning bridge. The dispositions made occupied the 30th, and as our whole force, 450 men, composed the brigade of Col. A. W. Reynolds, then serving on court martial, but naturally anxious to be in the field, I ordered him forward to Whiteside, a strong position fourteen miles towards Bridgeport, on the 1st inst. He was directed to observe the enemy, and to retard his advance if practicable. In the mean time I had been advised by Col. Glenn, under date of the 30th, at Dalton, that he would bring on his unarmed regiment as soon as transportation could be procured, and he was confidently expected on the 1st instant. It was necessary to collect the arms belonging to the sick of the 39th and 40th Georgia regiments, and with them to arm Col. Glenn's command. This I undertook, with the purpose of moving on promptly to Col. Reynolds' support. Col. Glenn arrived on the 2d, and was soon armed and supplied with ammunition, but the tenor of Col. Reynolds' dispatches during the day was such, as to lead me to think it judicious to hold the regiment disposable, lest the enemy should move up on the west side, and attempt to cross near Chattanooga. About 10 o'clock that night, I received from him the following dispatch:

General Leadbetter:

Scouts came in from Kelly's Ferry, reported on reliable information that the enemy, five thousand strong, had crossed at Shell Mound.

A. W. REYNOLDS, *Colonel commanding.*

I answered: If you are satisfied your information is reliable, burn all the bridges on the railroad and country roads, and fall back with your command to Lookout Mountain. I will meet you there with Col. Glenn's regiment.

W. LEADBETTER, *Brigadier-general.*

The point indicated is close to the Tennesse river, where the railroad and all the country roads intersect each other. To this dispatch, the Colonel replied that he would move accordingly. About

4 o'clock A. M., of the 3d, we met there, and having selected the best line of defence, too extensive, however, for our force, I placed the men in position, and a bridge on the country road over Lookout creek, in front, was burned. I also ordered the railroad bridge over the same creek to be burned, as soon as our pickets should have come in. Col. Reynolds then proceeded to town. This railroad bridge was actually not burned till late in the day, but I was on the mountain, and supposed it had been destroyed early. After receiving positive information, therefore, at 1 P. M., that the force of the enemy on this side of the river was small, the order for the destruction of the bridge was not countermanded. It will be restored by means of trestle work in a few days.

The series of events, thus related, has excited the utmost indignation of a terrified people, and no abuse, whether of a personal or official bearing, has been spared me. Aware, as I am, that all the troops under your command were required at other points, and that you expected the approach of the enemy to be retarded in this quarter, mainly by the destruction of the bridges, I shall endeavor to endure this storm of obloquy, with such equanimity as may be vouchsafed to me.

On Saturday morning, the enemy set fire to the west bridge at Bridgeport, and it was wholly destroyed. Soon after, they evacuated the place precipitately, and at the last advices from Stevenson, were hastening their departure from that point.

I am, sir, very respectfully,
Your obedient servant,
D. LEADBETTER,
Brigadier-general.

REPORT OF THE AFFAIR AT PRINCETON.

REPORT OF BRIG.-GEN. HUMPHREY MARSHALL.

CAMP NEAR JEFFERSONVILLE, VA.,
May 22, 1862.

To R. E. LEE,
Commanding, &c., Richmond:

GENERAL: In my last letter I advised you that the opportune return of Brig.-gen. Heth with his force to Dublin depot rendered it unnecessary for me to proceed in that direction. But I ventured to suggest to that officer, that a lateral movement, by me, cutting the line of the enemy's communication at Princeton, might assist him materially in clearing the country of the column which was endeavoring to penetrate to the railroad. Gen. Heth approving the idea, I moved my whole force at once, via Saltville, towards this place, arriving here on the 12th instant. I took the responsibility of ordering to the field some skeleton companies, just recruited, and intended to form part of a new regiment, authorized by an order of the Secretary of War, of 9th April, issued to Major McMahon, formerly Gen. Floyd's Aid-de-camp. This corps, composed of seven companies, so called, did not number more than four hundred men, and none of them were trained at all. Under my order, they elected a lieutenant-colonel, for the time, only to lead them on this expedition. I also took the responsibility of placing in their hands the old muskets turned in to Gen. Dimmock by Col. Trigg, which I found at Abingdon. I left Abingdon with a force composed of the 54th Virginia, six hundred men; the 29th Virginia, four hundred and twenty men; (four companies, wholly recruits, three raised by me this spring, and one by Lieut. March); the 5th Kentucky, five hundred men; Dunn's battalion of recruits, four hundred men; Bradley's Mounted Kentucky Rifles, about two hundred and seventy-five men, making an aggregate of two thousand one hundred and ninety-five men, to which, add Jeffree's battery of six pieces, manned by recruits almost entirely.

Gen. Heth desired a delay of a day or two to reorganize the companies in Floyd's brigade, which were under his command. Having dispatched couriers to Col. Wharton, directing him to meet me in Princeton, on the night of the 16th, by advancing from Rocky Gap; and, having informed Gen. Heth (who was in position at the mouth of Wolf creek), that he should attack the enemy at the mouth of East river, on the morning of the 17th, I put my column in motion on the 15th, and reached Princeton on the night of the 16th. My advance was unexpected by Brig.-gen. Cox, who had his head-quarters and body guard at Princeton at the time, with a force variously estimated at from five hundred to twelve hundred men—the former probably nearer the truth than the latter. The pickets of the enemy were encountered by my advance guard about four miles from Princeton, and a skirmish continued from that place, through the woodlands and brushwood, to a point something over one mile from the court-house. This skirmish was conducted by the 5th Kentucky, from which I lost Capt. Leonidas Elliott, who fell mortally wounded (since dead) at the head of his company, while bravely beating the enemy back. In this skirmish the enemy lost some sixteen or twenty, who were left on the field. We had only four wounded, including Capt. Elliott. None killed. I directed Col. Trigg to move on the right of the 5th Kentucky and take the enemy in flank, and so to press on to Princeton. Arriving at the hill (subsequently occupied by me), from which the land drops into the level vale, in which Princeton stands, a halt was ordered by Brig.-gen. Williams, and a line of battle formed, with a view of bringing up the artillery to shell the town from that point. I thought it best to take the place by small arms, and though daylight was now nearly gone, I ordered the battalions forward; Trigg leading to the right; May next; Moore's and Bradley's men next, so as to move on the place through the meadows and by the road we had travelled. In half an hour, a sharp, hot fire on the right, announced Col. Trigg in contact with the enemy. Fire, from a regiment, is seldom more steady than this I refer to. Succeeded by a general shout, and then by absolute silence, which lasted at least an hour and a half before I received any message from the troops in front, really, I did not know but that we had met a check, and that regimental commanders were arranging for a new assault. As every thing had to be left to them, under such circumstances, I waited about half a mile from town, placing my battery in position, at once, to command the town and our road. I supported the battery with Dunn's battalion. After a while I was informed that the enemy had fled before us, leaving his tents, clothes, swords, officers' uniforms, and even the lights burning in his tents.

It is probable had we not halted before nightfall, we might have captured many prisoners, possibly the General himself; for I was informed he did not leave town until twilight. But none of us could foresee, and so far as I know, every one acted for the best. The regiments went in with hearty good will and promptly. Major Bradley lost one of his men, Weeden, of Halladay's company. Trigg had some six men wounded, one of whom, private Carter of company I, was mortally wounded. So the town of Princeton fell into my hands about 10 P. M., on the 16th of May; the line of the enemy's communication with Raleigh was cut, and the head-quarters of the "Kanawa Division" was abruptly stampeded. A mass of correspondence fell into my hands. Letters and orders, dated from the 10th down to the 16th of May, fully disclose the intentions of the enemy and his strength. I send you several of these for your perusal. I learned from the inhabitants of Princeton that on the morning of the 15th, the two regiments, about 900 men each, had passed through town towards East river, and that two regiments had been expected to arrive at 8 P. M., from Raleigh, the very evening I came. I had a knowledge that one or more regiments had passed on to the mouth of East river, by the road from Dunlap, without coming through Princeton. Combining the information I had from the letters captured with the news I received from the people in Princeton, I learned that I was in the neighborhood of at least four regiments, of which Gen. Heth had no knowledge. My own position had suddenly become very critical. I had only heard from Col. Wharton that he had not passed East river mountain on the morning of the 15th. He had not arrived at Princeton on the night of the 16th, as I had directed and desired. I did not know the direction in which Gen. Cox had retired, whether to East river or Raleigh; but whether in the one or the other direction, I had no assurance but that the morrow would find me struggling with my force, more than half of whom were undrilled recruits, against largely superior numbers of well trained troops, of every arm. Casting about as well as I could at night, to catch an idea of the topography, I found that the ruins of Princeton occupy a knoll in the centre of some open level meadows, entirely surrounded by woodlands, with thick undergrowth, which fringe the open grounds, and that through the entire circuit about the town, the central position at the court-house can be commanded by the Enfield rifle. Roads lead in through these woods in several directions. My men had marched 19 miles during the day, had slept none, and were scattered among the houses and tents, to discover what had been left by the enemy. I at once determined to withdraw from the ruins before dawn, and to take position within range of the town site, so as to cover the road by which I entered. This I effected, the dawn finding me in the act of completing the operation. My force was marched from the town. After daylight I received a dispatch from Col. Wharton, dated the 16th, at the cross roads, eleven miles from Princeton, promising to come to town by 9 A. M. on the 17th. Before he arrived, the enemy had re-entered the town, a force I could not estimate, but which was provided with artillery, and displayed more than two full regiments. Col. Wharton arrived in the neighborhood by the road leading in from the cross roads, a little after 9 A. M. The enemy was at the time throwing forward his skirmishers, to dispute with mine the woods and points overhanging the road, which led in from the cross roads to Princeton, which road ran nearly parallel to the one by which I had advanced. I had written to Col. Wharton to press on, and he would have the enemy in flank. The Col. opened with his single piece of artillery, a little after nine, upon my right, and the batteries in town and at my position at once opened upon each other at long range. Col. Wharton soon came to me to report his position and force. The force was about 800 men. My estimate is, I now had some 2,800 men, of whom one-half were raw recruits. A regiment of the enemy coming down from the direction of the cross roads to Princeton, about this time, appeared in the rear of Col. Wharton's command, and were attacked by it furiously. The struggle lasted but a short time. The havoc in the enemy's ranks was terrible. Col. W. reports to me 211 as the dead and wounded of the enemy. I understand that more than 80 bodies were buried on the field. The enemy appeared with a flag of truce, asking to bury their dead, and to remove their wounded. I refused, but hearing, after about an hour, *that some officer had allowed it*, and that the enemy were then engaged in burying, I directed Brig.-gen. Williams to permit the ambulances of the enemy to pass along my right, for the purpose of carrying away the wounded, also. There was no further battle. I waited for news from Brig.-gen. Heth, or to learn of his approach to Princeton, as the signal for a general engagement with the enemy. If Brig.-gen. Heth had successfully attacked at the mouth of East river in the morning, as requested to do, he might be hourly expected to communicate his approach to Princeton, by his couriers or his artillery. If he had not attacked, but was still at the mouth of Wolf creek, it would be imprudent in me to assail the enemy, for the probability was strong that he would hazard the assault himself against any position, attempting to beat me, while he preserved his front against Heth.

If Gen. Heth could, by means of my diversion, get through the narrows of New river, our forces should join the night of the 17th, and then, combined, we could fight on the 18th the whole force of the enemy, and, if successful, could pursue his vanquished column to Raleigh, burn his stores, and press our advantage as far as we desired. This was my reasoning. I would not move upon the town in the evening of the 17th; 1st, because the result would then be problematical, and that problem would likely be favorably solved on the arrival of Gen. Heth's command. A grand result would then be easily obtained. Had I attacked under the circumstances, and had I failed, nothing could have shielded me from condemnation as a rash officer, who perilled all and lost all, when a few more hours would have doubled his force. I confidently expected at nightfall on the 17th, that the enemy, in superior force, would attack me in the morning, or that a junction with Gen. Heth would enable me to attack his whole force, which was apparently concentrated around Princeton. He was in plain view under my glass—his wagons deliberately parked, his regiments exercising, and all the appearances given which indicate the purpose to give battle. My forces were masked to him. He could have no idea of its amount. In this fact was my safety, until Heth could come up. It seems Brig.-gen. Heth did advance to the mouth of the East river, and found the enemy had abandoned tents and camp equipage, both there and at French's, where he had been fortifying. The Gen. passed on until he came within four or five miles of Princeton, on the evening of the 17th, when, hearing in the country from somebody that I had been repulsed and was retreating, he fell back in the night to the mouth of East river. His courier arrived at my position, (one mile from the court-house) about 9 A. M., on the 18th, conveying to me the information that Gen. Heth's force was now so required in another direction as to forbid further pursuit of the enemy, with a request to return Col. Wharton to a post in the district of New river, indicated by the General commanding said district. The enemy had, during the night, vacated Princeton, taking the Raleigh road, his rear passing Blue Stone river about sun-rise. I ordered my battalion of Mounted-Rifles to follow him. I ascertained that on the night of the 18th he encamped about 10 miles from Princeton, in a very strong position, having some seven-regiments with him in retreat, in all from five to seven thousand men. On the 19th I again sent forward on his line of retreat, and ascertained that he had passed the Flat Top mountains, had burned some of his caissons and gun-carriages, and had abandoned some of his wagons the preceding night. He was now twenty-five miles from Princeton. Nothing was now left to me but to return to the district whose interests are under my charge. I left a company of mounted men at Princeton, with orders to remain until Gen. Heth could relieve them, and with the rest of my command I returned to this point. I left 71 of the enemy wounded in hospital at Princeton, too badly shot to be moved at all. His surgeons were left in attendance, and a chaplain was permitted to be with them. I return a list of 29 prisoners. The men themselves have been marched to Abingdon, where three others from the same army have been confined, whose names you have already. My quarter-master has made return of our captures, among which I may mention about 35 miles of telegraph wire, horses, mules, saddles, pack-saddles, medical instruments, medicines in panniers, tents, a few stores, 18 head of cattle, a number of wagons, and some excellent muskets and rifles. These last have been taken in charge by my ordnance officers, and will be issued to my command, unless otherwise ordered.

Reviewing the whole movement, I have only to regret that Brig.-gen. Heth did not join me on the 17th, and did not communicate to me his whereabouts during the day or night. All was accomplished that I anticipated from the movement, *except the capture of prisoners.* The invasion has been signally repulsed, and the enemy has been demoralized and broken. The country he threatened so imminently has been relieved. It is a triumph of strategy merely, without loss on our part. My list of casualties will only exhibit two killed on the field, and two seriously wounded, who will die; and some ten or twelve wounded, but not dangerously. The enemy has lost largely; and indeed I should not be surprised if, in killed and wounded, his loss reaches four hundred. One of his regiments scattered in the woods, threw away guns and uniforms, and its members are daily picked up by the country people.

Your obedient servant,

H. MARSHALL,

Brigadier-general, commanding.

ARTICLES CAPTURED FROM THE ENEMY AT PRINCETON, VIRGINIA.

CAMP AT TIFFANY'S, May 21, 1862.

Brigadier-general MARSHALL, *commanding, &c.:*

GENERAL: I have to report the following articles captured from the enemy at Princeton, Va., on the 16th and 17th instant, viz:

12 bell tents.
2 wall tents and flies.
5 horses.
18 mules.
35 pack saddles.
4 wagons.

A lot of incomplete harness.

Respectfully

W. F. FISHER,
Major and Chief Q. M., Army E. Ky.

LIST OF PRISONERS CAPTURED AT PRINCETON, MERCER COUNTY, VIRGINIA.

MAY 16, 17, 18, 1862.

Of the 28th Ohio, Colonel Moore:

Private Charles Cross........................Company G.
" Daniel Chantemp...................... "
" John Yagel........................Company H.
" H. A. Miller...................... "
" Charles Hertwick....................Company F.
" Christian Ludwig....................Company C.
Corpor'l John Keen...................... "

12th Ohio, Colonel White:

Private John Klein........................Company E.

37th Ohio, Colonel Seiber.

Private Frederick Rock......................Company A.
" M. Kohl...................... "
" Thomas Kemper....................Company C.
" Frank Krobs....................Company K.
" Henry Bergeichen....................Company F.

Private Paul Kapff .... Company H.
" Charles Groth .... "
Corpor'l Jacob Rauft .... "
Private Henry Rothenberg .... Company K.

23d Ohio, Colonel Scammon.

Private Leonard Beck .... Company C.
" W. B. Waterhouse .... "

34th Ohio, Colonel Pratt.

Captain O. P. Evans .... Company B.
Private George W. Thompson .... Company K.
" David Coleman .... Company C.
" Frank M. Curl .... Company F.
" Anthony Eblehart .... "
" Michael Kelly .... Company I.
" Jacob Fasnacht .... "
" M. A. Blakeman .... Company D.

2d Virginia Cavalry, Colonel Bowles.

Private Robert Murphy (Irishman) .... Company K.

CAMP NEAR JEFFERSONVILLE, VA.

The above is a list of prisoners, except one wounded man, in hospital, whose name I have not yet learned. They consist of seventeen Germans, one Irishman, and ten native Ohioans. Some of the Germans are not naturalized. Besides these, there are two citizens of Mercer county, not reported herein, taken up on charge of disloyalty.

HIRAM HAWKINS,
Major and Officer of the Day.

General MARSHALL.

LETTERS FOUND IN GEN. COX'S CAMP

HEAD-QUARTERS 23D REG'T O. V. INF., U. S. A.
ADJ'TS OFFICE, CAMP AT MOUTH OF EAST RIVER,
May 14th, 1862.

MY DEAR PARENTS:—I again sit down, pen in hand, to inform you of my *whereabouts*. I wrote you a letter while I was at Princeton, inclosing you $10, and, I believe, informing you that the regiment had left Princeton for Giles Court House, (or, as it is more properly called, Pearisburg.) I was left behind to take care of the tents and office, until the train could come back, and move us on. I left there on the 10th inst., and we had not proceeded but a few miles, when we met a courier with dispatches, saying that our regiment had been attacked at Pearisburg, and driven back. He said they had retreated about five miles. The rebel force was about 4000, and 6 pieces of artillery. They drove in our pickets about daylight, and as our men had no artillery with them, were obliged to retreat. Therefore, Col. Hayes ordered the regiment to fall back, which was done in good order, our men fighting as they fell back, and fairly mowing the rebels down. As soon as they could get their cannon to bear on us, they commenced shelling us, but they were very poor artillerists, as most of their shells burst 30 feet over the boys' heads. As it was, there was only one man killed, and a number wounded. The regiment would never have been driven back, if our artillery had been sent up when it ought to have been. Our regiment is now encamped about 12 miles from Pearisburg. We will have a very strong force when we move forward again—enough to take Pearisburg, and go right on to Newbern. There are now here 3 regiments, viz.: 23d, 12th, and 30th, which form the 1st brigade, under Col. E. P. Scammon.

There are 6 more regiments expected up here in a day or two, the 26th, 34th, 27th, 48th, 47th, and 25th, which will form the 2d and 3d brigades, besides, about 4 regiments of cavalry, and a number of batteries of artillery—in all, about 12,000 effective men, commanded by Brig.-gen. Cox. The 23d will have the post of honor—*the advance*. Our boys captured a quantity of secesh money—Jeff Davis' scrip, at Pearisburg, in the bank. The people around there would not take our Treasury notes, they had rather have Jeff Davis' scrip. You may bet we were willing. We go out into the country and buy chickens with it, and they will give us silver in exchange, if our purchases do not come to the full amount of the bill. I will inclose you one of them.

I received a letter from Helen, while at Princeton, the day after I had written one to her. I will write again, soon. Direct your next letter to Pearisburg, Va. Be sure and write the number of the regiment plain, as there are so many of us here, now, there will be a good many mistakes. Write as soon as you can. Remember me to everybody, and believe me,

Your affectionate son,

H. O. LOOMIS,

Care of Lieut. M. C. Avery, Adj't 23d regiment O. V., Pearisburg Va.

PRINCETON, W. VA.,
May the 16th, 1862.

DEAR SISTER:—I take my pen in hand, to write you a few lines, to let you know where, and how I am. I am well, and I hope you are the same. I have received three letters from you since I have written one. The reason I don't write oftener is, that I don't have time. I am now in Princeton, Mercer county, Virginia. *There are six thousand soldiers here.* We expect to have a big battle in two or three days. The secesh are only ten miles from us, well fortified, and ten thousand strong, and they can be reinforced in twelve hours, while we can't get reinforced in twelve days. I think we will have a hard fight of it. If we take them, the fight may be over before you get this. We have marched fifty miles in two days. Our company ain't with the regiment now, but we will be to-morrow; then we will march in on them. The regiments are the 34th, 37th, 28th, 30th, 23d, and 12th, and one battalion cavalry, and two batteries. Henry Secrist is in one of the batteries. I saw all the boys in company H; they are all well. I haven't heard from Marcus or Andrew Griffiin, since I left Barboursville. I would like to hear from them, but I don't know where they are now. Dave Lemon is working on the telegraph, helping to put it up. I am glad to hear that Georgia is well, and that mother got the money I sent her. Send me a dollar's worth of postage stamps. I havn't time to write any more.

Direct to

LEWIS BOYD,

Co B, 34th regiment, Western Va., by way of Gauley Bridge.

CAMP EAST RIVER, IN THE MOUNTAINS,
May 14th, 1862.

DEAR FRIEND ABNER:—You will please pardon me for not writing to you sooner, in answer to yours trom Washington. I did not, however, get it till it was an old letter, as it was directed to Charleston, and not in care of the regiment, and lay in the post office for some time before I got it. So I thought best to wait till we got on the march, and I might, perhaps, have more of interest to tell you.

Well, here we are, within three miles of the enemy, in force, and strongly fortified, with a much larger force than we have now, from what we can learn, and can receive reinforcements at any time, by rail road from Richmond. They would only have to march about twenty-five miles, to get here from Newbern depot. Besides, we are without tents, and but very little provisions, and raining. So, you see, we are in a deplorable fix, "ain't we?" But we are active foragers, and as long as there is any thing in the mountains to eat, we are not going to starve. And we have got so used to the rain, that we can sleep about as well when the rain is pouring down upon us, as when it is clear star-light. So that, notwithstanding the discouraging appearance of things, we are in good spirits, and expect to be in Newbern in a few days, and then we will have plenty to eat, tents to sleep in, and ride on the railroad, "perhaps." We left Charleston on the 3d, leaving every thing behind, except what we really had to have. The road, most of the way, is rather rough, being up one mountain side and down the other, the entire way. We found the country very poor, and but few inhabitants on the route; the houses being of the very poorest description, and many of them being deserted, having been occupied by secesh. We came through Fayetteville, Berkley, and Princeton—the latter town had been burned by the rebels, on the approach of our advance, they having had several skirmishes on the way. The 23d O. V. I. were in advance, with the 2d battalion, V. V. M. R., and had advanced to Giles, the next county seat, aud had captured a large amount of provisions, etc., but being without artillery support, were driven out the day previous to our arrival, and had to fall back to this point, the mouth of East river, (that is, if I have been correctly informed as to the name of the stream, which empties into New river here.) We are within about eight miles of Giles, and we have to go through what is called the Narrows—a passage through a very high mountain range, through which New river runs—the road running with the river. At this place, the rebels are now fortified, and receiving reinforcements, and seem determined to prevent our going through. But I guess we will not go back from here without a little fight, even should we not get to our destination (Newbern). The object of this expedition is to cut off the retreat of the enemy from Richmond. It is rather a dangerous undertaking, as the enemy can turn all the force against us, if they have a mind to, it being their direct route southward by railroad. If we don't have to lay here too long waiting for our other force, I have no fear of our success. All depends upon our getting there before the rebels can reinforce sufficient to keep us back. I am fearful, however, that we have been laying here too long now, but we were almost worn out on arriving here, having made a forced march of nearly a hundred and fifty miles in 8 days, and being destitute, as I before said, of every thing, it was impossible to go any further with an enemy, at the same time to drive him ahead of us, stronger than we were. *I think we'll move to-night; I dare not tell you what our force is till we get through.* We are in Col. Scammon's brigade, and in Gen. Cox's division. I have no idea what is going on any where in the world but here. I am in hopes, however, that Richmond is in our possession by this time, and, also, the Mississippi valley, to the Gulf. If so, the rebellion is killed, and if there is any more fighting, it will be guerrilla warfare.

But I must conclude this disconnected scrawl. I thought, perhaps, I could write a letter when I undertook it, but I am in a wagon loaded with feed, and a little almost of every thing else, with horses hitched to it, and a lot of teamsters climbing in and out, and gassing and cursing around me so, that it is impossible for me to write. I will try and do better next time, when I will try and find time to write when it ain't raining. My love to my folks at home, and everybody else. Please write soon. Direct to Charleston, Va., to follow the regiment.

Yours, respectfully,
LEM. M. MICHAEL.

REPORT

Of engagement with small boat of the enemy on Crooked River.

CAPTAIN HALEY T. BLOCKER, COMMANDING.

HEAD-QUARTERS CAMP GLADDEN,
WAKULLA COUNTY, May 21, 1862.

Brig.-gen. JOSEPH FINEGAN,
Com'dg Dep't of Middle and East Florida, Tallahassee, Fla.:

GENERAL:—I have the honor to report that on yesterday morning, at 3½ o'clock, I left this camp with a detachment of thirty-three men for Crooked river, at which point we arrived at 1 o'clock P. M. In a short time after our arrival, I discovered a boat leaving the blockading vessel, and approaching the mouth of said river. I immediately placed my men in ambush on Carr's hill, and when the boat came opposite, we opened fire on the enemy, and killed or wounded all the party of twenty-one, except four. It gives me pleasure to state that my men acted gallantly throughout the whole affair. There was no one hurt on our side, although our fire was returned from the boat. Had my men been properly armed, not one of the enemy could have escaped.

I have the honor to be, general,
Your obedient servant,
H. T. BLOCKER,
Captain commanding Beauregard Rangers.

REPORT

Of the Evacuation of Corinth, and Retreat to Tupelo Mississippi.

G. T. BEAUREGARD, GENERAL COMMANDING.

HEAD-QUARTERS WESTERN DEPARTMENT,
TUPELO, MISS., June 13, 1862.

GENERAL:—In relation to the recent military operations in this quarter, I have to submit the following for the information of the War Department:

The purposes and ends for which I had held and occupied Corinth having been mainly accomplished by the last of May, and by the 25th of that month having ascertained definitely that the enemy had received large accessions to his already superior force, whilst ours had been reduced day by day by disease, resulting from bad water and inferior food, I felt it clearly my duty to evacuate that position without delay. I was further induced to this step by the fact that the enemy had declined my offer of battle, twice made him, outside of my intrenched lines, and sedulously avoided the separation of his corps, which he advanced with uncommon caution, under cover of heavy guns, strong intrenchments, constructed with unusual labor, and with singular delay, considering his strength, and our relative inferiority in numbers.

The transparent object of the Federal commander had been to cut off my resources by destroying the Mobile and Ohio, and the Memphis and Charleston railroads. This was substantially foiled by the evacuation and withdrawal along the line of the former road; and, if followed by the enemy, remote from his base, I confidently anticipated opportunity for resumption of the offensive, with chances for signal success.

Under these plain conditions, on the 26th ult., I issued verbally several orders, copies of which are herewith, marked A, B, and C, partially modified subsequently, as will be seen by the papers, etc., herewith, marked D, E, F, and G. These orders were executed, I am happy to say, with singular precision, as will be found fully admitted in the correspondence, from the scene, of the Chicago "Tribune," herewith transmitted.

At the time finally prescribed, the movement commenced, and was accomplished without the knowledge of the enemy, who only began to suspect the evacuation after broad daylight on the morning of the 30th May, when, having opened on our lines from his formidable batteries of heavy and long range guns, erected the night previously, he received no answer from any direction. But as our cavalry pickets still maintained their positions of the previous day, he was not, apparently, fully satisfied of our movements, until some stores, of little value in the town, were burned, which could not be removed.

It was then, to his surprise, the enemy became satisfied that a large army, approached and invested with such extraordinary preparations, expense, labor, and timidity, had disappeared from his front, with all its munitions and heavy guns, leaving him without knowledge, as I am assured, whither it had gone; for his scouts were scattered in all directions, as I have since ascertained, to inquire what directions our forces had taken. Even now, indeed, I have reason to believe, the Federal commander has little knowledge of the position and disposition of my main forces.

But for the unfortunate and needless delay, on the Memphis and Charleston Railroad, of some five trains of box cars, (three miscellaneously freighted, and two empty,) in passing beyond the bridges over the Hatchie river and its branches, which in the plan of evacuation had been directed to be destroyed, at a certain hour, on the morning of the 30th ultimo, not an incident would have marred, in the least, the success of the evacuation, in the face of a force so largely superior. It was, however, through a too rigid execution of orders that these bridges were burned, and we were obliged to destroy the trains, as far as practicable, and burn the stores, including some valuable subsistence, to what extent will be more precisely reported as soon as practicable.

The troops moved off in good spirits and order, prepared to give battle, if pursued, but no serious pursuit was attempted. Remaining in rear of the Tuscumbia and its affluents, some six miles from Corinth, long enough to collect stragglers incident to new levies, my main forces resumed the march, and were concentrated on Baldwin, with rear guards left to hold the bridges across the Tuscumbia and tributaries, which were not drawn back until the evening of the 2d instant.

Whilst at Rienzi, half way to Baldwin, I was informed that on the morning of the 30th ult., a detachment of the enemy's cavalry had penetrated to Boonville, eight miles south of Rienzi, and had captured and burned a railroad train of ammunition, baggage, and subsistence, delayed there forty-eight hours by some mismanagement. I regret to add that the enemy also burned the railroad depot, in which were, at the moment, a number of dead bodies, and at least four sick soldiers of this army, who were consumed; an act of barbarism scarcely credible, and without a precedent, to my knowledge, in civilized warfare.

Upon the opportune appearance in a short time, however, of an inferior force of cavalry, the enemy left in great haste and confusion, after having received one volley. Only one of our men was carried away by him. Quite a considerable number of stragglers, and of our sick and convalescent, *en route* to southern hospitals, who for a few moments had fallen into the enemy's hands, were rescued. These are the 2,000 men untruthfully reported by Gens. Pope and Halleck to their War Department, as "captured and parolled" on that occasion.

I desire to record that one Col. Elliott, of the Federal army, commanded in this raid, and is responsible for the cruel death of our sick.

As for the 10,000 stand of small arms, also reported by these officers as destroyed, the truth is, that not to exceed 1,500, mostly inferior muskets, were lost on that occasion.

I had intimations of this expedition the day before the evacuation, and had detached immediately suitable commands of infantry and cavalry to foil its purposes, and to protect the bridges on the line of my march. Unfortunately the infantry passed through and south of Booneville, but a little while before the enemy made his descent; the cavalry, as before said, reached there in time only to rescue our men who had been captured.

Equally inaccurate, reckless, and unworthy are the statements of these Federal commanders in their several official reports by telegraph, bearing dates of the 30th and 31st of May, and of 1st, 2d and 4th of June, as published in Cincinnati and Chicago journals, touching the amount of property and stores destroyed by us at Corinth, and Gen. Pope's alleged pressing pursuit.

Major-gen. Halleck's dispatch, of 4th June, may particularly be characterized as disgracefully untrue; possibly, however, he was duped by his subordinate. Nothing, for example, can be wider from the truth than that 10,000 men and 15,000 small arms of this army were captured or lost. In addition to those destroyed at Booneville, some 500 inferior small arms were accidentally left by convalescents in a camp, four miles south of Corinth.

No artillery of any description was lost; no clothing. No tents worth removal were left standing. In fine the letters of newspaper correspondents, inclosed, give a correct statement, both as to the conduct of the retreat, the scanty spoils of war left behind, the actual barrenness of substantial results to the enemy, and exhibit his doubt, perplexity, and ignorance, concerning the movements of this army.

Baldwin was found to offer no advantages of a defensive character, and being badly provided with water, I determined to fall back upon this point, some 20 miles south, 52 miles from Corinth, and here to await the developments of the enemy's plans and movements.

Accordingly, leaving Baldwin on the 7th (see papers appended, marked H), the main body of my forces was assembled here on the 9th inst., leaving all the approaches from Corinth carefully guarded by a competent force of cavalry under an efficient officer, who occupied a line 15 miles north of this place.

Supported by my general officers, I am doing all practicable to organize for defensive operations, whensover any movement of the enemy may give the opportunity, which I anticipate as not remote.

I feel authorized to say, by the evacuation, the plan of campaign of the enemy was utterly foiled, his delay of seven weeks, and vast expenditures, were of little value, and he has reached Corinth to find it a barren locality, which he must abandon as wholly worthless for his purposes.

I have the honor to be, respectfully,
Your obedient servant,
(Signed) G. T. BEAUREGARD,
General commanding.

To General Sam. Cooper,
Adjutant-gen., and Inspector-gen., C. S. A., Richmond, Va.

P. S.—My effective force on the morning of the evacuation, 30th May, 1862, did not exceed 47,000 men of all arms; that of the enemy, obtained from the best source of information, could not have been less than 90,000 men of all arms.

(Signed) G. T. BEAUREGARD,
General commanding.

(A.)

Strictly Confidential.)

HEAD-QUARTERS CAVALRY, W. D.,
CORINTH, MISS., May 26th, 1862.

SPECIAL ORDERS, No. 30.

I. Capt. Mauldin, commanding company cavalry at Bear creek bridge, will hold his command in readiness to move at a moment's notice towards Baldwin or Guntown, on the M. and O. R. R. He will, when orders to remove are received, thoroughly destroy all bridges, both of railroads and ordinary roads, on Bear creek and its tributaries, and all bridges on his line of march. Should the enemy force him to fall back, before orders to do so have been received, he will burn all bridges as above instructed.

II. The commanding officer of the cavalry on and near the Tennessee river, will, if compelled by the enemy to fall back, move in the direction of Tuscaloosa, Ala., or Columbus, Miss.

III. The commanding officer of cavalry, at or near Rienzi, will follow the movements of the army when they pass Rienzi, with his entire force.

IV. The commanding officer of the cavalry forces at or near Jacinto, will report at once, in person, to Gen. Van Dorn, for orders, and will, until further orders, receive all of his orders from Gen. Van Dorn.

V. The commanding officer of the troops at Chewalla and Cypress, will hold their commands in readiness to move on short notice, by the most direct route, to Kossuth. When commencing this movement, they will thoroughly destroy the Cypress bridge, and all the railroad and mud road bridges in their rear, and all bridges that might be of service to the enemy; they will take their artillery with them, and on reaching Kossuth, will follow up the general movement of the army and protect its rear.

VI. The commanding officer of the cavalry at Pocahontas, will hold his command in readiness to move on short notice to Ripley. On commencing the move, he will destroy all the railroad and mud road bridges in his rear, and all other bridges that may be of service to the enemy will be destroyed. He will take all of his artillery with him, and move from Ripley to Pantotoc, and will protect the rear of the forces moving in that direction

When at Ripley, he will communicate with general head-quarters at Baldwin, for orders.

By order of Brig.-gen. W. N. R. BEALL.

(Signed) BEALL HAMPSTEAD,
Captain and Assistant Adjutant-general.

(B.)

MEMORANDUM OF ORDERS.

HEAD-QUARTERS WESTERN DEPARTMENT,
CORINTH, MISS., May 27th, 1862.

The following memorandum is furnished to Gen. Bragg, for the intended movement of his army from this place to Baldwin, at the time hereinafter indicated:

1st. Hardee's corps will move on the direct road from his position to Danville, by Cleburni camp, which lies on the east of the Mobile and Ohio railroad, part of the way, thence to Rienzi and to Baldwin.

2d. Bragg's corps, via the turnpike to Kossuth, until it reaches the south side of the Tuscumbia, thence by the Rienzi and Black Land road to Carrollsville and Baldwin.

3d. Breckinridge's corps (or reserve), via the turnpike to Kossuth, thence to Black Land, Carrollsville, and Baldwin.

4th. Polk's corps, via the turnpike to Kossuth, thence by the Western road to Black Land, Carrollsville, and Baldwin.

5th. The baggage train of these corps must leave their position at 12 M., precisely, on the 28th inst., and stop for the night on the south side of the Tuscumbia, on the best available ground. The provision trains will follow the baggage trains.

6th. The ammunition and ambulance trains must be parked at the most convenient point to their brigades, and moved in rear of the provision trains to the south side of the Tuscumbia, where they will await further orders. All of these trains are to be accompanied by one pioneer company and two infantry companies, properly distributed per brigade. The brigade and regimental quarter-master must accompany and be responsible for their trains.

7th. The officers in charge of the baggage trains, will receive sealed orders as to their point of destination, which they will open at the first mentioned stopping place.

8th. As it may become necessary to take the offensive, the troops will take their position in the trenches, as soon as practicable, after disposing of their baggage in the wagon trains. One brigade per corps will be put in line of battle, in the best position for the offensive, in front of the trenches. The reserve will remain in position as already indicated to its general commanding. These troops will all bivouac in position, and at 3 o'clock A. M., on the 29th inst., if not attacked by the enemy, will take up their line of march to Baldwin by the routes indicated in Article I, leaving properly distributed cavalry pickets in front of their lines, to guard and protect this retrograde movement. These pickets will remain in position until recalled by the chief of cavalry, who will remain in Corinth, for the purpose of directing the retrograde movement of cavalry, when each regiment must follow the route taken by the corps to which it shall have been temporarily assigned, for the protection of its rear and flanks.

9th. Under no circumstance will these cavalry regiments abandon their position in front of the line (unless compelled by overpowering numbers), until the rear of the columns of the army of the Mississippi shall have crossed the Tuscumbia; when the general commanding each corps will communicate that fact to the chief of cavalry for his information and guidance.

10th. The cavalry pickets will continue the usual skirmishing with the enemy in front of the lines, and when retiring they will destroy the roads and bridges in their rear, as far as practicable; and after having crossed the Tuscumbia, they will guard the crossings until recalled by the general commanding.

11th. The chief of cavalry will order, if practicable, one regiment to report to Major-gen. Polk, one to Major-gen. Hardee, one to Gen. Bragg, and one to Major-gen. Van Dorn, independently of the regiment now at Jacinto, already ordered to report to the latter officer.

12th. After the departure of the troops from the intrenched line, a sufficient number of drums from each brigade must be left to beat at "reveille" at the usual hour, after which they can rejoin their commands.

13th. The commanding officer of corps of the army of the Mississippi, will leave, on the south side of the Tuscumbia, five hundred infantry and two pieces of artillery, to guard the four crossings of that stream, and to effectually destroy the bridges and obstruct the roads after the passage of the cavalry.

14th. On arriving at Baldwin, the best defensive position will be taken by the army of the Mississippi, due regard being had to a proper and sufficient supply of wood and water for the troops and horses of the different commands.

G. T. BEAUREGARD,
General commanding.

(C.)

MEMORANDUM OF MOVEMENTS ON BALDWIN FOR GENERAL VAN DORN.

HEAD-QUARTERS WESTERN DEPARTMENT,
Corinth, Miss., May 27, 1862.

1. The baggage trains of his army must leave their position at daybreak on the 28th instant, by the road on the east of the Mobile and Ohio railroad, to stop temporarily at about six miles from his head-quarters, but with secret orders to the officers in charge of them to continue rapidly on the direct road to the vicinity of Baldwin. The provision trains will follow the baggage trains.

2. The ammunition and ambulance trains must be parked at the most convenient point to their brigades, or near the general head-quarters, where they will remain until the troops shall have been moved to the front to take up their line of battle, when these trains will be ordered to follow the provision trains.

All of these trains must be accompanied by one pioneer company and two infantry companies (properly distributed) per brigade. The brigade and regimental quarter-masters must accompany and be responsible for their trains.

The officers in charge of the baggage trains will receive sealed orders as to their point of destination, which they will open at the already mentioned stopping-place.

3. As it may become necessary to take the offensive, the troops will take their position in line of battle as soon as practicable after disposing of their baggage in the wagon trains.

These troops will bivouac in position, and at 3 o'clock A. M. on the 29th instant, if not attacked by the enemy, will take up their line of march to Baldwin by the route indicated (Article I.), leaving properly distributed cavalry pickets in front of their lines to guard and protect this retrograde movement.

These pickets shall remain in position until recalled by the chief of cavalry, who will remain in Corinth for the purpose of directing the retrograde movement of the cavalry, when each regiment will follow the route taken by the corps to which it shall have been temporarily assigned, for the protection of its rear and flanks.

4. Under no circumstances will the cavalry regiments abandon their position in front of the lines (unless compelled by overpowering numbers), until the rear of the column of the Army of the West shall have crossed Clear creek, when the generals commanding shall communicate the fact to the chief of cavalry for his information and guidance.

5. The cavalry pickets will continue the usual skirmishing with the enemy in front of the lines, and when retiring will destroy, as far as practicable, the roads and bridges in their rear, and after having crossed Clear creek, they will guard the crossing until recalled by the general commanding.

6. The chief of cavalry will order, if practicable, one regiment to report to Major-gen. Polk and one to Major-gen. Hardee, one to Gen. Bragg and one to Major-gen. Van Dorn, independently of the regiment now at Jacinto, already ordered to report to the latter officer.

7. After the departure of the troops from the intrenched lines, a sufficient number of drums from each brigade must be left to beat "reveille" at the usual hour, after which they can join their commands.

8. The commanding officer of the Army of the West will leave, if necessary, on the south side of Clear creek, about five hundred infantry and two pieces of artillery, to defend the crossing of said stream, and to effectually destroy the bridges and obstruct the road after the passage of the cavalry.

9. On arriving in the vicinity of Guntown, the best defensive position will be taken in rear of Twenty-mile creek, due regard being had to a proper and sufficient supply of wood and water for the troops.

(Signed) G. T. BEAUREGARD,
General commanding.

(D.)

(Confidential.)

CORINTH, *May 28th* 1862.

To Gen. B. BRAGG,
Commanding Army of the Mississippi, Corinth:

GENERAL:—Considering that we have yet still so much to be removed from this place, I have decided that the retrograde movement shall not take place until the 30th instant, at the hours appointed, instead of the 29th.

You will please issue all necessary orders to that effect to the forces under your command.

It would be advisable to stop at once the ammunition and provision trains at convenient points to this place.

Respectfully, your obedient servant,
(Signed) G. T. BEAUREGARD,
Gen. commanding.
(Signed) GEORGE WM. BRENT,
Acting Chief of Staff.

(E.)

CORINTH, *May 28th*, 1862.

To Major-gen. E. VAN DORN,
Danville road:

GENERAL:—I approve of your request to leave at 12 h (not 11) to-night, if it be clear. Send artillery at sundown two miles back, so as to be beyond reach of sound to the enemy. Be careful, however, not to send it too far.

As Bragg's rear guard will not leave until 3 h A. M., yours ought not to leave before 2 1-2 h, for Hardee's left would then be uncovered whilst moving in rear of your present position and before crossing the railroad.

Hardee will destroy the bridges (dirt and railroad) on Tuscumbia, provided he is guarding them. But have the matter clearly understood with him, so as to admit of no error. I referred in my note to the small bridge on Clear creek, one which you must pass.

You, must, of course, have out as few details as possible. You must be the sole judge of that.

The telegraph operator must remain at his post as long as possible, say until your main forces move to the rear, for at any moment we may be called upon to move forward.

I am glad to hear of the sham balloon. I hope it is so, for I fear that more than their artillery at this moment.

Your obedient servant,

(Signed) G. T. BEAUREGARD,

Gen. commanding.

P. S.—You must not forget to obstruct thoroughly the road across Clear creek, near Gen. Jones' lines. You or Hardee must keep a strong guard of infantry and two pieces of artillery at the Clear creek railroad bridge, until the last cars shall have left the depot here. Please arrange this matter distinctly with him.

Would it not be prudent to send one regiment, two pieces of artillery, and some cavalry to protect your train?

I think I would keep Price back in best position, to move either to the rear to protect the train, if necessary, or to the front, in case of battle.

George W. Brent, *Acting Chief of Staff.*

(F.)

Corinth, *May* 25, 1862.

Gen. B. Bragg, *Corinth:*

General:—From information received, Guntown, four miles and a half below Baldwin, is considered a better position for the defensive; hence we will go there. Please give the necessary orders.

Small details must be kept in or about old camps, to keep up usual fires, on account of balloon, with orders to join their commands at 10 hour, on the march to the rear, or in front, in case of battle.

Not too many fires must be kept on the lines to-night, so as not to reveal too clearly our position. A brigade (the best one) from each corps will be selected to guard and bring up the rear of each column, to move off about two hours after the rest of the column, and from which, a small detail will be left at each bridge to destroy it after passage of cavalry. Detail to be in proportion to importance of bridge.

Would it not be advisable for the main forces to start at the 1 h, and the rear guards at 3 h A. M.?

No rockets must be fired to night.

Your obedient servant,

(Signed) G. T. BEAUREGARD,

George Wm. Brent,

Acting Chief of Staff.

(G.)

HEAD-QUARTERS WESTERN DEPARTMENT,
CORINTH, May 1862.

To Gen. B. BRAGG and Major-gens. E. VAN DORN, L. POLK, W. J. HARDEE, J. C. BRECKINRIDGE:

GENERALS:—The following modifications have been made in the order relative to the retrograde movement from this place:

1st. At sundown, the light batteries must be sent to about *one mile* from the intrenched lines, in order to avoid communicating to the enemy any information of the movement. These batteries must be so placed outside of the road as to follow their brigades at night without any difficulty.

2d. At 8 o'clock P. M., the heavy batteries of the lines must be removed, without noise, to the cars and sent to the Central depot.

3d. At 10 o'clock P. M., the retrograde movement of the forces is to commence, as already instructed.

4th. At 12 o'clock P. M., or as soon thereafter as possible, the rear guard is to follow the movement.

5th. As soon as the army of the Mississippi shall have got beyond the *Tuscumbia*, and the army of the West beyond *Ridge creek*, Gen. Beall, at Corinth (Chief of Cavalry), shall be informed of the facts, and the position in the rear of said stream shall be held until the train shall be considered beyond the reach of the enemy.

6th. Camp-fires must be kept up all night by the troops in position, and then by the cavalry.

7th. Three signal rockets shall be sent up at three o'clock in the morning by the cavalry pickets of Gens. Van Dorn, Bragg, and Polk.

8th. All Artesian and other wells must be destroyed this evening, by a detachment from each brigade. All Artesian well machinery must be sent, forthwith, to the depot for transportation to Saltillo.

9th. Whenever the railroad engine shall whistle through the night, near the intrenched line, the troops in the vicinity shall cheer repeatedly, as though reinforcements had been received.

(Signed) G. T. BEAUREGARD,
General commanding.
GEO. WM. BRENT,
Acting Chief of Staff.

(H.)

MEMORANDUM OF ORDERS.

HEAD-QUARTERS WESTERN DEPARTMENT,
BALDWIN, June 6, 1862, 5 h, P. M.

I. Gen. Van Dorn's army will start at 3 h, A. M., on the 7th instant, on its way to Tupelo, via the road from Baldwin to Priceville. It will halt for the night at Sand creek, a distance of about (17) seventeen miles from Baldwin. It will resume the line of march the next morning at 3 h, A. M., and will take position, for the present, at Priceville, leaving a brigade at the cross of the road, with the Ripley and the Cotton Gin road, near Smith or Brooks' house, and a cavalry force at or about the steam saw-mill. One brigade will be sent to Morrisville or vicinity, and a force of cavalry to guard the (20) mile creek ferry, on the road from Fulton, with a strong picket at the latter place. The cavalry regiment at Marietta, will not leave that position until the 8th instant, at 4 A. M.

II. General Hardee's corps will start for Tupelo, at 4 h, P. M., on the 7th instant, via the same road as Gen. Van Dorn's army, stopping for the night at a creek, about nine miles from its present position. He will send at 4 h, A. M., on that day, one regiment and two pieces of artillery, to the cross-road with the Natchez railroad, to guard the Twenty-mile creek crossing.

His corps will resume its line of March at 4 h, A. M., on the 8th instant, and will get to Tupelo that night if practicable. His rear guard of cavalry, will remain in its present position, until 12 P. M., on the 7th instant, and afterwards in the vicinity of Baldwin, (guarding the rear of Hardee's corps,) until about 4 h, A. M., on the 8th instant.

III. General Breckinridge's corps of reserve, will leave for Tupelo, via Carrollsville and Birmingham, at 3 h, A. M., on the 7th instant, stopping for the night at Yanoby creek, a few miles beyond the latter town, and will resume its line of march at 3 h, A. M., on the 8th instant.

IV. Gen. Bragg's corps will leave by the same road as Gen. Breckinridge's (passing to the westward of Carrollsville), at 2 h, P. M., on the 7th instant, stopping for the night at or near Birmingham; leaving there at 3 h, A. M., for Tupelo.

His cavalry will follow on the same road, the movement from where it is now posted, at 2 h., A. M., on the 8th instant. The regiment at Ripley will move on the road from that place to Tupelo, and all said cavalry will be posted as already indicated to Gen. B. on the map.

V. Gen. Polk's corps will conform its movements to that of Gen. Bragg, starting at 2 h, P. M., on the 8th instant, on the direct road to Saltillo, west of the railroad, halting at that place until further orders. His cavalry will remain where at present posted, and will follow his movements along the same road (guarding his rear), at 3 h, A. M., on the 8 instant.

VI. All infantry outposts should be recalled in time to join their command.

VII. All finger boards and mile posts should be taken down by the cavalry of the rear guards.

(Signed) G. T. BEAUREGARD,
General commanding.

(Official) THOS. JORDAN,
A. A.-general.

Northern Newspaper Correspondence, and Official Telegraphic Dispatches of Gens. Halleck and Pope, touching Evacuation of Corinth.

LETTER FROM CORINTH.

[Correspondence of Cincinnati Commercial.]

General McCook's Division, preliminary to the Evacuation of Corinth.

EDITORS COMMERCIAL: I have only time for a very brief epistle before the mail goes, and, luckily, I have not much to say. On Wednesday night breastworks were thrown up, and Terrells' battery planted on an eminence in the woods, about 700 yards from the rebel works. The position being secured, it was enlarged upon and strengthened yesterday. W. S. Sherman's (late Thomas) division, moving up in a line on the right, and Nelson's on the left of McCook. On the day the second division moved out, advances, with heavy cannonading, were made by Thomas on the right, and Pope on the left, but not a response in kind was elicited from the enemy. During the night, we could hear teams being driven off, and boxes being nailed, in the rebel camp. Deserters, however (I understand), reported that they were making "a stand," and would fight the next day.

Considerable cannonading was done by our forces, and yet no response, and yesterday the same. Last night the same band sounded retreat, tattoo, and taps all along the rebel lines, moving from place to place, and this morning suspicion was ripened into certainty, when we saw dense columns of smoke arise in the direction of Corinth, and heard the report of an exploding magazine. Corinth was evacuated; Beauregard had achieved another "triumph!"

I do not know how the matter strikes abler military men, but I think we have been "fooled." The works are far from being invulnerable; and the old joke of quaker guns has been played off on us. They were real wooden guns, with stuffed "paddies" for gunners. I saw them. We approached clear from Shiloh, in line of battle, and made preparations to defend ourselves, compared with which, the preparations of Beauregard sunk into insignificance.

This morning we could have poured shot and shell from over three hundred guns into works that never saw the day, when Gen. McCook could not have taken his division into them. The indications are that the rebel force here did not exceed 60,000 men. With what light I had, I regarded the mode of our advance upon Corinth as deep wisdom; with the light I now have, I do not.

The 1st Ohio was among the first to mount the works; but, I believe, the 24th Ohio was the very first; and their new flag, lately received from the 6th, was the first to wave in triumph over the now famous village of Corinth. When we got into Corinth, I suppose the fires kindled by the rebels had destroyed all they meant to destroy, (which was every thing movable that they could not remove,) but much more damage would have been done but for our timely arrival. The place is entirely deserted, except by one or two families.

(Signed) KAPPA.

WASHINGTON, May 30th.

The following dispatch was received at the War Department this morning;

HEAD-QUARTERS NEAR CORINTH, May 30.

Hon. E. M. STANTON,
Secretary of War:

The enemy's position and works, in front of Corinth, were exceedingly strong. He cannot occupy a stronger position in his flight. This morning he destroyed an immense amount of public and private property, stores, provisions, wagons, tents, &c. For miles out of town, the roads are filled with arms, haversacks, &c., thrown away by his fleeing troops.

A large number of prisoners and deserters have been captured, estimated by Gen. Pope at 2000.

Gen. Beauregard evidently distrusts his army, or he would have defended so strong a position. His troops are generally much discouraged and demoralized.

For the last few days their resistance has been slight.

(Signed) H. W. HALLECK,
Major-gen. commanding.

WASHINGTON, June 2.

The following dispatch has been received at the War Department, in reply to an inquiry of Gen. Meigs:

CORINTH, May 31, 1862.

To M. C. C. MEIGS,
Q. M.-general:

If Beauregard has been at Richmond, others have forged his signature, as I have received letters from him about the exchange of prisoners nearly every day for the last fortnight.

The evacuation of Corinth commenced on Wednesday, and was completed on Thursday night, but in great haste, as an immense amount of property was destroyed and abandoned. No troops have gone from here to Richmond, unless within the past two days.

(Signed) H. W. HALLECK,
Major-gen. commanding.

The Retreat of the Enemy from Corinth—Great Destruction of Property—A bold Cavalry Reconnoissance.

WASHINGTON, June 2.

The following dispatch was received at the War Department this morning:

HALLECK'S HEAD-QUARTERS,
CAMP NEAR CORINTH, June 1, 1862.

"Hon. E. M. STANTON,
Secretary of War:

"The following dispatch has been received from Gen. Pope:

"To Maj.-gen. HALLECK:

"It gives me pleasure to report, to-day, the brilliant success of the expedition sent out on the 28th instant, under Col. Elliott, with the second Iowa cavalry.

"After forced marches, day and night, through a very difficult country, and obstructed by the enemy, he finally succeeded in reaching the Mobile and Ohio railroad, at Boonville, at 2 o'clock A. M., on the 30th. He destroyed the track in many places south and north of the town, blew up one culvert, destroyed the switch and track, burned up the depot and a locomotive, and a train of 26 cars, loaded with supplies of every kind, destroyed 10,000 stand of small arms, three pieces of artillery, and a great quantity of clothing and ammunition, and parolled 2000 prisoners, which he could not keep with his cavalry.

"The enemy had heard of his movements, and had a train of box and flat cars, with flying artillery, and five thousand infantry, running up and down the road, to prevent him from reaching it.

"The whole road was lined with pickets for several days.

"Col. Elliott's command subsisted on meat alone, such as they could find in the country. For daring and dispatch this expedition has been distinguished in the highest degree, and entitles Col. Elliott and his command to high distinction.

"The result will be embarrassing to the enemy, and contribute greatly to their loss and demoralization. He reports the roads full of small parties of the retreating enemy, scattering in all directions.

(Signed) "Major-gen. POPE."

WASHINGTON, June 4.

The following dispatch was received this morning at the War Department:

HALLECK'S HEAD-QUARTERS, June 4.

Hon. E. M. STANTON,
Secretary of War:

Gen. Pope, with 40,000 men, is thirty miles south of Florence, pressing the enemy hard. He already reports 10,000 prisoners and deserters from the enemy, and 15,000 stand of arms captured. Thousands of the enemy are throwing away their arms. A farmer says that when Beauregard learned that Col. Elliot had cut the railroad, on his line of retreat, he became frantic, and told his men to save themselves the best way they could.

We captured nine locomotives, and a number of cars. One of the former is already repaired, and is running to-day. Several more will be in running order in a few days. The result is all that I could possibly desire.

(Signed) H. W. HALLECK,
Major-gen. commanding.

[Special Correspondence of the Chicago Tribune.]

PITTSBURG LANDING, May 30th, 1862.

Just after I had written my letter, dated this morning, a dispatch was received from Gen. Halleck's head-quarters, stating that our flag waved over the Court-House at Corinth. The news caused much surprise here, as it was wholly unexpected, for the rebels had been disputing the ground with us, inch by inch, during the past few days, and with a stubbornness that indicated an intention to make a desperate resistance behind the main works of defence. Whether the reasons of the evacuation were merely strategical, or that the supply of provisions was running short, yet remains to be seen. I learn from a professed union man, a deserter from the rebels, that they had been for some time on short rations, the men getting only a quarter ration and the horses three ears of corn per day. Their animals are said to be in very bad condition. The water in and around Corinth is also very bad. It smells so offensively that the men have to hold their noses while drinking it. As our men advanced, they found the water much deteriorated, and very difficult to obtain.

When our forces entered the place about 7 A. M., after shelling it for some time, they found but two or three men and a few women and children in it. These were gathered around the little heaps of furniture they had snatched from the burning buildings. Whether the buildings were set on fire by our shells or the retreating rebels, is not known. During the night, our pickets, and indeed the entire advance of the army, heard repeated explosions, doubtless caused by the blowing up of the magazines. Nothing of any use to us, whatever, was found, not even a Quaker gun. These were of no use, however, at Corinth, as they could not have been seen by us.

The retreat of the enemy was conducted in the best order. Before our men had entered the place, all had got off safely. Gen. Halleck has thus achieved one of the most barren triumphs of the war. In fact it is tantamount to a defeat. It gives the enemy an opportunity to select a new position as formidable as that at Corinth, and in which it will be far more difficult for us to attack him, on account of the distance our army will have to transport its supplies. Supposing the enemy take up their second position of defence at Grand Junction, about sixty miles from here, 4,000 additional wagons will be required. At $113 each, this would involve an expense of nearly half a million of dollars, to say nothing of mules, pay of teamsters, forage, &c. Then there is the fatigue to our men, the attacks of guerilla parties in our rear, &c.

I look upon the evacuation there as a victory to Beauregard, or, at least, as one of the most masterly pieces of strategy that has been displayed during this war. It prolongs the contest in the southwest for at least six months.

It is rumored that the main body of the rebels is stationed at Kossuth, a few miles from Corinth, while some 25,000 have gone on to Grand Junction, which the enemy have been fortifying for some time past.

Up to last night the enemy kept up a display of force along his whole line, thus completely deceiving our generals.

I learn that the lines of fortification at Corinth are numerous and formidable, but I have no authentic statement of their real strength and condition.

Gen. Halleck must feel deeply mortified at the evacuation. It clearly shows that he knew nothing of the position and strength of the enemy, and of his ulterior designs. This, in a great measure, arises from the exclusion of contrabands from camp. If this war is ever to be brought to a close, it must be by making use of the negro in every possible way.

(Signed) F.

Letter of Gen. Beauregard.

Head-quarters Western Department,
Tupelo, Miss., June 15, 1862.

Gen. Samuel Cooper,
A. G., C. S. A., Richmond, Va.:

General:—After delaying, as long as possible, to obey the oft repeated recommendations of my physicians, to take some rest, for the restoration of my health, I have concluded to take advantage of the present lull in the operations of this army, due to the necessity of attending to its organization and discipline, and to the uncertain movements of the enemy, for absenting myself a short while from here, hoping to be back in time to assume the offensive at the earliest moment practicable. Meanwhile, I will transfer the command of the forces, &c., of this department, to the next officer in rank, Gen. Bragg, furnishing him with such instructions as will enable him to give all orders required during my absence.

I propose leaving here to-morrow at 12 M., for Mobile, where I will remain a day or two, inspecting the condition of its defences, and will offer to Brig.-gen. Forney such advice as in my judgment may be necessary, and he may be willing to accept. I will then repair to Bladen Springs on the Tombigbee river, about seventy-five miles north of Mobile, where I will remain about one week or ten days, or long enough to restore my shattered health.

Very respectfully,
Your obedient servant,
(Signed) G. T. BEAUREGARD,
General commanding.

HEAD-QUARTERS WESTERN DEPARTMENT,
TUPELO, June 14th, 1862.

We hereby certify, that after attendance upon Gen. Beauregard for the past four months, and treatment of his case, that in our professional opinion, he is incapacitated physically for the arduous duties of his present command, and we urgently recommend rest and recreation.

(Signed) R. L. BRODIE,
Surgeon, P. A. C. S.
(Signed) SAMUEL CHOPPIN,
Surgeon, P. A. C. S.

True Copy,
(Signed) A. R. CHISHOLM,
Aid-de-camp.

REPORT OF THE ENGAGEMENT ON JAMES ISLAND.

MAJOR-GEN. PEMBERTON, COMMANDING.

HEAD-QUARTERS DEPARTMENT SO. CA. AND GEO.,
CHARLESTON, *June*, 1862.

To Gen. S. COOPER,
Adjutant and Inspector-general:

GENERAL:—I trust it will not be considered irrelevant in officially reporting the action of the 16th June, 1862, between our forces and those of the United States, on James Island, to refer briefly to the connection which this affair had with certain alterations I had adopted in the plan of defence established prior to my assignment to the command of this department. After a thorough personal examination of Coles Island, its defences and approaches, I was convinced that however desirable in many respects it might be to continue its occupation, there were disadvantages not to be overcome. With the means at my disposal, I deemed it therefore essential to the safety of Charleston, that the batteries on Coles battery island should be transferred to a more defensible position on the James Island side of the Stono river.

This change would draw in our lines to the best supporting distance, and compel a land attack upon our intrenched position across James Island, flanked on the right by the proposed fort on the Stono, and on the left by the advanced work at Secessionville.

This design was carried into execution. A strong and commanding work was erected on the Stono, completely controlling that river in the direction of the inlet of the same name, as well as the approach through North Edisto inlet, on the mouth of Wappoo cut. The intrenched lines to the east of James Island creek were also greatly strengthened by a system of interior redoubts and redans.

Early in May, the guns were removed from Coles battery island. On the 13th of the same month, the abduction of the steamer Planter by her negro crew gave the enemy information of the abandonment of Coles island. The services of skilful pilots among these negroes were immediately availed of, and the enemy's gunboats entered the river about the 17th. Under cover of their fire, he commenced landing his troops on James Island on the 2d June. His force was gradually increased, until it was believed to have amounted to from ten to twelve thousand of all arms. Between the 2d and 15th June, several skirmishes occurred, the results of which were duly reported by the immediate commander, and the reports forwarded to the War Department. The enemy kept up at intervals a heavy fire from his gunboats, varying from five to eight in number, against Secessionville, from positions on the Stono, and a branch of Folly river, as also from a land battery established under cover of his boats on a point distant about a mile from our own battery at Secessionville. No injury was, however, done to our works. One man was killed in his tent, and several wounded. A few shells were thrown in the direction of the new fort on the Stono at long range, but no attempt was made to engage at the fort a less distance than two and a half miles.

About 4 A. M. on the 16th, the enemy drove in or captured our pickets, some 800 yards in front of the battery at Secessionville, and advancing rapidly upon this work in line of battle, arrived within a few hundred yards of it before our guns could open upon him. To the culpable negligence of the pickets is to be attributed the near approach of the enemy before he was discovered. The men, however, were at their guns, which were at once well and rapidly served. Lieut.-col. Gaillard's and Smith's battalions, (Charleston and Pee Dee), were moved promptly into position under the orders of Col. J. C. Lamar, the heroic commander of the post. The enemy was driven back in confusion, and with great loss. A second attempt, after he had received reinforcements, met with a similar result, and a third was equally unsuccessful.

A flank movement was then attempted against the right of the battery, but was repulsed by the Charleston battalion, aided by the Louisiana battalion, under Lieut.-col. McEnery, which had been promptly dispatched by Col. Johnson Hagood, the immediate commander, to the support of Secessionville, on the first intimation of the enemy's advance upon that position, and which arrived in time to participate in the dangers and glory of this admirable repulse. On the evening of the 15th, I directed Brig.-gen. Evans to send sufficient reinforcements to Secessionville to relieve the garrison of the arduous duties in which it had been engaged for a number of days previous. A detachment of four officers, (Capt. J. Jamison, commanding), and one hundred men of Col. Goodlet's 22d S. C. volunteers, came up just in time to meet the first onset of the enemy, performing most excellent service, and sustaining a loss of 10 killed and 7 wounded. For further details of the action immediately in front of Secessionville, I respectfully refer to the reports, (herewith), of Brig.-gen. Evans, Col. J. G. Lamar, and his subordinate commanders; and for those details resulting from the enemy's flank movement upon Secessionville, Brig.-gen. Evans' report, to that of Col. Johnson Hagood, 1st S. C. volunteers, who had been assigned to the command of an advanced corps, composed of his own regiment; the 24th S. C., Col. C. H. Stevens; the Eutaw battalion, Lieut.-col. Simonton; and the Louisiana battalion, Lieut.-col. Mc Enery. The latter, as before stated, was early dispatched to the support of Secessionville; the remaining corps greatly aiding in the final and complete defeat of the enemy. The report of each of the above named subordinate commanders is respectfully forwarded herewith.

Not having been an eye-witness of this well-fought contest, it is impossible for me, perhaps, to commend where commendation is most due. Many of the best and bravest have fallen: among them Capt. J. J. Reed, Lamar's regiment; Capt. Henry King, Charleston battalion; 1st Lieut. John Edwards, of the same command; 2d Lieut. R. W. Green, Eutaw battalion, and 1st Sergeant James M. Baggott, who fell whilst serving his piece as No. 1, and was immediately succeeded by his company commander, the gallant and lamented Reed.

My estimation of the conduct of Col. J. G. Lamar, is fully expressed in my General Orders, No. —, of June 17th. His undaunted courage was an example well followed by those who surrounded him.

Lieut.-cols. P. C. Gaillard, A. D. Smith, and James McEnery. Major D. Ramsey, Captain J. Jamison, were each in command of their respective corps, during the whole, or a part of the action, and are highly commended in the report of Col. Lamar. I refer to his, and to the reports of the officers above-named, for records of further instances of individual gallantry.

In like manner, I refer to the reports of Brig.-gen. Evans, to Col. C. H. Stevens, Lieut.-col. Simonton, and to Col. Hagood's, and to his subordinate commanders, and Col. Goodlet, who, all deserving high praise themselves, have doubtless bestowed it where it is best deserved.

I inclose, herewith, a list of the killed, wounded, and missing—amounting in the aggregate to 204. Many of those reported as wounded, have been slightly so.

I also inclose a list of those most highly commended by commanders.

From the best information I have received, I estimate the loss of the enemy to have been between seven and eight hundred.

Very respectfully,

your obedient servant,

J. C. PEMBERTON,

Major-gen. commanding.

Report of Brig.-gen. N. G. Evans.

HEAD-QUARTERS SECOND MILITARY DIVISION, S. C.
ADAMS' RUN, June 19,'1862.

To Major J. R. WADDY,
Assistant Adjutant-general, Charleston, S. C.:

MAJOR:—I have the honor to submit the following report of the action of the troops under my command on James Island on the 16th instant.

On the afternoon of the 15th instant, I was informed by Col. T. G. Lamar, 1st artillery, that from his observation of the movements of the enemy, he was convinced that Secessionville would, doubtless, be attacked either on that night or on the morning of the 16th. I directed him to hold his position, that he would be reinforced if necessary. At 2 o'clock on the morning of the 16th inst., I received a note from him, informing me that the enemy were advancing. I repaired to Clark's house as soon as possible, where I arrived at fifteen minutes past 4 o'clock, A. M., when I found Col. Johnson Hagood, 1st S. C. V., had, in his untiring vigilance, ordered three regiments to be in readiness for an immediate attack, and had already sent a detachment of Col. Goodlett's regiment to the support of Col. Lamar, watching closely the movements of the enemy in front of Secessionville. I determined to reinforce the place to two thousand strong, and immediately ordered the 4th Louisiana battalion and Col. Goodlett's regiment to repair at double-quick and report to Col. Lamar at Secessionville. Lieut.-col. McEnery, with his battalion, arrived just in time to receive the second assault of the enemy and to materially aid in repulsing him. At this time, I received a message from Col. Hagood, that the enemy were approaching on our right, and asking reinforcements. I directed him to attack the enemy, and immediately ordered the 51st Georgia and Col. Williams' regiment to repair to his assistance. The engagement now became general on both wings. Col. C. H. Stevens, who was with Col. Hagood, seeing that the 24-pound battery, near Clarke's house, was not being fired, directed Lieut.-col. Capers, of his regiment, to take command of his battery and to fire on the enemy, with which, though one piece was dismounted, he did gallant and effective service, firing constantly into the flank of the enemy. On the third assault of the enemy, Lieut.-col. Capers was very successful with his piece, piercing the columns of the enemy eleven times.

For the details of the gallant defence of the works at Secessionville, I would respectfully refer the major-general commanding to the official reports of the immediate commanders herewith submitted. Three times did that heroic band repulse (often at the point of the bayonet) a force thrice their strength, under the fire of three gunboats and four stationary or land batteries. About 10 o'clock, the enemy retreated in great confusion, leaving their dead and wounded on the field, a number lying in our trenches. The loss of the enemy I have been unable to ascertain, but, from what I saw, was at least four hundred in killed, wounded, and prisoners. The dead of the enemy immediately in front of the Secessionville works, numbered one hundred and sixty-eight, while forty-two wounded had been brought within the works. The dead I directed to be immediately buried, and the wounded to be removed to the hospital. A considerable number of arms and accoutrements were captured, a partial return of which will be found in the paper marked "G." A full report of these arms I directed Capt. Reary, ordnance officer, to make to the chief of ordnance in Charleston. At 12 o'clock M., I received a note from the major-general commanding, that he was at Brig.-gen. Gist's head-quarters, asking if I wished reinforcements, that they were ready. I replied, through my aid-de-camp, that I thought the enemy was leaving his position, as he was burning the houses he had first occupied. I then joined the major-general commanding and accompanied him to Secessionville, to inspect the works as well as to ascertain our loss, and the situation and condition of our troops. After giving instructions relative to the wounded and dead, also as to the arms captured I returned to my head-quarters, and, in accordance with instructions from the major-general commanding, ordered Col. P. P. Colquitt to repair with his regiment of Georgia volunteers as soon as possible, and relieve Col. Goodlett, in command of Secessionville. Col. Goodlett and his command were completely worn down and exhausted. I would here state that I had before directed Col. Lamar to send all of his exhausted men to the rear on the arrival of Col. Goodlett's command, which order left him but one hundred and fifty men for duty.

The troops at Secessionville, on the morning of the 16th, were much fatigued, as they had been engaged at work in the intrenchments during the entire night, and many were entirely worn out when the action commenced in the morning.

In reference to the action on our right, I would respectfully refer for particulars to the reports of Cols. Hagood and C. H. Stevens, herewith inclosed.

To my personal staff, 1st Lieut. W. H. Rodgers, special aid-de-camp, Capts. R. E. Elliott and Samuel J. Corrie, and H. W. Carr, I am much indebted for their untiring exertions in transmitting my orders under fire. Assistant Surgeon James Evans, of my staff, rendered material aid to the wounded, who were brought to the rear. In conclusion, I would add that, at 8 o'clock A. M., Brig.-gen. W. D. Smith joined me at Clarke's house, where I directed him to take command of the right wing, and attack the enemy vigorously. I have received no report from him, but take it for granted the reports of Cols. Hagood and Stevens cover the action of the troops on the right.

To the dauntless Lamar and the troops under his command, at the commencement of the assault, the Charleston battery, Lieut.-col. Gaillard, Lieut.-col. Smith's battalion, and companies of Lamar's regiment engaged, the country, and South Carolina in particular, owe a debt of gratitude and thanks, which I know a grateful people will acknowledge. For the gallant dead, the country will ever mourn.

The intrepid Reed fell whilst cheering his men to victory, just as the enemy was repulsed.

The reports herewith inclosed will give casualties on our side, thirty-nine killed, ninety-three wounded and two missing. Total, one hundred and thirty-four.

No report has been received from Lieut.-col. Smith's battalion. Col. T. G. Lamar's report will be forwarded as soon as received.

Herewith I also inclose you a copy of a letter from Brig.-gen. Stevens, commanding the Federal forces, and also a copy of my reply.

Very respectfully,
Your obedient servant,
N. G. EVANS,
Brig.-gen. commanding.

Report of Colonel Lamar.

To Major-General J. C. PEMBERTON,
Commanding Department of S. Carolina and Georgia:

GENERAL: Through the interposition of Providence, it became my duty to report to you that the forces under my command gained a complete victory over the enemy on the 16th instant, at Secessionville Neck.

On the morning of the 16th of June, about four o'clock, my pickets were driven in, and reported to me that the enemy were advancing in force, and had already passed Rives' house, distant from my batteries about three-fourths of a mile. I immediately dispatched a courier to Lieut.-cols. Gaillard and Smith, ordering them to move up their battalions at once; and to Gen. Evans, to inform him of the advance of the foe, and I then proceeded to my batteries, where I found a detachment at each gun, having ordered such to be the case day and night.

When I arrived at the batteries, I found that the enemy were within seven hundred yards, in line of battle, and advancing on me at the double-quick. I ordered the 8-inch columbiad to be loaded with grape, which order was promptly obeyed by Lieut. Mosely, of company I, whom I found at the battery on my arrival. I mounted the chassis, and pointed the gun myself. In the mean time, Sergeant James M. Baggott, of Capt. Reed's company B, fired upon the advancing line from the rifled 24-pound gun, to the left of the columbiad, and of which he was the gunner. My reason for pointing the columbiad myself, was to fire at the centre of the line, and thereby break it, in order to cause confusion and delay, so that I might get my infantry into position previous to their reaching my lines. The shot had the desired effect; they immediately flanked to the right and left.

I then ordered the columbiad to be loaded with canister, which was promptly done, and I again pointed it. I then left the battery to get my infantry into position. On leaving the battery I met Lieut. Humbert, of company I (under whose command the columbiad was), within two or three paces of the battery, and directed him to give them canister freely, which he did. I then ordered Capt. T. Y. Simons to go to Lieut.-cols. Gaillard and Smith, and tell them to hurry up their battalions.

Lieut.-col. Smith, of the Pee Dee battalion, first attracted my attention, whereupon I ordered him to take position on the left. Although the enemy had then reached the left flank, and were pouring in a murderous fire on my men at the guns, Lieut.-col. Smith obeyed with promptness, and soon drove them from their position. I then ordered Lieut.-col. Gaillard to take position on my right and centre, which was promptly done. It was not long after getting my infantry into position, that the enemy were driven back in confusion. They were soon, however, reinforced, and made another desperate charge, when I again drove them back; a third time they came, but only to meet with a most determined repulse.

They then made a flank movement on my right on the west of Secessionville, and on the other side of the creek, where they were gallantly met by the Charleston battalion, which was soon reinforced by the Louisiana battalion, commanded by Lieut.-col. McEnery, who also gallantly met them with a cheer. At this time I was so much exhausted from loss of blood, from having been wounded in the head by a minié ball on the second charge, that the command was turned over to Lieut.-col. Gaillard, and afterwards to Lieut.-col. Wagner, although I never ceased to give orders to my batteries. We achieved a great victory, yet it was at a considerable loss, both in numbers and personal worth. Capt. Samuel J. Reed, of Barnwell district, and commanding company B, fell while gallantly fighting at his gun. I may safely say that his place cannot be filled. He was every thing that could be desired in an officer, and as brave, true, and gallant a man as ever sacrificed his life on a field of battle. Peace to his ashes!

Lieuts. Lancaster and Johnson, of company B, who were in command of the two rifled 24-pounders, did great execution, although not having grape or canister. Lieut. Bellinger, of the same company, who commanded the 18-pounder, poured a murderous fire into the approaching line, and, in connection with the columbiad, did more than any thing else for the fortunes of the day. These gallant officers deserve the thanks of the country, and I commend them to your notice. Capt. G. D. Keitt, and Lieuts. Humbert, Barton, Oliver, and Mosely, all acted with great bravery and determination.

I cannot close this report without bringing to further notice, Senior First Lieut. J. B. Humbert, of company I, who acted with so much gallantry and determination in managing his gun, to which may be mainly attributed the fortunes of the day, not only on account of its calibre and weight of metal, but to its well-directed fire, and to the skill with which it was managed; and also Second Lieuts. T. P. Oliver and J. W. Mosely, of the same company, who rendered valuable assistance to Lieut. Humbert. First Lieut. Barton, of the same company, displayed great skill and coolness in the management of the mortar, which had considerable effect upon the enemy. Too much praise cannot be given to these gallant officers, and to the detachments under their command. Capt. F. T. Miles, of the Calhoun Guard, Charleston battalion, who was stationed at my batteries during the previous night, and whose command was the first placed in position, has my sincere thanks. He and his men fought like heroes, and did all that men could do.

Lieut.-col. P. C. Gaillard, and Major David Ramsey, conducted themselves with the utmost coolness, and were as gallant as officers could be. They both, as well as their entire command, acted with commendable courage and determination, and deserve the thanks of the country.

Lieut.-col. A. D. Smith, commanding the Pee Dee battalion, and a most gallant officer, was the first that attracted my attention when the infantry were coming up to the engagement, and to him I am indebted for having relieved my left flank at a very critical time. I noticed that several of his men were shot down before he could get into position, and that, after the enemy had been driven back the first time, and while they were on their second charge, Lieut.-col. Smith went out upon the field in front of the battery, gathered up as many of the small arms of the enemy as he could carry, and gave them to his own men, whose guns had refused to fire. I commend him to your favorable notice. His command acted with great courage. My thanks are also due to Major Hudson, who acted with decided gallantry. I must also speak in high terms of the actions of Lieut. W. H. Kitchings, of company H, who was in command of the Reed battery at Clark's house, which battery consisted of two smooth bore 24-pound guns, and also of my adjutant, Lieut. E. J. Frederick, who, seeing that the enemy's sharpshooters were concealed on my right flank, over the marsh, and were picking off my men, proceeded immediately to the above battery, when he and Lieut. Kitchings soon dislodged them, and poured well-directed shots into them as they retreated.

To Capt. McCreery, of the ordnance department, as well as to Capt. Bonneau, and Lieuts. Matthews and Hall, of our gunboat, I return my sincere thanks, for their valuable service at the columbiad battery.

The casualties in the two companies of my regiment that were engaged, are as follows:

Company B, Barnwell district. Killed—Capt. S. J. Reed, 2d Sergeant James M. Baggott. Privates Elbert Bates, R. R. Bates, H. H. Dycles, W. J. Nix, W. Redmond, D. J. Reilly, and J. Watson.

Mortally wounded and since dead—privates Chesley Bates and Jeff. C. Eaves.

Wounded severely—Sergeant R. F. Nevills, and privates V. W. Bellinger, W. Fleming, Redick Pitts, W. J. Chitly, F. M. King, L. L. Cox, H. H. Nevills, S. H. Nevills; H. L. Baggott, Thomas Ursery, W. D. Elkins, J. W. Gillam, J. G. Mitchel, B. H. Dyches, J. W.

Phillips, D. P. Hutson, W. J. Martin, J. B. Corbit, J. R. Wains, and M. Whaley.

Wounded slightly—Corporal N. A. R. Walker, and privates A. O. Houser, J. J. Walker, D. Holden, W. R. Delk, and J. Templeton.

Missing—W. P. Hair, (previously wounded.)

Company I, Orangeburg District. Killed—privates W. H. Amaker, J. A. R. Shuler, H. A. Hoover, Daniel Kelly, J. W. Gibson, and Jno. Jones.

Wounded severely—Sergeant George Bolivar, private J. C. Evans. Slightly—Sergeants J. Marchant and S. C. L. Miller. Privates J. C. Stevenson, N. A. Whetstone, G. J. Bonnett, G. J. Parlor, John Robinson, and G. W. Golson.

RECAPITULATION:

Killed	15
Since dead	2
Wounded	37
Missing	1
Total	55

I estimate the loss of the enemy, as near as I can, at from six to eight hundred; 341 of their dead are buried in front of my batteries; 107 were taken prisoners, many wounded, and who have since died, and I conjecture that some were drowned. Large quantities of their wounded were carried off by their ambulances. About 400 stand of small arms fell into our hands, together with one horse wounded in the mouth, and numerous smaller articles.

For the casualties in the Charleston battalion, Lieut.-col. Gaillard, and the Pee Dee battalion, Lieut.-col. Smith, together with their reports concerning the behavior of officers and men, I beg leave to refer you to the accompanying documents, marked respectively A and B.

It is proper to state, that the forces under my command did not amount to more than 500 men, until the arrival of the Louisiana battalion. But this small force manfully stood their ground against an assaulting force of from one to five thousand men, among whom were the picked regiments of the enemy—the 79th New York Highlanders, and the 8th Michigan—notwithstanding that they had for fourteen days and nights been subjected to the most arduous duties.

On Sunday night, the 15th inst., I received orders from Brig.-gen. Evans, to the effect, that although it might require superhuman exertions, he expected me to take the guns off the gunboat, and place them in battery on land. This was impossible, unless I had had a force and the means under my control that were necessary to move these guns. I therefore had to have the gunboat moved up to Secessionville, where there was a wharf. In the mean time, I, with the two companies of my own regiment, proceeded to throw up the earthworks of the batteries, which were not completed until 3 o'clock the next morning. My men were so much fatigued, not only from the night work, but from a very spirited engagement the day previous, which lasted several hours, against the gunboats and land batteries of the enemy, that I allowed them to lay down to rest. They had hardly fallen asleep when the alarm was given, and this was the first time that any man was allowed to sleep without his arms in his hand, and at the spot that he would have to use them, during the time that I had been in command of the post.

In conclusion, I would state that the great victory achieved on the 16th June, over such a superior force of the enemy, is owing entirely to the patriotism, love of freedom, and indomitable courage of the officers and men under my command. Every man did his duty!

I have the honor, general, to be,
With sentiments of high regard,
Your obedient servant,
F. G. LAMAR,
Col. commanding Post.

Report of Major David Ramsey.

SECESSIONVILLE, June 21, 1862.

Colonel T. G. LAMAR:

COLONEL: I beg leave to forward to you a list of casualties in the Charleston battalion, in the engagement of the 16th instant:

Field and Staff.—Wounded—Lieut.-col. P. C. Gaillard, slightly in knee; Capt. R. Press. Smith, A. Q. M., severely.

Company A, Charleston Riflemen.—Wounded—Capt. Julius A. Blake, slightly; Lieut. F. Lynch, slightly.

Company B, Charleston Light Infantry.—Killed—Private J. B. W. Hammett. Wounded, mortally—private P. Gilhooly. Wounded, slightly—Privates M. Lacy and W. H. Lutcliffe. Missing—J. R. Gibbes and J. P. Johnson.

Company C, Irish Volunteers.—Killed—Private Dan. Howard. Wounded, severely—John May. Wounded, slightly—Lieut. John Burke, private J. P. Murphy.

Company D, Sumter Guard.—Killed—Capt. H. C. King, Lieut. J. J. Edwards, Corporal J. Volentine, privates G. Poznanski and S. F. Edgerton. Wounded—Sergeant J. J. Wells; privates R. C. Evans, A. Roumillat, E. L. Terry, W. W. Johnson, H. Neufoille, H. Volentine, E. S. Tennent, G. W. Dingle, T. P. Lockwood.

Company E, Calhoun Guard.—Killed—Private Thomas Parker. Wounded—Capt. F. T. Miles, Lieut. J. W. Axon, Sergeant S. C. Black; privates C. P. Brown, C. B. Buist, Isaac Holmes, H. C. Choate, J. E. Smith.

Company F, Union Light Infantry.—Killed—Sergeant R. J. Henry; private James Davis. Wounded—Lieut. George Brown; private Wm. Cummins.

RECAPITULATION:

Killed 10. Wounded 30. Missing 2. Total 42.

It is hardly possible to enumerate the individual instances of valor and good conduct. All did their duty, and the list of dead and wounded will testify with what devotion. Out of about one hundred men, forty, besides the two of the field and staff, were killed or wounded. You are aware of the distinguished conduct and skill of Lieut.-col. Gaillard, in command after you were wounded, until the arrival of Lieut.-col. McEnery, and I only mention, as peculiarly noticeable, Lieut. Campbell, of company F, who repulsed, personally, a storming party, using a handspike, until he seized a rifle. Also, Mr. Josiah Tennent, of the Calhoun Guard, who felled no less than six of the enemy. Capt. William Ryan's good service at a gun you can appreciate yourself. Lieut. George Brown and Sergeant Hendrick, of company F, deserve mention for bringing ammunition through a heavy fire; and most particularly Lieut. Alexander A. Allemory, of the Irish volunteers, who passed and repassed a severe fire of musketry and cannon several times with ammunition in his arms. I have mentioned those especially noticeable, but can only repeat that I refrain from enumerating others, simply because it would be to furnish a roll of those engaged.

Very respectfully,

Your obedient servant,

DAVID RAMSAY,

Major commanding C. Battalion.

Report of Lieut.-col. A. D. Smith.

SECESSIONVILLE, JAMES ISLAND,
June 19th, 1862.

Col. LAMAR:

The following is a correct list of the casualties in my command, in the engagement of the 16th instant:

Company A, Capt. Smart.—Killed, none; wounded seriously, private H. Cooper and Alexander Bourn; wounded slightly, sergeant W. T. Smith; Lieut. T. Starvis, and privates Wm. Buss and F. M. Jordan, were captured on picket.

Company B, Capt. Evans.—Killed, Private Duncan Deas; wounded seriously, sergeant W. L. McFarland, (since dead,) private Jesse Pierce; slightly, privates R. D. Moore, John R. Threat and Isaac Hurst.

Company C, Capt. Davis.—Killed, none; wounded seriously privates Wm. Cole and Thomas Driggers; slightly, private Leonard Oxendieu; corporal John Roller, arm shot off.

Company D, Capt. Best.—Killed—Privates J. T. Alford and J H. Lay; wounded seriously, first Lieut. J. G. Beauty; slightly privates S. Jones and M. Stalvey.

Company F, Capt. Carter.—Killed, none; wounded seriously, private C. C. Anderson; slightly, corporal E. F. Sandsbury, and privates W. D. Rollins and J. E. P. Hickson.

Company G, Capt. Graham.—Killed, none; wounded seriously, privates L. Stricken and Wm. Eliot; slightly, orderly sergeant John H. Williamson, and private J. W: Tripps.

RECAPITULATION.

Killed, 3; since died, 1; wounded, 22; captured, 3. Total, 29.

Your obedient servant,

A. D. SMITH,

Lieut.-col. commanding Smith's Battalion.

Report of Col. Johnson Hagood, 1st regiment S. C. Volunteers.

HEAD-QUARTERS ADVANCED FORCES,
JAMES ISLAND, June 18, 1862.

Capt MALLORY P. KING,
A. A.-general:

CAPTAIN: I am required to report the operations of the troops under my command on the 16th inst.

Some days previously, I had had the honor to be placed in command of a corps, composed of the 1st and 24th South Carolina volunteers, the Eutaw battalion, and McEnery's Louisiana battalion, to which were assigned the duties of the advanced guard. The force at Secessionville, however, continued to keep out in front of that position its own outposts, which were not under my command, and made no direct report to me. This has since been changed. On the night of the 15th and 16th, the troops on outpost duty, under my command, consisted of seven companies of Stevens' 24th S. C. regiment, six companies of Hagood's 1st S. C. volunteers, and one company of the 47th Georgia volunteers (Col. Williams,), all under the immediate charge of Col. Stevens. They covered the whole front of our lines, from Secessionville road to New Town cut. The pickets from Secessionville covered the space from the Secessionville road to the marsh on the left of our lines.

At 4.30 A. M. on the 16th, I received a dispatch from Col. Stevens, that the Secessionville pickets had been driven in, and that the enemy was advancing in force upon that position. I immediately ordered under arms the portion of the 1st regiment not on picket, and Col. Simonton's Eutaw battalion, directing them to proceed down the Battery Island road, in front of our intrenchments, to the flank of the enemy's advance, and ordered Col. McEnery's Louisiana battalion to proceed in rear by the bridge to Secessionville, delivering these orders in person.

Proceeding in advance down the Battery Island road, I ordered forward one of the two 6-pounders of Boyce's battery, stationed at the crossing of the Fort Johnson road, and, arriving at the scene of action, found the enemy making their second advance upon the post at Secessionville. A thicket of felled trees ran parallel with their line of advance, and about four hundred yards west of it, on the edge of which, next the enemy, Col. Stevens had deployed about one hundred men, who had been on picket duty near that point. These men were from the companies of Capts. Tompkins, Pearson, (Lieut. Hammeter, commanding,) and Gooding, (Lieut. Beckham, commanding,) of the 24th regiment S. C. volunteers. The Battery Island road, so obstructed, as to be impassable by troops or vehicles, ran between this felled thicket and a dense wood, stretching towards Grimball's, on the Stono. Simonton's battalion, coming up, was placed behind the felled thicket in line of battle, its right resting near the Battery Island road, and the detachment of the 1st regiment S. C. volunteers was placed in reserve in the Battery Island road, throwing a strong line of skirmishers toward the Stono, which runs nearly parallel with this road, to guard against an advance from that point. Boyce's piece, under Lieut. Jeter, was placed on Simonton's left, at the extremity of the felled thicket. The object of this disposition was chiefly defensive, as a general advance upon our lines seemed imminent. Three regiments of infantry advanced in front of us, but beyond musket range, to attack the west flank of the work at Secessionville, being supported by a battery of field artillery, near the Battery Island road, in front, and beyond Simonton's right. Lieut. Jeter was directed to open upon these regiments, which he did with effect. I immediately sent to the general commanding, asking to be supported in making an attack upon the rear and flank of these regiments. When the permission to attack, and the assurance of support arrived, the enemy had retreated. In the mean while, the fire of Jeter's piece drew upon us a heavy fire from the enemy's field battery, which, from the sheltered position of our troops, did but little damage, and four companies of the 3d Rhode Island regiment were sent as skirmishers to seize the felled woods, and capture the piece. Stevens' skirmishers gallantly repelled them. A portion of the enemy, however, penetrated to Simonton's line of battle, and one of his companies, and a platoon of another, were for a few minutes engaged in driving them back. A few casualties in other portions of his line occurred from the random fire of the enemy engaged with our skirmishers, and one man in the detachment from the 1st regiment was wounded in the same way. The enemy, in retiring, were seen carrying off their wounded. Six men were left dead in front of our skirmishers, twelve were left dead further on toward Secessionville, where the three regiments spoken of were fired upon by Lieut. Jeter, making their loss in this part of the field eighteen killed. Eleven prisoners were captured, of whom eight were wounded. Sixty-eight small arms, mostly Enfield rifles, were abandoned by them, and recovered by this command. Our loss was eight killed, twenty-two wounded, and two missing. Appended is a detailed list of casualties.

I have the honor to be,

Very respectfully,

JOHNSON HAGOOD,

Colonel 1st S. C. Volunteers, commanding.

Report of Col. C. W. Stevens, 24th Regiment S. C. Volunteers.

HEAD-QUARTERS 24TH REGIMENT S. C. VOLUNTEERS,
JAMES ISLAND, June 18, 1862.

To Col. JOHNSON HAGOOD,
1st Regiment S. C. Volunteers,
Commanding Advanced Forces:

COLONEL:—In obedience to orders, I beg to submit the following report of the part taken by my regiment in the battle of Secessionville, on the morning of the 16th instant.

Seven companies of the 24th regiment S. C. volunteers, with six companies of the 1st regiment S. C. volunteers, and one from the 47th Georgia regiment, constituted the picket force placed under my command, and with which I went on duty on Sunday, 15th instant. This force covered our whole picket line, except that in front of Secessionville, which was guarded by pickets from the force stationed at that post.

All remained quiet along the line during the day and night, and at day-light I rode to New Town cut, with a view to visit and inspect the pickets. On reaching that point, I distinctly heard the guns of the enemy in front of Secessionville, and started on my return to that point. On my way, I encountered a courier with the intelligence that the enemy had advanced in large force to storm our works at Secessionville. This information I immediately forwarded to yourself and to the head-quarters of the brigadier-general commanding, proceeding myself to the front to verify the statement. In passing I took portions of four companies of my regiment, which happened to be on duty in that vicinity, and moved them in the direction of the abatis of felled timber, extending on the left of the Battery Island road.

I ordered Capt. Weaver, company I, to occupy this abatis, to prevent the enemy from penetrating it with his skirmishers. The detachments of my other three companies, viz.: company D, Capt. Gooding; company G, Lieut. Hammeter, and company K, Capt. Tompkins, numbering less than one hundred men, were posted in a heavy thicket, extending from the abatis to the marsh on the left. On taking this position, I found the enemy drawn up in line of battle at Hill's house, to my right and front. With my weak force this position could only be defensive, and I rode back to ask for artillery and support, which were brought up by you. As all of the subsequent events passed under your own observation, it is unnecessary to report them, except that I would especially mention Capt. Tompkins, company K, and Lieut. Beckham, of company G, and the detachments from these two companies, who held their position gallantly in the front and did excellent service, until ordered to withdraw.

Lieut.-col. Capers, my second in command, having been sent by you to order fire to be opened from the new twenty-four pounder battery, in advance of our lines, was retained by Gen. Evans at that post, and directed the fire of the battery with his usual gallantry and efficiency.

Major Hammond remained at his post in charge of the pickets on the hill road and New Town cut. After the enemy had left the field, I returned to my picket duties until regularly relieved. I append a list of the casualties in my own regiment.

I have the honor to be,

Very respectfully,

C. H. STEVENS,

Colonel 24th Regiment S. C. Volunteers.

LIST OF CASUALTIES IN THE 24TH REGIMENT S. C. VOLUNTEERS.

Company G, Lieut. Hammeter, commanding.—Killed, privates M. Dawkins and John Morrell.

Wounded, private Joel Hunt.

Company K, Capt. Tompkins, commanding.—Killed, private J. E. Bussy.

Wounded, Lieut. F. W. Anderson, Sergeant S. W. Burton, privates James Horn, R. P. Germain, and Pickens New.

Missing, private James Collins.

Company D, Capt. Gooding, commanding.—Wounded, Sergeant D. U. Bowers.

Company I, Capt. L. B. Weaver, commanding.—Missing, private John Duncan.

RECAPITULATION:

Killed,...	3
Wounded,	7
Missing,	2
Total,	12

Report of Lieut.-colonel Charles H. Simonton.

HEAD-QUARTERS EUTAW REGIMENT,
25TH S. C. V., June 17th, 1862.

To Capt. JOSEPH WALKER,
A. A. A.-general:

CAPTAIN:—I have the honor to make the following report of the results of the engagement of yesterday to my regiment.

Having been ordered to move at reveille, I formed and marched my regiment to the field in rear of Hill's house, and having there reported to Col. Hagood, was placed by him in position behind a hedge. Upon being placed in position, I was informed that Col. Stevens had a portion of his regiment deployed as skirmishers in our front, and was ordered to take all precautions to prevent our men firing into them.

Shortly after we took position, we were put under a heavy fire of small arms, directed principally against my left wing. In obedience to orders, I kept my men under restraint, and prevented any firing, until feeling satisfied that the enemy were actually in my front. I then gave orders to fire. After a brisk fire of about a half hour, they were driven off. During their retreat, we were exposed to an enfilading fire from a field battery on our flank.

Below, I append a list of casualties. The behavior of my regiment was such as I could have wished.

Lieut. Blum, of the Washingtonton Light Infantry, company B, whose company was chiefly under fire, distinguished himself by his extreme coolness, encouraging his men. He rendered most efficient aid in restraining their natural desire to return the fire of the enemy. The conduct of his men could not be surpassed. They were under my eye all the time. Two of his men, privates J. Campbell Martin and T. Grange Simons, Jr.—the first wounded in the head and leg, and the other in three places, with his clothes riddled—continued to fire until taken from the field.

A large number of arms and accoutrements were recovered from the field, and several prisoners were captured.

With this, I inclose the reports of Lieut. Blum and of Capt. Adger, Quarter-master. The arms and accoutrements are in the hands of the latter, subject to your order.

Very respectfully,

Your obedient servant,

(Signed) CHARLES H. SIMONTON,

Lieut.-col. commanding.

CASUALTIES TO EUTAW REGIMENT—(25TH S. C. V.)

Killed.

Second Lieut. Richard W. Greer,	Washington	Light	Infantry,	co. B.
First Serg't F. Lanneau, Jr.,	"	"	"	"
Private Samuel Salters,	"	"	"	"
Private T. N. Gadsden, Jr.,	"	"	"	"

Wounded.

Private J. H. Taverner,	Washington	Light	Infantry,	co. B,	mortally.
Private J. C. Martin,	"	"	"	"	severely.
Bat. 2d Lieut. S. J. Burger,	"	"	"	"	"
Private J. H. Deveaux,	"	"	"	"	"
" J. B. Glover,	"	"	"	"	"
" T. G. Simons, Jr.,	"	"	"	"	"
" A. S. Trumbo,	"	"	"	"	slightly.
" R. S. McCutchen,	"	"	"	"	"
" J. H. Shulte,	"	"	"	"	"
" J. P. Gibbes,	"	"	"	"	"
" E. V. Shuler,	St. Matthews	Rifles,	slightly.		
" G. M. Dantzler,	"	"	"		
" J. W. Wannamaker,	"	"	"		

Sergeant R. A. Horton, Yeadon Light Infantry, slightly.

Respectfully submitted,

(Signed) CHARLES H. SIMONTON,

Lieut.-col. cammanding Eutaw regiment,

25th South Carolina Volunteers.

Report of Lieutenant R. A. Blum.

CAMP PETTIGREW, JAMES ISLAND, S. C.,
June 16th, 1862.

Lieut.-col. SIMONTON,

I beg leave to report the following casualties and incidents of this morning's engagement:

Shortly after our regiment had taken its position, my company was subjected to repeated volleys discharged from the thicket, immediately in our front, which we had been informed was held by a company from Col. Stevens' regiment. On this account, in obedience to orders from Col. Hagood, we did not reply for several minutes. Soon after our first volley, which was briskly returned by the enemy, Lieut. R. W. Greer, and 1st Sergeant Fleetwood Lanneau, Jr., with the following members of my company, fell dead upon the field:

T. N. Gadsden, Jr., and Samuel Satters, J. H. Tavener and J. Campbell Martin, supposed mortally wounded,

The following were severely wounded:

Second battalion, Lieut. Samuel J. Burger; privates H. B. Glover, A. S. Trumbo, T. Grange Simons, Jr., J. H. Deveaux, James P. Gibbes, R. S. McCutchen, J. H. Shulte.

It is impossible for me to single out individual instances, where all behaved with the utmost coolness and bravery, but I feel that it is but just to report the conduct of John Campbell Martin and T. Grange Simons, Jr., as worthy of special notice. After being severely wounded, they persisted in reloading and firing until overcome by exhaustion.

I am, yours respectfully,

(Signed) R. A. BLUM,
Lieut. commanding W. L. I. Co. B., I. R.

Report of Capt. J. E. Adger.

CAMP PETTIGREW, JAMES ISLAND,
June 16, 1862.

Lieutenant-colonel SIMONTON,
Commanding Eutaw Regiment, 25th S. C. V.

COLONEL: I beg leave to make the following return of arms and accoutrements, &c., recovered from the field during, and subsequent to, this morning's engagement with the enemy:

Enfield rifles, in order	54	
" " needing repair	3	
" " not repairable	3–	60
Minié " in order		8
Total number of arms	68	
Cartridge boxes	44	
" " and belts	26	
Waist belts	28	
" " clasps wanting	9–	37
Bayonet scabbards	38	
Cap boxes	24	
Cartridges (Enfield)	950	

Very respectfully,
Your obedient servant,
J. E. ADGER,
Quarter-master Eutaw regiment and Acting Ordnance Officer.

Report of Lieutenant-Colonel J. McEnery.

SECESSIONVILLE, June 20, 1862.

To Captain MALLORY P. KING,
Assistant Adjutant-general.

CAPTAIN: I have the honor to submit the following report of the part taken in the battle of the 16th of June, near Secessionville, by my battalion.

A little after dawn, on the morning of the 16th instant, Col. Hagood, commanding 1st regiment, S. C. V., came in person to my quarters, about two miles and a half distant from this place, and ordered me to have my battalion under arms and march immediately to the Secessionville battery, at which place an engagement with the enemy was being had. With promptness the battalion was formed, and the march, at double-quick, was begun in the direction of Secessionville. When arrived at the first cross roads, some little delay ensued, arising from my ignorance of the road leading to Secessionville. After the lapse of a few moments I was assured as to the right road, and instantly the battalion was moved off at double-quick for the scene of action. Arriving at Secessionville, I was informed that the enemy in force were advancing on the right of the battery on the opposite side of the marsh, directly up the marsh to the bridge. I hastened my command, at a run, through an open ground to the woods on the marsh. In crossing this open marsh, and while placing the battalion in position in the outer edge of the woods, it was exposed to a terrific fire from the enemy's gunboats, siege battery, field batteries, and small arms. I then ordered the men to advance in the skirt of woods, the better to view the enemy, and afford it protection from the incessant fire of the enemy. At this point, for half an hour, the fire on both sides was indeed terrific. Finally, the enemy waned, fell back, and there begun his precipitate retreat on the right in front. The gallant Lamar being struck down, and being the senior officer present, I caused an incessant volley of grape and canister to be poured into the broken and retreating columns of the enemy, until they passed beyond view. Col. Goodlett, my senior officer, arriving about 12 M., assumed command.

I cannot speak in terms of too high praise of the coolness, bravery, and gallantry of the officers and men of my little command. I went into the action with two hundred and fifty men, and succeeded in putting to rout twice that force of the enemy on the right. I think that the force of the enemy would undoubtedly have completely flanked the battery but for our timely arrival.

The small band of brave men in the fort, exhausted and broken down in their almost superhuman exertions in repelling the foe in front, must have been unequal to the task of successfully engaging the enemy in front and on the right.

It is impossible to arrive at a correct list of the slain and wounded of the enemy, as in his retreat he bore off the field many of his dead and wounded. One hundred and sixty-eight of the enemy were buried on the field. My battalion brought from the battle-field in front the following arms and accoutrements, which have been delivered to the ordnance office, viz.:

Enfield rifles (in good condition),	27
" " (damaged),	4
Rifled muskets (in good condition),	83
Springfield muskets (in good condition),	62
" " (damaged),	6
Total,	182
Cartridge boxes,	78
Saddles,	2

These are arms and accoutrements we gathered on that part of the field in front. Troops belonging to other commands, I understand, picked up a great many arms and accoutrements on the right across the marsh. I suppose the above arms are about one-third of the number captured.

The following is a list of casualties in my battalion, to wit:

Company A.—None killed. Wounded, R. Vaughn and J. Williams.

Company B.—Killed, J. B. Williams and Jno. Gleason. Wounded, Sergeant B. Thomas, privates J. McClendon, S. W. Robinson, W. J. Blyth, A. N. Packer, and J. B. Honeycutt.

Company C.—Killed, J. W. Ragan. Wounded, R. Porter, F. Carroll, and J. D. Montgomery.

Company D.—Killed, H. L. Berry. Wounded, R. W. Childers, W. Scarborough, J. W. Upshaw, and J. L. Smith.

Company E.—Killed, B. C. Campbell, J. Lenier. Wounded, 1st Sergeant Perryman, 2d Sergeant Carpenter, privates F. Poyler, J. Muckey, Jno. Stockman, and F. Guice.

Company F.—Wounded (dangerously), Capt. Walker.

Total killed,	6
" wounded,	22
Total casualties,	28

This report would have been made earlier, but now is the first opportunity since the battle that I have had to write it.

I am, captain,
Your obedient servant,
J. McENERY,
Lieut.-col. commanding 4th Louisiana battalion.

Report of Col. S. D. Goodlett.

HEAD-QUARTERS 22D REGIMENT S. C. V.,
CAMP ON JAMES ISLAND, S. C.,
June 18, 1862.

Gen. EVANS,
James Island, S. C.:

GENERAL:—I have the honor to make the following report of the casualties in my command, originating from the fight of the 16th instant:

In obedience to an order from head-quarters, I detailed one hundred picket men, ten from each company, to go as a fatigue party about 1 o'clock A. M., of the 16th instant, to Secessionville. I placed Capt. Joshua Jamison in command of the detail, and Lieuts. L. S. Hill, H. H. Sally, and J. B. Cobb, were detailed as Lieuts., thus completing a command as one company.

This detail arrived at Secessionville in time to meet the first onset of the enemy. Capt. Jamison, and Lieuts. Hill, Sally, and Cobb, acted with great coolness, courage, and determination, and sustained and supported Capt. Reid's battery to the last. The ranks of this detail, as will be seen by the exhibit "A," accompanying this, were decimated. Killed ten, wounded seven.

The balance of my command were ordered to support the battery to the right of Secessionville, when a galling fire was opened upon us from the enemy's artillery, without damage.

We were then ordered to the support of Secessionville, and arrived there at the close of the engagement.

I am happy to state that my command throughout acted with coolness and determination; and that too much praise cannot be bestowed upon Capt. Jamison and the lieutenants and detail before alluded to, for the manner in which they demeaned themselves in the fight.

I would state one fact, before bringing this report to a close, that according to the number actively engaged, that the detail of one hundred men made from my command, under Capt. Jamison, suffered more in proportion than any of the forces on our side.

I have the honor to be, sir,
Your obedient servant,
S. D. GOODLETT,
Col. commanding 22d regiment S. C. V

Letter of Brig.-gen. Isaac I. Stevens, commanding Federal forces.

HEAD-QUARTERS 2D DIVISION, N. D. D. S.,
JAMES ISLAND, S. C., *June* 18, 1862.

To the Commanding General of the Confederate Forces on James Island, S. C.:

SIR:—In the action of the 16th it is known that some of our dead, and, it is probable, that a few of our wounded were left at, or in rear of, your works. In compliance with the urgent wishes of friends, and in accordance with my own convictions of propriety and of duty, I have determined to send a flag of truce to ascertain the names of the killed and of the wounded, and, if practicable, to recover the bodies of the dead.

It will be ever my determination to conform, in the most ample manner, to the usages of civilized and Christian warfare, and I have seen to it that all of your men, who are now prisoners in our hands, have been treated with courtesy and respect. I am glad to learn that, on your part, the same course has been taken towards the prisoners recently taken by you.

The bearers of the flag of truce I now send to you are my division Surgeon, Dr. George S. Kemble, and my aid-de-camp, Capt. Wm. T. Lusk, and I trust you will find it consistent with your duty to extend to them every proper facility to procure information in regard to their missing comrades, and, if possible, to recover the remains of the dead.

We shall be glad to send money and clothing to our prisoners in your hands, and in return will see that articles of necessity and comforts, which their friends desire to send, safely reach your men, prisoners with us.

I am, sir, very respectfully,
Your obedient servant,
ISAAC I. STEVENS,
Brig.-gen. commanding.

Reply of Brig.-general N. G. Evans.

HEAD-QUARTERS JAMES ISLAND,
June 18, 1862.

Brig.-gen. STEVENS, *Commanding Federal Forces, &c.:*

GENERAL:—Your communication, through a flag of truce, borne by Dr. Geo. S. Kemble and Capt. Wm. T. Lusk, has just been received, and, in reply thereto, I have the honor to state that the information desired as to the names and condition of your wounded, in the engagement of the 16th instant, will be cheerfully furnished you at an early hour. The wounded having been sent to the city of Charleston, it is necessary to communicate with that place first.

I have also to state that your dead, as far as found, have been decently interred.

It has ever been the custom of our armies to conform to the "usages of civilized and Christian warfare," and our wounded and prisoners have been, and are being, well cared for in all respects.

I send this by my aid-de-camp, Capt. W. H. Rodgers.

Very respectfully, your obedient servant,
N. G. EVANS,
Brig.-gen. commanding Confederate Forces.

List of Killed, Wounded and Missing in the different corps engaged in the fight of the 16*th day of June*, 1862, *at Secessionville, South Carolina, James Island.*

LAMAR'S REGIMENT OF ARTILLERY, S. C.

Wounded, Col. T. G. Lamar.

Company B.—Killed, Capt. S. J. Reed, 2d Sergeant James M. Baggott; privates Elbert Bates, R. R. Bates, H. H. Lyches, W. J. Nix, W. Redmond, D. J. Reiley, and G. W. Watson.

Mortally wounded, (since dead), privates Chesley Bates and Jeff. C. Eaves.

Severely wounded—Sergeant R. F. Nevills; privates W. W. Bellinger, W. Flemming, Reddick Pitts, W. J. Chitty, F. M. King, L. L. Cox, H. H. Nevills, S. H. Nevills, H. L. Baggott, Thomas Ursery, W. D. Elkins, J. W. Gillam, S. G. Mitchell, B. H. Dyches, J. W. Philips, D. P. Hutson, W. J. Martin, J. B. Corbit, J. R. Mairs, and W. Whaley.

Slightly wounded—Corporal N. A. K. Walker; privates A. O. Houser, J. J. Walker, D. Holder, W. R. Delk, and J. Templeton.

Missing—Private W. P. Hair, previously wounded.

Company I.—Killed, privates W. H. Arnaker, J. A. R. Shuter, H. A. Hoover, Daniel Kelly, J. W. Gibson, and J. Jones.

Wounded severely—Sergeant Geo. Boliver; private J. C. Evans.

Wounded slightly—Sergeants J. Marchant, S. C. L. Miller; privates J. C. Stephenson, N. A. Whetitone, G. J. Bonnett, G. J. Parlor, J. Robinson, and J. W. Golson.

RECAPITULATION:

Killed,	15
Since dead,	2
Wounded,	38
Missing,	1
Total,	56

22d Regiment S. C. Volunteers.

Company A.—Killed, privates R. A. Cowan, and Benjamin Harris.

Company B.—Wounded, private John Wheeler.

Company C.—Wounded, private Edward Sigemore.

Company D.—Killed, privates William Roach, and Henry Pressure.

Company E.—Killed, private J. J. Spivay.

Wounded, privates W. F. Connell, and Francis Connell.

Company F.—Wounded, private William Gilstrap.

Company G.—Killed, privates Thomas A. Stribling, and Henry Orr.

Company H.—Wounded, private Thomas Bowers.

Company I.—Killed, privates Liona Justus, and Duman Wooley

Wounded, private P. Tar.

Company K.—Killed, private Alfred Cawer.

Wounded, private E. P. Campbell.

RECAPITULATION:

Killed	10
Wounded	8
Total	18

Smith's Battalion S. C. Volunteers.

Company A.—Seriously wounded, privates Henry Cooper, and Alexander Brown.

Slightly wounded, Lieut. W. T. Jarvis, and Sergeant W. T. Smith.

Missing, privates William Russ, and F. M. Jordan, captured on picket.

Company B.—Killed, private Duncan Deas.

Seriously wounded (since dead), Sergeant W. L. McFarland.

Seriously wounded, private Jesse Pierce.

Slightly wounded, privates R. D. Moore, John R. Threat, and Isaac Hurst.

Company C.—Seriously wounded, privates William Cole, and Thos. Driggers.

Slightly wounded, Corporal John Roller, and private Leonard Orxendien.

Company D.—Killed, privates J. T. Alford and H. Lay.

Seriously wounded, 1st Lieut. J. G. Beaty.

Slightly wounded, privates S. Jones and M. Stalrey.

Company F.—Seriously wounded, private C. C. Anderson.

Slightly wounded, Corporal E. F. Sandsbury, and privates W. D. Collins, and J. E. P. Hickson.

Company G.—Seriously wounded, privates L. Stricken and Wm. Elliott.

Slightly wounded, 1st Sergeant J. H. Williamson, and private J. W. Tripp.

RECAPITULATION:

Killed	3
Since dead	1
Wounded	22
Missing	3
Total	29

Charleston Battalion—Field and Staff.

Wounded slightly, Lieut.-col. P. C. Gaillard.

Wounded severely, Capt. R. Press Smith, A. Q. M.

Company A.—Wounded slightly, Capt. Julien A. Blake, and Lieut. F. Lynch.

Company B.—Killed, private J. B. W. Hammett.

Wounded mortally, private P. Gilhooly.

Wounded slightly, privates M. Lacy, J. P. Johnson, and W. H Sutchliffe.

Missing, private J. R. Gibbs.

Company C.—Killed, private Dan Howard.

Wounded severely, private John May.

Wounded slightly, Lieut. John Burke and private J. P. Murphy.

Company D.—Killed, Capt. H. C. King, Lieut. J. J. Edwards, Corporal J. Volentine; privates G. Poynauski and J. F. Edgarton.

Wounded, Sergeant J. J. Wells; privates R. C. Evans, A. Roumillat, E. L. Terry, W. W. Johnson, H. Neofuille, H. Volentine, E. S. Tennent, G. W. Dingle and T. P. Lockwood.

Company E.—Killed, private Thomas Parker.

Wounded, Capt. F. T. Miles. Lieut. J. W. Axson, sergeant S. C. Black; privates C. P. Brown, C. B. Buist, Isaac Holmes, H. E. Choate, and J. E. Smith.

Company F.—Killed, Sergeant R. J. Henery and private James Davis.

Wounded, Lieut. George Brown and private William Commins.

RECAPITULATION:

Killed	10
Wounded	30
Missing	2
Total	42

Eutaw Battalion.

Company B.—Killed, 2d Lieut. R. W. Greer, Sergeant Fleetwood Launeau, Jr.; privates Samuel Salters and Thomas N. Gadsden, Jr.

Wounded mortally, privates J. H. Tavener and J. C. Martin.

Wounded severely, 2d Lieut, S. J. Burger; privates J. H. Devaux, A. B. Glover, and T. G. Simons.

Wounded slightly, privates A. S. Trumbo, Robert G. McChutchen, J. H. Shulte, and J. P. Gibbs.

Lieutenant Mathews' Rifles.

Wounded slightly, privates E. V. Shuler, G. M. Dantzler, and J. W. Wannamaker.

Zeadon Light Infantry.

Wounded slightly, Sergeant R. A. Wharton.

RECAPITULATION:

Killed	4
Wounded	14
Total	18

24th Regiment S. C. Volunteers.

Company D.—Killed, none.

Wounded, Sergeant D. W. Bowers.

Company G.—Killed, privates M. Dawkins and John Mowells.

Wounded, private Joel Hunt.

Company I.—Wounded and missing, private John Duncan.

Company K.—Killed, private J. E. Bussy.

Wounded, Lieut. F. W. Anderson, Sergeant G. W. Benton; privates James Hern, K. P. Gomain, and Pickens New.

Missing, private John Duncan.

RECAPITULATION:

Killed	3
Wounded	7
Missing	2
Total	12

47th Regiment Georgia Volunteers.

Company B.—Killed, Lieut. B. A. Graham.

RECAPITULATION:

Killed	1
Total	1

1st Regiment S. C. Volunteers.

Company H.—Wounded, private John A. Nichole.

RECAPITULATION:

Wounded	1
Total	1

4th Louisiana Battalion.

Company A.—Wounded, privates R. S. Vaughan and James Williams.

Company B.—Killed, privates J. B. Williams and John Gleason.

Wounded, Sergeant B. Thomas; privates Jeff. McClendon, S. W. Robinson, W. J. Blythe, A. N. Packer, and J. B. Honeycutt.

Company C.—Killed, private J. W. Ragan.

Wounded, privates P. Porter, F. Carrol, and J. D. Montgomery.

Company D.—Wounded, privates H. L. Berry, R. W. Childers, T. Mehan, W. Scarborough, J. W. Upshan, and J. L. Smith.

Company E.—Killed, privates B. P. Campbell and Joseph Lanier.

Wounded, Sergeants W. J. Perryman and A. D. Carpenter privates F. Taylor, J. Mulkey, John Stopman, and J. Gryce.

Company F.—Wounded, Capt. James H. Walker.

RECAPITULATION:

Killed	5
Wounded	24
Total	29

TOTAL CASUALTIES.

Killed	51
Wounded	144
Missing	9
Since dead	3
Total	207

Names of Individuals reported by Commanders, as Distinguished for Gallant Conduct in the Affair at James Island.

In the report of Brig.-gen. N. G. Evans:

Col. T. G. Lamar, Lamar's regiment S. C. artillery, for gallant and meritorious conduct.

Lieut.-col. Gaillard, Charleston battalion S. C. V. (mentioned particularly in report of Col. T. G. Lamar), gallant conduct.

Lieut.-col. A. D. Smith, Smith's battalion S. C. V. (mentioned particularly in report of Col. T. G. Lamar), gallant conduct.

Capt. Samuel J. Reed, company B, Lamar's regiment artillery, fell gallantly fighting one of his guns, again mentioned in report of Col. T. G. Lamar.

Personal staff:

1st Lieut. W. H. Rogers, special aid-de-camp, rendered valuable service in transmitting orders under fire.

Capts. R. E. Elliott, Samuel J. Corrie, and H. W. Carr, volunteer aids-de-camp, rendered valuable service in transmitting orders under fire.

Assistant Surgeon James Evans, rendered material aid to the wounded.

In the report of Col. T. G. Lamar:

Lieut.-col. A. D. Smith, Smith's battalion S. C. V., gallant and meritorious conduct (mentioned in report of Brig.-gen. N. G. Evans).

Lieut.-col. C. P. Gaillard, Charleston battalion, gallant conduct, mentioned in report of Brig.-gen. N. G. Evans, stationed in the centre and on the right of battery, at Secessionville, and subsequently in command of the battery.

Major David Ramsey, Charleston battalion, meritorious conduct on the right of the battery at Secessionville. Major Hudson, Smith's battalion, meritorious conduct, on the left of the battery at Secessionville.

Capt. Samuel J. Reed, company B, Lamar's regiment artillery, fell fighting at one of his guns on the battery at Secessionville (mentioned in Brig.-gen. Evans' report).

Capt. F. T. Miles, Calhoun Guard, Charleston battalion, gallant conduct, stationed on battery at Secessionville.

Capt. G. D. Keitt, Lamar's regiment artillery, great bravery.

Lieuts. Barton, Oliver, and Mosley, same regiment, great bravery.

Senior 1st Lieut. J. B. Humbert, company I, Lamar's regiment artillery, specially mentioned for great bravery and valuable service, stationed in battery at Secessionville, 8-inch columbiad.

Lieuts. Lancaster and Johnson, company B, Lamar's regiment, and Lieut. Bellinger, of same company, gallant conduct, in battery at Secessionville.

Lieut. W. H. Ketchings, company H, Lamar's regiment, gallant conduct, Reed's battery, Clarke's house.

Adjutant E. J. Frederick, Lamar's regiment, gallant conduct, battery at Secessionville, and Reed's battery at Clarke's house.

Capt. W. W. McCreery, ordnance department, C. S. A., rendered valuable service at the eight-inch columbiad in the battery at Secessionville.

Capt. Bonneau, Lieuts. Mathews and Hall, C. S. N., rendered valuable service at the eight-inch columbiad in the battery at Secessionville.

In the report of Col. S. D. Goodlett, 22d regiment S. C. V.:

Capt. Joshua Jamison, Lieut. L. S. Hill, H. H. Lally, and J. B. Cobb, valuable service and gallant conduct in sustaining the battery at Clarke's house.

In the report of Col. Stephens, 24th regiment S. C. V.:

Lieut.-col. Capers, 24th regiment S. C. V., gallant conduct in defending advanced battery of 24-pound guns.

Capt. Tompkins, company K, and Lieut. Beckham, company G. gallant conduct in holding advanced position until ordered to withdraw.

In the report of Lieut.-col. A. W. Smith, Smith's battalion S. C. V.:

Lieut. Campbell, company F, gallant conduct in personally repulsing an assaulting party on the left of the battery at Secessionville.

Capt. W. H. Ryan, valuable service in battery at Secessionville.

Lieut. E. Brown, company F, and Lieut. Alexander A. Allemory, Irish volunteers, valuable service in carrying ammunition through fire of artillery and infantry.

Sergeant Hendricks, valuable service in carrying ammunition under heavy fire, in battery at Secessionville.

Private Joseph Tennent, of the Calhoun Guard, gallant conduct on the left of battery at Secessionville.

In report of Lieut.-col Simonton, "Eutaw battalion:"

Lieut. Blum, Washington Light Infantry, company B, gallant conduct, advanced position, on the right flank.

Privates J. Campbell Martin and George Simons. Jr., gallant conduct, both severely wounded, but still fought until exhausted and carried off, mentioned in report of Lieut. Blum.

In report of Lieut. Blum, commanding detachment of Eutaw battalion:

Privates J. Campbell Martin and Grange Martin, Jr., gallant conduct (mentioned in report of Col. Simonton).

REPORT OF THE EXPEDITION INTO KENTUCKY.

BRIGADIER-GENERAL MORGAN COMMANDING.

HEAD-QUARTERS MORGAN'S COMMAND,
KNOXVILLE, TENN., July 30, 1862.

To R. A. ALLSTON,
Assistant Adjutant-general:

GENERAL: I have the honor to report, that upon the day of the engagement at Tomkinsville, a full report of which I have already sent you, I moved my command, consisting of my own regiment, the Georgia regiment of Partizan Rangers, commanded by Col. A. A. Hunt, and Major Gano's Texas squadron, to which was attached two companies of Tennessee cavalry, in the direction of Glasgow, which place I reached at 12 o'clock that night.

There were but few troops in the town, who fled at our approach. The commissary stores, clothing, &c., together with a large supply of medical stores, found in Glasgow, were burned, and the guns were distributed among my command, about two hundred of which were unarmed when I left Knoxville. From Glasgow, I proceeded along the main Lexington road to Barren river, halting for a short time at a point near Cave city, my object being to induce the belief that I intended destroying the railroad bridge between Bowling Green and Woodsonville. I caused wires connecting with the portable battery that I carried with me to be attached to the telegraph line near Horse cave, and intercepted a number of dispatches. At Barren river, I detached three companies under Capt. Jack Allen, to move forward rapidly and destroy the Salt river bridge, that the troops along the line of railroad might be prevented from returning to Louisville. On the following morning I moved on towards Lebanon, distant thirty-five miles from Barren river. At 11 o'clock at night I reached the bridge over Rolling Fork, six miles from Lebanon. The enemy had received information of my approach from their spies, and my advance guard was fired upon at the bridge. After a short fight the force at the bridge was dispersed, and the planks which had been torn up having been replaced, the command moved forward to Lebanon.

About two miles from the town, a skirmish commenced between two companies I caused to dismount and deploy, and a force of the enemy posted upon the road, which was soon ended by its dispersion and capture. Lieut.-col. A. Y. Johnson, commanding the troops in the town, surrendered, and I entered the place. The prisoners taken, in number about sixty-five, were parolled. I took immediate possession of the telegraph, and intercepted a dispatch to Col. Johnson, informing him that Col. Owens, with the 60th Indiana regiment, had been ordered to his assistance. So I at once dispatched a company of Texas rangers, under Major Gano, to destroy the railroad bridge on the Lebanon branch, which he successfully accomplished in time to prevent the arrival of the troops. I burned two long buildings full of commissary stores, consisting of upwards of five hundred sacks of coffee and a large amount of all other supplies in bulk, marked for the army at Cumberland Gap. I also destroyed a very large amount of clothing, boots, &c. I burned the hospital buildings, which appeared to have been recently erected and fitted up, together with about thirty-five wagons and fifty-three new ambulances. I found in the place a large store of medicines, five thousand stand of arms, with accoutrements, about two thousand sabres, and an immense quantity of ammunition, shells, &c. I distributed the best arms among my command, and loaded one wagon with them, to be given to recruits that I expected to join me. I also loaded a wagon with ammunition. The remainder of the arms, ammunition, and the hospital and medical stores, I destroyed. While in Lebanon, I ascertained from telegraphic dispatches that I intercepted, that the force which had been started from Lebanon junction to reinforce Lieut.-col. Jonnson, had met and driven back the force under Capt. Jack Allen, killing one of the men, and preventing him from accomplishing the purpose for which he had been detached. I proceeded from Lebanon on the following day, through Springfield to Macksville, at which point I was attacked by home guards. Two of my men were taken prisoners, and one severely wounded. I remained at Macksville that night to recover the prisoners, which I did the next morning. I then left for Harrodsburg, capturing a Federal captain and lieutenant on the road. Reached Harrodsburg at half-past twelve o'clock; found that the home guard of all that portion of country had fled to Lexington. A force was also stationed on the bridge where the Lexington road crosses the Kentucky river. My reception at this place was very encouraging; the whole population appeared to turn out and vie with each other as to who should show us most attention. I left Harrodsburg at six o'clock the same evening, and moved to Lawrenceburg, twenty miles distant, threatening Frankfort, in order to draw off the troops from Georgetown. I remained there until the return of the courier from Frankfort, who brought the information that there was a force in Frankfort of two or three thousand men, consisting of home guards collected from the adjacent counties, and a few regular troops. From Lawrenceburg I proceeded to Shrykes' ferry, on the Kentucky river, raised the boat which had been sunken, and crossed that evening, reaching Versailles at seven o'clock. I found this place abandoned by its defenders, who had fled to Lexington. Remained there that night, and on the next morning marched towards Georgetown.

While at Varsailles, I took about three hundred Government horses and mules. I passed through Midway on the way to Georgetown, and was informed, just before reaching the place, that a train from Frankfort was nearly due, with two regiments of Federals. I tore up the track, and posted the howitzers to command it, and formed my command along the line of the road, but the train was warned of our presence, and returned to Frankfort. Having taken possession of the telegraph office, I intercepted a dispatch, asking if the road was clear, and if it would be safe to start the train from Lexington. I replied to send the train, and made preparations to receive it, but it was also turned back and escaped. I reached Georgetown, 12 miles from Lexington, that evening. Just before entering the town, I was informed that a small force of home guards had mustered to oppose us. I sent them word to surrender their arms, and they should not be molested, but they fled. The people of Georgetown also welcomed us with gladness, and provided my troops with every thing they needed. I remained at Georgetown two days, during which time I sent out a company, under Capt. McMillan, to destroy the track between Midway and Lexington, and Midway and Frankfort, and to blow up the stone bridge on that road, which he successfully accomplished. Hearing that a company of home guard were encamped at Stamping grounds, thirteen miles distant, I dispatched a company, under Capt. Hamilton, to break up their encampment, burn the tents and stores, and destroy the guns. This was also accomplished, Capt. Hamilton taking fifteen prisoners and all their guns, and destroying a large amount of medical and commissary stores. I also, while at Georgetown, sent Capt. Castleman, with his company, to destroy the railroad bridges between Paris and Lexington, and report to me at Winchester. This was done.

Determining to move on Paris, with a view of returning, and hearing that the place was being rapidly reinforced from Cincinnati, I deemed it of great importance to cut off the communication from that place, while I drew off the troops that were already there by a feint on Lexington. I therefore dispatched a portion of two companies towards Lexington, with instructions to drive the pickets to the very entrance of the city, while I moved the command towards Cynthiana. When I arrived within three miles of this place, I learned that it was defended by a considerable force of infantry, cavalry and artillery. I dispatched the Texas squadron, under Major Gano, to enter the town on the right, the Georgia regiment to cross the river and get in the rear, while I moved my own regiment, with the artillery, under the command of Lieut. J. E. Harris, down the Georgetown pike. A severe engagement took place, which lasted about an hour and a half before the enemy were driven into the town and compelled to surrender. I took four hundred and twenty prisoners, including about seventy home guard. I regret to have to mention the loss of eight of my men in killed, and twenty-nine wounded. The enemy's loss was 194 in killed and wounded, according to their own account. Their excess in killed and wounded is remarkable, as they fought us from behind stone fences, and fired at us from buildings as we charged through the town. We captured a very fine 12-pounder brass piece of artillery, together with a large number of small arms, and about three hundred Government horses. I found a very large supply of commissary and medical stores, tents, guns, and ammunition at this place, which I destroyed. The parolled prisoners were sent under an escort to Falmouth, where they took the train for Cincinnati. I proceeded the next morning towards Paris, and was met on the road by the bearer of a flag of truce, offering the unconditional surrender of the place. I reached Paris at 6 o'clock, remained there that night, and started towards Winchester the next morning. As my command was filing out of Paris on the Winchester pike, I discovered a large force of Federals coming towards the town from the direction of Lexington. They immediately counter-marched, supposing, no doubt, that my intention was to get in their rear. This enabled me to bring off my entire command without molestation, with the exception of two of my pickets, who were probably surprised. Reached Winchester that day at 12 o'clock, remained until 4 o'clock, when I proceeded towards Richmond. At Winchester I found a number of arms, which were destroyed. I arrived at Richmond at 12 o'clock that night, and remained until the next afternoon, when I proceeded to Crab Orchard. I had determined to make a stand at Richmond, and await reinforcements, as the whole people appeared ready to rise and join me, but I received information that large bodies of cavalry, under Gen. Clay Smith and Cols. Woolford, Metcalf, Mundy, and Wynkop, were endeavoring to surround me at this place, so I moved on to Crab Orchard. There I attached my portable battery to the telegraph leading from Stanford to Louisville, and learned the exact position of the enemy's forces, and directed my movements accordingly. Leaving Crab Orchard at 11 o'clock, I arrived at Somerset, distant 28 miles, at sun-down. I took possession of the telegraph, and countermanded all the previous orders that had been given by Gen. Boyle to pursue me, and remained here in perfect security all night. I found a very large supply of commissary stores, clothing, blankets, shoes, hats, &c., at this place, which were destroyed. I also found the arms that had been taken from Gen. Zollicoffer, together with large quantities of shell and ammunition, all of which were destroyed. I also burned at this place and Crab Orchard about one hundred and twenty government wagons.

From Somerset, I proceeded to Monticello, and from thence to a point between Lexington and Sparta, where my command is now encamped. I left Knoxville on the 4th day of this month, with about nine hundred men, and returned to Lexington on the 28th inst., with nearly twelve hundred, having been absent just twenty-four days, during which time I travelled over a thousand miles, captured seventeen towns, destroyed all the Government supplies and arms in them, dispersed about fifteeen hundred home guard, and parolled nearly twelve hundred regular troops. I lost in killed, wounded, and missing, of the number that I carried into Kentucky, about ninety. I take great pleasure in testifying to the gallant bravery and efficiency of my whole command. There were individual instances of daring so conspicuous that I must beg the privilege of referring to them. Private Moore, of Louisiana, a member of company A, of my regiment, particularly distinguished himself by leading a charge, which had an important effect in winning the battle. The report of the regimental commanders, which are inclosed, are respectively referred to for further instances of individual bravery and efficiency. I feel indebted to all my aids for the promptness with which my orders were executed, and particularly to Col. St. Leger Grenfel, for the assistance which his experience afforded me.

All of which is respectfully submitted,

(Signed) JOHN H. MORGAN,

Acting Brig.-gen. C. S. A.

Report of Lieut.-col. B. W. Duke.

CYNTHIANA, July 17th, 1862.

Capt. R. A. ALSTON,

Assistant Adjutant-general:

SIR: During the engagement to-day, the regiment engaged the enemy on the Georgetown pike, and after a desperate fight of about an hour and a half, succeeded in driving them into the town, where a hot street fight occurred, lasting until near dark. We took the 12-pound brass piece that had so annoyed us during the early part of the action.

Where all engaged acted so nobly, 'tis difficult to particularize; but it is generally conceded that company A covered itself with glory, which is acknowledged by the regiment.

P. H. THORP, *Adjutant.*

Capt. R. A. ALSTON,

Assistant Adjutant-general:

In the action referred to above, my regiment was deployed upon the Georgetown pike, companies A and B upon the right, companies E and F upon the left. After a stubborn fight, the enemy were driven from all the positions in the edge of the town. Company B was then sent to the extreme, to engage a force which threatened our right flank, and succeeded in dispersing it. Companies E and F charged up to the bank of the river, under a severe fire of musketry and grape, and were prevented from entering the town only by the depth of the water at that point. Company A crossed the river at a ford near the bridge, charged across the bridge, and, after a very severe contest, drove the enemy from the houses near the bridge. Company C, previously held in reserve, charged through the town on horseback, and forced the enemy to abandon their artillery, and cleared that street. The two last-named companies, then uniting with the Georgians, who had dashed in upon the left, forced the enemy to abandon the depot, and subsequently the town.

It is almost impossible to speak in terms too high of the different officers under my command; good conduct and individual gallantry were so common, that it almost ceased to be a matter of remark.

Capts. Hutchingson and Webber led their companies in perfect order through a fire that was unusually severe. Lieut. J. A. Smith and Bowyer, of company A, were both severely wounded in front of that company, and in the midst of the enemy.

Capt. Bowles and Lieut. Myers, of company C, behaved with great gallantry; the latter was struck from his horse, but fortunately the wound was but slight.

Lieut. White, commanding company B, performed the duty assigned him, and kept his company in front of a superior force for nearly an hour, finally dispersing it.

I have the pleasure to report the gallant and efficient conduct of Capt. Thorpe, adjutant of my regiment, and my thanks are due him for the manner in which he superintended the execution of every order. I cannot too highly compliment Col. St. Leger Grenfel, who acted with my regiment, for the execution of an order, which did, perhaps, more than any thing else to gain the battle. His example gave new courage to every one who witnessed it. I have the honor to report that every one in my regiment gave satisfaction to myself and their respective commanders.

B. W. DUKE,

Lieut.-col. commanding regiment.

Report of Lieut.-col. F. M. Nix.

HEAD-QUARTERS CAMP SMITH,
NEAR KNOXVILLE, TENN., July 30, 1862,

R. A. ALSTON,
A. A. A.-gen. Morgan's Brigade:

SIR: I have the honor to submit the following report of the action of the 1st regiment Georgia Partizan Rangers, in the battle of Cynthiana, on Thursday, 17th inst.:

On Thursday, the 17th inst., when the brigade had arrived within a few miles of Cynthiana, I was ordered by Gen. Morgan to detach my regiment, and attack the town on the west side, at the report of the cannon. Having made a circuit of five or more miles, through plantations, and over many obstructions not anticipated, with all possible dispatch, I arrived in the suburbs, and formed a line a few minutes after the signal of attack was heard, when I observed a body of the enemy's cavalry advancing towards my line, which were promptly repulsed by a volley from my command. Having advanced a short distance, I ordered Capt. Jones to deploy his company (A) to the right of the pike, in order to cover the whole or the rear of the town, and prevent the escape of the enemy in case of their defeat. Before the whole of company A, however, could be deployed, it encountered a body of cavalry advancing on the pike, which were repulsed, after a sharp contest. Advancing further, Capt. Jones encountered a force of artillery with one brass field piece, which he charged and repulsed, the enemy, having the piece behind them, still advancing, and completing the deployment to the right of the pike. Company A captured sixty-eight prisoners, marched them to a corner of the main street, and left them in charge of a squad under command of Lieut. R. H. Chapman. At this juncture, intelligence having reached Capt. Jones, through a prisoner, that a reinforcement of seven hundred men was coming in by railroad, he ordered Quarter-master-sergeant John C. Allen to take a file of men, and burn a long railroad bridge in his rear, which was promptly executed, the remainder of the company advancing until the firing ceased.

Company B, advancing along Main street, driving before it a body of the enemy, killed some and captured many. Lieut. Meadows and a private of said company, and private S. T. Moore, of company A, being the first to approach the brass field piece, which was captured. Advancing along Main street, this company was ordered to dislodge a party of the enemy from a garden, which was promptly executed. Companies B and C, and a portion of company A, were then ordered to charge the depot and a neighboring brick building, from which the enemy was pouring an incessant fire. After a severe conflict they drove the enemy from both these strongholds, killing and capturing several of them, and afterwards pursuing the enemy to the corn-field, in which they made their last stand. The only casualty in company B was one man wounded; in company C, two killed and six wounded, three slightly and three severely; among the latter was 2d Lieut. Thomas E. Pitts. The left wing, viz.: companies D, E, and F, under command of Major Samuel J. Winn, advanced steadily on the left of the pike, engaging the enemy at several points, and driving them into the centre of the town, having killed and captured a number of them, and not halting until the enemy was routed. The left wing sustained no loss either in killed or wounded. I feel that many thanks and much praise are due to the officers and soldiers of my command for their highly creditable and heroic conduct on the occasion of this battle. All of which is respectfully submitted.

F. M. NIX,
Lieut.-col. commanding 1st regiment Georgia Partizan Rangers.

Report of Major R. M. Gano, commanding battalion cavalry in Morgan's brigade.

To JOHN H. MORGAN,
Brig.-gen. commanding brigade in the Kentucky expedition of July, 1862.

HONORED SIR:—I have the pleasure of reporting to you the action of the battalion under my command in the recent expedition to Kentucky. This report is intended to embrace only the action of the battalion while separated from the other troops under your command. The battalion was composed of four companies—two Texas companies under my command, known as the Texas squadron; company A, commanded by Lieut. Speen, and company B, by Capt. Hauffman, and two Tennessee companies, viz.: company C, commanded by Capt. McMillan, and company D, by Capt. Hamilton, having left Knoxville on the morning of the 4th of July, 1862. We reached Walden's ridge on the evening of the 5th, where the bushwhackers fired upon our foraging party, mortally wounding Mr. J. N. O'Brien, of company A, of the Texas squadron. He lived 24 hours, suffered much, was a model soldier, a fond husband, affectionate father, and a worthy man in all the relations of life. Cut down in the prime of life, he died in a noble cause, the defence of his country from the invader.

We reached Tompkinsville on the morning of the 8th, about sunrise. I was then ordered to the right of the town, on the Old Mill road, to attack from that point and cut off all retreat from that quarter. I proceeded as directed, and drove in the pickets, giving the alarm in the enemy's camp. When we came in sight of the enemy, they were forming on horseback, apparently with the intention of attacking us, not dreaming of the reception prepared before breakfast for them. I arranged my command to receive them, but only had the opportunity of firing a few long range guns at them, as the well-aimed shell from your howitzers drove them back from their position, and I then thought, from their movements, that they would retreat on the Burksville road, and I immediately ordered Capt. Huffman through the woods upon our right, with two companies, to intercept them there, but the rapid and well-aimed fire from the Georgians, under Col. Hunt, from one point, and of your regiment from another, drove the enemy into such a hasty retreat, that they passed out through a woodland trail some half mile or more, and then falling into the Burksville road, put their horses to their utmost speed. The Texans, so famous for horsemanship, started in pursuit, and a portion of the squadron, on faster horses, soon came up with some 75 of the enemy under Major Jordan and two lieutenants, trying to cover their hasty retreat. They did not surrender to our demand, but fired back at us, wounding Thomas Huffhines. Then commenced a running fight, 75 Yankees against about one dozen Texans, and many an invader bit the dust. Among the number one lieutenant, one sergeant, and two corporals. We captured Major Jordan, one lieutenant, one sergeant, and four privates. Our casualties were, in this running fight, two wounded, viz.: J. Huffman, flesh wound in the thigh, and J. Loose, a sabre cut in the head, severing the outer table of the skull—neither dangerous. The enemy lost 9 killed, 7 captured; number of wounded unknown.

At Bear Wallow, on the 9th, Capt. Huffman's company was detailed from my command, upon an expedition under Capt. Jack Allen. For their movements, I refer you to his report.

After the bushwhacking from New Market to Lebanon on the

night of the 10th, and after the surrender of Col. Johnson and his forces, he having stated that the home guards would fire upon us from the houses if we entered the town, you will recollect how nobly the three companies of my battalion at the still hour of the night marched through to receive their fire. Lieut. Spears in front, Capt. McMillan next, and Capt. Hamilton third; but the fire came not, the women waived their handkerchiefs, and the place was ours, as witnessed by the shout that rent the air, and then, without rest, having been in saddle 24 hours, how cheerfully we posted off five miles in the country, in compliance with the order to burn the bridges, which we did, capturing the guard. Capt. Huffman and his company rejoined us at Macksville, the night of the 11th, and next morning I was ordered forward to take possession of Harrodsburg. The home guards had assembled at this place to drive us back, but before we came in sight they had fled precipitately to the Kentucky cliffs to reinforce Joshua Bell, who was collecting all the home guards at the bridge on the Danville and Lexington road, and the aforesaid militia general (Bell) was exhorting his assemblage to deeds of heroism and valor, when a party of 65 home guards came from Lancester to reinforce them. They came shouting and waving their hats. Bell's pickets fled and reported Morgan coming with his forces at full gallop. Their heroic leader then announced that they could not possibly make a stand there, and every man must take care of himself, and they all fled in the direction of Lexington, some on horseback, some on foot—(the author of this, Mike Chrisman, made several miles on foot and fainted by the wayside). The wicked flee when no man pursueth. The excitement and dread at Harrodsburg, on the part of the Unionists, was intense. Strange that any persons in Kentucky could be deluded by the lies of Geo. D. Prentice to believe that the Southern people, noted for their chivalry, liberality, and sympathy, could be guilty of the baseness ascribed to us by those base hirelings of the North. But now they have been shown better by actions, which speak louder than words. A few words guaranteeing respect to persons and and property quieted their fears, and all united in preparing us a repast. But the ladies—God bless them!—true and loyal to their native South, are bright examples of patriotism and fidelity to our country, our instructions, and the liberties vouchsafed to us by the struggles of our forefathers.

From Harrodsburg, per order, I proceeded towards Paris, intending to avoid the pickets at Lexington (having only 92 men with me), but accidentally coming upon them, I feigned an attack, and crossing several roads, and frightening in their pickets, they reported a large rebel force coming in from different roads. The greatest excitement prevailed, and with cannon and huge proclamation, they prepared for defence, compelling every man, of whatever sentiment, to take up arms. I did not attack the city with my small force, but leaving Lexington to my right, and passing in by Paynes' depot, on the Frankfort road, I halted my company at the residence of John Payne, near Georgetown, for dinner. Mrs. P., not knowing any better, sent word to her husband in town, that a body of Union cavalry were there. He immediately called upon the Provost Marshal to accompany him home. He could not go, but sends his deputy, Alex. Long. Soon another messenger arrived in the person of Oliver Gaines, with an order to me to take my forces over to the Frankfort road and cut off Morgan's forces, as the rebels were certainly coming that way. I answered, "all right," and administered the oath of secrecy and non-interference to the two messengers, with three others that had assembled there by accident.

I then passed up the iron works road, followed, as I afterwards learned, at long distance, by a party of home guards, mounted upon such horses as they had been able to pick up on the streets of Georgetown, some riding with bridles, and some with halters, but when they came in the rear of our little column, they concluded discretion the better part of valor, and turned off on another road. We passed through the farm of Victor Flournoy, stopping to refresh ourselves at the spring of the Rev. R. J. Breckinridge, where the ladies came out, and one, whose bright eyes bespoke a Southern heart, was very curious to know what party we belonged to. This accidental call was construed into an attempt to arrest the doctor, and his son, Capt. Will. Breckinridge, whom we had not seen, was accused of being accessory. It is not surprising they should judge thus, meting by their own measure. The enemy may feel the effect of Capt. William's steel upon the field of battle, but they will never find a man of his noble Southern soul trying to secure his father's arrest. Taking tea at my father's, I proceeded on to Kizers' station, on the Paris and Covington road, and fired the bridge. The burning bridge fired an old shed beneath, which I afterwards learned was Mr. K.'s distillery. I regretted the loss of private property, but as it did happen, better be a distillery than any thing else. I here lost seven pickets, through their mistaking the road, and we hunted them until day, and, consequently did not destroy the Town send bridge, as I had contemplated.

We then proceeded towards Georgetown, and while encamped

in a woodland near that place, R. P. Tannehill, of company A, Texas squadron, was, by the accidental discharge of a gun, launched into eternity. Robert was a brave soldier boy, always ready, devoted to the Southern cause, and the main prop of his widowed mother; but we laid our bold soldier boy to rest more than a 1,000 miles from his fond mother, who little dreams of the removal of her boy. On this, the evening of the 15th, we rejoined you in Georgetown, and by order, arrested Mr. Sam Thompson, the Provost Marshal of that place.

On the 17th instant, near Cynthiana, in accordance with your order, I proceeded with my command across to the Millersburg pike, arresting the guard at the bridge, driving in the pickets and commencing the fight on the side of the town. We drove the enemy back from that portion of the town. They soon returned in pretty large force, waving their hands. I ordered to cease firing, thinking they wished to surrender, but they had taken us for home guards, and commenced cursing us for firing on our own men. I ordered them to lay down their arms, when they fired and ran. We opened a brisk fire, and they dropped their guns for two squares down the street. We killed some ten or twelve, wounding many, and capturing as many more in town, and when they retreated from the town, we pursued on horseback, capturing many more. The loss from my battalion was 1 killed in Capt. Hamilton's company, 3 badly wounded, viz.: Lieut. R. Speer, of company A, of the Texas squadron, Clarke Aldridge, of Capt. Hoffman's company. There were two others slightly wounded. Capt. H. is of a brave stock, and is an honor to the name. On all other occasions, the forces were together, and your report will embrace the whole.

My command conducted themselves with the bravery that has alway characterized them, securing lasting honors to themselves, while rendering such efficient service to their country; and to their honor be it said, they have never failed to show kindness to the captured and wounded of the enemy, and respect to the rights of others. I think the kindness of your entire command to the enemy, when in their power, will be a good example to those of our enemies who have, throughout the State of Kentucky, busied themselves with tyrannizing over and oppressing those who honestly differ with them in political opinion. Let all those who wish to serve their country, join the army, and show to the world they are not cowards, and not employ their time in trying, in a cowardly manner, to secure the arrest of those neighbors who differ with them in political sentiment.

We are now, on the 29th instant, again at Knoxville, Tenn., having returned from one of the most daring and adventurous expeditions on record, with a very small loss in numbers, but having struck a blow from which the enemy will not soon recover.

Yours,

R. M. GANO,

Major, commanding Battalion Cavalry in Morgan's Brigade.

Report of Lieut. Harris.

MORGAN'S BRIGADE, CYNTHIANA, KY.,
July 18, 1862.

Capt. ALLETON,

A. A.-gen., Morgan's Legion:

SIR:—In obedience to special instructions, I have to report that my battery entered the engagement of the 17th instant, on the Turnpike road, leading to this place, about 300 yards, from the bridge, at — o'clock, and commenced shelling the enemy, who were occupying the latter position, which was kept up under showers of musketry, balls, and grape, from the enemy's artillery, for an hour, at which time they retired before a charge of cavalry. By order of the General, the pieces were then manned, by hand, to the front, across the bridge, again coming under galling fire of the enemy's sharpshooters, who occupied the depot and surrounding buildings, about 80 yards distant.

I regret here to have to report the inefficiency of my command, for a short time, resulting mainly from a want of discipline and drill, which you know I have scarcely had time to produce. Under these difficulties, however, the firing continued slowly until the enemy evacuated his final position. The casualties in this command are as follows, viz.:

Wounded—Cannonier W. B. Shelton, slightly in the head; cannonier Thomas Shanks, flesh wound in leg. Three horses killed.

In conclusion, I cannot but mention the gallant conduct of cannonier W. B. Shelton, as setting an emulous example to others, who, when having been wounded in the head, and lain senseless for ten minutes, on recovering himself, resumed his post, where he continued throughout the engagement.

I am, captain, your obedient servant,

JOS. C. HARRIS

First Lieut. commanding Artillery, Morgan's Legion.

George Elsworth's Dispatches.

KNOXVILLE, July 30, 1862.

Capt. A. R. ALSTON,

A. A.-general:

SIR: On July 10th, Gen. Morgan, with a body-guard of fifteen men and myself, arrived at a point half a mile below Horse Cave, on the Louisville and Nashville railroad, where I took down the telegraph line and connected my pocket instrument, for the purpose of taking off all dispatches as they passed through. Owing to a heavy storm prevailing south, the atmospheric electricity prevented me from communicating with Bowling Green or Nashville. The first I heard was Louisville calling Bowling Green. I immediately put on my ground wire south, and noticed particularly, at the same time, what change it would make in the circuit. It did make it stronger but owing to the storm mentioned above, affecting telegraphs more or less, Louisville did did not suspicion any thing wrong, and I answered for Bowling Green, when I received the following message:

LOUISVILLE, July 10, 1862.

To S. D. Brown,

Commanding Bowling Green:

You and Col. Houghton move together. I fear the force of Col. Houghton is too small to venture to Glasgow. The whole force should move together, as the enemy are mounted. We cannot venture to leave the road too far, as they may pass around and ruin it.

J. T. BOYLE,

Brig.-gen., commanding.

I returned the usual signal, after receiving the message, of O. K.

Louisville immediately called Nashville, and I answered for Nashville, receiving business for two hours. This business was mostly of a private nature, and I took no copies. It could be plainly seen, by the tenor of the messages, that Morgan was in the country, and all orders to send money and valuables by railroad were countermanded (as they supposed); but little did the operator at Louisville think that all of his work would have to be repeated the next day. Louisville also sent the news of the day, and thus all were furnished with New York and Washington dates of that day. During the whole of the time it was raining heavy. My situation was any thing but an agreeable one—sitting in the mud, with my feet in the water up to my knees.

At 11 o'clock P. M., the general being satisfied that I had drained Louisville of all the news, concluded to close for the night, and he verbally gave me the following message to send, dating and signing it as below:

NASHVILLE, July 10, 1862.

To Henry Dent,
Provost Marshal, Louisville:

Gen. Forrest, commanding brigade, attacked Murfreesboro', routing our forces, and is now moving on Nashville. Morgan is reported to be between Scottsville and Gallatin, and will act in concert with Forrest, it is believed. Inform general commanding.

STANLEY MATTHEWS.
Provost Marshal.

I am not aware that Gen. Morgan claims to be a prophet, or a son of a prophet, but Forrest did attack Murfreesboro', and rout the enemy.

On arriving at Lebanon, July the 12th, I accompanied the advance guard into town, and took charge of the telegraph office immediately. This was, as you know, at 3:30 A. M. I adjusted the instrument and examined the circuit. No other operator on the line appeared to be on hand this early. I then examined all the dispatches of the day previous. Among them I found the following:

LEBANON, July 11, 1862.

To General Boyle,
Louisville, Ky.:

I have positive information that there are 400 marauders in 20 miles of this place, on the old Lexington road, approaching Lebanon. Send reinforcements immediately.

A. Y. JOHNSON,
Lieut.-col., commanding.

At 7:30 A. M. an operator, signing Z, commenced calling B, which I had ascertained, by the books in the office, was the signal for Lebanon office. I answered the call, when the following conversation between Z and myself ensued:

To B:

What news? Any more skirmishing after your last message?

Z.

To Z:

No; we drove what little cavalry there was away. B.

To B:

Has the train arrived yet? Z.

To Z:

No. About how many troops on train? B.

To B:

Five hundred. Z.

My curiosity being excited as to what station Z was; and to ascertain, without creating any suspicion, I adopted the following plan:

To Z:

A gentleman here in the office bets me the cigars you cannot spell the name of your station correctly.

To B:

Take the bet. Lebanon Junction. Is this not right? How did he think I would spell it?

To Z:

He gives it up. He thought you would put two b's in Lebanon.

B.

To B:

Ha! ha! He is a green one. Z.

To Z:

Yes; that's so. B.

To Z:

What time did train with soldiers pass? B.

To B:

At 8.30 last night. Z.

To Z:

Very singular where the train is. B.

To B:

Yes, it is. Let me know when it arrives. Z.

At 8.20 Z called me up, and said:

To B:

The train has returned. They had a fight with the rebels at New Hope. The commanding officer awaits orders here. Z.

To Z:

Give us the particulars of the fight. Col. Johnson is anxious to know all about it. B.

To B:

I will as soon as possible. Z.

To B:

Here is Moore's message to Gen. Boyle. Z.

LEBANON JUNCTION, July 12, 1862.

To General Boyle,
Louisville, Ky.:

At 11 o'clock last night, part of my command encountered a force of rebel cavalry posted on the county road, half a mile south of the railroad. After a brisk fire of musketry for twenty minutes, the enemy was routed, and fled. Skirmishers were sent out in different directions, but were unable to find the enemy. At three this morning, apprehending that an effort might be made to destroy the bridges in our rear, we moved down to New Haven, and remained until after daylight, when the train went back to the scene of the skirmish.

A Mr. Forman, of Owen county, was found mortally wounded. He reported the rebel force at 450, under command of Capt. Jack Allen, and that they had fallen back towards Greensburg. One horse was killed and three captured. The books of the company were found. In the field, blood was found at different places, showing that the enemy was severely punished. No casualties on our side. Here, with train, waiting orders.

O. F. MOORE,
Commanding.

Lebanon Junction being the repeating station for Louisville business, he forwarded the following telegrams, just from Louisville, 9 A. M.:

LOUISVILLE, July 12, 1862.

To Col. Johnson,
Lebanon:

Leave good guard and join Col. Owen. Pursue the enemy and drive him out. Be cautious and vigorous. Make no delay.

J. T. BOYLE,
Brig.-gen. commanding.

LOUISVILLE, July 12, 1862.

To Col. Owen,
Lebanon:

You will move after the enemy and pursue him.

J. T. BOYLE,
Brig.-gen. commanding.

You will see by the above message that Col. Owen must have been *en route* for Lebanon.

Up to the time of our leaving Lebanon, which was about noon, Col. Moore, in command of those 500 troops at Lebanon Junction, had not received his orders, or I could furnish you with them. This I greatly regretted; but Gen. Morgan, having no fears of "Lincoln's web-footed soldiery," told me I could close my office, and to allay all suspicion at not being able to communicate with Lebanon during the afternoon, I told the operator at Lebanon junction, as follows:

To Z.:

I have been up all night, and am very sleepy; if you have no objection, I will take a nap until 2 or 3 oclock. B.

To B.:

All right, don't oversleep yourself. Z.

Wonder if I did!

Arrived at Midway, on the Lexington and Louisville railroad, about 10 A. M. At this place I surprised the operator, who was quietly sitting on the platform of the depot, enjoying himself hugely. Little did he suspicion that Morgan was in his vicinity.

I asked him to call Lexington, and to ask Lexington the time of day. He did so. I demanded this for the purpose of getting his style of handling the key, which corroborated my first impression, from the fact that I noticed paper in the instrument. To use a telegraphic phrase, he was a "plug operator." I adopted his style of writing, and commenced operations.

In this office I found a signal book, which, by the way, became very useful. It contained the calls for all the offices. Dispatch after dispatch was going to and fro from Lexington, Georgetown, Paris, and Frankfort. All contained something in reference to Morgan. I tested the line, and found by applying my ground wire it made no difference with the circuit, and as Lexington was head-quarters, I cut Frankfort off.

I omitted to state, that on commencing operations at this place, I discovered that there were two wires on this railroad. One was what we term a through wire, running direct from Lexington to Frankfort, and not entering any of the way offices. I found that all military business was sent over that wire, and as it did not enter Midway office, I ordered it cut, thus forcing Lexington on the wire that did run into this office.

Midway was called and I answered, when I received the following:

LEXINGTON, July 15th, 1862.

To J. W. Woolums,
Operator, Midway:

Will there be any danger in coming to Midway? Is every thing right?

TAYLOR,
Conductor.

I inquired of my prisoner if he knew a man by the name of Taylor. He said Taylor was conductor. I immediately gave Taylor the following reply:

MIDWAY, July 15th, 1862.

To Taylor,
Lexington:

All right. Come on. No signs of any rebels here.

WOOLUMS.

The operator in Cincinnati then called Frankfort. I answered, and received about a dozen of unimportant dispatches. He had no sooner finished, when Lexington called Frankfort, and again I answered, receiving the following message:

LEXINGTON, July 15th, 1862.

To Gen. Finnell,
Frankfort:

I wish you to move the forces at Frankfort, on the line of the Lexington railroad, immediately, and have the cars follow, and take them up as soon as possible. Further orders will await them at Midway. I will, in three or four hours, move forward on the Georgetown road. Will have most of my men mounted. Morgan left Versailles this morning at 8, with 800 men, on the Midway road, moving in the direction of Georgetown.

Brig.-gen. WARD.

This being our position and intention exactly, it was thought proper to throw Gen. Ward on some other track, so in the course of half an hour, I manufactured the following dispatch, which was approved by Gen. Morgan, and I sent it:

MIDWAY, July 15, 1862.

To Brig.-gen. Ward,
Lexington:

Morgan, with upwards of one thousand men, came within a mile of here, and took the old Frankfort road, bound, as we suppose, for Frankfort. This is reliable

WOOLUMS,
Operator.

In about 10 minutes, Lexington again called Frankfort, and as I was doing the work of two or three offices, I answered the call, and received the following:

LEXINGTON, July 15, 1862.

To Gen. Finnell,
Frankfort:

Morgan, with more than one thousand men, came within a mile of here, and took the old Frankfort road. This dispatch received from Midway, and is reliable. The regiment from Frankfort had better be recalled.

Gen. WARD.

I receipted for this message, and again manufactured a message to confirm the information Gen. Ward had received from Midway, and not knowing the tariff from Frankfort to Lexington, I could not send a formal message. I waited until the circuit was occupied, and then broke in, appearing greatly excited, and told those using the wire I must have the circuit, and commenced calling Lexington. He answered with as much gusto as I called. I telegraphed as follows:

To Lexington:

Tell Gen. Ward our pickets have just been driven in. Great excitement. Pickets say the force of the enemy must be 2,000.

FRANKFORT.

It was now 2 P. M., and Gen. Morgan wished to be off for Georgetown. I run a secret ground connection, and opened the circuit on the Lexington end. This was done to leave the impression that the Frankfort Operator was "skedaddling," or that Morgan's men had destroyed the telegraph.

We arrived at Georgetown at sundown. I went to the telegraph office; found it locked; inquired for the operator; he was pointed out to me. I hailed him and demanded admission into his office. He very courteously showed me into his office. I discovered the instruments had been removed. I asked where they were; he replied, that he had sent them to Lexington. I asked him what time he had Lexington last. He said 9 o'clock, since that time the line had been down. I remarked that it must be an extraordinary line to be in working condition *when it was down*, as I heard him sending messages to Lexington when I was at Midway at 1 o'clock. This was a stunner, he had nothing to say. I immediately tested the line by applying the ends of the wire to my tongue, and found the line O. K. I said nothing to him, but called for a guard of two men to take care of Wm. Smith until I got ready to leave town.

I did not interrupt the line until after tea, when I put in my own instruments, and after listening for an hour or two at the Yankees talking, I opened the conversation as follows: signing myself Federal Operator, as I had done before successfully at other places.

To Lexington:

Keep mum. I am in the office, reading by the sound of my magnet in the dark. I crawled in when no one seen me. Morgan's men are here, camped on Dr. Ganos' place. GEORGETOWN.

To Georgetown:

Keep cool. Don't be discouraged. About how many rebels are there?

LEXINGTON.

To Lexington:

I don't know. I did not notice, as Morgan's operator was asking me about my instruments. I told him I sent them to Lexington. He said "damn the luck," and went out. GEORGETOWN.

To Georgetown:

Be on hand and keep us posted. LEXINGTON

To Lexington:

I will do so. Tell Gen. Ward I'll stay up all night if he wishes. GEORGETOWN.

To Georgetown:

Mr. Fulton wishes to know if the rebels are there. CINCINNATI.

To Cincinnati:

Yes. Morgan's men are here. GEORGETOWN.

To Georgetown:

How can you be in the office and not be arrested? CINCINNATI.

To Cincinnati:

Oh! I am in the dark, and reading by sound of the magnet. GEORGETOWN.

This settled Cincinnati.

Question after question was asked me about the rebels, and I answered to suit myself. Things had been going on this way about two hours, when Lexington asked me where my assistant was? I replied, "Don't know." He then asked me, have you seen him today? I replied, "No." Well, from this time out, no telegraphing could I do in the beautiful city of Georgetown.

Wishing to keep myself busy, and make myself useful, I concluded to call on Mr. Smith, the operator, who was under guard in my room. I did so. I informed Mr. Smith that I would furnish him with a mule in the morning, and I should be pleased to have him accompany me to Dixie, as I understood he was in the employ of the United States Government. This was any thing but agreeable to the said Smith.

It seemed to me I had hit the young man in the right place, and I remarked that if he had not sent his instruments to Lexington, I would have taken them in preference to his person. His face brightened, and an idea struck him very forcibly that he would make a proposition. He did so, and it was to furnish me the instruments, if I would release him. This I agreed to, as telegraph instruments are of much more value to the Southern Confederacy than Yankee telegraphers. I accompanied Mr. Smith to the servant's room, and there, under the bed, in a chest, were the instruments. After Mr. Smith giving me his word of honor not to leave town for twenty-four hours, he was at liberty to visit his wife and young Smiths.

On arriving at Cynthiana, I found that the operator had "skedaddled." I tested the wires, and found no fluid from either Cincinnati or Lexington, nor were the wires in working condition when I left the next day. At Paris the operator had made a clean sweep. He left the night before, taking all his instruments. At Crab Orchard there was no office, and I put in my pocket magnet. This was at 11 A. M., and the first message I heard was the following:

LOUISVILLE, July 21.

To Col. Woolford,
Danville:

Pursue Morgan. He is at Crab Orchard, going to Somerset.

BOYLE.

No sooner had the Danville operator receipted for this, than the operator at Lebanon suggested the following:

To Lebanon Junction:

Would it not be well for Danville and offices below here to put on their ground wires, when they send or receive important messages, as George Elsworth, the rebel operator, may be on the line between here and Cumberland Gap.

LEBANON.

The operator at the Junction agreed with him, and said it would be a good idea, but it was not carried into effect.

Arrived at Somerset that morning, I took charge of the office. I ascertained from citizens that the office had been closed for three weeks up to the very hour our advance guard arrived in town, and then it was opened by the operator from London, who came to work the instrument, for the purpose of catching Morgan, but, unfortunately for Uncle Sam, the operator had no time to either send or receive a message. But I am glad to say he had it in fine working condition for me. I had been in the office some time, when Stanford called Somerset, and said, "I have just returned from Crab Orchard, where I have been to fix the line. The rebels tore it down. I left there at 8 o'clock. The 9th Pennsylvania cavalry had not then arrived. What time did you get in from London?"

STANFORD.

To Stanford:

"Just arrived, and got my office working finely."

SOMERSET.

To Somerset:

"Any signs of Morgan yet? He left Crab Orchard at 11.30 A. M. to-day.

STANFORD.

To Stanford:

"No. No signs of him as yet."

SOMERSET.

To Somerset:

"For fear they may take you by surprise, I would suggest we have a private signal. What say you?"

STANFORD.

To Stanford:

"Good. Before signing, we will make the figure 7."

SOMERSET.

This was mutually agreed upon.

I asked when would Woolford be at Somerset, and he said Woolford had telegraphed Boyle that his force was green and insufficient to attack Morgan. Seeing there was no use of my losing a night's rest, I told Sandford I would retire, and that I had made arrangements with the pickets to wake me up in case Morgan came in. The operator at Lebanon Junction urged me to sit up, but I declined on the ground of being unwell. This did not satisfy him, but after arguing with him for some time I retired.

JULY 22.

Opened office at 7 o'clock. Informed Stanford operator that Morgan had not yet arrived. Made inquiries about different things, and after every thing in town belonging to the United States government was destroyed, the general gave me the following messages to send:

SOMERSET, July 22.

To George D. Prentice,
Louisville:

Good morning, George D. I am quietly watching the complete destruction of all of Uncle Sam's property in this little burg. I regret exceedingly that this is the last that comes under my supervision on this route. I expect in a short time to pay you a visit, and wish to know if you will be at home. All well in Dixie.

JOHN H. MORGAN,
Commanding brigade.

SOMERSET, July 22.

Gen. J. T. Boyle,
Louisville:

Good morning, Jerry. This telegraph is a great institution. You should destroy it, as it keeps me too well posted. My friend Elsworth has all of your dispatches since the 10th of July on file. Do you wish copies?

JOAN H. MORGAN,
Commanding brigade.

Hon. George Dunlop,
Washington, D. C.:

Just completed my tour through Kentucky; captured 16 cities; destroyed millions of dollars worth of United States property; passed through your country, but regret not seeing you. We parolled 1,500 Federal prisoners.

Your old friend,
JOHN H. MORGAN,
Commanding brigade.

The following is an order I issued to all operators while at Georgetown:

HEAD-QUARTERS TELEGRAPH DEPARTMENT OF KENTUCKY,
CONFEDERATE STATES OF AMERICA,
GEORGETOWN *July* 16, 1862.

GENERAL ORDER, No. 1.

When an operator is positively informed that the enemy is marching on his station, he will immediately proceed to destroy the telegraph instruments and all materials in his charge. Such instances of carelessness as exhibited on the part of the operators at Lebanon, Midway, and Georgetown, will be severely dealt with.

By order of G. A. ELSWORTH,
General Military Superintendant C. S. Telegraph Department.

The above report contains but a few of the dispatches I received and sent during Gen. Morgan's late expedition through Kentucky. Those of the greatest interest and importance are respectfully submitted.

I remain, your obedient servant,
GEORGE A. ELSWORTH,
Morgan's telegrapher.

REPORT OF OPERATIONS ON THE PENINSULA.

MAJOR-GEN. J. B. MAGRUDER, COMMANDING.

HEAD-QUARTERS DEPARTMENT PENINSULA,
LEE'S FARM, May 3, 1862.

Gen. S. COOPER,
A. and I. G., C. S. A.:

GENERAL:—Deeming it of vital importance to hold Yorktown, on York river, and Mulberry Island, on James river, and to keep the enemy in check by an intervening line, until the authorities might take such steps as should be deemed necessary to meet a serious advance of the enemy in the Peninsula, I felt compelled to dispose my forces in such a manner as to accomplish these objects with the least risk possible, under the circumstances of great hazard which surrounded the little army I commanded.

I had prepared, as my real line of defence, positions in advance at Harwood's and Young's Mills. Both flanks of this line were de fended by boggy and difficult streams and swamps.

In addition, the left flank was defended by elaborate fortification at Ship Point, connected by a broken line of redoubts crossing the heads of the various ravines emptying into York river and Wormley's creek and terminating at Fort Grafton, nearly in front of Yorktown. The right flank was defended by the fortifications at the mouth of Warwick river, and at Mulberry Island Point, and the redoubts extending from the Warwick to the James river.

Intervening between the two lines was a wooded country, about two miles in extent. This wooded line, forming the centre, needed the defence of infantry in a sufficient force to prevent any attempt on the part of the enemy to break through it.

In my opinion, this advanced line, with its flank defences, might have been held by twenty thousand troops. With twenty-five thousand, I do not believe it could have been broken by any force the enemy could have brought against it. Its two flanks were protected by the "Virginia" and the works on one side, and the fortifications at Yorktown and Gloucester Point on the other.

Finding my forces too weak to attempt the defence of this line, I was compelled to prepare to receive the enemy, on a second line, on Warwick river. This line was incomplete in its preparations, owing to the fact that a thousand negro laborers, whom I had engaged in fortifying, were taken from me and discharged, by superior orders, in December last; and a delay of nine weeks consequently occurred, before I could reorganize the laborers for the engineers.

Keeping, then, only small bodies of troops at Harwood's and Young's Mills, and at Ship Point, I distributed my remaining forces along the Warwick line, embracing a front from Yorktown to Minor's farm, of twelve miles, and from the latter place to Mulberry Island Point, one and a half miles. I was compelled to place in Gloucester Point, Yorktown, and Mulberry Island, fixed garrisons, amounting to six thousand men, my whole force being eleven thousand. So that it will be seen that the balance of the line, embracing a length of thirteen miles, was defended by about five thousand men.

After the reconnoissances in great force from Fortress Monroe and Newport News, the enemy on the 3d April, advanced and took possession of Harwood's Mill. He advanced in two heavy columns, one along the Old York road, and the other along the Warwick road, and on the 5th of April, appeared simultaneously along the whole front of our line from Minor's farm to Yorktown. I have no accurate data, upon which to base an exact statement of his force, but from various sources of information, I was satisfied that I had before me the enemy's army of the Potomac, under the command of Gen. McClellan, with the exception of the two *corps d'armée* of Banks and McDowell, respectively. Forming an aggregate number of certainly not less than one hundred thousand, since ascertained to have been one hundred and twenty thousand men.

On every portion of my lines, he attacked us with a furious cannonading and musketry, which was responded to with effect, by our batteries and troops of the line. His skirmishers were also well thrown forward on this and the succeeding day, and energetically felt our whole line, but were everywhere repulsed by the steadiness of our troops. Thus, with five thousand men, exclusive of the garrisons, we stopped and held in check over one hundred thousand of the enemy. Every preparation was made in anticipation of another attack by the enemy. The men slept in the trenches and under arms, but to my utter surprise, he permitted day after day to elapse without an assault.

In a few days, the object of his delay was apparent. In every direction, in front of our lines, through the intervening woods, and along the open fields, earthworks began to appear. Through the energetic action of the government, reinforcements began to pour in, and, each hour, the army of the Peninsula grew stronger and stronger, until anxiety passed from my mind as to the result of an attack upon us.

The enemy's skirmishers pressing us closely in front of Yorktown, Brig.-gen. Early ordered a sortie to be made from the redoubts for the purpose of dislodging him from Palmentary's peach orchard. This was effected in the most gallant manner by the 2d Florida, Col. Ward, and 2d Mississippi battalion, Lieut.-col. Taylor, all under the command of Col. Ward. The quick and reckless charge of our men, by throwing the enemy into a hasty flight, enabled us to effect, with little loss, an enterprise of great hazard against a superior force, supported by artillery, when the least wavering or hesitation, on our part, would have been attended with great loss.

The Warwick line, upon which we rested, may be briefly described as follows:

Warwick river rises very near York river, and about a mile and a half to the right of Yorktown. Yorktown and redoubts Nos. 4 and 5, united by long curtains, and flanked by rifle-pits from the left of the line, until at the commencement of the military road it reaches Warwick river—here a sluggish and boggy stream, twenty or thirty yards wide, and running through a dense wood fringed by swamps.

Along this river are five dams, one at Wynne's mill, and one at Lee's mill, and three constructed by myself. The effect of these dams is to back up the water along the course of the river, so that nearly three-fourths of its distance its passage is impracticable for either artillery or infantry. Each of these dams is protected by artillery and extensive earthworks for infantry.

After eleven days of examination, the enemy seems very properly to have arrived at the conclusion that Dam No. 1, the centre of our line, was the weakest point in it, and hence on the 16th April he made what seems to have been a serious effort to break through at that point.

Early on that morning he opened, at that dam, a most furious attack of artillery, filling the woods with shells, while his sharpshooters pressed forward close to our lines.

From 9 A. M. to 12 M., six pieces were kept in constant fire against us, and by 3 P. M. nearly three batteries were directing a perfect storm of shot and shell on our exposed position. We had only three pieces in position at that point, but two of them could not be used with effect, and were rarely fired, so that we were constrained to reply with only one 6-pounder, of the Troupe Artillery, Cobb's Georgia legion, Capt. Stanley, under the particular charge of Lieut. Pope.

This piece was served with the greatest accuracy and effect, and by the coolness and skill with which it was handled, the great odds against us were almost counterbalanced.

By 3.30 P. M., the intensity of the cannonading increasing, heavy masses of infantry commenced to deploy in our front, and a heavy musketry fire was opened upon us. Under the cover of this continuous stream of fire, an effort was made by the enemy to throw forces over the stream and storm our 6-pounder battery, which was inflicting such damage upon them.

This charge was very rapid and vigorous, and before our men were prepared to receive it, several companies of a Vermont regiment succeeded in getting across and occupying the rifle-pits of the 15th N. C. volunteers, who were some hundred yards to the rear, throwing up a work for the protection of their camp.

This regiment immediately sprang to arms, and engaged the enemy with spirit, under the lead of their brave but unfortunate commander, McKinney, and, aided by the 16th Georgia regiment, repulsed the enemy; but when the gallant McKinney fell, a temporary confusion ensued, which was increased by an unauthorized order to fall back. The enemy renewed the attack with great force.

At this moment, the 7th and 8th Georgia, under command or Cols. Wilson and Lamar, respectively, the left of the 16th Georgia, under command of Col. Goode Bryan, and the two companies of Capts. Martin and Burke, of the 2d Louisiana, under Col. Norwood, accompanied by the 15th North Carolina, with fixed bayonets and the steadiness of veterans, charged the rifle-pits and drove the enemy from them with great slaughter.

Col. Anderson, commanding his brigade, and the commanding officers of the troops above mentioned, deserve great praise for the promptness with which they rushed to the conflict and repelled this serious attempt of the enemy.

Subsequently, the enemy massed heavier bodies of troops, and again approached the stream. It was evident that a most serious and energetic attack, in large force, was being made to break our centre, under, it is believed, the immediate eye of McClellan himself; but Brig.-gen. Howell Cobb, who was in command at that point, forming the 2d Louisiana, 7th and 8th Georgia, of Col. Anderson's brigade, the 15th North Carolina, 14th Georgia, and Cobb's legion in line of battle on our front, received the attack with great firmness, and the enemy recoiled, with loss, from the steady fire of our troops, before reaching the middle of the water.

Brig.-gen. McLaws, commanding the 2d division, of which Cobb's command formed a part, hearing the serious firing, hastened to the scene of action, and exhibited great coolness and judgment in his arrangements. The 10th Louisiana, 15th Virginia, a part of the 17th Mississippi, and the 11th Alabama, were ordered up as reserves, and were placed in position, the 10th Louisiana marching to its place with the accuracy of a parade drill. The other regiments were assigned positions out of the range of fire.

In addition, Gen. McLaws placed the whole of his division under arms, ready to move as circumstances might require.

Col. Anderson had led two of his regiments, the 7th and 8th Georgia, into action, and held two others in reserve, while Brig.-gen. Toombs advanced with his own brigade, under the immediate command of Brig.-gen. Semmes, close to the scene of action, and by my order (having just arrived), placed two regiments of this brigade in action, retaining the rest as reserves.

These dispositions rendered our position perfectly secure, and the enemy suffering from his two repulses, darkness put an end to the contest.

The dispositions of Gen. McLaws were skilfully made. His whole bearing and conduct is deserving of the highest commendation. I cannot designate all the many gallant officers and privates who distinguished themselves, and respectfully call the attention of the commanding general to the accompanying reports; but I would fail to do my duty, if I did not specially mention some particular instances. Brig.-gen. Cobb, commanding at this point, exhibited throughout the day the greatest courage and skill, and when once, at a critical moment, some troops in his line of battle wavered, he, in person, rallied the troops under a terrible fire, and by his voice and example, entirely re-established their steadiness.

Brig.-gen. Toombs had in the morning, by my order, detached from this division Col. Anderson's brigade, to support Brig.-gen. Cobb, and late in the evening, when ordered forward by me, promptly and energetically led the remainder of his command under fire, arriving just before the enemy ceased the vigor of his attack, and in time to share its dangers.

Brig.-gen. P. J. Semmes commanded Toombs' brigade, the latter being in command of the division, and showed his usual promptness and courage.

Col. Levy, of 2d Louisiana regiment, was the colonel commanding at Dam No. 1, and evinced judgment, courage, and high soldierly qualities, in his conduct and arrangements, which I desire specially to commend.

Capt. Stanley was in command of two pieces of artillery, including the 6-pounder, so effectively served. Both he and Lieut. Pope conducted themselves with skill and courage.

Capt. Jordan's piece was in a very exposed place, and was soon disabled after a few rounds, and was promptly withdrawn. Both he and his men exhibited great steadiness, under the terrible fire which swept over them.

The enemy's loss, of course, cannot be accurately estimated, as the greater part of it occurred over on their side of the stream, but I think it could have scarcely been less than six hundred killed and wounded.

Our loss was comparatively trivial, owing to the earthworks, which covered our men, and did not exceed seventy-five in killed and wounded.

All the reinforcements which were on their way to me had not yet joined me, so that I was unable to follow up the action of the 16th of April by any decisive step.

The reinforcements were accompanied by officers who ranked me, and I ceased to command.

I cannot too highly commend the conduct of the officers and men of my whole command, who cheerfully submitted to the greatest hardships and deprivations. From the 4th of April to the 3d of May, this army served almost without relief in the trenches.

Many companies of artillery were never relieved during this long period. It rained almost incessantly. The trenches were filled with water; the weather was exceedingly cold; no fires could be allowed; the artillery and infantry of the enemy played upon our men almost continuously day and night; the army had neither coffee, sugar, nor hard bread, but subsisted on flour and salt meat, and that in reduced quantities; and yet no murmurs were heard. Their gallant commanders of the army of the Potomac, and the Department of Norfolk, though not so long a time exposed to these sufferings, shared these hardships and dangers with equal firmness and cheerfulness. I have never seen, and I do not believe that there ever has existed, an army (the combined army of the Potomac, Peninsula, and Norfolk) which has shown itself, for so long a time, so superior to all hardships and dangers.

The best drilled regulars the world has ever seen, would have mutinied under a continued service in the trenches for twenty-nine days, exposed every moment to musketry and shells, in water to their knees, without fire, sugar, or coffee, without stimulants, and with an inadequate supply of cooked flour and salt meats. I speak of this in honor of those brave men, whose patriotism made them indifferent to suffering, to disease, to danger, and death. Indeed, the conduct of the officers and men was such as to deserve throughout the highest commendation.

I beg leave to invite the attention of the department to the reports which accompany this, and to commend the officers and men there named to the most favorable consideration of the Government.

I cannot close this report without publicly bearing testimony to the great and devoted services of the cavalry of the Peninsula, so long under my command, always in the presence of superior forces of the enemy. I owe much of the success, which attended my efforts to keep them within the walls of their fortresses, to the alacrity, daring, vigilance, and constancy of the 3d Virginia cavalry, and the independent companies from James City, Matthews, Gloucester, and King and Queen counties.

The services rendered by the officers of my staff have been invaluable. To these I owe my acknowledgments: Capts. Brayn and Dickinson, of the adjutant-general's department; Majors Magruder and Brent, of the commissary and ordnance departments respectively; Capt. White, acting chief quarter-master; Col. Cabell, chief of artillery; Lieut.-col. Cary, acting inspector-general; Lieut. Douglas, of the engineers; Lieuts. Eustis and Alston, aids-de-camp; Dr. George W. Milden, acting staff officer; Mr. J. R. Bryan, Mr. H. M. Stanard, Mr. D. T. Brashear, and Mr. Henry A. Doyce, who, as volunteer aids, have rendered most important services, and to private E. P. Turner, of the New Kent cavalry, on duty sometimes in the field, at others in the assistant adjutant-general's office.

My thanks are due to Lieut.-col. Ball, of the Virginia cavalry, who for several weeks during the siege acted as a volunteer aid. His conduct on the 5th, in my immediate presence, and under a severe fire of the enemy, was very gallant, and worthy of the high reputation which he won at Manassas.

I am also greatly indebted to Major George Neay, of the 115th Virginia militia, who has aided me in the administration, civil as well as military, of the affairs of the Peninsula, and to Lieuts. Joseph Phillips and Causey, of the Confederate army. The local knowledge of these officers has been of great advantage to the service, whilst their intrepidity and enterprise have been in the highest degree conspicuous on every occasion.

I cannot express too strongly my estimate of the services rendered by my chief quarter-master, Major Bloomfield. Soon after he took charge, he introduced order, promptness, and economy, in the management of his department.

The scarcity of supplies and materials was so great as to make it almost impossible to procure them.

The genius, energy, and extraordinary industry of Major Bloomfield, however, overcame all obstacles, and enabled the army of the Peninsula to move, to march, and to fight, with the regularity of a machine.

This statement is made in justice to Major Bloomfield, who is absent, on account of sickness, at the time that I write.

I ask the attention, also, of the Government to the valuable services rendered by Mr. Wm. Morris, of Baltimore, the signal officer, in charge of the signal service of the Peninsula, and to those of his efficient assistant, Lieut. Lindsay, of the 15th Virginia regiment.

It is but just to Col. Charles A. Crump, that I should bear testimony to the zeal, gallantry, and decided ability with which he performed the various duties of commander of the post at Gloucester Point, during the year in which he was under my command. He was worthily supported, on all occasions, by Lieut.-col. P. R. Page, and the other officers and men constituting his force.

That accomplished officer, Capt. Thomas Jefferson Page, of the navy, successfully applied the resources of his genius and ripe experience to the defence of Gloucester Point, whilst the important work opposite was commanded with devoted zeal and gallantry by Brig.-gen. Rains.

My thanks are due to Capt. Chatard, of the navy, for valuable services as inspector of batteries, and to Lieut.-col. Noland, late of the navy, the efficient commander of the batteries at Mulberry Island Point.

That patriotic and scientific soldier, Col. B. S. Ewell, rendered important services to the country during my occupation of the Peninsula, as did Col. Hill Carter, the commander at Jamestown, and his successor, Major J. R. C. Lewis.

I should fail in my duty to the country, and especially to the State of Virginia, if I neglected to record the self-sacrificing conduct of Capt. Wm. Allen, of the artillery.

At the very commencement of the war, this gentleman erected, at his own expense, on Jamestown Island, extensive fortifications for the defence of the river, and from that time until he was driven from his home, he continued to apply the resources of his large estate to the benefit of his country. And so great and disinterested were his zeal and devotion as an officer, that he lost almost the whole of his immense possessions in endeavoring to remove the public property committed to his charge, and that of the commanding officers. I cannot commend his conduct as an officer too highly to the government, nor his patriotism as a citizen too warmly to the love and respect of his countrymen.

To Capt. Rives, Capt. St. John, Capt. Clark, and Capt. Dimmock of the Engineers, and their able assistants, the country is greatly indebted for the formidable works which enabled me to meet and repulse with a very small force the attack of an army of over one hundred thousand well-drilled men, commanded by the best officers in the service of the enemy.

The steadiness and heroism of the officers and men of the artillery of the Peninsula, both heavy and light, were very conspicuous during the attack on the 5th April, and throughout the siege which followed. The high state of efficiency of this arm of the service was mainly due to Col. George W. Randolph, chief of artillery on my staff, who applied to its organization, discipline, and preparation for the field, the resources of his great genius and experience.

To this intrepid officer and distinguished citizen, the country is indebted for the most valuable services, from the battle of Bethel, where his artillery principally contributed to the success of the day, to the period when he was removed from my command by promotion. He was ably assisted by Lieut.-cols. Cabell and Brown, of the same corps. The medical officers deserve the highest commendation for the skill and devotion with which they performed their duty in this sickly country.

To Capt. Ben Harrison, and Lieut. Hill Carter, Jr., and their admirable troop, the Charles City cavalry, I am also indebted for meritorious services under my own eye on numerous occasions.

I have the honor to be,
Very respectfully,
Your obedient servant.
J. BANKHEAD MAGRUDER,
Major-general.

Report of Brig.-gen. McLaws, commanding Division.

HEAD-QUARTERS 2D DIVISION,
RIGHT FLANK LEE'S FARM, April 30, 1862.

To Capt. A. G. DICKINSON,
Assistant Adjutant-general:

On the 16th inst., between 2 and 3 P. M., my attention was attracted by an increase in the intensity of fire which had been heard during the morning from the direction of Dam No. 1. Thinking that perhaps a real attack was intended at that point, I ordered forward the 10th Louisiana, 15th Virginia, and four companies of the 17th Mississippi, and rode towards the dam, ordering up on my way the 11th Alabama, also, to act as reserve to Dam No. 2, and directed my whole command, artillery, infantry, and dragoons, to be under arms, and ready to obey any order at once. I then joined Gen. Cobb. The firing at this time, from both cannon and small arms, was very heavy and constant, convincing me that the attack was intended as a real one, and I became exceedingly anxious for the reserves to come forward, for Gen. Kershaw's brigade, of the 3d, 4th, 7th, and 8th S. C., were in position some four and a half miles on my right, down the Peninsula, and should the line be broken at this point of attack by a large body of the enemy, that position would be a critical one, and Lee's farm have to be abandoned, unless a considerable force of our troops were on hand to oppose them. I heard from Gen. Cobb that Gen. G. T. Anderson's brigade had been ordered to his support by Gen. Magruder, and sent off by Lieut. Stanard, who offered his services to bring it forward, and sent others to hasten those regiments I had previously ordered up.

A body of the enemy succeeded in crossing the pond below the dam, and were in our lower rifle-pits. Col. McKinney, of the 15th North Carolina, was killed while gallantly leading his regiment to repuls ethem. His death, and the sudden dash of the enemy, created some confusion, which was, however, promptly corrected by Gen. Cobb, who, riding in among the men, they recognized his voice and person, and promptly retook their positions. Col. Anderson's brigade, at this time came forward most opportunely, and the 7th Georgia, Col. Wilson, followed by the 8th, Col. L. M. Lamar, charging the enemy with the bayonet, and assisted by the 5th Louisiana and others, drove them back across the pond, killing a large number. A few minutes after this, one of the artillery pieces was reported as disabled, and I ordered up a section of Capt. Palmer's battery, which was in reserve on Lee's farm, and Capt. Thos. Jeff. Page, of the Magruder Light Artillery, being near me, offered his battery, and I directed him to bring it. Soon after this, the regiments I had ordered forward came rapidly up. The 10th Louisiana, Col. Marigny, was ordered to the main point of attack, and the others halted within a few hundred yards. Capt. Page's and Capt. Palmer's batteries came dashing forward at full speed, and I felt my position secure. The firing ceased as night came on, and the assault was not renewed.

I refer you to the reports of Gen. Cobb, and of Cols. Levy, Bryan, T. R. R. Cobb, Lamar, and Wilson, and of Capt. Stanley, of the Troupe Artillery, Cobb's legion, accompanying this, for further particulars, and for their notice of individual merit. In the death of Col. McKinney, the service has lost one who was pure in all his thoughts and just in all his acts. A brave and skilful officer, who, in his death, as in his life, reflected honor upon both his native and his adopted State, and illustrated the Christian gentleman.

Major James M. Goggin, A. A. and Inspector-general, Major A. H. McLaws, Dr. Master, Capt. McIntosh, A. A.-general, and Lieut Tucker, aid-de-camp, were with me, and were of signal service.

Very respectfully, T. McLAWS,

Brigadier-general commanding.

Report of Colonel William M. Levy.

CAMP OF 2ND LOUISIANA REGIMENT VOLS.,
DAM NO. 1, April 18th, 1862.

To Capt. JAMES BANN,
Assistant Adjutant-general Brigade:

SIR:—On the 16th instant, at about 8 o'clock A. M., the enemy appeared in considerable force in the woods, and rear portion of Gannon's field, opposite the position occupied by the 2d Louisiana regiment. In a few minutes, two pieces of artillery were put in position, and opened a fire of shell upon us. This was briskly replied to by the 6-pounder field-piece of the Troupe artillery, belonging to Col. Cobb's Georgia Legion, and by a few shots from the 12-pounder howitzer (Capt. Jordan's battery). During the morning, and up to about 3 o'clock, sharp artillery firing was kept up on both sides, and the infantry were engaged in skirmishing at pretty long range.

A little after 3 o'clock, the enemy brought up more artillery, and displayed 6 pieces (2 rifled Parrot) and opened a furious cannonade, which they kept up with scarcely the slightest intermission for three hours. While showering their shell upon us, a bold rush was made across the river, or creek, by a considerable body of the enemy's infantry, who suddenly dashed through the water, and, under cover of the woods, reached the rifle-pits, in front of the position of the 15th North Carolina regiment. This regiment, with the exception of its picket, was at work intrenching its camp; and while leading his men to charge the enemy, Col. McKinney fell and died instantly, gallantly pressing forward at the head of his command. The unfortunate death of Col. McKinney threw the 15th into momentary confusion, and the enemy was then at the rifle-pits, and about to cross them. At this time, companies B, (Capt. A. H. Martin), and D, (Capt. R. E. Burke), of the 2d Louisiana regiment, under the direction of Major Norwood, of that regiment, threw themselves from their position at the redoubt and curtain at the crest of the hill, and attacked the enemy along the left of the rifle-pits, while the 7th Georgia vigorously attacked them along the rest of the line, and the 8th Georgia came up on the right of the 7th Georgia. Company I, (Capt. Flournoy,) and company K, (Capt Kelso,) 2d Louisiana regiment, stationed at the lower redoubt (near Dam No. 1), opened fire upon the enemy from their position, at the redoubt. The rapid and vigorous attack of our troops at once checked the enemy, and in a few minutes they precipitately retreated, recrossed the creek, and sought shelter from the havoc which pursued them, under cover of their field-pieces.

Shortly afterwards, the movements of the enemy showed that, with a larger force, they intended to renew their effort to break our lines; and, with a largely increased force, they again attempted to cross, but were speedily repulsed, retreating in disorder. I have no means of ascertaining the number of killed and wounded on the part of the enemy, but from the bodies left on this side, and the removal, from the field on the other side, of bodies, I am certain it must have amounted to at least two hundred.

I cannot refrain from mentioning, that as falling under my immediate observation, while the conduct of all our troops was most satisfactory, the 7th Georgia regiment, the section of the Troupe Artillery, (Capt. Stanley), and the companies of the 2d Louisiana regiment, which I have enumerated, manifested the most praiseworthy alacrity and intrepidity.

After this second repulse, the enemy retired their infantry from the field, and night coming on, the contest ceased, leaving us in full possession of our position, from which we had not moved except to drive back and pursue the enemy, and in the enjoyment of the pleasing knowledge that we had repulsed a foe largely exceeding us in numbers.

I have the honor to remain, sir,
Very respectfully,
Your obedient servant,
WM. M. LEVY,
Col. comd'g 2d La. regiment and Dam No. 1.

Report of Col. Goode Bryan.

BIVOUAC SALLIE FERIGG'S,
16TH GEORGIA REG'T,
April 19, 1862.

Capt. JOHN A. COBB,
A. A.-general:

SIR:—I have the honor to report that on the morning of the 16th, under orders from head-quarters 2d brigade, company D, (Capt. Montgomery,) of this regiment, was sent to rifle-pits of 15th

North Carolina regiment to act as sharpshooters, and protect a working party of that regiment. About half past three o'clock, heavy firing being heard in that direction, the 16th Georgia regiment advanced and took position in the trenches, on the right of the battery opposite Dam No. 1, at which point a considerable force of the enemy had crossed and occupied our rifle-pits. They were soon driven back across this by the 15th North Carolina, 7th Georgia, and a portion of the 16th Georgia regiments, stationed near the dam. A heavy fire was kept up by the North Carolina 7th and 16th Georgia regiments until dark, at which time the enemy retired. I cannot close this report without an expression of great gratification in the coolness and gallantry displayed by both officers and men of my command during the engagement, and particular mention should be made of Capt. Montgomery, of company D. Being down from the rifle-pits with only three of his men (the others being deployed as skirmishers), he gave warning to the 15th North Carolina of the advance of the enemy, and joining that regiment with the few men of his company that could be collected, charged with that command and drove the enemy from their pits.

I am, sir, your obedient servant,

GOODE BRYAN,

Col. 16th Georgia regiment.

Report of Lieut.-col. Ihue.

HEAD-QUARTERS 15TH REG'T N. C. V.,
NEAR LEE'S FARM,
April 19, 1862.

JOHN A. COBB,
A. A.-general:

I hereby transmit a report of the action of the 15th North Carolina volunteers, in the engagement of the 16th instant, near Dam No. 1, on Warwick creek.

On the morning of the 16th, cannonading along the line towards Wynn's Mill, and also some of the enemy's guns being brought to bear upon our batteries at Dam No. 1, and as the day progressed other indications of an attack by the enemy upon our line, induced Col. McKinney to call the regiment into line on the military road running in front of where the regiment was lying.

About 10 o'clock A. M., calling in a working party of a hundred men, and keeping the regiment in this state of readiness for two hours or more, he ordered the arms stacked, and had the whole regiment detailed for work upon a heavy intrenchment, which he had been ordered to have erected in front of the encampment, and about two hundred yards in the rear of the rifle-pits skirting the water thrown back by Dam No. 1, making arrangements for carrying on the work the whole of the ensuing night. Our pickets were in front of the rifle-pits, close along the water's edge. From the best information I have, at the point where the enemy charged, the depth of the water was about four feet, and its width from one hundred and fifty to two hundred yards, and covered with heavy timber and thick undergrowth.

About three o'clock P. M., the regiment being engaged upon the works alluded to, the pickets gave the alarm that the enemy were charging rapidly across the water and making to our rifle-pits. The regiment was immediately thrown in line of battle, and being ordered by Col. McKinney, advanced at a double-quick and with a yell upon the enemy, who had taken partial shelter behind the earth thrown from our pits before the regiment could reach them, and opened a terrible fire upon us as we advanced. Their fire was returned with promptness and with deadly effect upon the enemy. Volley after volley in rapid succession immediately followed from both sides, amidst which Col. McKinney gallantly fell, in the early part of the engagement, shot through the forehead. He fell near the centre of the line, and his death was not known to either officers or men for some time after it occurred, and a deadly fire was kept up by both sides till about five o'clock P. M.

Not knowing the strength of the enemy at the commencement of the engagement, Col. McKinney dispatched an orderly to Brig.-gen. Cobb for reinforcements, and after having been engaged in close conflict, the enemy having given way on our right, the 7th Georgia regiment, under Col. Wilson, came to our assistance, and at this moment the enemy gave way in precipitate retreat, and did not again rally at any point on our line.

The regiment had about five hundred men engaged. I have no means of definitely ascertaining the force of the enemy, but it must have been superior to ours. Prisoners report that they belonged to the 3d Vermont regiment, commanded by Col. Hyde. We captured eight of them. The number of killed of the enemy, in front of where the regiment was engaged, has been ascertained to be thirty. How many fell in the water is not known. Our loss in killed is as follows:

Col. R. M. McKinney.

Privates Wm. Yandles, of company B, Joseph Tonery and Wm Finch, of company D, and Francis Gilbert, of company F; sergeant H. M. Clendenin, and privates Elmsley Steel and Hardy Wood, of company H, private J. H. Parker, of company I, private Wm. Boon, of company K, and privates J. S. Foushee and M. H. Bennett, of company K, making in all twelve men.

The wounded are as follows:

Capt. Samuel T. Stancell, of company A, sergeant A. V. Helms, mortally; corporal B. G. Coon, and privates Thomas Mills, (since dead,) Francis Cuthberston, W. C. Wolf and F. R. Barcman, of company B; private Joseph Downs, (since dead,) of company D; private John Sherrod, of company E; privates Wm. A. Avera and Jno. McDonald, and Francis Morrison, of company F; private Samuel D. Gordon, of company G; privates W. G. C. Bradshaw, C. C. McMurrey, John T. Ray, W. H. Guthrie and Fred. R. Marze, of company H; private R. S. Green, of company I; 2d Lieut. J. J. Reid, sergeants R. W. Thomas, S. H. Griffin, and J. B. Armstrong; corporals John Dillard and W. Thompson, (since dead); privates S. R. Hilliard, J. W. T. Melton, J. W. Bates and J. H. Freeman, of company K; 2d. Lieut. J. L. Merritt, and private S. M. Riggshee, of company K, making in all thirty-one.

I regret that I cannot make a more detailed report of the engagement and its incidents, under present circumstances.

Too much cannot be said in commendation of the gallant bearing of both officers and men, under a terrific fire of musketry for the space of two hours, and the fate of the gallant dead call the living to other deeds of daring for their country's cause.

It is with peculiarly deep feelings of regret that I report the death of Col. Robert M. McKinney, a conscientious, brave, just and skilful officer, and a Christian gentleman.

Your obedient servant,

P. R. IHUE,

Lieut.-col. commanding.

To Brig.-gen. Howell Cobb,

Commanding 2d Brigade, 2d Division.

H. A. Dowd, *Adj't.*

Report of Colonel H. C. Cabell.

MAY 10, 1862.

To Major-gen. J. B. MAGRUDER,

GENERAL: I have the honor to submit the following report of the artillery under my command, from the 5th of April, till the evacuation of the Peninsula. Our line of defence consisted of the fortifications at Yorktown, the redoubts, Nos. 4 and 5, near Yorktown, and the line of the head waters of Warwick river, and the Warwick river itself. The narrow Peninsula, formed by the junction of the Warwick and the James rivers, was abandoned up to a point about five miles from the mouth of Warwick river, and at this point, called Minor's farm, a series of redoubts, extending from the right bank of this river, nearly to Mulberry Island fort, were constructed to check any assault of the enemy upon our right flank, coming up by the way of Land's End. The Warwick river had also obstructions placed in it to prevent the approach of the enemy's gunboats up this river, and we were further protected by our gunboat Teazer, which was placed near the mouth of the Warwick. From the topography of the ground it was absolutely necessary to occupy the whole of this line in the then condition of our forces. Our forces were so few in number that it was essential to the safety of the command that the whole should be defended, as the breaking of our lines at any point would necessarily have been attended by the most disastrous results; the centre broken or our flank turned, compelling a precipitate retreat to Yorktown or Mulberry Island, to stand a siege of the enemy's land force, assisted by the whole naval force, with but little prospect of relief or reinforcements, when the enemy occupied the intermediate country. The left bank of the York river was protected by the fortifications at Gloucester point. The force of infantry was very small. The cavalry consisted of one and a half regiments. The artillery force was very large. Heavy guns were mounted at Gloucester point, at Yorktown, at redoubt No. 4, and at Mulberry Island. From deserters, prisoners, and other sources, we were convinced that the enemy was advancing in very large force. He had been collecting his troops and munitions of war for several weeks, and it was certain that he would commence his march with a vastly superior force. Our advanced regiments retired before the enemy, according to orders, and took their positions upon and in rear of the Warwick river line, in perfect order. Reinforcements had been promised us from Richmond, and the determination of the commanding general to defend the position against assault met the cordial approval and co-operation of the army of the Peninsula. Three roads led up from the Peninsula and crossed the line of our defences. The first on our right was the Warwick road, that crossed at Lee's mill. The second crossed at Wynne's mill, and the third was commanded by the redoubts, Nos. 4 and 5, near Yorktown. The crossing at Lee's mill was naturally strong, and fortifications had been erected there and at Wynne's mill. Below Lee's mill the Warwick river, affected by the tides and assisted by swamps on each side, formed a tolerable protection, but the marshes could easily be made passable and the river bridged. Between Lee's mill and Wynne's mill, an unbroken forest extended on the right bank of the stream, a distance of about three miles. Two additional dams were constructed, the one, dam No. 1, nearest to Wynne's mill, the outer, dam No. 2.

A dam, called the upper dam, was constructed in the stream above Wynne's mill. This detailed description of the line of defence seems necessary to explain the positions of the artillery of the Peninsula. The whole force of artillery were placed in position. Capt. Young's battery and a portion of Major ——— battery, occupied Minor's farm. A 12-pounder of Capt. Cosnihan's and a Parrott piece of Capt. Sands', under the command of Lieut. Ritter, were placed in the extreme right redoubt at Lee's mill, the battery under the charge of Capt. Cosnihan. Capt. Sands' three pieces, and Capt. Garrett's and Read's battery, each consisting of three pieces, occupied the remaining positions at Lee's mill. One gun of Capt. Nelson's battery, under the command of Lieut. Nelson, was placed at dam No. 1. (The Donaldsonville battery) 6 pieces, Capt. Moran, Capt. Macon's battery (the Fayette artillery), 6 pieces, three pieces of the Howitzers, Capt. Herdnall, and a portion of Capt. Southall's battery, were stationed at Wynne's mill. A piece of Capt. Herdnall's, and a piece of Capt. Southall's artillery were placed at the upper dam. Capts. Smith's, Armistead's, Richardson's, and Page's, and the remaining pieces of Capt. Nelson's and Southall's batteries, occupied positions at redoubts Nos. 4 and 5, the curtain connecting these reboubts, Yorktown, and the intermediate positions. The enemy came up and opened fire upon the morning of the 5th of April. From that time till our evacuation of the Peninsula, the firing was continued with slight intermissions. I have been thus particular in noticing the batteries in position on the 5th of April, because I think it due to all who first stare the advance of the enemy, in force at least seven times greater than ours, and confident in superior numbers, should have a place in this report. It is a tribute due to their courage, firmness, and patriotic purpose to defend our position to the last, no matter in what superior numbers he should come. The defence was gallantly and most successfully made, and our pieces all along the line from Minor's farm to Yorktown were fired at the enemy. My duties called me along the whole lines, and I can bear willing testimony to the bravery of the infantry and cavalry, all of whom were acting as skirmishers along the line. Wherever the enemy appeared, and they appeared all along the lines, our muskets and artillery opened upon them. The enemy after a few days seemed to change their purpose of breaking our lines by assault, and commenced to erect batteries in front of our lines. They seemed determined to forego the gallant charge and resort to the spade and their rifled guns, under the cover of intrenchments, to dislodge us from our position. No other course afforded a more ennobling tribute to our small force, or a more damaging slur upon the boasted arrogance of the enemy. On the 16th of April, Gen. McClellan laid aside his "ill-timed prudence," and ventured an assault at dam No. 1, one of the weakest positions on our line. It was of great danger and consummate importance to us. A small clearing in the woods had been made on the one side, opening upon a large field upon the other. The cleared space did not permit us to employ but few guns at this position.

The enemy had erected three batteries, and opened upon us with a converging fire of sixteen guns. A 24-pounder howitzer of Capt. Enders' battery occupied the front and most exposed position, immediately at Dam No. 1. Two pieces of the Troupe artillery, (Capt. Stanley,) occupied positions at the left and right redoubts about two hundred yards to the rear upon rising ground. The enemy made an assault in force upon this position and attempted to cross. I refer to the reports of Capt. Stanley and Capt. Jordan for a detailed account of their conduct in the fight. The charge was signally repulsed by our infantry. Our artillery did all that could be done in sustaining our infantry force and dispersing the enemy. It gives me great pleasure to bear tribute to the alacrity with which Capt. Page and Capt. Palmer hurried up to this position when sent for by me. It was a critical point in the engagement, but by the daring assaults of our infantry, the enemy were quickly dispersed, before their guns could be brought up. After this signal repulse no further assault was made on our lines. But the fire of the enemy was incessant from artillery and musketry. During this time our artillery had to be changed frequently at Dam No. 1.

This position was occupied by four pieces of Capt. Rosser's battery, Capt. Richardson's battery, a section of Capt. Palmer's howitzers, and a section of Capt. Rogers' battery, at the redoubt to the right of Dam No. 1. The positions of the artillery had also to be shifted at other points. All these movements were made at night, necessarily.

I was much indebted to Lieut.-col. Brown for his disposition of the batteries of the left flank. His report will give a more detailed account of these batteries, as my supervision over them ceased upon the arrival of Gen. Pendleton, chief of artillery, on Gen. Johnson's staff, and was confined necessarily to the command of Major-gen. Magruder. Up to that time I witnessed the courage and skill they displayed. Capt. Stanard's battery arrived and was placed in position below Lee's mill on the 8th of April, Capt. Kemper's battery arrived a few days after, and was also put in position.

From the 5th April to the of , many of our batteries were not once relieved. Until reserves came, relief was impossible, yet officers and men exhibited as much perseverance and ability to bear exposure and labor without murmur, as they did courage in resisting the enemy. Our defences, which were as strong as they could be made by the limited force at your command, were necessarily extremely imperfect, and much work had to be done after the enemy was upon us. But our men held their positions, while our works were being perfected, and until a sufficient force arrived to make us secure.

The God of battles, that ever sides with a just cause, and a wise disposition of our forces, and courage and discipline of our army, has insured us one of the most gallant defences against apparently overwhelming numbers, that history gives any record of.

The fidelity and promptness with which my orderlies, Wm. O. Duke, of the Richmond Fayette artillery, and , of the Charles City troop, conveyed my orders, deserve attention.

I cannot close this report without calling attention to the batteries of light and heavy artillery in the several garrisons of Gloucester Point, Yorktown, and Mulberry Island. The very small force constituting the army of the Peninsula, on the fifth of April, required the withdrawal of the whole infantry and cavalry force from Gloucester Point, to move the line of defence between the York and James rivers. The heavy artillery was thus left without any support for several days, and most nobly and efficiently did they maintain their position. When the line of defence was contracted, Mulberry Island was thrown out of the lines of defence several miles, to stand, if necessary, a siege. Capt. Garrett's and Young's batteries were withdrawn to this fort, thus isolated. The efficiency and skill of the cannoniers at Yorktown were attested during the whole defence. The firing was continued until 2 o'clock at night, the night of the evacuation, by which time many of our troops had arrived at Williamsburg. The skill and efficiency of our cannoniers was not only attested by my own observation, but by the accounts that have been published in the Northern papers. I ascribe their superior efficiency to the entire calmness and courage of our cannoniers, and their superior intelligence. They have had but little opportunity for practising, though they have been taught the principles and science of firing. Their entire self-possession, united with courage, intelligence, and patriotic zeal, enabled them to practice the best rule for firing, "fire with deliberate promptness," and ensure their success.

I beg leave particularly to call attention to the efficiency of Lieut. Wm. B. Jones, who acted most efficiently as my adjutant during the greater portion of the defence, and of my adjutant Richard M. Venable, who relieved him from duty to enable Lieut. Jones to return to his company, all the other officers having become incapacitated from service by arduous and constant exposure at the batteries. I deeply regret to have to state that one of these officers, Lieut. Shields, a gallant and chivalrous spirit, who had distinguished himself in action, has since died.

Very respectfully,

H. C. CABELL,

Col. 1st regiment artillery, and Chief of Artillery.

Report of Capt. M. Stanley.

To Col. T. R. R. COBB,

Commanding Georgia Legion:

COLONEL: I have the honor to report as follows, in reference to the part taken by the battery under my command (Troupe Artillery), in the engagement of the 16th instant, at Dam No. 1. I had but two of my pieces in position at that point, and a 6-pounder army howitzer, under Lieut. Lumpkin. The former was on the right, in an earthwork of but little strength, and the latter in an earthwork somewhat stronger, on the left. Both works are unfortunately placed, being in too low a position to command the field on the opposite side of the dam. Beside my own piece one other was there—a 24-pounder iron howitzer, belonging to Capt. Jordan's battery—placed behind the work just at the dam, and in a position to command scarcely more than the dam itself. Our horses, in charge of their drivers, were placed in a bottom to the right and rear of our position. Our 12-pound howitzer took no part in the engagement, because the direction of the enemy was such that it could not be fired without endangering the lives of our own men in the intrenchments at the dam. In front of the dam, on the opposite side from us, is a broad field in which the ground rises gradually from the water's edge to the crest of a hill, 600 or 700 yards distant, and then slopes up gradually to the woods beyond. This conformation gave the enemy an admirable position in which to place his artillery, and it indicates how unfortunate for us is the position of our works, and of the dam itself. At about 9 o'clock A. M. on the 16th instant, the enemy brought up, under cover of the hill, a battery of six pieces, and placed them just beyond the crest, so as to fire, and yet be, to a large extent, protected. Judging from the balls thrown, of which a large number have been gathered up, the most of their guns were rifled. There were, however, some 12-pounder round shell, and 12-pounder round shot, indicating a smooth bore.

Against this formidable array, the only piece which could be used with any effect, or without endangering the lives of our men near the dam, was the smooth-bore 6-pounder, under Lieut. Pope. For several hours did this piece maintain the unequal conflict. Capt. Jordan's piece fired a few rounds, but, from its disadvantageous position, could not command the enemy's position, and therefore exhibited sound judgment in not prolonging its fire.

A little before noon there was a mutual cessation of the fire. Soon after dinner the conflict was renewed. An attempt was made by the enemy's infantry to carry our rifle-pits by fording the stream in the woods, some distance below the dam; and during this assault the fire of their artillery upon our works was terrific. The whole atmosphere was filled with the exploding shell and shrapnel. As before, the piece under Lieut. Pope replied steadily and effectively, and not until the cannoniers were exhausted did the firing on our side cease. It was after night when the conflict closed.

Though several of my men were struck with fragments of shell and spent minié balls, and though our works were repeatedly penetrated by the enemy's shot, not one behind the works was seriously injured.

One of our drivers, W. P. Meeler, a brave and faithful young man, who was with the horses, had his right leg shot off below the knee by a cannon ball. Seven of our horses were killed in the fight; five of them by minié balls in the engagement of the infantry. That the casualties among my men were so few, I ascribe to the merciful providence of Almighty God.

The men, with hardly an exception, exhibited great coolness and courage.

Although the howitzer detachment took no active part in the conflict, their position was exposed to a very fierce fire.

I mention, with special commendation, Lieut. A. F. Pope, gunner J. F. Dillard, and private J. C. Strickland.

The following, also, are worthy of particular notice:—Sergeant R. K. Pridgeon and privates A. C. Sorrell and George B. Atkinson.

In conclusion, I would suggest that our position at Dam No. 1 is very inferior to that of the enemy, and that in view of his powerful and numerous artillery, special attention be given to that point.

I have the honor to be,
Very respectfully,
Your obedient servant,
M. STANLEY,
Captain, commanding Troupe Artillery, Georgia Legion.

REPORT OF EXPEDITION TO PINCKNEY ISLAND.

J. C. Pemberton, Major-gen. Commanding.

Head-quarters Department S. C. and Ga.,
Charleston, Aug. 27th, 1862.

To Gen. S. Cooper,
Adjutant and Inspector-general, C. S. A.:

General:—I have the honor to forward the inclosed reports of Col. W. S. Walker and Capt. Stephen Elliott, Beaufort Light Artillery, of an expedition against the enemy, stationed on Pinckney Island. In forwarding these reports, I would respectfully call your attention to the gallant and good conduct of Capts. Stephen Elliott and Mickler, who conducted the expedition with complete success to our arms.

I am, general, very respectfully.
J. C. PEMBERTON,
Major-gen. commanding Dep't S. C. and Ga.

Report of Col. W. S. Walker.

HEAD-QUARTERS 3D MILITARY DISTRICT,
MCPHERSONVILLE, Aug. 22d.

To Major J. R. WADDY,
A. A.-general,
Department S. C. and Ga.:

MAJOR:—I have the honor to report that, from the reconnoissance of Lieut.-col. Colcoch, of the 2d battalion cavalry, and Capt. J. M. Mickler, 11th infantry, and the information obtained from three deserters, I was persuaded that a force of the enemy, stationed on the northeastern point of Pinckney Island, and believed not to exceed one hundred men, could be surprised and captured. For this purpose, I ordered Capt. Stephen Elliott, of the Beaufort Artillery, with Capt. J. H. Mickler, 11th infantry, to organize a boat expedition.

I refer you to the inclosed report of Capt. Elliott for a clear and unreserved statement of his operations.

For a due understanding of the hazardous nature of the undertaking, it is necessary to state, that a gunboat cruises in that immediate neighborhood, and her masts were seen through the trees from the enemy's encampment. There was not only the danger attending an attack upon an enemy nearly equal in force, but the still greater risk of being intercepted by the powerful batteries of a war steamer. The conception of the expedition required daring and great rapidity of execution. A prolonged contest, even if successful, would have been fatal in its results. I knew that the high qualities of the leaders and their men would secure the prompt execution, and the result has amply justified my confidence.

While great credit is due to every officer and man engaged, I must specially mention the conspicuous services of Capts. Elliott and Mickler.

My position, in front of an enemy occupying islands, and commanding their approach with powerful war steamers, as well as the character of my force, consisting mainly of cavalry, armed with shot guns, has disabled me from undertaking any large operations against the enemy. I believe, however, I have succeeded in impressing him with an exaggerated estimate of my force, by means of repeated attacks upon his pickets at various points, which would seem to indicate the confidence and audacity of a strong and threatening force.

I have been indebted to Capt. Stephen Elliott, who is a sailor as well as a soldier, for the organization, and largely for the execution of these affairs. With great zeal and enterprise, he has contributed a sagacity and prudence which have invariably secured success.

His officers and men have proved worthy of their commander. They have borne exposure, fatigue, and hunger, with unshrinking courage and alacrity.

Capt. Mickler has but recently been under my command, but, in that short time, his boldness as a scout and his gallantry as a leader have sustained his well-earned reputation.

I would commend all the officers and men engaged in the expedition to the most favorable notice of the general commanding.

I inclose a copy of the only order of special interest among those captured. I will send the prisoners to Charleston as soon as I have examined them.

I have the honor to be, very respectfully,
Your obedient servant,
W. S. WALKER,
Colonel commanding.

Report of Captain Stephen Elliott.

McPHERSONVILLE, S. C., August 22, 1862.

Lieut. E. H. BARNWELL,
A. A.-general, 3d Military District, Department S. C.:

SIR:—I have the honor to submit the following report of an expedition to Pinckney Island, organized in pursuance to orders from District head-quarters:

On the 18th, in company with Capt. Mickler, I made a careful reconnoissance of the island, and formed my plan of attack. I extended orders to Capt. Mickler to transport four boats from Horton's to Bear Island, and to join me there on the evening of the

21st, with one hundred men. I also directed that fifty men of the Beaufort artillery, with muskets, and a four-pounder boat gun, should meet me at Boyd's Landing on the 19th, in order to take six boats to Foot Point and Bear Island, by the way of Broad river. The dispositions were successfully accomplished within the required time.

On the 21st, at 3 A. M., I left Bear Island with detachments of Capts. Mickler's, Leadbetter's, and Westcoat's companies, under the commands of their captains, and of the Beaufort artillery, under Lieut. Stuart, amounting in all to one hundred and twenty men (120), thirty-six (36) of whom acted as oarsmen, and remained in the boats—nine in number.

Passing down a creek two miles in length, I landed, at early dawn, on Pinckney Island, three hundred (300) yards in rear of the dwelling-house, which is situated at the apex of an angle, whose sides include about forty (40) degrees. Deploying rapidly across the base, I moved forward toward the point, over ground on one side open and on the other covered by a dense thicket, up to the camp of company H., 3d regiment New Hampshire volunteers, surprising them, killing, according to the most careful estimate, fifteen, and capturing thirty-six, four of whom were wounded. Six were seen to escape, and five are known to have been absent. These, with the previous numbers named, give sixty-two (62), the number on their morning report book. The Lieutenant in command, the only officer present, either escaped or was killed. There is good reason to believe the latter.

To avoid delay in so exposed a position, I forbade the men to touch an article, and we returned, bringing off the company records and two fine boats, having remained on the island fifteen minutes.

Eight of my men were wounded, six of them, I regret to say, by their own men. This is the more provoking, as I earnestly and repeatedly warned both officers and men against this very danger. Some palliation may exist in the fact that some of the men were engaged for the first time, that the disaster sprung from an excess of zeal and courage, and that there was not light enough to distinguish persons at any distance. The mixture of small detachments too, at all times an element of confusion, is especially so in surprises at night, when the necessity of silence demands the most rigid discipline and uniformity of action.

I take pleasure in saying that the whole command acted with great spirit and determination. It is a just tribute to a gallant officer to say that Capt. Mickler, by his ceaseless energy and labor for days and nights previously, as well as by his valuable suggestions, contributed in no small degree to the success of the enterprise; while, by his impetuous courage, he rendered complete the surprise of he enemy.

Inclosed are lists of our wounded and of the prisoners. I send, also, the books and papers captured.

Very respectfully, your obedient servant,

STEPHEN ELLIOTT, Jr.,

Capt. Beaufort Artillery, commanding expedition.

List of Prisoners at McPhersonville. S. C.

1	Jerome B. McQueslan,	Sergeant	company H,	3d	N. H.
2	George W. Bumham,	"	"	"	"
3	Chas. F. French,	"	"	"	"
4	Wm. Godd,	Corporal	"	"	"
5	Charles Schenner,	"	"	"	"
6	George Cluff,	"	"	"	"
7	Wm. Robinson,	Private	"	"	"
8	Eben Adams,	"	"	"	"
9	Asa B. Perry,	"	"	"	"
10	Jeremiah Dogan,	"	"	"	"
11	James C. Roach,	"	"	"	"
12	Patrick Welch,	"	"	"	"
13	David A. Paige,	"	"	"	"
14	John Locklan,	"	"	"	"
15	John B. Davis,	"	"	"	"
16	H. C. Paige,	"	"	"	"
17	John Brady,	"	"	"	"
18	Thos. Adams,	"	"	"	"
19	Edw'd Bickford,	"	"	"	"
20	Levy McDuffie,	"	"	"	"
21	Walker J. Rupards,	"	"	"	"
22	John A. Smith,	"	"	"	"
23	Alden E. Metcalf,	"	"	"	"
24	Chas. F. Bumham,	"	"	"	"
25	Timothy Parker,	"	"	"	"
26	Wm. Butterfield,	"	"	"	"
27	James Callahan,	"	"	"	"
28	Geo. A. Turner,	"	"	"	"

List of Prisoners at Hardeeville, S. C.

1	Chas. Harvey, Sergeant	company H,	3d,	N. H.	
2	Enoch Harvey, Private	"	"	"	(Wounded in arm.)
3	Dan'l Jepperson, "	"	"	"	"
4	Cyrus Hunt, "	"	"	"	(Sick.)
5	Elbert Blood, "	"	"	"	"
6	Frank Ferrin, "	"	"	"	"
7	America Briggs, "	"	"	"	(W'd'd in head.)
8	James O'Neal, "	"	"	"	(Sick.)

The above is a correct list of the prisoners captured at Pinckney Island.

STEPHEN ELLIOTT, Jr.,
Capt. Beaufort Artillery, com'd'g expedition.

LIST OF WOUNDED.

Company C, 11th regiment, S. C. V.—Private ——, wounded in leg, severely.

Company E, 11th regiment S. C. V.—Capt. Mickler, wounded in leg, not dangerous. Sergeant Jesse Smith, body, dangerously. Corporal J. Nix, wounded in body, since died. Private D. B. Goyhagen, wounded in leg, slightly. Private J. Horton, leg, slightly.

Company G, 11th regiment S. C. V.—Private M. Bradley, wounded in ankle, slightly.

Capt. Howard's cavalry.—Private Vergneur, wounded in arm, severely.

The above is a correct list of our wounded.

STEPHEN ELLIOTT, Jr.,
Capt. Beaufort Artillery, com'd'g expedition.

ORDER OF MAJOR-GEN. D. HUNTER.

HEAD-QUARTERS DEPARTMENT OF THE SOUTH,
HILTON HEAD, PORT ROYAL, S. C.
August 17th, 1862.

GENERAL ORDERS, No. 27.

I. The 7th regiment of New Hampshire volunteers, Col. Putnam, will be held in readiness to embark for St. Augustine, Florida, of which place it will hereafter form the garrison. Lieut.-col. Sleeper, of the 4th regiment of New Hampshire volunteers, on being relieved by Col. Putnam, will embark with the several companies of his regiment, now at Saint Augustine, for this place.

II. It is with deep regret that the general commanding the department has received several reports against officers for returning fugitive slaves, in direct violation of a law of Congress. It will hardly be believed, when it is announced that a New England colonel is to-day, in the second year of the rebellion, in arrest for having been engaged in the manly task of turning over a young woman, whose skin was almost as white as his own, to the cruel lash of her rebel master!

III. Numerous acts of pilfering from the negroes have taken place in the neighborhood of Beaufort, committed by men wearing the uniform of the United States. I cannot and will not call them soldiers. To enable Gen. Saxton to have these petty thieves arrested and sent to this post for punishment, the three companies of the 4th regiment of New Hampshire volunteers, now at Beaufort, will be placed exclusively under his command, for service on the plantations. Major Drew, or the officer commanding these three companies, will be directed by Gen. Brannan to report immediately to Gen. Saxton for orders.

IV. All the furniture left by the rebels on the islands, including that left in the city of Beaufort, is hereby placed under the exclusive jurisdiction of Gen. Saxton.

By command of Major-gen. D. Hunter,

(Signed) ED. W. SMITH,

1st Lieut. 15th Infantry, Act'g Ass't Adj't-gen'l.

REPORT OF THE AFFAIR NEAR GALLATIN.

Col. John H. Morgan commanding.

Head-quarters Morgan's Regiment.
Hartsville, August 22, 1862.

To Adjutant-general:

General:—I beg to confirm my dispatch of the 20th inst., announcing the result of yesterday's expedition.

My command, consisting of my own regiment, 700 strong, and a squadron of Texas rangers, numbering about 100 men, returned that day, worn out, to Gallatin.

At 11 P. M., I received information from one of my friendly scouts that the enemy's cavalry were encamped on the roadside, between Castilian Springs and Hartsville, a distance of only 12 miles from my camp.

Judging from the fact that they had halted by the roadside, I concluded that they intended to march at night, and attack early in the morning, and I made my preparations accordingly, dispatching scouts upon whom I could depend, to bring me positive information as to the enemy's movements.

At day-break my column was on the move, and as the advanced guard reached the head of the town, my pickets came galloping in, followed by my principal scout, who reported that he was closely pursued by a large body of cavalry.

Not wishing, on account of the inhabitants, to make Gallatin the scene of our contest, I advanced my column, and was greeted, on reaching the Hartsville pike, by a heavy fire from that direction.

I dismounted the two leading companies to fight, and threw them into the woods, on the left of the road. The enemy increased his fire, and I gradually had my whole command engaged.

The fight began at half-past 6 o'clock, and was maintained without much advantage on either side—the enemy having, perhaps, rather the best of it at first—until about half-past 8, when they began to fall back, and my men to redouble their efforts. At half-past 9, I had driven them four miles, and was preparing for a final charge, when a flag of truce was brought, proposing an armistice, in order to bury their dead.

My reply was, that I could entertain no proposition, except unconditional surrender.

I learned that the troops were commanded by Brig.-gen. Johnson. During the parley, the enemy had formed into line of battle, and were, evidently, ready to defend themselves from any fresh attack.

I divided my force into three divisions, leading one myself in the direction which I thought Gen. Johnson had taken. Major Morgan had five companies under his orders, on my left. Lieut.-col. Duke, on my right, had three companies and his advance guard.

Some delay was occasioned by the non-arrival of my gallant Texas rangers, who formed part of the body under my own immediate orders. They had been separated from their horses during the preceding fight, and had not been able to recover them in time to come to the front. On their arrival, we marched on in the direction of the enemy, and Col. Duke's division coming within sight, advanced at a canter, and opened fire.

Gen. Johnson's forces being on a good pike, retreated for some time, faster than my men, who were on difficult ground, could follow, but, after a pursuit of some two miles, they were overtaken, and compelled to fight.

They were dismounted and formed behind their horses. The position they had selected was a very good one, especially as they considerably out-numbered Col. Duke's force, which was the only one opposed to them, Major Morgan and my own detachment, in the eagerness of pursuit, having taken too far to the left.

Col. Duke reports that on perceiving that the enemy had halted, he formed his three companies and the advance guard into columns of squadrons, preserving the regular distances between each, so as to be able to form into line at command, and attack.

This was done with admirable precision and coolness by his men, and nothing could exceed their gallantry.

The enemy were formed under the brow of a hill, and my men were drawn up above them, so that their fire told with effect on my line, whilst that of the attacking party went over their heads.

After a very sharp engagement of about fifteen minutes, they broke and ran.

Gen. Johnson, his Adj.-gen. Capt. Turner, Major Winfrey, and a number of privates were captured, but the main body escaped to the hills, through the woods and high corn, making for the Cumberland river.

Thus ended an action in which my command, not exceeding 700 men, (one whole company being in the rear with prisoners) succeeded in defeating a brigade of 1,200 chosen cavalry, sent by Gen. Buell expressly to take me or drive me out of Tennessee, killing and wounding some 180, and taking 200 prisoners, including the Brig.-gen. commanding, and the greater part of the regimental officers.

My loss in both actions amounted to 5 killed and 18 wounded, 2 missing. Amongst the wounded was Capt. Huffman, who had his arm shattered by a ball whilst leading gallantly on his brave Texan rangers—a small body of men, commanded by Major Gano, of whom I cannot speak too highly, as they have distinguished themselves ever since they joined my command, not only by their bravery, but their good soldier-like conduct.

To all my officers and men my best acknowledgments are due; nothing but hard fighting carried them through.

To my personal staff I am deeply indebted—Col. St. Leger Grenfell, Acting Adjt.-gen., ably supported me; Capt. Lewellen, my quarter-master, and Capt. Green Roberts, who acted as my Aides-de-camp, were most active and fearless in carrying my orders, and the Captains of companies cool and collected in the performance of them.

Lieut.-col. Duke led on his regiment, if possible, with more than his usual gallantry, and contributed, by the confidence with which he has inspired his men, to insure the success of the day.

Lieut.-col. Duke makes particular mention of the cool and determined manner in which Lieut. Rogers, commanding advanced guard, Capts. Hutchinson, Castle, and Lieut. White, respectively commanding the three companies composing his division, behaved; in fact, the conduct of both officers and men deserves the highest praise.

I received every assistance from the patriotism and zeal of the neighboring citizens, amongst whom Major Duffey, and Capt. R. A. Bennet, were pre-eminent.

I have also to report that I have received a dispatch from Gen Forrest, stating that he has encamped within eight miles of me, with a reinforcement of 800 men, but no artillery—the want of this arm cripples my movements and prevents my advance with that certainty of effect which a battery would afford.

Recruits are daily and hourly arriving. The population seems at last to be thoroughly aroused, and to be determined on resistance.

I hope shortly, general, to be able to report further successes, and rest assured that no exertions on my part shall be wanting—no sacrifices on that of my officers and men will prevent our giving as good an account of the enemy as our small numbers will admit of.

I have the honor to be,

With the greatest respect, general,

Your most obedient servant,

JOHN H. MORGAN,

Colonel commanding Cavalry, C. S. A.

P. S.—This morning I received positive information as to Gen. Nelson's intentions and movements. He is retreating from Nashville to reinforce Bowling Green, at the head of 1,500 infantry, 200 cavalry, and 12 cannon. It is evidently the intention of the Federals to attempt the defence of the line at Bowling Green and Lebanon.

J. H. M.

PROCLAMATION.

HEAD-QUARTERS MORGAN'S BRIGADE,
HARTSVILLE, TENN., August 22, 1862.

SOLDIERS: Your gallant bearing during the last two days will not only be inscribed in the history of the country and the annals of this war, but is engraven deeply in my heart.

Your zeal and devotion on the 20th, at the attack of the trestle-work at Saundersville, and of the Springfield Junction Stockade—your heroism during the two hard fights of yesterday, have placed you high on the list of those patriots who are now in arms for our Southern rights.

All communication cut off betwixt Gallatin and Nashville—a body of 300 infantry totally cut up or taken prisoners—the liberation of those kind friends arrested by our revengeful foes—for no other reason than their compassionate care of our sick and wounded, would have been laurels sufficient for your brows. But, soldiers, the utter annihilation of Gen. Johnson's brigade—composed of twenty-four picked companies of regulars, and sent on purpose to take us, raises your reputation as soldiers, and strikes fear into the craven hearts of your enemies. Gen. Johnson and his staff, with 200 men taken prisoners, sixty-four killed and 100 wounded, attests the resistance made, and bears testimony to your valor.

But our victories have not been achieved without loss. We have to mourn some brave and dear comrades. Their names will remain in our breasts, their fame outlives them. They died in defence of a good cause. They died like gallant soldiers—with their front to the foe.

Officers and men! Your conduct makes me proud to command you! Fight always as you fought yesterday, and you are invincible.

JOHN H. MORGAN,
Colonel commanding Cavalry.

REPORT OF OPERATIONS AT BRIDGEPORT AND BATTLE CREEK.

BRIG.-GEN. S. B. MAXEY COMMANDING.

HEAD-QUARTERS C. S. FORCES, NEAR GRAHAM'S,
OPPOSITE MOUTH OF BATTLE CREEK, Aug. 30, 1862.

To Capt. C. S. STRINGFELLOW,
Assistant Adjutant-general.

CAPTAIN: I have the honor to submit the following report of the affairs in which a portion of the troops under my command were engaged on the 27th instant:

Early in the morning I ordered Capt. P. H. Rice, commanding company A, Howard's battalion, Georgia and Alabama cavalry, to ford the Tennessee river, about two and a half miles below Bridgeport, and cautiously approach that place and attack the enemy. Capt. Rice found, however, that the enemy had precipitately evacuated the night before.

This being communicated to me, I ordered the 32d Alabama regiment of infantry, Col. McKinstry, which was concealed on the bank of the river, to cross. Capt. Rice was, in the mean time, ordered to throw his cavalry well out on the Battle creek and Stevenson roads.

Scarcely had the 32d crossed, when the cavalry reported enemy's infantry and cavalry approaching in force, the truth of which was made apparent from the clouds of dust in the roads.

I immediately ordered the 32d to be formed in line of battle, near the crest of the hill in the town. And in a few moments the enemy's cavalry (4th Ohio and one other, name not known), dashed up in full speed, and were permitted to come within less than fifty yards of the infantry before a gun was fired, when a galling fire was poured into them, and they retreated in great confusion. In a short time clouds of dust warned me of the enemy's approach on our left, and to meet it, I had the front of the left wing changed forward in time to receive another dash of cavalry, which was again thrown in confusion by another volley more effective than the first, and he again retreated, but re-formed, and by the dust I soon saw he was approach ing the centre. A company of the 32d Alabama, armed with the Enfield rifle, commanded by Lieut. Sellers, was placed in the centre in ambush, and as the enemy came up the hill, in very close range, this company rose and delivered its deadly fire simultaneously with the wings, separated for cover, and this time the enemy broke and fled in perfect confusion.

Whilst this portion of the fight was going on, my batteries, consisting of Capt. Freeman's and Capt. Dunn's artillery, and one 24-pounder rifle-gun, opened (by previous agreement) out on the enemy's works, at the mouth of Battle creek, about five miles distant up the river, and continued incessantly during the entire day. The heavy columns of dust bearing towards Stevenson from the enemy's camps around there, showed a general commotion.

At night I ordered the battery commanders to keep the fire up, believing the enemy, if properly managed, would evacuate before day. At about two o'clock in the morning the work was abandoned in great confusion, the enemy burning most of his commissary stores, but leaving in our possession some $30,000 worth of valuable property, embracing some commissary stores, ordnance stores, quartermaster stores, clothing, all his tents, thirty-two horses and four mules, a few wagons and ambulances, and some few medicines, and a splendid case of surgical instruments, besides some sutler's stores, a number of officers' trunks, many of the post commander's papers, and some very valuable maps. It is proper to observe, that after the fight commenced at Bridgeport, the 3d Georgia cavalry and 25th Tennessee infantry were ordered across, but did not reach the place in time to participate. Indeed, it was only after the fight had opened that I received notice that the 3d Georgia was placed at my disposal temporarily.

I was informed by the major-general commanding, several days ago, that some cavalry, under Col. Lay, would move down the Sequachie Valley, and I had hoped to have its assistance. At 10 P. M. on the 27th, I received a note from Col. Lay, dated Jasper, 5½ P. M., informing me that he was there with 550 cavalry, and desired me to inform him of my movements, stating that he heard the cannonading, &c. This I did, with an expression of belief that the enemy would be shelled out before morning, and saying to him (in substance) that if he would take his position about the mouth of Sweeden's cove about daylight, he would probably get them.

It is unfortunate that these suggestions were not acted on, for if they had been, the enemy being panic-stricken by throwing cavalry in his front, the hills on either side, and my forces in rear, would have been easy prey. I am indebted to Capt. S. M. Scott, Assistant Adjutant-gen., Capt. C. G. Schultz, Assistant Inspector-gen., Capt. M. H. Lewis, ordnance officer of my staff, and my aid, Lieut. R. C. Andrews, for valuable and efficient aid. The work between the two points kept the first three constantly busy—Capt. Scott personally superintending the throwing forward reinforcements. My aid, Lieut. Andrews, was with me at Bridgeport, and did his duty coolly and well.

The 32d Alabama did nobly, fighting like veterans, under their able colonel (McKinstry), seconded by Lieut.-col. Maney, distinguished for gallantry and coolness on the field. Capts. Freeman and Dure, and the officers under them, did their whole duty. Lieut. Holtzclaw, of Capt. Dure's battery, worked the siege gun most of the time and splendidly. It was handled part of the time by Capt. McCreery. Capt. Rice and his command acted in a manner worthy of all praise. In short, I never saw troops behave better than did the 32d Alabama, Rice's cavalry, Freeman's and Dure's batteries, and the detachment with siege guns. I particularly call your attention to the boldness of this regiment of infantry in wading a broad sheet of water, such as the Tennessee, up to their arm-pits, with retreat cut off, and the enemy known to be strong in front. Should I be furnished with sufficient cavalry to reap the fruits of this movement, our cause will be greatly benefited. The work out of which the enemy was shelled, is a splendidly constructed field work, admirably executed, is the key to the Sequachie Valley, and its possession completely breaks the enemy's chain up the Tennessee river. With cavalry to operate from that point toward Stevenson and Huntsville, the enemy could be kept in constant alarm. I neglected in this appropriate place, to say, which I do with gratitude, that our loss was trifling, only six wounded—one missing—thus small owing to the fact that the grounds on which the fight took place at Bridgeport were perfectly well known to me, and the men, most of the time, had the advantage of cover. The enemy's loss, for such an affair, was heavy, variously estimated from fifty to seventy-five killed and wounded in the two engagements, certainly not less than fifty, and the indications are it was greater.

Very respectfully,

your obedient servant,

S. B. MAXEY,

Brig.-gen. commanding.

REPORT
Of the three engagements with the enemy, near Richmond, Ky.

MAJOR-GENERAL E. KIRBY SMITH COMMANDING.

HEAD-QUARTERS ARMY OF KENTUCKY,
RICHMOND, KY., August 30th, 1862.

Gen. S. COOPER,
Adjutant and Inspector-general C. S. A., Richmond Va.:

SIR:—It is my great pleasure to announce to you that God has thrice blessed our arms to-day. After a forced march, almost day and night, for three days, over a mountain wilderness, destitute alike of food and water, I found the enemy drawn up in force to oppose us, at a point eight miles from this place. With less than half my force, I attacked and carried a very strong position at Mount Zion Church, after a hard fight of two hours. Again, a still better position at White's farm, in half an hour; and finally, in this town, just before sunset, our indomitable troops deliberately walked (they were too tired to run) up to a magnificent position, manned by 10,000 of the enemy, many of them perfectly fresh, and carried it in fifteen minutes. It is proper for me now to give you the exact results of these glorious battles. Our loss is comparatively small. That of the enemy, many hundred killed and wounded, and several thousand prisoners. We have captured artillery, small arms, and wagons. Indeed, every thing indicates the almost entire annihilation of this force of the enemy. In the first two battles they were commanded by Gen. Manson, in the last by Gen. Nelson.

Reinforcements *must* be sent up to me at once. We have large numbers of adherents here, who, if we can show an ability to maintain *ourselves*, will flock to our standard.

I am, sir, respectfully,
Your obedient servant,
(Signed) E. KIRBY SMITH,
Major-general commanding.

AUGUST 31st.

GENERAL:—I have only time to add that the commander of the enemy, Gen. Nelson, was wounded in the thigh. The second in command, Gen. Manson (and staff), a prisoner in this place, and Gen. Miller killed. All their artillery taken, some 3,500 prisoners, and their whole force dispersed in every direction. The cavalry continues to bring in prisoners.

Respectfully, and in haste,

(Signed) E. KIRBY SMITH,

Major-general.

Report of Maj.-gen. E. Kirby Smith.

HEAD-QUARTERS ARMY OF KENTUCKY,
LEXINGTON, KY., Sept. 16, 1862.

Gen. S. COOPER,
Adjutant and Ins.-gen.,
Richmond, Va.:

GENERAL:—In my short letter of the 30th ultimo, I gave you the results of my actions of that day, of which I have the honor now to make a more detailed report.

Before leaving Barboursville for this part of Kentucky, I wrote to you, fully explaining the reasons that prompted me to take that step. Until my advance descended the Big Hill, it met with no opposition from the enemy. Here, on the morning of the 29th, the enemy was discovered to be in force in our front, and a bold reconnoissance of the cavalry, under Col. Scott, in the afternoon, indicated a determination to give us battle. Although Churchill's division did not get up until quite late in the afternoon, and then in an apparently exhausted state, I determined to march to Richmond the next day, even at the cost of a battle with the whole force of the enemy. The leading division, under Gen. Cleburne, was moved early the next morning, and after marching two or three miles, they found the enemy drawn up in line of battle in a fine position near Mount Zion Church, six miles from Richmond. Without waiting for Churchill's division, Cleburne at once commenced the action, and when I arrived on the field, half-past 7 o'clock, the fire of artillery was brisk on both sides. As my force was almost too small to storm the position in front without a disastrous loss, I sent Gen. Churchill, with one of his brigades, to turn the enemy's right

While this move was being executed, a bold and well-conducted attempt on the part of the enemy to turn Cleburne's right, was admirably foiled by the firmness of Col. Preston Smith's brigade, who repulsed the enemy with great slaughter. It was about this time, and while he was riding from his right to his left, that Gen. Cleburne was badly wounded in the face, and thus, at a critical moment, I was deprived of the services of one of the most gallant, zealous, and intelligent officers of the whole army.

The command of this division then devolved upon Col. Preston Smith. In the mean time, Gen. Churchill had been completely successful in his movement upon the enemy's right flank, where, by a bold charge, his men completed a victory already partially gained by the gallantry of our troops on the right.

In this action our loss was quite heavy on the right, but in comparison with that of the enemy, was small.

It being reported that the enemy had taken up a new position, on White's farm, two miles in front, I ordered Churchill, with one brigade, to again turn his right, intending to bring up Preston Smith on the other flank. But a desperate attempt on the part of the enemy to crush Churchill, caused the action to commence before the arrival of Smith's division, and so this gallant brigade (Col. McCray's), of Texans and Arkansians had to fight the battle alone. Although the odds opposed to them were fearful, yet, by reserving their own fire, under the deafening roar of the enemy's guns, and by a well-timed and dashing charge upon the advancing lines, they completely routed and put to flight the hosts of the enemy, just as the cheers of Smith's division announced their arrival in the field. The loss of the enemy here was very great, including one piece of artillery; ours, almost nothing. Scott's cavalry having been around to our left by another road, to get in the rear of Richmond, I felt during the whole day much in need of cavalry to follow up our different successes. It was then, that in this second repulse of the enemy, I ordered Capt. Nelson, commanding a company of Partizan Rangers, to charge the retreating masses of the enemy. This was promptly and admirably obeyed, the results being the capture of numerous prisoners. In passing a deserted camp of the enemy, I found from some of the wounded that Gen. Nelson, with reinforcements, had arrived after the second battle. A march of two miles brought us within sight of the town, in front of which, and on a commanding ridge, with both flanks resting upon woods, Nelson had determined to make a final stand. For a third time, Churchill, with a brigade (McNair's), was sent off to the left, when a deafening roar of musketry soon announced the raging of a furious combat. In the mean while, Preston Smith, bringing up his division at a double-quick, formed with wonderful decision and rapidity in front of the enemy's centre and left. Almost without waiting the command of the officers, this division coolly advanced under the murderous fire of a force twice their number, and drove them from the field in the greatest confusion, and with immense slaughter. Owing to the open character of the country, our loss in the last fight was quite heavy, including some valuable regimental officers. The exhausted condition of my men, together with the closing in of night, prevented the pursuit of the enemy more than a mile beyond Richmond. But the timely arrival of Col. Scott, with his cavalry, upon their two lines of retreat, enabled him greatly to increase the fruits of the hard labors of the day, by capturing large numbers of prisoners, including Gen. Manson and staff, as also eight pieces of artillery, and a number of wagons, and while my whole force was not more than five thousand, that of the enemy was more than ten. In this last engagement, we took prisoners from thirteen regiments. Our loss in killed and wounded is about 400; that of the enemy is about 1,000, and his prisoners 5,000. The immediate fruits of the victory were 9 pieces of artillery and 10,000 small arms, and a large quantity of supplies. These latter were greatly increased by the capture of this place and Frankfort, the whole number of cannon taken being about twenty. I regret that I am unable to forward with this the reports of all the different commands of the forces engaged.

Those inclosed (Gen. Churchill's and Col. Scott's), will show you how much cause the Confederacy has to be proud of her sons. I almost fear to particularize, lest I do not full justice to all; but I cannot close this report without expressing my admiration at the promptness and intelligence with which Gens. Churchill and Cleburne, and Col. Preston Smith, executed the orders given them. My thanks are due to the following members of my staff, who were with me on the field, for their active assistance to me during the day, viz.: Cols. Pegram and Boggs, Lieut.-col. Brent, Majors J. A. Brown, McElrath, and Thomas, Capt. Merse, Lieuts. Cunningham and Pratt, and Capts. Walworth, and Hammond, and McFrevet, volunteer aids. Too much praise cannot be given to the medical director, Surgeon S. A. Smith, and to his assistants, for their untiring devotion to the arduous labors that devolved upon them.

As regards the intrepid behavior of the true patriots, the men in the ranks, I can only say, that as long as the destinies of the South remain in such hands, we need never fear Northern subjugation. But even more than their noble courage before the enemy, are we called upon to admire that higher courage, which enabled them to undergo, without murmur, the fatigues and hardships of one of the most difficult marches of this war. For several days, and parts of the nights, through a country almost entirely without water, over stony roads, with their almost bare feet, and with green corn and beef, without salt, as their only food, did these gallant men trudge along, inspired only with the desire of being led against the invaders of their homes, and the oppressers of their liberties.

I refer you to the reports of the division and brigade commanders, only a part of which I am now able to forward, for notice of special cases of good behavior.

I remain, general,
Very respectfully,
Your obedient servant,
E. KIRBY SMITH.

Report of Brig.-gen. Churchill.

HEAD-QUARTERS 3D DIVISION, A. K.,
CYNTHIANA, KY., September 8th, 1862.

To Major-gen. E. KIRBY SMITH:

GENERAL:—I have the honor to report, that on the morning of the 30th ultimo, according to instructions, I moved my division, composed of the first and second brigades, commanded by Cols. McCray and McNair respectively, up the road in the direction of Richmond. When I arrived in the neighborhood of Kingston, I heard the artillery open on our right, showing that Gen. Cleburne had met the enemy.

It was now about 8 o'clock A. M. It was at this time you arrived on the field, and ordered me to hold one of my brigades in reserve, while, with the other, I was to make a flank movement on the enemy's right. In accordance with these instructions, I left Col. McNair, with his brigade, as a reserve force, and proceeded with Col. McCray's brigade, composed of Arkansas and Texan troops, to execute the movement on the enemy's flank, and, by proceeding cautiously through a corn field and a ravine, had almost perfected the move, when the enemy, pressed by our forces on our right, commenced to give way; but, after falling back some distance, they formed in a skirt of timber, when my forces fired and charged upon them. Then, for the first time discovering my position, they commenced a precipitate retreat, but not before we had killed a great many, and taken a number of prisoners.

I was again ordered to move up on the left, with the same brigade, while Gen. Cleburne was to move on the right. After proceeding some two miles in the direction of Richmond, I found the entire force of the enemy, numbering eight or ten thousand, in a strong position on the left of the road, concealed by a cornfield and a skirt of timber. I then sent Gen. Cleburne word to move up, that I was ready to engage the enemy. I then placed one section of Capt. Humphrey's battery, under command of Lieut. ———, on my right, about two hundred yards from the enemy, to more effectually rake his lines. Before Gen. Cleburne's division came up, the fight had commenced in earnest.

The fire of the enemy's artillery and musketry was most terrific, while we replied only with artillery. I then ordered my command to lie down, protected by a fence and ditch, and, for full five minutes, we did not fire a gun in response to their terrible fire.

The enemy were at this time advancing in heavy force, and when they had arrived within fifty yards of my line, the order was given to rise, fire, and charge, which order was promptly and gallantly obeyed. The enemy could not withstand the desperate courage of my men, but still, for a while they contested every inch of ground as they were driven from it, until finally, finding it impossible to check this gallant charge, they gave way in every direction.

The victory was complete. The field was covered with the dead and wounded of the enemy, and some (though comparatively few) of the gallant sons of Arkansas and Texas fell martyrs to the cause of liberty. Here we captured a large number of prisoners, guns and equipments of all kinds. In this charge one splendid rifle cannon was taken. This was, perhaps, the most severely contested fight of the day. Finding this brigade worn down by incessant fighting, I ordered up Col. McNair to follow in pursuit of the now flying enemy. After pursuing them some two miles, we found them again drawn up in line, near the outskirts of Richmond, having collected their whole force for a last and final struggle.

Here I took position on the right of the enemy's line. Soon my skirmishers engaged those of the enemy, which was soon followed by a general engagement of my forces. I was driving back the enemy's right wing, when I heard firing on my right, showing that

Gen. Cleburne had engaged the enemy on their left. The engagement then became general throughout the entire line.

For a time the contest was sharp, and the rattle of the musketry almost deafening, but again, for the third and last time, the enemy fled in great confusion through the streets of Richmond, as night closed upon our victorious army.

I captured in this engagement a large amount of ordnance and ordnance stores, together with four or five hundred prisoners.

I cannot speak too highly of the gallantry and coolness displayed by Cols. McNair and McCray throughout the entire day, and I have to thank them for the promptness and skill with which they executed orders. Of the two batteries in my division, the one commanded by Capt. Douglas was ordered the evening previous to report to Gen. Cleburne for orders. The other, commanded by Capt. Humphreys, was with my division during the whole day, and it gives me great pleasure to say that his pieces were handled with surprising skill and ability, and did great execution in the ranks of the enemy.

My loss during the entire day in killed, wounded, and missing, was two hundred and twenty-four.

Before closing, I must particularly mention the daring bravery and gallant bearing, on the battle-field, of the following members of my staff: Capt. B. S. Johnson, Adj.-gen.; Capt. B. F. Blackburn, Inspector-gen.; Capt. John Renwick, volunteer aid; Capt. Jones, Signal Corps, and Lieut. J. M. Rose, Ordnance officer. These officers were ever seen bearing orders through the thickest of the fight, and, at times, in the front of the battle, cheering on my men to victory. My Division Surgeon, Dr. C. H. Smith, in addition to his professional services upon the field to the wounded, rendered me many valuable services. The officers and men of my entire division always met the enemy with unflinching gallantry, and were the proud victors of every field; and for the privations, hardships, and almost unequalled marches, all of which they have borne without a murmur, they deserve the thanks of their country.

I have the honor to be, general, very respectfully,

Your most obedient servant,

Y. J. CHURCHILL,

Brig.-gen. commanding 3d Division Army of Kentucky.

Report of Col. E. McNair.

HEAD-QUARTERS 2D BRIGADE
Sept. 6, 1862.

GENERAL:—I have the honor to report the following loss and casualties in the 2d brigade, 3d division, army of Kentucky, in the action near Richmond, 30th August, viz.:

1st Arkansas mounted riflemen.—Killed,	8
" " " Wounded,	18
Total,	26
4th Arkansas regiment.—Killed,	6
" " Wounded,	17
Total,	23
Baltimore mounted riflemen.—Killed,	1
" " " Wounded,	10
Total,	11
30th regiment.—Killed,	1
" Wounded,	9
Total,	10
4th battalion.—Wounded,	6

In regard to the part my brigade took in the battle near Richmond, Ky., I will only say that officers and men did their duty, their whole duty. I will not particularize, lest I do some injustice, but will leave you and the country to judge of us.

I am, your most obedient servant,

E. McNAIR,
Col. commanding 2d brigade, 3d division, Army Kentucky.

Report of Col. J. S. Scott.

HEAD-QUARTERS KIRBY SMITH'S BRIGADE,
LEBANON, KY., *Sept.* 11, 1862.

To Major-gen. E. KIRBY SMITH,
Commanding Army of Kentucky,
LEXINGTON, KY.:

The evening of the 13th August I left Kingston, Tenn., with the 1st cavaley, Lieut. Nixon Conoly, 1st Georgia cavalry, Col. Morrison, and the Buckner Guards, Capt. Jarrett, numbering in the aggregate 896, and passing through Montgomery, and Jamestown, Tenn., Monticello, and Somerset, Ky., reached London on the 17th.

During the night of the 16th, when 25 miles from London, I learned that five companies of the 3d Tennessee volunteers, Col. W. S. A., were stationed there. I selected 500 men from the command and made a forced march, reaching the town about 7 o'clock the next morning, when I attacked the place, and after a brief resistance by the enemy I captured it, killing 13, wounding 17, and taking 111 prisoners. My loss was one officer and one private killed, none wounded.

I took a large number of wagons laden with quarter-masters' and commissary's stores, a number of horses and mules, and several hundred stands of arms, all of which I have forwarded to you.

After leaving London, I employed my command gathering mules, horses, and wagons, that had been left along the road by the affrighted Federals, from London to Mt. Vernon and Richmond. The evening of the 22d, learning that a train was coming (intended for the Pass), guarded by infantry and cavalry, I moved my command to meet them. My advance came upon them at Big Still, 17 miles from Richmond, where the fight commenced and resulted as stated in my former report.

After driving in their pickets within two miles of Richmond, the morning of the 24th, and gathering up all the trains, horses, and mules, I fell back slowly to the junction of the Wild-cat and Richmond roads, which I reached the evening of the 25th.

On the 27th, the 3d Tennessee cavalry, Col. Starns, was added to my command, and I moved on in the direction of Richmond.

On the 27th, I made a reconnoissance of the enemy with my whole command, and finding them in position about three miles from Richmond, I fell back four miles to the infantry and reported to Gen. Cleburne, who was in command of the advanced division.

On the morning of the 30th, in obedience to your orders, I passed around to the west of Richmond, and took possession of the roads leading to Lexington. The majority of my forces were posted on the Lexington road, and one company on the Lancaster road, the remainder between the two roads. About 4 o'clock, stragglers from the battle-field commenced passing into my lines, and gradually increased in numbers until 6 o'clock, when the main body of the enemy, apparently about 5000 strong, with 9 pieces of artillery, came upon us.

My forces, being well ambuscaded, poured a destructive fire into their ranks, killing about 60, and wounding a large number. The firing commenced, in obedience to my orders, on the extreme left, extending to the right, which was nearest Richmond; after which, almost the entire force immediately surrendered.

Owing to the smallness of my force (about 850), I was unable to still guard the roads and remove all the prisoners to the rear, consequently, a large number escaped, wandering through the cornfields and woodlands, it being now too dark to distinguish them, when a few paces ahead or distant. I am unable to state the number of prisoners taken by my command, owing to the fact that they were captured principally after dark, and during the same night were turned over to Gen. Preston Smith, in obedience to your orders, but am confident they could not fall short of 3500. I captured, also, nine pieces of artillery, a large number of small arms, and wagons loaded with army supplies.

Among the prisoners captured, was Brig.-gen. Manson, and a number of field and staff officers.

On the morning of the 31st, I moved to the Kentucky river, and drove the rear guard of the enemy from the opposite bank.

On the 1st September, I moved on, and camped near Lexington, and on the 2d, moved around Lexington and camped near Georgetown, and the 3d ultimo, we moved on to Frankfort, and hoisted the battle flag of the 1st " Louisiana" cavalry, in default of a Confederate flag, on the Capitol of the State, while the rear guard of the enemy, about 8000 strong, were quiet spectators from the opposite hills. The same evening, I detailed all my command, with horses in condition to travel (1450 in number), to pursue the enemy and harass his rear. The next morning, September 4th, they came upon the enemy about sunrise, near Shelbyville, and drove them into and through the town, and then crossed over to the railroad and destroyed the bridges, in obedience to your orders, and returned to camp near Frankfort. The 6th and 7th remained in camp near Frankfort. My loss, since leaving Kingston, is one officer and 6 privates killed, 21 wounded, and 9 taken prisoners.

Since reaching London, I have captured four thousand prisoners, (including those turned over to Gen. Smith and those parolled by me,) about 375 wagons, mostly laden with provisions and army stores, near 1500 mules, and a large number of horses. It has been impossible to keep an account of the wagons recaptured by my command, owing to the rapidity of my movements.

I cannot close this report without bearing testimony to the soldierly conduct of my command. They have endured unusual privations and fatigues without murmur. I cannot compliment the commanders of the brigades too highly for the assistance rendered me. I would mention, that the first 106 miles of our march, over a rough and barren country, was made in 42 hours, having been delayed one day, on account of getting our horses shod.

The statement of the property captured at Frankfort was handed in to your head-quarters by me, in person, on Saturday last.

My forces have been materially reduced by the numerous details which I found it necessary to make, in order to remove wagons and stock to the rear, and I shall use my utmost endeavors to concentrate my command at as early a day as possible.

Hoping that the results achieved by the "Kirby Smith brigade" may prove satisfactory to you, general,

I remain, very respectfully,

Your obedient servant,

J. S. SCOTT,

Colonel commanding brigade.

[The following reports having been inadvertently omitted in their regular order, and being a part of the history of the operations on the Cumberland and Tennessee rivers, are therefore inserted as a supplement:]

COL. HEIMAN'S LETTER, INCLOSING REPORT IN REGARD TO BOMBARDMENT AND SURRENDER OF FORT HENRY.

RICHMOND, August 11, 1862.

Adj.-gen. COOPER:

SIR: Inclosed herewith please find my report in regard to bombardment and surrender of Fort Henry.

I prepared this report at Fort Donelson, immediately after the fall of Fort Henry, but my imprisonment after the surrender of the troops at Fort Donelson prevented me from forwarding it to the proper authorities before now. I have now the honor to submit it to you with my high regards.

Your most obedient servant,

(Signed) A. HEIMAN,

Colonel 10th Tennessee regiment.

Col. Heiman's Report.

FORT DONELSON,
February 8th, 1862.

Col. W. W. MACKALL,
Assistant Adj.-gen:

In the absence of Gen. Tilghman, who is a prisoner in the hands of the enemy, being next in command of his division, it becomes my duty, and I have the honor to submit to you the following report in regard to the bombardment and surrender of Fort Henry, and the subsequent retreat of its garrison to Fort Donelson.

The armament of the fort consisted of ten 32-pounders, two 42-pounders, two 12-pounders, one .24-pounder rifle-gun, and one 10-inch columbiad. The garrison consisted of my regiment, (10th Tennessee,) under command of Lieut.-col. McGavock; the 4th Mississippi, Col. Drake; two companies of the 3d Alabama battalion, Major Garvin; a company of artillery, commanded by Capt. Taylor; one company of Forrest's cavalry, Capt. Milner, and forty mounted men, acting Capt. Melton, stationed as picket and rocket guard, at Bailey's landing, three miles below the fort; Capt. Culbertson's light battery, (four six-pounders and one six-pounder rifle-gun,) amounting in all to an aggregate of 1,885 men.

The heights on the opposite side of the river, with the unfinished works of Fort Heiman, were occupied by the 27th Alabama regiment, Col. Hughes; the 15th Arkansas, Col. Gee; two companies of Alabama cavalry, commanded by Capts. Hubbard and Houston, and an unorganized company of forty men, Kentucky cavalry, Capt. Padgett, and a section of a light battery, commanded by Lieut. Hankinicz, amounting in all to 1,100 men.

At Paris landing, five miles above the fort, the 48th Tennessee, Col. Voorhies, and the 51st Tennessee, Col. Browder, were stationed. These were skeleton regiments, containing, together, not more than four hundred men.

With the exception of the 10th Tennessee and the 4th Mississippi, these were all new troops, who had just entered the service. They were not drilled, were badly equipped, and very indifferently armed with shot guns and Tennessee rifles. None of the cavalry had either sabres or pistols, and were only partly armed, with double-barrelled shot-guns; no other equipments whatever. There was much sickness among the new troops, so that the forces for the defence of Fort Henry and Fort Heiman did not amount to more than 2,600 effective men. There were also at Fort Henry the steamers Dunbar, Capt. Fowler; Lynn Boyd, Capt. Smedley; Appleton Belle, Capt. Heffernan, (regular packet from the fort to Danville,) the Samuel Orr and the Patton. The latter two boats were used for hospitals.

General Tilghman's division head-quarters being at Fort Donelson, where he was untiring in his exertions to complete the defences of that post, Fort Henry, during his absence, was under my command. On the morning of the 4th instant, at half-past four o'clock, the sentinel at our three-gun battery announced a rocket signal from the picket at Bailey's landing, which was immediately answered by a rocket from the fort, when three more rockets went up from the picket, announcing the approach of three of the enemy's gunboats. The eleven guns bearing on the river were immediately manned and shotted, and every thing held in readiness for an attack. The steamers were all moved out of range of the enemy's gunboats, and the Dunbar and Boyd were dispatched to Paris landing for the two regiments stationed there. I sent a courier to Gen. Tilghman, at Fort Donelson, informing him of these facts. Shortly after daylight, the pickets on both sides of the river reported a large fleet coming up, and the smoke from several gunboats now became visible over the island. I directed Capt. Ellis, of the 10th, with a small escort of mounted men, to proceed down on the right bank of the river, and Capt. Anderson, of the same regiment, on the opposite bank, to reconnoitre, and ascertain whether the enemy was landing troops. I directed Capt. Milner, with his company of cavalry, to occupy the several roads leading from Bailey's landing to the fort, and throw forward a sufficient number of pickets and videttes. I directed Col. Drake to send two companies of his regiment and a section of Culbertson's battery to the rifle-pits, for the defence of the Dover road, about three-quarters of a mile from the fort, while Major Garvin occupied the rifle-pits across the road, leading to Bailey's landing. Twelve torpedoes were sunk in the chute of the river at the foot of the island. For want of powder and time, none were sunk in the main channel. Those sunk were rendered utterly useless by the heavy rise in the river. At about nine o'clock, the gunboats commenced throwing shells at the quarters of our pickets and other buildings in the neighborhood of Bailey's landing.

Capt. Ellis returned, reporting eight gunboats and ten large transports in the river, and that they were landing their cavalry. He also stated that he had seen two light batteries or barges, but that no troops were at that time landing on the opposite side of the river. I again sent a courier to Gen. Tilghman, informing him of these facts. During all this time he had a large force at work on the epaulments, and trying to keep the water out of the fort. The lower magazine had already two feet of water in it, and the ammunition had been removed to a temporary magazine above ground, which had but very little protection, but we had been at work day and night for the last week, to cover it with sand-bags and to protect it by a traverse. At about 12 o'clock, five gunboats came in sight in the main channel. All the troops, except the heavy artillery force, were marched out of range of the enemy's guns. The gunboats formed in line of battle across the channel, about two miles below the fort, beyond the range of our 32-pounders. I gave positive orders that none of these guns should be fired, unless the boats came within their range; therefore, we had only to depend on the 24-pounder rifle-gun, and the 10-inch columbiad, the latter gun with an iron carriage on an iron chassie, had, on previous trials of firing with twenty-pound charges, proved defective, owing to the too great recoil for the length of the chassie, or other defects. This was, however, remedied by clamping the carriage to the chassie, and even then it recoiled with such tremendous force against the hurters, that in almost every instance it disarranged the pintle. I have since learned that this defect was common to these guns.

At about one o'clock, the gunboats opened fire with shell and shot, which was immediately returned by our rifled gun, and 10-inch columbiad. The former fired archer shells. At the third or fourth fire, one of the clamps of the columbiad broke, and fearing that another fire would upset the gun, it was not fired again. The rifled gun was fired in quick succession, and with good effect; meanwhile the gunboats kept up a constant fire with good practice. As the boats advanced, we opened fire with the eleven guns bearing on the river, which was kept up for about half an hour, when the enemy withdrew. Their shot fell in and around the fort. Some of their shells fell a quarter of a mile beyond the fort, showing a range superior to our own. None of the shells which fell in the fort exploded, and but one man was wounded. I reported the result to Gen. Tilghman, and that the enemy was landing a large force, and that additional transports were arriving. I was satisfied that we could not hold the heights opposite the fort, and that it would be prudent to move the forces from there to Fort Henry, but did not like to take the responsibility, without the order of Gen. Tilghman, as a previous order from you stated positively that these heights must be held. However, these troops were held in readiness to move at a moment's warning. At five o'clock I sent another courier, with an escort, to the general, stating my views in regard to the troops at Fort Heiman, and requesting his orders, " or what I desired more, his presence," and cautioned him not to come without a strong escort, and by the upper road, believing that the enemy had already cavalry pickets on the main Dover road. Before night, I reinforced the outposts on the Dover road with two companies of the 10th Tennessee, under Capts. Morgan and Ford, and the 6-pounder rifled gun. At half-past eleven, Gen. Tilghman and Major Gilmer's corps of engineers arrived, with three companies of Lieut.-col. Gantt's cavalry, from Fort Donelson. At daylight, on the morning of the 5th, Gen. Tilghman directed the removal of the troops from Fort Heiman to Fort Henry, with the exception of the cavalry. Gen. Tilghman now formed the troops at the fort into two brigades. The first commanded by myself, consisting of the 10th Tennessee, Lieut.-col. McGavock, 48th Tennessee, Col. Browder, 51st Tennessee, Col. Voorhies, Col. Gantt's battalion of Cavalry, and Capt. Culbertson's light battery. The second brigade, under command of Col. Drake, consisted of the 4th Mississippi, Major Adair, 27th Alabama, Col. Hughes, Alabama battalion, Major Garvin, Capts. Milner's and Melton's cavalry, and section of light battery, Capt. Clare. He appointed Major McComice assistant-adj.-gen., and Lieut. Phar aid-de-camp, his own staff having remained at Fort Donelson. Gen. Tilghman assigned each brigade its position at the rifle-pits, and all preparations were made to receive the enemy by land and water.

A reconnoitring party of cavalry met the enemy, and in a skirmish one man of Capt. Milner's company was killed. Gen. Tilghman then ordered out a battalion of the 10th Tennessee, a battalion of the 4th Mississippi, and Milner's cavalry, and proceeded in person with them to the scene of the skirmish, but the enemy had retired.

During the night, Col. Milton A. Haynes, of the artillery, arrived from Fort Donelson to give his aid in the coming engagement, and brought information that in obedience to orders from Gen. Tilghman, Col. Head would send two regiments to Kirkman's furnace from Fort Donelson next morning, which is half way between the forts, to act as a reserve. Early on the morning of the 6th, heavy volumes of black smoke rose over the island, manifesting that the fleet was not to remain idle long; and judging from the number of transports in the river, they must have landed a very large force during the two days and nights; and, as it was afterwards ascertained, Gen. Grant had 12,000 men between the fort and Bailey's landing, and Gen. Smith 6,000 men on the opposite bank of the river. At about ten o'clock in the morning, Gen. Tilghman and Major Gilmer came in a small boat from the steamer Dunbar, which was lying during the night at Fort Heiman, and prepared for the engagement on hand. At eleven o'clock the gunboats made their appearance in the chute, seven in number, and formed in line of battle two miles from the fort. Gen. Tilghman ordered the troops to be marched out of range of the enemy's guns. None were permitted to remain in the fort but those on duty with the artillery, who were under the command of Capt. Taylor.

Gen. Tilghman, with his staff, took position at the centre battery to observe the movements of the gunboats, and direct the firing of our batteries. The enemy opened fire with shot and shell, which was returned by our 10-inch columbiad and 24-pounder rifled gun, until they came in range of the lighter guns, when the whole eleven guns bearing on the river opened fire. The enemy's practice improved as they advanced. The firing on both sides was without a moment's intermission. Shot after shot were exchanged, with admirable rapidity and precision, and the enemy's shell struck and exploded in every direction. Unfortunately, our most reliable gun, the 24-pounder rifle, bursted, wounding all the men who served it. Shortly afterwards the vent of the 10-inch columbiad closed, and could not be opened. Our reliance was now on the 32 and 42-pounders, and, I regret to state, for the latter we had not the proper ammunition. Shortly afterwards, a premature explosion of one of the guns killed two men. By this time we had lost the use of five guns, but a constant fire was kept up on both sides, the gunboats nearing all the time; their point-blank range telling fearfully on the fort, while we had to depress our guns and change our range after every shot. This unequal fire was kept up with an energy which does great credit to the officers and men at the guns.

This fearful cannonading had lasted now over an hour, and it was evident the fort could not hold out much longer. Major Gilmer called my attention to the state of affairs, requesting me to state to Gen. Tilghman that it was useless to hold out longer; to keep up this useless contest would cost the lives of many more, without any possible advantage to the result. I replied to Major Gilmer that these were my views, but that I would not like to make any suggestions to the general; that he must be his own judge in regard to this affair. When Gen. Tilghman was shortly after reminded of the state of affairs, he would not entertain the idea of a surrender, stating that he had as yet lost but few men, and inquired the reason why some of the guns had ceased firing. He was told that several of the men were killed, many wounded, and all the rest exhausted, and that we had no men to relieve them. The general threw off his coat, sprang on the chassie of the nearest gun, stating that he would work it himself, ordering, at the same time, fifty men of my regiment to the fort to assist the gunners. Seeing nobody whom I could send for them, I started myself, the bombardment still going on unabated; but, before I could reach the command, the boats were so close to the fort that further resistance was impossible. The flag was hauled down, and the firing ceased.

I returned, in person, immediately to the fort for further orders. Gen. Tilghman informed me that he had surrendered, believing that it was his duty to do so, as every military man would see the impossibility of holding the fort against such fearful odds, and stating to me that I was not included in the surrender, as I was not in the fort at the time the flag was struck, and directed me to continue the retreat according to orders at Fort Donelson, by the upper road, having gained all the time necessary for a safe retreat. Owing to bad roads, the high water, and the close pursuit of the enemy's cavalry, I found it a physical impossibility to save the light artillery.

About three miles from the fort, our rear was attacked by the enemy's cavalry. Their fire was handsomely returned by Col. Gee and Major Garvin. Major Lee, of the 15th Arkansas, and Captain Leach, of the Alabama battalion, were surrounded and made prisoners. We sustained no other loss.

I may be permitted to state, that the self-sacrificing heroism displayed by Gen. Tilghman in this terrible and most unequal struggle, challenges the admiration of all gallant men, and entitles him to the gratitude of the whole people of the Confederate States. The tact, skill, and untiring energy which characterized his whole course, while in command of the defence of the Tennessee and Cumberland rivers, proved him a most skilful and gallant leader.

During the bombardment of Fort Henry, Gen. Tilghman was ably assisted by Major Gilmer, Col. Haynes, Major McComice, Capts. Miller and Haydon (Engineers), Capt. Taylor, Lieuts. Watts and Weller, and Capt. G. R. G. Jones, and the men under their command deserve particular credit for the effective and energetic manner in which they managed their guns.

My thanks are eminently due to Col. Drake, and the regimental and detachment commanders, for the able and orderly manner in which they conducted their commands.

The events which followed so closely upon the fall of Fort Henry —the surrender of the troops at Fort Donelson, and my own imprisonment (from which I have just been released), have prevented me from forwarding this report at an earlier date.

Very respectfully, your obedient servant,

(Signed) A. HEIMAN,

Col. commanding 1st Brigade, Tilghman's Division.

Answer of Col. Forrest to Interrogations propounded by the Special Committee of the House of Representatives of the Confederate Congress, charged with the duty of inquiring into the management of the Quarter-master and Commissary Department, about the time of the surrender of the City of Nashville.

Interrogatory 1st.—I was not at the city of Nashville at the time of its surrender, but was there at the time the enemy made their entrance into that part of the city known as Edgefield, having left Fort Donelson, with my command, on the morning of its surrender, and reached Nashville on Tuesday, February 18th, about 10 o'clock A. M. I remained in the city up to the Sunday evening following.

Interrogatory 2d.—It would be impossible to state from the data before me, the value of the stores, either in the quarter-master or commissary departments. Having no papers then, nor any previous knowledge of the stores. The stores in the quarter-master's department consisted of all stores necessary to the department—clothing, especially, in large amounts, shoes, harness, etc., with considerable unmanufactured material. The commissary stores, were meat, flour, sugar, molasses, and coffee. There was a very large amount of meat in store, and on the landing, at my arrival, though large amounts had already been carried away by citizens.

Interrogatory 3d.—A portion of these stores had been removed before the surrender. A considerable amount of meat on the landing, I was informed, was thrown into the river on Sunday, *before my arrival*, and carried off by the citizens. The doors of the commissary depot were thrown open, and the citizens, in dense crowds, were packing and hauling off the balance, at the time of my arrival, on Tuesday. The quarter-master's stores were also open, and the citizens were invited to come and help themselves, which they did, in larger crowds, if possible, than at the other department.

Interrogatories 4th and 5th.—On Tuesday morning, I was ordered by Gen. Floyd to take command of the city, and attempted to drive the mob from the doors of the departments, which mob was composed of straggling soldiers and citizens of all grades. The mob had taken possession of the city to that extent, that every species of property was unsafe. Houses were closed, carriages and wagons were concealed, to prevent the mob from taking possession of them. Houses were being seized everywhere. I had to call out my cavalry, and after every other means failed, charge the mob, before I could get it so dispersed as to get wagons to the doors of the departments, to load up the stores for transportation. After the mob was partially dispersed and quiet restored, a number of citizens furnished wagons and assisted in loading them. I was busily engaged in this work on Friday, Saturday, and Sunday. I transported 700 large boxes of clothing to the Nashville and Chattanooga railroad depot, several hundred bales osnaburgs and other military goods from the quarter-master's department, most, if not all the shoes having been seized by the mob. I removed about 700 or 800 wagon loads of meat. The high water having destroyed the bridges, so as to stop the transportation over the Nashville and Chattanooga railroad, I had large amounts of this meat taken over the Tennessee and Alabama railroad. By examination on Sunday morning, I found a large amount of fixed ammunition, in the shape of cartridges and ammunition for light artillery, in the magazine, which, with the assistance of Gen. Harding, I conveyed over seven miles on the Tennessee and Alabama railroad, in wagons, to the amount of 30 odd wagon loads, after the enemy had reached the river. A portion was sent on to Murfreesboro' in wagons. The quarter-master stores which had not already fallen into the hands of the mob, were all removed, save a lot of rope, loose shoes, and a large number of tents. The mob had already possessed themselves of a large amount of these stores. A large quantity of meat was left in store, and on the river bank, and some at the Nashville and Chattanooga railroad depot, on account of the break in the railroad. I cannot estimate the amount, as several storehouses had not been opened up to the time of my leaving. All stores left fell into the hands of the enemy, except forty pieces of light artillery, which were burned and spiked by order of Gen. Floyd, as were the guns at Fort Zollicoffer. My proposition to remove these stores, made by telegraph, to Murfreesboro', had the sanction of Gen. A. S. Johnston.

Interrogatory 6*th*. No effort was made, save by the mob, who were endeavoring to possess themselves of these stores, to prevent their removal, and a very large amount was taken off before I was placed in command of the city.

Interrogatory 7*th*. It was (eight days) from the time the quarter-master left the city before the arrival of the enemy—commissaries and other persons connected with these departments leaving at the same time. With proper diligence on their part, I have no doubt all the public stores might have been transported to places of safety.

Interrogatory 8*th*. Up to Saturday the railroads were open, and might have been used to transport these stores. Saturday the bridges of the Nashville and Chattanooga railroad gave way. Besides these modes of conveyance, a large number of wagons might have been obtained, had the quiet and order of the city been maintained, and large additional amounts of stores might, by these means, have been transported to places of safety.

Interrogatories 9*th and* 10*th*.—I saw no officer connected with the quarter-master or commissary departments, except Mr. Patton, who left on Friday. I did not, at any time, meet or hear of Major J. K. Stevenson in the city during my stay there.

Interrogatories 11*th*, 12*th and* 13*th*.—From my personal knowledge, I can say nothing of the manner in which Major Stevenson left the city. Common rumor and many reliable citizens informed me that Major Stevenson left by a special train, Sunday evening, February the 16th, taking personal baggage, furniture, carriage, and carriage horses; the train ordered by himself, as President of the railroad.

Interrogatory 14*th*. All the means of transportation were actually necessary for the transportation of Government stores, of sick and wounded soldiers—many of whom fell into the hands of the enemy for want of it, and who might have been saved by the proper use of the means at hand. The necessity for these means of transportation for stores will be seen by the above answers which I have given. I have been compelled to be as brief as possible, in making the above answers, my whole time being engaged, as we seem to be upon the eve of another great battle. The city was in a much worse condition than I can convey the idea of, on paper, and the loss of public stores must be estimated by millions of dollars. The panic was entirely useless, and not at all justified by the circumstances. Gen. Harding and the Mayor of the city, with Mr. Williams, deserve special mention for assistance rendered in removing the public property. In my judgment, if the quartermaster and commissary had remained at their post, and worked diligently, with the means at their command, the Government stores might all have been saved between the time of the fall of Fort Donelson and the arrival of the enemy in Nashville.

Respectfully submitted by

A. B. FORREST,

Colonel commanding Forrest's Brigade Cavalry.

INDEX.

www.ingramcontent.com/pod-product-compliance
Lightning Source LLC
LaVergne TN
LVHW021227110826
845150LV00002B/268

* 9 7 8 1 4 2 5 5 6 3 2 2 6 *